D0903266

HOLT McDOUGAL

New York

United States History

and New York History: Post–Civil War to the Present

William Deverell
Deborah Gray White

HOLT McDOUGAL
a division of Houghton Mifflin Harcourt

Copyright © 2010 by Houghton Mifflin Harcourt Publishing Company

All rights reserved. No part of this work may be reproduced or transmitted in any form or by any means, electronic or mechanical, including photocopying or recording, or by any information storage and retrieval system, without the prior written permission of the copyright owner unless such copying is expressly permitted by federal copyright law. Requests for permission to make copies of any part of the work should be addressed to Houghton Mifflin Harcourt Publishing Company, Attn: Contracts, Copyrights, and Licensing, 9400 SouthPark Center Loop, Orlando, Florida 32819.

Printed in the U.S.A.

If you have received these materials as examination copies free of charge, Houghton Mifflin Harcourt Publishing Company retains title to the materials and they may not be resold. Resale of examination copies is strictly prohibited.

Possession of this publication in print format does not entitle users to convert this publication, or any portion of it, into electronic format.

ISBN-13: 978-0-554-02469-1

ISBN-10: 0-554-02469-1

123456789 1421 15 14 13 12 11 10 09

Authors

William Deverell

William Deverell is Professor of History at the University of Southern California. He is the author of *Railroad Crossing: Californians and the Railroad, 1850-1910* and *Whitewashed Adobe: The Rise of Los Angeles and the Remaking of the Mexican Past*. He is the editor of the *Blackwell Companion to the American West*. With Greg Hise, he co-authored *Eden by Design: The 1930 Olmsted-Bartholomew Plan for the Los Angeles Region* and co-edited *Land of Sunshine: The Environmental History of Metropolitan Los Angeles*. He is the former chairman of the California Council for the Humanities.

Deborah Gray White

Deborah Gray White, a former New York City school teacher, is Distinguished Professor of History at Rutgers University in New Brunswick, New Jersey. A specialist in American history and the history of African Americans, she is the author of several books including: *Ar'n't I A Woman? Female Slaves in the Plantation South; Too Heavy a Load: Black Women in Defense of Themselves, 1894-1994*; and *Let My People Go, African Americans 1804-1860*, Volume 4 in the *Young Oxford History of African Americans*.

Program Consultants

Contributing Author

Kylene Beers, Ed.D.
Senior Reading Researcher
School Development Program
Yale University
New Haven, Connecticut

A former middle school teacher, Dr. Beers has turned her commitment to helping struggling readers into the major focus of her research, writing, speaking, and teaching. She is the current editor of the National Council of Teachers of English literacy journal *Voices from the Middle* and the author of *When Kids Can't Read: What Teachers Can Do* (Heinemann, 2002).

General Editor

Frances Marie Gipson
Secondary Literacy
Los Angeles Unified School
   District
Los Angeles, California

In her current position, Frances Gipson guides reform work for secondary instruction and supports its implementation. She has designed curriculum at the district, state, and national levels. Her leadership of a coaching collaborative with Subject Matter Projects of the University of California at Los Angeles evolved from her commitment to rigorous instruction and to meeting the needs of diverse learners.

Senior Literature and Writing Specialist

Carol Jago
English Department Chairperson
Santa Monica High School
Santa Monica, California

An English teacher at the middle and high school levels for 26 years, Carol Jago also directs the reading and literature project at UCLA and writes a weekly education column for the Los Angeles Times. She has been published in numerous professional journals and has authored several books, including *Cohesive Writing: Why Concept is Not Enough* (Boynton/Cook, 2002).

New York Program Advisors

Tim Backus
K-12 Supervisor of Social Studies
Colonie Central High School
Albany, New York

Ann-Jean Paci
Retired Assistant Principal
Social Studies Department
Sheepshead Bay High School
Brooklyn, New York

Anthony Powell
Social Studies Department Chair
Edmund Miles Middle School
Amityville, New York

Walter Robertson
Social Studies Department Chair
Dunkirk High School
Dunkirk, New York

Bob Van Amburgh
Instructional Supervisor
City School District of Albany
Albany, New York

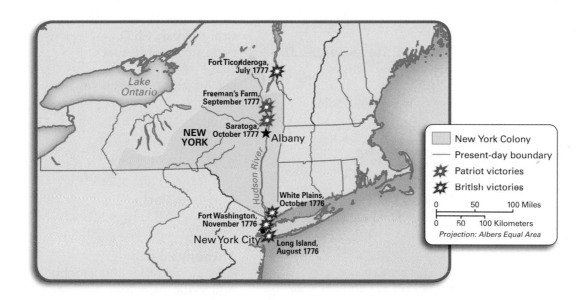

Legend:
- New York Colony
- Present-day boundary
- ✸ Patriot victories
- ✸ British victories

0   50   100 Miles
0   50   100 Kilometers
Projection: Albers Equal Area

Consultants

Martha H. Ball, M.A.
Religion Consultant
Utah 3Rs Project Director
Utah State Office of Education
Salt Lake City, Utah

John Ferguson, M.T.S., J.D.
Senior Religion Consultant
Assistant Professor
Political Science/Criminal Justice
Howard Payne University
Brownwood, Texas

J. Frank Malaret
Senior Consultant
Dean, Downtown and West
    Sacramento Outreach Centers
Sacramento City College
Sacramento, California

Kimberly A. Plummer, M.A.
Senior Consultant
History-Social Science Educator/
    Advisor
Holt, Rinehart & Winston

Galit Reichlin
Associate Director
Middle Eastern Affairs and
    International Analysis
Anti-Defamation League
(Reviewed Chapter 30 for
    Middle East content)

Andrés Reséndez, Ph.D.
Senior Consultant,
Assistant Professor
Department of History
University of California at Davis
Davis, California

Academic Reviewers

Anne C. Bailey, Ph.D.
Spelman College
Atlanta, Georgia

Albert Camarillo, Ph.D.
Department of History
Stanford University

Larry Conyers, Ph.D.
Department of Anthropology
University of Denver

Willard Gatewood, Ph.D.
Emeritus Alumni Distinguished
    Professor, Department of
    History
University of Arkansas

Christopher Hendricks, Ph.D.
Department of History
Armstrong Atlantic State
    University
Savannah, Georgia

Skip Hyser, Ph.D.
Department of History
James Madison University
Harrisonburg, Virginia

Yasuhide Kawashima
Department of History
University of Texas at El Paso

Brenda E. Stevenson, Ph.D.
Department of History
UCLA
Los Angeles, California

David Switzer, Ph.D.
Department of Social Studies
Plymouth State University
Plymouth, New Hampshire

Jessica Wang, Ph.D.
Department of History
UCLA
Los Angeles, California

Nan Woodruff, Ph.D
Department of History
Pennsylvania State University

Craig Yirush, Ph.D.
Department of History
UCLA
Los Angeles, California

Educational Reviewers

Henry Assetto
Twin Valley High School
Elverson, Pennsylvania

John Bilsky
Linton Middle School
Penn Hills, Pennsylvania

Julie Chan, Ed.D.
Director, Literacy Instruction
Newport-Mesa Unified School
    District
Costa Mesa, California

Kermit Cummings
Cockeysville Middle School
Baltimore County Public Schools
Baltimore, Maryland

Katherine A. DeForge
Social Studies Chair
Marcellus Central School
Marcellus, New York

Sandra Eades
Ridgely Middle School
Lutherville, Maryland

Ed Felten
Coopersville Public School
    District
Coopersville, Michigan

Tim Gearhart
Daniel Lewis Middle School
Paso Robles, California

Stacy Goldman
Lincoln Middle School
Berwyn, Illinois

Joseph P. Macary
Supervisor of Social Studies
Waterbury Public Schools
Waterbury, Connecticut

Carol Eiler Moore
Dundalk Middle School
Dundalk, Maryland

Tina Nelson
Baltimore County Public School
    District
Baltimore, Maryland

Ann-Jean Paci
Sheepshead Bay High School
Brooklyn, New York

Anthony Powell
Edmund W. Miles Middle School
Amityville, New York

Linda Prior
Floyd T. Binns Middle School
Culpeper County, Virginia

Wendy Schanberger
Hereford Middle School
Monkton, Maryland

Sue A. Shinn
Culpeper Middle School
Culpeper, Virginia

Kathleen Torquata
Lincoln Middle School
Berwyn, Illinois

Contents

UNIT 1 A Growing America (1850–1914) 1

Deadwood, South Dakota

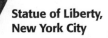

**Statue of Liberty,
New York City**

UNIT 2 The Beginning of Modern America (1867–1920)

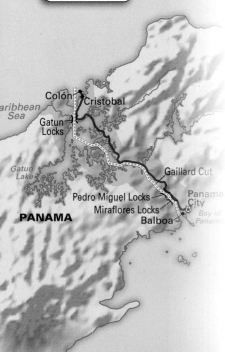

Canal zone
Canal route
Railroad
Locks
0   10   20 Miles
0   10   20 Kilometers

Colón   Cristobal
Caribbean Sea
Gatun Locks
Gatun Lake
Gaillard Cut
Pedro Miguel Locks
Miraflores Locks
Panama City
Bay of Panama
PANAMA   Balboa

New Yorker
Theodore Roosevelt

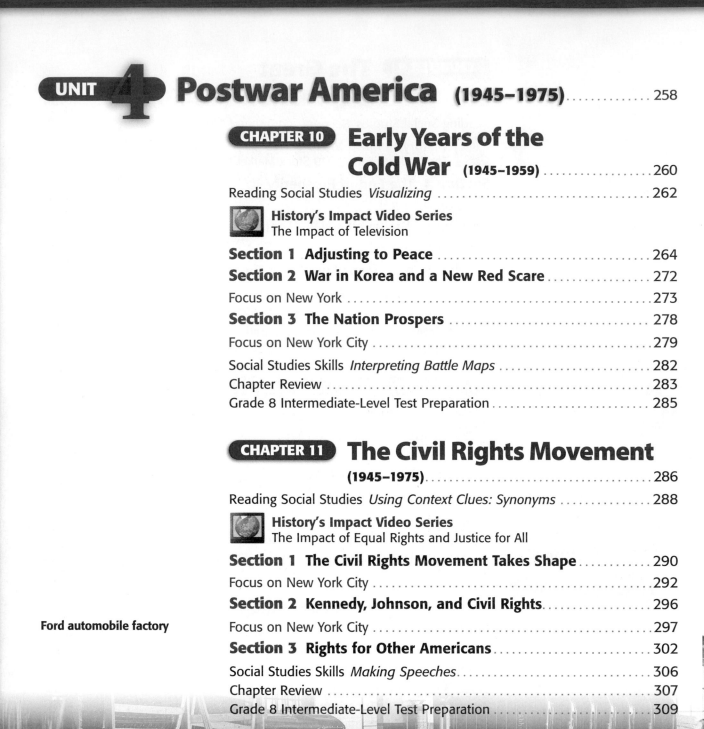

Ford automobile factory

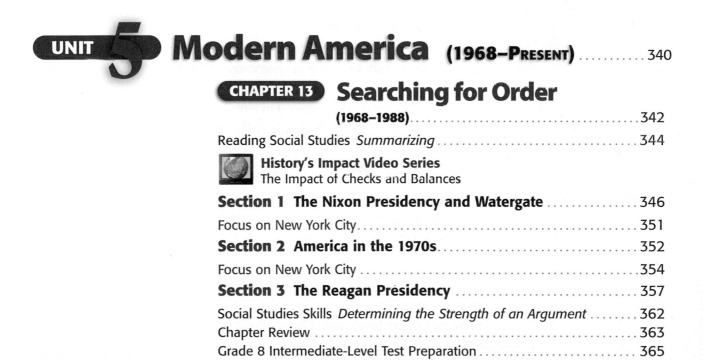

From the Collections of Henry Ford Museum and Greenfield Village

March on Washington

Features

**New Yorker
Eleanor Roosevelt**

LINKING TO TODAY

Link people and events from the past to the world you live in today.

QUICK FACTS

Examine key facts and concepts quickly and easily with graphics.

Charts, Graphs, and Tables

Analyze information presented visually to learn more about history.

CHARTS

INFOGRAPHICS

Analyze and interpret information from graphics.

TIME LINES

See how key events are related in time.

Points of View

See how different people have interpreted historical issues in different ways.

Historic Documents

Examine key documents that have shaped U.S. history.

Literature in History

Learn about the beliefs and experiences of people who lived in other times and places through literature pieces.

Social Studies Skills

Learn, practice, and apply the skills you need to study and analyze history.

**New York City's
Flatiron Building**

Primary Sources

Read and analyze the exact words of important people and documents as related to the study of U.S. history.

Cesar Chavez

Former New York City Mayor Rudolph Giuliani

Maps

Interpret maps to see where important events happened and analyze how geography has influenced history.

Interactive Maps

Program Maps

Interactive Map

The Dust Bowl

New York Social Studies Middle School Standards

What are the New York Social Studies Middle School Standards?

Learning standards are simply the things you are expected to know, understand, and be able to do as a result of your education. Learning standards are usually organized by subject and grade. So standards for your United States history course, for example, focus on the knowledge and skills you will need to gain in your social studies class this school year.

How can New York Social Studies Middle School Standards help me?

These learning standards are helpful because they give you a clear picture of what you will be expected to learn. This can help you to focus on key material as you work through the school year. You can think of the standards as a kind of checklist—and you can even check off important subjects and skills as you master them. Another advantage of becoming familiar with the standards is that teachers often base lesson plans and tests on these standards. That means that the standards can give you a preview of what to expect in this course.

How are the New York Social Studies Middle School Standards organized?

New York educators have organized the teaching of social studies by creating different kinds of standards at several levels. At the top level are New York State Learning Standards for Social Studies. These are very broad standards—each one covers a large amount of learning. Because they are so broad, there are only five of them, and only one refers to the study of United States and New York history. You can read it below. On the next page, you will read more detailed parts of the standard.

Each Standard is divided into Key Ideas. These Key Ideas give you a description of the main categories of information you will be learning, as well as the kinds of skills you will be practicing.

Standard 1—History of the United States and New York

Students will use a variety of intellectual skills to demonstrate their understanding of major ideas, eras, themes, developments, and turning points in the history of the United States and New York.

1. The study of New York State and United States history requires an analysis of the development of American culture, its diversity and multicultural context, and the ways people are unified by many values, practices, and traditions.

Central Park, New York City

2. Important ideas, social and cultural values, beliefs, and traditions from New York State and United States history illustrate the connections and interactions of people and events across time and from a variety of perspectives.

3. Study about the major social, political, economic, cultural, and religious developments in New York State and United States history involves learning about the important roles and contributions of individuals and groups.

4. The skills of historical analysis include the ability to: explain the significance of historical evidence; weigh the importance, reliability, and validity of evidence; understand the concept of multiple causation; understand the importance of changing and competing interpretations of different historical developments.

Standard 2—World History

Students will use a variety of intellectual skills to demonstrate their understanding of major ideas, eras, themes, developments, and turning points in world history and examine the broad sweep of history from a variety of perspectives.

1. The study of world history requires an understanding of world cultures and civilizations, including an analysis of important ideas, social and cultural values, beliefs, and traditions. This study also examines the human condition and the connections and interactions of people across time and space and the ways different people view the same event or issue from a variety of perspectives.

2. Establishing timeframes, exploring different periodizations, examining themes across time and within cultures, and focusing on important turning points in world history help organize the study of world cultures and civilizations.

3. Study of the major social, political, cultural, and religious developments in world history involves learning about the important roles and contributions of individuals and groups.

4. The skills of historical analysis include the ability to investigate differing and competing interpretations of the theories of history, hypothesize about why interpretations change over time, explain the importance of historical evidence, and understand the concepts of change and continuity over time.

Brooklyn Bridge

Standard 3—Geography

Students will use a variety of intellectual skills to demonstrate their understanding of the geography of the interdependent world in which we live—local, national, and global—including the distribution of people, places, and environments over the Earth's surface.

1. Geography can be divided into six essential elements which can be used to analyze important historic, geographic, economic, and environmental questions and issues. These six elements include: the world in spatial terms, places and regions, physical settings (including natural resources), human systems, environment and society, and the use of geography. (Adapted from The National Geography Standards, 1994: Geography for Life)

2. Geography requires the development and application of the skills of asking and answering geographic questions; analyzing theories of geography; and acquiring, organizing, and analyzing geographic information. (Adapted from The National Geography Standards, 1994: Geography for Life)

Standard 4—Economics

Students will use a variety of intellectual skills to demonstrate their understanding of how the United States and other societies develop economic systems and associated institutions to allocate scarce resources, how major decision-making units function in the U.S. and other national economies, and how an economy solves the scarcity problem through market and nonmarket mechanisms.

1. The study of economics requires an understanding of major economic concepts and systems, the principles of economic decision making, and the interdependence of economies and economic systems throughout the world.

2. Economics requires the development and application of the skills needed to make informed and well-reasoned economic decisions in daily and national life.

Grand Central Station New York

Standard 5—Civics, Citizenship, and Government

Students will use a variety of intellectual skills to demonstrate their understanding of the necessity for establishing governments; the governmental system of the U.S. and other nations; the U.S. Constitution; the basic civic values of American constitutional democracy; and the roles, rights, and responsibilities of citizenship, including avenues of participation.

1. The study of civics, citizenship, and government involves learning about political systems; the purposes of government and civic life; and the differing assumptions held by people across time and place regarding power, authority, governance, and law. (Adapted from The National Standards for Civics and Government, 1994)

2. The state and federal governments established by the Constitutions of the United States and the State of New York embody basic civic values (such as justice, honesty, self-discipline, due process, equality, majority rule with respect for minority rights, and respect for self, others, and property), principles, and practices and establish a system of shared and limited government. (Adapted from The National Standards for Civics and Government, 1994)

3. Central to civics and citizenship is an understanding of the roles of the citizen within American constitutional democracy and the scope of a citizen's rights and responsibilities.

4. The study of civics and citizenship requires the ability to probe ideas and assumptions, ask and answer analytical questions, take a skeptical attitude toward questionable arguments, evaluate evidence, formulate rational conclusions, and develop and refine participatory skills.

New York City Harbor

Reading like a Historian

Historians and other social scientists use specific methods to systematically study human cultures in the past and present. Paintings and other artifacts can be used to help understand the past. The famous painting on the next page, *Washington Crossing the Delaware*, captures the determination of Patriot leaders and soldiers to endure brutal conditions in the hope of winning their struggle for liberty. As you study United States history, you too will learn how to use different historical sources to **Read like a Historian.**

To find out more about reading like a historian and the historical sources that follow, visit

go.hrw.com
More Online
KEYWORD: HISTORIAN

By Frances Marie Gipson
Secondary Literacy Coordinator
Los Angeles Unified School District, Los Angeles, California

What Does It Mean to Read like a Historian?

In your history class you will be doing a lot of reading, thinking, and problem-solving. Much of your reading and thinking will center on different types of texts or materials. Since you are in a history class reading all sorts of things, a question to consider is, "What does it mean to think, read, and solve problems like a historian?"

Historians work with different types of sources to understand and learn from history. Two categories of sources are **primary** and **secondary** sources.

Primary Sources are historical documents, written accounts by a firsthand witness, or objects that have survived from the past. A study of primary sources might include letters, government documents, diaries, photographs, art objects, stamps, coins, and even clothing.

Secondary Sources are accounts of past events created by people some time after the events happened. This textbook and other books written about historical events are examples of secondary sources.

As you learn more about your work as a historian, you will begin to ask questions and analyze historical materials. You will be working as a detective, digging into history to create a richer understanding of the mysteries of the past.

How to Analyze Written Sources

"Spain's Victory of Peace"

To five hundred thousand Cubans starved or otherwise murdered have been added an American battleship and three hundred American sailors lost as the direct result of the dilatory [delaying] policy of our government toward Spain. If we had stopped the war in Cuba when duty and policy alike urged us to do the *Maine* would have been afloat today, and three hundred homes, now desolate, would have been unscathed.

– New York Journal, February 17, 1898

26.23 SPANISH-AMERICAN WAR, 1898.
Credit: The Granger Collection, New York

Asking questions can help you determine the relevance and importance of written primary sources, such as this newspaper editorial about the sinking of an American warship. As you analyze the primary source above and the primary and secondary sources included in this textbook, ask yourself questions like the ones below.

- Who created the source and why?

- Did the writer have firsthand knowledge of the event, or does he report what others saw or heard?

- Was the writer a neutral party, or did the author have opinions or interests that might have influenced what was recorded?

- Did the writer wish to inform or persuade others?

- Was the information recorded during the event, immediately after the event, or after some lapse of time?

The Attack on Lawrence, Kansas

"Sheriff Jones, again at the head of an army of Missourians, marched into Lawrence. In broad daylight, they threw the printing presses of two newspapers into a river. They burned down the Free State Hotel and other buildings. Antislavery Kansans seethed with rage. Here is how one eyewitness described the attack: *Sheriff Jones, after looking at the flames rising from the hotel and saying that it was 'the happiest day of his life,' dismissed the troops and they began their lawless destruction.*"

–John A. Garraty, from *The Story of America*, 1994

When reading secondary sources, such as the description of the attack on Lawrence, Kansas, historians ask additional questions to seek understanding. They try to source the text, build evidence, and interpret the message that is being conveyed. For historians, reading is a quest to find evidence to answer or challenge a historical problem. As you study secondary sources, ask questions like the ones below.

- Who is the author? What do I know about this author?
- Did the author have firsthand information? What is the author's relationship to the event?
- What might be the author's motivation in writing this piece?
- What type of evidence did the author look at?
- Are any assumptions or biases present?
- How does this document fit into the larger context of the events I am studying?
- What kind of source is it?
- Is the source an original?
- Is the content probable or reasonable?
- What does the date tell me about the event?
- What do I already know about this topic that will help me understand more of what I am reading?

How to Analyze an Artifact

Artifacts, such as this phonograph invented by Thomas Edison, take many forms. They might be coins, stone tools, pieces of clothing, or even items found in your backpack. As you study artifacts in this textbook, ask yourself questions like the ones below.

- Why was this object created?

- When and where would it have been used?

- What does the artifact tell me about the technology available at the time it was created?

- What can it tell me about the life and times of the people who used it?

- How does the artifact help to make sense of the time period?

How to Analyze a Historical Map

Maps, such as this one from 1719 of New France, are symbolic representations of places shown in relation to one another. All maps necessarily include some details and leave out others. As you study maps in this textbook, ask questions like the ones below.

- When and where was the map produced?

- What details has the mapmaker chosen to include (or exclude) on this map?

- Why was the map drawn?

- How can I determine if the map is accurate?

- How are maps used to analyze the past, present, and future?

How to Analyze a Photograph

Photographs, like the one above of African American soldiers during the Civil War, are another important source for historians. One way to study a photograph is to write down everything you think is important about it. Then divide the image into four sections and describe the important elements from each section. As you study photographs in this textbook, ask questions like the ones below.

- What is the subject of the photograph?
- What does the image reveal about its subject?
- What is the setting for the photograph?
- What other details can I observe?
- When and where in the past was the photograph created?
- How can I describe the photographer's point of view?

How to Analyze a Political Cartoon

In 1871 Thomas Nast published this cartoon—"Who Stole the People's Money?"—poking fun at corruption in politics. As you study political cartoons in this textbook, use the following helpful tips and questions.

- List the parts of the political cartoon and the importance of each part.

- Describe the focus or significance of the political cartoon.

- Do the captions and call-out boxes clarify the political cartoon's purpose?

- Does the cartoon help me understand the information that I am studying in my textbook better?

Become an Active Reader

by Dr. Kylene Beers

Did you ever think you would begin reading your social studies book by reading about reading? Actually, it makes better sense than you might think. You would probably make sure you learned some soccer skills and strategies before playing in a game. Similarly, you need to learn some reading skills and strategies before reading your social studies book. In other words, you need to make sure you know whatever you need to know in order to read this book successfully.

Tip #1
Use the Reading Social Studies Pages

Take advantage of the two pages on reading at the beginning of every chapter. Those pages introduce the chapter themes; explain a reading skill or strategy; and identify key terms, people, and academic vocabulary.

Themes

Why are themes important? They help our minds organize facts and information. For example, when we talk about baseball, we may talk about types of pitches. When we talk about movies, we may discuss animation.

Historians are no different. When they discuss history or social studies, they tend to think about some common themes: Economics, Geography, Religion, Politics, Society and Culture, and Science and Technology.

Reading Skill or Strategy

Good readers use a number of skills and strategies to make sure they understand what they are reading. These lessons will give you the tools you need to read and understand social studies.

Key Terms, People, and Academic Vocabulary

Before you read the chapter, review these words and think about them. Have you heard the word before? What do you already know about the people? Then watch for these words and their meanings as you read the chapter.

Tells which theme or themes are important in the chapter

Explains a skill or strategy good readers use

Gives you practice in the reading skill or strategy

Identifies the important words in the chapter

Tip #2
Read like a Skilled Reader

You will never get better at reading your social studies book—or any book for that matter—unless you spend some time thinking about how to be a better reader.

Skilled readers do the following:

- They preview what they are supposed to read before they actually begin reading. They look for vocabulary words, titles of sections, information in the margin, or maps or charts they should study.

- They divide their notebook paper into two columns. They title one column "Notes from the Chapter" and the other column "Questions or Comments I Have."

- They take notes in both columns as they read.

- They read like **active readers**. The Active Reading list below shows you what that means.

- They use clues in the text to help them figure out where the text is going. The best clues are called signal words.

> **Chronological Order Signal Words:** *first, second, third, before, after, later, next, following that, earlier, finally*
>
> **Cause and Effect Signal Words:** *because of, due to, as a result of, the reason for, therefore, consequently*
>
> **Comparison/Contrast Signal Words:** *likewise, also, as well as, similarly, on the other hand*

Active Reading

Successful readers are **active readers**. These readers know that it is up to them to figure out what the text means. Here are some steps you can take to become an active, and successful, reader.

Predict what will happen next based on what has already happened. When your predictions don't match what happens in the text, reread the confusing parts.

Question what is happening as you read. Constantly ask yourself why things have happened, what things mean, and what caused certain events.

Summarize what you are reading frequently. Do not try to summarize the entire chapter! Read a bit and then summarize it. Then read on.

Connect what is happening in the part you're reading to what you have already read.

Clarify your understanding. Stop occasionally to ask yourself whether you are confused by anything. You may need to reread to clarify, or you may need to read further and collect more information before you can understand.

Visualize what is happening in the text. Try to see the events or places in your mind by drawing maps, making charts, or jotting down notes about what you are reading.

Tip #3
Pay Attention to Vocabulary

It is no fun to read something when you don't know what the words mean, but you can't learn new words if you only use or read the words you already know. In this book, we know we have probably used some words you don't know. But, we have followed a pattern as we have used more difficult words.

Key Terms and People

At the beginning of each section you will find a list of key terms or people that you will need to know. Be on the lookout for those words as you read through the section.

> Some 6,000 lives were lost during the American construction of the **Panama Canal**. It was finally opened to ships on August 15, 1914, linking the Atlantic and Pacific oceans. The opening ceremony was held the next y...

Revolution in Panama
No one was a stronger supporter of a Central American canal than President Theodore Roosevelt. Roosevelt knew that the best spot for the canal was the Isthmus of Panama, which at the time was part of the nation of Colombia. But he was unable to convince the Colombian senate to lease a strip of land across Panama to the United States.

Roosevelt considered other ways to gain control of the land. He learned that Panamanian revolutionaries were planning a revolt against Colombia. On November 2, 1903, a U.S. warship arrived outside Colón, Panama. The next day the revolt began. Blocked by the U.S. warship, Colombian forces could not reach Panama to stop the rebellion. Panama declared itself an independent country. The United States then recognized the new nation.

The new government of Panama supported the idea of a canal across its land. The United States agreed to pay Panama $10 million plus $250,000 a year for a 99-year lease on a 10-mile-wide strip of land across the isthmus.

Building the Canal
Canal construction began in 1904. The first obstacle to overcome was tropical disease. The canal route ran through 51 miles of forests and swamps filled with mosquitoes, many of which carried the deadly diseases malaria and yellow fever.

Dr. William C. Gorgas, who had helped Dr. Walter Reed stamp out yellow fever in Cuba, organized a successful effort to rid the canal route of disease-carrying mosquitoes. If Gorgas had not been successful, the canal's construction would have taken much longer. It also would have cost much more in terms of both lives and money.

Even with the reduced risk of disease, the work was very dangerous. Most of the canal had to be blasted out of solid rock with explosives. Workers used dozens of steam shovels to cut a narrow, eight-mile-long channel through the mountains of central Panama. Sometimes workers died when their shovels struck explosive charges. "The flesh of men flew in the air like birds every day," recalled one worker from the West Indies.

Some 6,000 lives were lost during the American construction of the **Panama Canal**. It was finally opened to ships on August 15, 1914, linking the Atlantic and Pacific oceans. An opening ceremony was held the next year. It had taken 10 years to complete, and the cost was $375 million. In the end, however, the world had its "highway between the oceans."

READING CHECK Drawing Conclusions Why did building the canal cost so many lives?

FOCUS ON NEW YORK
Theodore Roosevelt's strong support for the Panama Canal has had far reaching effects for his home state of New York. In 2003, the Port Authority of New York and New Jersey collaborated with the Panama Canal Authority on a plan to help boost the two states' trade with Asia.

THE IMPACT TODAY
Today the Panama Canal Zone is threatened by deforestation and erosion because of heavy use. Decreased rainfall is also hurting the canal.

The massive Gatun Locks, shown here under construction in 1914, raise ships 85 feet onto Gatun Lake, an inland waterway on the Panama Canal.

125

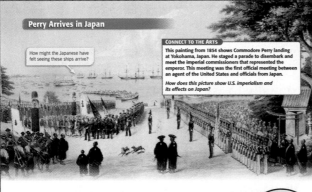

Perry Arrives in Japan

How might the Japanese have felt seeing these ships arrive?

CONNECT TO THE ARTS
This painting from 1854 shows Commodore Perry landing at Yokohama, Japan. He staged a parade to disembark and meet the imperial commissioners that represented the emperor. This meeting was the first official meeting between an agent of the United States and officials from Japan.

How does this picture show U.S. imperialism and its effects on Japan?

Some Japanese leaders welcomed trade with the United States. In 1868 people who favored the industrialization process came to power in Japan, beginning a 40-year period of modernization. By the 1890s Japan was becoming a major imperial power. It defeated China in the Sino-Japanese War from 1894 to 1895. As a result, Japan gained new territory and enjoyed the same trading privileges in China as European countries. In 1904 Japan attacked Russian forces stationed in China. President Theodore Roosevelt helped to negotiate a peace treaty to end the Russo-Japanese War a year later. Japan gained control of Korea, a lease on Port Arthur in China, and other rights. Japan had become a world power.

Foreign Powers in China
After Japan defeated China, other countries took advantage of China's weakness by seizing **spheres of influence** — areas where foreign nations controlled resources. Germany, Great Britain, France, Japan, and Russia all took control of areas within China.

Some U.S. leaders feared that the United States would be closed out of Chinese markets. In 1899 Secretary of State John Hay sent notes to Japan and many European countries announcing the **Open Door Policy**. This policy stated that all nations should have equal access to trade in China. The policy was neither rejected nor accepted by European powers and Japan but made U.S. intentions clear.

Meanwhile, many Chinese resented the power and control held by foreign nations. This hostility sparked the **Boxer Rebellion**. The Boxers were Chinese nationalists who were angered by foreign involvement in China. In their language, the group was called the Fists of Righteous Harmony. Westerners called them Boxers because they used a clenched fist as their symbol. Although officially denounced, they were secretly supported by the Chinese government.

In June 1900 the Boxers took to the streets of Beijing, China's capital, and laid siege to the walled settlement where foreigners lived. They killed more than 200 people.

ACADEMIC VOCABULARY
process a series of steps by which a task is accomplished

AMERICA AS A WORLD POWER **115**

ACADEMIC VOCABULARY

process a series of steps by which a task is accomplished

Academic Vocabulary

When we use a word that is important in all classes, not just social studies, we define it in the margin under the heading *Academic Vocabulary*. You will run into these academic words in other textbooks, so you should learn what they mean while reading this book.

Words to Know

As you read this social studies textbook, you will be more successful if you know or learn the meanings of the words on this page. There are two types of words listed here. The first list contains academic words, the words we discussed at the bottom of the previous page. These words are important in all classes, not just social studies. The second list contains words that are special to this particular topic of social studies, U.S. history.

Academic Words

abstract	expressing a quality or idea without reference to an actual thing
acquire	to get
advocate	to plead in favor of
affect	to change or influence
agreement	a decision reached by two or more people or groups
aspects	parts
authority	power, right to rule
cause	the reason something happens
circumstances	surrounding situation
classical	referring to the cultures of ancient Greece or Rome
complex	difficult, not simple
concrete	specific, real
consequences	the effects of a particular event or events
contemporary	existing at the same time
contract	a binding legal agreement
criteria	rules for defining
develop/ development	1. the process of growing or improving 2. Creation
distinct	separate
distribute	to divide among a group of people
effect	the result of an action or decision
efficient/ efficiency	productive and not wasteful
element	part
establish	to set up or create
execute	to perform, carry out
explicit	fully revealed without vagueness
facilitate	to bring about
factor	cause
features	characteristics
function	use or purpose
ideal	ideas or goals that people try to live up to
impact	effect, result
functions	uses or purposes
implement	to put in place
implications	effects of a decision
implicit	understood though not clearly put into words
incentive	something that leads people to follow a certain course of action
influence	change or have an effect on
innovation	a new idea or way of doing something
logic/logical	1. reasoned, well thought out 2. well thought out ideas
method	a way of doing something
motive	a reason for doing something
neutral	unbiased, not favoring either side in a conflict
policy	rule, course of action

primary	main, most important
principle	basic belief, rule, or law
procedure	a series of steps taken to accomplish a task
process	a series of steps by which a task is accomplished
purpose	the reason something is done
reaction	response
rebel	to fight against authority
role	1. a part or function 2. Assigned behavior
strategy	a plan for fighting a battle or war
structure	the way something is set up or organized
traditional	customary, time-honored
values	ideas that people hold dear and try to live by
vary/various	1. To be different 2. of many types

Social Studies Words

AD	refers to dates after Jesus's birth
anthropology	the science of human beings, especially their physical characteristics and cultures
BC	refers to dates before the birth of Jesus
BCE	refers to "Before Common Era," dates before the birth of Jesus
CE	refers to "Common Era," dates after Jesus's birth
century	a period of 100 years
civilization	the culture of a particular time or place
climate	the weather conditions in a certain area over a long period of time
culture	the knowledge, beliefs, customs, and values of a group of people
custom	a repeated practice; tradition
democracy	governmental rule by the people, usually on a majority rule principle
economics	a social science concerned with the production, distribution, and consumption of goods and services
geography	the study of the earth's physical and cultural features
monarchy	governmental rule by one person, a king or queen
political science	the study of government and politics
psychology	the study of mind and behavior
society	a group of people who share common traditions
sociology	the science of society, social institutions, and social relationships

Mapping the Earth

A **globe** is a scale model of the earth. It is useful for showing the entire earth or studying large areas of the earth's surface.

A pattern of lines circles the globe in east-west and north-south directions. It is called a **grid**. The intersection of these imaginary lines helps us find places on the earth.

The east-west lines in the grid are lines of **latitude**. Lines of latitude are called **parallels** because they are always parallel to each other. These imaginary lines measure distance north and south of the **equator**. The equator is an imaginary line that circles the globe halfway between the North and South Poles. Parallels measure distance from the equator in **degrees**. The symbol for degrees is °. Degrees are further divided into **minutes**. The symbol for minutes is ´. There are 60 minutes in a degree. Parallels north of the equator are labeled with an N. Those south of the equator are labeled with an S.

The north-south lines are lines of **longitude**. Lines of longitude are called **meridians**. These imaginary lines pass through the Poles. They measure distance east and west of the **prime meridian**. The prime meridian is an imaginary line that runs through Greenwich, England. It represents 0° longitude.

Lines of latitude range from 0°, for locations on the equator, to 90°N or 90°S, for locations at the Poles. Lines of longitude range from 0° on the prime meridian to 180° on a meridian in the mid-Pacific Ocean. Meridians west of the prime meridian to 180° are labeled with a W. Those east of the prime meridian to 180° are labeled with an E.

Lines of Latitude

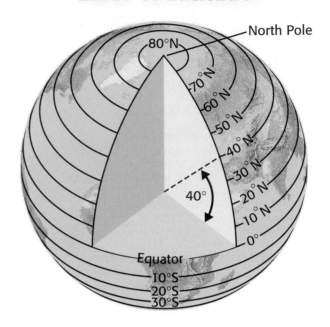

Lines of Longitude

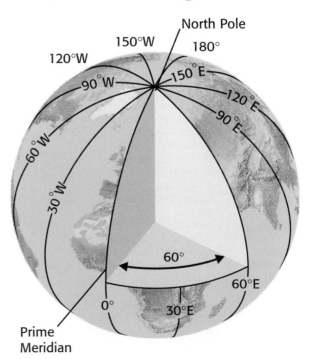

Northern Hemisphere

The equator divides the globe into two halves, called **hemispheres**. The half north of the equator is the Northern Hemisphere. The southern half is the Southern Hemisphere. The prime meridian and the 180° meridian divide the world into the Eastern Hemisphere and the Western Hemisphere. However, the prime meridian runs right through Europe and Africa. To avoid dividing these continents between two hemispheres, some mapmakers divide the Eastern and Western hemispheres at 20°W. This places all of Europe and Africa in the Eastern Hemisphere.

Our planet's land surface is divided into seven large landmasses, called **continents**. They are identified in the maps on this page. Landmasses smaller than continents and completely surrounded by water are called **islands**.

Geographers also organize Earth's water surface into parts. The largest is the world ocean. Geographers divide the world ocean into the Pacific Ocean, the Atlantic Ocean, the Indian Ocean, and the Arctic Ocean. Lakes and seas are smaller bodies of water.

Southern Hemisphere

Western Hemisphere

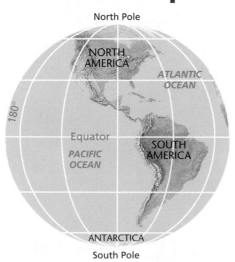

Eastern Hemisphere

Mapmaking

A **map** is a flat diagram of all or part of the earth's surface. Mapmakers have created different ways of showing our round planet on flat maps. These different ways are called **map projections**. Because the earth is round, there is no way to show it accurately in a flat map. All flat maps are distorted in some way. Mapmakers must choose the type of map projection that is best for their purposes. Many map projections are one of three kinds: cylindrical, conic, or flat-plane.

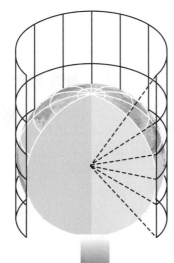

Paper cylinder

Cylindrical Projections

Cylindrical projections are based on a cylinder wrapped around the globe. The cylinder touches the globe only at the equator. The meridians are pulled apart and are parallel to each other instead of meeting at the Poles. This causes landmasses near the Poles to appear larger than they really are. The map below is a Mercator projection, one type of cylindrical projection. The Mercator projection is useful for navigators because it shows true direction and shape. However, it distorts the size of land areas near the Poles.

Mercator projection

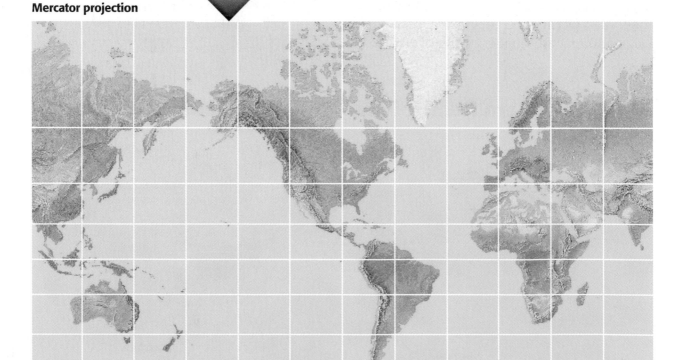

Conic Projections

Conic projections are based on a cone placed over the globe. A conic projection is most accurate along the lines of latitude where it touches the globe. It retains almost true shape and size. Conic projections are most useful for showing areas that have long east-west dimensions, such as the United States.

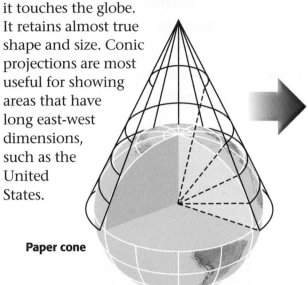

Paper cone

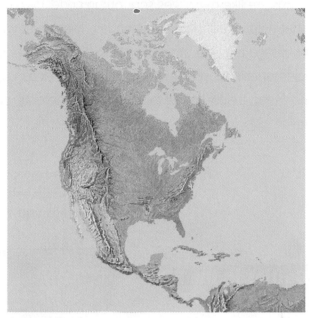

Conic projection

Flat-Plane Projections

Flat-plane projections are based on a plane touching the globe at one point, such as at the North Pole or South Pole. A flat-plane projection is useful for showing true direction for airplane pilots and ship navigators. It also shows true area. However, it distorts the true shapes of landmasses.

Flat plane

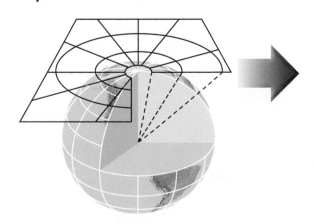

Flat-plane projection

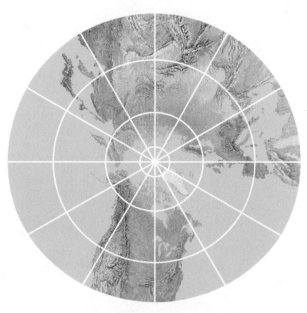

Map Essentials

Maps are like messages sent out in code. Mapmakers provide certain elements that help us translate these codes. These elements help us understand the message they are presenting about a particular part of the world. Of these elements, almost all maps have titles, directional indicators, scales, and legends. The map below has all four of these elements, plus a fifth—a locator map.

❶ Title

A map's **title** shows what the subject of the map is. The map title is usually the first thing you should look at when studying a map, because it tells you what the map is trying to show.

Battles in the East

Legend:
- Union state
- West Virginia (Separated from Virginia in 1861 and joined the Union in 1863)
- Confederate state
- Union forces
- Union victory
- Confederate forces
- Confederate victory

0   15   30 Miles
0   15   30 Kilometers

PENNSYLVANIA

MARYLAND

WEST VIRGINIA

Shenandoah Valley

Potomac River

Antietam Sep. 1862

Washington

Manassas Junction

Bull Run July 1861 & Aug. 1862

Fair Oaks May – June 1862

Richmond

James River

Seven Days June 1862

Yorktown

York R.

Chesapeake Bay

ATLANTIC OCEAN

VIRGINIA

LEE
McCLELLAN
POPE

N W E S

❷ Compass Rose

A directional indicator shows which way north, south, east, and west lie on the map. Some mapmakers use a "north arrow," which points toward the North Pole. Remember, "north" is not always at the top of a map. The way a map is drawn and the location of directions on that map depend on the perspective of the mapmaker. Most maps in this textbook indicate direction by using a compass rose. A **compass rose** has arrows that point to all four principal directions, as shown.

❸ Scale

Mapmakers use scales to show the distances between points on a map. Scales may appear on maps in several different forms. The maps in this textbook provide a bar **scale**. Scales give distances in miles and kilometers.

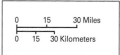

To find the distance between two points on the map, place a piece of paper so that the edge connects the two points. Mark the location of each point on the paper with a line or dot. Then, compare the distance between the two dots with the map's bar scale. The number on the top of the scale gives the distance in miles. The number on the bottom gives the distance in kilometers. Because the distances are given in large intervals, you may have to approximate the actual distance on the scale.

❹ Legend

The **legend**, or key, explains what the symbols on the map represent. Point symbols are used to specify the location of things, such as cities, that do not take up much space on the map. Some legends, such as the one shown here, show colors that represent certain elevations. Other maps might have legends with symbols or colors that represent things such as roads. Legends can also show economic resources, land use, population density, and climate.

❺ Locator Map

A locator map shows where in the world the area on the map is located. The area shown on the main map is shown in red on the locator map. The locator map also shows surrounding areas so the map reader can see how the information on the map relates to neighboring lands.

Working with Maps

The Atlas at the back of this textbook includes both physical and political maps. Physical maps, like the one you just saw and the one below, show the major physical features in a region. These features include things like mountain ranges, rivers, islands, and plains. Political maps show the major political features of a region, such as countries and their borders, capitals, and other important cities.

Topographic Maps

Some maps are topographic maps. A topographic map, like this one, shows the shape of the earth's surface using contour lines. Contour lines are imaginary lines connecting points of the same elevation above sea level. The distance between the lines represents the distance between points on the earth's surface. If the lines are close together, the feature is more steep than if the lines are far apart. Symbols on topographic maps represent natural and manmade features such as rivers, mountains, roads, and even buildings. Name five symbols you see on this topographic map.

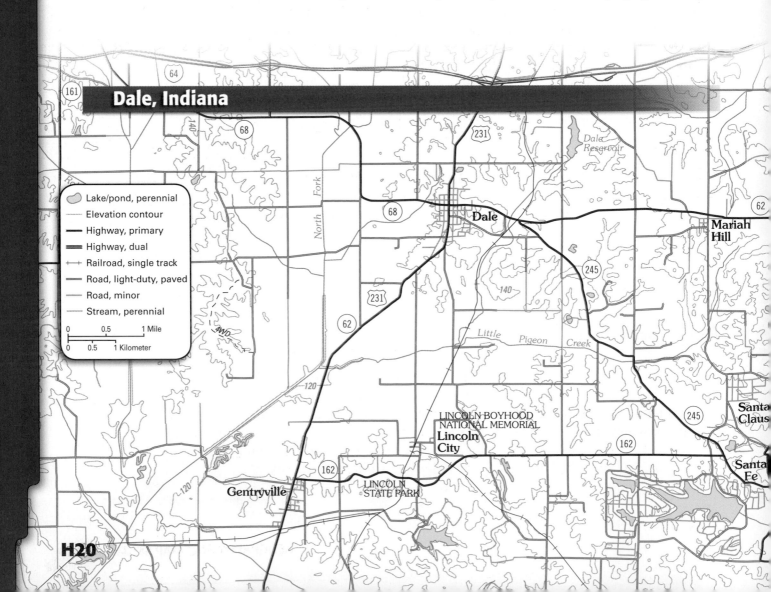

Dale, Indiana

Lake/pond, perennial
Elevation contour
Highway, primary
Highway, dual
Railroad, single track
Road, light-duty, paved
Road, minor
Stream, perennial

0   0.5   1 Mile
0   0.5   1 Kilometer

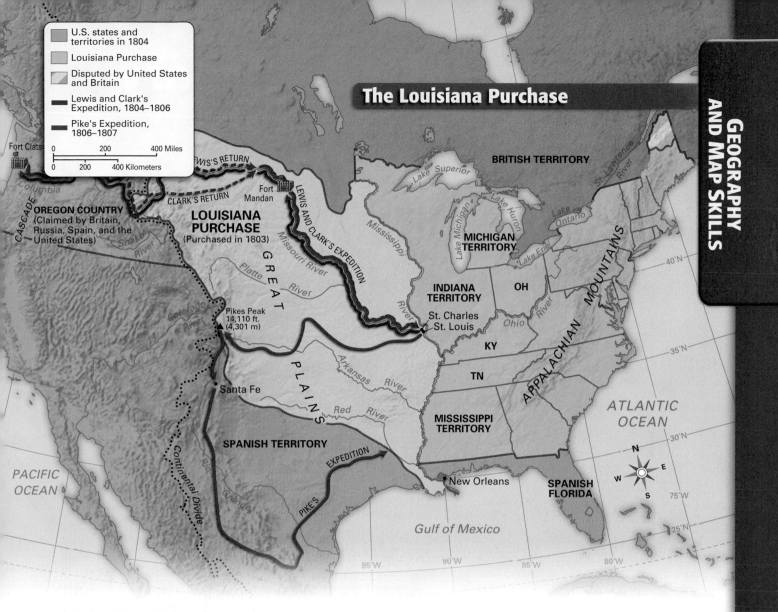

The Louisiana Purchase

U.S. states and territories in 1804
Louisiana Purchase
Disputed by United States and Britain
Lewis and Clark's Expedition, 1804–1806
Pike's Expedition, 1806–1807

Historical Map

In this textbook, most of the maps you will study are historical maps. Historical maps, such as this one, are maps that show information about the past. This information might be which lands an empire controlled or where a certain group of people lived. Often colors are used to indicate the different things on the map. What does this map show?

Route Map

One special type of historical map is called a route map. A route map, like the one above, shows the route, or path, that someone or something followed. Route maps can show things like trade routes, invasion routes, or the journeys and travels of people. If more than one route is shown, several arrows of different colors may be used. What does this route map show?

The maps in this textbook will help you study and understand history. By working with these maps, you will see where important events happened, where empires rose and fell, and where people moved. In studying these maps, you will learn how geography has influenced history.

Geographic Dictionary

OCEAN
a large body of water

CORAL REEF
an ocean ridge made up of skeletal remains of tiny sea animals

GULF
a large part of the ocean that extends into land

PENINSULA
an area of land that sticks out into a lake or ocean

BAY
part of a large body of water that is smaller than a gulf

ISLAND
an area of land surrounded entirely by water

ISTHMUS
a narrow piece of land connecting two larger land areas

DELTA
an area where a river deposits soil into the ocean

STRAIT
a narrow body of water connecting two larger bodies of water

SINKHOLE
a circular depression formed when the roof of a cave collapses

WETLAND
an area of land covered by shallow water

RIVER
a natural flow of water that runs through the land

LAKE
an inland body of water

FOREST
an area of densely wooded land

COAST
an area of land near the ocean

MOUNTAIN
an area of rugged land that generally rises higher than 2,000 feet

VALLEY
an area of low land between hills or mountains

VOLCANO
an opening in Earth's crust where lava, ash, and gases erupt

CANYON
a deep, narrow valley with steep walls

GLACIER
a large area of slow-moving ice

HILL
a rounded, elevated area of land smaller than a mountain

PLAIN
a nearly flat area

DUNE
a hill of sand shaped by wind

OASIS
an area in the desert with a water source

DESERT
an extremely dry area with little water and few plants

PLATEAU
a large, flat, elevated area of land

The Five Themes of Geography

Geography is the study of the world's people and places. As you can imagine, studying the entire world is a big job. To make the job easier, geographers have created the Five Themes of Geography. They are: **Location, Place, Human-Environment Interaction, Movement,** and **Region**. You can think of the Five Themes as five windows you can look through to study a place. If you looked at the same place through five different windows, you would have five different perspectives, or viewpoints, of the place. Using the Five Themes in this way will help you better understand the world's people and places.

❶ Location The first thing to study about a place is its location. Where is it? Every place has an absolute location—its exact location on Earth. A place also has a relative location—its location in relation to other places. Use the theme of location to ask questions like, "Where is this place located, and how has its location affected it?"

❷ Place Every place in the world is unique and has its own personality and character. Some things that can make a place unique include its weather, plants and animals, history, and the people that live there. Use the theme of place to ask questions like, "What are the unique features of this place, and how are they important?"

❸ Human-Environment Interaction People interact with their environment in many ways. They use land to grow food and local materials to build houses. At the same time, a place's environment influences how people live. For example, if the weather is cold, people wear warm clothes. Use the theme of human-environment interaction to ask questions like, "What is this place's environment like, and how does it affect the people who live there?"

❹ Movement The world is constantly changing, and places are affected by the movement of people, goods, ideas, and physical forces. For example, people come and go, new businesses begin, and rivers change their course. Use the theme of movement to ask questions like, "How is this place changing, and why?"

❺ Region A region is an area that has one or more features that make it different from surrounding areas. A desert, a country, and a coastal area are all regions. Geographers use regions to break the world into smaller pieces that are easier to study. Use the theme of region to ask questions like "What common features does this area share, and how is it different from other areas?"

1

LOCATION
The United States is located in the Western Hemisphere. Forty-eight of the states are located between Mexico and Canada. This location has good farmland, many resources, and many different natural environments.

Canada

United States

Mexico

PLACE
New York City is one of the most powerful cities in the world. The people of New York also make the city one of the most ethnically diverse places in the world.

HUMAN-ENVIRONMENT INTERACTION
People near Las Vegas, Nevada, transform the desert landscape by building new neighborhoods. Americans modify their environment in many other ways—by controlling rivers, building roads, and creating farmland.

REGION
The United States is a political region with one government. At the same time, smaller regions can be found inside the country, such as the Badlands in South Dakota.

MOVEMENT
People, goods, and ideas are constantly moving to and from places such as Seattle, Washington. As some places grow, others get smaller, but every place is always changing.

How to Make This Book Work for You

Studying U.S. history will be easy for you using this textbook. Take a few minutes to become familiar with the easy-to-use structure and special features of this history book. See how this U.S. history textbook will make history come alive for you!

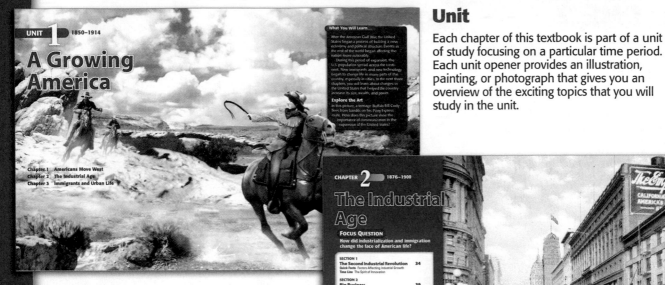

Unit

Each chapter of this textbook is part of a unit of study focusing on a particular time period. Each unit opener provides an illustration, painting, or photograph that gives you an overview of the exciting topics that you will study in the unit.

Chapter

Each chapter begins with a chapter-opener introduction where the sections of the chapter are listed out, and ends with Chapter Review pages and a Standardized Test Practice page.

Reading Social Studies These chapter-level reading lessons teach you skills and provide opportunities for practice to help you read the textbook more successfully. Within each chapter there is a point-of-reference *Focus on Reading* note in the margin to demonstrate the reading skill for the chapter. There are also questions in the Chapter Review activity to make sure that you understand the reading skill.

Social Studies Skills The Social Studies Skills lessons, which appear at the end of each chapter, give you an opportunity to learn and use a skill that you will most likely use again while in school. You will also be given a chance to make sure that you understand each skill by answering related questions in the Chapter Review activity.

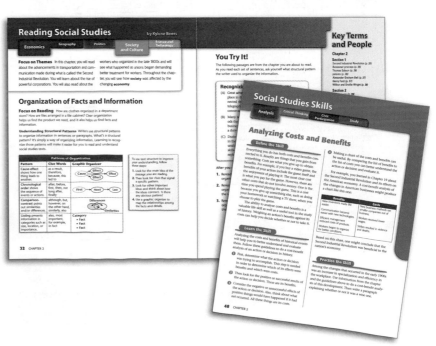

Section

The Section opener pages include: Main Idea statements, an overarching Big Idea statement, and Key Terms and People. In addition, each section includes the following special features.

If You Were There . . . introductions begin each section with a situation for you to respond to, placing you in the time period and in a situation related to the content that you will be studying in the section.

Building Background sections connect what will be covered in this section with what you studied in the previous section.

Short sections of content organize the information in each section into small chunks of text that you should not find too overwhelming.

The **Taking Notes** feature allows you to write down the most important information from the section in a usable format.

Big Business

SECTION 2

If YOU were there...

It is 1895, and your town is home to a large corporation. The company's founder and owner, a wealthy man, lives in a mansion on a hill. He is a fair employer but not especially generous. Many townspeople work in his factory. You and other town leaders feel that he should contribute more to local charities and community organizations.

How could this business leader help the town more?

BUILDING BACKGROUND Advanced technology along with the use of oil and electric power helped American businesses grow. Soon, the shape of the American economy changed. Some companies grew so large that they began to dominate entire industries.

Dominance of Big Business

In the late 1800s many entrepreneurs formed their businesses as **corporations**, or businesses that sell portions of ownership called stock shares. The leaders of these corporations were some of the most widely respected members of American society in the late 1800s. Political leaders praised prosperous businesspeople as examples of American hard work, talent, and success.

New sales techniques like those taught by John H. Patterson helped change business practices.

What You Will Learn...

Main Ideas

1. The rise of corporations and powerful business leaders led to the dominance of big business in the United States.
2. People and the government began to question the methods of big business.

The Big Idea

The growth of big business in the late 1800s led to the creation of monopolies.

Key Terms and People

corporations, p. 39
Andrew Carnegie, p. 40
vertical integration, p. 40
John D. Rockefeller, p. 40
horizontal integration, p. 41
trust, p. 41
Leland Stanford, p. 41
social Darwinism, p. 41
monopoly, p. 42
Sherman Antitrust Act, p. 42

TAKING NOTES As you read this section, take notes on the new business practices you learn about. Keep them organized in a chart like the one below.

New Business Practice

THE INDUSTRIAL AGE **39**

Hoover Elected

With the economy booming, public support for the Republican Party remained strong. When President Coolidge decided not to run for reelection in 1928, the party chose his secretary of commerce, **Herbert Hoover**, as its nominee. Hoover had gained national attention during World War I as head of the U.S. Food Administration. He organized the nation's food supply so more food could be sent to soldiers overseas. After the war, he headed the American Relief Administration, which sent food and supplies to the war-torn countries of Europe. The Democrats nominated New York governor Alfred E. Smith.

Hoover told voters that he was the right choice to maintain economic prosperity. Hoover boldly claimed that "we in America today are nearer to the final triumph over poverty than ever before in the history of any land."

Smith's campaign focused mainly on issues facing city dwellers. This concerned some rural voters. Smith's religious faith also became an issue. He was the first Catholic to run for president. His opponents stirred up fears that

FOR PRESIDENT HOOVER

...defeated Democrat Alfred E. Smith in the 1928 presidential election.

Smith would be controlled by the pope and other church officials. In the end, Hoover won easily, gaining 58 percent of the popular vote.

READING CHECK Drawing Conclusions What helped Herbert Hoover win the presidency in 1928?

SUMMARY AND PREVIEW In this section you learned about politics and the economy in the 1920s. In the next section you will learn more about how society changed during the decade.

FOCUS ON NEW YORK CITY
After losing to Herbert Hoover in the 1928 presidential election, Al Smith became the president of Empire State, Inc., which built and operated the Empire State Building in New York City. Smith was also involved with the 1934 modernization of the Central Park Zoo.

Section 1 Assessment

Reviewing Ideas, Terms, and People

1. **a. Describe** What was the result of the 1920 presidential election, and why?
   b. Summarize What did the **Teapot Dome scandal** reveal about **Warren G. Harding**'s administration?
2. **a. Identify** Who succeeded Harding as president, and what were his main policies?
   b. Analyze What was the main weakness of the **Kellogg-Briand Pact**?
3. **a. Recall** Why did American businesses grow during the 1920s?
   b. Explain Why were Model T prices low?
4. **a. Recall** Why was **Herbert Hoover** elected?
   b. Elaborate Who would you have voted for in the 1928 election? Explain your answer.

Critical Thinking

5. **Summarizing** Review your notes on the presidents from the 1920s. Then copy the

graphic organizer below and expand on your notes by summarizing the main ideas or achievements of each president.

President	Ideas/Achievements

FOCUS ON WRITING

6. **Taking Notes on Consumer Goods** Make a list of new products people had access to in this decade, including cheaper automobiles and appliances for the home. Be sure to note how these products improved the lives of Americans. Use the information about advertising in this section to help you with ideas for your radio advertisement.

THE ROARING TWENTIES **177**

Focus on New York City features highlight events in New York City history, while **Focus on New York** features offer additional information about New York state history.

Reading Check questions end each section of content so that you can test whether or not you understand what you have just studied.

Summary and Preview statements connect what you have just studied in the section to what you will study in the next section.

Section Assessment boxes provide an opportunity for you to make sure that you understand the main ideas of the section. We also provide assessment practice online!

A Review of New York History

BUILDING BACKGROUND The first settlers in the Americas came in small groups from Asia over the course of thousands of years. These people spread to the farthest points of North and South America, forming communities along the way. Many similarities and differences arose between Native American groups in different regions of the continents, including what is today New York State.

New York Harbor in 1850

Early New York

Reading Focus *As you read, think about what life might have been like for a colonial New Yorker.*

Archaeologists believe that people began living in what is now New York about 10,000 years ago. By about A.D. 1200, two major Native American cultures had developed in this region—the Algonquin and the Iroquois. Algonquin groups built villages near the Atlantic coast and along the rivers and streams of southern New York. Iroquois groups lived mainly in central and western New York. Both Algonquin and Iroquois groups made use of the natural resources of the Eastern Woodlands. Wood was used to build canoes and tools, and areas of forest land were cleared to plant corn and other crops.

In about 1570, five Iroquois nations—the Seneca, Cayuga, Onondaga, Oneida, and Mohawk—joined to form a powerful alliance that became known as the Iroquois Confederacy. Representatives from the five met often to select leaders, resolve disputes, and decide on policies. The Iroquois Confederacy remained an influential force in the region well into the 1700s.

Colonial New York

Italian explorer Giovanni da Verrazano sailed into what is now New York Harbor in 1524, becoming the first European to see New York. In 1609 Henry Hudson, sailing for the Dutch, explored the river that was soon named for him. Hudson's explorations led the Dutch government to claim New York. The Dutch named their colony New Netherland.

The Dutch and English

Dutch traders were attracted to New Netherland by the abundance of valuable resources, especially fur. In 1624 the Dutch established Fort Orange,

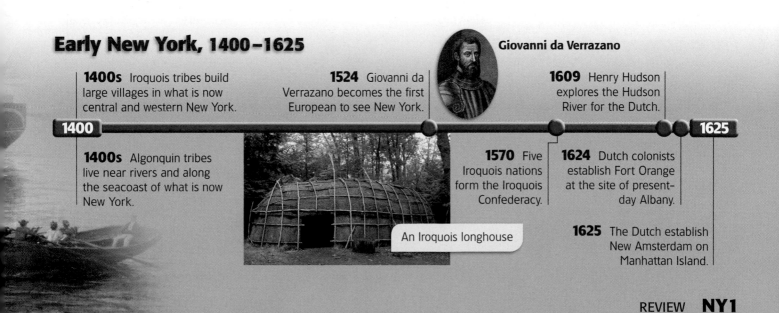

Early New York, 1400–1625

Giovanni da Verrazano

1400s Iroquois tribes build large villages in what is now central and western New York.

1524 Giovanni da Verrazano becomes the first European to see New York.

1609 Henry Hudson explores the Hudson River for the Dutch.

1400

1625

1400s Algonquin tribes live near rivers and along the seacoast of what is now New York.

1570 Five Iroquois nations form the Iroquois Confederacy.

1624 Dutch colonists establish Fort Orange at the site of present-day Albany.

An Iroquois longhouse

1625 The Dutch establish New Amsterdam on Manhattan Island.

KEY FACTS

- **1625** Dutch New Amsterdam is established on Manhattan.
- **1664** New Amsterdam is renamed New York by the English.
- **1763** The French and Indian War breaks out.
- **1776** The thirteen American colonies declare independence.

a fur-trading post on the Hudson River. The following year, Dutch settlers established New Amsterdam at the southern end of the island of Manhattan. From its earliest days, New Amsterdam was home to a diverse mix of cultures—a visitor in the 1640s reported hearing 18 different languages in the growing city. Outside of the towns, huge tracts of fertile land were granted to wealthy landowners called patrons. Patrons then rented sections of their land to farmers.

Eager to build an empire of its own, England conquered New Netherland in 1664, renaming the colony New York. The city of New Amsterdam became New York City, and Fort Orange was renamed Albany.

Native Americans and Colonists

By 1700 a diverse mix of about 20,000 European settlers lived in the New York colony. In some ways, these colonists were similar to the Native Americans who also lived in New York. Cultural traditions and family ties were very important in both societies. Both developed systems of organizing communities and choosing leaders. Both worked to be as self-sufficient as possible.

Differences between Native Americans and colonists included the social roles of men and women in each community. Iroquois women had more influence than most women in colonial societies. In addition, in Iroquois communities, women could select and remove tribal leaders and also did much of the farming.

Native Americans and colonists spoke different languages and often addressed each other by different names. Dutch settlers, for example, named Algonquian groups according to nearby geographic features. That explains how the Lenape people, who lived along the Delaware River, became known to Europeans as the Delaware. "Iroquois" was also a name used by Europeans. The Iroquois referred to themselves as Haudenosaunee, meaning "people of the longhouse."

From Colony to State, 1625–1800

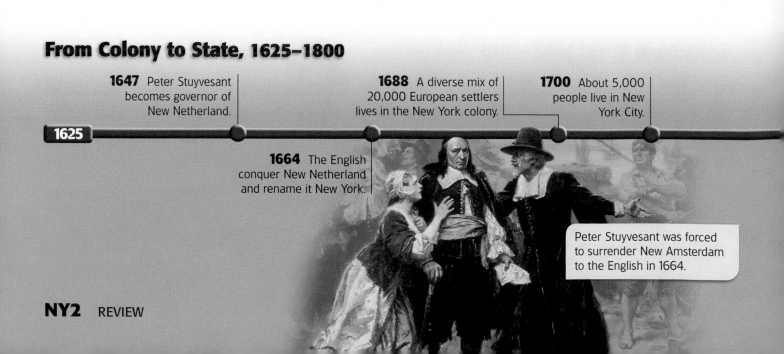

1647 Peter Stuyvesant becomes governor of New Netherland.

1688 A diverse mix of 20,000 European settlers lives in the New York colony.

1700 About 5,000 people live in New York City.

1625

1664 The English conquer New Netherland and rename it New York.

Peter Stuyvesant was forced to surrender New Amsterdam to the English in 1664.

From Colony to State

New York continued to grow under British rule, with industries such as farming and shipbuilding gaining importance. By 1733 New York was one of 13 British colonies along the east coast of what is now the United States.

Declaring Independence

In the 1760s, Britain decided to raise the tax on American colonists. New Yorkers joined the protests that soon led to the American Revolution.

The Revolution created challenges for the new states. New Yorkers had to organize a new state government, recruit soldiers, help finance the war effort, and deal with issues such as slavery. Citizens were divided over these important issues, as well as over support for the war. New York City, captured by the British in 1776, became a refuge for Loyalists. In other parts of the state, Loyalists were attacked or had their property confiscated.

New York and the Revolution

New York State witnessed many important battles during the war. In 1775 Patriots seized Fort Ticonderoga, capturing badly needed cannons for the Continental Army. The British invasion of New York in 1777 ended with an American victory at Saratoga—a victory that became known as the "turning point" of the war. New York also saw fierce fighting between Patriots and Iroquois groups, several of which sided with Britain. The war destroyed the power of the Iroquois Confederacy in New York.

When the war finally ended in 1783, George Washington and his officers held a farewell ceremony at Fraunces Tavern in New York City. Many Loyalists fled to Canada. This migration changed the balance between British and French settlers in Canada, resulting in a strengthening of ties to Great Britain.

Participation in the struggle for independence changed the way New Yorkers thought about government. Many now expected to become active citizens in their government. Republican ideals, which emphasized the sharing of power, began to influence politics in the new state.

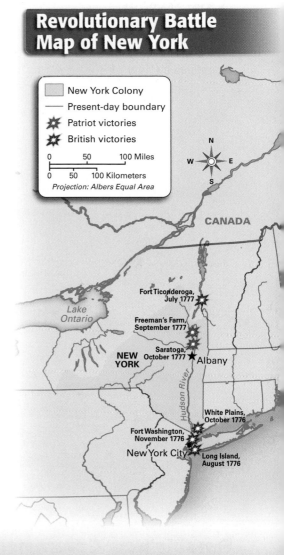

Revolutionary Battle Map of New York

New York Colony
Present-day boundary
Patriot victories
British victories

0   50   100 Miles
0   50   100 Kilometers
Projection: Albers Equal Area

CANADA

Lake Ontario

Fort Ticonderoga, July 1777

Freeman's Farm, September 1777

NEW YORK

Saratoga, October 1777   Albany

Hudson River

White Plains, October 1776

Fort Washington, November 1776

New York City   Long Island, August 1776

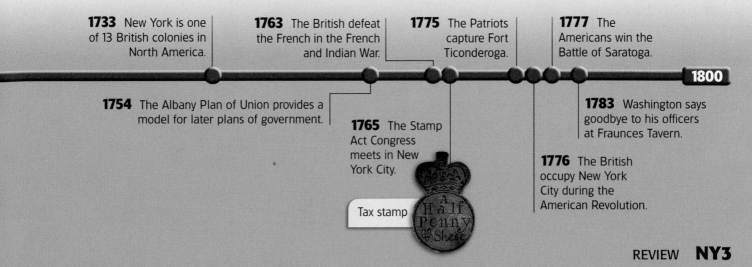

1733 New York is one of 13 British colonies in North America.

1754 The Albany Plan of Union provides a model for later plans of government.

1763 The British defeat the French in the French and Indian War.

1765 The Stamp Act Congress meets in New York City.

1775 The Patriots capture Fort Ticonderoga.

1776 The British occupy New York City during the American Revolution.

1777 The Americans win the Battle of Saratoga.

1783 Washington says goodbye to his officers at Fraunces Tavern.

1800

Tax stamp

KEY FACTS

- **1777** New York's first state constitution is written.
- **1786** The Annapolis Convention takes place.
- **1788** The Poughkeepsie Convention is held.
- **1788** The U.S. Constitution is ratified by New York.

Forming New Governments

Twenty years before the Revolution, New Yorkers were involved in an early attempt to organize a government with other colonies. This happened in Albany in 1754, when leaders from several colonies met and drafted the Albany Plan of Union. The Albany Plan called for the 13 colonies to work closely together in a central government. Though the plan was not adopted, its ideas would influence later attempts to form a national government.

After declaring independence in July 1776, New Yorkers began work on a state constitution. Led by John Jay, Robert Livingston, and Gouverneur Morris, New York leaders completed drafting a New York constitution in 1777. The constitution, which included the text of the Declaration of Independence, was approved by representatives at the constitutional convention in Kingston, New York. It was not submitted to a popular vote. The constitution set up a government that was similar to New York's colonial government, with several important changes.

The plan of government was based on the principle of majority rule, with protections for the rights and liberties of the minority. A governor with limited authority served a three-year term. New York's legislature had two houses: the Senate and the Assembly. Senators served four-year terms, while Assembly members served a one-year term. New York's first system of state courts was also established by the constitution. The right to vote for elected leaders was limited to men who owned property. New York's new constitution was in effect from 1777 to 1822.

New York's early state government functioned fairly well—more smoothly, in fact, than the national government under the Articles of Confederation. For this reason, the New York constitution became a model for the new national plan of government.

Forming New Governments, 1750–1800

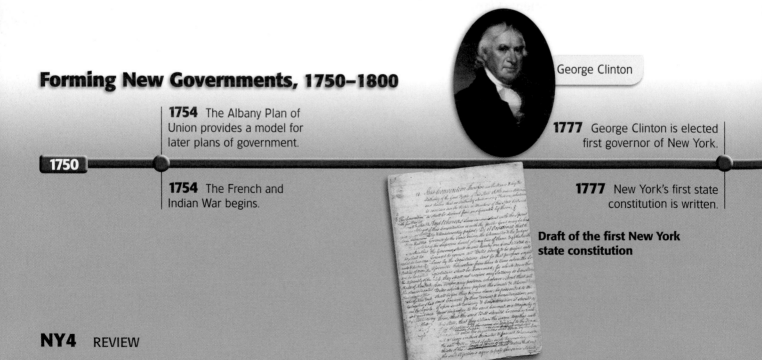

1754 The Albany Plan of Union provides a model for later plans of government.

1754 The French and Indian War begins.

George Clinton

1777 George Clinton is elected first governor of New York.

1777 New York's first state constitution is written.

Draft of the first New York state constitution

New York and the U.S. Constitution

The national government under the Articles of Confederation was clearly unable to solve the young country's problems. In 1786 Alexander Hamilton represented New York at the Annapolis Convention in Annapolis, Maryland. Hamilton and leaders from other states discussed ways to improve the effectiveness of the national government while maintaining key elements of the new philosophy of self-rule. This meeting led to the Constitutional Convention the following year in Philadelphia. Hamilton influenced the debate in Philadelphia with his ideas for a powerful national government. The United States Constitution was completed and signed by delegates in September 1787.

Each state now had to decide whether or not to ratify the new Constitution. This sparked heated debate between Federalists, who supported the Constitution, and Antifederalists, who worried that it gave the federal government too much power. New York governor George Clinton was an outspoken Antifederalist, and it looked as if the Constitution would be rejected by this important state. To try to prevent this, Alexander Hamilton and John Jay joined James Madison of Virginia to write the *Federalist Papers*, a series of articles arguing in favor of ratification. First published in New York City newspapers, the *Federalist Papers* greatly influenced the debate in New York and other states.

New York's ratification convention was held in Poughkeepsie in June 1788. The delegates approved the Constitution in a close vote of 30 to 27. Several Antifederalists voted for ratification based on the promise that a bill of rights would be added to Constitution.

New York City served as the first national capital under the new constitution. George Washington traveled to New York City and was sworn in as the nation's first president on April 30, 1789. Washington chose Alexander Hamilton for the key position of secretary of the treasury.

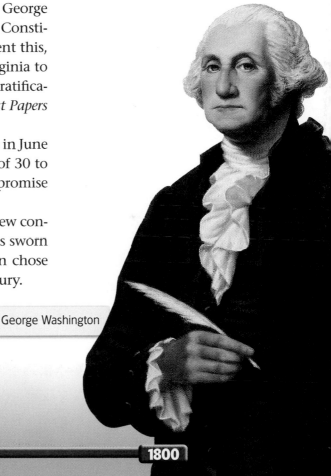

George Washington

1789 George Washington is sworn in as president in New York City.

1789 Alexander Hamilton becomes the nation's first secretary of the treasury.

1800

1786 New York leaders attend the Annapolis Convention.

1787–1788 Alexander Hamilton and John Jay help write the *Federalist Papers*.

The *Federalist Papers*

1788 Delegates to the Poughkeepsie Convention discuss New York's ratification of the Constitution.

1788 New York becomes the eleventh state to ratify the Constitution.

The Empire State

KEY FACTS

- **1807** The *Clermont* makes its first voyage.
- **1825** The Erie Canal is completed.
- **1831** New York's first railroad between Albany and Schenectady opens.

Reading Focus *As you read, notice how life changed for New Yorkers during the early and mid-1800s.*

At the time of the American Revolution, New York ranked just seventh in population among the original 13 states. This changed quickly after independence, as New York experienced explosive growth. By 1810 New York had the largest population in the nation and was among the leaders in manufacturing, transportation, and trade. In the early 1800s, people began referring to New York by a new nickname: "the Empire State." The name comes from a quotation by George Washington, who called New York State "the seat of empire." Washington hoped the young nation would prosper as New York had done.

Transportation and Manufacturing

The Transportation Revolution of the 1800s was a major factor in New York's rapid rise. In 1807 Robert Fulton successfully tested his steamboat *Clermont* on the Hudson River. In 1825 the 363-mile Erie Canal was completed, connecting Buffalo, on Lake Erie, with Albany, on the Hudson River. The Erie Canal greatly lowered the cost of transporting goods from the Midwest to the East. Cities along the canal boomed, and New York City became the busiest port in the country. By 1850 a growing network of railroads replaced canals in importance. As canals had done, railroads lowered the cost of moving large quantities of goods between New York and other parts of the country.

Robert Fulton's *Clermont*

The Empire State, 1785–1835

1785

1807 Robert Fulton's steamboat *Clermont* makes its first voyage.

1810 New York City is the biggest city in the United States.

1810 New York State has the largest population of any state.

New York City in 1810

Improvements in transportation helped farmers earn more money—money they wanted to spend on manufactured goods. New York cities became major manufacturing centers as the Industrial Revolution changed life in the United States. By 1860, for example, nearly half of the nation's clothing was being manufactured in New York City.

A Wave of Immigration

The rapid growth of American industry attracted millions of immigrants to the United States in the mid-1800s. Economic and political troubles in Germany and a devastating potato famine in Ireland contributed to this large wave of immigration. Most of these immigrants entered the United States at the port of New York City. Many then used the Erie Canal or New York railroads to travel west in search of farmland or factory jobs. Many also settled in New York City. In fact, New York City was not only the nation's largest city—it was also home to the nation's largest population of immigrants. By 1860, 48 percent of New York City's 1 million residents were foreign born.

This large wave of immigration led to tensions in New York, as in other states. The majority of New York's immigrants, especially those form Ireland, were Catholic. Prejudice toward Catholics sparked anti-immigrant feelings in some New Yorkers. Others worried they might lose their jobs to immigrants who would work for lower wages. Opponents of immigration were known as nativists. Nativists formed an organization known as the Know-Nothing Party, which briefly gained influence in New York politics in the 1850s.

Lockport, on the Erie Canal

Nineteenth century locomotive

1825 The Erie Canal opens.

1827 Sojourner Truth escapes from slavery to a New York farm.

1827 Slavery ends in New York State.

1831 New York's first railroad connects Albany and Schenectady.

1835

Sojourner Truth

KEY FACTS

- **1827** Slavery is abolished in New York.
- **1848** The Seneca Falls Convention is held.

Reform Movements

Like many states, New York saw an expansion of voting rights during the Age of Jackson. New York leaders revised the state constitution in 1822, changing the old law that only property owners could vote. All white men who paid taxes were granted the right to vote. Black men, however, were still required to own property in order to vote.

As more New Yorkers became actively involved in the democratic process, many began participating in reform movements. A Protestant religious revival known as the Second Great Awakening inspired reformers in New York. Revivals in central and western New York were so intense, this region became known as the "Burned-Over District" because of the heated sermons given. Inspired by the Second Great Awakening, many New Yorkers worked to solve social problems in the United States.

Abolition Movement

In 1799 New York passed a law calling for the gradual abolition of slavery in the state. Slavery was finally ended once and for all in 1827. Many New Yorkers, both black and white, were active in the movement to abolish slavery everywhere in the United States. Abolitionist Frederick Douglass moved to Rochester, New York, where he began publishing the *North Star*, an abolitionist newspaper. Harriet Tubman, who escorted hundreds of slaves to freedom on the Underground Railroad, also moved to New York. Several important Underground Railroad routes passed through New York and continued into Canada.

Women's Rights

New Yorker Elizabeth Cady Stanton organized the nation's first women's rights convention, which was held in Seneca Falls, New York, in 1848. The Seneca Falls Convention launched the women's rights movement. Stanton, along with Susan B. Anthony and other New York activists, helped lead a national campaign for women's property rights and voting rights.

Reform Movements and the Civil War, 1820–1860

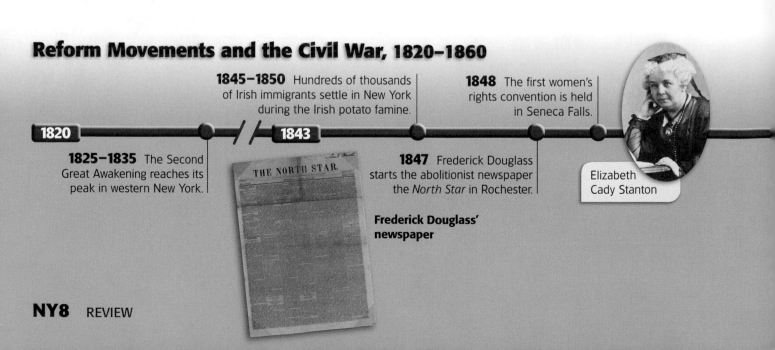

1845–1850 Hundreds of thousands of Irish immigrants settle in New York during the Irish potato famine.

1848 The first women's rights convention is held in Seneca Falls.

1820

1843

1825–1835 The Second Great Awakening reaches its peak in western New York.

THE NORTH STAR.

Frederick Douglass' newspaper

1847 Frederick Douglass starts the abolitionist newspaper the *North Star* in Rochester.

Elizabeth Cady Stanton

Civil War and Reconstruction

Reading Focus *As you read, explore how the Civil War affected New York state and New York City.*

In the presidential election of 1860, New York voted for Abraham Lincoln, a Republican who opposed the expansion of slavery. The state's 35 electoral votes helped Lincoln win the presidency without receiving a single electoral vote from the South. Seven southern states, protesting his election, quickly seceded from the Union and formed the Confederate States of America. In April 1861 Confederate forces launched an attack on Union troops at Fort Sumter in South Carolina, starting the Civil War. Four more Southern states soon seceded and joined the Confederacy.

New York and the Civil War

Some New Yorkers had economic and political ties to the South, and a large part of New York City's economy relied on the port there and its shipments of Southern cotton to Europe. There was therefore some support for the South in the city. The mayor of New York City even expressed a desire to secede from the Union. With the firing on Fort Sumter, however, support for the Union surged. New Yorkers immediately answered Lincoln's call for troops, and a large pro-Union rally was held at Union Square in New York City. Eventually the state would send more troops, more supplies, and more food than any other state in the nation, north or south. New York sent 500,000 soldiers to the Civil War, and more than 4,000 of these were African Americans. Its soldiers also suffered more casualties than any other state. New York factories contributed to the Union victory by producing war supplies. The Union's

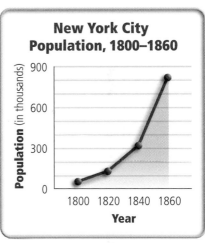

New York City Population, 1800–1860

The population of New York City rose dramatically during the first half of the nineteenth century.

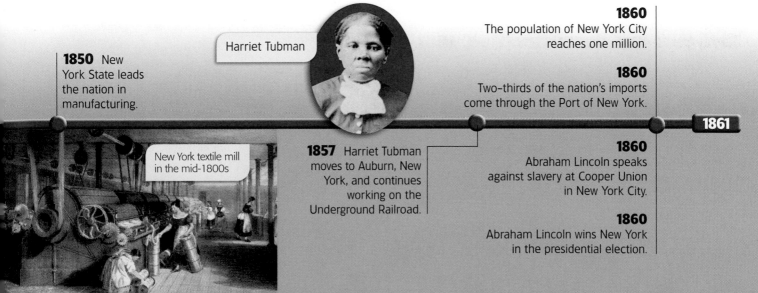

1850 New York State leads the nation in manufacturing.

New York textile mill in the mid-1800s

Harriet Tubman

1857 Harriet Tubman moves to Auburn, New York, and continues working on the Underground Railroad.

1860 The population of New York City reaches one million.

1860 Two-thirds of the nation's imports come through the Port of New York.

1860 Abraham Lincoln speaks against slavery at Cooper Union in New York City.

1860 Abraham Lincoln wins New York in the presidential election.

1861

KEY FACTS

- **1861** The Civil War begins.
- **1863** Draft riots take place in New York City.

best known ironclad warship, the USS *Monitor*, was built in a Brooklyn shipyard.

Although no Civil War battles were fought in New York, the war did bring violent conflict to the state. In July 1863, just days after the Battle of Gettysburg, a massive riot broke out in New York City. The direct cause of the riot was the federal government's plan to draft soldiers into the Union army. The plan allowed wealthy citizens to avoid the draft by paying $300 to buy a substitute. Many poor, recent Irish immigrants could not afford the $300 and thought that free African Americans would take the jobs that immigrants wanted. During the public announcement of draftees, people began to violently attack government offices and African American workers and businesses. In five days of rioting, more than 100 people were killed and at least $1 million in damages occurred, including the arson of an African American church and orphanage. The violence finally came to an end when troops were recalled from Gettysburg and dispersed the rioters.

Though New York was too far distant from the South to be invaded by Confederate troops, more than 12,000 captured Confederate soldiers were held in a prisoner of war camp in Elmira, New York. Prisoners were sent to Elmira from other overcrowded camps, but their situations did not improve. Conditions at the camp were largely unsanitary, and much-needed supplies rarely arrived, despite the efforts of the camp's commander. Due to overcrowding and disease, about one-fourth of the prisoners in Elmira died.

Despite the support that most New Yorkers showed for the Union, some continued to sympathize with the cause of the South. As in other Northern states, they were called Copperheads. In 1864 several Copperheads, along with Confederate agents, planned revolts in several Northern cities including New York City. On Election Day, the Confederate agents started fires in more than a dozen important New York buildings. The fires were extinguished by city authorities, and the agents fled to Canada.

Civil War and Reconstruction, 1861–1877

1861 The Civil War begins.

1864 A prisoner camp for captured Confederate soldiers opens at Elmira.

1865 President Lincoln is assassinated. He will lie in state in Washington and New York City before being buried in Illinois.

1861

1861 The 79th New York Cameron Highlanders Regiment mutinied against a new commander.

1863 Draft riots break out in New York City.

The New York City draft riot

1868 The Fourteenth Amendment guarantees all citizens equal protection of the law.

New York in the Era of Reconstruction

Once the war was over, Americans began the process of rebuilding the nation. Republican political leaders at both state and national levels tried to pass legislation that would allow African Americans equal political and economic opportunities, and they sometimes succeeded. More often, however, laws attempting to bring equality to African Americans were thwarted by opposing politicians. In New York, a Republican-led state legislature ratified the Fifteenth Amendment in 1869, granting black men the right to vote. But the next legislature that was elected, made up of a majority of Democrats, reversed this decision. The amendment went into effect anyway when enough other states approved it. Despite the new law, black New Yorkers were subjected to racial discrimination in social, economic, and political arenas.

The political life of New York City during this period was dominated by the Democratic political machine known as Tammany Hall. Tammany Hall leaders appealed to the large population of Irish immigrants in the city. Tammany Hall offered jobs and security to recent immigrants who had few opportunities, but it was not above using prejudice against African Americans or stealing from the city. From 1863 until his conviction in 1873, Tammany Hall was led by William Marcy Tweed. Although the city began large public works projects, such as parks and sewers during Tweed's reign, Tammany Hall politicians used these projects to hide their theft of millions of dollars from the city. Tweed was eventually caught and sent to jail, but the political machine continued to dominate city politics for another 60 years.

In New York City, industries that had benefited from the Civil War, such as banking and clothing manufacture, were able to expand even further. The city is still the most important center for these industries in the United States today. The war and its aftermath also strengthened the city's economic ties with the growing Midwest, as the region's farm products and manufactured goods increasingly flowed through New York City to the rest of the world.

Campaign banner for Samuel J. Tilden

January, 1870 New York reverses its ratification of the Fifteenth Amendment.

March, 1870 New York again ratifies the Fifteenth Amendment

1869 New York ratifies the Fifteenth Amendment.

1869 The Transcontinental Railroad is completed.

1877

1876 New Yorker Samuel J. Tilden is defeated in the disputed presidential election.

The Transcontinental Railroad

Industrial and Urban Growth

Reading Focus *As you read, draw conclusions about the changes that took place in New York during the late 1800s and early 1900s.*

KEY FACTS

- **1882** The first electric power station opens in Manhattan.
- **1886** The Statue of Liberty opens.
- **1892** Ellis Island opens.

The rise of corrupt political machines was a serious problem throughout New York in the years following the Civil War. Reformers, including lawyer Samuel J. Tilden, worked to fight political corruption. Known as an effective reformer, Tilden was elected governor of New York in 1874 and was chosen to be the Democratic candidate for president in 1876. Tilden faced Republican Rutherford B. Hayes in one of the most intensely disputed presidential elections in U.S. history. Though Tilden won the popular vote, the electoral vote was contested in several states. After weeks of bitter debate, Hayes was declared the winner.

New York Industry

New York's economy continued to grow in the second half of the 1800s. One major development was the increasing importance of the New York Stock Exchange, based on Wall Street in Manhattan. By selling shares on Wall Street, companies raised money to expand their businesses. New York City became the financial capital of the country, a position it still holds today.

New York entrepreneurs made key contributions to the nation's rapid industrial expansion. Cornelius Vanderbilt bought several railroad companies, consolidating them in an efficient network that made train travel faster and easier. George Eastman began selling Kodak cameras in 1888, making photography widely accessible. John D. Rockefeller built Standard Oil into a massive company that controlled 90 percent of the country's oil refining business by 1880. While the state's industries boomed, local farmers were

Industrial and Urban Growth, 1870–1920

John D. Rockefeller

1876 Samuel J. Tilden is defeated in the disputed presidential election.

1885 John D. Rockefeller opens his new Standard Oil headquarters in New York City.

1888 George Eastman begins selling Kodak cameras.

1870

1882 Thomas Edison opens the nation's first electric power station in downtown Manhattan.

Thomas Edison's Manhattan power station

1886 The Statue of Liberty opens to the public.

The Statue of Liberty

unable to compete with the huge wheat and corn farms of the Midwest. Some New York farmers responded by diversifying their crops, producing dairy products, fruits, and vegetables.

New Immigrants

The Statue of Liberty, a gift from France, opened to the public in October 1886. This huge copper-covered statue on Liberty Island in New York Harbor became a symbol of American freedom and opportunity—the very things that were attracting millions of immigrants to the United States. For many of these immigrants, the first stop was the Ellis Island immigration station, which opened in 1892.

New Wave of Immigration

From the 1870s to the 1920s, more than 20 million immigrants arrived in this country. These immigrants became known as "new immigrants," to distinguish them from the "old immigrants" who had arrived in the mid-1800s. The new immigrants came largely from Italy, Austria-Hungary, Poland, Russia, and other parts of Eastern and Southern Europe. About 2 million Jews, escaping persecution at home, were part of this massive wave of immigration. Several hundred thousand French Canadians also came, often settling in northern New York and New England.

Arriving with little money, many immigrants crowded into poor urban neighborhoods throughout New York. Buffalo's Italian and Polish communities grew rapidly. New York City's Lower East Side was home to a variety of ethnic neighborhoods. Nearby Chinatown provided a haven for Chinese immigrants, who often faced discrimination in the United States.

Becoming American

Immigrants began the process of Americanization—adjusting to the language, economy, government, and traditions of the United States. While

Madame C. J. Walker

1900 The first electric bus begins running along New York City's Fifth Avenue.

1916 Entrepreneur Madame C. J. Walker moves to New York City.

1920

1892 Ellis Island immigration station opens.

1880s-1920s Millions of immigrants settle in New York.

Immigrants arrive at Ellis Island

KEY FACTS

- **1882** New Yorkers hold the first Labor Day celebration.
- **1883** The Brooklyn Bridge is completed.
- **1901** Theodore Roosevelt is elected president.
- **1905** The Supreme Court hears *Lochner* v. *New York*.
- **1911** Fire breaks out at the Triangle Shirtwaist factory.
- **1917** New York women gain suffrage.

adapting to American life, immigrants also influenced their new country with their own cultures and traditions. The process of change that takes place when one culture comes in contact with another is known as acculturation.

City Life

By the year 1900, the population of New York State topped 7 million. More than half of the state's population lived in just four cities: New York City, Buffalo, Rochester, and Syracuse. New York's urban areas offered both exciting opportunities and serious challenges.

Urban Attractions

New York City was home to more than 3 million people in 1900, making it twice as big as the next-largest American city, Chicago. As the city grew, new types of construction helped improve city life. Skyscrapers, for example, made efficient use of crowded city streets. The Flatiron Building, opened in 1902, was one of the city's first skyscrapers. One of the innovations that made skyscrapers possible was the safety elevator, invented by Elisha Graves Otis in his Yonkers workshop. Another development that changed city life was the opening of the New York City subway in 1904. Subway lines eased crowding in lower Manhattan neighborhoods by allowing families to move farther from their jobs.

Urban Problems

One major problem facing New York was the continuing influence of corrupt political machines. New York City's Tammany Hall, led by Boss Tweed, used payoffs and bribes to influence both city and state government. Unhealthy living conditions in many urban neighborhoods presented another major challenge. Overcrowding, poor sanitation, disease, and crime were all common in areas like New York City's Lower East Side.

New Yorker Theodore Roosevelt

City Life and Reform, 1880–1920

1882 New York workers hold the nation's first Labor Day celebration.

1890 Jacob Riis publishes *How the Other Half Lives*, describing terrible living conditions in New York City tenements.

1901 Theodore Roosevelt becomes president.

1880

1883 Construction of the Brooklyn Bridge is completed.

1902 The Flatiron Building becomes one of New York City's first skyscrapers.

Brooklyn Bridge

Progressive Reforms

A group of investigative reporters known as muckrakers wrote about political corruption, unhealthy living conditions, and other problems facing American society. By describing these issues to the public, muckrakers hoped to inspire change. In 1904, for example, New York City–based *McClure's Magazine* published Ida Tarbell's description of the unfair business practices of Rockefeller's Standard Oil Company.

Progressives

A reform movement known as the Progressive Movement began addressing many of these problems in the late 1800s and early 1900s. One of New York's leading Progressives was Theodore Roosevelt, who served as New York City police commissioner and state governor before serving as president from 1901 to 1909.

Progressives in New York government helped pass the Tenement House Act of 1901, which required tenements to have better plumbing and ventilation. New York State also took the lead in passing labor laws, including a law limiting bakers to a 10-hour workday. This law was challenged in the case *Lochner* v. *New York*, in which the Supreme Court overturned New York's labor law.

Labor and Suffrage

New York was also at the center of the labor and women's suffrage movements. New York workers established the holiday that became Labor Day when they held a huge parade in September 1882. In 1886 Samuel Gompers, a union leader at a New York City cigar factory, helped found the American Federation of Labor. Meanwhile, a new generation of suffrage activists continued the work of Elizabeth Cady Stanton and Susan B. Anthony, holding rallies around the state. Women gained the right to vote in New York in 1917. Three years later, the Nineteenth Amendment became law, granting the vote to all American women.

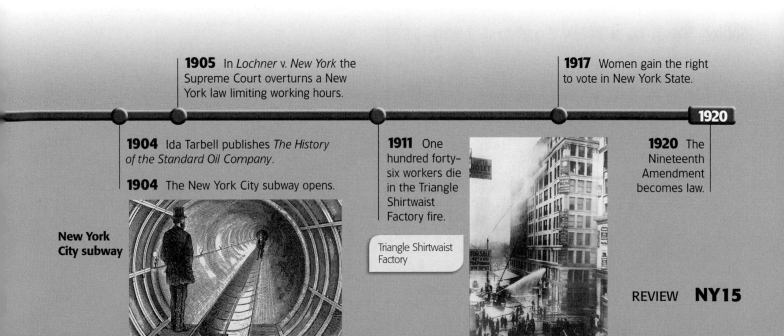

1905 In *Lochner* v. *New York* the Supreme Court overturns a New York law limiting working hours.

1917 Women gain the right to vote in New York State.

1904 Ida Tarbell publishes *The History of the Standard Oil Company*.

1904 The New York City subway opens.

1911 One hundred forty-six workers die in the Triangle Shirtwaist Factory fire.

1920 The Nineteenth Amendment becomes law.

1920

New York City subway

Triangle Shirtwaist Factory

New York and the Modern World

KEY FACTS

- **1929** The stock market crashes.
- **1932** Franklin Roosevelt is elected president.
- **1941** The Japanese bomb Pearl Harbor.
- **1942** The Manhattan Project begins.

Reading Focus *As you read, notice how history has affected the lives of modern New Yorkers.*

New York played a central role in the cultural life of the United States in the early 1900s. Babe Ruth, who began playing for the New York Yankees in 1920, helped make baseball a nationally popular sport. Lillian and Dorothy Gish and Rudolph Valentino were among the many movie stars who got their start in New York theaters.

Literature and Music

In the 1800s New York was home to some of the nation's most accomplished writers, including Washington Irving, Herman Melville, and Walt Whitman. In the early 1900s, Edith Wharton helped continue this tradition of great literature. Though she grew up in a time when women were discouraged from becoming serious writers, Wharton wrote dozens of successful short stories and novels—and in 1921 became the first woman to win the Pulitzer Prize for fiction.

Great literature was also being produced in New York City's Harlem, the largest African American neighborhood in the country. In the 1920s poet Langston Hughes was part of the creative movement known as the Harlem Renaissance. More than just a literary movement, the Harlem Renaissance witnessed a celebration of African American culture. The brilliant jazz composer and band leader Duke Ellington also moved to New York in the 1920s. People packed into New York City clubs to hear the exciting and innovative music that give this decade the nickname the Jazz Age.

New York in a New Century, 1920–1950

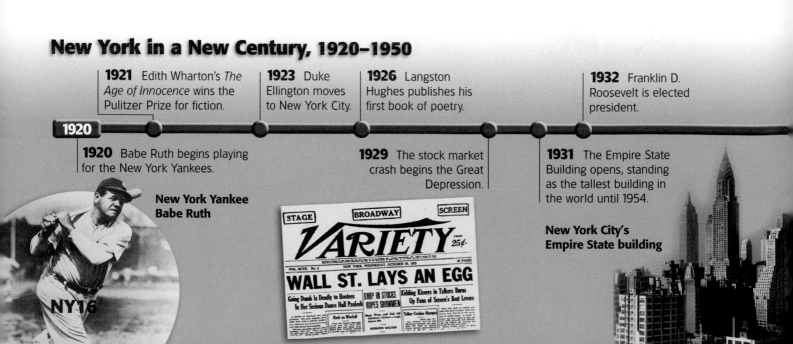

1921 Edith Wharton's *The Age of Innocence* wins the Pulitzer Prize for fiction.

1923 Duke Ellington moves to New York City.

1926 Langston Hughes publishes his first book of poetry.

1932 Franklin D. Roosevelt is elected president.

1920

1920 Babe Ruth begins playing for the New York Yankees.

1929 The stock market crash begins the Great Depression.

1931 The Empire State Building opens, standing as the tallest building in the world until 1954.

New York Yankee Babe Ruth

New York City's Empire State building

STAGE BROADWAY SCREEN
VARIETY PRICE 25¢.
WALL ST. LAYS AN EGG

The Great Depression and the New Deal

During the boom years of the 1920s, people and business from all over the country invested heavily in the stock market. Americans dreamed of making a quick fortune on Wall Street. When the stock market crashed in 1929, the entire national economy crashed with it. Franklin D. Roosevelt was governor of New York during the start of the Great Depression. Roosevelt developed state government programs designed to help people through the hard times. These programs gained national attention, helping Roosevelt win the presidential election of 1932. As president, Roosevelt expanded the ideas he had tried in New York into the New Deal, a broad series of programs designed to battle the Great Depression.

World War II

Another of President Roosevelt's policy goals was to improve U.S. relations with Latin American countries. As part of what he called the Good Neighbor policy, Roosevelt announced that the United States would intervene less frequently in Latin American affairs.

Roosevelt's main foreign policy challenge was World War II. As it had done in previous wars, New York contributed more soldiers to the war effort than any other state. New York factories and shipyards pumped out supplies for the Allied armies. Another vital part of the war effort was the Manhattan Project, the American-led program to build an atomic bomb. It was named the Manhattan Project because scientists began working on the effort at Manhattan's Columbia University.

After World War II, world leaders formed the United Nations, which established its headquarters in New York City in 1946. Representing the United States at the UN, Eleanor Roosevelt headed the United Nations Commission on Human Rights. She helped draft the Universal Declaration of Human Rights, which was passed by the UN in 1948.

Atomic bomb

1942-1945 The Manhattan Project produces the world's first atomic bombs.

1946 The United Nations establishes its headquarters in New York City.

1947 Joe DiMaggio of the New York Yankees wins his third American League Most Valuable Player award.

1950

1941 The United States enters World War II.

1946 Eleanor Roosevelt is chosen to lead the UN Commission on Human Rights.

KEY FACTS

- **1947** Major-league baseball is integrated.
- **1969** The Woodstock festival is held.
- **1971** The Pentagon Papers are published.
- **2001** Terrorists destroy the World Trade Center.

Modern Issues and Challenges

The American economy boomed in the years after World War II, and life in New York continued to change. One significant development was the rapid growth of suburbs. Levittown, a 17,000-home suburban community on Long Island, became a model for other suburbs around the country.

Diversity in New York

On April 15, 1947, Jackie Robinson took the field for the Brooklyn Dodgers, ending decades of segregation in major-league baseball. In addition to becoming a Hall of Fame ballplayer, Robinson was as a key figure in the growing African American civil rights movement. Native Americans also struggled for their rights. The Onondaga, Oneida, and other Iroquois nations filed land claims, demanding the return of parts of their traditional lands in New York. Some of these land claims are still unresolved today.

In the 1960s, women who had been calling for equality since the founding of the nation and had won the right to vote in 1920, began a new movement to increase their rights. Many had grown dissatisfied with the expectation that they should be only wives and mothers. Women, like Bronx-born Bella Abzug, became vocal in the fight for equality. In 1970 Abzug ran for the U.S. House of Representatives on a platform of women's rights and peace. She won, becoming one of only 12 women in the House of Representatives.

The Vietnam Era

Bitter debate over the Vietnam War caused deep divisions in American society in the 1960s. Violent protests broke out in New York and in other parts of the nation. In 1968, for example, student protesters occupied several buildings on the campus of Columbia University in New York City. The police used force to remove the protesters. Some 700 students were arrested.

Shirley Chisholm

Modern New York, 1945–today

1947 Jackie Robinson begins playing for the Brooklyn Dodgers, ending segregation in baseball.

1968 Shirley Chisholm becomes the first African American woman elected to the U.S. Congress.

1945

1947 The suburb of Levittown is established on Long Island.

1969 The Woodstock festival is held on a New York farm.

1971 The *New York Times* begins publishing the Pentagon Papers.

Woodstock poster

Some young people protested mainstream American culture by forming a rebellious counterculture. In 1969 more than 300,000 people gathered at the Woodstock Music and Art Fair, held at a Bethel, New York, farm. Woodstock became a lasting symbol of the counterculture's idealistic spirit.

In June 1971, two years after Woodstock, the *New York Times* began publishing the Pentagon Papers. These secret U.S. government documents made it clear that government officials had been misleading the public about the progress of the Vietnam War. The Nixon Administration went to court to block publication of these documents, leading to the Supreme Court case *New York Times* v. *United States*. The Supreme Court ruled that the First Amendment protected the newspaper's right to publish the controversial documents.

September 11 and Beyond

As the 20th century came to a close, the United States faced challenges different from any the country had faced before. International terrorism was a growing danger in the 1990s. This reality was brought home to New Yorkers in February 1993, when terrorists exploded bombs beneath the World Trade Center in downtown Manhattan. Terrorists struck New York City again on September 11, 2001, crashing two hijacked jet planes into the Twin Towers of the World Trade Center. The towers were destroyed, and nearly 3,000 people were killed.

People from all over the state and country responded by pulling together to find ways to help. In the years since September 11, New York City has begun the long process of rebuilding. Rudolph Giuliani, who was mayor of New York at the time of the attacks, believes the city is even stronger today than it was before the attacks. "The city is more vital," he said, "the city is rebuilding, the city is even more diverse."

Rescue workers at the World Trade Center

1973 World Trade Center's Twin Towers are completed.

1982 Mario Cuomo is elected governor and serves three terms.

1994 George Pataki is elected governor.

1989 David Dinkins becomes New York City's first African American mayor.

1993 Terrorists bomb the World Trade Center.

1993 New York's population of 18.1 million is the nation's third-largest, behind California and Texas

2001 Terrorist attacks destroy the World Trade Center.

Today

World Trade Center Towers

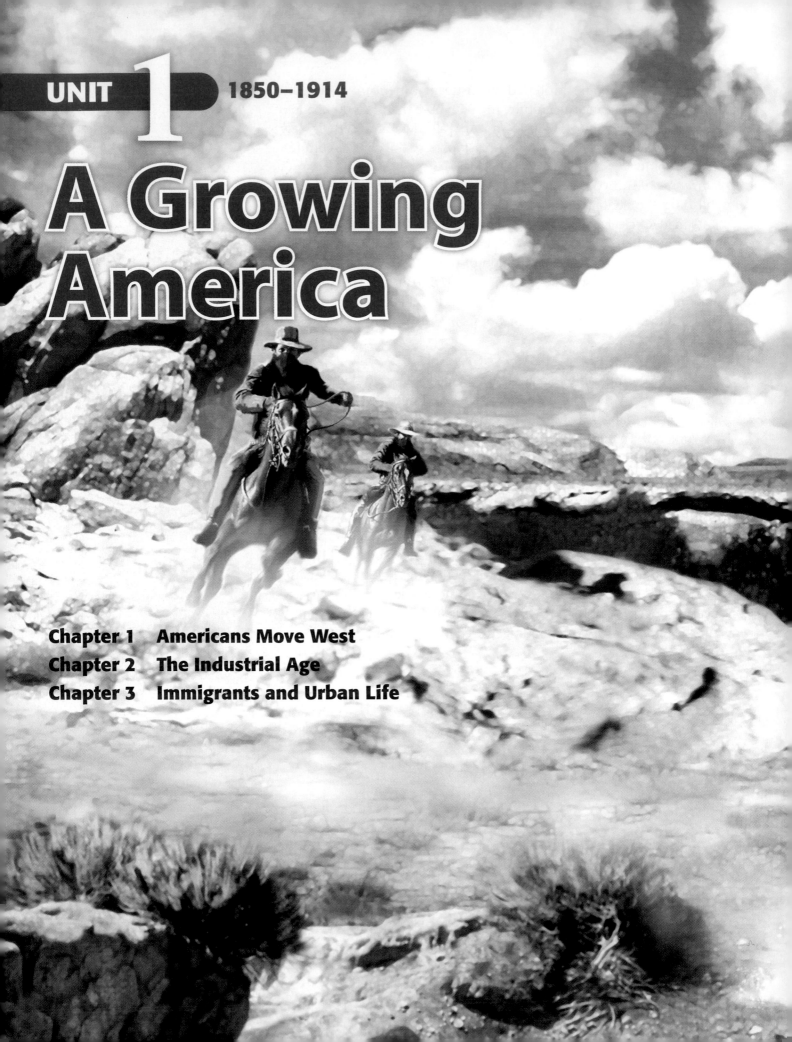

UNIT 1 1850–1914

A Growing America

What You Will Learn...

After the American Civil War, the United States began a process of building a new economy and political structure. Events in the rest of the world began affecting the nation more noticeably.

During this period of expansion, the U.S. population spread across the continent. New immigrants and new technology began to change life in many parts of the country, especially in cities. In the next three chapters, you will learn about changes in the United States that helped the country increase its size, wealth, and power.

Explore the Art

In this picture, a teenage Buffalo Bill Cody flees from bandits on his Pony Express route. How does this picture show the importance of communication in the expansion of the United States?

Americans Move West

FOCUS QUESTION

How did industrialization and immigration change the face of American life?

FOCUS ON WRITING

Writing a Letter Before telephones and e-mail, one way to communicate with people far away was by letter. In this chapter, you will read about the settlement of the West by European Americans. Suppose you were an Irish immigrant working on a railroad that crossed the Great Plains. What might you have seen or experienced? After you read the chapter, you will write a letter to your sister in Ireland telling her about your experiences.

UNITED STATES

1860 The Pony Express begins delivering mail between East and West.

1850   1860

WORLD

1855
Paris holds a World's Fair.

HOLT
History's Impact
▶video series
Watch the video to understand the impact of the West on American culture.

What You Will Learn...

In this chapter you will learn about how the great American West changed in the late 1800s. Settlers poured into the region and built mines, ranches, farms, and railroads. In this photo, modern pioneers re-create a wagon journey from the 1800s.

1873
Susan B. Anthony is convicted of voting illegally in Canandaigua, New York.

NY

10 MILES OF TRACK, LAID IN ONE DAY. APRIL 28TH 1869.

1869 The first transcontinental railroad is completed.

1874 Gold is discovered in the Black Hills of the Dakotas.

1879 Thousands of African Americans migrate from the South to Kansas.

1890 The Massacre at Wounded Knee occurs.

1870

1880

1890

1864 French scientist Louis Pasteur invents the purification process of pasteurization.

ORIENT-EXPRESS

1883 The Orient Express railway makes its first run from Paris to Istanbul.

1888 Brazil abolishes slavery.

PARIS · VIENNE · CONSTANTINOPLE

Reading Social Studies

Economics | Geography | Politics | Society and Culture | Science and Technology

Focus on Themes In this chapter you will follow the development of the United States from the mid-1800s through the 1890s. You will learn that California was admitted to the Union in 1850. You will find out about the struggles that people faced as the movement West continued and people settled the Great Plains. You will learn about the **technological** advancements made during this time as well as the difficult **geographical** obstacles miners and ranchers faced in the West.

Understanding through Questioning

Focus on Reading When newspaper reporters want to get to the heart of a story, they ask certain questions: who, what, when, where, why, and how. When you are reading a history book, you can use the same questions to get to the heart of what happened in the past.

Hypothetical Questions You can also use questions to dig deeper than what is in the text. You can ask hypothetical, or what if, questions. These questions ask what might have happened had events occurred differently. Sometimes asking such questions can help history come alive.

Who?
Congress

Where?
the West

How?
Congress gave land to anyone who agreed to settle on it for five years.

In 1862 Congress passed two important land acts that helped open the West to settlers. The Homestead Act gave government-owned land to small farmers. Any adult who was a U.S. citizen or planned to become one could receive 160 acres of land. In exchange, homesteaders promised to live on the land for five years. The Morrill Act granted more than 17 million acres of federal land to the states. *(p. 20)*

What if?
If Congress had not passed these laws, U.S. citizens might not have moved West. The United States might not have grown as quickly as it did.

What?
encouraged new settlement

When?
1862

Why?
Perhaps Congress feared what would happen to western lands if they remained unsettled by U.S. citizens.

You Try It!

Read the following passage and then answer the questions below.

Building Communities

From Chapter 1, p. 22

Women were an important force in the settlement of the frontier. They joined in the hard work of farming and ranching and helped build communities out of the widely spaced farms and small towns. Their role in founding communities facilitated a strong voice in public affairs. Wyoming women, for example, were granted the vote in the new state's constitution, which was approved in 1869. Annie Bidwell, one of the founders of Chico, California, used her influence to support a variety of moral and social causes such as women's suffrage and temperance.

Answer these questions based on the passage you just read.

1. Who is this passage about?

2. What did they do?

3. When did they do this?

4. How do you think they accomplished it?

5. Why do you think they were able to accomplish so much?

6. How can knowing this information help you understand the past?

7. What if women in the West had been given more rights? Fewer rights? How might the West have been different?

As you read Chapter 1, ask questions like *who, what, when, where, why, how,* and *what if* to help you analyze what you are reading.

Key Terms and People

Chapter 1

Section 1
frontier *(p. 6)*
Comstock Lode *(p. 7)*
boomtowns *(p. 8)*
Cattle Kingdom *(p. 9)*
cattle drive *(p. 9)*
Chisholm Trail *(p. 9)*
Pony Express *(p. 10)*
transcontinental railroad *(p. 10)*

Section 2
Treaty of Fort Laramie *(p. 14)*
reservations *(p. 15)*
Crazy Horse *(p. 15)*
Treaty of Medicine Lodge *(p. 15)*
buffalo soldiers *(p. 16)*
George Armstrong Custer *(p. 16)*
Sitting Bull *(p. 16)*
Battle of the Little Bighorn *(p. 16)*
Massacre at Wounded Knee *(p. 17)*
Long Walk *(p. 17)*
Geronimo *(p. 17)*
Ghost Dance *(p. 18)*
Sarah Winnemucca *(p. 18)*
Dawes General Allotment Act *(p. 18)*

Section 3
Homestead Act *(p. 20)*
Morrill Act *(p. 20)*
Exodusters *(p. 21)*
sodbusters *(p. 21)*
dry farming *(p. 21)*
Annie Bidwell *(p. 22)*
National Grange *(p. 23)*
deflation *(p. 24)*
William Jennings Bryan *(p. 24)*
Populist Party *(p. 24)*

Academic Vocabulary

In this chapter, you will learn the following academic words:

establish *(p. 8)*
facilitate *(p. 22)*

Miners, Ranchers, and Railroads

What You Will Learn...

Main Ideas

1. A mining boom brought growth to the West.
2. The demand for cattle created a short-lived Cattle Kingdom on the Great Plains.
3. East and West were connected by the transcontinental railroad.

The Big Idea

As more settlers moved West, mining, ranching, and railroads soon transformed the western landscape.

Key Terms

frontier, *p. 6*
Comstock Lode, *p. 7*
boomtowns, *p. 8*
Cattle Kingdom, *p. 9*
cattle drive, *p. 9*
Chisholm Trail, *p. 9*
Pony Express, *p. 10*
transcontinental railroad, *p. 10*

TAKING NOTES As you read the following section, take notes on the kinds of economic opportunities that people found in the West. Organize your notes in a table like the one below.

Opportunities in the West

If YOU were there...

You are a cowboy in Texas in 1875. You love life on the open range, the quiet nights, and the freedom. You even like the hard work of the long cattle drives to Kansas. But you know that times are changing. Homesteaders are moving in and fencing off their lands. Some of the older cowboys say it's time to settle down and buy a small ranch. You hope that they're not right.

What would make you give up a cowboy's life?

BUILDING BACKGROUND In the years following the Civil War, the U.S. population grew rapidly. Settlements in the West increased. More discoveries of gold and silver attracted adventurers, while the open range drew others. Thousands of former Civil War soldiers also joined the move West.

Mining Boom Brings Growth

During the years surrounding the War, most Americans had thought of the Great Plains and other western lands as the Great American Desert. In the years following the Civil War, Americans witnessed the rapid growth of the U.S. population and the spread of settlements throughout the West. With the admission of the state of California to the Union in 1850, the western boundary of the American **frontier**—an undeveloped area—had reached the Pacific Ocean.

The frontier changed dramatically as more and more people moved westward. Settlers built homes, fenced off land, and laid out ranches and farms. Miners, ranchers, and farmers remade the landscape of the West as they adapted to their new surroundings. The geography of the West was further changed by the development and expansion of a large and successful railroad industry that moved the West's natural resources to eastern markets. Gold and silver were the most valuable natural resources, and mining companies used the growing railroad network to bring these precious metals to the East.

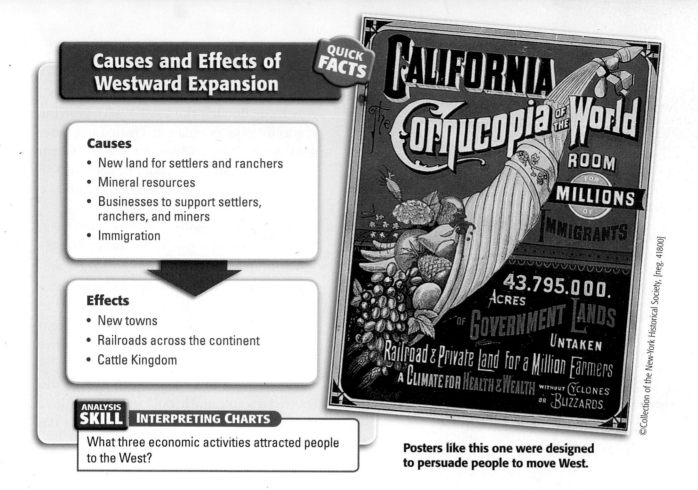

Causes and Effects of Westward Expansion

QUICK FACTS

Causes
- New land for settlers and ranchers
- Mineral resources
- Businesses to support settlers, ranchers, and miners
- Immigration

Effects
- New towns
- Railroads across the continent
- Cattle Kingdom

ANALYSIS SKILL INTERPRETING CHARTS

What three economic activities attracted people to the West?

©Collection of the New-York Historical Society, [neg. 41800]

Posters like this one were designed to persuade people to move West.

Big Business

Most of the precious metals were located in western Nevada. In 1859 miner Henry Comstock discovered a huge deposit of gold and silver in Nevada that became called the **Comstock Lode**. The deposit was incredibly rich and deep. In just the first year after its discovery, the Comstock Lode lured thousands of California miners to Nevada. Over the next 20 years, the Comstock Lode produced more than $500 million worth of gold and silver.

Expensive equipment was needed to remove the silver and gold that were trapped within quartz rock. Larger mining companies bought up land claims from miners who could not afford this machinery. As a result, mining became a big business in the West.

As companies dug bigger and deeper mines, the work became more dangerous. Miners had to use unsafe equipment, such as elevator platforms without protective walls. They worked in dark tunnels and breathed hot, stuffy air. They suffered from lung disease caused by dusty air. Miners often were injured or killed by poorly planned explosions or by cave-ins. Fire was also a great danger. Mining was therefore one of the most dangerous jobs in the country. In the West, worries about safety and pay led miners to form several unions in the 1860s.

Settlers

People from all over the world came to work in the western mines. Some miners came from the eastern United States. Others emigrated from Europe, Central and South America, and Asia. Many Mexican immigrants and Mexican Americans were experienced miners. They were skilled in assaying, or testing, the contents of valuable ore. One newspaper reporter wrote, "Here were congregated the most varied elements of humanity . . . belonging to almost every nationality and every status of life."

New Towns

Mining booms also produced **boomtowns**, communities that grew suddenly when a mine opened. Most disappeared just as quickly when the mine closed. Some, such as Denver, Colorado, and Helena, Montana, endured. Most boomtowns had general stores, saloons, and boardinghouses.

Few women or families lived in boomtowns. "I was never so lonely and homesick in all my life," wrote one young woman. Women washed, cooked, made clothes, and chopped wood. They also raised families, **established** schools, and wrote for newspapers. Their work helped turn some mining camps into successful, permanent towns.

ACADEMIC VOCABULARY

establish to set up or create

READING CHECK **Summarizing** What risks did miners face?

The Cattle Kingdom

The cattle industry was another area of rapid growth. Following the Civil War, a growing economy and population created a greater demand for beef in the East. Cattle worth $3 to $6 each in Texas could be sold for $38 each in Kansas. In New York, they could be sold for $80 each.

The most popular breed of cattle was the longhorn. The longhorn spread quickly throughout western Texas. Because these animals needed very little water and could survive harsh weather, they were well-suited to the dry, desert-like environment of western Texas. But how could Texas ranchers move the longhorns to eastern markets?

In 1867 businessman Joseph McCoy discovered a solution. He built pens for cattle in the small town of Abilene, Kansas. The Kansas

Myth and Reality in the Wild West

No episode in American history has given rise to as many myths as the Wild West. Writers of dime novels, popular in the East, helped created the myths in the years after the Civil War. Even today, popular books, television shows, and movies continue to portray the West in ways that are more myth than reality.

Myth: The cowboy was a free-spirited individual.

Reality: Most cowboys were employees. Many joined labor unions and even went on strike.

Myth: Western cowtowns were wild places where cowboys had gunfights, and there was little law and order.

Reality: Most were orderly cities with active law enforcement. Showdowns rarely, if ever, occurred.

Myth: Almost all cowboys were Anglo Americans.

Reality: About 25 percent of cowboys were African Americans, and 12 percent were Hispanic.

Pacific Railroad line went through Abilene. As a result, cattle could be shipped by rail from there. Soon, countless Texas ranchers were making the trip north to Abilene to sell their herds of cattle.

Around the same time, cattle ranching began to expand in the Midwest. The Great Plains from Texas to Canada, where many ranchers raised cattle in the late 1800s, became known as the **Cattle Kingdom**. Ranchers grazed huge herds on public land called the open range. The land had once been occupied by Plains Indians and buffalo herds.

Importance of Cowboys

The workers who took care of the ranchers' cattle were known as cowhands or cowboys. They borrowed many techniques and tools from vaqueros (bah-KER-ohs), Mexican ranch hands who cared for cattle and horses. From vaqueros came the western saddle and the lariat—a rope used for lassoing cattle. The cowboys also borrowed the vaqueros' broad felt hat. However, they changed it into the familiar high-peaked cowboy hat.

One of the cowboy's most important and dangerous duties was the **cattle drive**. On these long journeys, cowboys herded cattle to the market or to the northern Plains for grazing. The trips usually lasted several months and covered hundreds of miles. The **Chisholm Trail**, which ran from San Antonio, Texas, to the cattle town of Abilene, Kansas, was one of the earliest and most popular routes for cattle drives. It was blazed, or marked, by Texas cowboy Jesse Chisholm in the late 1860s.

At times, rowdy cowboys made life in cattle towns rough and violent. There were rarely shoot-outs in the street, but there was often disorderly behavior. Law officials such as Wyatt Earp became famous for keeping the peace in cattle towns.

End of the Open Range

As the cattle business boomed, ranchers faced more competition for use of the open range. Farmers began to buy range land on the Great Plains where cattle had once grazed. Small ranchers also began competing with large ranchers for land. Then in 1874, the invention of barbed wire allowed westerners to fence off large amounts of land cheaply. The competition between farmers, large ranchers, and small ranchers increased. This competition led to range wars, or fights for access to land.

Making matters worse, in 1885 and 1886, disaster struck the Cattle Kingdom. The huge cattle herds on the Plains had eaten most of the prairie grass. Unusually severe winters in both years made the ranching situation even worse. Thousands of cattle died, and many ranchers were ruined financially. The Cattle Kingdom had come to an end.

FOCUS ON READING
Ask yourself questions about the information in this paragraph to help you understand the competition between farmers and ranchers.

READING CHECK Drawing Conclusions
Why did the Cattle Kingdom come to an end?

Marshal Wyatt Earp

Deadwood, South Dakota

The Transcontinental Railroad

FOCUS ON NEW YORK CITY

In 1854 so-called orphan trains organized by the New York Children's Aid Society began moving homeless and neglected children from the streets of New York City to foster families in western rural areas. By the time the program ended in 1929, more than 100,000 children had been placed by the society. The program helped these children to realize a happy and productive life beyond the grim city streets.

As more Americans began moving West, the need to send goods and information between the East and West increased. Americans searched for ways to improve communication and travel across the country.

In 1860 a system of messengers on horseback called the **Pony Express** began to carry messages west. The messengers carried mail between relay stations on a route about 2,000 miles long. However, telegraph lines, which sent messages faster, quickly put the Pony Express out of business.

Some Americans wanted to build a **transcontinental railroad**—a railroad that would cross the continent and connect the East to the West. The federal government, therefore, passed the Pacific Railway Acts in 1862 and in 1864. These acts gave railroad companies loans and large land grants that could be sold to pay for construction costs. Congress had granted more than 131 million acres of public land to railroad companies. In exchange, the government asked the railroads to carry U.S. mail and troops at a lower cost. Many railroad companies were inspired to begin laying miles of tracks.

Great Race

Two companies, the Central Pacific and the Union Pacific, led the race to complete the transcontinental railroad. In February 1863, the Central Pacific began building east from Sacramento, California. At the end of the year, the Union Pacific started building west from Omaha, Nebraska.

The Union Pacific hired thousands of railroad workers, particularly Irish immigrants. Chinese immigrants made up some 85 percent of the Central Pacific workforce. The railroad's part-owner Leland Stanford praised them, but he paid them less than other laborers. Chinese crews also were given the most dangerous tasks and had to work longer hours than other railroad laborers. They took the job, however, because the $30 a month

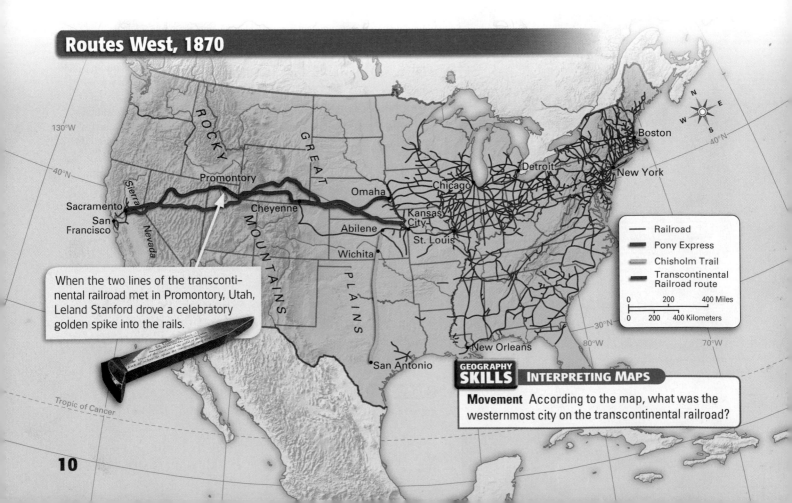

Routes West, 1870

When the two lines of the transcontinental railroad met in Promontory, Utah, Leland Stanford drove a celebratory golden spike into the rails.

Railroad
Pony Express
Chisholm Trail
Transcontinental Railroad route

0   200   400 Miles
0   200   400 Kilometers

GEOGRAPHY SKILLS   INTERPRETING MAPS

Movement According to the map, what was the westernmost city on the transcontinental railroad?

that the Central Pacific paid was as much as 10 times what they could earn in China.

Railroad companies faced many geographic challenges. For example, workers for Central Pacific struggled to cross the Sierra Nevada mountain range in California. Breaking apart its rock formations required setting carefully controlled explosions using large amounts of blasting powder and the explosive nitroglycerin. And in the winter of 1866, snowdrifts more than 60 feet high trapped and killed dozens of workers. Faced with these obstacles, the Central Pacific took four years to lay the first 115 miles of track.

Meanwhile, Union Pacific workers faced harsh weather on the Great Plains. In addition, the company pressured them to work at a rapid pace—at times laying 250 miles of track in six months.

For both railroad companies, providing food and supplies for workers was vital. This job became more difficult in remote areas. The railroad companies consequently often relied on local resources. Professional hunters, such as William "Buffalo Bill" Cody, shot thousands of buffalo to feed Union Pacific workers.

Golden Spike

Congress required the two completed rail lines to connect at Promontory, Utah. On May 10, 1869, a golden spike was used to connect the railroad tie joining the two tracks. Alexander Toponce witnessed the event.

" Governor Stanford, president of the Central Pacific, took the sledge [hammer], and the first time he struck he missed the spike and hit the rail. What a howl went up! Irish, Chinese, Mexicans, and everybody yelled with delight. 'He missed it'... Then Stanford tried it again and tapped the spike. "

—Alexander Toponce, quoted in
A Treasury of Railroad Folklore,
edited by B. A. Botkin and Alvin F. Harlo

The railroad companies were not finished, though. Following completion of the transcontinental railroad, companies continued building railroads until the West was crisscrossed with rail lines.

The Central Pacific and Union Pacific connected their tracks at Promontory, Utah, in 1869, completing the transcontinental railroad.

Effects of the Transcontinental Railroad

- Increased settlement of the West
- Increased business activity and East-West trade
- Helped make the railroad industry one of the most powerful in the country

Results of the Railroad

The transcontinental railroad increased both economic growth and the population in the West. Railroad companies provided better transportation for people and goods. They also sold land to settlers, which encouraged people to move West.

New railroads helped businesses. Western timber companies, miners, ranchers, and farmers shipped wood, metals, meat, and grain east by railroad. In exchange, eastern businesses shipped manufactured goods to the West. As trade between regions increased, the idea that the U.S. economy was inter-

THE IMPACT TODAY

Today's businesses ship goods across the country using railroads, the interstate highway system, and airplanes.

dependent became more widespread. Even perceptions of time became more formal as railroad schedules began to unite areas that had before existed under different times. Four continental time zones were established in 1883.

Railroad companies encouraged people to put their money into the railroad business, which they did—sometimes unwisely. Railroad speculation and the collapse of railroad owner Jay Cooke's banking firm helped start the Panic of 1873. By the 1880s, many small western railroads were deeply in debt. Despite such setbacks, Americans remained interested in railroad investments. By 1890 there were about 164,000 more miles of track in operation than in 1865. Railroads had become one of the biggest industries in the United States.

READING CHECK **Finding Main Ideas** How did the railroad affect the development of the West?

SUMMARY AND PREVIEW In this section you learned about the increased settlement of the West. In the next section you will learn about conflicts with Native Americans.

go.hrw.com
Online Quiz

Section 1 Assessment

Reviewing Ideas, Terms, and People

1. **a. Recall** Why did Americans move West in the years following the Civil War?
   b. Draw Conclusions What effect did the discovery of the **Comstock Lode** have on the West?
   c. Evaluate Do you think women were important to the success of mining towns? Why or why not?
2. **a. Recall** What led to the cattle boom in the West?
   b. Analyze Why was there competition between ranchers and farmers to settle in the Great Plains?
   c. Evaluate What played the biggest role in ending the **Cattle Kingdom**? Why?
3. **a. Recall** When and where did the Union Pacific and Central Pacific lines meet?
   b. Make Generalizations How do you think the **transcontinental railroad** improved people's lives?

Critical Thinking

4. **Comparing** Review your notes about opportunities in the West. Then use a graphic organizer like the one below to list the effects of these opportunities.

Opportunity	Effect

FOCUS ON WRITING

5. **Taking Notes on Mining, Ranching, and the Railroads** As you read this section, take notes on how mining, ranching, and railroads changed the West. How might a railroad worker feel about these changes?

Wars for the West

If YOU were there...

You are a member of the Sioux nation, living in Dakota Territory in 1875. These lands are sacred to your people, and the U.S. government has promised them to you. But now gold has been found here, and the government has ordered you to give up your land. Some Sioux leaders want to fight. Others say that it is of no use, that the soldiers will win.

Would you fight to keep your lands? Why?

> **BUILDING BACKGROUND** Miners, ranchers, and farmers all moved West in the years after the Civil War. The arrival of settlers and the U.S. army to the Great Plains meant the end of the way of life of the Indians who lived there. The coming of the railroad began this destruction, with the killing of thousands of buffalo. Treaties were made but did not protect Indian lands from settlers.

Settlers Encounter the Plains Indians

As miners and settlers began crossing the Great Plains in the mid-1800s, they pressured the federal government for more access to western lands. To protect these travelers, U.S. officials sent agents to negotiate treaties with the Plains Indians.

The Plains Indians lived in the Great Plains, which stretch north into Canada and south into Texas. Indian groups such as the Apache and the Comanche lived in and around Texas and

What You Will Learn...

Main Ideas

1. As settlers moved to the Great Plains, they encountered the Plains Indians.
2. The U.S. Army and Native Americans fought in the northern plains, the Southwest, and the Far West.
3. Despite efforts to reform U.S. policy toward Native Americans, conflict continued.

The Big Idea

Native Americans and the U.S. government came into conflict over land in the West.

Key Terms and People

Treaty of Fort Laramie, *p. 14*
reservations, *p. 15*
Crazy Horse, *p. 15*
Treaty of Medicine Lodge, *p. 15*
buffalo soldiers, *p. 16*
George Armstrong Custer, *p. 16*
Sitting Bull, *p. 16*
Battle of the Little Bighorn, *p. 16*
Massacre at Wounded Knee, *p. 17*
Long Walk, *p. 17*
Geronimo, *p. 17*
Ghost Dance, *p. 18*
Sarah Winnemucca, *p. 18*
Dawes General Allotment Act, *p. 18*

TAKING NOTES As you read this section, take notes on the major events in Native Americans' loss of land rights. Organize them in a chart like the one below.

Date	Event

The Plains Indians depended on two animals—the horse and the buffalo.

what is now Oklahoma. The Cheyenne and the Arapaho lived in different regions across the central Plains. The Pawnee lived in parts of Nebraska. To the north were the Sioux. These groups spoke many different languages. However, they used a common sign language to communicate and they shared a similar lifestyle.

Hunting Buffalo

For survival, Plains Indians depended on two animals—the horse and the buffalo. The Spanish brought horses to America in the 1500s. Plains Indians learned to ride horses, and hunters used them to follow buffalo herds year-round. While on horseback, most Plains Indian hunters used a short bow and arrows to shoot buffalo from close range.

Plains Indians used buffalo for food, shelter, clothing, utensils, and tools. Women dried buffalo meat to make jerky. They made tepees and clothing from buffalo hides, and cups and tools from buffalo horns. As one Sioux explained, "When our people killed a buffalo, all of the animal was utilized [used] in some manner; nothing was wasted." The Plains Indians prospered. By 1850, some 75,000 Native Americans lived on the Plains.

Struggle to Keep Land

Miners and settlers were also increasing in numbers—and they wanted Indians' land. The U.S. government tried to avoid disputes by negotiating the **Treaty of Fort Laramie**, the first major treaty between the U.S. government and Plains Indians. Two years later, several southern Plains nations signed a treaty at Fort Atkinson in Nebraska. These treaties recognized Indian claims to most of the Great Plains. They also allowed the United States to build forts and roads and to travel across Indian homelands. The U.S. government promised to pay for any damages to Indian lands.

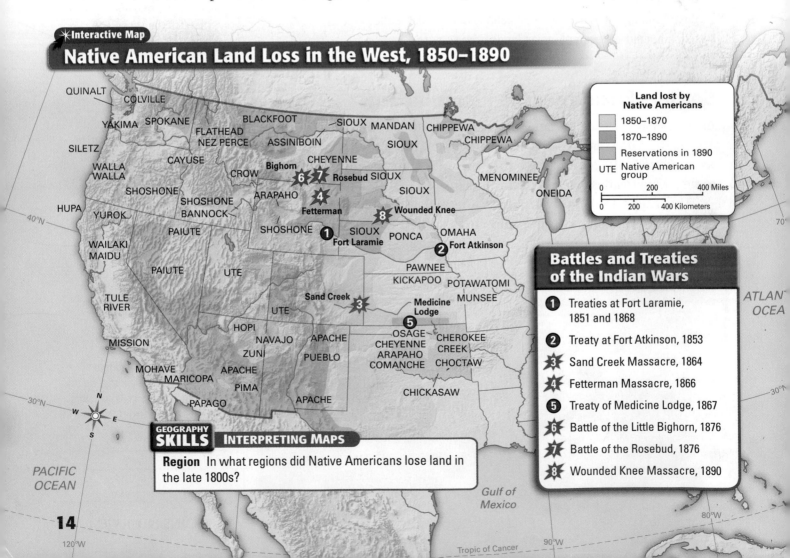

Interactive Map

Native American Land Loss in the West, 1850–1890

Land lost by Native Americans
- 1850–1870
- 1870–1890
- Reservations in 1890
- UTE Native American group

0   200   400 Miles
0   200   400 Kilometers

Battles and Treaties of the Indian Wars
1. Treaties at Fort Laramie, 1851 and 1868
2. Treaty at Fort Atkinson, 1853
3. Sand Creek Massacre, 1864
4. Fetterman Massacre, 1866
5. Treaty of Medicine Lodge, 1867
6. Battle of the Little Bighorn, 1876
7. Battle of the Rosebud, 1876
8. Wounded Knee Massacre, 1890

GEOGRAPHY SKILLS INTERPRETING MAPS

Region In what regions did Native Americans lose land in the late 1800s?

Tribal Councils

Native Americans have long held tribal councils to make decisions on behalf of the group. Today this tradition of Native American government continues. There are more than 500 tribal governments in the United States. Tribal governments provide a wide range of services, including law enforcement, health care, and education. Here, a member of the Blackfoot Tribal Council addresses the Montana state legislature.

ANALYSIS SKILL **ANALYZING INFORMATION**

What types of services do tribal governments provide?

The treaties did not keep the peace for long. In 1858 the discovery of gold in what is now Colorado brought thousands of miners to the West. They soon clashed with the Cheyenne and the Arapaho. In 1861 the U.S. government negotiated new treaties with Plains Indians. These treaties created **reservations**, areas of federal land set aside for Native Americans. The government expected Indians to stay on the reservations, which made hunting buffalo almost impossible.

Pioneers and miners continued to cross the Great Plains. Many miners used the Bozeman Trail. To protect them, the U.S. Army built forts along the trail, which ran through favored Sioux hunting grounds. The Sioux responded with war. In late 1866, **Crazy Horse** and a group of Sioux ambushed and killed 81 cavalry troops.

In 1868, under the Second Treaty of Fort Laramie, the government agreed to close the Bozeman Trail, abandon the forts, and provide reservation land to the Sioux.

The U.S. government also negotiated for southern Plains Indians to move off their land. In the 1867 **Treaty of Medicine Lodge**, most southern Plains Indians agreed to live on reservations. However, many Indians did not want to give up their hunting grounds. Fighting soon broke out between the Comanche and Texans. The U.S. Army and the Texas Rangers were unable to defeat the Comanche, so they cut off the Comanche's access to food and water. In 1875 the last of the Comanche war leaders surrendered.

READING CHECK **Summarizing** What was the federal policy toward the Plains Indians in the 1860s and 1870s?

Two Views of a Historic Battle

CONNECT TO THE ARTS

Art historians have identified about 1,000 paintings of the Battle of the Little Bighorn. The painting on this page was painted in 1899. The painting on the next page is one of the many colored-pencil drawings of the battle done by Red Horse, who participated in the fight. He drew them five years after the battle.

How do these paintings show the influences of different cultures?

The Native Americans are shown surrounding a small force of U.S. soldiers.

General Custer is shown standing among his men as he fires.

Fighting on the Plains

In the northern Plains, Southwest, and Far West, Native Americans continued to resist being moved to and confined on reservations. The U.S. government sent troops, including African American cavalry, who the Indians called **buffalo soldiers**, into the area to force the Indians to leave.

Battles on the Northern Plains

As fighting on the southern Plains came to an end, new trouble started in the north. In 1874 Lieutenant Colonel **George Armstrong Custer**'s soldiers discovered gold in the Black Hills of the Dakotas. **Sitting Bull**, a leader of the Lakota Sioux, protested U.S. demands for the land.

"What treaty that the whites have kept has the red man broken? Not one. What treaty that the white man ever made with us have they kept? Not one."
—Sitting Bull, quoted in *Touch the Earth* by T. C. McLuhan

Other Sioux leaders listened to Sitting Bull and refused to give up land. Fighting soon broke out between the army and the Sioux.

On June 25, 1876, Custer's scouts found a Sioux camp along the Little Bighorn River in Montana Territory. Leading 264 of his soldiers, Custer raced ahead without waiting for any supporting forces. In the **Battle of the Little Bighorn**, Sioux forces led by Crazy Horse and Sitting Bull surrounded and defeated Custer and his troops. Newspapers called the battle "Custer's Last Stand" because his entire command was killed. It was the worst defeat the U.S. Army suffered in the West. The Battle of the Little Bighorn was also the Sioux's last major victory.

In 1881 Sitting Bull and a few followers returned from Canada where they had moved. They had run out of food during the hard winter. They joined the Sioux on Standing Rock Reservation in Dakota Territory.

These are wounded men.

The U.S. Army is shown on horseback in this painting.

Almost a decade later, in 1890, while following orders to arrest Sitting Bull, reservation police killed him. Many Sioux left the reservations in protest. Later that year, the U.S. Army shot and killed about 150 Sioux near Wounded Knee Creek in South Dakota. This **Massacre at Wounded Knee** was the last major incident on the Great Plains.

Southwest

The Navajo lived in what became Arizona and New Mexico. In 1863 the Navajo refused to settle on a reservation. In response, U.S. troops made raids on the Navajo's fields, homes, and livestock.

When the Navajo ran out of food and shelter, they started surrendering to the U.S. Army. In 1864 the army led Navajo captives on the **Long Walk**. On this 300-mile march the Navajo were forced to walk across the desert to a reservation in Bosque Redondo, New Mexico. Along the way, countless Navajo died.

Far West

The United States had promised to let the peaceful Nez Percé keep their land in Oregon. Within a few years, however, the government ordered the Nez Percé to a reservation in what is now Idaho. Before leaving, a few angry Nez Percé killed some local settlers and tried to escape to Canada. Near the border, U.S. troops overtook them and sent them to a reservation in what is now Oklahoma.

Final Battles

By the 1880s, most Native Americans had stopped fighting. The Apache of the Southwest, however, continued to battle the U.S. Army. A Chiricahua Apache named **Geronimo** and his band of raiders avoided capture for many years. In September 1886 Geronimo surrendered, ending the Apache armed resistance.

READING CHECK **Contrasting** How did the Apache resistance differ from that of the Navajo?

Conflict Continues

By the 1870s, many Native Americans lived on reservations, where land was usually not useful for farming or buffalo hunting. Many Indians were starving.

A Paiute Indian named Wovoka began a religious movement, the **Ghost Dance**, that predicted the arrival of paradise for Native Americans. In this paradise, the buffalo herds would return and the settlers would disappear.

U.S. officials did not understand the meaning of the Ghost Dance. They feared it would lead to rebellion, so they tried to end the movement, which had spread to other groups, including the Sioux. After the massacre in 1890 at Wounded Knee, the Ghost Dance movement gradually died out.

In the late 1870s, a Paiute Indian named **Sarah Winnemucca** called for reform. She gave lectures on problems of the reservation system. In 1881 Helen Hunt Jackson published a book entitled *A Century of Dishonor* that urged reform of U.S. Indian policy.

Sarah Winnemucca spoke out for the fair treatment of her people.

Some reformers believed that Native Americans should adopt the ways of white people. The **Dawes General Allotment Act** of 1887 tried to lessen traditional influences on Indian society by making land ownership private rather than shared. The act also promised—but failed to deliver—U.S. citizenship to Native Americans. After breaking up reservation land, the government sold the acreage remaining. The Act took about two-thirds of Indian land.

READING CHECK **Evaluating** How did reformers try to influence Native Americans' lives?

SUMMARY AND PREVIEW In this section you read about conflict in the settlement of the West. In the next section you will learn more about Great Plains settlers.

Section 2 Assessment

go.hrw.com
Online Quiz

Reviewing Ideas, Terms, and People

1. **a. Describe** What animals did Plains Indians depend on, and how did they use those animals?
   b. Analyze How did U.S. policy toward the Plains Indians change in the late 1850s?
   c. Elaborate Would you have agreed to move to a **reservation**? Why or why not?
2. **a. Describe** What events led to the **Battle of the Little Bighorn**?
   b. Elaborate Why do you think most Indian groups eventually stopped resisting the United States?
3. **a. Describe** How did the **Dawes General Allotment Act** affect American Indians?
   b. Predict What effect do you think the **Massacre at Wounded Knee** would have on relations between Plains Indians and the United States?

Critical Thinking

4. **Identifying Cause and Effect** Review your notes about Native American land losses. Organize the events in a time line like the one below.

   1851   1864   1867   1887

FOCUS ON WRITING

5. **Reading about the Wars for the West** As you read this section, take notes on the wars between the U.S. government and the Plains Indians. How might a railroad worker have experienced these conflicts?

Chief Joseph

What would you do to protect your home and your ways of life?

When did he live? 1840–1904

Where did he live? Chief Joseph lived in the Wallowa Valley, the Nez Percé homeland, in present-day Oregon.

What did he do? Chief Joseph led his people in an effort to hold on to the Nez Percé homeland and to avoid war with the United States. For years, Joseph and a band of Nez Percé refused to move as white settlers moved into the valley. Finally, after being threatened with attack, Joseph gave in. An army led by General Oliver Otis Howard eventually chased the Nez Percé across Idaho, Wyoming, and Montana. They were sent to a reservation in what is now Oklahoma, where many died.

Why is he so important? Chief Joseph's surrender speech earned him a place in American history. The band of 700 people, including only 200 warriors, made a courageous three-month, 1,400-mile trek, hoping to cross into Canada for protection. Exhausted, hungry, and freezing, Joseph's people collapsed just short of the Canadian border. In later years, the chief spoke about what had happened.

Cause and Effect What brought suffering to Chief Joseph and his people?

Chief Joseph of the Nez Percé nation tried to protect his people from the advancement of white settlers.

Speech

"I am tired of fighting. Our chiefs are killed … The old men are all dead … It is cold, and we have no blankets. The little children are freezing to death. My people, some of them, have run away to the hills, and have no blankets, no food. No one knows where they are—perhaps freezing to death. I want to have time to look for my children, and see how many of them I can find. Maybe I shall find them among the dead. Hear me, my chiefs! I am tired. My heart is sick and sad. From where the sun now stands I will fight no more forever."

—Chief Joseph of the Nez Percé, surrender speech, October 5, 1877

Farming and Populism

What You Will Learn...

Main Ideas

1. Many Americans started new lives on the Great Plains.
2. Economic challenges led to the creation of farmers' political groups.
3. By the 1890s, the western frontier had come to an end.

The Big Idea

Settlers on the Great Plains created new communities and unique political groups.

Key Terms and People

Homestead Act, *p. 20*
Morrill Act, *p. 20*
Exodusters, *p. 21*
sodbusters, *p. 21*
dry farming, *p. 21*
Annie Bidwell, *p. 22*
National Grange, *p. 23*
deflation, *p. 24*
William Jennings Bryan, *p. 24*
Populist Party, *p. 24*

TAKING NOTES As you read this section, take notes on the reasons for the rise of populism. Organize your notes in a graphic organizer like the one below.

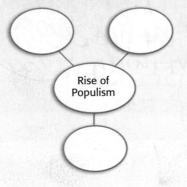

If YOU were there...

You are a female schoolteacher in Wisconsin in 1880. You live and teach in a small town, but you grew up on a farm and are used to hard work. Now you are thinking about moving West to claim free land from the government. You could teach in a school there, too. You think it would be an exciting adventure, but your family is horrified that a single woman would move West on her own.

Would you decide to become a homesteader?

BUILDING BACKGROUND By the 1870s and 1880s, the Great Plains had been "tamed" and made more welcoming to settlers. The end of the open cattle range was coming, and the Indian wars were nearly over. The government moved to encourage permanent settlements in the West by offering land to homesteaders.

New Lives on the Plains

In 1862 Congress passed two important land grant acts that helped open the West to settlers. The **Homestead Act** gave government-owned land to small farmers. Any adult who was a U.S. citizen or planned to become one could receive 160 acres of land. In exchange, homesteaders promised to live on the land for five years. The **Morrill Act** granted more than 17 million acres of federal land to the states. The act required each state to sell this land and to use the money to build colleges to teach agriculture and engineering.

Settling the Plains

People from all over the country moved West. Many farming families moved from areas where farmland was becoming scarce or expensive, such as New England. Many single women moved West. The Homestead Act granted land to unmarried women, which was unusual for the time.

The promise of land and a life free of discrimination also drew a large group of African Americans West. In 1879 some

20,000 to 40,000 southern African Americans moved to Kansas. Known as **Exodusters**, these southerners made a mass exodus, or departure, from the South. A number of black communities soon developed.

Western homesteads also were attractive to immigrants. Norwegian, Swedish, Danish, German, and Czech immigrants formed many small communities on the Great Plains.

Farming the Plains

Plains farmers had many unique challenges. The seasons were extreme. Weather could be extreme. Also, the root-filled sod, or dirt, beneath the Plains grass was very tough. The hard work of breaking up the sod earned Plains farmers the nickname **sodbusters**.

In the 1890s western Plains farmers began **dry farming**, a new method of farming that shifted the focus away from water-dependent crops such as corn. Instead, farmers grew more hardy crops like red wheat. In addition, by the 1880s mechanical farming was becoming common. By using machinery, farmers could work much more quickly on large fields with fewer workers. Farmers shipped their harvest east by train. From there, crops were shipped overseas. The Great Plains soon became known as the breadbasket of the world.

Primary Source

LETTER
Letter from the Plains, 1863

In a letter to her family in Norway, immigrant Gro Svendsen describes her new life as a farmer on the plains of Iowa.

"*I remember I used to wonder when I heard that it would be impossible to keep the milk here as we did at home. Now I have learned that it is indeed impossible because of the heat here in the summertime . . . It's difficult, too, to preserve the butter. One must pour brine [salt water] over it or salt it.*

The thunderstorms are so violent that one might think it was the end of the world . . . Quite often the lightning strikes down both cattle and people, damages property, and splinters sturdy oak trees into many pieces."

—quoted in *Sources in American History*

ANALYSIS SKILL **ANALYZING PRIMARY SOURCES**

What might be some of the differences between Norway and Svendsen's new home in Iowa?

Pioneers like this family often lived in houses made of sod because there were few trees for lumber on the Plains.

Building Communities

Women were an important force in the settlement of the frontier. They joined in the hard work of farming and ranching and helped build communities out of the widely spaced farms and small towns. Their role in founding communities **facilitated** a strong voice in public affairs. Wyoming women, for example, were granted the vote in the new state's constitution, which was approved in 1869. **Annie Bidwell**, one of the founders of Chico, California, used her influence to support a variety of moral and social causes such as women's suffrage and temperance.

Many early settlers found life on their remote farms to be extremely difficult. Farmers formed communities so that they could assist one another in times of need. One of the first things that many pioneer communities did was establish a local church and school.

Children helped with many chores around the farm. Author Laura Ingalls Wilder was one of four children in a pioneer family. Wilder's books about settlers' lives on the prairie are still popular today.

READING CHECK Comparing and Contrasting
How were settlers' lives alike and different from their lives in the East?

ACADEMIC VOCABULARY
facilitate to make easier

FOCUS ON NEW YORK

Today, agriculture is an important part of New York's economy. About one quarter of the state's land is used for farming, and its 36,000 farms produce products such as milk, meat, poultry, fruits, vegetables, and field crops such as corn, oats, and wheat.

Farmers' Political Groups

From 1860 to 1900, the U.S. population more than doubled. To feed this growing population, the number of farms tripled. With modern machines, farmers in 1900 could harvest a bushel of wheat almost 20 times faster than they could in 1830.

Farm Incomes Fall

The combination of more farms and greater productivity, however, led to overproduction. Overproduction resulted in lower prices for crops. As their incomes decreased, many farmers found it difficult to pay bills. Farmers who could not make their mortgage payments lost their farms and homes. Many of these homeless farmers became tenant farmers who worked land owned by others. By 1880 one-fourth of all farms were rented by tenants, and the number continued to grow.

The National Grange

Many farmers blamed businesspeople—wholesalers, brokers, grain buyers, and especially railroad owners—for making money at their expense. As economic conditions worsened, farmers began to follow the example of other workers. They formed associations to protect and help their interests.

Time Line

Farming and the Rise of Populism

1862 President Lincoln signs the bill that authorizes the transcontinental railroad.

1867 The National Grange is founded.

1879 Exodusters move to Kansas.

22

One such organization was founded by Oliver Hudson Kelley, who toured the South in 1866 for the U.S. Department of Agriculture. Kelley saw firsthand how the country's farmers suffered. Afterward, Kelley and several government clerks formed the National Grange of the Patrons of Husbandry in 1867. The **National Grange** was a social and educational organization for farmers. (*Grange* is an old word for granary.) Local chapters were quickly founded, and membership grew rapidly.

The Grange campaigned for political candidates who supported farmers' goals. The organization also called for laws that regulated rates charged by railroads. The U.S. Supreme Court ruled in 1877 that the government could regulate railroads because they affected the public interest. In 1886 the Court said that the federal government could only regulate companies doing business across state lines. Rate regulation for railroad lines within states fell to the state governments.

In February 1887 Congress passed the Interstate Commerce Act, providing national regulations over trade between states and creating the Interstate Commerce Commission to ensure fair railroad rates. However, the commission lacked power to enforce its regulations.

Agricultural Supply and Demand

CONNECT TO ECONOMICS

Supply is the amount of a good that is available. *Demand* is the amount of a good that people want to buy. When supply exceeds demand, prices fall.

What happened to the price of wheat as the supply increased?

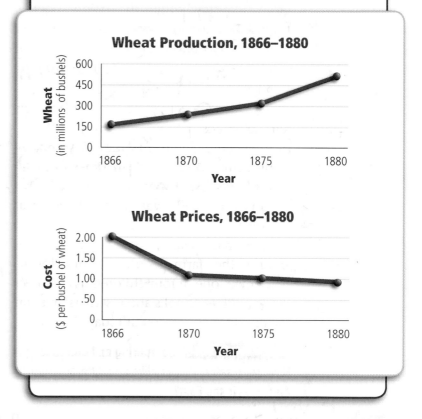

Wheat Production, 1866–1880

Wheat Prices, 1866–1880

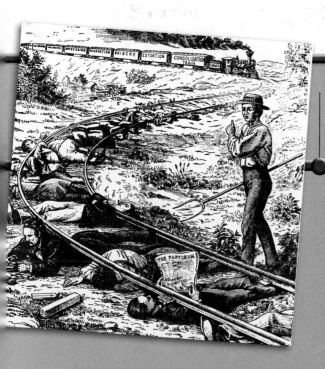

1887 The Interstate Commerce Commission is formed to regulate railroad prices.

1896 The Populist Party backs William Jennings Bryan as the Democratic presidential candidate.

1892 The national Populist Party is formed.

ANALYSIS SKILL READING TIME LINES

How many years after the authorization of the transcontinental railroad was the Interstate Commerce Commission created?

Free Silver Debate

Money issues also caused problems for farmers. Many farmers hoped that help would come from new laws affecting the money supply.

Since 1873 the United States had been on the gold standard, meaning that all paper money had to be backed by gold in the treasury. As a result, the money supply grow more slowly than the nation's population and led to **deflation**—a decrease in the money supply and overall lower prices. One solution was to allow the unlimited coining of silver and to back paper currency with silver. This was the position of those in the Free Silver movement.

During the late 1870s, there was a great deal of support for the Free Silver movement. Many farmers began backing political candidates who favored free silver coinage. One such candidate was **William Jennings Bryan** of Nebraska.

The two major political parties, however, largely ignored the money issue. After the election of 1888, the Republican-controlled Congress passed the Sherman Silver Purchase Act. The act increased the amount of silver purchased for coinage. However, this did not help farmers as much as they had hoped.

Populist Party

To have greater power, many farmers organized to elect candidates that would help them. These political organizations became known as the Farmers' Alliances.

In the 1890 elections the Alliances were a strong political force. State and local wins raised farmers' political hopes. At a conference in Cincinnati, Ohio, in 1891, Alliance leaders met with labor and reform groups. Then, at a convention in St. Louis in February 1892, the Alliances formed a new national political party.

The new party was called the **Populist Party**, and it called for the government to own railroads and telephone and telegraph systems. It also favored the "free and unlimited coinage of silver." To gain the votes of workers, the Populists backed an eight-hour workday and limits on immigration.

The concerns of the Populists were soon put in the national spotlight. During the Panic of 1893, the U.S. economy experienced a crisis that some critics blamed on the shortage of gold. The failure of several major railroad companies also contributed to the economic problems.

The Panic of 1893 led more people to back the Populist call for economic reform. In 1896 the Republicans nominated William McKinley for president. McKinley was firmly against free coinage of silver. The Democrats nominated William Jennings Bryan, who favored free coinage.

The Populists had to decide between running their own candidate, and thus splitting the silver vote, or supporting Bryan. They decided to support Bryan. The Republicans had a well-financed campaign, and they won the election. McKinley's victory in 1896 marked the end of both the Populist Party and the Farmers' Alliances.

READING CHECK Summarizing Why did farmers, laborers, and reformers join to form the Populist Party?

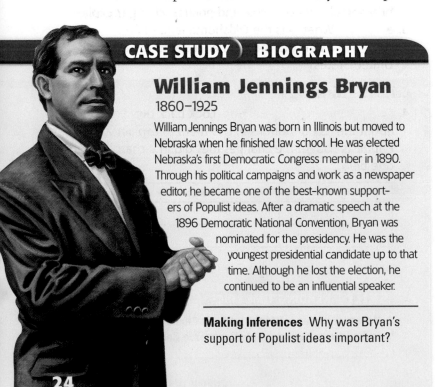

CASE STUDY) BIOGRAPHY

William Jennings Bryan
1860–1925

William Jennings Bryan was born in Illinois but moved to Nebraska when he finished law school. He was elected Nebraska's first Democratic Congress member in 1890. Through his political campaigns and work as a newspaper editor, he became one of the best-known supporters of Populist ideas. After a dramatic speech at the 1896 Democratic National Convention, Bryan was nominated for the presidency. He was the youngest presidential candidate up to that time. Although he lost the election, he continued to be an influential speaker.

Making Inferences Why was Bryan's support of Populist ideas important?

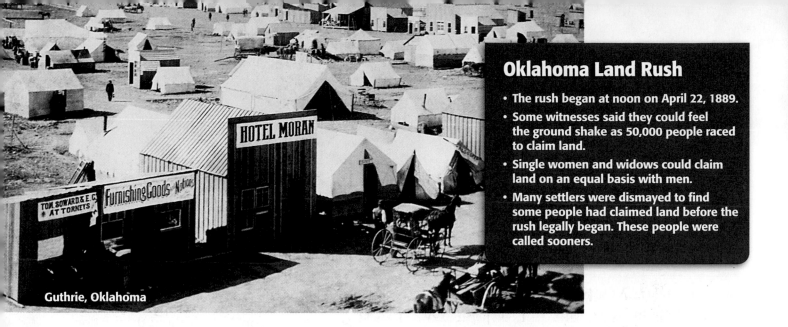

HOTEL MORAN

TOM SOWARD & E.C.
AT TORNEYS

Furnishing Goods

Guthrie, Oklahoma

Oklahoma Land Rush

- The rush began at noon on April 22, 1889.
- Some witnesses said they could feel the ground shake as 50,000 people raced to claim land.
- Single women and widows could claim land on an equal basis with men.
- Many settlers were dismayed to find some people had claimed land before the rush legally began. These people were called sooners.

End of the Frontier

By 1870 only small portions of the Great Plains remained unsettled. For most of the next two decades, this land remained open range.

In March 1889, government officials announced that homesteaders could file claims on land in what is now the state of Oklahoma. This land had belonged to Creek and Seminole Indians. Within a month, about 50,000 people rushed to Oklahoma to stake their claims.

In all, settlers claimed more than 11 million acres of former Indian land in the famous Oklahoma land rush. This huge wave of pioneers was the last chapter of the westward movement. By the early 1890s, the frontier had ceased to exist in the United States.

READING CHECK Finding Main Ideas
What event signaled the closing of the frontier?

SUMMARY AND PREVIEW In this section you read about the challenges settlers faced. In the next chapter you will read about the growth of America's industrial power and how that growth affected American lives.

go.hrw.com
Online Quiz

Section 3 Assessment

Reviewing Ideas, Terms, and People

1. **a. Describe** What groups settled in the Great Plains?
   b. Explain How did the U.S. government make lands available to western settlers?
   c. Elaborate Would you have chosen to settle on the frontier? Why or why not?
2. **a. Recall** What was the goal of the **National Grange**?
   b. Make Inferences Why did the **Populist Party** want the government to own railroads and telegraph and telephone systems?
   c. Evaluate Do you think farmers were successful in bringing about economic and political change? Explain.
3. **a. Recall** What was the Oklahoma land rush?
   b. Explain Why did the frontier cease to exist in the United States?

Critical Thinking

4. **Comparing and Contrasting** Look back over your notes about the rise of populism. Use them to explain why Populists sought the changes they did in a chart like the one below.

Change sought	Reason why

FOCUS ON WRITING

5. **Farming the Great Plains** As you read this section, take notes on the growth of farming on the Great Plains. How did farmers interact with the railroads? What changes might have been apparent to a railroad worker?

Social Studies Skills

Comparing Migration Maps

Define the Skill

One of the best ways of using geography to learn history is by comparing maps. This skill allows you to see changes over time. It also helps you see relationships between one factor, such as population growth, and another factor, such as transportation routes or economic activities in an area.

Learn the Skill

Follow these steps to compare information on maps.

1 Apply basic map skills by reading the title and studying the legend and symbols for each map.

2 Note the date of each map and the area it covers. Maps compared for changes over time should include the same areas. Those used to look for relationships should have similar dates.

3 Note similarities or differences. Closely examine and compare each map's patterns and symbols.

4 Apply critical thinking skills. Make generalizations and draw conclusions about the relationships you find.

Practice the Skill

Use the maps below to answer the following questions.

1. What present-day state was unsettled by Americans in 1850 and almost completely settled in 1890?

2. Which other two present-day states show the most settlement by Americans from 1850 to 1890?

3. Why do you think the West coast was settled before the interior of the United States?

4. According to the maps, how might rivers have shaped the settlement of the West?

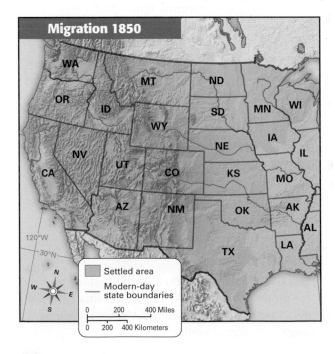

Migration 1850

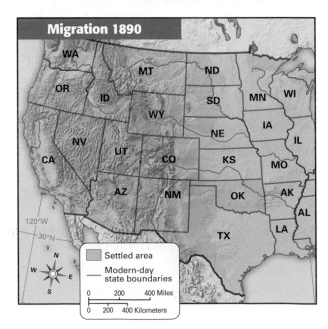

Migration 1890

Chapter Review

HOLT
History's Impact
▶ video series
Review the video to answer the closing question:
How was a cowboy's job essential to the American economy?

Visual Summary

Use the visual summary below to help you review the main ideas of the chapter.

QUICK FACTS

The American West

As settlers moved West, they came into conflict with American Indians. The U.S. government defeated Indian resistance and moved many tribes to reservations.

The completion of the transcontinental railroad in 1869 opened the West to more settlement. Gold and silver strikes also drew people hoping to get rich.

The railroads helped make the rise of the Cattle Kingdom possible. Cowboys drove huge herds of cattle from ranches to railway stations to be shipped to the East.

Farmers settled the Great Plains in large numbers. They overcame many hardships to make the Plains the breadbasket of America.

Reviewing Vocabulary, Terms, and People

1. Who was the leader of the 7th Cavalry in the Battle of the Little Bighorn?

a. Cyrus McCormick
c. William Jennings Bryan
b. Leland Stanford
d. George Armstrong Custer

2. What act gave millions of acres of federal lands to the states, which were to sell them and use those funds to build agricultural and engineering colleges?

a. Morrill Act
c. Pacific Railway Act
b. Sherman Act
d. Interstate Commerce Act

3. Which frontier woman was instrumental in supporting reform efforts in the West?

a. Sarah Winnemucca
c. Annie Bidwell
b. Laura Ingalls Wilder
d. Lucretia Mott

Comprehension and Critical Thinking

SECTION 1 *(Pages 6–12)*

4. a. Recall Why were many Americans eager to move to the western frontier?

b. Analyze How did railroads and ranching change the landscape of the West?

c. Elaborate In your opinion, which made the greatest changes to the West—mining, ranching, or railroads? Explain your answer.

SECTION 2 *(Pages 13–18)*

5. a. Describe What was life like for the Plains Indians before and after the arrival of large numbers of American settlers?

b. Draw Conclusions Why did the spread of the Ghost Dance movement cause concern for U.S. officials?

c. Elaborate What do you think about the reservation system established by the United States?

SECTION 3 *(Pages 20–25)*

6. **a. Identify** What political organizations did western farmers create? Why did farmers create these organizations?

b. Analyze How did women participate in the settling of the American frontier?

c. Predict How might the end of the frontier in the United States affect the nation?

Reviewing Themes

7. **Geography** What geographic obstacles did miners, ranchers, and railroad workers face in the West?

8. **Science and Technology** What types of technology did farmers on the Great Plains use? How did it benefit them?

Using the Internet   go.hrw.com

9. **Activity: Creating a Presentation** Our view of the settlement of the West is heavily influenced by popular culture. Writers, painters, and illustrators provided a steady flow of words and images that sensationalized life in the American West. Later, film makers and television producers also contributed to the myth of the Wild West. "When legend becomes fact," said one actor in the classic western movie *The Man Who Shot Liberty Valance*, "print the legend." How does legend affect our view of this part of our history? Enter the activity keyword. Analyze the myths and realities of the West and the ways in which they shaped our view of that time period. Then create a visual display or PowerPoint presentation to present your research.

Reading Skills

Understanding Through Questioning *Use the Reading Skills taught in this chapter to answer the question about the reading selection below.*

> For survival, Plains Indians depended on two animals—the horse and the buffalo. The Spanish brought horses to America in the 1500s. Plains Indians learned to ride horses, and hunters used them to follow buffalo herds year-round. *(p. 14)*

10. Write two or three questions you have about the information in the passage above. Remember to use the five W's—Who? What? When? Where? and Why?

Social Studies Skills

Comparing Migration Maps *Use the Social Studies Skills taught in this chapter to answer the questions about the map below.*

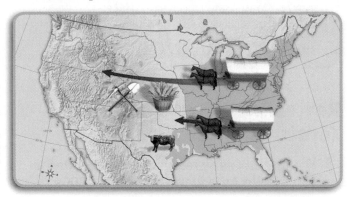

11. According to the map above, for what reasons did settlers migrate to the West?

a. for mining, ranching, and farming

b. for jobs in manufacturing

c. for the homes in the major cities there

d. for the fishing industry

FOCUS ON WRITING

12. **Writing Your Letter** Review your notes. Then write a letter to your sister back in Ireland about your experiences on the Great Plains. Describe all the changes you have seen. Use colorful language and precise details to make your sister feel as though she were there.

Grade 8 Intermediate-Level Test Preparation

Directions (1-5): For each statement or question, write on the separate answer sheet the *number* of the word or expression that, of those given, best completes the statement or answers the question.

Base your answer to question 1 on the list below and on your knowledge of social studies.

> - Government ownership of railroads
> - Free and unlimited coinage of silver
> - An eight-hour day for industrial workers
> - Strict limits on foreign immigration
> - Election of officials who will help farmers

1 Which of the following intended to accomplish the changes listed above in American society?

(1) the Morrill Act
(2) the Populist Party
(3) the National Grange
(4) the Homestead Act

2 The goal of many reformers who wanted to help Native Americans in the late 1800s was to

(1) get Indians to adopt the ways of white people.
(2) return to Indians all the land that had been taken from them.
(3) relocate all the nations to create an American Indian state in Oklahoma.
(4) negotiate treaties to bring peace to the frontier.

3 What played the *most* important part in the growth of the West's population and economy between 1865 and 1900?

(1) the mining industry
(2) the Cattle Kingdom
(3) the Populist Party
(4) the railroad

4 In general, the policy of the United States government toward Native Americans in the West was to

(1) send the army to track them down and engage them in battle.
(2) move them onto reservations and open their homelands to white settlers.
(3) kill all the buffalo so that they could not continue their traditional way of life.
(4) drive them into Canada or Mexico to settle.

5 The biggest problem facing western farmers in the late 1800s was

(1) a scarcity of good, cheap land to farm.
(2) their lack of organization to achieve change.
(3) overproduction and low crop prices.
(4) the threat of attacks by Native Americans.

Base your answer to question 6 on the text below and on your knowledge of social studies.

> "You said that you wanted to put us upon a reservation, to build us houses and make us medicine lodges [places of religious practice]. I do not want them. I was born upon the prairie, where the wind blew free and there was nothing to break the light of the sun. I was born where there were no enclosures and where everything drew a free breath. I want to die there and not within walls."
>
> —Ten Bears, quoted in *Eyewitnesses and Others*

6 Constructed-Response Question Why does Ten Bears not want to move to a reservation?

The Industrial Age

FOCUS QUESTION

How did industrialization and immigration change the face of American life?

FOCUS ON WRITING

A Business Plan You are an inventor in the late 1800s, and you want to start a business to sell your new inventions. Write a business plan for investors that will encourage them to lend you money to start your business. As you read this chapter, gather information about the new business practices that you can use to run your business. Then write your plan. Include information about what you will sell, how you will make it, and how you can avoid conflicts with the workers who make your product.

UNITED STATES

1879
Thomas Edison invents the first lightbulb.

1870

WORLD

1876
German engineer Nikolaus A. Otto perfects a gasoline-powered engine.

HOLT

History's Impact
▶ video series
Watch the video to understand the impact of the United States as the world's most powerful industrial nation.

What You Will Learn...

In this chapter you will learn about how the United States became an industrial power in the late 1800s. A new wave of immigrants provided the labor, and the combination of industry and immigration led to increased urbanization of the country. Cities like San Francisco, shown here, began to take the shape that they still have today. In fact, much of what we know as modern America developed during this important period.

1883
The Brooklyn Bridge opens.

NY

1886
The American Federation of Labor is formed on December 8.

1890
Congress passes the Sherman Antitrust Act.

1892
On June 29 the Homestead strike begins. Carnegie Steel Company refuses to negotiate with the union.

1880

1883 The island volcano of Krakatau in the Pacific Ocean erupts in one of the world's greatest natural disasters.

1889 The Eiffel Tower is built in Paris.

1890

1898 French scientists Pierre and Marie Curie discover radium.

1900

31

Reading Social Studies

by Kylene Beers

Economics | Geography | Politics | Society and Culture | Science and Technology

Focus on Themes In this chapter, you will read about the advancements in transportation and communication made during what is called the Second Industrial Revolution. You will learn about the rise of powerful corporations. You will also read about the workers who organized in the late 1800s and will see what happened as unions began demanding better treatment for workers. Throughout the chapter, you will see how **society** was affected by the changing **economy**.

Organization of Facts and Information

Focus on Reading How are clothes organized in a department store? How are files arranged in a file cabinet? Clear organization helps us find the product we need, and it also helps us find facts and information.

Understanding Structural Patterns Writers use structural patterns to organize information in sentences or paragraphs. What's a structural pattern? It's simply a way of organizing information. Learning to recognize those patterns will make it easier for you to read and understand social studies texts.

Patterns of Organization		
Pattern	**Clue Words**	**Graphic Organizer**
Cause-effect shows how one thing leads to another.	as a result, therefore, because, this led to	Cause → Effect, Effect, Effect → Effect
Chronological order shows the sequence of events or actions.	after, before, first, then, not long after, finally	First → Next → Last
Comparison-contrast points out similarities and/or differences.	although, but, however, on the other hand, similarly, also	Differences / Similarities
Listing presents information in categories such as size, location, or importance.	also, most important, for example, in fact	Category • Fact • Fact • Fact

To use text structure to improve your understanding, follow these steps:

1. Look for the main idea of the passage you are reading.
2. Then look for clues that signal a specific pattern.
3. Look for other important ideas and think about how the ideas connect. Is there any obvious pattern?
4. Use a graphic organizer to map the relationships among the facts and details.

You Try It!

The following passages are from the chapter you are about to read. As you read each set of sentences, ask yourself what structural pattern the writer used to organize the information.

Recognizing Structural Patterns

(A) Great advances in communication technologies took place in the late 1800s. By 1861, telegraph wires connected the East and West coasts. Five years later, a telegraph cable on the floor of the Atlantic Ocean connected the United States and Great Britain. *(p. 37)*

(B) Many business leaders justified their business methods through their belief in social Darwinism . . . Other business leaders, however, believed that the rich had a duty to aid the poor. *(p. 41)*

(C) During the late 1800s, several factors led to a decline in the quality of working conditions. Machines run by unskilled workers were eliminating the jobs of many skilled craftspeople. These low-paid workers could be replaced easily. *(p. 44)*

After you read the passages, answer the questions below:

1. Reread passage A. What structural pattern did the writer use to organize this information? How can you tell?

2. Reread passage B. What structural pattern did the writer use to organize this information? How can you tell? Why do you think the writer chose this pattern?

3. Reread passage C. What structural pattern did the writer use to organize this information? How can you tell? Why do you think the writer chose this pattern?

As you read Chapter 2, think about the organization of the ideas. Ask yourself why the writer chose to organize the information in this way.

Key Terms and People

Academic Vocabulary

In this chapter, you will learn the following academic words:
implement *(p. 37)*
acquire *(p. 40)*

The Second Industrial Revolution

What You Will Learn...

Main Ideas

1. Breakthroughs in steel processing led to a boom in railroad construction.
2. Advances in the use of oil and electricity improved communications and transportation.
3. A rush of inventions changed Americans' lives.

The Big Idea

The Second Industrial Revolution led to new sources of power and advances in transportation and communication.

Key Terms and People

Second Industrial Revolution, *p. 35*
Bessemer process, *p. 35*
Thomas Edison, *p. 36*
patents, *p. 36*
Alexander Graham Bell, *p. 37*
Henry Ford, *p. 37*
Wilbur and Orville Wright, *p. 38*

TAKING NOTES As you read this section, take notes on the inventors of the Second Industrial Revolution. Organize your notes in a table like the one below.

Inventor

If YOU were there...

You live in a small town but are visiting an aunt in the city in the 1890s. You are amazed when your aunt pushes a button on the wall to turn on electric lights. At home you still use kerosene lamps. You hear a clatter outside and see an electric streetcar traveling down the street. You are shocked when a telephone rings, and your aunt speaks to someone miles away!

Which of these inventions would you find most amazing?

BUILDING BACKGROUND The first Industrial Revolution in America began in the early 1800s. It changed the way products were made, from handwork to machines. It moved the workplace from cottages to factories. Later, it brought advances in transportation and communication. The Second Industrial Revolution built on these changes, introducing new technology and new sources of power.

Breakthroughs in Steel Processing

Technological advances were important to the **Second Industrial Revolution**, a period of rapid growth in U.S. manufacturing in the late 1800s. By the mid-1890s, the United States had become the world's industrial leader.

The Steel Industry

Some of the most important advances in technology happened in the steel industry. Steel is iron that has been made stronger by heat and the addition of other metals. In the mid-1850s Henry Bessemer invented the **Bessemer process**, a way to manufacture steel quickly and cheaply by blasting hot air through melted iron to quickly remove impurities. Before, turning several tons of iron ore into steel took a day or more. The Bessemer process took only 10 to 20 minutes.

The Bessemer process helped increase steel production. U.S. mills had produced 77,000 tons of steel in 1870. By 1879 production had risen to more than 1 million tons in one year.

Riding the Rails

As steel dropped in price, so did the cost of building railroads. Companies built thousands of miles of new steel track. The design of elegant passenger and sleeping cars improved passenger service. Manufacturers and farmers sent products to market faster than ever by rail in newly invented refrigerated shipping cars. Cities where major rail lines crossed, such as Chicago, grew rapidly. Railroads also increased western growth by offering free tickets to settlers. Finally, as rail travel and shipping increased, railroads and related industries began employing more people.

 **READING CHECK** **Identifying Cause and Effect** How did steel processing change in the 1850s? How did this affect the United States?

QUICK FACTS

Factors Affecting Industrial Growth

- Greater ability to use natural resources
- A growing population
- Transportation advances
- Rising immigration
- Inventions and innovations
- Increasing business investment
- Government policies assisting business, such as protective tariffs

Homestead Steel Mill

Steel mills like this one in Homestead, Pennsylvania, were the center of the new steel industry that led to advancements in rail travel. Workers used the Bessemer process to make steel more quickly.

How do you think mills like this one affected the surrounding area?

35

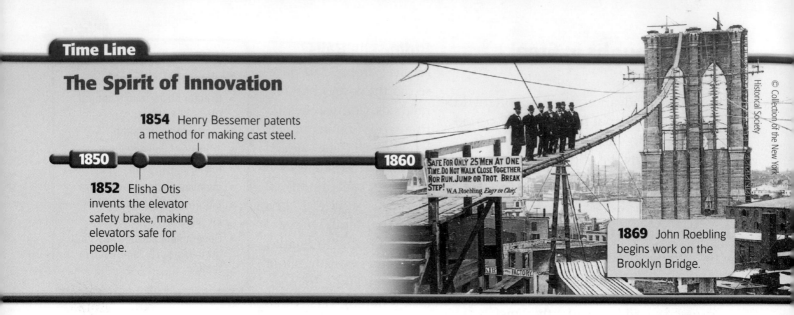

1854 Henry Bessemer patents a method for making cast steel.

1850

1860

1852 Elisha Otis invents the elevator safety brake, making elevators safe for people.

SAFE FOR ONLY 25 MEN AT ONE TIME. DO NOT WALK CLOSE TOGETHER NOR RUN, JUMP OR TROT. BREAK STEP! W.A.Roebling *Engr in Chief.*

1869 John Roebling begins work on the Brooklyn Bridge.

© Collection of the New York Historical Society

Use of Oil and Electricity

The Second Industrial Revolution was characterized by dramatic developments in the use and distribution of oil and electricity. These power sources fueled other changes.

Oil as a Power Source

An important technological breakthrough in the late 1800s was the use of petroleum, or oil, as a power source. People had known about oil for many years but had discovered few ways to use it. However, in the 1850s, chemists invented a way to convert crude, or unprocessed, oil into a fuel called kerosene. Kerosene could be used for cooking, heating, and lighting. Suddenly, there was a demand for oil.

FOCUS ON READING

How does this paragraph show the cause-and-effect structure?

As demand grew, people began searching for a reliable source for oil. In 1859 Edwin L. Drake proved that it was possible to pump crude oil from the ground. Soon, wildcatters, or oil prospectors, drilled for oil in Ohio, Pennsylvania, and West Virginia. Oil became a big business as these states began producing millions of barrels per year. Oil companies built refineries to turn the crude oil into finished products like kerosene. One oil company supervisor referred to oil workers as "men who are supplying light for the world."

Electricity Spreads

In addition to kerosene, electricity became a critical source of light and power during the Second Industrial Revolution. The possible uses of electricity interested inventors like **Thomas Edison**. His research center in Menlo Park, New Jersey, was called an invention factory. Edison explained his practical approach to science.

"I do not regard myself as a pure scientist, as so many persons have insisted that I am. I do not search for the laws of nature ... for the purpose of learning truth. I am only a professional inventor ... with the object [goal] of inventing that which will have commercial utility [use]."

—Thomas Edison, quoted in *American Made,* by Harold C. Livesay

Edison eventually held more than 1,000 **patents**, exclusive rights to make or sell inventions. Patents allowed inventors to protect their inventions from being manufactured by others.

In 1878 Edison announced that he would soon invent a practical electric light. By the end of 1879 Edison and his team of inventors had created the electric lightbulb. The public was excited. However, Edison had a problem. At the time, few homes or businesses could get electricity. Edison therefore built a power plant that began supplying electricity to dozens of New York City buildings in

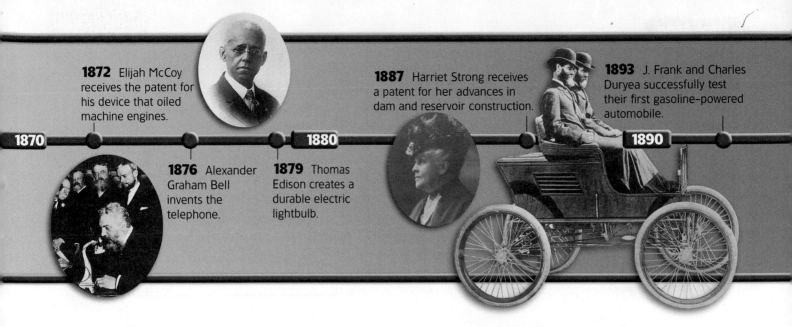

1872 Elijah McCoy receives the patent for his device that oiled machine engines.

1876 Alexander Graham Bell invents the telephone.

1879 Thomas Edison creates a durable electric lightbulb.

1887 Harriet Strong receives a patent for her advances in dam and reservoir construction.

1893 J. Frank and Charles Duryea successfully test their first gasoline-powered automobile.

1870   1880   1890

September 1882. The *New York Times* reported that with electric lighting in the newspaper offices, "it seemed almost like writing by daylight." However, Edison's equipment could not send electricity over long distances. As a result, his power company, Edison Electric, provided electricity mainly to central cities.

In the late 1880s, George Westinghouse built a power system that could send electricity across many miles. As Edison and Westinghouse competed, the use of electricity spread rapidly in the nation's cities. After a while, electricity soon lit homes and businesses and powered city factories. Electricity also was used to power streetcars in cities across the nation.

READING CHECK Drawing Conclusions
Why did people begin to pump oil from the ground?

Rush of Inventions

In the late 1800s, inventors focused on finding solutions to practical problems. Communication and transportation took the lead.

Advances in Communication

Great advances in communication technologies took place in the late 1800s. By 1861, telegraph wires connected the East and West coasts. Five years later, a telegraph cable on the floor of the Atlantic Ocean connected the United States and Great Britain.

However, the telegraph carried only written messages and was difficult for untrained people to use. These problems were solved in March 1876, when inventor **Alexander Graham Bell** patented the telephone. Bell was a Scottish-born speech teacher who studied the science of sound. He called the telephone a "talking telegraph."

Telephone companies raced to lay thousands of miles of phone lines. By 1880 there were about 55,000 telephones in the United States, and by 1900 there were almost 1.5 million.

Automobiles and Planes

In 1876 a German engineer invented an engine powered by gasoline, another fuel made from oil. In 1893 Charles and J. Frank Duryea used a gasoline engine to build the first practical motorcar in the United States. By the early 1900s, thousands of cars were being built in the United States.

At first, only the wealthy could buy these early cars. **Henry Ford** introduced the Model T in 1908. Ford was the first to **implement** the moving assembly line in manufacturing, a process that greatly reduced the cost of building a product, thus making cars more affordable.

THE IMPACT TODAY

AT&T Corporation is a direct descendant of Bell's original company. AT&T pioneered the use of telephone cables across the oceans, satellite communications, and a radar system for the U.S. Defense Department.

ACADEMIC VOCABULARY

implement
to put in place

The Spirit of Innovation

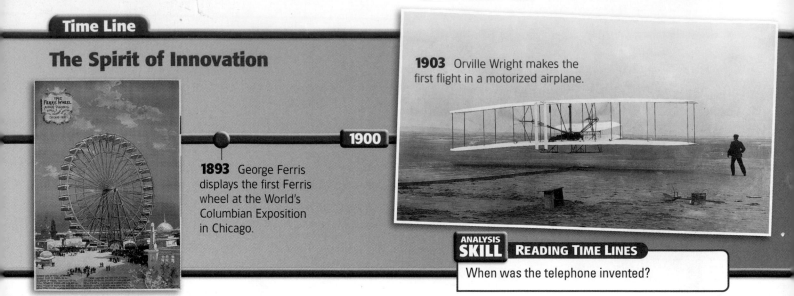

1903 Orville Wright makes the first flight in a motorized airplane.

1893 George Ferris displays the first Ferris wheel at the World's Columbian Exposition in Chicago.

1900

ANALYSIS SKILL **READING TIME LINES**

When was the telephone invented?

New engine technology helped make another breakthrough in transportation possible—air flight. Brothers **Wilbur and Orville Wright** built a lightweight airplane that used a small, gas-powered engine. In Kitty Hawk, North Carolina, Orville Wright made the first piloted flight in a gas-powered plane on December 17, 1903. This invention would change the way that many Americans traveled in the future and would increase the demand for oil production.

READING CHECK **Comparing** What new inventions excited the public in the 1800s? How were they used?

SUMMARY AND PREVIEW The Second Industrial Revolution led to advances in energy sources, communication, and transportation. In the next section you will learn about the growth of big business.

go.hrw.com
Online Quiz

Section 1 Assessment

Reviewing Ideas, Terms, and People

1. **a. Describe** What was the **Bessemer process**?
   b. Summarize How did improvements to railroads affect the economy and transportation in the United States?
   c. Elaborate What do you think was the most important effect of the Bessemer process? Why?
2. **a. Identify** What is kerosene, and for what could it be used?
   b. Explain What problem did **Thomas Edison** face regarding the use of electricity, and how did he solve it?
3. **a. Recall** What contribution did **Wilbur and Orville Wright** make to transportation?
   b. Draw Conclusions How did **Alexander Graham Bell**'s invention improve life in the United States?
   c. Elaborate Why do you think there was a rush of inventions in the late 1800s?

Critical Thinking

4. **Analyzing** Look over your notes on inventors. Use them to complete a table like the one below about inventors and their inventions.

Inventor	Invention

FOCUS ON WRITING

5. **Information on a Product** In your notes, list what kinds of new products became available at this time. What do you think would be a good thing to make and sell during the late 1800s?

Big Business

If **YOU** were there...

It is 1895, and your town is home to a large corporation. The company's founder and owner, a wealthy man, lives in a mansion on a hill. He is a fair employer but not especially generous. Many townspeople work in his factory. You and other town leaders feel that he should contribute more to local charities and community organizations.

How could this business leader help the town more?

BUILDING BACKGROUND Advanced technology along with the use of oil and electric power helped American businesses grow. Soon, the shape of the American economy changed. Some companies grew so large that they began to dominate entire industries.

Dominance of Big Business

In the late 1800s many entrepreneurs formed their businesses as **corporations**, or businesses that sell portions of ownership called stock shares. The leaders of these corporations were some of the most widely respected members of American society in the late 1800s. Political leaders praised prosperous businesspeople as examples of American hard work, talent, and success.

What You Will Learn...

Main Ideas

1. The rise of corporations and powerful business leaders led to the dominance of big business in the United States.
2. People and the government began to question the methods of big business.

The Big Idea

The growth of big business in the late 1800s led to the creation of monopolies.

Key Terms and People

corporations, *p. 39*
Andrew Carnegie, *p. 40*
vertical integration, *p. 40*
John D. Rockefeller, *p. 40*
horizontal integration, *p. 41*
trust, *p. 41*
Leland Stanford, *p. 41*
social Darwinism, *p. 41*
monopoly, *p. 42*
Sherman Antitrust Act, *p. 42*

TAKING NOTES As you read this section, take notes on the new business practices you learn about. Keep them organized in a chart like the one below.

New Business Practice

New sales techniques like those taught by John H. Patterson helped change business practices.

Corporations Generate Wealth

Successful corporations reward not only the people who found them but also investors who hold stock. Stockholders in a corporation typically get a percentage of profits based on the amount of stock they own. Although stockholders actually own the corporation, they do not run its day-to-day business. Instead, they elect a board of directors that chooses the corporation's main leaders, such as the president.

While many companies kept traditional ways of doing business, corporations provided several important advantages over earlier business forms. Stockholders in a corporation are not responsible for business debts. If a corporation fails financially, the stockholders lose only the money that they invested. Stockholders are also usually free to sell their stock to whomever they want, whenever they want. As a result, corporations encouraged more investment in businesses. By 1900 more than 100 million shares per year were being traded on the New York Stock Exchange.

Business Leaders

Business leaders used new decision-making strategies to help them build wealthy and powerful companies. **Andrew Carnegie** was one of the most admired businesspeople of the time. Born in Scotland, Carnegie came to the United States as a poor immigrant. As a teenager he took a job with a railroad company and quickly worked his way up to the position of railroad superintendent.

In 1873 he focused his efforts on steel-making. Carnegie expanded his business by buying out competitors when steel prices were low. By 1901 Carnegie's mills were producing more steel than all of Great Britain's mills combined. Carnegie's businesses succeeded largely through **vertical integration**, or ownership of businesses involved in each step of a manufacturing process. For example, to lower production costs, Carnegie acquired the iron ore mines, coalfields, and railroads needed to supply and support his steel mills.

John D. Rockefeller was also successful in consolidating, or combining, businesses. By age 21, while a partner in a wholesale business, he decided to start an oil-refining company. In only 10 years Rockefeller's Standard Oil Company was the country's largest oil refiner. Like Carnegie, Rockefeller used

FOCUS ON NEW YORK

In addition to a rise in big businesses, the second half of the 1800s also saw the rise of banking and financial institutions. One of the most successful bankers was J. P. Morgan, who began his career in New York in the 1850s and 1860s. His firm, JP Morgan & Co., was established in 1895 and became one of the most powerful banks in the world. At the turn of the century, Morgan was the richest man in the United States.

ACADEMIC VOCABULARY

acquire to get

The Rise of Investing

Investors purchased stock in corporations in record numbers in the late 1800s. They received stock certificates, like the one shown here, to document their part ownership in corporations. Corporations used the money raised by selling stocks to expand. Standard Oil Company financed the building of this refinery in Richmond, California, by selling stock.

Why did investors buy stock?

POLITICAL CARTOON
Trusts

The wealth and size of trusts such as Standard Oil made many Americans fear the influence of business leaders over government.

What do you think the smokestacks on the Capitol building represent?

What does the position of the White House suggest?

ANALYSIS SKILL **ANALYZING PRIMARY SOURCES**

How does the cartoonist show Rockefeller's power?

vertical integration. For example, the company controlled most of the pipelines it used.

Rockefeller's company also developed **horizontal integration**, or owning all businesses in a certain field. By 1880 Rockefeller's companies controlled about 90 percent of the oil refining business in the United States. Rockefeller also formed a **trust**, a legal arrangement grouping together a number of companies under a single board of directors. To earn more money, trusts often tried to get rid of competition and to control production.

Leland Stanford was another important business leader of the late 1800s. He made a fortune selling equipment to miners. While governor of California, he became one of the founders of the state's Central Pacific railroad. Stanford also founded Stanford University.

Late in life, Stanford argued that industries should be owned and managed cooperatively by workers. He believed this would be the fulfillment of democracy.

READING CHECK Comparing and Contrasting
Why did Andrew Carnegie use vertical integration?

Questioning the Methods of Big Business

By the late 1800s, people and the government were becoming uncomfortable with child labor, low wages, and poor working conditions. They began to view big business as a problem.

Social Darwinism

Many business leaders justified their business methods through their belief in **social Darwinism**, a view of society based on scientist Charles Darwin's theory of natural selection. Social Darwinists thought that Darwin's "survival of the fittest" theory decided which human beings would succeed in business and in life in general.

Other business leaders, however, believed that the rich had a duty to aid the poor. These leaders tried to help the less fortunate through philanthropy, or giving money to charities. Carnegie, Rockefeller, Stanford, and other business leaders gave away large sums. Carnegie gave away more than $350 million to charities, about $60 million of which

FOCUS ON NEW YORK CITY

Wealthy businesspeople of the late 1800s such as Andrew Carnegie, John D. Rockefeller, and J. P. Morgan were behind many of the philanthropic and business efforts that still help define New York City. Carnegie Hall, Rockefeller Center, and the Metropolitan Museum of Art all owe much to these wealthy men. Foundations first organized by the men still support art and education programs across the nation.

went to fund public libraries to expand access to books.

The Antitrust Movement

Critics of big business said that many business leaders earned their fortunes through unfair business practices. These criticisms grew stronger in the 1880s as corporations became more powerful. Large corporations often used their size and strength to drive smaller competitors out of business. Carnegie and Rockefeller, for example, pressured railroads to charge their companies lower shipping rates. Powerful trusts also arranged to sell goods and services below market value. Smaller competitors went out of business trying to match those prices. Then the trusts raised prices again.

Some people became concerned when a trust gained a **monopoly**, or total ownership of a product or service. Critics argued that monopolies reduced necessary competition. They believed competition in a free market economy kept prices low and the quality of goods and services high.

Some Americans also worried about the political power of wealthy trusts. Many citizens and small businesses wanted the government to help control monopolies and trusts. People who favored trusts responded that trusts were more efficient and gave the consumer dependable products or services.

Many members of Congress favored big business. However, elected officials could not ignore the concerns of voters. In July 1890 Congress passed the **Sherman Antitrust Act**, a law that made it illegal to create monopolies or trusts that restrained trade. It stated that any "attempt to monopolize . . . any part of the trade or commerce among the several States" was a crime. However, the act did not clearly define a trust in legal terms. The antitrust laws were therefore difficult to enforce. Corporations and trusts kept growing in size and power.

The federal government also began regulating interstate commerce, or the movement of goods between states. The Interstate Commerce Commission, established in 1887, regulated the railroad industry by setting the rates railroads could charge for different routes.

READING CHECK **Analyzing** How did concerns about trusts lead to the Sherman Antitrust Act?

SUMMARY AND PREVIEW In the late 1800s some corporations became monopolies that dominated industries such as oil. In the next section you will learn about how industrial workers organized to improve working conditions.

go.hrw.com
Online Quiz

Section 2 Assessment

Reviewing Ideas, Terms, and People

1. **a. Identify** What are **horizontal** and **vertical integration**?
   b. Explain What are the benefits of investing in **corporations**?
   c. Evaluate What do you think about the business methods of **Carnegie**, **Rockefeller**, and **Stanford**?
2. **a. Describe** What is **social Darwinism**?
   b. Summarize What concerns did critics of big business have regarding **trusts**?
   c. Evaluate Was the **Sherman Antitrust Act** successful? Why or why not?

Critical Thinking

3. **Contrasting** Look back over your notes about new business practices. Find examples of the new business practices. Use them to complete a graphic organizer like the one below.

New Practices	Example

FOCUS ON WRITING

4. **Gathering Information on Business** Look back over your notes and determine what new practices helped businesses expand during this time. Which practices could you use to start your business? Where would you try to sell your product?

Andrew Carnegie, John D. Rockefeller, and Leland Stanford

How would you go about building an industry?

Andrew Carnegie (1835–1919) Born in Scotland, Carnegie rose to become a multibillionaire in the steel industry. He brought new technologies to his steel mills and made them extremely efficient. In 1901 he sold Carnegie Steel Company for $250 billion, making him the richest man in the world.

John D. Rockefeller (1839–1937) Rockefeller got his start in the oil business in Cleveland, Ohio. Rockefeller's Standard Oil Company quickly bought out its competitors throughout the United States. To better control oil production and delivery, Rockefeller also bought railroad rights, terminals, and pipelines.

Leland Stanford (1825–1893) Leland Stanford was born to a New York farming family that sent him to excellent private schools. After practicing law in Wisconsin, he made his career in California. Stanford was instrumental in building the western section of the transcontinental railroad. He then plunged into politics, serving one term as governor. His political connections helped him obtain huge state land grants and other benefits for his railroad companies. As president of Central Pacific and Southern Pacific, he oversaw the laying of thousands of miles of track throughout the West.

Why are they so important? Carnegie, Rockefeller, and Stanford helped make America the world's greatest industrial power by the end of the 1800s. They built giant industries that made goods cheaply by keeping workers' wages low. They also engaged in ruthless business practices to defeat their competition and create monopolies. The Sherman Antitrust Act was passed in reaction to the Standard Oil monopoly. Later in life, all three men became philanthropists, people devoted to charity work. Rockefeller's philanthropies gave out $500 million in his lifetime. Carnegie spent $350 million, funding educational grants, concert halls, and nearly 3,000 public libraries. Stanford founded Stanford University in 1884.

Finding Main Ideas
Why are these three men important figures in U.S. history?

Carnegie

Rockefeller   Stanford

Industrial Workers

What You Will Learn...

Main Ideas

1. The desire to maximize profits and become more efficient led to poor working conditions.
2. Workers began to organize and demand improvements in working conditions and pay.
3. Labor strikes often turned violent and failed to accomplish their goals.

The Big Idea

Changes in the workplace led to a rise in labor unions and workers' strikes.

Key Terms and People

Frederick W. Taylor, *p. 44*
Knights of Labor, *p. 45*
Terence V. Powderly, *p. 45*
American Federation of Labor, *p. 45*
Samuel Gompers, *p. 45*
collective bargaining, *p. 46*
Mary Harris Jones, *p. 46*
Haymarket Riot, *p. 46*
Homestead strike, *p. 47*
Pullman strike, *p. 47*

TAKING NOTES As you read this section, take notes about the problems workers faced in the new economy. Organize your notes in a chart like the one below.

Problems of Workers

If YOU were there...

You run a button machine in a clothing factory in the 1890s. You work from 7:00 in the morning until 6:00 at night, every day except Sunday. Your only break is 15 minutes for lunch. Now you hear about a movement to start a workers' union to bargain with your employer. Union members will ask for an eight-hour workday. But you think your employer might fire you if you join.

Would you join the union?

BUILDING BACKGROUND The rise of corporations and the establishment of monopolies gave big business a great deal of power. An antitrust movement arose to try to limit the power of trusts. Workers themselves began to organize and take action against bad working conditions and other problems.

Maximizing Profits and Efficiency

During the late 1800s, several factors led to a decline in the quality of working conditions. Machines run by unskilled workers were eliminating the jobs of many skilled craftspeople. These low-paid workers could be replaced easily. Factories began to focus on specialization, or workers repeating a single step again and again. Specialization brought costs down and caused production to rise. But it also made workers tired, bored, and more likely to be injured. Specialization allowed for Henry Ford's idea of a moving assembly line to speed production. Ford's use of the moving assembly line allowed automobiles to be made more quickly and cheaply. Automobiles soon became available to a wider segment of the population than ever before.

In 1909 **Frederick W. Taylor**, an efficiency engineer, published a popular book called *The Principles of Scientific Management*. He encouraged managers to view workers as interchangeable parts of the production process. In factories, managers influenced by Taylor paid less attention to working conditions. Injuries increased, and as conditions grew worse, workers looked for ways to bring about change.

READING CHECK **Identifying Cause and Effect** Why did companies begin to use scientific management? How did it affect workers?

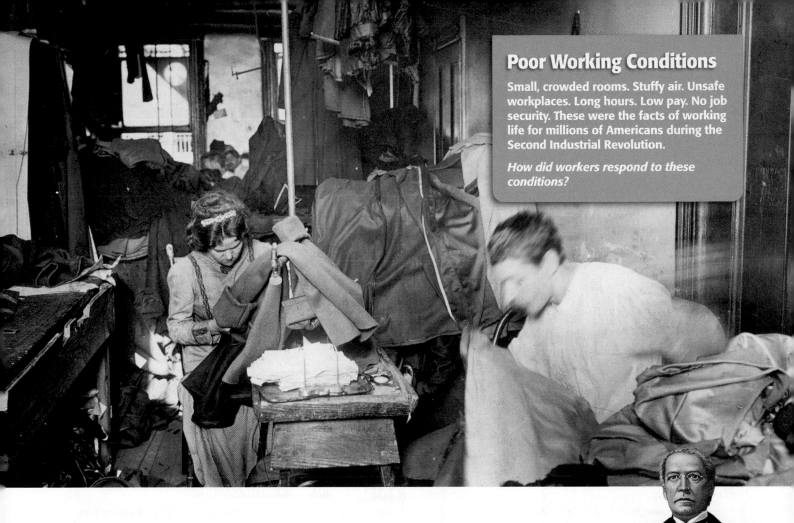

Poor Working Conditions
Small, crowded rooms. Stuffy air. Unsafe workplaces. Long hours. Low pay. No job security. These were the facts of working life for millions of Americans during the Second Industrial Revolution.

How did workers respond to these conditions?

Workers Organize

Workers formed labor unions to get better wages and working conditions for all workers in a factory or industry. The first national labor union, the **Knights of Labor**, was founded in the 1870s. It pushed for an eight-hour workday, equal pay for equal work, and an end to child labor. Union members also wanted the government to regulate trusts. Unlike most unions at the time, the Knights included both skilled and unskilled workers. The Knights of Labor was originally organized much like a secret society. In 1879 **Terence V. Powderly** became leader of the Knights. He ended all secrecy, creating the first truly national labor union in the United States.

Another early labor union was the **American Federation of Labor (AFL)**, led by **Samuel Gompers**. Unlike the Knights, the American Federation of Labor organized individual national unions, such as the mineworkers' and steelworkers' unions. The AFL

CASE STUDY ⟩ **BIOGRAPHY**

Samuel Gompers
1850–1924

Samuel Gompers was born in London. He came to the United States with his parents in 1863 at age 13. He worked as a cigar maker and joined a local union, eventually becoming its president. The Cigarmakers Union was reorganized and later joined the American Federation of Labor. Gompers became the AFL's first president and remained so, except for the year 1895, until his death. He campaigned for basic trade-union rights, such as the right to picket and to organize boycotts and strikes. His efforts on behalf of workers helped organized labor to gain respect.

Summarizing How did Samuel Gompers help the labor-union movement?

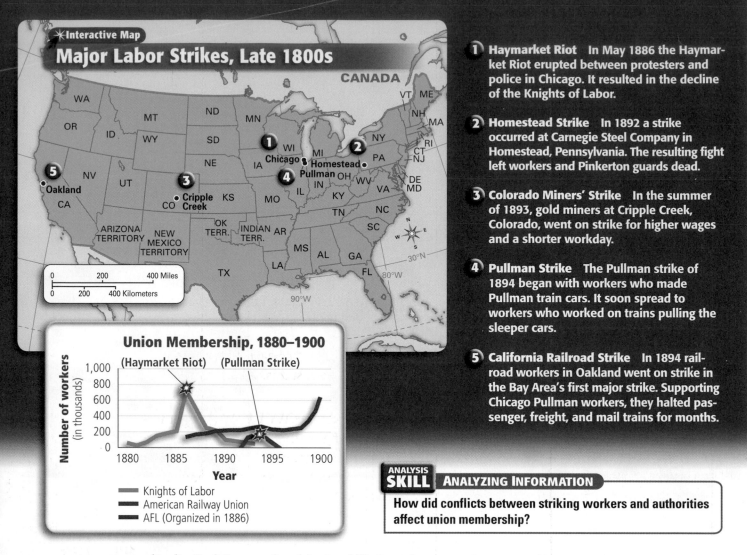

Major Labor Strikes, Late 1800s

CANADA

1 **Haymarket Riot** In May 1886 the Haymarket Riot erupted between protesters and police in Chicago. It resulted in the decline of the Knights of Labor.

2 **Homestead Strike** In 1892 a strike occurred at Carnegie Steel Company in Homestead, Pennsylvania. The resulting fight left workers and Pinkerton guards dead.

3 **Colorado Miners' Strike** In the summer of 1893, gold miners at Cripple Creek, Colorado, went on strike for higher wages and a shorter workday.

4 **Pullman Strike** The Pullman strike of 1894 began with workers who made Pullman train cars. It soon spread to workers who worked on trains pulling the sleeper cars.

5 **California Railroad Strike** In 1894 railroad workers in Oakland went on strike in the Bay Area's first major strike. Supporting Chicago Pullman workers, they halted passenger, freight, and mail trains for months.

Union Membership, 1880–1900

Number of workers (in thousands)

(Haymarket Riot) (Pullman Strike)

Year

- Knights of Labor
- American Railway Union
- AFL (Organized in 1886)

ANALYSIS SKILL **ANALYZING INFORMATION**

How did conflicts between striking workers and authorities affect union membership?

also limited its membership to skilled workers. This gave the union great bargaining power but left out most workers. The AFL appealed to the growing number of skilled workers such as engineers, machinists, and managers. By 1890 the AFL's membership was larger than that of the Knights. With **collective bargaining**—all workers acting collectively, or together—workers had a much greater chance of success in negotiating with management. Most employers opposed collective bargaining. One company president said, "I shall never give in. I would rather go out of business."

Many women took active roles in unions. For example, **Mary Harris Jones**, an Irish immigrant, worked for better conditions for miners. A fiery speaker, she organized strikes and helped educate workers.

THE IMPACT TODAY

In 1955 the AFL merged with the Congress of Industrial Organizations to become the AFL-CIO. Today the organization has more than 10 million members.

READING CHECK **Contrasting** How did the Knights of Labor and the AFL differ?

Labor Strikes

By the late 1800s, other unions were gaining strength. Major workers' strikes swept the country and included miners in Colorado, steel workers in Pennsylvania, and railroad workers in Illinois and California. The first major labor strike began in 1886 in Chicago.

In May 1886, thousands of union members in Chicago went on strike because they wanted an eight-hour workday. Two strikers were killed in a fight with police. The next night, workers met at Haymarket Square to protest the killings. In what became known as the **Haymarket Riot**, someone threw a bomb that wounded many police officers and killed eight. The police fired into the crowd, killing several people and wounding 100 others.

Eight people, some of whom were not at the riot, were arrested and convicted of conspiracy. One of them had a Knights of Labor membership card. Though Knights leadership had not supported the strike, several local chapters had. Membership in the Knights fell quickly.

Sometimes, business owners succeeded in breaking up unions. In 1892 a violent strike called the **Homestead strike** took place at Andrew Carnegie's Homestead steel factory in Pennsylvania. Union members there protested a plan to buy new machinery and cut jobs. The company refused to negotiate with the union and locked workers out of the plant, hiring strike breakers to perform their jobs. The workers responded by seizing control of the plant. Gunfire erupted on July 6, when Pinkerton detectives hired by the company tried to enter the plant. A fierce battle raged for 14 hours, leaving 16 people dead. The governor called out the state militia to restore order. Continuing for four more months, the union was eventually defeated.

Another major strike happened at George Pullman's Pullman Palace Car Company in the company town of Pullman, Illinois. Most of the company workers lived there, paying high rents. During a financial depression that began in 1893, Pullman laid off about half of the workers and cut pay for those that were left, without lowering their rents. On May 11, 1894, workers began the **Pullman strike**, which stopped traffic on many railroad lines until federal courts ordered the workers to return to their jobs. President Grover Cleveland sent federal troops to Chicago to stop the strike. Such defeats seriously damaged the labor movement for years.

READING CHECK **Analyzing** What were the effects of early major strikes on workers?

SUMMARY AND PREVIEW Workers formed unions to fight for better conditions and to keep their jobs. In the next section, you will learn about a new wave of immigrants in the late 1800s.

Section 3 Assessment

Reviewing Ideas, Terms, and People

1. **a. Recall** Why did conditions in factories begin to decline?
   b. Draw Conclusions How were workers affected by specialization and scientific management?
   c. Evaluate Do you think scientific management made businesses more successful? Explain.
2. **a. Identify** What role did **Mary Harris Jones** play in the labor movement?
   b. Analyze Why did workers demand **collective bargaining**, and why did business owners oppose it?
   c. Elaborate Do you think the demands made by labor unions were reasonable? Explain your answer.
3. **a. Describe** What major labor strikes took place in the late 1800s?
   b. Evaluate Do you think President Cleveland was right to use federal troops to end the **Pullman strike**? Explain.

Critical Thinking

4. **Analyzing** Review your notes about the problems workers faced. Use them to complete a table like the one below about how workers tried to solve the problems they faced.

Problem	Solution

FOCUS ON WRITING

5. **Taking Notes on Working Conditions** In your notebook, list some reasons why industrial workers were unhappy with working conditions. Can you think of ways to run your business so that you can avoid the problem of strikes?

Social Studies Skills

Analyzing Costs and Benefits

Define the Skill

Everything you do has both costs and benefits connected to it. *Benefits* are things that you gain from something. *Costs* are what you give up to obtain benefits. For example, if you buy a video game, the benefits of your action include the game itself and the enjoyment of playing it. The most clear cost is what you pay for the game. However, there are other costs that do not involve money. One is the time you spend playing the game. This is a cost because you give up something else, such as doing your homework or watching a TV show, when you choose to play the game.

The ability to analyze costs and benefits is a valuable life skill as well as a useful tool in the study of history. Weighing an action's benefits against its costs can help you decide whether or not to take it.

Learn the Skill

Analyzing the costs and benefits of historical events will help you to better understand and evaluate them. Follow these guidelines to do a cost-benefit analysis of an action or decision in history.

1. First, determine what the action or decision was trying to accomplish. This step is needed in order to determine which of its effects were benefits and which were costs.

2. Then look for the positive or successful results of the action or decision. These are its benefits.

3. Consider the negative or unsuccessful effects of the action or decision. Also, think about what positive things would have happened if it had *not* occurred. All these things are its costs.

4. Making a chart of the costs and benefits can be useful. By comparing the list of benefits to the list of costs you can better understand the action or decision and evaluate it.

For example, you learned in Chapter 2 about the Second Industrial Revolution and its effects on the American economy. A cost-benefit analysis of the changes in American businesses might produce a chart like this one:

Benefits	Costs
New inventions made life easier.	New business methods ran smaller companies out of business.
Communication became easier with new technologies.	Workers received lower wages.
Efficient management reduced costs of products.	Strikes resulted in violence and deaths.
Workers began to organize for better conditions.	

Based on this chart, one might conclude that the Second Industrial Revolution was beneficial to the nation's economy.

Practice the Skill

Among the changes that occurred in the early 1900s was an increase in specialization and efficiency in the workplace. Use information from the chapter and the guidelines above to do a cost-benefit analysis of this development. Then write a paragraph explaining whether or not it was a wise one.

Chapter Review

HOLT
History's Impact
▶ video series
Review the video to answer
the closing question:
*What advantages and disad-
vantages did the assembly line
create? Do you think assembly
lines still exist today?*

Visual Summary

QUICK FACTS

*Use the visual summary below to help you review
the main ideas of the chapter.*

Inventions
- Bessemer process
- Lightbulb
- Automobile

Big Business
- Growth of corporations
- Wealthy business owners
- Antitrust movements

Labor Movement
- Knights of Labor
- American Federation of Labor
- Haymarket Riot
- Homestead strike

Reviewing Vocabulary, Terms, and People

*Identify the descriptions below with the correct term or
person from the chapter.*

1. Labor organization that represented both skilled
   and unskilled laborers and was the first national
   labor union in the United States

2. Inventor who patented the telephone in 1876

3. A way of making steel quickly and cheaply by
   blasting hot air through melted iron to quickly
   remove waste

4. A system of business in which one company
   owns businesses in each step of the
   manufacturing process

5. Powerful business leader who helped to found
   the Central Pacific Railroad

6. Union speaker who worked to better the lives of
   mine workers

7. A method of negotiating for better wages or
   working conditions in which all workers act
   together to ensure a better chance for success

Comprehension and Critical Thinking

SECTION 1 *(Pages 34–38)*

8. **a. Identify** What was the Second Industrial
   Revolution?

   b. Draw Conclusions Why were advances in
   transportation and communication important
   to the Second Industrial Revolution?

   c. Elaborate Which invention do you think had
   the greatest effect on people's lives in the late
   1800s? Explain your answer.

SECTION 2 *(Pages 39–42)*

9. **a. Recall** What criticisms were made of business
   leaders and trusts?

   b. Analyze How did the rise of corporations and
   powerful business leaders lead to the growth of
   big business?

   c. Evaluate Do you think the growth of big
   business helped or hurt ordinary Americans?
   Explain your answer.

10. **a. Recall** What led to poor working conditions in factories during the Second Industrial Revolution?

   b. Make Inferences Why did labor unions have a better chance of improving working conditions than laborers did on their own?

   c. Evaluate Did the strikes of the 1880s and 1890s hurt or help the labor movement in the long run? Explain your answer.

Reviewing Themes

11. **Economics** How did the rise of big business affect consumers in the United States?

12. **Society and Culture** What changes in society were brought about by the organization of labor?

Using the Internet   go.hrw.com

13. **Activity: Creating a Time Line** Technology in some sense has been part of human history since we began to write history. All tools are, in a sense, technology. In this chapter you read about new scientific discoveries that had positive and negative effects. Enter the activity keyword. Then choose one technological innovation mentioned in the chapter and trace its development to the present day. Create an illustrated time line to present your research.

Reading Skills

Organization of Facts and Information *Use the Reading Skills taught in this chapter to answer the question about the reading selection below.*

> Corporations provided several important advantages over earlier business forms. Stockholders in a corporation are not responsible for business debts. If a corporation fails financially, the stockholders lose only the money that they invested. Stockholders are also usually free to sell their stock to whomever they want, whenever they want. *(p. 40)*

14. By which structural pattern is the above passage organized?

   a. Listing

   b. Cause-effect

   c. Chronological order

   d. Comparison-contrast

Social Studies Skills

Analyzing Costs and Benefits *Use the Social Studies Skills taught in this chapter to answer the question below.*

15. Write two costs and two benefits of the Pullman strike from the point of view of the workers who participated.

FOCUS ON WRITING

16. **Writing Your Business Plan** Collect your notes and determine a good product to sell during the late 1800s. Decide which business practices you would use and which you would not. Write two to three paragraphs in which you explain why your product would sell, which business practices you can use to make your product, and how to avoid conflicts with workers. Remember to explain to the investors why your plan will work.

Grade 8 Intermediate-Level Test Preparation

Directions (1-6): For each statement or question, write on the separate answer sheet the *number* of the word or expression that, of those given, best completes the statement or answers the question.

Base your answer to question 1 on the map below and on your knowledge of social studies.

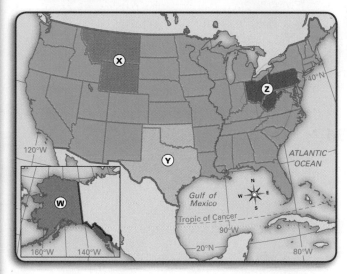

1 Which area on the map provided the petroleum for the oil-refining industry that arose in the United States in the mid- to late 1800s?

(1) the area labeled W   (3) the area labeled Y

(2) the area labeled X   (4) the area labeled Z

2 The person *most* responsible for making the steel industry a big business in the United States is

(1) John D. Rockefeller.

(2) Andrew Carnegie.

(3) Henry Bessemer.

(4) Leland Stanford.

3 Which strategy helped labor unions, such as the AFL, achieve their goals?

(1) collective bargaining

(2) government intervention

(3) increased output

(4) continued child labor

4 The development of corporations in America was helped by

(1) suburbs.

(2) vertical integration.

(3) the Sherman Antitrust Act.

(4) social Darwinism.

5 Buildings in New York City were among the first to have electric lights. Which inventor was responsible?

(1) Andrew Carnegie

(2) Thomas Edison

(3) Leland Stanford

(4) John D. Rockefeller

6 One cause of labor strikes in the late 1800s was that workers sought

(1) shorter workdays.

(2) vertical integration.

(3) social Darwinism.

(4) lower wages.

Base your answer to question 7 on the text below and on your knowledge of social studies.

"Machinery is now recognized as essential to cheap production. Nobody can produce effectively and economically without it, and what was formerly known as domestic manfacture is now almost obsolete. But machinery is one of the most expensive of all products, and its extensive purchase and use require an amount of capital far beyond the capacity [ability] of the ordinary individual to furnish."

—David Wells, quoted in *Voices of the American Past*

7 **Constructed-Response Question** How might the large amounts of money needed for machinery affect the future of business?

CHAPTER 3 1872–1914

Immigrants and Urban Life

FOCUS QUESTION

How did industrialization and immigration change the face of American life?

FOCUS ON WRITING

A Memo You are a writer at a television network, and you have an idea for a TV drama series set in the late 1800s. Draft a memo telling your boss about your story idea. As you read this chapter, gather information about the people, places, and events of this time period. Tell about the cast of characters, the setting, and the basic plot of your series.

UNITED STATES

1873
Olmsted designs the U.S. Capitol grounds.

1876
The Centennial Exposition opens in Philadelphia.

1870

WORLD

1878
Electric streetlights are introduced in London.

HOLT

History's Impact
▶ video series
Watch the video to understand the impact of immigrants on the United States.

What You Will Learn...

Millions of immigrants from Europe came through Ellis Island, shown here. They came in search of jobs, freedom, and better lives for their families. Most settled in New York, Chicago, and other growing cities. American cities began to take the shape they still have today. In this chapter you will learn about the wave of immigration that changed the United States in the late 1800s and early 1900s.

1886
Workers complete the Statue of Liberty.

NY

1889
Jane Addams founds Hull House in Chicago.

1893 The Ferris Wheel is introduced at the 1893 Columbian Exposition in Chicago.

1880

1890

1900

1910

1886
Impressionists' exhibit opens in Paris.

1891 Construction begins on Russia's Trans-Siberian Railroad.

1901 The first Nobel Prizes are awarded in Stockholm, Sweden.

IMMIGRANTS AND URBAN LIFE **53**

Focus on Themes In this chapter, you will read about the changes in **society and culture** in the late 1800s. Among these changes was an increase in immigration. New immigrants to America found a society full of **economic** opportunities and hardships. Immigration and technology combined to change the way of life in cities.

Understanding Historical Fact versus Historical Fiction

Focus on Reading When you read a book like *The Red Badge of Courage* or see a movie about World War II, do you ever wonder how much is fiction and how much is fact?

Distinguishing Fact from Fiction Historical fiction gives readers a chance to meet real historical people and real historical events in the framework of a made-up story. Some of what you read in historical fiction could be verified in an encyclopedia, but other parts existed only in the author's mind until he or she put it on paper. As a good reader of history, you should know the difference between facts, which can be proved or verified, and fiction.

Notice how one reader determined which details could be verified or proved.

> That was a *woman filling her pail by the hydrant* you just bumped against. The *sinks are in the hallway,* that all the tenants may have access—and all be poisoned alike by their summer stenches. Hear the pump squeak! It is the lullaby of tenement house babes. In summer, when *a thousand thirsty throats pant for a cooling drink in this block,* it is worked in vain ...
>
> — From *How the Other Half Lives,* by Jacob Riis

> The woman filling her pail isn't a fact I can check. He's just using her as an example of what women did.

> We could probably check city records to see whether the buildings really had sinks in the hallways.

> The writer is generalizing here. We probably can't prove 1,000 thirsty throats. We could find out whether the city's water pumps actually went dry in the summer. That's verifiable.

You Try It!

The following passage is from *Bread Givers* by Anzia Yezierska, a young immigrant to New York. After you read it, answer the questions below.

> Mashah [Anzia's sister] came home with stories that in rich people's homes they had silver knives and forks, separate, for each person. And new-ironed tablecloths and napkins every time they ate on them. And rich people had marble bathtubs in their own houses, with running hot and cold water all day and night long so they could take a bath any time they felt like it, instead of having to stand on a line before the public bath-house, as we had to do when we wanted a bath for the holidays. But these millionaire things were so far over our heads that they were like fairy tales.
>
> That time when Mashah had work hemming towels in an uptown house, she came home with another new-rich idea, another money-spending thing, which she said she had to have. She told us that by those Americans, everybody in the family had a toothbrush and a separate towel for himself.
>
> —Anzia Yezierska, *Bread Givers*

1. Which facts from the paragraph above can be confirmed?

2. What sources might you check to confirm some of these facts?

3. List two things from the passage that could not be confirmed.

4. Why are these two things not able to be confirmed?

As you read **Chapter 3,** notice which facts you could easily confirm.

A New Wave of Immigration

What You Will Learn...

Main Ideas

1. U.S. immigration patterns changed during the late 1800s as new immigrants arrived from Europe, Asia, and Mexico.
2. Immigrants worked hard to adjust to life in the United States.
3. Some Americans opposed immigration and worked to restrict it.

The Big Idea

A new wave of immigration in the late 1800s brought large numbers of immigrants to the United States.

Key Terms and People

old immigrants, *p. 56*
new immigrants, *p. 56*
steerage, *p. 57*
benevolent societies, *p. 59*
tenements, *p. 59*
sweatshops, *p. 60*
Chinese Exclusion Act, *p. 61*

TAKING NOTES As you read, look for information about new immigrants' lives in the United States. Take notes on the benefits and challenges immigrants found. Use a diagram like the one below.

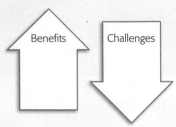

Benefits   Challenges

If YOU were there...

You live with your family on a small farm in Italy in the 1890s. You want to earn some money to help your parents, but there are not many jobs nearby. You have heard that jobs are easy to find in the booming factories of the United States. But you speak no English and know no one in America.

Would you travel to the United States in search of new opportunities?

BUILDING BACKGROUND From its beginnings, America has attracted people from many parts of the world. They came for many reasons, including religious freedom, the chance to start new lives, and land. In the late 1800s, jobs created by the rapid growth of the U.S. economy drew millions of new immigrants.

Changing Patterns of Immigration

Millions of immigrants came to the United States from northern Europe in the mid-1800s. They came mainly from Great Britain, Germany, Ireland, and the countries of Scandinavia. Except for the Irish, who were Roman Catholics, most were Protestants. Many were skilled workers. Others settled in rural areas and became farmers. By the late 1800s immigrants from northern Europe were known as **old immigrants**. A newer and larger wave of immigration—from different parts of the world—was arriving in the United States.

New Immigrants

During the 1880s more than 5 million immigrants arrived in the United States—about the same number of people as had arrived during the six decades from 1800 to 1860 combined. The majority of these **new immigrants** were from southern and eastern Europe. Thousands of Czechs, Greeks, Hungarians, Italians, Poles, Russians, and Slovaks came to the United States to find new opportunities and better lives. A young woman from Russia spoke for many of her fellow immigrants when she said she hoped "for all manner of miracles in a strange, wonderful land!"

New immigrants came from many different cultural and religious backgrounds. They included Orthodox Christians, Roman Catholics, and Jews. Some were escaping political or religious persecution. They were eager for the job opportunities created by the U.S. industrial boom of the late 1800s.

Arriving in a New Land

Immigrants often faced a difficult journey by ship. Most traveled in **steerage**—an area below deck near the rudder. Tickets in steerage were the cheapest on the ship, but still seemed expensive to many immigrants. Steerage was hot, smelly, and cramped. As many as 2,000 people traveled in long narrow compartments, often sleeping in berths three bunks high. Rolling and crashing waves made many seasick, some for the entire trip. Some died of diseases they caught during the journey.

Once in the United States, new arrivals were processed through government-run immigration centers. The busiest center on the East Coast was Ellis Island, which opened in New York Harbor in 1892. The first immigrant processed through Ellis Island was Annie Moore Schayer, a 14 year old from Ireland. Over the next 40 years, millions of European immigrants came through Ellis Island.

At immigration centers officials interviewed and examined immigrants to decide whether to let them enter the country. People with contagious diseases or legal problems could be turned away. "There was this terrible anxiety that one of us might be rejected," remembered one immigrant traveling with his family. "And if one of us was, what would the rest of the family do?" This rarely happened, however. Less than 2 percent of the people who arrived at Ellis Island were not allowed into the country.

On the West Coast, immigrants from Asia entered the country through Angel Island, which opened near San Francisco in 1910. Angel Island became a detention center for many Chinese

Primary Source

AUTOBIOGRAPHY
An Immigrant's Story

Mary Antin and her family were Jewish. They moved from Russia to Boston in the 1890s to find religious freedom. Here, Antin writes about their journey.

> What do you think *fugitive* means here?

For sixteen days the ship was our world ... [It] pitched and rolled so that people were thrown from their berths [beds] ... All this while the seasickness lasted. Then came happy hours on deck, with fugitive sunshine, birds atop the crested waves, band music and dancing and fun ...And so suffering, fearing, brooding [worrying], rejoicing, we crept nearer and nearer to the coveted [wished for] shore, until, on a glorious May morning, six weeks after our departure from Polotzk our eyes beheld the Promised Land [the United States].

—Mary Antin, *The Promised Land*

> Antin describes a mix of emotions.

ANALYSIS SKILL **ANALYZING PRIMARY SOURCES**

Why do you think Antin was both "fearing" and "rejoicing" during her trip?

immigrants. Laws limited immigration from China. Only Chinese whose fathers were U.S. citizens could enter the country. The process of proving their right to enter took two to three weeks and sometimes months, compared to hours or days at Ellis Island.

Mexican immigrants also came to the United States in large numbers in the late 1800s. The main processing center for immigrants from Mexico was in El Paso, Texas. Most settled in the Southwest. They found work in construction, steel mills, and mines, and on large commercial farms.

READING CHECK **Contrasting** How was the experience of immigrants at Ellis Island different from that of immigrants at Angel Island?

THE IMPACT TODAY

Almost half of all Americans today are related to someone who passed through Ellis Island. Visitors can now research their family origins at the Ellis Island Immigration Museum.

ASIA

NORTH AMERICA

New York City

40°N

San Francisco

El Paso

PACIFIC OCEAN

Equator

160°W

SOUTH AMERICA

In this photo, Japanese men and Chinese women leave the detention center on Angel Island in San Francisco Bay. Angel Island was the processing center for many immigrants from Asia.

Augustin and Maria Lozano and their two children are shown after moving from Mexico to California. Many Mexican immigrants moved into the Southwest.

Adjusting to a New Life

FOCUS ON NEW YORK CITY

New York City is famous for its ethnic neighborhoods, such as Chinatown, Little Italy, and the Lower East Side.

FOCUS ON READING

How could you verify the facts in this paragraph?

Once they entered the United States, immigrants began the hard work of adjusting to life in a new country. They needed to find homes and jobs. They had to learn a new language and get used to new customs. This was all part of building a new life.

Immigrant Neighborhoods

Many immigrants moved into neighborhoods with others from the same country. In these neighborhoods, they could speak their native language and eat foods that reminded them of home. Immigrants could also practice the customs that their families had passed down from generation to generation. An Italian immigrant remembered that in his new neighborhood, "cheeses from Italy, sausage, salamis were all hanging in the window."

In their newly adopted neighborhoods, many immigrant groups published newspapers in their own languages. They founded schools, clubs, and places of worship to help preserve their customs. In New York City, for example, Jewish immigrants founded a theater that gave performances in Yiddish—the language spoken by Jews from central and eastern Europe.

Immigrants often opened local shops and small neighborhood banks. Business owners helped new arrivals by offering credit and giving small loans. Such aid was important for newcomers because there were few commercial banks in immigrant neighborhoods. In 1904 Italian immigrant Amadeo Peter Giannini started the Bank of Italy in San Francisco. This bank later grew and became the Bank of America.

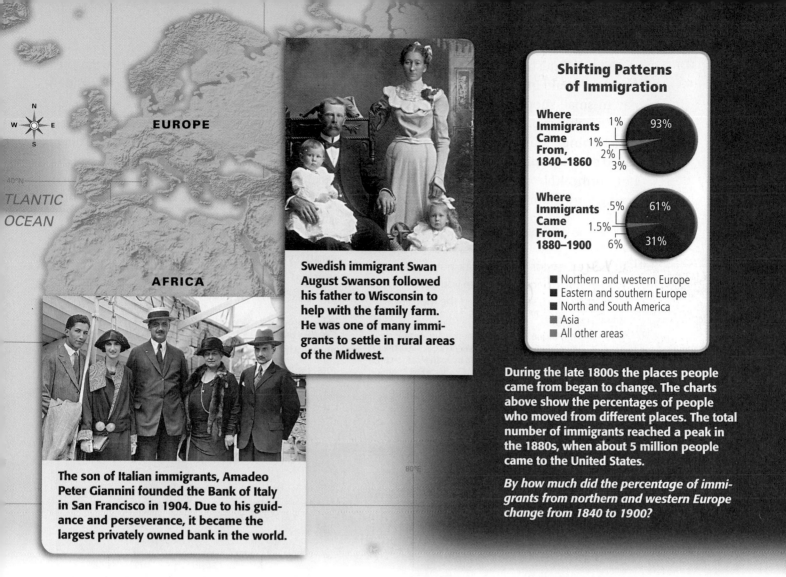

Shifting Patterns of Immigration

Where Immigrants Came From, 1840–1860
93%
1%
1%
2%
3%

Where Immigrants Came From, 1880–1900
61%
.5%
1.5%
6%
31%

- ■ Northern and western Europe
- ■ Eastern and southern Europe
- ■ North and South America
- ■ Asia
- ■ All other areas

Swedish immigrant Swan August Swanson followed his father to Wisconsin to help with the family farm. He was one of many immigrants to settle in rural areas of the Midwest.

The son of Italian immigrants, Amadeo Peter Giannini founded the Bank of Italy in San Francisco in 1904. Due to his guidance and perseverance, it became the largest privately owned bank in the world.

During the late 1800s the places people came from began to change. The charts above show the percentages of people who moved from different places. The total number of immigrants reached a peak in the 1880s, when about 5 million people came to the United States.

By how much did the percentage of immigrants from northern and western Europe change from 1840 to 1900?

Some immigrant communities formed **benevolent societies**. These aid organizations offered immigrants help in cases of sickness, unemployment, or death. At that time, few national government agencies provided such aid.

Even with neighborhood support, however, immigrants often found city life difficult. Many immigrants lived in **tenements**—poorly built, overcrowded apartment buildings. One young woman in New York City described the difference between her hopes and reality in the new land:

" [I dreamed] of the golden stairs leading to the top of the American palace where father was supposed to live. [I] went 'home' to ... an ugly old tenement in the heart of the Lower East Side. There were stairs to climb but they were not golden. "
– Miriam Shomer Zusner, *Yesterday: A Memoir of a Russian Jewish Family*

Immigrants worked hard to adjust to their new country. Children often learned American customs more quickly than their parents. In public schools immigrant children learned English from *McGuffey's Readers*—illustrated textbooks that taught reading and writing.

Finding Work

Many new immigrants had worked on farms in their homelands. Few could afford to buy land in the United States, however. Instead, they found jobs in cities, where most of the country's manufacturing took place.

Having come from rural areas, few new immigrants were skilled in modern manufacturing or industrial work. They often had no choice but to take low-paying, unskilled jobs in garment factories, steel mills, or construction. Long hours were common.

FOCUS ON NEW YORK

New York City has always attracted immigrants. However, other parts of the state have had large waves of immigration as well. In the 1840s, 1850s, and 1860s, many French Canadians migrated to northern New York.

Not all industrial labor took place in large factories. Some immigrants worked for little pay in small shops or mills located in their own neighborhoods. Often associated with the clothing industry, these workplaces were called **sweatshops** because of long hours and hot, unhealthy working conditions. One young immigrant worker remembered:

"When the shirtwaists were finished at the machine … we were given scissors to cut the threads off. It wasn't heavy work, but it was monotonous [boring], because you did the same thing from seven-thirty in the morning till nine at night."

– Pauline Newman, quoted in *American Mosaic: The Immigrant Experience in the Words of Those Who Lived It,* by Joan Morrison and Charlotte Fox Zabusky

Immigrants with skills that were in demand sometimes found work outside factories and sweatshops. For example, some immigrants worked as bakers, carpenters, masons, or skilled machinists. Others saved or borrowed money to open small businesses such as laundries, barbershops, or street vending carts. New immigrants often opened the same types of businesses in which other immigrants from the same country were already succeeding. They worked hard for long hours to become successful themselves.

READING CHECK **Summarizing** How did new immigrants help themselves and others to try to make successful lives in the United States?

LINKING TO TODAY

Asian Americans Today

Today more than 12 million people in the United States are of Asian origin. They account for nearly 5 percent of the U.S. population—or about 1 in 20 Americans. Asian Americans trace their roots to various countries, including China, India, the Philippines, and, like this family, Vietnam. Most Asian Americans live in the West. California has by far the largest Asian American population of any state.

ANALYSIS SKILL **ANALYZING INFORMATION**

Why have so many people moved to the United States?

Opposition to Immigration

Some Americans welcomed immigrants. Many business leaders, for example, wanted immigrant workers who were willing to work for low pay. In general, however, anti-immigrant feelings grew along with the rise in immigration in the late 1800s. Some labor unions opposed immigration because their members believed immigrants would take jobs away from native-born Americans.

Other Americans called nativists also feared that too many new immigrants were being allowed into the country. Many nativists held racial and ethnic prejudices. They thought that the new immigrants would not learn American customs, which might harm American society.

Some nativists were violent toward immigrants. Others **advocated** laws to stop or limit immigration. For example, in 1880 about 105,000 Chinese immigrants lived in the United States. Two years later, Congress passed the **Chinese Exclusion Act**, banning Chinese people from immigrating to the United States for 10 years. This law marked the first time a nationality was banned from entering the country. Although the law violated treaties with China, Congress continued to renew the law for decades to come. In 1892 another law was passed restricting convicts, immigrants with certain diseases, and those likely to need public assistance from entering the country.

Despite such opposition immigrants continued to arrive in large numbers. They worked for low pay in factories and built buildings, highways, and railroads. Their labor helped power the continuing industrial growth of the late 1800s and early 1900s. Although they did not always achieve their dreams as quickly as they had hoped, most immigrants were still confident about the future for themselves and their families in the United States. An immigrant from Russia named Abraham Hyman expressed this idea, saying, "Your feeling is that a better time is coming, if not for yourself, for your families, for your children."

READING CHECK **Analyzing** Why did nativists oppose immigration?

ACADEMIC VOCABULARY

advocate to plead in favor of

SUMMARY AND PREVIEW Immigrants helped build the nation's economy and cities, but they met resistance from some native-born Americans. In the next section you will learn about what life was like in urban America.

Section 1 Assessment

go.hrw.com
Online Quiz

Reviewing Ideas, Terms, and People

1. **a. Identify** What was Ellis Island?
   b. Contrast What differences existed between the **old immigrants** and the **new immigrants**?
2. **a. Identify** What job opportunities were available to new immigrants?
   b. Summarize How did immigrants attempt to adapt to their new lives in the United States?
   c. Elaborate Why do you think many immigrants tolerated difficult living and working conditions?
3. **a. Recall** What was the purpose of the **Chinese Exclusion Act**?
   b. Explain Why did some labor unions oppose immigration?
   c. Predict How might the growing opposition to immigration lead to problems in the United States?

Critical Thinking

4. **Categorizing** Review your notes on the benefits and challenges new U.S. immigrants faced. Then use the following graphic organizer to categorize the challenges into different areas of life.

Education:

Work:

Challenges faced by new immigrants

Culture:

Living Conditions:

FOCUS ON WRITING

5. **Writing about Immigrants and Their Lives** Make a list of potential characters for your TV series, and be sure to include new immigrants. Take notes about what life was like for them.

The Growth of Cities

If YOU were there...

The year is 1905 and you have just come to the city of Chicago from the small town where you grew up. People rush past as you stop to stare up at the skyscrapers. Elevated trains roar overhead, and electric streetcars clatter along streets already crowded with pushcarts and horse-drawn wagons.

Will you stay and look for work in this big city?

BUILDING BACKGROUND Industrial growth and a new wave of immigration swelled the populations of American cities in the late 1800s. Cities changed quickly to accommodate so many new people, offering urban residents excitement and new kinds of entertainment.

Growth of Urban Areas

In 1850 New York City was the only U.S. city with a population of more than 500,000. By 1900 New York City, Chicago, Philadelphia, Saint Louis, Boston, and Baltimore all had more than half a million residents. More than 35 U.S. cities had populations greater than 100,000. About 40 percent of Americans now lived in urban areas.

As you have read, new immigrants were responsible for a lot of this urban growth. So were families from rural areas in the United States. As farm equipment replaced workers in the countryside, large numbers of rural residents moved to the cities in search of work. African Americans from the rural South also began moving to northern cities in the 1890s. They hoped to escape discrimination and find better educational and economic opportunities. Cities such as Chicago; Cleveland, Ohio; Detroit, Michigan; and New York saw large increases in their African American populations during the late 1800s and early 1900s.

Perhaps the most dramatic example of urban growth was the rise of Chicago. The city's population exploded from 30,000 in 1850 to 1.7 million in 1900. Chicago passed Saint Louis as the

What You Will Learn...

Main Ideas

1. Both immigrants and native-born Americans moved to growing urban areas in record numbers in the late 1800s and early 1900s.
2. New technology and ideas helped cities change and adapt to rapid population growth.

The Big Idea

American cities experienced dramatic expansion and change in the late 1800s.

Key Terms and People

mass transit, *p. 64*
suburbs, *p. 64*
mass culture, *p. 64*
Joseph Pulitzer, *p. 65*
William Randolph Hearst, *p. 65*
department stores, *p. 65*
Frederick Law Olmsted, *p. 65*

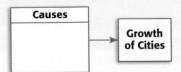

TAKING NOTES As you read, take notes on the causes of the growth of cities.

Causes → Growth of Cities

POSTCARD
Chicago, 1900

Postcards like this one were one way people shared the experience of visiting or living in a big city like Chicago. This scene shows a bustling street corner at which modern transportation like streetcars mingle with horse-drawn carts.

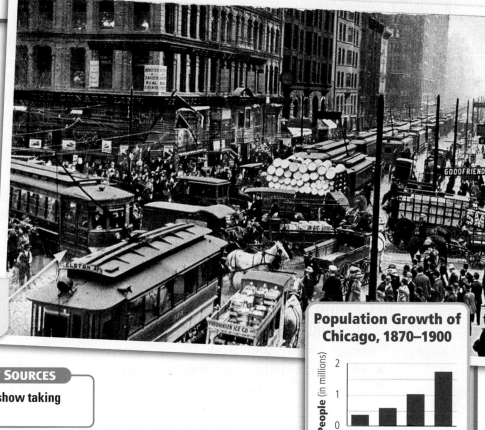

Streetcars move large numbers of people through the crowded cities.

Population Growth of Chicago, 1870–1900

People (in millions)

2

1

0

1870 1880 1890 1900

Year

ANALYSIS SKILL **ANALYZING PRIMARY SOURCES**

What changes does this picture show taking place in cities at the time?

biggest city in the Midwest. Along with the large numbers of African Americans moving to the city, many of Chicago's new residents were immigrants from southern and eastern Europe. In 1900 immigrants and their children made up three-quarters of Chicago's population.

Chicago's location was another **factor** in its rapid growth. Many of the new railroad lines connecting the East and West coasts ran through Chicago. This put Chicago at the heart of the nation's trade in lumber, grain, and meat. Thousands of new Chicago residents found work in the city's huge slaughterhouses and meatpacking plants. Here, meat from the West and Midwest was packed into refrigerated train cars and shipped to the growing cities of the East, where it could be sold in shops to customers.

READING CHECK Identifying Cause and Effect
What factors led to massive population growth in urban areas during the late 1800s and early 1900s?

Changing Cities

American cities such as Chicago were ill-prepared for the rapid urban growth of the late 1800s and early 1900s. Where was everyone going to live? How were people going to get from home to work on crowded city streets? Several new technologies helped cities meet these challenges. These technologies forever changed the look and function of U.S. cities.

Building Skyscrapers

With so many people moving to urban areas, cities quickly ran out of building space in downtown areas. One solution would be to build taller buildings. Typical city buildings in the mid-1800s were only five stories tall, but taller structures were impossible to construct because the building materials available were either too weak or too heavy.

This changed with the rise of the American steel industry in the late 1800s.

ACADEMIC VOCABULARY
factor cause

THE IMPACT TODAY

Skyscrapers today use much of the same technology that was developed in the late 1800s—steel skeletons and elevators. Chicago's Sears Tower, with 110 stories, is one of the tallest buildings in the world.

Mills began producing tons of strong and inexpensive steel. Soon, architects such as Louis Sullivan of Chicago began designing multistory buildings called skyscrapers. Architects used steel beams to make sturdy frames that could support the weight of tall buildings. This allowed builders to use limited city space more efficiently.

The safety elevator, patented by Elisha Otis in the 1850s, helped make skyscrapers practical. Previous elevators had been unsafe because they would crash to the ground if the elevator cable snapped. Otis's safety elevator included a device to hold the elevator in place if the cable broke.

Getting Around

Taller buildings made it possible for more people to live and work in city centers. This increased the need for **mass transit**, or public transportation designed to move many people. By the late 1860s New York City had elevated trains running on tracks above the streets. Chicago followed in the 1890s.

Some cities built underground railroads, known as subways. In 1897 the first subway in the United States opened in Boston. In 1904 the first line of the New York City subway system began operation. Cable cars and electric trolleys also became common. These streetcars cheaply and quickly carried people in the cities to and from work.

Many Americans who could afford it moved to **suburbs**, residential neighborhoods outside of downtown areas that had begun springing up before the Civil War. Mass transit networks made such moves possible. People could live in the suburbs and take trolleys, subways, or trains into the cities.

New Ideas

In the late 1800s the United States also began to develop forms of **mass culture**, or leisure and cultural activities shared by many people. One factor contributing to mass culture was a boom in publishing. The invention of the Linotype, an automatic typesetting machine, greatly reduced the time and cost of printing. In 1850

Frederick Law Olmsted

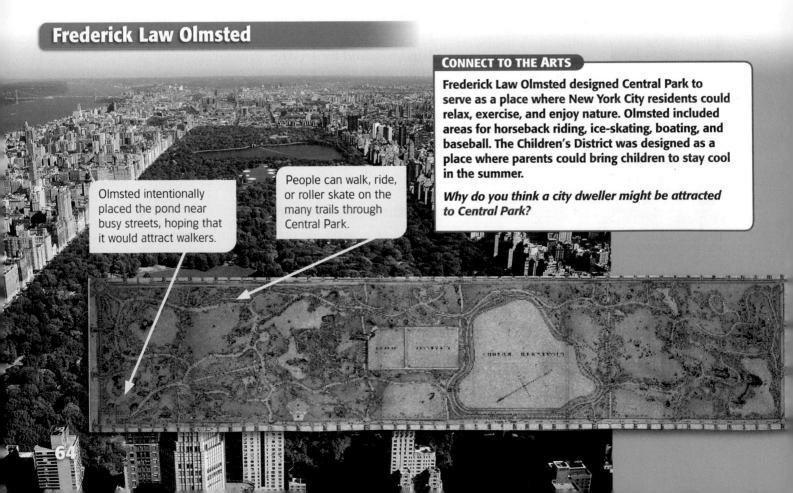

Olmsted intentionally placed the pond near busy streets, hoping that it would attract walkers.

People can walk, ride, or roller skate on the many trails through Central Park.

CONNECT TO THE ARTS

Frederick Law Olmsted designed Central Park to serve as a place where New York City residents could relax, exercise, and enjoy nature. Olmsted included areas for horseback riding, ice-skating, boating, and baseball. The Children's District was designed as a place where parents could bring children to stay cool in the summer.

Why do you think a city dweller might be attracted to Central Park?

there were fewer than 300 daily newspapers in the country. Because of the use of Linotype machines, by 1900 there were more than 2,000 newspapers.

Big cities often had many newspapers, so publishers had to compete for readers. In 1896 **Joseph Pulitzer** added a color comic to his *New York World* newspaper. More people started buying Pulitzer's paper. **William Randolph Hearst**, publisher of the *New York Journal*, saw that comics helped sell newspapers. So he added a color comic strip to the *Journal*. Soon, newspapers across the country were adding comic strips.

Mass culture affected how people shopped as well. Giant retail shops, or **department stores**, appeared in some cities during the late 1800s. An early one was Marshall Field in Chicago, which offered low prices and large quantities of products. It also was the first department store to offer its customers a restaurant where they could eat while shopping. Newspaper advertising was used to bring in customers. American's rising expectations rose along with their standard of living and level of consumption.

World fairs were another example of mass culture. Fairs brought merchants together, which sometimes resulted in new ideas and products. At the 1904 Saint Louis World's Fair, for example, a Syrian food vendor began making cones for a nearby ice cream vendor who had run out of dishes. Ice cream cones became popular throughout the country.

The demand for public entertainment also led to the creation of amusement parks, such as New York's Coney Island. The inexpensive entry tickets made Coney Island a favorite destination for children and families. For a nickel, visitors could ride a new invention called the Switchback Railway—the country's first roller coaster.

As cities grew, people became aware of the need for open public space. Landscape architect **Frederick Law Olmsted** became nationally famous. He designed Central Park in New York City as well as many state and national parks. Some of his other well-known projects include Prospect Park in Brooklyn, New York, and the U.S. Capitol grounds, which he worked on between 1874 and 1895.

READING CHECK **Summarizing** What forms of mass culture were available in urban areas?

SUMMARY AND PREVIEW Immigration and new technology helped cities grow in the late 1800s. In the next section you will learn about some of the problems caused by rapid urban growth.

go.hrw.com
Online Quiz

Section 2 Assessment

Reviewing Ideas, Terms, and People

1. **a. Identify** What groups of people began moving to cities in the late 1800s?
   b. Explain Why did African Americans begin to move to northern cities in the 1890s?
   c. Predict Do you think cities such as Chicago continued to grow in the 1900s? Why or why not?
2. **a. Define** What is **mass transit**? What made mass transit necessary?
   b. Explain How did new inventions make it possible for people to build skyscrapers?
   c. Evaluate Which improvement to urban living do you think had the greatest impact on people's lives? Explain your answer.

Critical Thinking

3. **Identifying Cause and Effect** Review your notes on the causes for the growth of cities. Then copy the following graphic organizer and use it to identify the effects of city growth. You may need to add more circles.

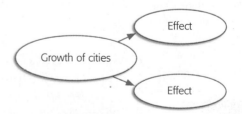

Growth of cities → Effect
Growth of cities → Effect

FOCUS ON WRITING

4. **Describing Setting** A city like those you have read about could serve as the setting of your TV series. How could you describe the city?

City Life

What You Will Learn...

Main Ideas

1. Crowded urban areas faced a variety of social problems.
2. People worked to improve the quality of life in U.S. cities.

The Big Idea

The rapid growth of cities in the late 1800s created both challenges and opportunities.

Key Terms and People

Jacob Riis, *p. 66*
settlement houses, *p. 68*
Jane Addams, *p. 68*
Hull House, *p. 68*
Florence Kelley, *p. 68*

TAKING NOTES As you read, take notes on problems facing city residents. You can organize your notes in a table like this one.

Urban Problems

If **YOU** were there...

You live in a fast-growing city in 1895. When you walk the streets, you meet families that are packed into run-down apartments in crowded, filthy neighborhoods. You meet immigrants who want to study English but have no money for classes. You are determined to help these city residents improve their lives.

What would you do to help improve life in your city?

BUILDING BACKGROUND Despite the new public parks, skyscrapers, and mass transit systems, many cities were not ready for the rapid population growth that began taking place in the late 1800s. Overcrowding and poor living conditions forced people to search for solutions to these problems.

Urban Problems

In the late 1800s and early 1900s, shortages of affordable housing forced many poor families to squeeze into tiny tenement apartments, which were frequently unsafe and unsanitary. Journalist and photographer **Jacob Riis** became famous for exposing the horrible conditions in New York City tenements. Riis wrote about one typical tenement family:

"There were nine in the family: husband, wife, an aged grandmother, and six children ... All nine lived in two rooms, one about ten feet square that served as parlor, bedroom, and eating-room, the other a small hall-room made into a kitchen."

— Jacob Riis, *How the Other Half Lives*

This kind of overcrowding caused sanitation problems. Most cities did not have a good system for collecting trash, so garbage often piled up outside apartment buildings. An article in the *New York Tribune* described the garbage in front of one tenement as a "mass of air poisoning, death-breeding filth, reeking in the fierce sunshine."

Unsafe conditions were also common in tenements. Before 1900 most cities did not have laws requiring landlords to fix their tenements or to maintain safety standards. A fire on one floor could easily spread, and fire escapes were often blocked or broken.

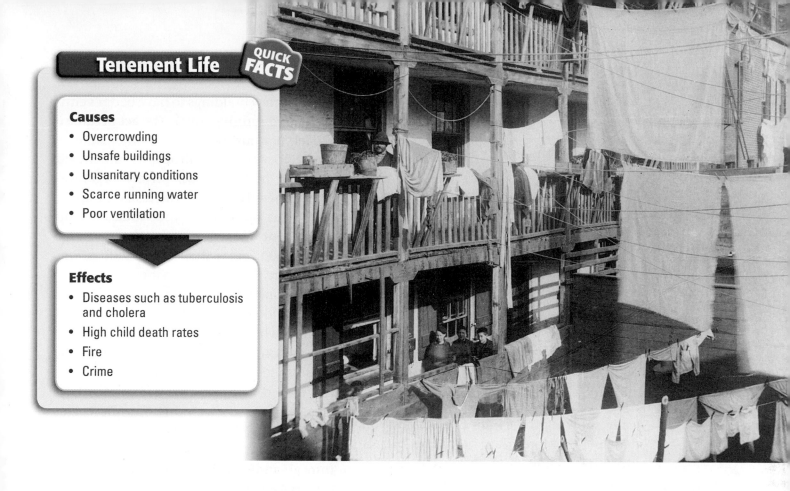

Tenement Life QUICK FACTS

Causes
- Overcrowding
- Unsafe buildings
- Unsanitary conditions
- Scarce running water
- Poor ventilation

Effects
- Diseases such as tuberculosis and cholera
- High child death rates
- Fire
- Crime

Tenement rooms had few or no windows to let in fresh air and sunshine. Comfort was also scarce, with so many people crowded into such small spaces. Running water and indoor plumbing were also scarce. So was clean water—cities often dumped garbage into local rivers that were used for drinking water.

Disease-causing bacteria grew easily in these conditions. Diseases such as cholera, typhoid, influenza, and tuberculosis spread quickly in crowded neighborhoods. Children were the most vulnerable to these diseases. For example, babies born in Chicago in 1870 had only a 50 percent chance of living to the age of five.

Air pollution was also a serious problem in many growing cities. This was a time when many business leaders were building huge oil refineries, steel mills, and other factories. The steel mills of Andrew Carnegie, for example, helped make Pittsburgh the nation's steel-making center in the late 1800s. Steel mills brought jobs and wealth to Pittsburgh, but they also caused some of the nation's worst air pollution. "Every street appears to end in a huge, black cloud," said one writer. "Pittsburgh is smoke, smoke, smoke—everywhere smoke." The air was so polluted at times that the city had to turn on outdoor lighting during the day.

The work of many city governments slowly helped to lessen some of these urban problems. By the late 1800s new sewage and water purification systems improved city sanitation. Many major cities also were hiring full-time firefighters and police officers. Police officers in cities were typically placed in one neighborhood. They knew the local residents and were frequently involved in local activities. They could spot local problems and, in many cases, provide help to immigrants.

READING CHECK **Summarizing** What challenges did many city residents face in the late 1800s?

THE IMPACT TODAY

Like many industrial cities, Pittsburgh has made great progress in cleaning its air and water. Today Pittsburgh is ranked as one of the cleanest American cities.

FOCUS ON NEW YORK CITY

Mary Mallon, or "Typhoid Mary," worked as a cook in numerous New York City households, unknowingly infecting people who ate the food she prepared with typhoid fever. Mallon spent the last 23 years of her life under quarantine and died in 1938.

Improving City Life

Jacob Riis hoped his book *How the Other Half Lives* would shock many Americans—and it did. A reformer named Lawrence Veiller helped lead the effort to improve conditions in tenements. Describing the effects of tenement living on children, he wrote:

> " A child living its early years in dark rooms, without sunlight or fresh air, does not grow up to be a normal, healthy person ... It is not of such material that strong nations are made. "
>
> – Lawrence Veiller, quoted in *Readings in American History, Vol. 2*

Veiller worked with an organization called the Charity Organization Society (COS) to get changes made to New York laws. In 1900 he and the COS sponsored an exhibit of photographs and maps graphically showing the conditions of New York tenements. More than 10,000 people visited the exhibit, and they were shocked by what they saw. The work of Veiller and the COS helped to get the 1901 New York State Tenement House Act passed. This law required new buildings to have better ventilation and running water. The act became a model for housing reform in other states.

Because there was little government aid available in the 1800s, private organizations generally took on the task of helping the urban poor. Some individuals set up **settlement houses**, or neighborhood centers in poor areas that offered education, recreation, and social activities.

Settlement houses were staffed by professionals and volunteers. Many were educated women who came from wealthy families. In 1886 Charles B. Stover and Stanton Coit established the first settlement house in the United States. It was called Neighborhood Guild and was located on the Lower East Side in New York City. In 1889 **Jane Addams** and Ellen Gates Starr moved into a run-down building in a poor Chicago neighborhood and turned it into **Hull House**, the most famous settlement house of the period.

The Hull House staff focused on the needs of immigrant families, and by 1893 Hull House was serving 2,000 people a week. It provided services such as English classes, day care, and cooking and sewing classes. Children and adults came to take part in club meetings, art classes, plays, and sports.

Jane Addams and the staff at Hull House also worked for reforms. They studied the problems facing immigrants and poor city dwellers, then searched for ways to improve conditions. **Florence Kelley** was one important reformer at Hull House. She visited sweatshops and wrote about the problems there. Her work helped convince lawmakers to take action. Illinois passed a law in 1893 to limit working hours for women and to prevent child labor.

Kelley became the state's chief factory inspector and helped enforce the law. Although she believed more reforms were needed, she did report some improvements:

Hull House

Neighborhood children attended kindergarten at Hull House. Their parents typically had low-paying jobs, and many were children of immigrants. Children like these had few other options for education.

How did Hull House try to improve the lives of children?

"Previous to the passage of the factory law of 1893, it was the rule of [a candy] factory to work the children ...from 7 A.M. to 9 P.M., with twenty minutes for lunch, and no supper, a working week of eighty-two hours ...Since the enactment of the factory law, their working week has consisted of six days of eight hours each, a reduction of thirty-four hours a week."

– Florence Kelley and Alzina P. Stevens, from *Hull House Maps and Papers*

As Hull House gained recognition, the settlement house movement spread to other cities. Most settlement houses continued to provide programs and services for city dwellers through the early 1900s. Some, such as Germantown Settlement in Pennsylvania, remain active today.

READING CHECK Drawing Conclusions
How did Hull House help improve city life?

SUMMARY AND PREVIEW Reformers in the late 1800s worked to solve urban problems. In the next chapter you will learn how Progressives pushed for further reforms.

CASE STUDY **BIOGRAPHY**

Jane Addams
1860–1935

Jane Addams was born in Cedarville, Illinois. Like many upper-class women of the era, she received a college education but found few jobs open to her. In 1888, on a visit to England with classmate Ellen Gates Starr, she visited a London settlement house. On their return to the United States, Addams and Starr opened a settlement house in Chicago. They started a kindergarten and a public playground. Addams also became involved in housing safety and sanitation issues, factory inspection, and immigrants' rights. In 1931 she shared the Nobel Peace Prize for her work with the Women's International League for Peace and Freedom.

Summarizing How did Jane Addams try to improve the lives of workers?

go.hrw.com
Online Quiz

Section 3 Assessment

Reviewing Ideas, Terms, and People

1. **a. Describe** What were conditions like in tenements?
   b. Summarize What problems resulted from the rapid growth of cities?
   c. Draw Conclusions Why do you think people lived in tenements?
2. **a. Define** What is a **settlement house**?
   b. Explain How did settlement houses help city dwellers?
   c. Evaluate Do you think settlement houses were successful? Why or why not?

Critical Thinking

3. **Categorizing** Review your notes on urban problems. Then copy the chart to the right onto your own sheet of paper and use it to identify the responses to those problems.

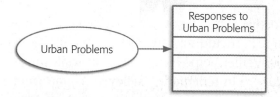

Urban Problems	→	Responses to Urban Problems

FOCUS ON WRITING

4. **Writing about Urban Problems** Finding solutions to problems is an important part of the plot of many stories. Take notes on scenes you could include in your TV series in which characters deal with the problems of urban life.

Social Studies Skills

Analysis   Critical Thinking   Civic Participation   Study

Making Comparisons

Define the Skill

Understanding similarities is important when studying history. Comparing two or more people, things, events, or ideas highlights the similarities between them. Making comparisons can help clarify larger historical issues. This is true when comparing different time periods or when comparing different things from the same time period. Making comparisons is important in identifying historical connections.

Learn the Skill

When you encounter similar people, things, events, or ideas in history, use the following guidelines to make comparisons.

1 Identify who or what you are going to compare.

2 Look for similarities between them. Find examples of what makes them alike. Note any differences as well.

3 Use comparison words such as *like, both,* and *similar* to point out similarities.

In this chapter, you have learned about several reformers, including Lawrence Veiller and Florence Kelley. Veiller helped lead the effort to improve conditions in tenements. Kelley was a reformer who worked at Hull House.

Lawrence Veiller and Florence Kelley were alike in many ways. Although Veiller focused on tenements and Kelley concentrated on factory work, both were concerned with problems that affected children. Both did research about their issues. Both then wrote about the poor conditions they found.

Both Veiller and Kelley worked successfully for laws that would improve those conditions. Kelley's work helped convince Illinois lawmakers to pass a law to limit child labor. Similarly, Veiller helped to get the 1901 New York State Tenement House Act passed.

Practice the Skill

Review the chapter to find two people, things, events, or ideas that are similar. Then apply the guidelines to answer the following questions.

1 Which people, events, or ideas will you compare? Why is each of them important?

2 How are they alike? How are they different?

3 Using your new skills, write a brief comparison of the experiences of a European immigrant and an enslaved African. Include information about how these experiences might have affected the culture of the United States.

Chapter Review

HOLT
History's Impact
▶ video series
Review the video to answer the closing question:
Why do you think the United States had stricter immigration regulations for Asian immigrants?

Visual Summary

QUICK FACTS

Use the visual summary below to help you review the main ideas of the chapter.

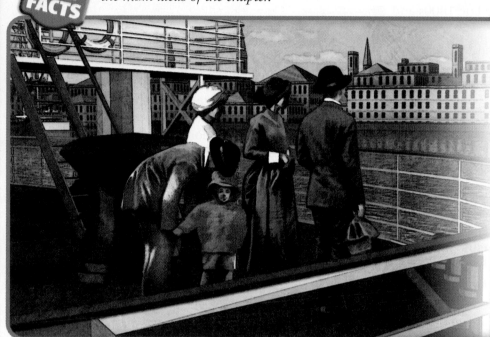

People Arrived
• New immigrants, mostly from southern and eastern Europe
• Came for new opportunities and better lives
• Mostly found jobs in cities
• Faced opposition from some Americans

Cities Grew
• Massive urban growth
• New technologies emerged—skyscrapers and mass transit
• New urban culture

Problems Developed
• Overcrowded tenements
• Unsanitary conditions

Reviewing Vocabulary, Terms, and People

Identify the descriptions below with the correct term or person from the chapter.

1. Public transportation systems built to move many people and ease traffic in crowded cities

2. Founded Hull House with Ellen Gates Starr in 1889

3. Organizations created by immigrants to help each other in times of sickness, unemployment, or other troubles

4. Law banning Chinese people from moving to the United States

5. Neighborhood centers in poor urban areas that offered education, recreation, and social activities

6. Landscape architect who designed New York City's Central Park

7. Small shops or mills where immigrants worked for long hours in hot, unhealthy conditions

Comprehension and Critical Thinking

SECTION 1 *(Pages 56–61)*

8. **a. Identify** From what parts of the world did the wave of new immigrants come?

   b. Analyze In what ways did immigration patterns in the United States change in the late 1800s?

   c. Elaborate In your opinion, were the difficulties that immigrants faced worth the benefits of life in the United States? Explain.

SECTION 2 *(Pages 62–65)*

9. **a. Recall** Why did U.S. cities experience such rapid growth in the late 1800s?

   b. Analyze How did new technologies help cities deal with population growth?

   c. Elaborate Would you have preferred to live in a city or in a suburb? Why?

10. a. Recall What were conditions like in tenements in the late 1800s?

b. Make Inferences Why did rapid population growth cause problems in cities?

c. Elaborate Why do you think the settlement house movement grew in the late 1800s and early 1900s?

Reviewing Themes

11. Economics What role did economics play in the growth of cities?

12. Society and Culture How did the lives of city dwellers change with the rise of mass culture?

Reading Skills

Understanding Historical Fact versus Historical Fiction *Use the Reading Skills taught in this chapter to answer the question about the reading selection below.*

> Mass culture affected how people shopped as well. Giant retail shops, or department stores, appeared in some cities during the late 1800s. One of the earliest was Marshall Field in Chicago, which offered low prices and large quantities of products. It also was the first department store to offer its customers a restaurant where they could eat while shopping. Newspaper advertising was used to bring in customers. The public was also attracted by fancy window displays. *(p. 65)*

13. Which facts above can be verified? Where would you look to verify them?

Social Studies Skills

Making Comparisons *Use the Social Studies Skills taught in this chapter to answer the question below.*

14. Choose two reforms that were discussed in this chapter. Make a comparison between the two.

Using the Internet go.hrw.com

15. Activity: Investigating Culture Mass culture developed in the late 1800s and early 1900s as a result of new and broader forms of communication taking root. Enter the activity keyword and explore some of the early influences on mass culture. Then research the ways in which modern culture is influenced by the media, the Internet, and other forms of mass communication. How does today's society experience mass culture? Create a visual display or computer-based presentation that compares mass culture then and now.

FOCUS ON WRITING

16. Writing Your Memo Look back over your notes about the people, places, and events of the late 1800s. Decide which of these you will include in your television drama series. Then draft a one- to two-paragraph memo to your boss describing the series. Remember to describe the basic plot, setting, and characters.

Grade 8 Intermediate-Level Test Preparation

DIRECTIONS (1–8): For each statement or question, write on the separate answer sheet the *number* of the word or expression that, of those given, best completes the statement or answers the question

1 **Which of the following is associated with providing a better life for urban immigrants in the late 1800s and early 1900s?**

(1) the department store

(2) the suburb

(3) the tenement

(4) the settlement house

2 **The nature of immigration to the United States changed in the late 1800s and early 1900s because**

(1) more immigrants came from southern and eastern Europe.

(2) immigrants began arriving from China for the first time.

(3) restrictions were put on the number of immigrants who could come from northern and western Europe.

(4) Protestant immigrants outnumbered Roman Catholic immigrants.

3 **Ellis Island and Angel Island were both**

(1) locations of settlement houses.

(2) immigration processing centers.

(3) centers of shipping and industry.

(4) amusement parks.

4 **Mass culture affected life in the United States by**

(1) contributing to the growth of department stores through advertising.

(2) enabling more people to move to suburbs.

(3) contributing to the buildling of skyscrapers.

(4) reducing disease in crowded neighborhoods.

5 **Which journalist and photographer exposed the horrible condition in New York City tenements?**

(1) William Randolph Hearst

(2) Joseph Pulitzer

(3) Maria Lozano

(4) Jacob Riis

6 **Anti-immigrant feeling resulted in**

(1) benevolent societies.

(2) the Chinese Exclusion Act.

(3) tenements.

(4) the Tenement House Act.

7 **What famous landmark did Frederick Law Olmstead design?**

(1) The Brooklyn Bridge

(2) Central Park

(3) The Washington Monument

(4) The Statue of Liberty

Base your answer to question 8 on the text below and on your knowledge of social studies.

> *"*lack of family privacy … lack of light and air, and of sanitary accommodations, insuring a large death rate, and danger from fire … [These places are] infested with vermin [insects] and infected with disease germs, they are a disgrace to humanity and a menace, not only to the health of the unfortunate residents therein, but to the health of the whole community.*"*
>
> —*The New York Times*, 1896

8 **Constructed-Response Question** Based on this description, to what was this article most likely referring?

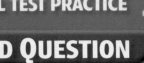
The Country Expands

Part A: Short-Answer Questions

Directions: Read and examine the following documents. Then, on a separate sheet of paper, answer the questions using complete sentences.

DOCUMENT 1

During the 1800s, immigrants from all over Europe poured into the United States. They often settled in places that were similar to their home countries. Even so, life here was very different. Letters to the "old country," like this one from a Norwegian immigrant named Gro Svendsen, described how difficult day-to-day life could be as a new immigrant to the United States.

> I remember I used to wonder when I heard that it would be impossible to keep the milk here as we did at home. Now I have learned that it is indeed impossible because of the heat here in the summer time . . . It's difficult, too, to preserve the butter. One must pour brine [salt water] over it or salt it. The thunderstorms are so violent that one might think it was the end of the world . . . Quite often the lightning strikes down both cattle and people, damages property, and splinters sturdy oak trees into many pieces.
>
> —**Gro Svendsen,** quoted in *Sources in American History*

1a. What problems does Svendsen specifically mention?

_____

1b. Why did immigrants continue to settle on the plains, even though it was a difficult life?

_____

DOCUMENT 2

Some people arrived in the United States dreaming of riches and an easy life. Yet many immigrants, especially those in cities, lived in crowded, run-down buildings. Miriam Shomer Zusner, whose family left Russia and came to the United States in 1890, later wrote about this experience.

> [I dreamed] of the golden stairs leading to the top of the American palace where father was supposed to live. [I] went 'home' to . . . an ugly old tenement in the heart of the Lower East Side. There were stairs to climb but they were not golden.
>
> —**Miriam Shomer Zusner,** *Yesterday: A Memoir of a Russian Jewish Family*

2a. How does Zusner describe the place where "father was supposed to live"?

_____

2b. What parts of the quotation show the difference between what Zusner dreamed of and what she found?

_____

DOCUMENT 3

During the 1800s, American cities were growing fast. They were also becoming more crowded. However, they offered modern conveniences that were not to be found in rural areas.

3a. Why would electricity be especially important in cities like Chicago?

_____

3b. What do you think it was like to live in Chicago in 1900?

_____

DOCUMENT 4

By the late 1800s, big businesses had enormous power in the United States. There were few controls on businesses, and some people believed the government should step in and regulate the corporations. Political cartoons like this one reflected that sentiment.

4a. Why do you think the cartoonist chose to use Rockefeller in this cartoon?

_____

4b. How has the artist drawn Rockefeller? How does this help the artist make his point?

_____

Part B: Essay

Historical Context: After the Civil War, the country resumed its westward expansion. The documents on these two pages relate to this period of growth and to the problems that came with it.

TASK: Using information from the four documents and your knowledge of U.S. history, write an essay in which you:

- discuss the challenges the United States faced in the second half of the 19th century.
- describe solutions that Americans provided to these challenges.

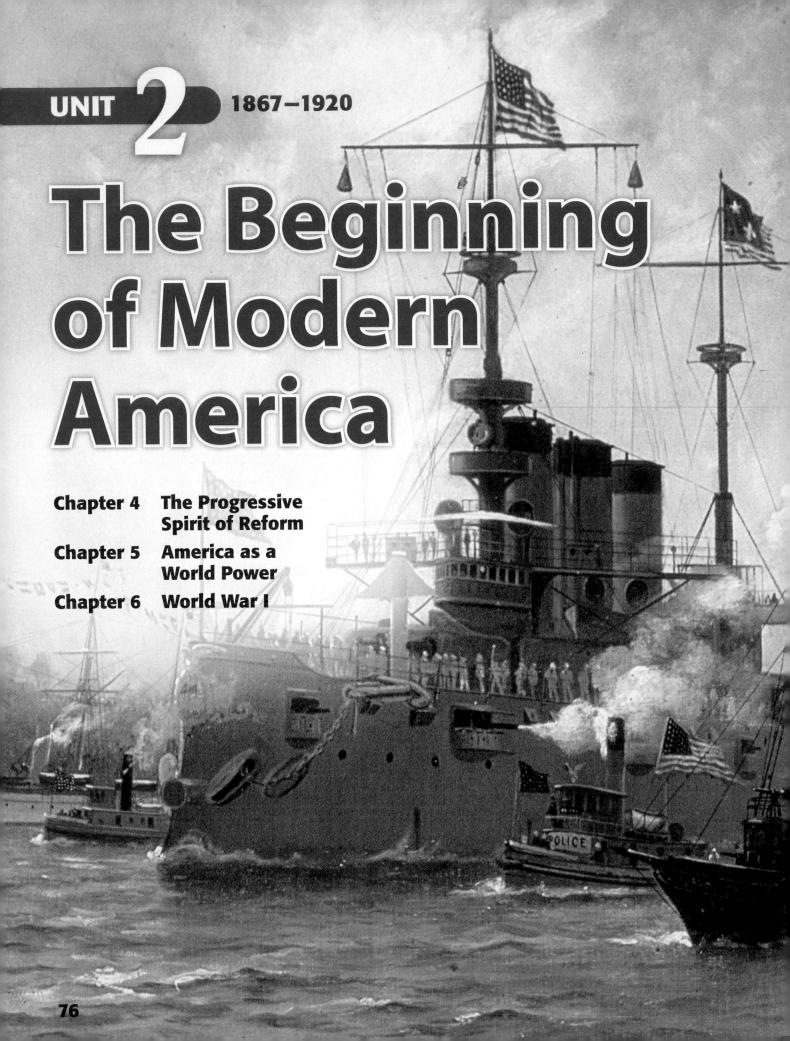

The Beginning of Modern America

As cities in the United States became more prosperous, people began to examine the inequalities in American society. A progressive spirit emerged that led to changes in American culture. The United States also began to expand its influence overseas.

Presidents were called upon to deal with many domestic and foreign challenges, including two wars that changed the landscape of international politics. During the Spanish-American War, the United States acquired overseas territories. During World War I, Americans fought in Europe for the first time.

Explore the Art

This painting shows the Great White Fleet, a group of U.S. ships that toured the world from 1907 to 1909. How might a tour of American ships affect foreign views of the United States?

The Progressive Spirit of Reform

FOCUS QUESTION

How do people affect change and reform?

FOCUS ON SPEAKING

Campaign Promises In this chapter you will read about the political corruption of the Gilded Age and the reform movements that followed. Serious problems face the nation, and you must convince voters that you should be the one to tackle those problems. Create and present a list of campaign promises that you would make if you were a politician running for office in the United States in the late 1800s or early 1900s.

UNITED STATES

1868
Ulysses S. Grant is elected president.

1865   1870

WORLD

1871 The British Parliament legalizes labor unions.

HOLT
History's Impact
▶ video series
Watch the video to understand the impact of women's suffrage.

What You Will Learn...

In this chapter you will learn about how reform movements swept across the United States in the late 1800s and early 1900s. These movements had a variety of aims, from ending government corruption to abolishing child labor. Ordinary citizens, like these women calling for their right to vote, participated in the movements.

1881
Charles Guiteau, a frustrated federal job seeker, assassinates President James A. Garfield.

1901 President William McKinley is assassinated, and Vice President Theodore Roosevelt becomes president.

NY
1911
The Triangle Shirtwaist Factory in New York City catches fire, killing 146 employees.

1920 Congress declares the Nineteenth Amendment ratified, giving women the right to vote.

| 1880 | 1890 | 1900 | 1910 | 1920 |

1888
Brazil officially ends slavery.

1912 The British luxury liner *Titanic* sinks after hitting an iceberg during its first voyage. About 1,500 passengers die.

1917
Mexico adopts a new constitution.

THE PROGRESSIVE SPIRIT OF REFORM **79**

Focus on Themes In this chapter, you will read about the corrupt **politics** of the Gilded Age, a time marked by attempts at reform. You will learn how **society and culture** reacted and responded to the problems of corruption and inequality. Finally, you will read about several presidents of the early 1900s who supported ideas and initiatives that promoted social reform.

Evaluating Sources

Focus on Reading Historical texts and current history books are good sources of information about the past. However, some sources can be more reliable than others to learn the truth.

Evaluating Texts Sometimes people write texts with a specific purpose or viewpoint in mind. Determining what the author's goal was in writing a passage can help you evaluate whether to believe all of the text, or merely some of it. Knowing which parts you can believe and which you cannot will help you understand what really happened in history.

Notice how one reader evaluated the source below.

> The man, therefore, who as the owner of newspapers, would corrupt public opinion is the most dangerous enemy of the State. We may talk about the perils incident [dangers attached] to the concentration of wealth, about the perils flowing from a disregard of fiduciary [financial] responsibility, about abuses of privilege, about exploiting the government for private advantage; but all of these menaces, great as they are, are nothing compared with a deliberate, persistent, artful, purchased endeavor to [change and direct] the public judgment.
>
> —*Harper's Weekly*, October 20, 1906, quoted in *Yellow Journalism* by W. Joseph Campbell

The author is using strong words to describe his viewpoint. Maybe he isn't being as objective as he should be.

The article lists several ideas that the author seems to think are bad. Are these things really bad? Can that help me determine the author's viewpoint?

This magazine was widely read when the article appeared. I think that makes the article a good source for some viewpoints of the time.

You Try It!

Read the passage below and evaluate whether you would use it as a source for a paper.

> Space is no intervention now between communication. [N]ot only do the wires of copper bind the world together in closer communication, but with the telephone it is possible to converse [talk] with friends a thousand miles away, hearing distinctly every word and recognizing the individual voice. Closer acquaintance has thus wrought [created] vast changes in public opinions and policies. The entire civilized world has been drawn more closely together, old ideas and prejudices have been wiped out.
>
> —*Cincinnati Times-Star*, January 1, 1900, quoted in *Yellow Journalism* by W. Joseph Campbell

1. What viewpoint of new technology is the author taking in this article? How can you tell?

2. Do you believe that the telephone brought about "changes in public opinions and policies"? Why or why not? Why might the author say this?

3. Can you trust the author when he says that "old ideas and prejudices have been wiped out"? Why or why not? Why might the author say this?

4. Did this article appear in a well-known newspaper? Does this make it more trustworthy or less?

5. Would you use this article as a source for writing a paper about how new inventions affected life in the early 1900s? Explain your answer.

As you read Chapter 4, evaluate the primary sources for their usefulness in understanding history.

Key Terms and People

Chapter 4

Section 1
political machines *(p. 82)*
Progressives *(p. 84)*
muckrakers *(p. 84)*
Seventeenth Amendment *(p. 86)*
recall *(p. 86)*
initiative *(p. 86)*
referendum *(p. 86)*
Robert M. La Follette *(p. 87)*

Section 2
Triangle Shirtwaist Fire *(p. 93)*
workers' compensation laws *(p. 93)*
capitalism *(p. 94)*
socialism *(p. 94)*
William "Big Bill" Haywood *(p. 94)*
Industrial Workers of the World *(p. 94)*

Section 3
Eighteenth Amendment *(p. 96)*
National American Woman Suffrage Association *(p. 96)*
Alice Paul *(p. 97)*
Nineteenth Amendment *(p.97)*
Booker T. Washington *(p. 97)*
Ida B. Wells *(p. 97)*
W. E. B. Du Bois *(p. 98)*
National Association for the Advancement of Colored People *(p. 98)*

Section 4
Theodore Roosevelt *(p. 100)*
Pure Food and Drug Act *(p. 101)*
conservation *(p. 101)*
William Howard Taft *(p. 102)*
Progressive Party *(p. 102)*
Woodrow Wilson *(p. 102)*
Sixteenth Amendment *(p. 103)*

Academic Vocabulary

In this chapter you will learn the following academic words:

motive *(p. 86)*
various *(p. 102)*

The Gilded Age and the Progressive Movement

What You Will Learn...

Main Ideas

1. Political corruption was common during the Gilded Age.
2. Progressives pushed for reforms to improve living conditions.
3. Progressive reforms expanded the voting power of citizens.

The Big Idea

From the late 1800s through the early 1900s, the Progressive movement addressed problems in American society.

Key Terms and People

political machines, p. 82
Progressives, p. 84
muckrakers, p. 84
Seventeenth Amendment, p. 86
recall, p. 86
initiative, p. 86
referendum, p. 86
Robert M. La Follette, p. 87

TAKING NOTES As you read, take notes on progressive reforms and the problems they addressed. Organize your notes in a chart like the one below.

Progressive reform	Problem it addressed

If YOU were there...

You live in a big-city neighborhood in the 1890s. You and your brother are both looking for jobs. You know that the man down the street is the "ward boss." He can always get city jobs for his friends and neighbors. But in return you'll have to promise to vote the way he tells you to in the upcoming election.

Would you ask the ward boss for a job? Why or why not?

BUILDING BACKGROUND The late 1800s were a time of contrasts in American life. Great wealth created through business ventures existed alongside poverty and the difficulties of tenement life. In politics, money led to corruption and dishonesty. Reacting to these conditions, reformers worked to improve many areas of American life.

Political Corruption

The late 1800s in the United States are often called the Gilded Age. The term came from a novel by that name. *The Gilded Age* highlights the inequality between wealthy business owners, who profited from the Industrial Revolution, and workers, who often labored under terrible conditions for little pay. Many people began to believe that the government should help fix this inequality. The first step was to get rid of corruption in politics.

Political Machines

In the late 1800s city and county politics were dominated by **political machines**—powerful organizations that used both legal and illegal methods to get their candidates elected to public office. For example, members of political machines sometimes stuffed ballot boxes with extra votes for their candidates. They also paid people to vote a certain way and then bribed vote counters. Through such actions, political machines could control local governments.

POLITICAL CARTOON
The Tammany Ring

William Marcy Tweed was the boss of the Tammany Hall political machine, which ran New York City politics during the second half of the 1800s. Tweed made illegal deals with gangs and other politicians that often involved large sums of money. He also took bribes for awarding contracts to specific companies. Tweed and the Tammany Ring were eventually forced out of power by lawsuits and public pressure such as political cartoons like the one on the right. Tweed is the man in the red vest.

The men have labels on their backs that show they represent different interests.

The Granger Collection, New York

ANALYSIS SKILL **ANALYZING PRIMARY SOURCES**

Why are the men shown standing in a circle?

Political machines were run by leaders called bosses. The machine's boss frequently traded favors for votes. For example, the boss might hand out city jobs to unqualified people or allow an illegal business to operate. The bosses drew much of their support from immigrants. They became popular among poor families because of the services they provided, including jobs and social services such as a fire brigade. A Boston politician said that the role of the machine boss was "to be . . . somebody that any bloke [man] can come to . . . and get help."

New York City's Democratic political machine, Tammany Hall, was one of the most notorious. After winning city elections in 1888, members of Tammany Hall rewarded their supporters with about 12,000 jobs. As boss of Tammany Hall, William Marcy Tweed may have stolen up to $200 million from the city. One man remembered how Tammany Hall stayed in power by intimidating voters:

" Father used to say, 'They know how you're voting. You can't fool them.' He was a Republican at heart, but he had to vote Democratic in order that they didn't find out and make it difficult for him. "

—Henry Fenner, quoted in *You Must Remember This,* edited by Jeff Kisseloff

Cleaning Up Political Corruption

Corruption was also a problem in the federal government. Many people thought that the corruption extended to the presidential administration of Ulysses S. Grant. During Grant's second term, federal officials were jailed for taking bribes from whiskey makers in exchange for allowing them to avoid paying taxes. Another scandal involved members of Congress who had taken bribes to allow the Union Pacific Railway to receive government funds. These scandals and others caused many Americans to question the honesty of national leaders.

In response, Americans began calling for changes in the civil service, the government job system. They disliked the spoils system, the practice of giving jobs to the winning candidates' supporters. Thomas Jefferson was the first to reward supporters with jobs. After his administration, each time a new party took power, it replaced many government officials. Many new employees were unqualified and untrained.

By the late 1800s government corruption was so widespread that reformers demanded that only qualified people be given government jobs. In response, President Rutherford B. Hayes

Gilded Age Presidents

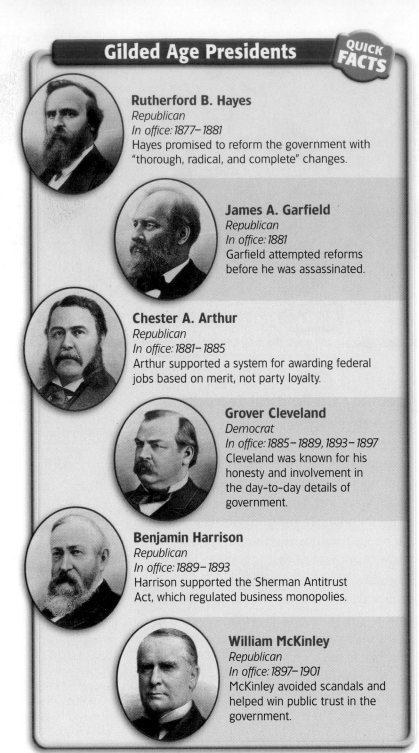

Rutherford B. Hayes
Republican
In office: 1877–1881
Hayes promised to reform the government with "thorough, radical, and complete" changes.

James A. Garfield
Republican
In office: 1881
Garfield attempted reforms before he was assassinated.

Chester A. Arthur
Republican
In office: 1881–1885
Arthur supported a system for awarding federal jobs based on merit, not party loyalty.

Grover Cleveland
Democrat
In office: 1885–1889, 1893–1897
Cleveland was known for his honesty and involvement in the day-to-day details of government.

Benjamin Harrison
Republican
In office: 1889–1893
Harrison supported the Sherman Antitrust Act, which regulated business monopolies.

William McKinley
Republican
In office: 1897–1901
McKinley avoided scandals and helped win public trust in the government.

THE IMPACT TODAY

Tests are still required for many federal jobs, including secretarial positions, air traffic control, and law enforcement.

made minor reforms, such as firing a powerful member of the New York Republican political machine. President James A. Garfield also attempted reforms. But on July 2, 1881, Garfield was attacked and shot twice by a mentally unstable federal job seeker named Charles Guiteau. The president later died from his wounds, and Vice President Chester A. Arthur became president.

Arthur continued the push for reforms by backing the Pendleton Civil Service Act, which was passed in 1883. This law set up a merit system for awarding federal jobs. Under the Pendleton Act, more than 10 percent of government job applicants had to pass an exam before they could be hired. It was a start to reforming other government practices.

READING CHECK **Analyzing** What factors led to civil-service reform?

Progressives Push for Reforms

A group of reformers known as **Progressives** were also working to improve society in the late 1800s. Progressives tried to solve problems caused by rapid industrial and urban growth. Their goals were to eliminate the causes of problems such as crime, disease, and poverty. They fought for reforms ranging from better working conditions to education programs in poor neighborhoods.

Muckrakers at Work

Some journalists urged Progressives to action by writing stories that vividly described problems in U.S. society. These journalists were nicknamed **muckrakers** because they "raked up" and exposed the muck, or filth, of society. Muckrakers wrote about troubling issues such as child labor, racial discrimination, slum housing, and corruption in business and politics.

In 1902 and 1903 Lincoln Steffens wrote a series of articles in *McClure's Magazine* exposing corruption in city government. In one article, he described how government officials in Saint Louis, Missouri, used their positions to earn extra money illegally:

"Men empowered to issue peddlers' licenses and permits to citizens who wished to erect awnings or use a portion of the sidewalk for storage purposes charged an amount in excess of the prices stipulated [set] by law, and pocketed the difference."
—Lincoln Steffens, *The Shame of the Cities*

PHOTOGRAPH
The Other Half

In 1890 Jacob Riis published How the Other Half Lives. *The book was a collection of photographs of residents and workers in New York City tenement buildings, including families and immigrants. The conditions of life that Riis showed in his photographs, like this one, shocked many wealthier Americans.*

Sweatshops turned out large amounts of clothing at low prices.

Sweatshops were located in tenements to avoid the labor laws that affected factories. Workers crowded into the small, stuffy spaces.

This 12-year-old boy said he was 16 in order to keep his job of pulling threads.

ANALYSIS SKILL **ANALYZING PRIMARY SOURCES**

How might this photograph encourage people to become reformers?

Another muckraker, Ida B. Tarbell, wrote articles criticizing the unfair business practices of the Standard Oil Company. Upton Sinclair exposed unsanitary practices in the meat-processing industry in his novel *The Jungle*.

Although such writing angered many politicians and business leaders, it also helped to unite Progressives. Muckrakers influenced voters, causing them to pressure politicians into backing reforms.

Reform Successes

A major goal of Progressive reformers was to help the urban poor. You have read about the work of housing reformers, which led to the 1901 New York State Tenement House Act. Other Progressives started settlement houses similar to Jane Addams's Hull House. People usually started settlement houses in poor areas in order to improve education, housing, and sanitation there.

The movement for urban reform also led to new professions, such as city planning and civil engineering. City planners helped design safer building codes and opened new public parks. Civil engineers improved transportation by paving streets and building bridges. Sanitation engineers tried to solve problems concerning pollution, waste disposal, and impure water supplies. Death rates dropped dramatically in areas where planners and engineers addressed these problems.

Progressives also believed that improving education would lead to a better society. In response to their demands for reform, states passed laws requiring all children to attend school. Some Progressives started kindergarten programs to help young city children learn basic social skills. In 1873 reformer Susan Blow opened the first American public kindergarten in Saint Louis. By 1898 more than 4,000 kindergartens had opened in the United States.

Philosopher John Dewey was a key supporter of early childhood education. His

FOCUS ON NEW YORK CITY

The Democratic political boss of Tammany Hall, William M. Tweed, was exposed by George Jones of the *New York Times*. Jones's series of investigative articles about the corruption of Tweed and his cronies led to the prosecution of Tweed. Tweed was convicted in 1872 and died in jail six years later.

<u>motive</u> was to help children learn problem-solving skills, not just memorize facts. This, he thought, would help them in everyday life. Dewey's teaching methods became a model for progressive education across the country.

Progressives also worked to improve the education of medical professionals. In the late 1800s the United States lacked a ready supply of well-trained and professionally organized doctors. Researchers knew the causes of diseases such as pneumonia and tuberculosis. However, there were few medical organizations that could help spread this knowledge.

Under the leadership of Joseph McCormack, the American Medical Association (AMA) brought together local medical organizations in 1901. The AMA supported laws designed to protect public health and showed how Progressives could organize to help improve society. Other organizations followed the AMA's lead.

READING CHECK **Finding Main Ideas** How did progressive reforms improve society?

CASE STUDY) BIOGRAPHY

Robert M. La Follette
1855–1925

Born in rural Wisconsin, Robert M. La Follette began his political career at a young age. He was elected to the U.S. House of Representatives in 1884, becoming the youngest member of Congress. He soon earned the nickname "Fighting Bob" for his energetic speaking style and his active support for progressive reforms.

After serving as Wisconsin's governor and as U.S. senator, La Follette ran for president as the Progressive Party candidate in 1924. He won his home state and received about 16 percent of the popular vote.

Drawing Conclusions Why might La Follette have been proud of the nickname "Fighting Bob"?

Expansion of Voting Power

Some Progressives worked to change state and local governments in order to reduce the power of political machines. In many places, reformers replaced corrupt ballots that listed only one party's candidates with government-prepared ballots that listed all candidates. Under pressure from reformers, many states adopted secret ballots, a measure that ensured the privacy of every voter.

Voting Reforms

Reformers also hoped to expand voting power. For example, they favored the **Seventeenth Amendment**, which allowed Americans to vote directly for U.S. senators. Before the constitutional amendment was passed in 1913, state legislatures had elected senators. Reformers also favored the direct primary, in which voters choose candidates for public office directly. Previously, party leaders had selected which candidates would run for office.

Other reform measures allowed voters to take action against corrupt politicians. Some states and cities gave unhappy voters the right to sign a petition asking for a special vote. The purpose of that vote was to **recall**, or remove, an official before the end of his or her term. If enough voters signed the petition, the vote took place. The official could then be removed from office if there were a majority of recall votes.

In California, Oregon, and states in the Midwest, Progressives worked on reforms to give voters direct influence over new laws. A procedure called the **initiative** allowed voters to propose a new law by collecting signatures on a petition. If enough signatures were collected, the proposed law was voted on at the next election. Another measure, called the **referendum**, permitted voters to approve or reject a law that had already been proposed or passed by a government body. This process gave voters a chance to overrule laws that they opposed.

Government Reforms

In addition to working for greater voter participation, Progressives attempted to change the way city government operated. Some reformers wanted city government to be run like a business. As a result of their efforts, several cities changed to council-manager governments. Under this system, voters elect a city council. The council then appoints a professional manager to run the city. Other business-minded reformers supported the commission form of government. Under this system, the city is headed by a group of elected officials. Each official manages a major city agency, such as housing or transportation.

One of the leaders of the effort to reform state government was Wisconsin's Republican governor **Robert M. La Follette**. La Follette decreased the power of political machines and used university professors and other experts to help write new laws and work in state agencies. He also made available to the public information on how politicians voted. That way, voters would know if leaders had

Expanding Democracy	QUICK FACTS
Direct Primaries	Voters choose candidates.
Recall	Voters can remove an official from office.
Initiatives	Voters can propose laws by petition.
Referendum	Voters can overrule a law.
17th Amendment	Senators are elected directly by voters.

kept their campaign promises. Called the Wisconsin Idea, La Follette's plan became a model for progressive reforms in other states.

READING CHECK **Evaluating** How did Progressives work to change voting procedures?

SUMMARY AND PREVIEW Progressives worked to reform government and improve city life. In the next section you will learn about reforms in working conditions.

Section 1 Assessment

Reviewing Ideas, Terms, and People

1. **a. Recall** What was the main goal of **political machines** during the Gilded Age?
   b. Draw Conclusions Why do you think some immigrants supported political machines?
   c. Predict Do you think the system of testing created by the Pendleton Civil Service Act would work to reduce corruption in the spoils system? Why or why not?
2. **a. Identify** Who were **muckrakers**? What effect did they have on reform?
   b. Explain How did **Progressives** try to improve education?
   c. Evaluate Which progressive reform do you think was most important? Why?
3. **a. Describe** What new ideas and practices were introduced to give voters more power?
   b. Draw Conclusions How did progressive reforms limit the power of political machines?

Critical Thinking

4. **Categorizing** Review your notes on the problems that progressive reforms addressed. Then copy the chart below and use it to categorize the various progressive reforms.

Progressive Reforms		
Social	Political	Urban

FOCUS ON SPEAKING

5. **Addressing Political and Social Problems** How would you address the problems of political corruption and urban growth during the late 1800s? Jot down notes about campaign promises you might make to assure voters that you would make the necessary reforms.

Reform Literature

from *How the Other Half Lives*
by Jacob Riis (1849–1914)

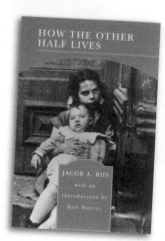

About the Reading How the Other Half Lives *describes the tenement houses where immigrants lived in New York City. Its author, Jacob Riis, was a newspaper reporter. His nonfiction book made Americans aware of the extremes of poverty suffered by working people. Riis believed that every human being deserved a decent, safe place to live.* How the Other Half Lives *led to reforms and new laws that improved housing conditions.*

AS YOU READ Look for details that help you see, hear, and smell Cherry Street.

Cherry Street. Be a little careful, please! ❶ The hall is dark and you might stumble over the children pitching pennies back there. Not that it would hurt them; kicks and cuffs are their daily diet. They have little else. Here where the hall turns and dives into utter darkness is a step, and another, another. A flight of stairs. You can feel your way, if you cannot see it. Close? Yes! What would you have? All the fresh air that ever enters these stairs comes from the hall door that is forever slamming, and from the windows of dark bedrooms that in turn receive from the stairs their sole supply of the elements God meant to be free . . . That was a woman filling her pail by the hydrant you just bumped against. The sinks are in the hallway, that all the tenants may have access—and all be poisoned alike by their summer stenches. Hear the pump squeak! It is the lullaby of tenement house babes. In summer, when a thousand thirsty throats pant for a cooling drink in this block, it is worked in vain . . . ❷

The sea of a mighty population, held in galling fetters, heaves uneasily in the tenements . . . If it rise once more, no human power may avail to check it. The gap between the classes in which it surges, unseen, unsuspected by the thoughtless, is widening day by day . . . I know of but one bridge that will carry us over safe, a bridge founded upon justice and built of human hearts.

GUIDED READING

WORD HELP

cuffs punches

utter complete

close stuffy

sole only

access right to use

stenches bad smells

in vain without success

galling causing pain; irritating

fetters chains

heaves rises and falls

avail help

❶ *The writer wants you to imagine that he is taking you on a tour of the building. Why do you think he chooses this way to describe the place?*

❷ *Find one detail that appeals to each sense: sight, sound, smell, taste, and touch. How would you sum up, in one sentence, the place that Riis describes?*

from *The Jungle*

by Upton Sinclair (1878–1968)

About the Reading The Jungle *focused the nation's attention on immigrant workers in the meatpacking industry. Upton Sinclair's novel showed bosses forcing human beings to live and work like animals. He also described, in shocking detail, how meat was handled. Sinclair published his book in 1906. Later that same year, the U.S. government passed the Pure Food and Drug Act and the Meat Inspection Act. Many Americans even gave up eating meat for a while.*

AS YOU READ Look for details that create one overwhelming effect.

There was never the least attention paid to what was cut up for sausage; there would come back from Europe old sausage that had been rejected, and that was mouldy and white—it would be dosed with borax and glycerine, and dumped into hoppers, and made over again for home consumption. There would be meat that had tumbled out on the floor, in the dirt and sawdust, where the workers had tramped and spit uncounted billions of consumption germs. ❶ There would be meat stored in great piles in rooms and the water from leaky roofs would drip over it, and thousands of rats would race about on it. It was too dark in these storage places to see well, but a man would run his hand over these piles of meat and sweep off handfuls of the dried dung of rats. ❷ These rats were nuisances, and the packers would put poisoned bread out for them; they would die, and then rats, bread, and meat would go into the hoppers together . . . ❸ There was no place for the men to wash their hands before they ate their dinner, and so they made a practice of washing them in the water that was to be ladled into the sausage. ❹

GUIDED READING

WORD HELP

borax white powder used in manufacturing and cleaning
glycerine sweet, sticky liquid
hoppers containers
consumption to eat or drink
consumption tuberculosis, a lung disease that was fatal at that time
ladled added with a large spoon

❶ *What overall effect or mood does Sinclair create?*

❷ *Based on the details in this passage, what were the packers most concerned about?*

❸ *Why do you think rats were considered nuisances?*

❹ *Find details that reveal how one improvement in working conditions might have resulted in healthier sausage.*

CONNECTING LITERATURE TO HISTORY

1. **Identify Cause and Effect** Jacob Riis and Upton Sinclair were both muckraking journalists. Why do you think so much muck existed in the tenements and in the meatpacking business? Why had people ignored those conditions for so long?

2. **Identify Cause and Effect** Both Riis and Sinclair believed that improving conditions for immigrants would benefit all of society. Explain how one specific change in the tenements might have a favorable effect on everyone. Then explain how one specific change in meat handling might affect everyone.

3. **Compare and Contrast** Both *How the Other Half Lives* and *The Jungle* inspired Progressives to work for reform. Which work do you think had the greater effect on its readers? Use details from each passage to explain your answer.

Reforming the Workplace

What You Will Learn...

Main Ideas

1. Reformers attempted to improve conditions for child laborers.
2. Unions and reformers took steps to improve safety in the workplace and to limit working hours.

The Big Idea

In the early 1900s, Progressives and other reformers focused on improving conditions for American workers.

Key Terms and People

Triangle Shirtwaist Fire, *p. 93*
workers' compensation laws, *p. 93*
capitalism, *p. 94*
socialism, *p. 94*
William "Big Bill" Haywood, *p. 94*
Industrial Workers of
    the World, *p. 94*

TAKING NOTES As you read, take notes on important labor problems and the workers they affected. You can organize your notes in a table like this one.

Problems in the Workplace

If YOU were there...

You have been working in a hat factory since 1900, when you were eight years old. Now you are experienced enough to run one of the sewing machines. You don't earn as much as older workers, but your family needs every penny you bring home. Still, the long hours make you very tired. One day you hear that people are trying to stop children from doing factory work. They think that children should be at school or playing.

Would you be for or against this social reform? Why?

BUILDING BACKGROUND Since the Second Industrial Revolution, more and more people were working long hours in difficult conditions. With adult workers earning low wages, many children had to work full time to help support their families. Progressive reformers began to focus on these problems.

Improving Conditions for Children

In the early 1900s a reformer named Marie Van Vorst took a series of jobs in factories and clothing mills around the country. She wanted to investigate working conditions for children by living and working alongside them. In a South Carolina textile mill, Van Vorst met children as young as seven years old. She described working with one young child:

"Through the looms I catch sight of ... my landlord's little child. She is seven; so small that they have a box for her to stand on ... I can see only her fingers as they clutch at the flying spools."
– Marie Van Vorst, quoted in *A History of Women in America,* edited by Carol Hymowitz

This girl—and other children like her—provided cheap labor for manufacturers. Some children were paid as little as 40 cents per day. Marie Van Vorst helped focus attention on the problem of child labor. Eliminating the problems of child labor became a major issue for Progressives and other reformers.

Children at Work

Children did many jobs in the late 1800s. Boys sold newspapers and shined shoes on the streets. Girls often cooked or cleaned for boarders staying with their families. Girls also worked at home with their mothers, sewing clothes or making handicrafts.

Like the child Van Vorst encountered, many children worked in industry. In 1900 more than 1.75 million children age 15 and under worked in factories, mines, and mills, earning very low wages.

Calls for Reform

As reporters published shocking accounts of working conditions for children, more people became aware of the problem. Progressives began to call for new reforms. You have read about Florence Kelley's work against child labor in Illinois. Kelley also served as a board member of the National Consumers' League, the major lobbying group for women's and children's labor issues. A lobbying group works to influence legislators in favor of a cause.

During the early 1900s, reformers finally got some laws passed to ease the conditions of child laborers. Some states raised the age at which students had to remain in school. In 1912 Massachusetts passed the first minimum wage law and created a commission to establish rates for child workers.

In 1916 and 1919 Congress passed federal child labor laws. The laws banned products made with child labor from being shipped from one state to another. The Supreme Court, however, ruled that the laws were unconstitutional. The Court argued that the laws went beyond the federal government's legal power to regulate interstate commerce.

In any case, laws alone could not end child labor. Some parents ignored child labor laws so that their children could continue contributing to the family income. Children were often instructed to lie about their age to government inspectors and tell them they were older than they really were.

FOCUS ON READING
What do you think the author's goal is in this paragraph?

READING CHECK Finding Main Ideas How did reformers try to improve child labor conditions?

Child Labor

Young children did much of the work in the American factories of the late 1800s. They were paid less than adult workers.

Why did some parents want their children to work?

History Close-up

Working Conditions for Children, Early 1900s

This illustration shows some of the jobs that children did in glass factories in the early 1900s. You can see that there were many ways for young workers to be injured on the job.

Hot air blew from the glass ovens into the working space.

Adult workers closely supervised child workers.

Workers wore no protection against the fires and machinery.

Temperatures in the ovens used to make glass were more than 2,000° Fahrenheit.

Bending and lifting often left young workers tired and sore after their long day's work.

ANALYSIS SKILL | **ANALYZING VISUALS**

Using the illustration, what can you tell about the life and work of these boys?

Safety and Working Conditions

Child labor reform was only part of the progressive effort to help American workers. Many Progressives also favored laws to ensure workers' safety, limit working hours, and protect workers' rights.

Workplace Safety

Workplace accidents were common in the 1800s and early 1900s. In 1900 some 35,000 people were killed in industrial accidents. About 500,000 suffered injuries. One child described how her sister was injured using a machine in a string factory. "You see you mustn't talk or look off a minute," she explained. "My sister was like me. She forgot and talked, and just that minute her finger was off, and she didn't even cry till she picked it up."

Accidents like this were not big news in the early 1900s, but in 1911 a much greater workplace tragedy shocked the nation. It took place at the Triangle Shirtwaist Company, a New York City clothing factory that employed mostly teenage immigrant women. On the afternoon of March 25, a fire started on the eighth floor of the factory. Workers tried to escape, but factory owners had locked the exit doors—to reduce theft of materials, they said.

By the time firefighters brought the fire under control, 146 workers had died. At a memorial service for the victims, union leader Rose Schneiderman called for action. "It is up to the working people to save themselves," she said. The **Triangle Shirtwaist Fire** and similar accidents led to the passage of laws improving factory safety standards.

Labor leaders and reformers also fought for **workers' compensation laws**, which guaranteed a portion of lost wages to workers injured on the job. In 1902 Maryland became the first state to pass such a law. However, new laws were not always strictly enforced. Working conditions remained poor in many places.

TRIAL TRANSCRIPT
Triangle Shirtwaist Fire

Ethel Monick was one of the teenage factory workers at the Triangle Shirtwaist Company. In the trial that followed the disaster, she described her experience in the fire. Rose Freedman, pictured, was the longest living survivor of the fire. She died in 2001.

I seen the fire and then I seen all the girls rushing down to the place to escape. So I tried to go through the Greene Street door, and there were quick girls there and I seen I can't get out there, so I went to the elevator, and then I heard the elevator fall down, so I ran through to the Washington Place side . . . I tried the door and I could not open it, so I thought I was not strong enough to open it, so I hollered girls here is a door, and they all rushed over and they tried to open it, but it was locked and they hollered "the door is locked and we can't open it!"

—Testimony of Ethel Monick, age 16

ANALYSIS SKILL **ANALYZING PRIMARY SOURCES**

According to Monick, what is the feeling in the factory?

The Courts and Labor

Not everyone supported the new workplace regulations. Some business leaders believed that the economy should operate without any government interference. They went to court to block new labor laws.

One important case began in New York in 1897, after the state passed a law limiting bakers to a 10-hour workday. Joseph Lochner, a bakery owner, challenged the law. The case eventually went to the U.S. Supreme Court in 1905. In *Lochner* v. *New York*, the Court ruled that states could not restrict the rights of employers and workers to enter into any type of labor agreement. The New York law was declared unconstitutional.

The Supreme Court did uphold some limits on working hours for women and children. In the 1908 *Muller* v. *Oregon* case, the Court upheld laws restricting women's work hours. The justices stated that such laws protected women's health, which was of public concern.

Labor Organizations

Labor unions were also a strong force for improving working conditions and paved the way for social reforms. Union membership rose from about 800,000 in 1900 to about 5 million in 1920. Led by Samuel Gompers, the American Federation of Labor (AFL) remained one of the strongest labor unions. The AFL focused on better working conditions and pay for skilled workers. Gompers supported the American system of **capitalism**, an economic system in which private businesses run most industries and competition determines the price of goods.

Some union members, however, believed in **socialism**—a system in which the government owns and operates a country's means of production. Socialists, led by Eugene V. Debs, hoped that the government would protect workers.

In 1905 a group of socialists and union leaders founded a union that welcomed immigrants, women, African Americans, and others not welcome in the AFL. Led by **William "Big Bill" Haywood**, this socialist union was called the **Industrial Workers of the World** (IWW). Its goal was to organize all workers into one large union that would overthrow capitalism. Staging strikes across the country, the IWW frightened many Americans with its aggressive tactics. Strong opposition led to its decline by 1920.

READING CHECK **Analyzing** How did reforms change the workplace?

SUMMARY AND PREVIEW Progressive reformers fought to improve working conditions. In the next section you will learn about how women and minorities struggled for their rights.

Section 2 Assessment

go.hrw.com
Online Quiz

Reviewing Ideas, Terms, and People

1. **a. Recall** What jobs did child laborers often hold?
   b. Explain Why did businesses employ children in factories?
   c. Elaborate Why do you think reformers began to demand improvements to child labor conditions?
2. **a. Identify** What events led to the movement to improve workplace safety?
   b. Make Inferences Why did the **Industrial Workers of the World** frighten some people?
   c. Predict What conflicts might arise between supporters of **capitalism** and **socialism**?

Critical Thinking

3. **Analyzing** Review your notes on labor reforms and workers. Then copy the graphic organizer shown below. Use it to give specific examples of how Progressives tried to reform child labor, women's labor, and workplace conditions.

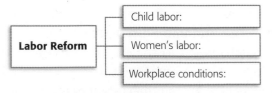

Labor Reform	Child labor:
	Women's labor:
	Workplace conditions:

FOCUS ON SPEAKING

4. **Addressing Problems in the Workplace** How would you address problems in the workplace? Make notes on campaign promises you might make to assure voters that you would address issues of child labor and workplace safety.

The Rights of Women and Minorities

If **YOU** were there...

You are a member of the graduating class of 1912 from an excellent women's college. You have always been interested in science, especially biology. You would like to be a doctor, but you know that medical schools accept very few women. One career path for you is to go into social work. Yet that's not what you really want to do.

How would you want to use your education?

BUILDING BACKGROUND The Progressives had a wide variety of goals. Besides attacking social problems such as child labor, they worked to reform government and make it more democratic. Changes in women's education affected the movement, as college-educated women often became leaders in working for reforms.

Women Fight for Temperance and Voting Rights

New educational opportunities drew more women into the Progressive movement. In the late 1800s, women began attending women's colleges, such as Smith College in Massachusetts and Vassar College in New York, in record numbers. In 1870 only about 20 percent of college students were women. By 1910 that number had doubled. The goal of female students was "to develop as fully as may be the powers of womanhood," said Sophia Smith, founder of Smith College.

Many women graduates entered fields such as social work and teaching. They found it much harder to enter professions such as law and medicine, which were dominated by men. With limited access to such professions, some women put their education to use by becoming more active in reform. Women's clubs campaigned for causes such as temperance, women's suffrage, child welfare, and political reform.

What You Will Learn...

Main Ideas
1. Women fought for temperance and the right to vote.
2. African American reformers challenged discrimination and called for equality.
3. Progressive reforms failed to benefit all minorities.

The Big Idea

The Progressive movement made advances for the rights of women and some minorities.

Key Terms and People
Eighteenth Amendment, *p. 96*
National American Woman Suffrage Association, *p. 96*
Alice Paul, *p. 97*
Nineteenth Amendment, *p. 97*
Booker T. Washington, *p. 97*
Ida B. Wells, *p. 97*
W. E. B. Du Bois, *p. 98*
National Association for the Advancement of Colored People, *p. 98*

TAKING NOTES As you read, take notes on the causes supported by different groups of progressive reformers. In each circle of a diagram like the one below, fill in details about one cause or goal. You may need to add more circles.

Progressive Reforms

The Temperance Movement

In the mid-1800s many of these reformers blamed social problems such as family violence and criminal behavior on a number of factors, including urbanization and immigration. They also blamed problems on alcohol consumption. As a result, many groups took up the cause of temperance, or avoidance of alcohol.

In 1874, reformers from many different backgrounds formed the Woman's Christian Temperance Union (WCTU), which fought for adoption of local and state laws restricting the sale of alcohol. Under the leadership of Frances Willard, the organization started 10,000 branches. More than 1,000 saloons were forced to shut down as a result of temperance supporters' efforts.

One especially radical temperance fighter chose more aggressive methods to fight for her cause. In the 1890s Carry Nation became famous for storming into saloons with a hatchet and smashing liquor bottles. Nation described destroying a Kansas saloon with bricks and rocks:

> " I threw as hard, and as fast as I could, smashing mirrors and bottles and glasses and it was astonishing how quickly this was done. "
>
> —Carry Nation, quoted in *Witnessing America: The Library of Congress Book of Firsthand Accounts of Life in America, 1600–1900*

FOCUS ON NEW YORK

National groups like NAWSA had the support of local and state groups such as the New York State Woman Suffrage Party and the Women's City Club of New York in their fight for women's suffrage. Both organizations supported the right of women to vote and worked to make women's voices heard in their communities.

In 1919 many years of temperance efforts led to the passage of the **Eighteenth Amendment**, banning the production, sale, and transportation of alcoholic beverages throughout the United States.

The Right to Vote

Women reformers also fought for suffrage, or the right to vote. Many people at this time opposed giving women the vote. Political bosses, for instance, worried about the anti-corruption efforts of women. Some business leaders worried that women voters would support minimum wage and child labor laws. Other people believed that women should only be homemakers and mothers and not politically active citizens.

In spite of such opposition, the women's suffrage movement began to gain national support in the 1890s. Elizabeth Cady Stanton and Susan B. Anthony founded the **National American Woman Suffrage Association** (NAWSA) in 1890 to promote the cause of women's suffrage. That same year, women

WE WERE VOTERS OUT WEST! WHY DENY OUR RIGHTS IN THE EAST?

Time Line

The Nineteenth Amendment

Women had been seeking the right to vote since 1776. Finally, in 1920 they achieved success with the passage of the Nineteenth Amendment.

1919

May 21, 1919 The House of Representatives passes the Nineteenth Amendment by a vote of 304 to 89.

June 4, 1919 The Senate passes the Nineteenth Amendment by a vote of 56 to 25.

June 10, 1919 Illinois, Michigan, and Wisconsin become the first states to ratify the Nineteenth Amendment.

won the right to vote in Wyoming. Colorado, Idaho, and Utah followed.

Carrie Chapman Catt became president of the NAWSA in 1900. Catt mobilized more than 1 million volunteers for the movement. She argued that women should have a voice in creating laws that affected them. "We women demand an equal voice," she said. "We shall accept nothing less."

Some women believed that NAWSA did not go far enough. In 1913 **Alice Paul** founded what would become the National Woman's Party (NWP). The NWP used parades, public demonstrations, picketing, hunger strikes, and other means to draw attention to the suffrage cause. Paul even organized picketing in front of the White House. Paul and other NWP leaders were jailed for their actions.

Suffragists finally succeeded in gaining the vote. In 1919 the U.S. Congress passed the **Nineteenth Amendment**, granting American women the right to vote. The Nineteenth Amendment was ratified by the states the following year, making it law.

READING CHECK **Analyzing** How did reformers draw attention to the temperance and women's suffrage movements?

African Americans Challenge Discrimination

White reformers often overlooked issues such as racial discrimination and segregation. African American reformers took the lead in addressing these problems.

One of the most important African American leaders was **Booker T. Washington**. Born into slavery, he became a respected educator while in his twenties. Washington's strategy was not to fight discrimination directly. Instead, he encouraged African Americans to improve their educational and economic well-being. This, he believed, would eventually lead to the end of discrimination.

Other African Americans spoke out more directly against discrimination. Journalist **Ida B. Wells** wrote about unequal educational opportunities available to African American children. In her Memphis newspaper *Free Speech*, Wells also drew attention to the lynching of African Americans. In a lynching, a person is hung by a mob. Sometimes a mob lynched people accused of a crime, denying them a fair trial, but other times, a lynching was just the result of hate. More than 3,000 African Americans were lynched between 1885 and 1915.

Although death threats forced Wells to move to the North, she continued campaigning against lynching. In 1900 she wrote:

" Our country's national crime is *lynching* … In fact, for all kinds of offenses—and, for no offenses— from murders to misdemeanors, men and women are put to death without judge or jury. "
—Ida B. Wells, from her article "Lynch Law in America"

FOCUS ON NEW YORK CITY

Ida Wells-Barnett began her speaking career in New York City, when she addressed 250 African American women on the subject of lynching. She would eventually speak on the topic in major cities across the United States and Great Britain. Her fight against racial discrimination and lynching included the strategy that publicizing atrocities outside the United States would bring pressure on the country to ban lynching.

August 26, 1920 The secretary of state officially declares the Nineteenth Amendment ratified by three-fourths of the states, making it law.

1920

1921

August 18, 1920 Tennessee becomes the thirty-sixth state to ratify the Nineteenth Amendment.

November 2, 1920 The first national election in which all women can vote is held.

Like Wells, **W. E. B. Du Bois** took a direct approach to fighting racial injustice. Born in Massachusetts, Du Bois was a college graduate who earned a doctorate from Harvard University. As part of his research, he studied and publicized cases of racial prejudice. Du Bois believed that African Americans should protest unjust treatment and demand equal rights.

In 1909 Du Bois and other reformers, including Ida B. Wells and Henry Moskowitz, founded the **National Association for the Advancement of Colored People** (NAACP), an organization that called for economic and educational equality for African Americans. The NAACP attacked discrimination by using the courts. In 1915 it won the important case of *Guinn* v. *United States,* which made grandfather clauses illegal. These laws were used in the South to keep African Americans from voting. Grandfather clauses imposed strict qualifications on voters unless their grandfathers had been allowed to vote. Many white voters met this requirement and were therefore permitted to vote in elections. However, most African Americans' grandfathers had been enslaved and could not vote.

Another important organization, the National Urban League, was formed in 1911 by Dr. George Edmund Haynes. This organization aided many African Americans moving from the South by helping them find jobs and housing in northern cities. The League addressed many of the same problems faced by other Progressives, such as health, sanitation, and education.

THE IMPACT TODAY

Today the NAACP claims around 2,200 adult branches and 1,700 branches for young people.

READING CHECK **Finding Main Ideas** What was the purpose of the NAACP?

Primary Source

POINTS OF VIEW
Fighting Discrimination

Booker T. Washington and W. E. B. Du Bois had very different views on how African Americans should handle discrimination.

❝Our greatest danger is that in the great leap from slavery to freedom we may overlook the fact that the masses of us are to live by the productions of our hands, and fail to keep in mind that we shall prosper in proportion as we learn to dignify and glorify common labour and put brains and skill into the common occupations of life . . . It is at the bottom of life we must begin, and not at the top.❞

—Booker T. Washington

❝Is it possible, and probable, that nine millions of men can make effective progress in economic lines if they are deprived of political rights, made a servile caste,* and allowed only the most meager chance for developing their exceptional men? If history and reason give any distinct answer to these questions, it is an emphatic No.❞

*lower social rank

—W. E. B. Du Bois

ANALYSIS SKILL **ANALYZING POINTS OF VIEW**

Finding Main Ideas What is the primary difference between the views of Washington and Du Bois?

Failures of Reform

Other minority groups felt left behind by the Progressive movement. Although some reformers tried to aid such groups, the aim of many was to encourage other ethnic groups to adopt the ways of mainstream American society. The Society of American Indians, formed in 1911, was one such attempt. Started by Native American doctors Carlos Montezuma and Charles Eastman, the society believed that integration into white society would end Native American poverty. Many Native Americans, however, wanted to preserve their traditional culture. They resisted the movement toward adopting white culture.

Immigrant groups from non-European countries also formed groups to help support their members. Chinese immigrants, for example, organized neighborhood associations. District associations, cultural groups, churches, and temples provided public services that white reformers ignored. Such groups provided the money for building San Francisco's Chinese hospital in 1925. Chinese immigration dropped, however, due in part to anti-Chinese riots that occurred in some western towns and cities.

While fewer Chinese immigrants came to the United States, the number of Mexican immigrants increased. The northern and southern borders between the United States and its neighbors were fairly easy to cross in this period. Many Mexican immigrants moved to the South and Southwest, where they became an important part of the societies and economies of these regions. Many Mexican immigrants found jobs in the mining and railroad industries. Others began farms or became migrant workers. Progressive labor laws and factory reforms did nothing to improve the poor living and working conditions of migrant farm workers.

READING CHECK **Summarizing** What were the limitations of progressive reforms?

SUMMARY AND PREVIEW Many U.S. citizens worked for progressive reforms. In the next section you will read about presidents who also worked for progressive goals.

go.hrw.com
Online Quiz

Section 3 Assessment

Reviewing Ideas, Terms, and People

1. **a. Identify** What did the **Eighteenth** and **Nineteenth Amendments** accomplish?
   b. Summarize How did **Alice Paul** and the National Woman's Party try to draw attention to the issue of women's suffrage?
2. **a. Identify** What role did **Ida B. Wells** play in reform efforts for African Americans?
   b. Contrast How did **Booker T. Washington** differ from other African American leaders?
   c. Evaluate Do you think the **National Association for the Advancement of Colored People** was successful in fighting discrimination? Explain.
3. **a. Describe** What discrimination did Chinese Americans face?
   b. Summarize How were some minority groups overlooked by the Progressive movement?

Critical Thinking

4. **Analyzing** Review your notes on Progressives' causes. Then copy the diagram shown and use it to identify the progressive reforms introduced by the temperance movement, the women's suffrage movement, and African Americans.

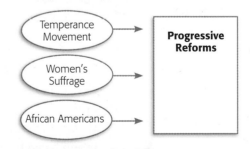

FOCUS ON SPEAKING

5. **Addressing the Rights of Women and Minorities** Review this section's material on education for women, women's suffrage, temperance, racial discrimination, and segregation. As a politician, what promises would you make regarding these issues? Think about how you would make your ideas acceptable to the American public. Would you be willing to compromise your ideals?

The Progressive Presidents

What You Will Learn...

Main Ideas

1. Theodore Roosevelt's progressive reforms tried to balance the interests of business, consumers, and laborers.
2. William Howard Taft angered Progressives with his cautious reforms, while Woodrow Wilson enacted far-reaching banking and antitrust reforms.

The Big Idea

American presidents in the early 1900s did a great deal to promote progressive reforms.

Key Terms and People

Theodore Roosevelt, *p. 100*
Pure Food and Drug Act, *p. 101*
conservation, *p. 101*
William Howard Taft, *p. 102*
Progressive Party, *p. 102*
Woodrow Wilson, *p. 102*
Sixteenth Amendment, *p. 103*

TAKING NOTES As you read, take notes on the achievements of each of the progressive presidents. Use a table like the one below to organize your notes.

Roosevelt	Taft	Wilson

If YOU were there...

It is 1912 and you're voting in your first presidential election. This election is unusual—there are three major candidates. One is the popular former president Theodore Roosevelt, who is running as a third-party candidate. He thinks the Republican candidate will not make enough progressive reforms. But the Democratic candidate is a progressive reformer, too.

How will you decide which candidate to support?

BUILDING BACKGROUND Political corruption was one early target of the progressive reformers. Some politicians who joined them believed that government—local, state, and national—should play an active role in improving society and people's lives.

Roosevelt's Progressive Reforms

During a summer tour after his second inauguration in 1901, President William McKinley met a friendly crowd in Buffalo, New York. Suddenly, anarchist Leon Czolgosz stepped forward and shot the president. A little more than a week later, McKinley died. Vice President **Theodore Roosevelt** took office.

Roosevelt's Square Deal

Roosevelt believed that the interests of businesspeople, laborers, and consumers should be balanced for the public good. He called this policy the Square Deal. He put the policy to the test in 1902 when faced by a coal miners' strike. Roosevelt knew the strike might leave the country without heating fuel for the coming winter. He threatened to take over the mines unless managers and strikers agreed to arbitration—a formal process to settle disputes. He felt this was the only fair way to protect Americans.

*"*The labor unions shall have a square deal, and the corporations shall have a square deal, and in addition all private citizens shall have a square deal.*"*

—President Theodore Roosevelt, quoted in *The Presidency of Theodore Roosevelt*, by Lewis L. Gould

The National Park System

In 1872 Yellowstone National Park, located mostly in Wyoming, became the first national park in the United States—and the world. Today there are 55 national parks in the United States. They are managed by the National Park Service (NPS), an agency of the federal government established in 1916. The National Park Service administers almost 84 million acres (133,000 square miles) of land.

President Theodore Roosevelt and conservationist John Muir in Yosemite National Park in California

Cathedral Rocks, Yosemite National Park

Regulating Big Business

Roosevelt made regulating big business a top goal of his administration. Muckrakers helped build support for this regulation. The public was shocked, for example, after reading Upton Sinclair's description of the meatpacking industry in *The Jungle*. Roosevelt opened an investigation and later convinced Congress to pass a meat inspection law.

In 1906 Congress passed the **Pure Food and Drug Act**. This law prohibited the manufacture, sale, and transport of mislabeled or contaminated food and drugs. Roosevelt also was the first president to successfully use the 1890 Sherman Antitrust Act to break up a monopoly. He persuaded Congress to regulate railroad shipping rates. The public largely supported this expansion of federal regulatory powers.

Conservation

Roosevelt's love of the outdoors inspired him to join other Progressives in supporting **conservation**, or the protection of nature and its resources. Roosevelt was the first president to consider conservation an important national priority.

People believed in conservation for various reasons. Preservationists such as John Muir thought that nature should be left untouched so that people could enjoy its beauty:

" Thousands of tired, nerve-shaken, over-civilized people are beginning to find out that going to the mountains is going home; that wildness is a necessity; and that mountain parks and reservations are useful not only as fountains of timber and irrigating rivers, but as fountains of life. "

—John Muir, *Our National Parks*

Other conservationists wanted to make sure the nation used its natural resources efficiently. Gifford Pinchot, the first head of the newly created Forest Service, valued forests for the resources they provided to build "prosperous homes." The disagreement between the two ideals of conservation eventually widened.

While Roosevelt was in office, the Forest Service gained control of nearly 150 million acres of public land. Roosevelt doubled the number of national parks, created 18 national monuments, and started 51 bird sanctuaries.

READING CHECK Summarizing What reforms did Roosevelt support?

Reforms of Taft and Wilson

Theodore Roosevelt hoped that his secretary of war, **William Howard Taft**, would take his place as president in 1908. Like Roosevelt, Taft favored business regulation and opposed socialism. With Roosevelt's assistance, Taft defeated William Jennings Bryan in the election of 1908.

Taft Angers Progressives

Despite their friendship, Roosevelt and Taft held different ideas about how a president should act. Taft thought Roosevelt had claimed more power than a president was constitutionally allowed.

ACADEMIC VOCABULARY

various
of many types

As president, therefore, Taft chose to move cautiously toward reform and regulation. This upset Roosevelt and **various** Progressives, who supported stricter regulation of big business. Although Taft's administration started twice as many antitrust lawsuits as Roosevelt's had, Progressives were not satisfied.

Taft angered Progressives further by signing the Payne-Aldrich Tariff of 1909. This tariff reduced some rates on imported goods, but it raised others. Progressives wanted all tariffs to be lowered in order to lower prices for consumers.

Furious with Taft, Roosevelt decided to run for president again in 1912. After Taft won the Republican nomination, Roosevelt and his followers formed the **Progressive Party**. It was nicknamed the Bull Moose Party because Roosevelt said he was "as strong as a bull moose." The split between Taft and Roosevelt divided the Republican vote, and Democratic candidate **Woodrow Wilson** won the electoral vote by a wide margin.

Wilson's Reforms

In his inaugural address, Wilson spoke of the terrible social conditions under which many working-class Americans lived. "We have been proud of our industrial achievements," he said, "but we have not hitherto [yet] stopped thoughtfully enough to count the human cost." Passing reform legislation was Wilson's top goal. He pushed for two measures soon after taking office: tariff revision and banking reform.

Wilson backed the Underwood Tariff Act of 1913, which lowered tariffs. The act also introduced a version of the modern

The Election of 1912

	Electoral Vote	Popular Vote
Wilson (Democrat)	435	6,286,214
T. Roosevelt (Progressive)	88	4,126,020
Taft (Republican)	8	3,483,922

*California cast 11 electoral votes for Roosevelt and 2 for Wilson.

WA 7, OR 5, MT 4, ND 5, MN 12, NH 4, VT 4, ME 6, MA 18, ID 4, SD 5, WI 13, NY 45, RI 5, WY 3, IA 13, MI 15, PA 38, CT 7, NV 3, NE 8, IL 29, IN 15, OH 24, NJ 14, CA 13*, UT 4, CO 6, KS 10, MO 18, KY 13, WV 8, VA 12, DE 3, MD 8, AZ 3, NM 3, OK 10, AR 9, TN 12, NC 12, SC 9, MS 10, AL 12, GA 14, TX 20, LA 10, FL 6

Wilson

Roosevelt

Taft

The Progressive Amendments, 1909–1920

QUICK FACTS

Number	Description	Proposed by Congress	Ratified by States
16th	Federal income tax	1909	1913
17th	Senators elected by people rather than state legislatures	1912	1913
18th	Manufacture, sale, and transport of alcohol prohibited	1917	1919
19th	Women's suffrage	1919	1920

income tax. The new tax was made possible in 1913 by the ratification of the **Sixteenth Amendment**. This amendment allows the federal government to impose direct taxes on citizens' incomes.

President Wilson next addressed banking reform with the 1913 Federal Reserve Act. This law created a national banking system called the Federal Reserve to regulate the economy.

Wilson also pushed for laws to regulate big business. The Clayton Antitrust Act of 1914 strengthened federal laws against monopolies. The Federal Trade Commission, created in 1914, had the power to investigate and punish unfair trade practices. Wilson's success in guiding reform programs through Congress helped him to win re-election in 1916.

READING CHECK Analyzing Why did Wilson win the election of 1912?

SUMMARY AND PREVIEW The Progressive presidents tried to change American society for the better. In the next chapter you will learn how they also helped the United States become a world power.

go.hrw.com
Online Quiz

Section 4 Assessment

Reviewing Ideas, Terms, and People

1. **a. Describe** How did **Theodore Roosevelt** support progressive reforms?
   b. Analyze Why did many Americans support **conservation**?
   c. Evaluate Do you think Roosevelt's reforms benefited the nation? Why or why not?
2. **a. Identify** What was the **Progressive Party**? Why was it created?
   b. Compare and Contrast How were the administrations of **William Howard Taft** and Roosevelt similar? How were they different?
   c. Evaluate Which president do you think had the biggest influence on progressive reform—Roosevelt, Taft, or **Woodrow Wilson**? Explain your choice.

Critical Thinking

3. **Comparing and Contrasting** Review your notes on the Progressive presidents. Then copy the diagram below and use it to compare and contrast the reforms of the Progressive presidents.

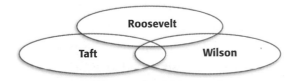

FOCUS ON SPEAKING

4. **The Ideas of Roosevelt, Taft, and Wilson** Do you agree or disagree with Presidents Roosevelt, Taft, and Wilson? Take notes on any of their ideas that you would include in your campaign promises.

Social Studies Skills

Short- and Long-term Causal Relationships

Define the Skill

Most historical events are the result of other events. When something happens as a result of other things that occur, it is an effect of those things. Some events take place soon after the things that cause them. Such events are called *short-term effects*. In contrast, *long-term effects* can occur years, decades, or even hundreds of years after the events that caused them. Being able to recognize short-term and long-term cause-and-effect relationships will help you to better understand historical events.

Learn the Skill

Clue words can sometimes reveal a cause-and-effect relationship between events. Often, however, such language clues may not be present. Therefore, when you study history, you should always look for other clues that might explain why an action or event occurred.

Short-term effects are usually fairly easy to identify. In historical writing they are often closely linked to the event that caused them. For example, consider this passage from Chapter 4.

" Some Progressives worked to change state and local governments in order to reduce the power of political machines. In many places, reformers replaced corrupt ballots that listed only one party's candidates with government-prepared ballots that listed all candidates. Under pressure from reformers, many states adopted secret ballots, giving every voter a private vote. "

This passage contains no clue words. Yet it is clear that cause-and-effect relationships exist. The power of political machines created corrupt voting practices. Reformers wanted to change this. One effect of this situation was the government-prepared ballot, and another was the secret ballot.

Recognizing long-term causal relationships is often more difficult. Since long-term effects take place well after the event that caused them, they may not be discussed at the same time as their cause. This is why you should always question why an event occurred as you learn about it. For example, in 1971 Congress passed the first federal law to protect the health and safety of all workers. This law was a long-term result of efforts begun years earlier by the progressives you read about in this chapter.

Many long-term effects result from major forces running through history that make things happen. They include economics, science and technology, expansion, conflict and cooperation among people, cultural clashes and differences, and moral and religious issues. Ask yourself if one of these forces is involved in the event being studied. If so, the event may have long-term effects that you should be on the lookout for when studying later events.

Practice and Apply the Skill

Review the information in Chapter 4 and answer these questions to practice recognizing short- and long-term causal relationships.

1. All packaged food today must have its contents listed on the container. This requirement is a long-term effect of what progressive reform?

2. Write a paragraph explaining the effects of the muckrakers on the news media today.

Chapter Review

HOLT
History's Impact
▶ video series
Review the video to answer the closing question:
How did the rights of women in individual states play a role in the women's suffrage movement?

Visual Summary

Use the visual summary below to help you review the main ideas of the chapter.

Progressives hoped to improve society through reform. Their goals included

- Temperance
- Women's suffrage
- Big business regulation
- Conservation
- Tariff and banking reform

PROSPERITY

Reviewing Vocabulary, Terms, and People

Identify the descriptions below with the correct term or person from the chapter.

1. System that proposed government ownership of the country's means of production

2. Republican governor who began a program to reform state politics in Wisconsin

3. Granted women in the United States the right to vote

4. Prohibited the manufacture, sale, and transport of mislabeled or contaminated food and drugs

5. Often dominated local politics and used corruption to get their candidates elected during the Gilded Age

6. Journalists who wrote about troubling issues such as child labor, tenement housing, and political corruption

Comprehension and Critical Thinking

SECTION 1 *(Pages 82–87)*

7. **a. Describe** What tactics did bosses and political machines use to gain control of local governments?

   b. Analyze What changes did Progressives make to city life?

   c. Elaborate Which progressive reform do you think had the greatest effect on Americans?

SECTION 2 *(Pages 90–94)*

8. **a. Identify** What reforms were made to improve working conditions? Who was affected by these reforms?

   b. Contrast What are the differences between capitalism and socialism?

   c. Elaborate If you were a business owner, would you have supported the progressive workplace reforms? Explain your answer.

SECTION 3 (Pages 95–99)

9. a. Recall What minority groups were overlooked by progressive reform efforts?

b. Analyze How did women's involvement in the Progressive movement lead to constitutional change?

c. Elaborate Do you agree with Booker T. Washington's approach to improving life for African Americans? Explain your answer.

SECTION 4 (Pages 100–103)

10. a. Describe How did William Howard Taft disappoint Progressives?

b. Compare In what ways were the reforms of Presidents Roosevelt, Taft, and Wilson similar?

c. Elaborate Would you have supported Wilson's progressive reforms? Explain your answer.

Reviewing Themes

11. Politics What role did political machines play in local politics during the Gilded Age?

12. Society and Culture How were children affected by the movement for workplace reforms?

Reading Skills

Evaluating Sources *Use the Reading Skills taught in this chapter to answer the question about the reading selection below.*

> The next day Rose went to town [Chicago] alone. The wind had veered [turned] to the south, the dust blew, and the whole terrifying panorama [view] of life in the street seemed some way blurred together, and forms of men and animals were like figures in tapestry. The grind and clang and clatter and hiss and howl of the traffic was all about her . . .
>
> —Hamlin Garland, from his novel *Rose of Dutcher's Coolly*, 1895

13. Is this a good source for understanding the experiences of Chicago in the late 1800s? Why or why not?

Social Studies Skills

Short- and Long-Term Causal Relationships *Use the Social Studies Skills taught in this chapter to answer the question about the reading selection below.*

> Despite their friendship, Roosevelt and Taft held different ideas about how a president should act. Taft thought Roosevelt had claimed more power than a president was constitutionally allowed.
>
> As president, therefore, Taft chose to move cautiously toward reform and regulation. (p. 102)

14. According to the passage above, what was a long-term cause of Taft's cautious reforms?

Using the Internet   go.hrw.com

15. Activity: Researching Progressives Rapid industrial and urban growth in America in the late 1800s resulted in a number of problems. Progressives worked to address these issues in many ways, including efforts to clean up political corruption, improve working conditions, and enact social reforms. Enter the activity keyword and explore the lives of some of the leaders of the Progressive movement. Then write a profile of a Progressive leader that outlines his or her life and impact on American reform.

FOCUS ON SPEAKING

16. Share Your Campaign Promises Review your notes about possible campaign promises. Which promises will be most helpful in getting you elected? Look at your promises to see whether they focus on issues important to voters. Then write a speech including your campaign promises that you can deliver to your class.

Grade 8 Intermediate-Level Test Preparation

Directions (1-5): **For each statement or question, write on the separate answer sheet the *number* of the word or expression that, of those given, best completes the statement or answers the question.**

Base your answer to question 1 on the photograph below and on your knowledge of social studies.

1 **The people in this photograph would probably have been *most* interested in which of the following reforms?**

(1) secret ballots

(2) the Pure Food and Drug Act

(3) child labor laws

(4) elimination of political machines

2 **Progressives were urged to action by the writings of journalists known as**

(1) Republicans.   (3) Capitalists.

(2) Muckrakers.   (4) Socialists.

3 **What was the *main* idea behind the creation of the civil-service system in the late 1800s?**

(1) Government jobs should be awarded to people who support the party in power.

(2) Government workers should be required to support the elected officials who hire them.

(3) Government employees should be qualified to do the jobs for which they were hired.

(4) Government jobs should not be filled with employees who serve in those jobs for life.

4 **The Nineteenth Amendment to the Constitution increased democracy in the United States by**

(1) granting women the right to vote.

(2) allowing the people of each state to elect their senators.

(3) establishing direct primary elections.

(4) enabling voters to remove elected officials from office before the end of their terms.

5 **The tragedy of the Triangle Shirtwaist Fire, in which 146 young women died, led to the passage of what laws?**

(1) child labor laws

(2) safety standard laws

(3) illegal immigrant laws

(4) minimum wage laws

Base your answer to question 6 on the text below and on your knowledge of social studies.

> There's only one way to hold a district: you must study human nature and act accordin' . . . To learn real human nature you have to go among the people, see them and be seen. I know every man, woman, and child in the Fifteenth District, except them that's been born this summer—and I know some of them, too. I know what they like and what they don't like, what they are strong at and what they are weak in, and I reach them by approachin' at the right side.
>
> —George Washington Plunkitt, quoted in *Eyewitnesses and Others*

6 **Constructed-Response Question** **How did Plunkitt say he kept his position in the political machine?**

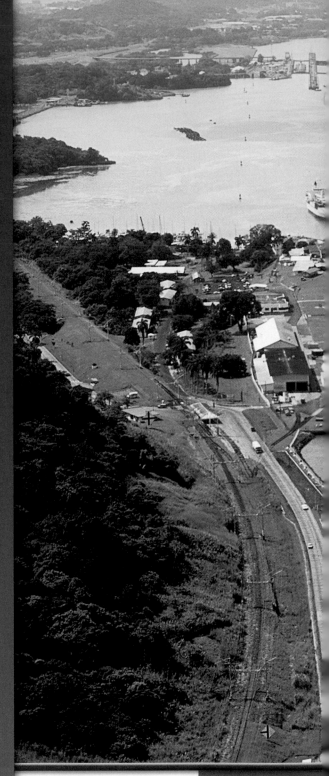

CHAPTER 5   1867–1920

America as a World Power

FOCUS QUESTION

How does a nation balance its own needs with the needs of the world?

FOCUS ON WRITING

A List of Pros and Cons In the last half of the 1800s, the United States became more involved in international affairs. As you read this chapter, you will analyze the nation's new role and use the results of your analysis to guide U.S. policy in the future. In order to analyze the advantages and disadvantages of an aggressive foreign policy, you will need to create a list of the pros and cons of U.S. involvement with other nations in the late 1800s and early 1900s. As you create your list, note which items are facts and which are opinions—either yours or someone else's.

UNITED STATES  **1867** The United States purchases Alaska.

1867

WORLD   **1868** Japan begins a time of modernization known as the Meiji Restoration.

HOLT

History's Impact
▶ video series
Watch the video to understand the impact of the United States as a world power.

What You Will Learn...

In this chapter you will learn about how the United States became a global power in the late 1800s and early 1900s. Through a combination of economic strength, military might, and aggressive foreign policy, America made its presence known in many parts of the world. One such place was Panama, where the United States built the Panama Canal, shown here. The United States has remained a powerful force on the international stage to this day.

NY

1901 President McKinley is assassinated in Buffalo, and New Yorker Theodore Roosevelt becomes president.

1890 Congress passes the McKinley Tariff, which gives a subsidy to U.S. sugar producers.

1898 The United States wins the Spanish-American War, gaining the Philippine Islands and Puerto Rico.

1914 The Panama Canal officially opens.

| 1880 | 1890 | 1900 | 1910 | 1920 |

1885 The Indian National Congress is formed in British-controlled India.

1895 Cubans rebel against Spanish rule.

1900 The Boxer Rebellion erupts in China.

1903 Panama declares itself an independent nation.

1910 The Mexican Revolution begins.

AMERICA AS A WORLD POWER **109**

Reading Social Studies

by Kylene Beers

Economics	Geography	Politics	Society and Culture	Science and Technology

Focus on Themes In this chapter, you will learn about how the physical **geography** of the United States changed as it acquired overseas territories. You will also read about how national and international **politics** affected foreign policy and brought new responsibilities to the government of the United States.

Comparing Historical Texts

Focus on Reading A good way to learn what people in the past thought is to read what they wrote. However, most documents will only tell you one side of the story. By comparing writings by different people, you can learn a great deal about various sides of a historical issue or debate.

Comparing Texts When you compare historical texts, you should consider two things: who wrote the documents and what the documents were meant to achieve. To do this, you need to find the writers' main point or points.

Document 1

"We have cherished the policy of non-interference with affairs of foreign governments wisely inaugurated [begun] by Washington, keeping ourselves free from entanglement, either as allies or foes, content to leave undisturbed with them the settlement of their own domestic concerns."

—President William McKinley, First Inaugural Address, 1897

Document 2

"Therefore, Mr. President, here is a war with terrible characteristics flagrant [obvious] at our very doors [in Cuba]. We have the power to bring it to an end. I believe that the whole American people would welcome steps in that direction."

—Senator Henry Cabot Lodge, Speech in Congress, 1896

Document 1	Document 2
Writer	
President William McKinley	Senator Henry Cabot Lodge
Main point	
The United States should not involve itself in the affairs of other countries.	The United States should go to war in Cuba.
Both Sides of the Issue	
Americans were torn over the war in Cuba. Some thought the United States should remain uninvolved as it always had. Others thought it was time for a change in foreign policy.	

You Try It!

Read the following passages, both taken from presidential addresses to Congress. As you read, look for the main point each president makes in his address.

Foreign Policy

In treating of our foreign policy and of the attitude that this great Nation should assume in the world at large, it is absolutely necessary to consider the Army and the Navy, and the Congress, through which the thought of the Nation finds its expression, should keep ever vividly in mind the fundamental fact that it is impossible to treat our foreign policy, whether this policy takes shape in the effort to secure justice for others or justice for ourselves, save as conditioned upon the attitude we are willing to take toward our Army, and especially toward our Navy.

—President Theodore Roosevelt,
Message to Congress, 1904

The diplomacy of the present administration has sought to respond to modern ideas of commercial intercourse [involvement]. This policy has been characterized as substituting dollars for bullets. It is one that appeals alike to idealistic humanitarian sentiments [feelings], to the dictates [rules] of sound policy and strategy, and to legitimate [make real] commercial aims.

—President William Howard Taft,
Message to Congress, 1912

After you read the passages, answer the following questions.

1. What was the main point Roosevelt made in his address?

2. What was the main point Taft made in his address?

3. How can a comparison of Roosevelt's and Taft's addresses to Congress help you understand the issues that shaped U.S. foreign policy in the early 1900s?

Key Terms and People

As you read Chapter 5, organize your notes to help you point out the similarities and differences among events or policies.

The United States Gains Overseas Territories

What You Will Learn...

Main Ideas

1. The United States ended its policy of isolationism.
2. Hawaii became a U.S. territory in 1898.
3. The United States sought trade with Japan and China.

The Big Idea

In the last half of the 1800s, the United States joined the race for control of overseas territories.

Key Terms and People

imperialism, *p. 112*
isolationism, *p. 113*
William H. Seward, *p. 113*
Liliuokalani, *p. 114*
spheres of influence, *p. 115*
Open Door Policy, *p. 115*
Boxer Rebellion, *p. 115*

TAKING NOTES As you read, make a list of examples of U.S. expansion in a chart like this one.

Areas or Trade Rights Gained

If YOU were there...

You are a Hawaiian living on Maui, one of the Hawaiian Islands, in 1890. Your parents work in a sugar mill owned by American planters. Although the mill supplies jobs, you don't trust the sugar planters. They have already made your king sign a treaty that gives them a lot of power in the islands. You are afraid they will take over the government.

What would you do if the planters took over your islands?

BUILDING BACKGROUND In the mid-1800s, most Americans had little interest in being involved with the rest of the world diplomatically. The Civil War and Reconstruction kept their focus on challenges at home. In the meantime, though, European nations were busily acquiring overseas territories. The United States would soon join them.

End of Isolation

In the 1800s powerful Western nations were busy building naval bases to protect their shipping routes around the world. This was an aspect of **imperialism**—building an empire by founding colonies or conquering other nations. Between 1870 and 1914, Europeans extended their colonial empires until they controlled most of Africa and Southeast Asia.

Roots of Imperialism

Several forces drove this wave of European imperialism. Countries wanted sources of raw materials—such as copper, rubber, and tin—to fuel industrial growth. Businesspeople wanted new markets for their manufactured goods. Also many

Europeans saw colonies as a source of power and national pride. The ethnocentric idea the Western nations could morally improve non-Western groups with their cultural influences encouraged many people to support imperialism.

In contrast, the United States followed a limited policy of **isolationism**—avoiding involvement in the affairs of other countries. In 1789 President George Washington had warned Americans "to steer clear of permanent alliances" with other countries. American leaders tried to follow this advice by staying out of overseas conflicts.

By the late 1800s, however, some Americans believed the United States needed to expand to keep its economy strong. In his 1890 book *The Influence of Sea Power upon History*, Alfred T. Mahan argued that the United States needed a strong navy to protect its economic interests. Mahan also explained that a strong navy needed overseas bases and coaling stations—places for ships to take on coal for fuel.

Seward's Folly

In 1867 the United States greatly expanded its North American territory when Secretary of State **William H. Seward** arranged the purchase of Alaska from Russia for $7.2 million. Some people thought Alaska was a frozen wasteland, calling the deal "Seward's Folly" [foolish act]. But Seward had purchased an area more than twice the size of Texas for two cents an acre. As he had hoped, Alaska became a source of valuable natural resources such as fur, timber, and minerals. Gold was found in Alaska in the 1890s, bringing miners and settlers to the area.

Based on Seward's belief that the United States "must continue to move on westward," the nation also annexed the Midway Islands in 1867. The islands' location about halfway between the U.S. West Coast and Japan made Midway an excellent coaling station for the U.S. Navy.

The United States wanted the island group of Samoa for similar reasons. The United States and Germany agreed to divide Samoa in 1899.

READING CHECK **Analyzing** Why did U.S. leaders end isolationist policies in the late 1800s?

THE IMPACT
TODAY

The United States still has hundreds of military bases in foreign countries.

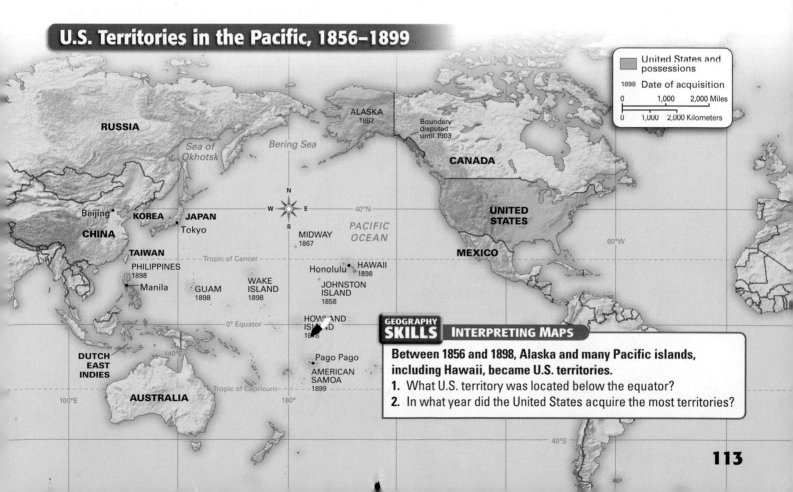

U.S. Territories in the Pacific, 1856–1899

United States and possessions

1898 Date of acquisition

0   1,000   2,000 Miles
0   1,000   2,000 Kilometers

RUSSIA

ALASKA
1867

Boundary disputed until 1903

CANADA

Sea of Okhotsk

Bering Sea

N
W ⊙ E
S

40°N

UNITED STATES

Beijing   KOREA   JAPAN
CHINA   Tokyo

MIDWAY
1867

PACIFIC
OCEAN

MEXICO

60°W

TAIWAN

Tropic of Cancer

PHILIPPINES
1898
Manila

GUAM
1898

WAKE
ISLAND
1898

Honolulu   HAWAII
1898
JOHNSTON
ISLAND
1858

0° Equator

HOWLAND
ISLAND
1856

DUTCH
EAST
INDIES

140°E

Pago Pago

AMERICAN
SAMOA
1899

Tropic of Capricorn

100°E   AUSTRALIA   180°

40°S

GEOGRAPHY SKILLS **INTERPRETING MAPS**

Between 1856 and 1898, Alaska and many Pacific islands, including Hawaii, became U.S. territories.
1. What U.S. territory was located below the equator?
2. In what year did the United States acquire the most territories?

113

Hawaii Becomes a Territory

Even more appealing than Samoa were the Hawaiian Islands. Hawaiians first saw Europeans in 1778. Trading and whaling ships in the Pacific soon began stopping in Hawaii. In the early 1800s American missionaries came and attempted to convert Hawaiians to Christianity. Missionaries opened businesses and raised crops, such as sugarcane. Some Americans became rich sugar planters.

By the 1840s most shops and shipyards in Hawaii were owned by Americans. Sugar became a leading export of the Hawaiian economy. An 1875 treaty allowed Hawaiian sugar to be shipped duty-free to the United States. (A duty is a tax on imported items.) This agreement helped the Hawaiian sugar industry prosper.

The planters used their power to force the Hawaiian king to sign a new constitution in 1887. It became known as the Bayonet Constitution because the king was forced to sign it at gunpoint. The constitution granted more power to the planter-controlled legislature. Many Hawaiians feared the foreigners' increase in power.

THE IMPACT TODAY

Today, sugarcane is Hawaii's most valuable crop.

In 1891 the king died, and his sister, **Liliuokalani** (li-LEE-uh-woh-kuh-LAHN-ee), became queen. She proposed a new constitution that would return power to the monarchy. The planters revolted. John L. Stevens, U.S. minister to Hawaii, called 150 marines ashore to support the revolt, and it succeeded without a battle. The planters formed a new government. Congress voted to annex the Hawaiian Islands in 1898.

READING CHECK **Identifying Cause and Effect** What effect did the growing power of the planters have on the Hawaiian monarchy?

United States Seeks Trade with Japan and China

Economic interest also drew the United States to Japan and China. The United States wanted to open and secure trade markets in both Asian countries.

Opening Trade with Japan

By the mid-1800s European powers had formed strong trade ties with most East Asian countries. However, the island nation of Japan had isolated itself from the rest of the world for hundreds of years.

The United States wanted to open up trade with Japan before Europeans arrived. President Millard Fillmore sent Commodore Matthew Perry to Japan to secure "friendship, commerce, [and] a supply of coal and provisions." Perry attempted a peaceful alliance in 1853, but he was not successful.

Perry returned to Japan in 1854 with seven warships. He gave Japanese leaders gifts and tried to show some of the benefits that Japanese-American trade would have. For instance, Perry presented them with a telegraph transmitter and a model train. This effort—and the presence of U.S. naval power—persuaded Japanese officials to open trade with the United States. The two countries signed a trade agreement in 1858.

CASE STUDY BIOGRAPHY

Liliuokalani
(1838–1917)
Born in Honolulu, Queen Liliuokalani was proud of Hawaiian traditions. Even after being driven from power in 1883, she continued speaking out on behalf of native–born Hawaiians. In 1887 she traveled to Washington, D.C., meeting with President Grover Cleveland to argue against the annexation of Hawaii by the United States. Until her death, Liliuokalani served as a symbol of Hawaiian pride and a reminder of the islands' history as an independent nation.

Drawing Conclusions Why do you think Liliuokalani was a symbol of Hawaiian pride?

Perry Arrives in Japan

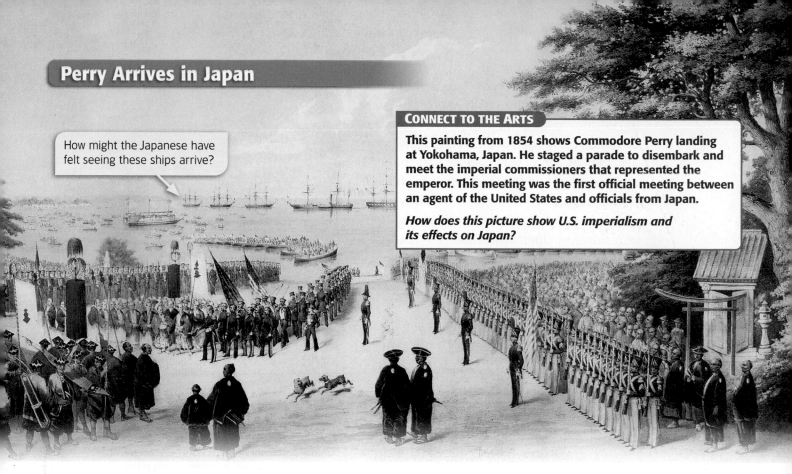

How might the Japanese have felt seeing these ships arrive?

CONNECT TO THE ARTS

This painting from 1854 shows Commodore Perry landing at Yokohama, Japan. He staged a parade to disembark and meet the imperial commissioners that represented the emperor. This meeting was the first official meeting between an agent of the United States and officials from Japan.

How does this picture show U.S. imperialism and its effects on Japan?

Some Japanese leaders welcomed trade with the United States. In 1868 people who favored the industrialization **process** came to power in Japan, beginning a 40-year period of modernization. By the 1890s Japan was becoming a major imperial power. It defeated China in the Sino-Japanese War from 1894 to 1895. As a result, Japan gained new territory and enjoyed the same trading privileges in China as European countries. In 1904 Japan attacked Russian forces stationed in China. President Theodore Roosevelt helped to negotiate a peace treaty to end the Russo-Japanese War a year later. Japan gained control of Korea, a lease on Port Arthur in China, and other rights. Japan had become a world power.

Foreign Powers in China

After Japan defeated China, other countries took advantage of China's weakness by seizing **spheres of influence**—areas where foreign nations controlled resources. Germany, Great Britain, France, Japan, and Russia all took control of areas within China.

Some U.S. leaders feared that the United States would be closed out of Chinese markets. In 1899 Secretary of State John Hay sent notes to Japan and many European countries announcing the **Open Door Policy**. This policy stated that all nations should have equal access to trade in China. The policy was neither rejected nor accepted by European powers and Japan but made U.S. intentions clear.

Meanwhile, many Chinese resented the power and control held by foreign nations. This hostility sparked the **Boxer Rebellion**. The Boxers were Chinese nationalists who were angered by foreign involvement in China. In their language, the group was called the Fists of Righteous Harmony. Westerners called them Boxers because they used a clenched fist as their symbol. Although officially denounced, they were secretly supported by the Chinese government.

In June 1900 the Boxers took to the streets of Beijing, China's capital, and laid siege to the walled settlement where foreigners lived. They killed more than 200 people.

ACADEMIC VOCABULARY

process a series of steps by which a task is accomplished

The siege continued for two months. Foreign military forces, including U.S. Marines, fought their way from the port of Tianjin to Beijing, where they invaded the Forbidden City. The Boxers were soon defeated. China was forced to make a cash payment of $333 million to foreign governments, $25 million of which went to the United States. Secretary of State Hay then sent another Open Door note to Japan and the European nations. The Open Door Policy remained in effect until World War II again closed China's borders to foreign influence.

READING CHECK Identifying Cause and Effect
What factors led to the Boxer Rebellion, and what was the result?

SUMMARY AND PREVIEW The United States greatly expanded its territory and influence in the Pacific. In the next section, you will learn about the causes and effects of the Spanish-American War.

Chinese nationalists attack the foreigners' compound in Beijing in this illustration of China's Boxer Rebellion.

go.hrw.com
Online Quiz

Section 1 Assessment

Reviewing Ideas, Terms, and People

1. **a. Describe** What policy had the United States followed regarding other countries before the late 1800s?
   b. Analyze Why did the United States expand to Alaska and to islands in the Pacific?
   c. Evaluate Do you think **William H. Seward**'s purchase of Alaska was a good decision? Explain.
2. **a. Recall** What became Hawaii's leading export?
   b. Sequence What events led to Hawaii's annexation as a U.S. territory?
   c. Elaborate What do you think about the planters' revolt against Queen **Liliuokalani**?
3. **a. Describe** How did the United States persuade Japanese leaders to sign a trade treaty?
   b. Contrast How was the U.S. experience establishing trade with China different from U.S. attempts to open trade with Japan?
   c. Evaluate Do you think Japan made the right decision in agreeing to open trade with the United States? Explain your answer.

Critical Thinking

4. **Generalizing** Review your notes on the areas or trade rights gained by the United States. Then use the chart below to identify the benefits of these areas and trade rights.

American Expansion

Areas or Trade Rights Gained	Benefits for United States

FOCUS ON WRITING

5. **Identifying Pros and Cons of U.S. Involvement Overseas** What did the United States gain from its involvement in these areas of the world? What were the disadvantages? As you read this section, identify pros and cons to add to your list.

The Spanish-American War

If **YOU** were there...

You live in New York City in 1898. Newspaper headlines are screaming about the start of war in Cuba. You hear that Theodore Roosevelt wants volunteers for a cavalry troop called the Rough Riders. You know how to ride a horse, and you've admired Roosevelt ever since he was New York's police commissioner. You know it will be dangerous, but it also sounds like a great adventure.

Would you join the Rough Riders? Why?

BUILDING BACKGROUND While the United States, Japan, and several European powers were gaining colonies, Spain's empire was declining. By the late 1800s Spain's once extensive American empire was reduced to two island colonies—Cuba and Puerto Rico. Eager for independence, some Cubans revolted against Spanish rule. Many Americans sympathized with Cuba's fight for independence—and some wanted to annex the nearby island.

War with Spain

You read earlier that newspaper publishers Joseph Pulitzer and William Randolph Hearst were in a fierce competition for readers. In the late 1890s their newspapers published stories from Cuba, where Cuban rebels were fighting for independence from Spain. To attract readers, Pulitzer and Hearst printed sensational, often exaggerated news stories. This technique is called **yellow journalism**. Vivid stories about Spanish brutality in Cuba convinced many Americans that the U.S. military should support the Cuban rebels.

What You Will Learn...

Main Ideas

1. In 1898 the United States went to war with Spain in the Spanish-American War.
2. The United States gained territories in the Caribbean and Pacific.

The Big Idea

The United States expanded into new parts of the world as a result of the Spanish-American War.

Key Terms and People

yellow journalism, *p. 117*
Teller Amendment, *p. 118*
Emilio Aguinaldo, *p. 119*
Anti-Imperialist League, *p. 120*
Platt Amendment, *p. 121*

TAKING NOTES As you read, use a graphic organizer like this one to list the results of the Spanish-American War.

Spanish-American War

↓

Results

Newspapers such as this one encouraged Americans to seek war with Spain.

Despite growing support for military action in Cuba, President Grover Cleveland was opposed to U.S. involvement. In 1896 William McKinley, a supporter of Cuban independence, was elected president. Several events soon led to war.

In February 1898 Hearst's newspaper published a letter written by the Spanish minister to the United States, Enrique Dupuy de Lôme. In it, de Lôme called McKinley "weak and a bidder for the admiration of the crowd." Many Americans were outraged.

In January 1898, even before de Lôme's letter became public, the United States sent the battleship USS *Maine* to Havana Harbor. The *Maine*'s mission was to protect U.S. citizens and economic interests in Cuba. On February 15 the *Maine* exploded and

sank, with a loss of 266 men. Although the cause of the explosion was unclear, the American press immediately blamed Spain. "Remember the *Maine!*" became a rallying cry for angry Americans.

President McKinley requested $50 million to prepare for war. Congress approved the money. Although Cuba was not a U.S. territory, Congress issued a resolution on April 20 declaring Cuba independent and demanding that Spain leave the island within three days. Attached to the resolution was the **Teller Amendment**, which stated that the United States had no interest in taking control of Cuba. In response to the resolution, Spain declared war on the United States. The next day, Congress passed, and McKinley signed, a declaration of war against Spain.

"Remember the *Maine!*"

Most of the men aboard the USS *Maine* were sleeping when a terrible explosion demolished the forward third of the ship at 9:40 p.m. on February 15, 1898. The rest of the ship sank quickly. Some 266 men were killed.

Who did the United States blame for the explosion?

War in the Philippines

While attention was focused on Cuba, the U.S. Navy won a quick victory nearly half-way around the world in the Philippines, a Spanish colony in the Pacific. Filipinos, like Cubans, were rebelling against Spanish rule.

As soon as the Spanish-American War began, American commodore George Dewey raced to the Philippines with four large warships and two small gunboats. On May 1, ignoring reports that mines beneath the water barred his way, he sailed into Manila Bay and destroyed the Spanish Pacific fleet stationed there. Dewey's forces sank or captured 10 ships. The Spanish lost 381 lives, but none of Dewey's men were killed.

Dewey had defeated the Spanish, but he did not have enough troops to occupy and secure the Philippines. Troops eventually arrived, and on August 13, U.S. troops and Filipino rebels led by **Emilio Aguinaldo** (ahg-ee-NAHL-doh) took control of the Philippine capital, Manila.

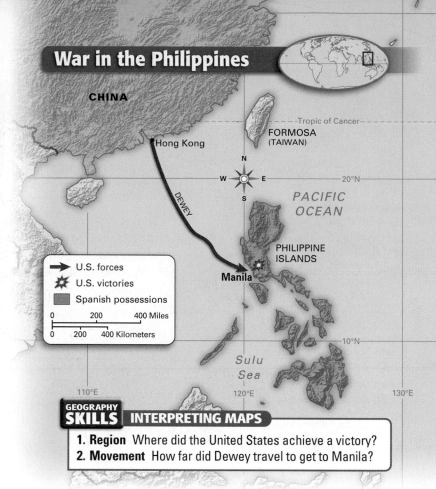

War in the Philippines

GEOGRAPHY **SKILLS** | **INTERPRETING MAPS**

1. **Region** Where did the United States achieve a victory?
2. **Movement** How far did Dewey travel to get to Manila?

War in the Caribbean

In contrast to the navy, the U.S. Army was unprepared for war. At the start of the conflict, the entire U.S. Army had only 28,000 soldiers. New volunteers quickly raised that figure to more than 280,000. The army did not have enough rifles or bullets for these soldiers. It did not even have appropriate clothing for the troops. Many soldiers received warm woolen uniforms to wear in Cuba's tropical heat.

The soldiers faced harsh living conditions in Cuba. They ate canned meat that one general called "embalmed beef," and many were stricken with yellow fever and other deadly diseases. More than 2,000 Americans died from diseases they contracted in Cuba. Fewer than 400 were killed in battle.

The most colorful group of soldiers was the Rough Riders. Second in command of this group was Lieutenant Colonel Theodore Roosevelt. Roosevelt had organized the Rough Riders to fight in Cuba. Volunteers included Native Americans, college athletes, cowboys, miners, and ranchers. Newspaper stories of their heroism earned the Rough Riders Americans' admiration. Four privates of the African American 10th Cavalry, who served with the Rough Riders, received the Congressional Medal of Honor.

Landing on June 22, 1898, the U.S. troops captured the hills around the main Spanish forces at Santiago. At the village of El Caney on July 1, some 7,000 U.S. soldiers, aided by Cuban rebels, overwhelmed about 600 Spanish defenders.

The main U.S. force then attacked and captured San Juan Hill. The Rough Riders and the African American 9th and 10th cavalries captured nearby Kettle Hill. The many accounts of the battle became popular with the American public back home. A journalist on the scene described the soldiers' charge:

FOCUS ON READING

How might accounts of the war written by these various soldiers have been different?

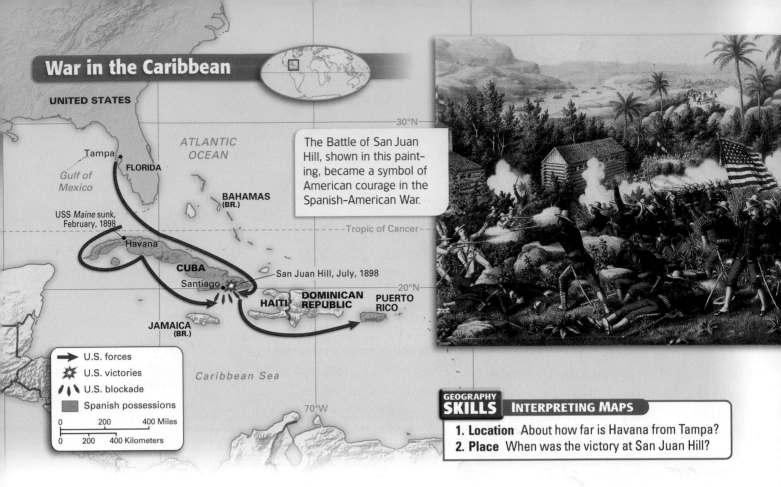

War in the Caribbean

UNITED STATES

ATLANTIC OCEAN

30°N

Tampa

FLORIDA

Gulf of Mexico

USS *Maine* sunk, February, 1898

BAHAMAS (BR.)

The Battle of San Juan Hill, shown in this painting, became a symbol of American courage in the Spanish–American War.

Tropic of Cancer

Havana

CUBA

San Juan Hill, July, 1898

Santiago

20°N

HAITI

DOMINICAN REPUBLIC

PUERTO RICO

JAMAICA (BR.)

Caribbean Sea

70°W

→ U.S. forces
✪ U.S. victories
⁄⁄ U.S. blockade
▪ Spanish possessions

0   200   400 Miles
0   200   400 Kilometers

GEOGRAPHY SKILLS INTERPRETING MAPS

1. **Location** About how far is Havana from Tampa?
2. **Place** When was the victory at San Juan Hill?

"It was a miracle of self-sacrifice, a triumph of bulldog courage …The fire of the Spanish riflemen …doubled and trebled [tripled] in fierceness, the crests of the hills crackled and burst in amazed roars and rippled with waves of tiny flame. But the blue line [of United States soldiers] crept steadily up and on."

—Richard Harding Davis, quoted in *The American Reader,* edited by Paul M. Angle

On July 3 the commander of the Spanish fleet decided to try breaking through the U.S. blockade. Though every Spanish ship was destroyed in the battle, American forces suffered only two casualties. Santiago surrendered two weeks later. President McKinley began peace negotiations with Spain, which was assured of defeat. A few days later, U.S. troops invaded Spanish-held Puerto Rico, which surrendered with little resistance. Spain signed a cease-fire agreement on August 12, 1898.

READING CHECK **Comparing** How was fighting in the Pacific and the Caribbean similar?

United States Gains Territories

The peace treaty placed Cuba, Guam, Puerto Rico, and the Philippines under U.S. control. In reaction, some Americans formed the **Anti-Imperialist League**, a group that opposed the treaty and the creation of an American colonial empire. They argued that the treaty threatened democracy because it denied self-government to the people living in the newly acquired territories. The Senate approved the peace treaty by a vote of 57 to 27—just one vote more than the two-thirds majority needed to ratify treaties.

Cuba

The Teller Amendment had declared that the United States would not annex Cuba. However, McKinley wanted to create stability and increase U.S. economic activity there, so he set up a military government. He appointed Leonard Wood, who had commanded the Rough Riders during the war, as governor.

Wood quickly began building schools and a sanitation system.

Even with the new sanitation system, disease remained a major problem. Dr. Walter Reed, head of the army's Yellow Fever Commission, was sent to Cuba in 1900 to help fight the disease. He and his volunteers conducted experiments, including allowing themselves to be bitten by infected insects. They soon proved that yellow fever was transmitted by mosquitoes. Getting rid of the standing water where mosquitoes lived helped health officials to control the disease.

Governor Wood also oversaw the writing of a Cuban constitution. The document included the **Platt Amendment**, which limited Cuba's right to make treaties and allowed the United States to intervene in Cuban affairs. It also required Cuba to sell or lease land to the United States. Cuban leaders compared the Platt Amendment to "handing over the keys to our house so that they [the Americans] can enter it at any time, whenever the desire seizes them." The Cubans reluctantly accepted the amendment, and U.S. troops withdrew. The amendment remained in force until 1934, and the U.S. government stayed actively involved in Cuban affairs until the late 1950s.

Puerto Rico

Like Cubans, Puerto Ricans had hoped for independence after the war. Instead, the U.S. government made the island a territory. On April 12, 1900, the Foraker Act established a civil government in Puerto Rico. It was headed by a governor and included a two-house legislature.

A debate over the new territory soon arose. People who lived in Puerto Rico were

Puerto Ricans Today

Today about 3.7 million Puerto Ricans live on the mainland United States. This is the second-largest Hispanic population in the country, behind people of Mexican descent. Puerto Ricans live throughout the United States, but about one-third live in New York State.

Puerto Rican culture is very strong in New York—the National Puerto Rican Day Parade in New York City is one of the largest parades for any ethnic group in the city.

Puerto Ricans in the Mainland United States

Puerto Rican Population (in millions)

Year: 1970 1980 1990 2000

ANALYSIS SKILL | **ANALYZING INFORMATION**

How are the people in the picture showing support for Puerto Rican culture?

considered citizens of the island but not of the United States. In 1917 the Jones Act gave Puerto Ricans U.S. citizenship and made both houses of the legislature elective. However, another 30 years passed before Puerto Ricans could elect their own governor. Today the island has its own constitution and elected officials but remains associated with the United States as what is known as a commonwealth.

The Philippines

Spain had surrendered the Philippines in return for a $20 million payment from the United States. Many Americans agreed with President McKinley, who said that the United States would benefit from the islands' naval and commercial value and that annexing the islands would keep Europeans from seizing them.

Filipino rebels, however, had expected to gain independence after the war. They had helped U.S. forces to capture Manila. When the United States decided instead to keep the islands, rebels led by Emilio Aguinaldo started a guerrilla war against the American forces. More than 4,200 U.S. soldiers and hundreds of thousands of Filipinos died before the conflict ended in 1902.

That same year, Congress passed the Philippine Government Act. It provided that an appointed governor and a two-house legislature would rule the Philippines. In 1946 the United States granted full independence to the Philippines.

READING CHECK **Summarizing** What areas did the United States control as a result of the war?

SUMMARY AND PREVIEW The United States fought a war with Spain and gained new territories in the Pacific and Caribbean regions. In the next section you will learn about U.S. interests in Latin America.

---

go.hrw.com
Online Quiz

Section 2 Assessment

Reviewing Ideas, Terms, and People

1. **a. Recall** What was the cause of the conflict between Cuba and Spain?
   b. Analyze How did **yellow journalism** affect public support for U.S. military action in Cuba?
   c. Elaborate Why do you think the United States was so successful in defeating Spain? Explain your answer.
2. **a. Identify** What territories did the United States gain as a result of the war?
   b. Analyze Why did some Americans oppose the annexation of the Philippines?

Critical Thinking

3. **Categorizing** Review your notes on the results of the Spanish-American War. Then copy the graphic organizer to the right. Use your notes to identify arguments for and against taking control of foreign territories.

Arguments for Imperialism		Arguments against Imperialism
	VS.	

FOCUS ON WRITING

4. **Identifying Pros and Cons of the Spanish-American War** As you read this section, add to your pros and cons list by identifying American losses and gains as a result of the Spanish-American War. What were the costs in human lives? What were the gains in territory? Can you identify any other losses and gains? For example, how did the United States handle the issues of self-rule involved in the war?

Theodore Roosevelt

What would you do to reform your country and make it stronger?

When did he live? 1858–1919

Where did he live? Theodore Roosevelt was born into a wealthy family in New York City. He spent two years on a ranch in the Dakota Territory, where he became an avid hunter and conservationist. His political career then took him to Albany, New York, where he served as state governor, and Washington, D.C., where he served as vice president and president.

What did he do? Roosevelt became a national hero while leading the Rough Riders in the Spanish-American War. After serving less than a year as vice president, the 42-year-old Roosevelt became the youngest president in U.S. history when President William McKinley was killed in 1901. As president, Roosevelt fought for progressive reforms and set aside millions of acres as national parks and forests. Roosevelt's aggressive foreign policy expanded American power in the world.

Why is he so important? "I believe in a strong executive," Roosevelt once declared. "While president, I have been president, emphatically [forcefully]; I have used every ounce of power there was in the office." As this quote suggests, Roosevelt was a strong leader who set a precedent for a more active and powerful presidency.

Drawing Conclusions What characteristics made Theodore Roosevelt a successful leader?

President Theodore Roosevelt and the Rough Riders

KEY EVENTS

1882
Elected to the New York State Assembly at age 23

1898
Becomes a hero in the Spanish-American War; elected governor of New York

1900
Elected vice president

1901
Becomes president when McKinley is assassinated

1903
Gains Panama Canal Zone for the United States

1906
Wins Nobel Peace Prize for helping to negotiate the Treaty of Portsmouth, ending a war between Russia and Japan

1919
Dies at home in New York

The United States and Latin America

What You Will Learn...

Main Ideas

1. The United States built the Panama Canal in the early 1900s.
2. Theodore Roosevelt changed U.S. policy toward Latin America.
3. Presidents Taft and Wilson promoted U.S. interests in Latin America.

The Big Idea

The United States expanded its role in Latin America in the early 1900s.

Key Terms and People

Panama Canal, *p. 125*
Roosevelt Corollary, *p. 127*
dollar diplomacy, *p. 128*
Mexican Revolution, *p. 128*
John J. Pershing, *p. 129*
Francisco "Pancho" Villa, *p. 129*

TAKING NOTES As you read, take notes on changing U.S. policies toward Latin America. List each policy in an outer circle of a web like this one.

U.S. policies toward Latin America

If YOU were there...

You are an engineer, and you've been working on the Panama Canal for almost eight years. Your work crews used huge steam shovels to slice through a ridge of mountains and built a huge artificial lake. You planned a system to move ships through different water levels. Now your work is done. You can watch massive ships travel from the Atlantic to the Pacific.

Which part of the work on the canal was the most challenging?

BUILDING BACKGROUND When the Spanish-American War began in 1898, the U.S. battleship *Oregon* set out from Washington State to join the fighting in Cuba. The approximately 12,000-mile trip around the southern tip of South America took more than two months. This delay convinced many U.S. leaders that the United States needed to build a canal linking the Atlantic and Pacific oceans.

Building the Panama Canal

A canal across the narrow neck of Central America would link the Atlantic and Pacific oceans and cut some 8,000 miles off the voyage by ship from the West to the East coasts of the United States. It would also allow the U.S. Navy to link its Atlantic and Pacific naval fleets quickly.

Revolution in Panama

No one was a stronger supporter of a Central American canal than President Theodore Roosevelt. Roosevelt knew that the best spot for the canal was the Isthmus of Panama, which at the time was part of the nation of Colombia. But he was unable to convince the Colombian senate to lease a strip of land across Panama to the United States.

Roosevelt considered other ways to gain control of the land. He learned that Panamanian revolutionaries were planning a revolt against Colombia. On November 2, 1903, a U.S. warship arrived outside Colón, Panama. The next day the revolt began. Blocked by the U.S. warship, Colombian forces could not reach Panama to stop the rebellion. Panama declared itself an independent country. The United States then recognized the new nation.

The new government of Panama supported the idea of a canal across its land. The United States agreed to pay Panama $10 million plus $250,000 a year for a 99-year lease on a 10-mile-wide strip of land across the isthmus.

Building the Canal

Canal construction began in 1904. The first obstacle to overcome was tropical disease. The canal route ran through 51 miles of forests and swamps filled with mosquitoes, many of which carried the deadly diseases malaria and yellow fever.

Dr. William C. Gorgas, who had helped Dr. Walter Reed stamp out yellow fever in Cuba, organized a successful effort to rid the canal route of disease-carrying mosquitoes. If Gorgas had not been successful, the canal's construction would have taken much longer. It also would have cost much more in terms of both lives and money.

Even with the reduced risk of disease, the work was very dangerous. Most of the canal had to be blasted out of solid rock with explosives. Workers used dozens of steam shovels to cut a narrow, eight-mile-long channel through the mountains of central Panama. Sometimes workers died when their shovels struck explosive charges. "The flesh of men flew in the air like birds every day," recalled one worker from the West Indies.

Some 6,000 lives were lost during the American construction of the **Panama Canal**. It was finally opened to ships on August 15, 1914, linking the Atlantic and Pacific oceans. An opening ceremony was held the next year. It had taken 10 years to complete, and the cost was $375 million. In the end, however, the world had its "highway between the oceans."

READING CHECK **Drawing Conclusions** Why did building the canal cost so many lives?

FOCUS ON NEW YORK

Theodore Roosevelt's strong support for the Panama Canal has had far reaching effects for his home state of New York. In 2003, the Port Authority of New York and New Jersey collaborated with the Panama Canal Authority on a plan to help boost the two states' trade with Asia.

THE IMPACT TODAY

Today the Panama Canal Zone is threatened by deforestation and erosion because of heavy use. Decreased rainfall is also hurting the canal.

The massive Gatun Locks, shown here under construction in 1914, raise ships 85 feet onto Gatun Lake, an inland waterway on the Panama Canal.

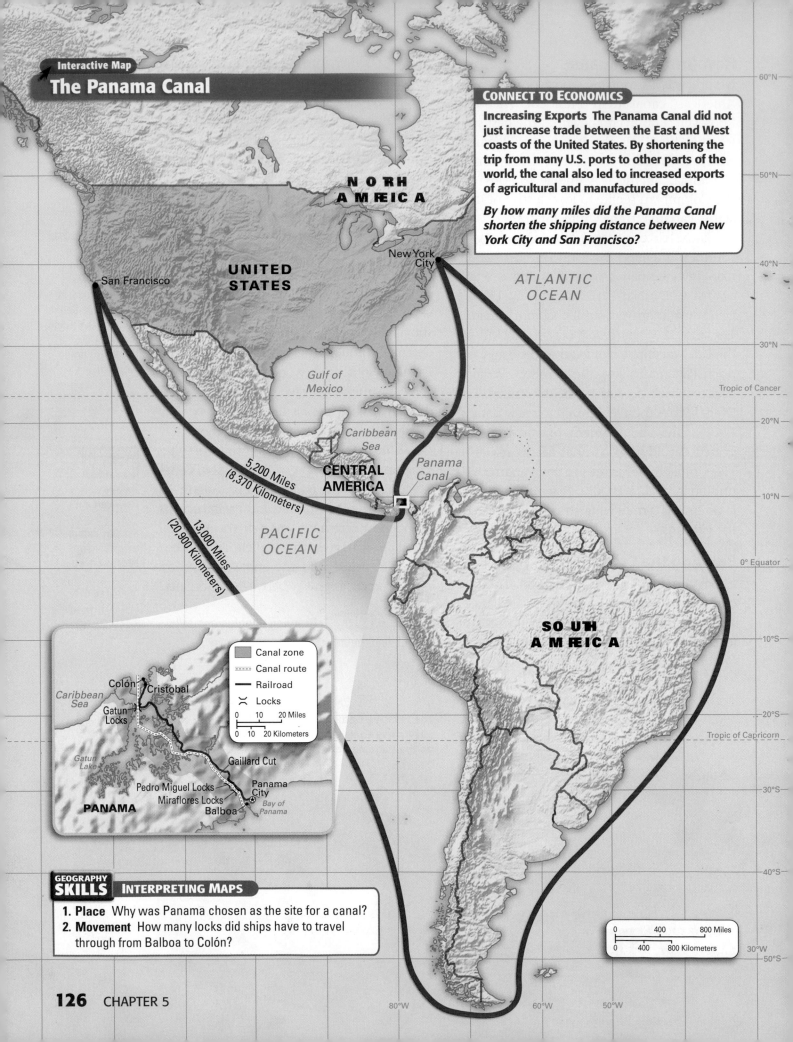

N O R T H
A M E R I C A

UNITED
STATES

San Francisco

New York
City

ATLANTIC
OCEAN

CONNECT TO ECONOMICS

Increasing Exports The Panama Canal did not just increase trade between the East and West coasts of the United States. By shortening the trip from many U.S. ports to other parts of the world, the canal also led to increased exports of agricultural and manufactured goods.

By how many miles did the Panama Canal shorten the shipping distance between New York City and San Francisco?

Gulf of
Mexico

Tropic of Cancer

Caribbean
Sea

Panama
Canal

5,200 Miles
(8,370 Kilometers)

CENTRAL
AMERICA

13,000 Miles
(20,900 Kilometers)

PACIFIC
OCEAN

S O U T H
A M E R I C A

0° Equator

Tropic of Capricorn

Inset map:

	Canal zone
	Canal route
	Railroad
	Locks

0   10   20 Miles

0   10   20 Kilometers

Caribbean
Sea

Colón   Cristobal

Gatun
Locks

Gatun
Lake

Gaillard Cut

Pedro Miguel Locks

Miraflores Locks

Panama
City

Balboa

Bay of
Panama

PANAMA

0   400   800 Miles

0   400   800 Kilometers

GEOGRAPHY SKILLS **INTERPRETING MAPS**

1. **Place** Why was Panama chosen as the site for a canal?
2. **Movement** How many locks did ships have to travel through from Balboa to Colón?

U.S. Policy Toward Latin America

As president, Theodore Roosevelt actively pursued progressive reforms at home. He also believed the United States should play a more active role in the Western Hemisphere. In 1900 Roosevelt said, "I have always been fond of the West African proverb: 'Speak softly and carry a big stick; you will go far.'" Roosevelt wanted everyone to know he would use a "big stick"—meaning U.S. military force—to protect U.S. interests in Latin America.

This was a change from the policies of previous presidents. In the 1823 Monroe Doctrine, President James Monroe had warned European nations not to interfere in the Western Hemisphere. While the Monroe Doctrine became a major principle of U.S. foreign policy, the United States did not have the military strength to enforce it. By the time Roosevelt became president, however, this situation was changing. The United States was growing stronger and expanding its influence. The United States was becoming a world power.

How should the United States use its new power in Latin America? This question came up often in the early 1900s. European banks had made loans to a number of Latin American countries. Venezuela, for example, fell deeply in debt to British and German investors. Venezuela refused to repay these debts in 1902. A similar situation arose in the Caribbean nation of the Dominican Republic in 1904. European powers prepared to use military force to collect the debts.

Roosevelt insisted the countries must repay their debts. But he did not want to allow Europeans to intervene in Latin America. The presence of European forces there would violate the Monroe Doctrine and threaten U.S. power in the region.

Roosevelt knew that U.S. officials would have to force debtor nations to repay their loans in order to keep European nations from directly intervening in Latin America. In December 1904 he announced what became known as the **Roosevelt Corollary** to the Monroe Doctrine. This addition warned that in cases of "wrongdoing" by Latin American countries, the United States might exercise "international police power."

The Roosevelt Corollary asserted a new **role** for the United States as an "international police power" in the Western Hemisphere. Roosevelt actively enforced the corollary throughout the rest of his presidency.

ACADEMIC VOCABULARY
role
assigned behavior

READING CHECK **Finding Main Ideas** Why did Roosevelt announce the Roosevelt Corollary?

Primary Source

POLITICAL CARTOON
Roosevelt's Imperialism

Theodore Roosevelt's foreign policy is shown visually in this cartoon. Roosevelt is the giant leading a group of ships that represent debt collection. The U.S. president is patrolling the Caribbean Sea and Latin American countries, trying to enforce the payment of debts to European countries.

What do you think this stick represents?

Why are these vessels warships?

ANALYSIS SKILL **ANALYZING PRIMARY SOURCES**

Analyzing How does the cartoonist portray the parts of the Roosevelt Corollary?

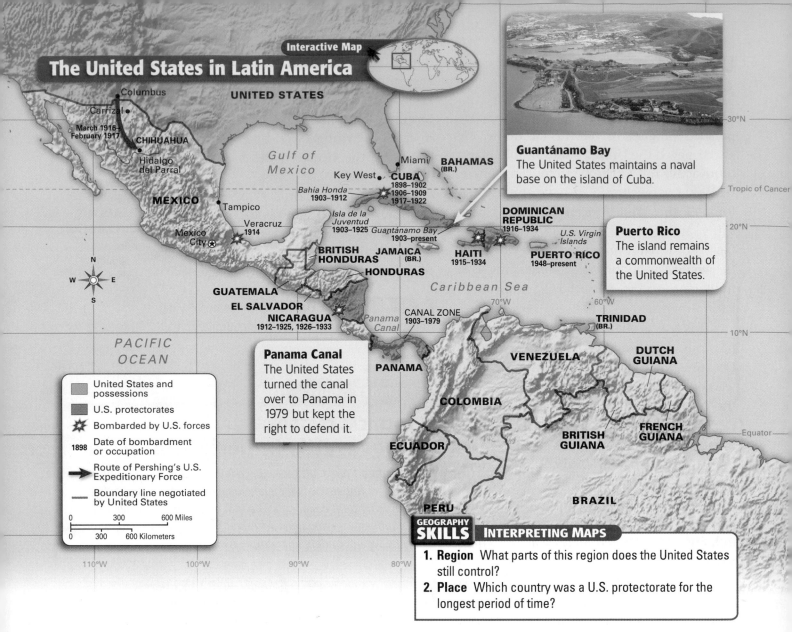

The United States in Latin America

Interactive Map

Guantánamo Bay
The United States maintains a naval base on the island of Cuba.

Puerto Rico
The island remains a commonwealth of the United States.

Panama Canal
The United States turned the canal over to Panama in 1979 but kept the right to defend it.

UNITED STATES

Columbus
Carrizal
March 1916–February 1917
CHIHUAHUA
Hidalgo del Parral

Gulf of Mexico

Miami
Key West
BAHAMAS (BR.)
CUBA
1898–1902
1906–1909
1917–1922
Bahia Honda 1903–1912

MEXICO
Tampico
Veracruz 1914
Mexico City

Isla de la Juventud 1903–1925
Guantánamo Bay 1903–present

DOMINICAN REPUBLIC 1916–1934
U.S. Virgin Islands
PUERTO RICO 1948–present

BRITISH HONDURAS
JAMAICA (BR.)
HONDURAS
HAITI 1915–1934

Caribbean Sea

GUATEMALA
EL SALVADOR
NICARAGUA 1912–1925, 1926–1933

CANAL ZONE 1903–1979
Panama Canal

TRINIDAD (BR.)

PACIFIC OCEAN

PANAMA

VENEZUELA

DUTCH GUIANA

COLOMBIA

ECUADOR

BRITISH GUIANA

FRENCH GUIANA

PERU

BRAZIL

Legend:
- United States and possessions
- U.S. protectorates
- ✦ Bombarded by U.S. forces
- 1898 Date of bombardment or occupation
- → Route of Pershing's U.S. Expeditionary Force
- — Boundary line negotiated by United States

0   300   600 Miles
0 300 600 Kilometers

30°N
Tropic of Cancer
20°N
10°N
Equator
70°W   60°W
110°W   100°W   90°W   80°W

GEOGRAPHY SKILLS | **INTERPRETING MAPS**

1. **Region** What parts of this region does the United States still control?
2. **Place** Which country was a U.S. protectorate for the longest period of time?

U.S. Interests in Latin America

William Howard Taft, who became president in 1909, also acted to protect U.S. interests in Latin America. Taft used a policy called **dollar diplomacy**—influencing governments through economic, not military, intervention.

President Taft described dollar diplomacy as "substituting dollars for bullets. It is . . . directed to the increase of American trade." He wanted to encourage stability and keep Europeans out of Latin America by expanding U.S. business interests there.

For example, in 1911 Nicaragua failed to repay a loan from British investors. American bankers lent Nicaragua $1.5 billion in return for control of the National Bank of Nicaragua and the government-owned railway. When local anger over this deal led to revolt in Nicaragua, Taft sent U.S. Marines to protect American interests.

When President Woodrow Wilson took office in 1913, he rejected Taft's dollar diplomacy. He believed the United States had a moral obligation to promote democracy in Latin America. Like Roosevelt, Wilson was willing to use military force to protect U.S. interests in the region.

In 1910 many Mexicans revolted against the harsh rule of Mexican dictator Porfirio Díaz. This was the start of the **Mexican Revolution**, a long, violent struggle for power in Mexico. The war affected U.S. interests

Departing from the example set by the nation's first president, George Washington, future presidents increased U.S. involvement around the world, particularly in Latin America.

Washington's Farewell Address
The United States will not become involved in European affairs.

Monroe Doctrine
The United States will defend its interests in the Western Hemisphere and keep European powers out.

Roosevelt Corollary
The United States will police wrongdoing by nations in the Western Hemisphere.

Taft's Dollar Diplomacy
The United States will use economic means to aid its interests in Latin America.

Wilson and Democracy
The United States will promote and protect democracy in the Western Hemisphere.

because Americans had invested more than $1 billion in Mexican land, mining, oil, and railways. American business leaders feared they would lose their investments.

In 1914 President Wilson learned that a German ship carrying weapons was headed to the port of Veracruz, Mexico. To keep the weapons from reaching the rebels, Wilson ordered the navy to seize Veracruz. Wilson acted again in 1916, sending General **John J. Pershing** and 15,000 U.S. soldiers into Mexico. Pershing's mission was to catch the rebel leader **Francisco "Pancho" Villa**, who had killed 17 Americans in New Mexico. Pershing failed to capture Villa, and Wilson recalled the troops.

In 1917 a new constitution began to bring order to Mexico. The violence caused more than 120,000 Mexicans to flee to the United States between 1905 and 1915.

READING CHECK **Summarizing** How did Wilson respond to events in Mexico?

SUMMARY AND PREVIEW The United States and Latin America established relationships through both conflicts and agreements. In the next chapter, you will learn how the United States became involved in conflict in Europe.

Section 3 Assessment

go.hrw.com
Online Quiz

Reviewing Ideas, Terms, and People

1. **a. Recall** Why did the United States want to build a canal?
   b. Analyze What challenges did the builders of the **Panama Canal** face? How did they overcome them?
   c. Elaborate Defend or criticize the U.S. decision to support the revolution in Panama.
2. **a. Describe** What problem was causing conflict between European and Latin American nations?
   b. Summarize How and why did Theodore Roosevelt change U.S. policy toward Latin America?
3. **a. Recall** What did Woodrow Wilson believe was the obligation of the United States to Latin America?
   b. Compare and Contrast How were the policies of Taft and Wilson toward Latin America similar? How were they different?

Critical Thinking

4. **Categorizing** Review your notes on U.S. policies toward Latin America. Then copy the web diagram below. Use it to identify American policies toward Latin America.

```
Roosevelt  ←→  U.S. Policy  ←→  Wilson
                   ↓
                  Taft
```

FOCUS ON WRITING

5. **Identifying Pros and Cons of U.S. Intervention** What were the pros and cons of the construction of the Panama Canal and interventionist U.S. policies toward Latin America? Take notes for your list as you read this section.

America's Global Influence
1900

By 1900 most of the current boundaries of the United States had been established. But the world had become a much smaller place. American inventions were spreading, changing daily life in countries around the world. In addition, U.S. troops stationed in China were displaying the increasing importance of the United States in global affairs.

ASIA

PACIFIC OCEAN

On July 5, 1900, William Jennings Bryan spoke out against U.S. involvement in China, saying, "Imperialism is the most dangerous of the evils now menacing [threatening] our country."

Asia Before 1898, U.S. troops had never been sent outside the Western Hemisphere. But in 1900, some 5,000 troops were in Asia, fighting alongside European troops.

Paris The Paris Exposition of 1900 showcased many U.S. inventions. One British writer claimed the exposition displayed "the Americanization of the world."

London

EUROPE

Paris

London In August 1900, English farmers protested in London against new farm equipment introduced from the United States that they feared would cause farmers to lose their jobs.

UNITED STATES

New York

ATLANTIC OCEAN

AFRICA

New York City Nearly 500,000 people immigrated to the United States in 1900. By 1920 more than 16 million had come. Many arrived in New York City.

SOUTH AMERICA

GEOGRAPHY SKILLS INTERPRETING MAPS

1. **Region** By 1900, what role was the U.S. military playing in China?
2. **Movement** In what ways did the U.S. influence other countries?

Social Studies Skills

Analysis | Critical Thinking | Civic Participation | Study

Continuity and Change in History

Define the Skill

A well-known saying claims that "the more things change, the more they stay the same." Nowhere does this observation apply better than to the study of history. Any examination of the past will show many changes—nations expanding or shrinking, empires rising and falling, changes in leadership, or people on the move, for example.

The reasons for change have not changed, however. The same general forces have driven the actions of people and nations across time. These forces are the threads that run through history and give it continuity, or connectedness. They are the "sameness" in a world of continuous change.

Learn the Skill

You can find the causes of all events of the past in one or more of these major forces or themes that connect all history.

1. **Cooperation and Conflict** Throughout time, people and groups have worked together to achieve goals. They have also opposed others who stood in the way of their goals.

2. **Cultural Invention and Interaction** The values and ideas expressed in peoples' art, literature, customs, and religion have enriched the world. But the spread of cultures and their contact with other cultures have produced conflict as well.

3. **Geography and Environment** Physical environment and natural resources have shaped how people live. Efforts to gain, protect, or make good use of land and resources have been major causes of cooperation and conflict in history.

4. **Science and Technology** Technology, or the development and use of tools, has helped humans across time make better use of their environment. Science has changed their knowledge of the world, and changed their lives, too.

5. **Economic Opportunity and Development** From hunting and gathering to herding, farming, manufacturing, and trade, people have tried to make the most of their resources. The desire for a better life has also been a major reason people have moved from one place to another.

6. **The Impact of Individuals** Political, religious, military, business, and other leaders have been a major influence in history. The actions of many ordinary people have also shaped history

7. **Nationalism and Imperialism** *Nationalism* is the desire of a people to have their own country. *Imperialism* is the desire of a nation to influence or control other nations. Both have existed across time.

8. **Political and Social Systems** People have always been part of groups—families, villages, nations, or religious groups, for example. The groups to which people belong shape how they relate to others around them.

Practice the Skill

Check your understanding of continuity and change in history by answering the following questions.

1. What forces of history are illustrated by the events in Chapter 5? Explain with examples.

2. How do the events in this chapter show continuity with earlier periods in U.S. history?

Chapter Review

Visual Summary

QUICK FACTS

Use the visual summary below to help you review the main ideas of the chapter.

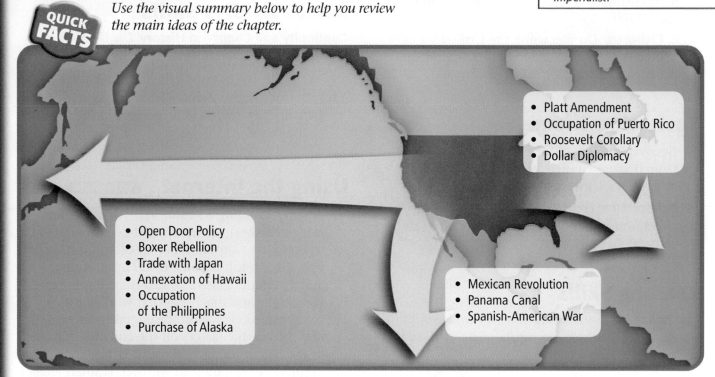

- Platt Amendment
- Occupation of Puerto Rico
- Roosevelt Corollary
- Dollar Diplomacy

- Open Door Policy
- Boxer Rebellion
- Trade with Japan
- Annexation of Hawaii
- Occupation of the Philippines
- Purchase of Alaska

- Mexican Revolution
- Panama Canal
- Spanish-American War

Reviewing Vocabulary, Terms, and People

1. In which of the following did the United States declare that it had no interest in taking control of Cuba?

a. Roosevelt Corollary   **c.** Open Door Policy

b. Monroe Doctrine   **d.** Teller Amendment

2. Which leader upset sugar planters in Hawaii by proposing a plan to return power to the monarchy?

a. Liliuokalani   **c.** Millard Fillmore

b. John L. Stevens   **d.** Woodrow Wilson

3. Which president supported Panama's revolt against Colombia in 1903?

a. Woodrow Wilson   **c.** William Howard Taft

b. William McKinley   **d.** Theodore Roosevelt

4. Who led U.S. forces into Mexico after attacks against U.S. citizens by Mexican rebels?

a. John Hay   **c.** John J. Pershing

b. William H. Seward   **d.** Theodore Roosevelt

Comprehension and Critical Thinking

SECTION 1 *(Pages 112–116)*

5. a. Identify Into what areas did the United States expand in the late 1800s?

b. Draw Conclusions How did the United States benefit from contact with foreign nations and territories?

c. Elaborate Which policy would you have supported—isolationism or imperialism? Explain your answer.

SECTION 2 *(Pages 117–122)*

6. a. Describe What events led the United States to declare war on Spain?

b. Analyze How did the United States benefit from the Spanish-American War?

c. Predict How might foreign countries view the actions of the United States in the Spanish-American War?

7. a. Identify In what ways did the United States become involved in Latin American affairs?

b. Draw Conclusions Why did the United States expand its role in Latin America in the early 1900s?

c. Elaborate Do you think the United States should have been as actively involved in Latin America as it was? Explain your answer.

Reviewing Themes

8. Geography How did the geography of the United States change after the end of its policy of isolationism?

9. Politics How did the policy of imperialism affect American politics in the late 1800s and early 1900s?

Reading Skills

Comparing Historical Texts *Use the Reading Skills taught in this chapter to answer the question about the reading selections below.*

A. "Sad to say, this most precious and sublime feature of the Yosemite National Park (Hetch Hetchy Valley), one of the greatest of all our natural resources for the uplifting joy and peace and health of the people, is in danger of being dammed and made into a reservoir to help supply San Francisco with water and light . . ."

—John Muir, *The Yosemite*, 1912

B. "As we all know, there is no use of water that is higher than the domestic use. Then, if there is, as the engineers tell us, no other source of supply that is anything like so reasonably available as this one; if this is the best, and, within reasonable limits of cost, the only means of supplying San Francisco with water, we come straight to the question of whether the advantage of leaving this valley in a state of nature is greater than the advantage of using it for the benefit of the city of San Francisco."

—Gifford Pinchot, address to Congress, 1913

10. How do the two men quoted to the left differ on the issue of building a dam in the Hetch Hetchy Valley?

Social Studies Skills

Continuity and Change in History *Use the Social Studies Skills taught in this chapter to answer the question below.*

11. Pick three of the themes listed on page 132. Explain how the themes connect to the history of the Panama Canal.

Using the Internet `go.hrw.com`

12. Activity: Creating a Poster The Panama Canal was opened on August 15, 1914. It took 10 years to build, cost a total of over $600 million, and had a death toll of some 6,000 lives. Human and geographic factors had a huge impact on the people and machines that worked on the canal project. Research the effects of human and geographic factors on the construction of the Panama Canal. Physical factors include landforms, climate, and weather. Human factors should focus on the use of technology and the reasons humans modified the environment, along with the hazards they faced. Then create a poster about the canal, highlighting the most important details.

FOCUS ON WRITING

13. Writing Your List of Pros and Cons Review your notes and choose the pros and cons to include in your final list. Decide whether you want to include only facts, only opinions, or some of each. How can your analysis of history help guide U.S. foreign policy in the future? When you have finished your list, use it as the basis for a paragraph recommending either that the United States continue to involve itself in the affairs of other nations or that it pull back from such involvement.

Grade 8 Intermediate-Level Test Preparation

DIRECTIONS (1–6): For each statement or question, write on the separate answer sheet the *number* of the word or expression that, of those given, best completes the statement or answers the question.

Base your answer to question 1 on the map below and on your knowledge of social studies.

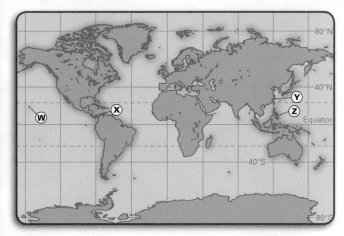

1 The only area in which the United States did not control territory in the late 1800s and early 1900s is shown on the map by which letter?

(1) W   (3) Y

(2) X   (4) Z

2 The practice of using U.S. businesses and economic aid to influence foreign governments and achieve U.S. goals in Latin America is known as

(1) imperialism.

(2) dollar diplomacy.

(3) isolationism.

(4) the big stick.

3 During the Mexican Revolution, President Wilson sent U.S. forces to Veracruz, Mexico. Which U.S. policy did this act best express?

(1) Roosevelt Corollary

(2) dollar diplomacy

(3) Teller Amendment

(4) isolationism

4 Which two nations did the United States hope to trade with rather than annex in the late 1800s?

(1) Hawaii and Japan

(2) Japan and China

(3) China and Cuba

(4) Cuba and Hawaii

5 How did American newspapers respond to the explosion of the USS *Maine* in Havana Harbor?

(1) They refused to report the story.

(2) They reported that the explosion was an accident.

(3) They blamed the explosion on Spain.

(4) They blamed the explosion on Cuban rebels.

6 In his book *The Influence of Sea Power upon History,* Alfred T. Mahan argued that the United States should

(1) avoid foreign conflicts.

(2) sell its naval bases.

(3) build a strong navy.

(4) remain isolationist.

Base your answer to question 7 on the text below and on your knowledge of social studies.

> "I am desirous that our two countries should trade with each other, for the benefit of both Japan and the United States. We know that the ancient laws of your imperial majesty's government do not allow of foreign trade, except with the Chinese and the Dutch; but as the state of the world changes . . . it seems to be wise, from time to time, to make new laws."
>
> —Letter from U.S. President Millard Fillmore to Japan, 1852

7 **Constructed-Response Question** What is President Fillmore asking the Japanese to do?

World War I

FOCUS QUESTION

How does a nation balance its own needs with the needs of the world?

FOCUS ON SPEAKING

Persuasive Speech Before the United States entered World War I in 1917, Americans heatedly debated joining the fight. Many were torn between either helping Britain and France or remaining isolated from world conflict. In this chapter, you will read about U.S. involvement in World War I. Then you will make a speech presenting your point of view on whether the United States should have entered the war.

UNITED STATES

WORLD

1914 President Wilson issues a proclamation of neutrality in the European war.

1914

1914 Archduke Francis Ferdinand is assassinated.

What You Will Learn...

In this chapter you will learn how an assassination in Europe sparked the deadliest war the world had ever seen. You will find out how the United States was drawn into the fighting and will read about new battle strategies, such as trench warfare. The photograph on this page shows the terrible conditions soldiers faced as they fought the enemy from their trench positions.

NY

1917
The Harlem Hellfighters arrive in France.

1916
Jeannette Rankin becomes the first woman elected to Congress.

I WANT YOU FOR U.S. ARMY
NEAREST RECRUITING STATION

1917
The Selective Service Act is passed, introducing the draft.

1918 President Wilson announces the Fourteen Points.

1919 The U.S. Senate refuses to approve the Treaty of Versailles.

1916

1918

1920

1915 A German U-boat sinks the *Lusitania*.

Steamships
CUNARD

EUROPE VIA LIVERPOOL
LUSITANIA
Fastest and Largest Steamer now in Atlantic Service Sails

1917 The United States declares war on Germany.

1918 Germany agrees to an armistice, ending World War I.

WORLD WAR I **137**

Focus on Themes In this chapter, you will read about World War I and the changes it brought to the United States and the world. Many of the **political** tensions that led to the war were caused by the rise of nationalism in European countries. You will read about how the war devastated European **economies** and how peace affected European countries.

Recognizing Fallacies in Reasoning

Focus on Reading As part of evaluating a historical argument, you can judge whether the reasoning is sound. A *fallacy* is a false or mistaken idea.

Recognizing Fallacies As you identify a main idea, judge its soundness. Look for cause-and-effect relationships that support the idea. Decide whether you think the argument is logical.

Notice how a reader explained the logical reasoning behind the main idea in the following paragraph.

Three main factors led to a shortage of labor in the United States during the war. First, American factories were working nonstop to produce weapons and supplies for the Allied forces. Factories needed new workers to meet this huge demand. Second, the war almost completely cut off immigration. As you know, immigrants had provided a steady source of labor to American industry. Third, many of the young men who would normally take factory jobs were off fighting in Europe.

From Chapter 6, p. 148

> If factories were working overtime, they would need more workers. This supports the main idea of a labor shortage.

> If factories were used to having immigrants to hire and there were fewer immigrants, it would make sense that there was a labor shortage.

> Here's a third reason for a labor shortage: Many men became soldiers. It makes sense that there was a labor shortage during the war.

You Try It!

The man who assassinated Archduke Francis Ferdinand was a Serb.

All Serbians wanted war with Austria-Hungary.

Wilson wanted to establish the League of Nations

because he thought it would help ensure peace.

Trench warfare was a new kind of warfare.

Therefore, trench warfare was more horrible than any other kind of warfare.

1. Is the first conclusion reasonable? Why or why not? How can you tell?

2. Do you think the second conclusion is logical or illogical? What makes you think so?

3. Is the third conclusion a fallacy of reason? What reasonable conclusions can you draw from the statement?

As you read **Chapter 6,** notice how the authors use logical reasoning to support their main ideas.

The Road to War

What You Will Learn...

Main Ideas

1. Many factors contributed to the outbreak of World War I.
2. European nations suffered massive casualties in the war's early battles.

The Big Idea

In 1914 tensions in Europe exploded into the deadliest war the world had ever seen.

Key Terms and People

militarism, *p. 141*
Archduke Francis Ferdinand, *p. 141*
mobilize, *p. 141*
Central Powers, *p. 141*
Allied Powers, *p. 141*
trench warfare, *p. 142*
stalemate, *p. 143*
U-boats, *p. 144*

TAKING NOTES As you read, identify the major battles of the beginning of World War I. In a chart like the one below, list the battles and where they were fought.

Battle	Location

If **YOU** were there...

You are walking past a newspaper stand when a headline catches your eye: "Austria–Hungary's Archduke Francis Ferdinand Assassinated in Sarajevo." Your first thought is, "Who's he?" You pick up the paper and read about the archduke and about the rising tensions in Europe related to his death. The article makes it sound like Europe is about to explode into war.

At this point, do you think the assassination will affect the United States? Why or why not?

BUILDING BACKGROUND European nations had not been involved in a major war in the region since the 1870s. Rising political tensions during the early 1900s threatened this peace, however, and nations began to build up their military forces. Even a small incident might trigger a major war.

Outbreak of War

Though Europe was at peace in the early 1900s, relations between European nations were not necessarily friendly. In fact, feelings of fear and distrust were growing among European powers such as Germany, France, Great Britain, Russia, and Austria-Hungary. This dangerous tension had several important causes.

Tensions in Europe

One cause of tension was the rise of nationalism in the 1800s. Nationalism is a strong sense of pride and loyalty to one's nation or culture. Nationalism inspired people who shared a language or culture to want to unite politically. In 1871, for example, Chancellor Otto von Bismarck and Kaiser Wilhelm I brought together several German states to form the nation of Germany.

While nationalism helped bring stability to Germany, it caused instability in other places. The empire of Austria-Hungary included people from many different cultural groups. One of these groups was the Slavs. Slavic nationalists wanted to break away from Austria-Hungary and join the independent Slavic country of Serbia on the

Balkan Peninsula. Leaders of Austria-Hungary reacted angrily, seeing this movement as a threat to their empire.

Another source of tension in Europe was imperialism. Britain's huge empire, stretching from Africa to Asia, brought it wealth and power. Eager to share in such benefits, other European powers competed for control of overseas territories. Fierce competition for territory took place within Europe as well. For example, Germany had taken the Alsace-Lorraine region from France in the Franco-Prussian War in 1871. France wanted it back.

In this competitive atmosphere, nations focused their resources on **militarism**—the aggressive strengthening of armed forces. European nations raced to build armies and navies that were larger than ever before.

As nations became more powerful, they sought to protect themselves by forming new alliances. Germany formed an alliance with Austria-Hungary in 1879. Each promised to defend the other in case of enemy attack. Concerned with Germany's growing power, France and Russia created their own alliance in 1893. Britain joined France and Russia in 1907.

The Spark

With so much hostility dividing European leaders, few efforts at diplomacy were made. A German general felt that "a European war is bound to come sooner or later." All that was needed was a spark to set Europe on fire. That spark flew from the Balkan province of Bosnia and Herzegovina.

Bosnia and Herzegovina had gained independence from Turkish rule in 1878. In 1908, however, Austria-Hungary annexed the province. Slavic nationalists resisted violently—they wanted the region to be part of Serbia.

On June 28, 1914, **Archduke Francis Ferdinand**, heir to the throne of Austria-Hungary, visited the province's capital of Sarajevo with his wife, Sophie. While riding through the streets, they were shot and killed by a 19-year-old Serb nationalist named Gavrilo Princip.

An End to Peace

The assassination of Archduke Francis Ferdinand and his wife, Sophie, by a Serb nationalist sparked the beginning of World War I.

How did the murder of the archduke bring war to Europe?

The assassination shattered Europe's fragile peace. Determined to crush Serbia and the Slavic nationalists, Austria-Hungary declared war on Serbia. Very quickly, other countries were pulled into the fighting. Russia had promised to support Serbia in case of war. It began to **mobilize**, or prepare its military for war. On August 1 Germany, Austria-Hungary's ally, declared war on Russia. Two days later, Germany also declared war on France, Russia's ally. To reach France quickly, the German army marched into Belgium on August 4. Britain, which had promised to support Belgium, then declared war on Germany.

As the fighting started, the alliance between Austria-Hungary and Germany came to be known as the **Central Powers**. Bulgaria and the Ottoman Empire later sided with the Central Powers. France, Russia, and Britain were known as the **Allied Powers**. Italy joined them in 1915. Over the next several years, soldiers from 30 nations and six continents would fight in what was then called the Great War. The conflict later became known as World War I.

READING CHECK **Identifying Cause and Effect**
How did nationalism contribute to political tensions in Europe?

Early Battles of the War

FOCUS ON READING
What mistake did the German leaders make in their reasoning?

Both sides expected the war to be over in a few months. German leaders planned to defeat France quickly, before Russia could join the fighting. But as the Germans marched toward France, they met fierce resistance from Belgian soldiers. This gave Britain and France time to mobilize their own troops.

The First Battle of the Marne

Belgian resistance slowed the German advance but could not stop it. On September 3 the German army was just 25 miles from Paris, the capital of France. The French army blocked the German advance at the Marne River, east of Paris. The First Battle of the Marne raged for several days before the Germans were pushed back.

By mid-September French and German troops faced each other along a long battle line called the western front. The western front stretched from the North Sea all the way to Switzerland. Meanwhile, the Russian and German armies were struggling back and forth along the eastern front, which reached from the Black Sea to the Baltic Sea. It quickly became clear that this war would be longer and deadlier than anyone had expected.

A New Kind of War

Part of what made World War I so long and deadly was a new technique called **trench warfare**—defending a position by fighting from the protection of deep ditches. When the French defeated the Germans in the First Battle of the Marne, the Germans did not retreat far. Instead, they dug trenches nearby. Opposite them, the French dug their own trenches. A 400-mile-long network of trenches soon stretched across the western front.

Soldiers fought in these cold, wet, and muddy ditches, sometimes for months at a time. The filthy trenches were perfect breeding

History Close-up

Trench Warfare

A series of trenches at the back was used to deliver food, ammunition, and mail to soldiers on the front lines.

Trenches were dug in a zigzag pattern so that the enemy could not stand at one end and fire down the length of a trench.

Some trenches served as first-aid posts where wounded soldiers were cared for until they could be evacuated.

grounds for germs, and soldiers on both sides died from disease. An American in the French army described life in the trenches:

"The impossibility of the simplest kind of personal cleanliness makes vermin [bugs] a universal ill, against which there is no remedy. Cold, dirt, discomfort, are the ever present conditions, and the soldier's life comes to mean …the most misery that the human organism [body] can support."
—Alan Seeger, *Letters and Diary of Alan Seeger*

The empty patch of ground between enemy trenches came to be known as no-man's-land. This area was quickly stripped of trees and blasted full of holes by artillery shells. Anyone who ventured into no-man's-land was likely to be killed by enemy fire.

Another factor that made World War I deadlier than previous wars was the use of modern technology. New machine guns, for example, could fire 400 to 600 bullets a minute. Enormous artillery guns fired shells over the trenches, where they exploded and sent speeding scraps of metal onto the soldiers below. Other shells spread poisonous gases. If soldiers were not wearing gas masks, the gas destroyed their lungs, causing slow, painful deaths. Poisonous gases were originally banned but came into use by both sides by the end of the war.

Other new weapons included tanks and airplanes. Tanks are armored combat vehicles that can cause heavy damage but cannot be destroyed easily. Airplanes were used to fire down on soldiers in trenches and to gather information about enemy locations. Airplanes also battled each other in fights called dogfights.

Land and Sea Battles

After a year of vicious fighting, the war had become a **stalemate**—a situation in which neither side can win a decisive victory. Determined to break the stalemate, both sides launched massive attacks in 1916. In February 1916 the Germans attacked the French city of Verdun, at the southern end of the western front. That summer, the Allies staged an attack along the Somme River, in northeastern

THE IMPACT TODAY

Many of the weapons first used in World War I, such as tanks and airplanes, are still used in warfare today. The use of poison gas, however, has been outlawed by international treaties.

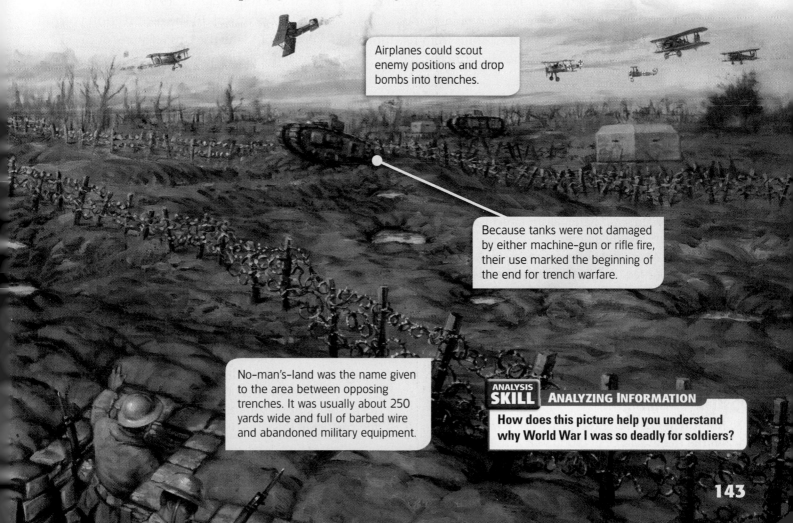

Airplanes could scout enemy positions and drop bombs into trenches.

Because tanks were not damaged by either machine-gun or rifle fire, their use marked the beginning of the end for trench warfare.

No-man's-land was the name given to the area between opposing trenches. It was usually about 250 yards wide and full of barbed wire and abandoned military equipment.

ANALYSIS SKILL **ANALYZING INFORMATION**

How does this picture help you understand why World War I was so deadly for soldiers?

German U-boats

Germany developed small submarines called U-boats as part of its war strategy. U-boats could strike Allied ships without being seen. They destroyed around 10 million tons of Allied and neutral ships and cargo from 1914 to 1918.

Why might U-boats have been so effective against the Allies?

France. Both battles raged for months, as the armies attacked and counterattacked.

By the end of the year, the Germans had failed to take Verdun. At the Somme River, the Allies had advanced just seven miles. Almost nothing had changed on the western front. But nearly 1 million men had been killed at Verdun and the Somme River.

As the stalemate on land dragged on, sea battles in the Atlantic Ocean and the North Sea became even more important. The powerful British navy blockaded the ports of the Central Powers and laid explosive mines in the North Sea. These could blow a huge hole in a ship, sinking it in minutes. The tactic effectively stopped ships from reaching German ports with needed supplies.

ACADEMIC VOCABULARY

neutral unbiased, not favoring either side in a conflict

The Germans responded by using submarines called **U-boats**. U-boats launched torpedoes against Allied supply ships, causing heavy losses. The Germans also attacked ships belonging to **neutral** countries they believed were helping the Allies. This would soon pull the United States into World War I.

READING CHECK **Categorizing** What new technologies did armies in World War I use?

SUMMARY AND PREVIEW World War I became a stalemate by 1916 as countries battled for control. In the next section you will find out why the United States decided to join the fighting.

---

go.hrw.com
Online Quiz

Section 1 Assessment

Reviewing Ideas, Terms, and People

1. **a. Describe** What factors contributed to the outbreak of World War I?
   b. Contrast How did nationalism affect Germany and Austria-Hungary differently?
   c. Predict What might have happened if Russia had not honored its agreement to defend Serbia?
2. **a. Identify** What were the outcomes of the early battles of the war?
   b. Explain How did Belgian resistance affect the German war plan?
   c. Evaluate How successful was **trench warfare** as a strategy?

Critical Thinking

3. **Identifying Cause and Effect** Review your notes on the major battles of World War I. Then copy

the graphic organizer below and use it to show the outcomes of these early battles and how they affected the war.

Battle	Outcome	Results

FOCUS ON SPEAKING

4. **Analyzing Rising Tensions** Start a list of ways that World War I might affect the United States. Was there sufficient reason for the United States to join the conflict at this time?

Americans Prepare for War

If YOU were there...

Everywhere you go people are talking about the war in Europe. The United States has just joined the fighting on the side of the Allied Powers. Many young men you know are volunteering to fight. Women are signing up to drive ambulances or work as nurses. You know that the situation in Europe is dangerous, but you want to serve your country.

Will you volunteer for service in World War I?

BUILDING BACKGROUND When World War I began, the United States had a long history of avoiding involvement in European conflicts. Most Americans wanted the United States to remain neutral in this war as well. But as tensions with Germany increased, it became clear that distance from Europe would not keep Americans out of battle.

The United States Enters World War I

Millions of Americans at this time were immigrants or children of immigrants. Many came from countries belonging to the Allied or Central Powers. They naturally sympathized with their former homelands. This did not change the fact that most Americans viewed World War I as a European conflict. They did not want American soldiers sent to the bloody battlefields of Europe. Shortly after World War I began, President Woodrow Wilson announced that the United States would remain neutral. Most Americans agreed that America should stay out of the war.

American Neutrality Threatened

Although the United States had a policy of neutrality, and both sides tried to prevent the United States from trading with the enemy, its merchants continued to trade with European nations. American ships carried supplies and war materials to the Allies. U.S. banks invested $2 billion in European war bonds, nearly all of it in Allied countries.

The Germans used U-boat attacks to try to stop supplies from reaching the Allies. Sometimes they attacked ships without warning.

What You Will Learn...

Main Ideas

1. The United States entered the war after repeated crises with Germany.
2. The United States mobilized for war by training troops and stepping up production of supplies.
3. Labor shortages created new wartime opportunities for women and other Americans.

The Big Idea

After entering World War I in 1917, Americans began the massive effort of preparing for war.

Key Terms and People

Lusitania, p. 146
Zimmermann Note, p. 146
Selective Service Act, p. 147
Liberty bonds, p. 147
National War Labor Board, p. 149

TAKING NOTES As you read, take notes on the new laws and government programs created to prepare for World War I. In each outer circle of this web, name one new law or program. You may need to add more circles.

New laws and government programs

In May 1915 a German U-boat sank the *Lusitania*, a British passenger liner. Nearly 1,200 people, including 128 Americans, were killed. The incident fueled anti-German feeling in the United States. Throughout the coming war, German Americans faced nativist attacks, including anti-German speeches, discrimination, and physical attacks. Other Americans of mixed heritage also had their loyalty questioned.

Secretary of State William Jennings Bryan resigned over President Wilson's handling of the affair. Bryan thought that Wilson's protest note to the Germans was designed to bring the United States into the war.

In March 1916 a U-boat attacked the *Sussex*, a French passenger ship. Several of the 80 casualties were Americans. Wilson demanded that the Germans stop attacking nonmilitary ships. German leaders responded with the *Sussex* pledge, agreeing not to attack merchant ships without warning.

Congress Declares War

When Wilson ran for reelection in 1916, the promise to remain neutral helped him win the election. Nearly a year after the *Sussex* pledge, however, the Germans again began launching attacks on ships, including American vessels. In response, Wilson broke off diplomatic relations with Germany and most Americans began supporting the entry of U.S. troops.

The United States stepped closer to war when Americans found out about the **Zimmermann Note**. This secret telegram to Mexico sent by the German foreign minister, Arthur Zimmermann, was decoded and then published by American newspapers in March 1917. In the note, Zimmermann proposed an alliance against the United States. He promised that Germany would help Mexico recapture areas that Mexico had lost during the Mexican-American War.

The American public was outraged by the telegram. Wilson knew that the United States would have little influence on the postwar peace if it remained neutral. "The world must be made safe for democracy," he proclaimed. Congress declared war on April 6, 1917.

READING CHECK Finding Main Ideas What events challenged U.S. neutrality?

FOCUS ON NEW YORK

Despite the large number of Germans in the United States around the time of World War I, many of them in New York, United States leaders felt closer to England than to Germany because Great Britain was a major trading partner. This feeling helped lead to the U.S. involvement in World War I on the side of the Allies.

Primary Source

NEWSPAPER ARTICLE
Sinking of the *Lusitania*

In 1915 German U-boats sank the Lusitania, *an event that pushed the United States toward entry into World War I. Newspapers quickly spread news of the disaster.*

The ship was treated as an enemy warship.

The accounts which have so far been received are fragmentary, and give no clear idea of the disaster. There is, however, no doubt that two torpedoes were fired without warning into the starboard side of the ship soon after 2 o'clock yesterday afternoon. There were conflicting accounts of the period during which the *Lusitania* remained afloat, but the Cunard Company states that she sunk 40 minutes after being struck.

—*The Register*, quoted in the *Times of London*

The ship sank before enough rescue ships could arrive.

ANALYSIS SKILL **ANALYZING PRIMARY SOURCES**

How might this disaster draw the United States into war with Germany?

SUPREME COURT DECISIONS

Schenck v. United States (1919)

Background of the Case Charles Schenck was arrested for violating the Espionage Act. He had printed and distributed pamphlets urging resistance to the draft. Schenck argued that the First Amendment, which guarantees freedom of speech and freedom of the press, gave him the right to criticize the government.

The Court's Ruling

The Supreme Court ruled that the pamphlet was not protected by the First Amendment and that the Espionage Act was constitutional.

The Court's Reasoning

The Supreme Court decided that under certain circumstances, such as a state of war, Congress could limit free speech. The Court created a test to distinguish between protected and unprotected speech. Unprotected speech would have to present "a clear and present danger" to national security. For example, the First Amendment would not protect a person who created a panic by yelling "Fire!" in a crowded theater.

Why It Matters

Schenck v. *United States* was important because it was the first case in which the Supreme Court interpreted the First Amendment. The Court concluded that certain constitutional rights, such as free speech, could be limited under extraordinary conditions, such as war. Later rulings by the Court narrowed the test of "clear and present danger" to speech advocating violence. The nonviolent expression of ideas and opinions—however unpopular—was thereby protected.

ANALYSIS SKILL **ANALYZING INFORMATION**

1. According to the Supreme Court, when could free speech be limited?
2. How do you think this case affected other people who opposed the war?

Mobilizing for War

In order to persuade the public to support the war effort, President Wilson formed the Committee on Public Information (CPI). The CPI organized rallies and parades and published posters and pamphlets. Speakers known as "four-minute men" gave short patriotic speeches in movie theaters and churches.

The U.S. government's war effort also involved limiting some freedoms in the United States. The Espionage Act of 1917 and the Sedition Act of 1918 restricted free speech and allowed the government to arrest opponents of the war. Antiwar mail was prohibited and seized. About 900 opponents of the war were jailed for violating these laws. The Sedition Act was later repealed, but the Espionage Act is still in effect today.

The United States was unprepared for war. To prepare the U.S. military, Congress passed the **Selective Service Act** in 1917. The act required men between the ages of 21 and 30 to register to be drafted. Almost 3 million Americans were drafted into service in World War I. A number of the draftees were African Americans. Altogether, about 400,000 African Americans served in the war. Their units were segregated from white forces and were commanded by white officers. Eventually, African Americans were trained as officers. During World War I, however, they were never placed in command of white troops.

Preparations for war were very expensive. Troops had to be trained, supplied, transported, and fed. Ships and airplanes had to be built and fueled. The government raised taxes and issued war bonds. Money from the sale of these **Liberty bonds** provided billions of dollars in loans to the Allies.

The government took other actions to supply the troops. The War Industries Board (WIB) oversaw the production and distribution of steel, copper, cement, and rubber. The Food Administration worked to increase food supplies for the troops. It guaranteed farmers high prices for their crops. To conserve food at home, citizens were encouraged to practice "meatless Mondays" and "wheatless Wednesdays." Many people also grew their own vegetables in "victory gardens" at home.

THE IMPACT TODAY

To conserve fuel used for lighting for the war effort, daylight saving time was first introduced in March 1918. The plan is still in effect today.

READING CHECK **Analyzing** How did the U.S. government gain public support for the war?

Women on the Battlefield

The role of women in World War I was much like their roles in previous wars—providing support for male troops. Women drove ambulances and entered the battlefield as nurses and medics. Red Cross volunteers were often responsible for the first stage of treatment of the wounded. Today women may also serve in the military as soldiers. They are not allowed to fight in ground combat, but they do serve as guards and pilots and in the navy.

Red Cross volunteers in World War I

Soldier on duty in Iraq

ANALYSIS SKILL **ANALYZING INFORMATION**

How have wartime roles for women changed since World War I?

New Wartime Opportunities

Three main factors led to a shortage of labor in the United States during the war. First, American factories were working nonstop to produce weapons and supplies for the Allied forces. Factories needed new workers to meet this huge demand. Second, the war almost completely cut off immigration. As you know, immigrants had provided a steady source of labor to American industry. Third, many of the young men who would normally take factory jobs were off fighting in Europe.

Women's War Efforts

This labor shortage created new opportunities for many workers. American women took on new roles to help the war effort. Some 1 million women joined the U.S. workforce during the war years. For many, this was their first experience working outside the home.

Women also worked for the war effort in Europe. About 25,000 American women volunteered as nurses, telephone operators, signalers, typists, and interpreters in France. Women were not given jobs in combat, but they braved gunfire at the front lines as nurses and ambulance drivers. One female driver described her World War I experiences:

❝We had our first air-raid work last night. I was the night driver on duty … Some bombs fell very near just as I got to the [hospital] … when shrapnel [metal fragments] whizzed past my head and there was a tremendous crash close beside … Then an ambulance call came and I tore off.❞
—Mrs. Guy Napier-Martin, quoted in *The Overseas War Record of the Winsor School, 1914–1919*

Other women, meanwhile, spoke out against U.S. participation in the war. Social reformer Jane Addams was against U.S. entry into the war. Jeannette Rankin of Montana, the first female member of Congress, was one of 50 House members to cast a vote against declaring war in 1917. "I want to stand by my country," she said, "but I cannot vote for war."

Labor and the War

Even with so many women joining the workforce, factories needed additional workers. New job opportunities encouraged Mexican Americans from the West and African Americans from the South to move to northern industrial cities.

Because labor was scarce, workers were in a good position to demand better wages and conditions. Union membership increased. More than 4 million unionized workers went on strike during the war. Because factory owners could not easily replace workers, they often agreed to demands.

President Wilson set up the **National War Labor Board** in April 1918. The board helped workers and management avoid strikes and reach agreements. The board settled more than 1,000 labor disputes. Its members were generally sympathetic to workers. They helped establish a minimum wage and limited work hours. They also required fair pay for women.

READING CHECK **Finding Main Ideas** How did war mobilization benefit American workers?

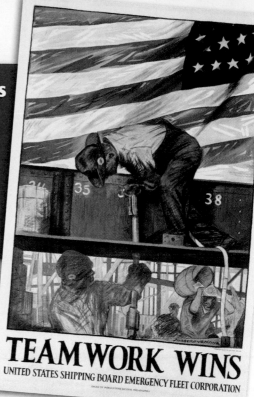

Patriotic Posters

Posters like this one encouraged American citizens to participate in the effort to provide weapons and food to soldiers fighting in World War I.

How does this poster inspire patriotism?

TEAMWORK WINS
UNITED STATES SHIPPING BOARD EMERGENCY FLEET CORPORATION

SUMMARY AND PREVIEW The war effort created new opportunities for women and other Americans. In the next section you will learn about what life was like for soldiers overseas.

Section 2 Assessment

go.hrw.com
Online Quiz

Reviewing Ideas, Terms, and People

1. **a. Explain** Why did the United States enter World War I?
   b. Evaluate Do you think the United States was right to stay neutral for so long? Why or why not?
2. **a. Explain** How did the United States prepare for war?
   b. Recall What was the purpose of the Committee on Public Information?
   c. Summarize How did the government exercise control over the economy during the war?
3. **a. Describe** How did women help the war effort abroad?
   b. Predict How do you think the end of the war affected labor unions? Explain your answer.

Critical Thinking

4. **Problem Solving** Review your notes on new laws and government programs during World War I.

Then copy the graphic organizer below and use it to identify the challenges the United States faced when mobilizing for World War I. List which new laws, government programs, and other changes responded to those challenges.

FOCUS ON SPEAKING

5. **Analyzing Wilson's Policies** Add to your list examples of causes of growing tension between Germany and the United States. What events led President Wilson to support war with Germany? Do you agree with his view? Why or why not?

Americans in World War I

What You Will Learn...

Main Ideas

1. American soldiers started to arrive in Europe in 1917.
2. The Americans helped the Allies win the war.
3. Germany agreed to an armistice after suffering heavy losses.

The Big Idea

American troops helped the Allies achieve victory in World War I.

Key Terms and People

American Expeditionary Force, *p. 150*
Communists, *p. 151*
armistice, *p. 154*

TAKING NOTES As you read, take notes on the achievements and victories of the American Expeditionary Force (AEF). Organize your notes in a chart like this one.

Achievements of the AEF

If **YOU** were there...

It is April 1918. You are marching into Paris with your army unit on your way to the front lines. Women and children throw flowers from windows and balconies as you pass through the city. You want to do whatever it takes to defend this city and its residents. You know that defeating Germany will be difficult and very dangerous.

Do you think American forces can help the Allies win the war?

BUILDING BACKGROUND Preparations for war helped make the United States a strong military power. By 1918 nearly 5 million Americans were serving in the army, navy, and marine corps. While this huge armed force was being trained, however, the fighting in Europe was going badly for the Allies. French and British leaders were eager for help from America.

American Soldiers Arrive

By the time U.S. troops started to arrive in Europe in 1917, the Allies were dangerously near defeat. German forces were advancing in France, once again driving toward Paris. The German navy was destroying Allied ships at sea. On the eastern front, the Russians were desperately struggling to hold back the Germans.

Joining the Fight

French and British generals called for immediate help on the front lines. They wanted the U.S. troops, known as the **American Expeditionary Force** (AEF), to join French and British units. But General John J. Pershing, leader of the American troops, insisted that the Americans join the fight as a separate force. He refused to have the AEF "scattered among the Allied forces where it will not be an American army at all."

Pershing also demanded that his troops be thoroughly trained for combat before rushing to the front lines. The AEF included many well-trained regular army and National Guard troops. But it also included a large number of inexperienced volunteers and draftees. Pershing gave the men three months of intense training in army discipline and trench warfare. He believed that taking the time to train his soldiers would help the Allies achieve victory.

Russia Leaves the War

While Pershing trained his troops, the Allies' position became even more dangerous. In November 1917 a group of Russians called the Bolsheviks overthrew the Russian government and seized power. The Bolsheviks were **Communists**—people who favor the equal distribution of wealth and the end of all forms of private property. The Bolsheviks thought workers should rule the country.

Led by Vladimir Lenin, the new Russian government faced a desperate situation. Around 8 million Russians had been killed or wounded during the war. Soldiers were deserting from the eastern front, and sailors were leaving naval bases. Food riots raged in the cities. The Russians could not keep fighting under these conditions. In March 1918 Russia signed the Treaty of Brest-Litovsk, a peace agreement with the Central Powers. A civil war then broke out in Russia between the Communists and forces loyal to the czar (ZAHR), Russia's emperor. The United States and other Allied countries sent aid to the czarist forces. Russia, however, one of the main Allied Powers, was out of World War I.

READING CHECK Drawing Inferences Why do you think General Pershing refused to put American troops in foreign units?

Winning the War

With Russia out of the fighting, German generals saw a chance to win the war. In the spring of 1918 Germany transferred many of its divisions of troops from the eastern front to the western front. Germany planned to smash the stalemate.

World War I U.S. Soldier

Soldiers carried a pack called a haversack, which held food, personal items, and extra socks.

The appearance of the Springfield rifles fooled the Germans into thinking the Americans had machine guns.

Gas masks were carried in a pouch around the neck.

A wool tunic was worn over a wool shirt and wool breeches.

A blanket could be carried at the bottom of the haversack with a special attachment.

Wool cloth strips called puttees were wrapped around the legs and tops of shoes for protection.

ANALYSIS SKILL ANALYZING VISUALS

How did clothing and supplies help a U.S. soldier in the battlefield?

The Final Battles

At the same time, American soldiers arrived. Even training had not prepared them for the realities of war. The troops lived on dried beef, hard biscuits, and canned emergency rations. The men shared the trenches with rats, lice, and sometimes the bodies of dead soldiers. A soldiers' song of the time described the situation:

❝ Sing me to sleep where bullets fall,
Let me forget the war and all;
Damp is my dug-out [trench], cold my feet,
Nothing but bully [canned meat] and biscuits to eat. ❞

—Quoted in *Great Push: An Episode of the Great War*, by Patrick MacGill

FOCUS ON NEW YORK CITY

Parades down Fifth Avenue in New York City became a common sight during World War I. Even before the United States entered the war, a "war preparedness" march took place. Ticker-tape parades continued during the war as a show of support for Red Cross volunteers and U.S. troops. After the war ended, returning soldiers were cheered along the way.

Interactive Map

World War I, 1914–1918

Legend:
- Allied Powers, 1916
- Central Powers, 1916
- Neutral Countries
- Allied Powers troop movements
- Central Powers troop movements
- British naval blockade
- Farthest Russian advance (1914)
- Farthest Central Powers advance
- Trench line, western front
- Armistice line, Nov. 11, 1918
- Allied victory
- Central Powers victory
- Undecided battle
- German submarine activity

0   200   400 Miles
0   200   400 Kilometers

ATLANTIC OCEAN

NORWAY

SWEDEN

FINLAND

Petrograd

GREAT BRITAIN

North Sea

DENMARK

Baltic Sea

RUSSIA

Lusitania sunk May 1915

London

Ypres Oct.–Nov. 1914 Apr.–May 1915

Berlin

Stebark Aug. 1914

EASTERN FRONT DEC. 1917

Sussex torpedoed March 1916

English Channel

NETHERLANDS

BELGIUM

GERMANY

LUXEMBOURG

Somme July–Nov. 1916

Paris

Battle of the Marne Sept. 1914, July 1918

Château-Thierry June 1918

Argonne Forest Sept.–Oct. 1918

Verdun Feb.–Dec. 1916

ALSACE-LORRAINE

WESTERN FRONT

SWITZERLAND

Vienna

AUSTRIA-HUNGARY

Budapest

Bay of Biscay

FRANCE

Kobarid Oct.–Nov. 1917

Adriatic Sea

BOSNIA and HERZEGOVINA

Sarajevo

SERBIA

ROMANIA

Black Sea

PORTUGAL

SPAIN

ITALY

Rome

MONTENEGRO

ALBANIA

BALKANS

BULGARIA

Bosporus

Constantinople

40°N

Mediterranean Sea

GREECE (Joined Allied Powers 1917)

Dardanelles

Gallipoli April 1915–Jan. 1916

OTTOMAN EMPIRE

GEOGRAPHY SKILLS   INTERPRETING MAPS

1. **Human-Environment Interaction** Why was the British naval blockade located where it was?
2. **Location** In which country were the most battles fought, according to this map?

On March 21, 1918, the Germans began blasting more than 6,000 heavy guns at Allied troops along the Somme River in northern France. German forces drove 40 miles into Allied lines before the advance stalled. Some 250,000 Germans had been killed or wounded. British and French casualties totaled 133,000.

The Germans then attacked farther south, advancing to the Marne River and pushing the French line back toward Paris. At this critical moment, General Pershing promised Allied commander Ferdinand Foch: "Infantry, artillery, aviation—all that we have . . . The American people would be proud to be engaged in the greatest battle of history." Two divisions of the AEF joined French forces.

The Germans were unprepared for the fresh energy and fighting skills of the Americans. The U.S. soldiers succeeded in stopping the German advance less than 50 miles from Paris. Then at Belleau Wood, the Allies attacked and gradually drove the Germans back.

German generals became desperate. In July 1918 they launched their final offensive— one last attempt to cross the Marne River. Terrible losses on the German side stopped the German offensive and protected Paris from invasion. Although they suffered about 12,000 casualties, American troops had helped force a major turning point in the war.

Driving the Germans Back

Now the Allies drove toward victory. There were more than 1 million U.S. troops in France, and they played a key role in the later battles of the war. In September 1918 Allied forces attacked and defeated the Germans at the town of Saint-Mihiel on the border of France and Germany. Along the Meuse River and in the Argonne Forest, near the French-Belgian border, American and Allied troops again attacked German forces.

Among the many heroes of these battles was a young man from Tennessee named Alvin York. In October 1918 York killed 25 German gunners and captured 132 prisoners. His heroism earned him fame and many awards, including the Congressional Medal of Honor. His life story even became the basis for a popular movie in 1941.

Also among the brave American troops were the African American soldiers of the 369th Infantry. Known as the Harlem Hellfighters, the 369th spent more time in combat than any other American unit. Its members were the first to reach the Rhine River on the German border. France awarded them the prized Croix de Guerre (Cross of War) medal for their bravery.

The Allies were also winning the war at sea. Allied war planners used a new **strategy** called the convoy system to protect their ships. This meant that destroyers capable of sinking U-boats escorted and protected groups of Allied merchant ships.

By November 1918, American soldiers were making rapid advances toward Germany. "For the first time the enemy lines were completely broken through," reported General Pershing.

ACADEMIC VOCABULARY
strategy a plan for fighting a battle or war

READING CHECK **Sequencing** Identify significant events leading to the turning of the tide in the war.

Armistice

At home and on the battlefield, Germans were tired of war. Food was so scarce in Germany that more than 800 German civilians were dying of starvation every day. In Germany and other nations of the Central Powers, food riots and strikes occurred. Germany was also running out of soldiers. In addition to those killed or wounded in 1918, one-quarter of Germany's fighting men had been captured by the Allies.

Germany's allies were also eager to end the war. Bulgaria and the Ottoman Empire quit the war in the fall of 1918. Austria-Hungary reached a peace agreement with the Allies on November 3. Seeing that his country was beaten, the German leader, Kaiser Wilhelm II, gave up his throne and fled to the Netherlands.

The 369th Infantry

The 369th Infantry spent 191 days in combat, longer than any other American force sent to Europe during World War I. Its members aided French forces at Château-Thierry and Belleau Wood, receiving the Croix de Guerre for their bravery. The "Harlem Hellfighters" became famous throughout Europe and America for their valor.

The Croix de Guerre was created by France in 1915 to reward bravery by members of the Allied armed forces—French citizens and foreigners alike.

The Germans then agreed to a cease-fire. The Allies demanded that Germany pull back from all its conquered territory. They insisted that Germany destroy its aircraft, tanks, and big guns and surrender its U-boats. The Germans had no choice but to accept these demands to disarm. The **armistice**, or truce, went into effect on the 11th hour of the 11th day of the 11th month of 1918. "At eleven o'clock everything got so quiet that the silence was nearly unbearable," remembered an American soldier. Then the silence was broken with shouts like "I've lived through the war!"

READING CHECK **Analyzing** How did Allied troops break the stalemate with Germany?

SUMMARY AND PREVIEW America's entry into World War I helped the Allies achieve victory. In the next section, you will learn about the effort to work out a permanent peace agreement.

go.hrw.com
Online Quiz

Section 3 Assessment

Reviewing Ideas, Terms, and People

1. **a. Define** What was the **American Expeditionary Force**?
   b. Analyze How did the Russian Revolution change the course of the war?
   c. Evaluate Why did Russia leave the war?
2. **a. Analyze** How did U.S. troops make a difference in the final battles of the war?
   b. Recall How was the Second Battle of the Marne a turning point in the war?
3. **a. Describe** What was Germany required to surrender in the **armistice**?
   b. Interpret Were the terms of the armistice fair? Explain your answer.

Critical Thinking

4. **Categorizing** Review your notes on the victories of the American Expeditionary Force. Then copy the graphic organizer below and use it to list challenges the Allies faced from 1917 to 1918. List the Allies' achievements during the same time period.

Allied Challenges	
Allied Achievements	

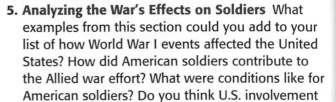

FOCUS ON SPEAKING

5. **Analyzing the War's Effects on Soldiers** What examples from this section could you add to your list of how World War I events affected the United States? How did American soldiers contribute to the Allied war effort? What were conditions like for American soldiers? Do you think U.S. involvement was justified?

Establishing Peace

If YOU were there...

Your older brother was drafted in 1917 and sent to fight on the western front in Europe. He has written home about the terrible conditions in the trenches and the horror of seeing men killed in battle. Now the war is over. You read in the newspaper that a peace treaty is being negotiated in Paris, France.

What do you hope the peace treaty will say?

BUILDING BACKGROUND After World War I, many questions about the future remained. Who would pay for the huge costs of the war? How should defeated powers' territories be divided? How could countries work together to avoid another world war? Leaders began discussing and debating these questions.

The Costs of War

While soldiers and civilians around the world celebrated the end of World War I in November 1918, the tragedy of war was never far from people's minds. When asked what the armistice meant, one British soldier simply said, "Time to bury the dead."

War Dead

The number of soldiers killed in World War I was beyond anything the world had ever experienced. About 5 million Allied soldiers and 3.5 million soldiers from the Central Powers died in combat. More than 20 million soldiers on both sides were wounded. The war devastated an entire generation of young men in many European nations. In France, for example, 90 percent of the healthy young men had served in World War I. More than 7 out of 10 of these men were killed or wounded. While the United States escaped this extreme level of devastation, American forces did suffer heavy losses. Some 116,000 U.S. troops died, and about 200,000 were wounded.

Financial Losses

Along with the shocking human losses, the war brought financial disaster to many parts of Europe. Factories and farms were left in ruins. "For mile after mile nothing was left," said one British visitor

What You Will Learn...

Main Ideas

1. The costs of war included millions of human lives as well as financial burdens.
2. President Woodrow Wilson and European leaders met to work out a peace agreement.
3. The U.S. Senate rejected the Treaty of Versailles.

The Big Idea

The United States and the victorious Allied Powers clashed over postwar plans.

Key Terms and People

League of Nations, *p. 157*
reparations, *p. 157*
Treaty of Versailles, *p. 158*
Henry Cabot Lodge, *p. 158*

TAKING NOTES As you read, take notes on the provisions of the Treaty of Versailles. You can use a graphic organizer like the one below to keep track of your notes.

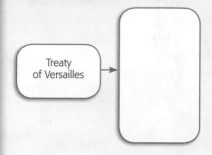

Treaty of Versailles →

THE IMPACT TODAY

Today vaccinations help prevent major outbreaks of the flu and other contagious diseases.

about the French countryside. "No building was habitable [livable] and no field fit for the plow." With farmers unable to raise crops, severe food shortages occurred.

The overall economic cost of the war was huge. Property worth $30 billion had been destroyed. The Allies had spent $145 billion on the war effort, and the Central Powers had spent $63 billion. France and Britain had borrowed large amounts of money to fight the war, and now they were deeply in debt to American banks. Germany was also in debt, and its people faced starvation.

The Influenza Epidemic

The world was in for another shock in 1918 when a worldwide epidemic of influenza, or flu, broke out. The virus was extremely contagious and deadly. Over the next two years, it spread around the world, killing approximately 30 million people—even more than the war itself.

The epidemic started in an army training camp in Kansas. Because the flu is transmitted through the air, it spread rapidly. American soldiers unknowingly spread the disease to other army camps, to American civilians, and eventually to soldiers and civilians in Europe. One American doctor said that seeing stacks of bodies at an army camp in Massachusetts "beats any sight they ever had in France after a battle." Half of the Americans who died during this period died from influenza.

The epidemic changed life everywhere in the United States. In Chicago, for example, the flu more than doubled the normal death rate in the fall of 1918. Many of those killed were young and strong. State and local governments took measures to prevent the spread of the disease. Kearney, Nebraska, imposed a quarantine, forbidding people who were ill from leaving their homes. Many cities banned public gatherings, including school classes. A man named Dan Tonkel remembered what life was like for children in his hometown of Goldsboro, North Carolina:

> "I felt like I was walking on eggshells. I was afraid to go out, to play with my playmates, my classmates, my neighbors …I remember I was actually afraid to breathe. People were afraid to talk to each other. It was like—don't breathe in my face, don't even look at me, because you might give me germs that will kill me."
>
> —Dan Tonkel, quoted in *Influenza 1918: The Worst Epidemic in American History,* by Lynette Lezzoni

Although there was no cure for the flu, people would try anything. One woman surrounded her daughter with raw onions. Another remembered, "We hung bags of . . . garlic about our necks. We smelled awful, but it was okay, because everyone smelled bad." By the time the influenza epidemic ended in 1919, it had killed 800,000 Americans at home and abroad.

READING CHECK Finding Main Ideas What made the influenza epidemic of 1918 so deadly?

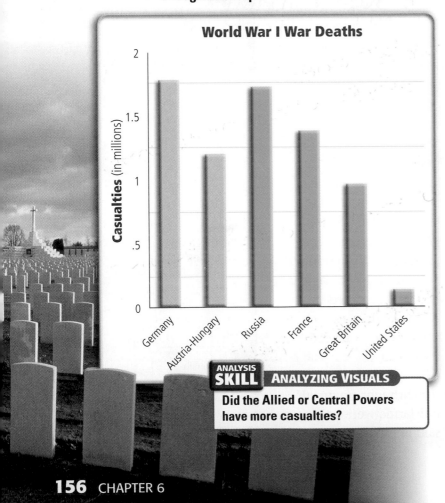

Memorials to soldiers killed in World War I, like this one at Somme, France, are located throughout Europe.

World War I War Deaths

Casualties (in millions)

Germany · Austria-Hungary · Russia · France · Great Britain · United States

ANALYSIS SKILL ANALYZING VISUALS

Did the Allied or Central Powers have more casualties?

The Peace Agreement

Even before the United States entered World War I, President Wilson began working to influence the postwar peace. In January 1917, he proposed a plan to end the war called "peace without victory." The plan was rejected by warring nations, however, and the United States soon entered the fighting. Now that American forces had helped win the war, Wilson was more determined than ever to shape the postwar peace. In January 1918, he outlined his vision for the postwar world in a plan known as the Fourteen Points.

Wilson's Fourteen Points

Wilson's Fourteen Points were a list of specific proposals for postwar peace. Several of the points would settle national border disputes. Others called for military cutbacks, proposed lower tariffs, and banned secret agreements between nations. Another proposed settlements for colonial peoples who wished to be independent. This reflected Wilson's strong belief in self-determination—the right of people to choose their own political status. The final point called for the creation of an international assembly of nations called the **League of Nations**. The League's mission would be to work to settle international disputes and encourage democracy.

European leaders disagreed with Wilson's vision for the peace settlement, wanting it to clearly punish Germany for its role in the war. They wanted to prevent Germany from ever again becoming a world power.

The Treaty of Versailles

President Wilson traveled to Europe to attend the Paris Peace Conference, which was held at the palace of Versailles (ver-SY), outside of Paris.

The leaders, called the Big Four—President Wilson, British prime minister David Lloyd George, French premier Georges Clemenceau, and Italian prime minister Vittorio Orlando—took control

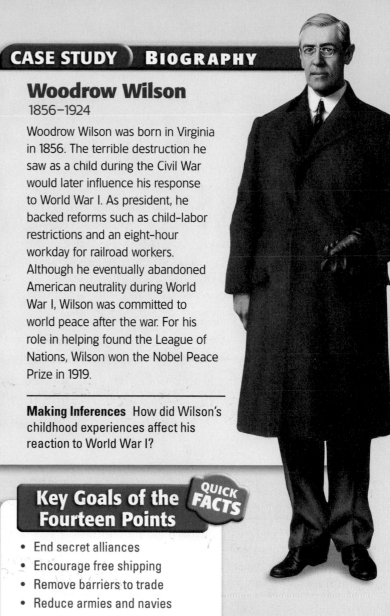

CASE STUDY) **BIOGRAPHY**

Woodrow Wilson
1856–1924

Woodrow Wilson was born in Virginia in 1856. The terrible destruction he saw as a child during the Civil War would later influence his response to World War I. As president, he backed reforms such as child-labor restrictions and an eight-hour workday for railroad workers. Although he eventually abandoned American neutrality during World War I, Wilson was committed to world peace after the war. For his role in helping found the League of Nations, Wilson won the Nobel Peace Prize in 1919.

Making Inferences How did Wilson's childhood experiences affect his reaction to World War I?

Key Goals of the Fourteen Points
QUICK FACTS

- End secret alliances
- Encourage free shipping
- Remove barriers to trade
- Reduce armies and navies
- Resolve colonial claims
- Support the right of people to choose their own government
- Settle border disputes
- Establish the League of Nations

of the conference. No representatives from Russia or the Central Powers attended.

Many Allied leaders defended their own country's interests and insisted on severe punishment for Germany. They wanted Germany to accept complete blame for the war and pay for the damage it had caused. These **reparations**, or payments for war damages, were set at $33 billion. France and the other Allies also wanted to take control of large parts of German territory.

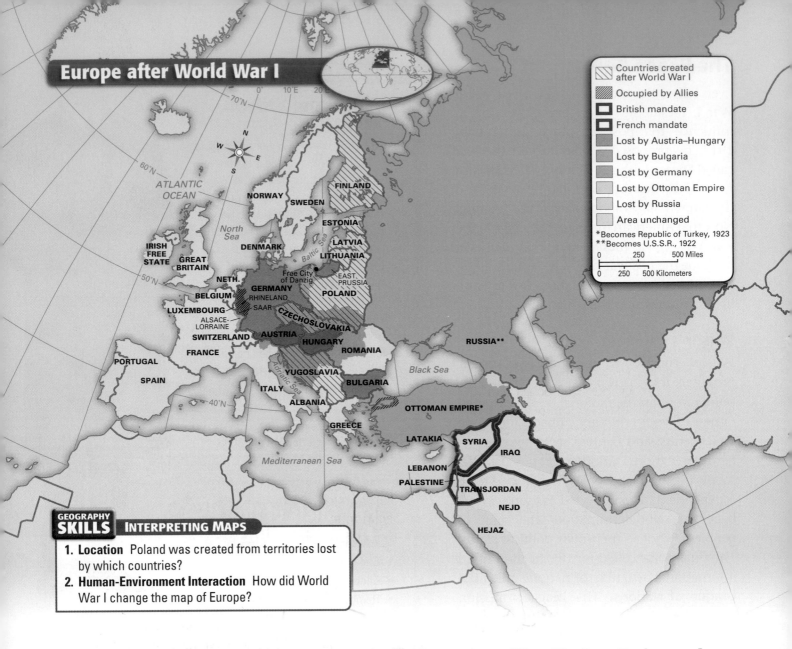

Europe after World War I

Legend:
- Countries created after World War I
- Occupied by Allies
- British mandate
- French mandate
- Lost by Austria–Hungary
- Lost by Bulgaria
- Lost by Germany
- Lost by Ottoman Empire
- Lost by Russia
- Area unchanged

*Becomes Republic of Turkey, 1923
**Becomes U.S.S.R., 1922

0   250   500 Miles
0   250   500 Kilometers

GEOGRAPHY SKILLS **INTERPRETING MAPS**

1. **Location** Poland was created from territories lost by which countries?
2. **Human-Environment Interaction** How did World War I change the map of Europe?

Wilson reluctantly agreed to the **Treaty of Versailles**, the peace settlement of World War I. In it, the League of Nations was established. Estonia, Finland, Latvia, Lithuania, Czechoslovakia, and Yugoslavia became independent countries. Poland was restored as a nation. The Central Powers turned over their colonies to the League of Nations, which assigned other European powers to rule. Though the Treaty of Versailles did not give Wilson everything he wanted, he hoped the League of Nations would solve remaining problems.

READING CHECK **Identifying Points of View**
Why did Allied leaders object to Wilson's plan?

Versailles Treaty Rejected

The U.S. Constitution states that treaties must be ratified by at least two-thirds of the members of the Senate. Wilson knew he was going to have a hard time convincing some senators to vote to ratify the Versailles Treaty. Republican senator **Henry Cabot Lodge** declared: "No peace that satisfied Germany in any degree can ever satisfy us." Lodge wanted the winners to set the terms of the peace.

Republicans insisted on changes to the treaty before they would ratify it. Their main objection was the League of Nations' power to use military force. They were worried that as a member of the League, the United States could be forced to send troops to war based on decisions made by the League of Nations. This, they argued, conflicted with Congress's constitutional power to declare war.

Wilson refused to compromise. He insisted that the treaty be ratified exactly as it was written. He traveled around the country, trying to convince the public to pressure Republican senators to vote for the treaty. Before he completed his tour, however, Wilson was weakened by a stroke.

Lodge announced that he was prepared to accept most of the treaty, though he still wanted to limit U.S. military commitment to the League of Nations. Wilson demanded that Democrats in the Senate refuse to change the treaty. When the vote was taken on November 19, 1919, neither the Democrats nor the Republicans would compromise. The Treaty of Versailles was defeated in the Senate.

It was a bitter disappointment for President Wilson. The United States signed separate peace treaties with Austria, Hungary, and Germany and never joined the League of Nations.

Causes and Effects of World War I

QUICK FACTS

Causes
- Nationalism
- Militarism
- Competition for territory
- Alliance system in Europe

Effects
- U.S. entry into the war in 1917
- Millions of deaths and wide-spread destruction in Europe
- Treaty of Versailles
- Creation of several new nations
- League of Nations

READING CHECK Supporting a Point of View
Do you think Wilson should have compromised with Republicans in the Senate on the Treaty of Versailles? Why or why not?

SUMMARY AND PREVIEW World War I changed the world map and affected the lives of millions. In the next chapter you will learn about American social, political, and economic conditions after the war.

Section 4 Assessment

go.hrw.com
Online Quiz

Reviewing Ideas, Terms, and People

1. **a. Recall** Approximately how many soldiers were killed or wounded in World War I?
   b. Draw Conclusions How did the war affect the European economy?
   c. Summarize How did Americans try to fight the influenza epidemic of 1918?
2. **a. Define** What was the **League of Nations**?
   b. Explain How did the **Treaty of Versailles** change the map of Europe?
   c. Elaborate Which countries did not attend the Paris Peace Conference? How do you think this affected the outcome?
3. **a. Identify** Who was **Henry Cabot Lodge**?
   b. Predict How might Wilson have ensured that the U.S. Senate would ratify the Treaty of Versailles?

Critical Thinking

4. **Identifying Points of View** Review your notes on the Treaty of Versailles. Then copy the graphic organizer below and use it to compare the positions of Woodrow Wilson, Allied leaders, and Senate Republicans. Fill in the results of each person's or group's goals.

	Goals	Results
Woodrow Wilson		
Allied Leaders		
Senate Republicans		

FOCUS ON SPEAKING

5. **Analyzing the Peace** Add to your list ways the United States was affected by World War I. How many American lives were lost? What were the results of the war? Do you think U.S. involvement in the war could have been avoided? Should the United States have joined the League of Nations?

Social Studies Skills

Analysis   Critical Thinking   Civic Participation   Study

Using Visual Resources

Define the Skill

A major part of history is understanding the events and ideas of the past. Visual resources are often good sources of information about the past. Visual resources include paintings, drawings, cartoons, posters, and photographs. The symbols and images in these resources tell us about the ideas and values of a time period. They often provide different information and points of view than do written documents.

Learn the Skill

Visual resources can have special purposes. For example, the poster above was produced by the U.S. government to inspire patriotism and encourage support for the war effort. It uses symbols and images to suggest that all Americans can contribute to the war effort.

You know from reading the chapter that conserving food to provide supplies for troops was an important part of the war effort. This poster encourages Americans to can fruits and vegetables. The pictures show canned tomatoes and peas in glass jars.

The poster also shows the German kaiser in a jar. He cannot reach his sword, which is outside the jar. He is helpless. This suggests that, by canning fruit and vegetables, Americans can help defeat the German leader.

Practice the Skill

Study the World War I poster below. Like the poster above, it was produced by the U.S. government to encourage support for the war effort. Write a paragraph describing the poster. Your paragraph should include the specific purpose of the poster, the symbols it uses, and whether it conveys its message effectively. You can use the text above as a model.

Chapter Review

Visual Summary

QUICK FACTS

Use the visual summary below to help you review the main ideas of the chapter.

The assassination of Archduke Francis Ferdinand threw Europe into a state of war.

Brutal fighting took place across Europe.

President Wilson thought a League of Nations would prevent future wars.

Reviewing Vocabulary, Terms, and People

Identify the descriptions below with the correct term or person from the chapter.

1. International assembly of nations designed to settle international disputes and encourage democracy

2. Strategy of defending a position by fighting from the protection of deep ditches

3. American fighting force trained and led by General John J. Pershing

4. Law that required men between the ages of 21 and 30 to register to be drafted into the armed forces

5. Senate leader who opposed the Treaty of Versailles

6. Truce between warring nations

7. Telegram from the German foreign minister proposing an alliance between Germany and Mexico against the United States

Comprehension and Critical Thinking

SECTION 1 *(Pages 140–144)*

8. **a. Identify** What event sparked World War I?

   b. Explain How did tensions in Europe lead to war?

   c. Draw Conclusions Why did the war in Europe become a stalemate?

SECTION 2 *(Pages 145–149)*

9. **a. Recall** What happened to the *Lusitania*? How did the American public react?

   b. Analyze How did the country's mobilization for war affect American women?

   c. Evaluate Do you think U.S. efforts to prepare for war were successful? Why or why not?

10. a. Define How did the American Expeditionary Force prepare for war?

b. Contrast How was the Second Battle of the Marne different from the First Battle of the Marne?

c. Draw Conclusions Do you think the Allies would have won World War I without American help? Explain your answer.

SECTION 4 *(Pages 155–159)*

11. a. Recall Which nations' leaders dominated the Paris Peace Conference?

b. Summarize What were the main ideas of Wilson's Fourteen Points?

c. Predict How effective do you think the League of Nations was? Why?

Using the Internet go.hrw.com

12. Activity: Researching the Technology of War
Many new technologies were introduced in World War I. The introduction of new weapons, like poison gas and machine guns, and combat vehicles, such as tanks and aircraft, made this war deadlier than any previous one. Enter the activity keyword. Research new battlefield technologies in World War I. Then write three journal entries from the point of view of a soldier in the trenches. Your entries should describe what the soldier who experienced these technologies and inventions for the first time saw, felt, and thought. Remember to use facts from your research in your journal entries.

Reviewing Themes

13. Economics How did World War I affect the economy of the United States?

14. Politics What lasting political changes were brought about by World War I?

Social Studies Skills

Using Visual Resources *Use the Social Studies Skills taught in this chapter to answer the question below.*

15. What parts of the U.S. war effort are shown in this poster?

Reading Skills

Recognizing Fallacies in Reasoning *Use the Reading Skills taught in this chapter to answer the question about the reading selection below.*

> The number of soldiers killed in World War I was beyond anything the world had ever experienced. About 5 million Allied soldiers and 3.5 million soldiers from the Central Powers died in combat. More than 20 million soldiers on both sides were wounded. *(p. 155)*

16. Which of the following is an example of a false conclusion drawn from the selection above?

a. More soldiers were killed in World War I than in any war up to that point.

b. World War I devastated the European population.

c. Europe would never recover from World War I.

d. The number of soldiers wounded was more than two times the number of soldiers killed.

FOCUS ON SPEAKING

17. Presenting Your Persuasive Speech
Review your notes and form an opinion on whether the United States should have entered World War I. You will have about five minutes to present your point of view. Use note cards to organize your ideas. Begin by writing a one-sentence introduction clearly stating your opinion. Then write several sentences with details and examples from the chapter that support your point of view. Conclude your speech with a sentence that summarizes your ideas. Practice your speech and then present it to the class.

Grade 8 Intermediate-Level Test Preparation

Directions (1–7): For each statement or question, write on the separate answer sheet the *number* of the word or expression that, of those given, best completes the statement or answers the question.

1 Which of the following was made up of Germany, Austria-Hungary, the Ottoman Empire, and Bulgaria?

(1) Central Powers

(2) Allied Powers

(3) League of Nations

(4) Big Four

2 Which of the following was an effect of the Communist takeover of the Russian government.

(1) The United States decided to join the Allies.

(2) The Germans began an offensive at the Marne River.

(3) Lenin received aid from the Allies.

(4) The Russians signed a peace agreement with the Central Powers.

3 During the war, many African Americans

(1) gained equal rights because of their military service.

(2) served in segregated units in the military.

(3) were removed from jobs in war industries and the military.

(4) volunteered to serve in the military without pay.

4 One reason the United States entered World War I was Germany's violation of

(1) the Treaty of Versailles.

(2) the Zimmermann Note.

(3) the *Sussex* pledge.

(4) Wilson's Fourteen Points.

5 A major opponent of the Treaty of Versailles was

(1) Otto von Bismarck.

(2) Woodrow Wilson.

(3) Henry Cabot Lodge.

(4) John J. Pershing.

6 Which of the following technologies was important to warfare at sea during World War I?

(1) U-boats

(2) bayonets

(3) ironclads

(4) poison gas

7 As the United States prepared for war, the government passed laws limiting some freedoms. These laws included:

(1) the Minutemen Act of 1917

(2) the Anti-Communist Act of 1918

(3) the Selective Service Act of 1917

(4) the Sedition Act of 1918

Base your answer to question 8 on the text below and on your knowledge of social studies.

*"*Adequate guarantees given and taken that national armaments [weapons] will be reduced to the lowest point consistent with domestic safety.*"*

—Woodrow Wilson, Fourteen Points

8 Constructed-Response Question Why do you think Wilson wanted to reduce the amount of weapons in nations around the world?

Reform and Change

Part A: Short-Answer Questions

Directions: Read and examine the following documents. Then, on a separate sheet of paper, answer the questions using complete sentences.

DOCUMENT 1

Many people read Jacob Riis's book about tenement life, *How the Other Half Lives*. One reason the book was so successful was its use of pictures, which let people see life in New York City slums for themselves. Here is one of Riis's photos.

1a. How does the photograph immediately communicate to the viewer that the boy has a difficult life?

1b. How does Riis position the people in the picture to make his point stronger?

DOCUMENT 2

Slavery had been abolished since 1862, but African Americans were still fighting to be treated fairly. W. E. B. Du Bois spoke out against discrimination and said that African Americans would make no social, political, or economic progress unless American society changed the way it thought about race.

> Is it possible, and probable, that nine millions of men can make effective progress in economic lines if they are deprived of political rights, made a servile caste, [lower social rank] and allowed only the most meager chance for developing their exceptional men? If history and reason give any distinct answer to these questions, it is an emphatic No.
>
> —W. E. B. Du Bois

2a. According to Du Bois, what four things are African Americans being denied?

2b. What is the tone of this statement?

DOCUMENT 3

John Muir was an explorer, writer, and conservationist who urged President Theodore Roosevelt to set aside land that would not be developed. Muir also established the Sierra Club. The following statement by Muir helps explain why he thought nature was so important.

> Thousands of tired, nerve-shaken, over-civilized people are beginning to find out that going to the mountains is going home; that wildness is a necessity; and that mountain parks and reservations are useful not only as fountains of timber and irrigating rivers, but as fountains of life.
>
> —**John Muir,** *Our National Parks*

3a. To what does Muir compare going to the mountains?

_____

3b. What does Muir mean when he says that people are "nerve-shaken" and "over-civilized"?

_____

DOCUMENT 4

The United States was able to stay neutral for most of World War I, but incidents like the sinking of the *Lusitania* pushed the country closer to entering the war. After the ship sank, pictures like this one made it all the more real for many Americans.

4a. What element on the right side of the picture makes it more dramatic?

_____

4b. How does the artist use the size of ship and the ocean to affect the viewer?

_____

Part B: Essay

Historical Context: The documents on these two pages are from the early part of the 20th century. For the United States, this was a period of reform at home and a time when the country was redefining its place in the world.

TASK: Using information from the four documents and your knowledge of U.S. history, write an essay in which you:

- discuss the reforms and changes of the early 20th century.
- identify leaders of the reform movement and their actions.

Boom Times and Challenges

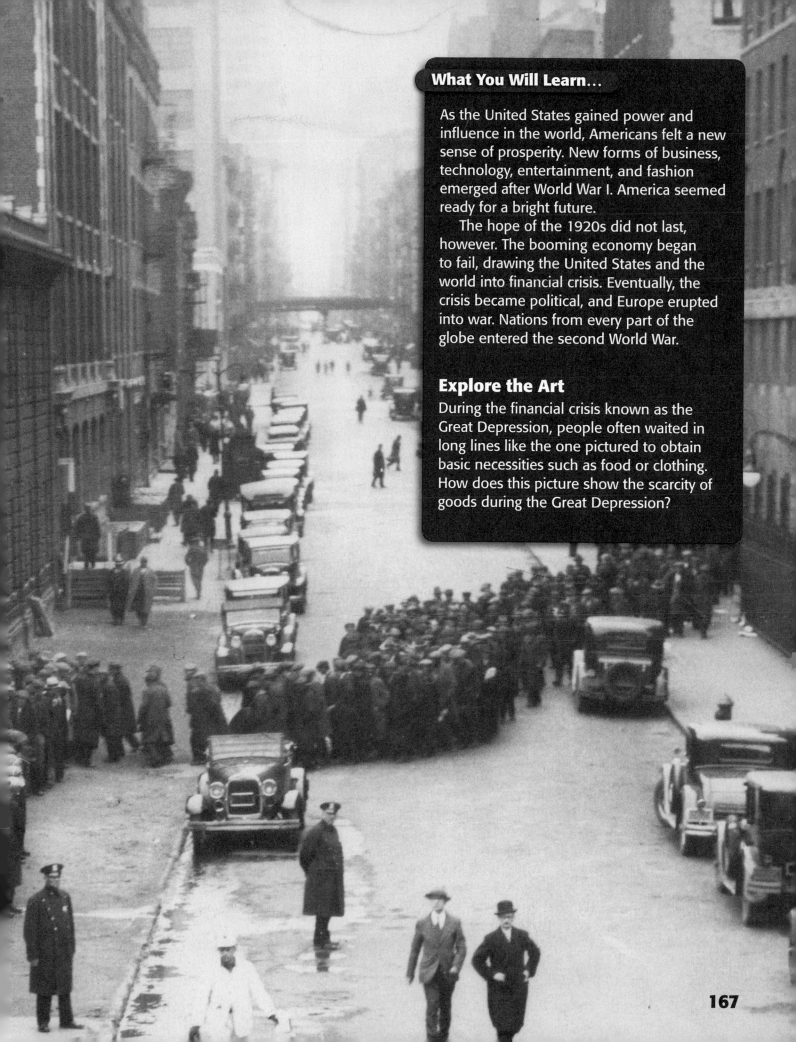

What You Will Learn…

As the United States gained power and influence in the world, Americans felt a new sense of prosperity. New forms of business, technology, entertainment, and fashion emerged after World War I. America seemed ready for a bright future.

The hope of the 1920s did not last, however. The booming economy began to fail, drawing the United States and the world into financial crisis. Eventually, the crisis became political, and Europe erupted into war. Nations from every part of the globe entered the second World War.

Explore the Art

During the financial crisis known as the Great Depression, people often waited in long lines like the one pictured to obtain basic necessities such as food or clothing. How does this picture show the scarcity of goods during the Great Depression?

The Roaring Twenties

FOCUS QUESTION

How does a nation respond to economic changes?

FOCUS ON WRITING

Radio Advertisement Radio stations began to air regular broadcasts in the 1920s. Radios linked Americans from coast to coast, allowing them to hear the same programs—and the same advertisements. In the 1920s Americans with means had new choices in entertainment, travel, fashion, and convenience. In this chapter, you will read about these new choices. You will then write a radio advertisement for a new product or form of entertainment of the 1920s.

UNITED STATES
1920
Warren Harding wins the presidency in a landslide victory.

1920

WORLD
1920
The League of Nations is established.

HOLT

History's Impact
▶ **video series**
Watch the video to understand the impact of younger generations on national culture.

What You Will Learn...

In this chapter you will learn about the ways that American life changed in the decade following World War I. With a booming economy, many people had money to spend on exciting new forms of entertainment. People flocked to bustling city centers like New York City's Times Square, shown in this painting.

NY

1923
Yankee Stadium opens, with Babe Ruth hitting a three-run home run in the first game there.

197 Native Americans are granted the right of U.S. citizenship.

1926 Ernest Hemingway publishes *The Sun Also Rises*.

THE SUN ALSO RISES

ERNEST HEMINGWAY

1929
Construction begins on the Empire State Building.

1922 **197** **1926** **1928** **1930**

1922 The tomb of King Tutankhamen is discovered.

197 Joseph Stalin becomes dictator of Communist Russia.

1926 Prince Hirohito becomes emperor of Japan.

1928 Alexander Fleming discovers penicillin.

169

Reading Social Studies

by Kylene Beers

| Economics | Geography | Politics | Society and Culture | Science and Technology |

Focus on Themes In this chapter, you will learn about the decade of the 1920s, a period called the Roaring Twenties. During this time, many in **society** thought that the Great War would be the last major war and that the future was bright. Also during this time, **science and technology** made leaps forward that would make life easier for millions of Americans.

Synthesizing Information

Focus on Reading Learning about history means synthesizing, or combining, many different sources about the past. When you read this textbook, you are reading a synthesis of other sources, accounts, and ideas about history.

Synthesizing Once you have identified the subject you are studying, you should try to read as many different accounts of the story as you can. Be sure to investigate the author of a source to learn what his or her goals might be. Compare and contrast the different sources and evaluate which ones you believe. Finally, use all the various stories you have read to form your own interpretation of what happened in history.

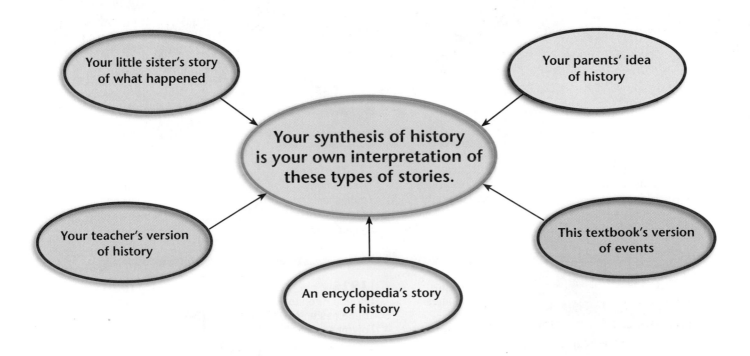

Your little sister's story of what happened

Your parents' idea of history

Your synthesis of history is your own interpretation of these types of stories.

Your teacher's version of history

This textbook's version of events

An encyclopedia's story of history

You Try It!

Read these varying accounts of the assassination of Archduke Francis Ferdinand and his wife, Sophie. Then write your own version of the story.

"Two bullets fired on a Sarajevo street on a sunny June morning in 1914 set in motion a series of events that shaped the world we live in today. World War One, World War Two, the Cold War and its conclusion all trace their origins to the gunshots that interrupted that summer day."

—Anonymous

"As the car came abreast he stepped forward from the curb, drew his automatic pistol from his coat and fired two shots. The first struck the wife of the Archduke, the Archduchess Sofia, in the abdomen . . . She died instantly. The second bullet struck the Archduke close to the heart. He uttered only one word, 'Sofia'—a call to his stricken wife. Then his head fell back and he collapsed. He died almost instantly."

—conspirator Borijove Jevtic

"As I was pulling out my handkerchief to wipe the blood away from his mouth, the duchess cried out to him, 'In Heaven's name, what has happened to you?' At that she slid off the seat and lay on the floor of the car ... I had no idea that she too was hit and thought she had simply fainted with fright. Then I heard His Imperial Highness say, "Sopherl, Sopherl, don't die. Stay alive for the children!"

—guard Count Franz von Harrach,
quoted in "Assassination of an Archduke," *Eyewitness to History*

1. What differences do you notice between accounts?

2. Why might these different authors have a different view of the assassination?

3. How can you tell what each author's viewpoint is?

4. Write your own version of what might have happened. Use details that you believe from the sources above.

As you read **Chapter 7,** notice any differing views from different sources.

Boom Times

What You Will Learn...

Main Ideas

1. President Harding promised a return to peace and prosperity.
2. Calvin Coolidge supported a probusiness agenda.
3. American business boomed in the 1920s.
4. In 1928 Americans elected Herbert Hoover, hoping he would help good financial times continue.

The Big Idea

American industries boomed in the 1920s, changing many Americans' way of life.

Key Terms and People

Warren G. Harding, *p. 172*
Calvin Coolidge, *p. 172*
Teapot Dome scandal, *p. 173*
Kellogg-Briand Pact, *p. 174*
Model T, *p. 175*
moving assembly line, *p. 175*
Herbert Hoover, *p. 177*

TAKING NOTES As you read, take notes on the presidents of the 1920s. Record your notes in a chart like this one.

President	Year Elected	Political Party

If YOU were there...

You have been working in a car factory for years, and now you have finally bought a car of your own—a shiny new 1920 Ford Model T. As you set out on your first drive, the car rattles and bounces over unpaved roads that were designed for horse-and-buggy travel. But you don't mind the rough ride. You now have the freedom to drive anywhere you want to go!

How will owning a car change your life?

BUILDING BACKGROUND The American economy boomed during World War I, as industries raced to produce weapons and supplies for the Allied armies. With more than 4 million men serving in the armed forces, there was a shortage of workers in American factories, and many people found jobs. When the war ended, however, conditions changed quickly, and the economy faced a difficult adjustment.

Return to Peace and Prosperity

The end of World War I had an immediate impact on the American economy. Because the government no longer needed war supplies, it canceled billions of dollars' worth of contracts with American factories. This meant that factories cut back on production at the very moment that millions of soldiers left the military and began looking for jobs. The result was a sharp rise in unemployment. Meanwhile, many people who did have jobs rushed to buy products they could not buy during the war. This caused prices to soar. Wages could not keep up with the rising prices, and thus workers could no longer afford to buy the goods they needed and wanted. Many went on strike for higher wages—more than 4 million in 1919 alone.

As the 1920 presidential election approached, the economic difficulties were bad news for the party in power, Woodrow Wilson's Democratic Party. Many voters blamed the Democrats for the hard times. Sensing the public's anger, the Republicans looked for a candidate who would offer new hope for American voters. They chose **Warren G. Harding**, a senator from Ohio. Harding picked Governor **Calvin Coolidge** of Massachusetts as his running mate.

Primary Source

POLITICAL CARTOON
Teapot Dome

During the Teapot Dome scandal, people began to question the judgment and honesty of government leaders. This cartoon, called "Juggernaut," was published in 1924 to show how harmful the scandal had been. A juggernaut is an indestructible force that crushes everything in its path.

How do the images in the cartoon illustrate the destructive force of the scandal?

ANALYSIS SKILL **ANALYZING PRIMARY SOURCES**

Why do you think the artist called this cartoon "Juggernaut"?

Harding based his campaign strategy on a promise to return the country to stability and prosperity, what he called "normalcy." His conservative policies contrasted with the reform-minded policies of the Progressive Era. Harding summed up his ideas in a campaign speech:

" America's present need is not heroics, but healing; not nostrums [uncertain cures] but normalcy [normal times]; not revolution, but restoration. "

—Warren G. Harding, 1920

Democrats believed there was still support for Wilson's ideas for reform. They ran Ohio governor James M. Cox for president and New York's Franklin D. Roosevelt for vice president. But Harding's promise of a return to normalcy captured the public's mood in 1920. Harding won a landslide victory with about 60 percent of the popular vote.

Harding worked quickly to help strengthen the economy. He put together a cabinet of experts who believed in reducing money owed by the government and limiting government involvement in the economy. Secretary of the Treasury Andrew Mellon pushed for tax cuts for wealthy Americans. Mellon believed that this policy would give the wealthy an **incentive** to invest in new businesses and create new jobs for other Americans. Mellon's opponents called

this idea the trickle-down theory, arguing that money would only "trickle down" in small drops to less-well-off Americans.

While Harding was president, businesses did in fact bounce back from the postwar recession. The economy created new, better-paying jobs, leading to an economic boom that lasted for most of the decade.

Harding faced problems in other areas, however. He had appointed many of his trusted friends to high positions. Some of these men used their positions to gain wealth through illegal means. "I have no trouble with my enemies," Harding once said. "But my . . . friends . . . keep me walking the floor nights."

What came to be known as the **Teapot Dome scandal** involved Secretary of the Interior Albert Fall, who accepted large sums of money and valuable gifts from private oil companies. In exchange, Fall allowed the companies to control government oil reserves in Elk Hills, California, and Teapot Dome, Wyoming. The U.S. Senate soon began investigating Fall, who was convicted of accepting bribes. He was the first cabinet member ever to be convicted of a crime for his actions while in office.

READING CHECK **Summarizing** What did Harding mean when he promised a return to normalcy?

ACADEMIC VOCABULARY
incentive something that encourages people to behave a certain way

Coolidge's Probusiness Administration

Just before details of the Teapot Dome scandal became public, President Harding died of a heart attack. In August 1923 Vice President Calvin Coolidge took charge. Coolidge had a strong reputation as an honest, serious, and trustworthy leader. These qualities helped him restore confidence in the government.

Coolidge acted quickly to fire all officials who had been involved in the bribery scandals of Harding's administration. This helped him win the presidential election in 1924. He received nearly twice as many votes as the Democratic candidate, John W. Davis.

Coolidge proved to be even more probusiness than Harding had been. Coolidge believed in a laissez-faire approach to business, which means little governmental regulation. He expanded the protectionist policies started under Harding. He also supported raising tariffs on foreign goods to decrease competition with domestic products. Despite higher tariffs, trade with other countries actually increased under Coolidge, mainly because many nations depended on trade with the United States to rebuild their economies after World War I.

Like the United States, European nations wanted a return to prosperity. Europeans also wanted to avoid another devastating war. In 1922 the United States, Japan, and several European powers signed treaties limiting the size of their naval forces and banning the use of poison gas. Another attempt at naval disarmament from 1924 failed, however, because France and Germany could not reach an agreement. In 1928 the United States and 14 other nations signed the **Kellogg-Briand Pact**, an agreement that outlawed war. Eventually 62 nations accepted the pact. There was no way to enforce the pact, however. One U.S. senator complained that the treaty would be "as effective to keep down war as a carpet would be to smother an earthquake." Still, it was a sign that most countries wanted to prevent another global conflict.

READING CHECK **Analyzing** How were Harding and Coolidge similar? How were they different?

THE IMPACT TODAY

Countries still try to prevent wars with international agreements. More than 180 nations have signed the Treaty on the Non-Proliferation of Nuclear Weapons, an agreement to prevent the spread of nuclear weapons.

The Model T Assembly Line

CONNECT TO SCIENCE AND TECHNOLOGY

Early assembly lines involved workers moving down a line of parts. On a moving assembly line, workers along the line specialize in one or two simple assembly tasks that they perform as parts move past them. The moving assembly line greatly increases the efficiency of mass production.

These workers are attaching the leather seat covers to the carriage and are stuffing them with horsehair.

Business Booms

The 1920s were years of rapid economic growth in the United States. Between 1921 and 1929, U.S. manufacturing nearly doubled. As jobs and wages increased, so did people's ability to buy new products. Some of these products changed the way Americans lived.

Ford's Model T

Today we think of cars as a major part of American life. In the early 1900s, though, cars were seen as luxury items that only the wealthy could afford. Henry Ford, an inventor and business leader from Detroit, helped to change this. Ford dreamed of building a car that most Americans could afford:

" I will build a motor car for the great multitude [most of the people]. It will be large enough for the family but small enough for the individual to run and care for. It …will be so low in price that no man making a good salary will be unable to own one. "

—Henry Ford, quoted in *Daily Life in the United States, 1920–1940,* by David E. Kyvig

Ford achieved his goal by building a sturdy and reliable car called the **Model T**, nicknamed the Tin Lizzie. In 1908 the Model T sold for $850. By 1925 it cost just $290. Ford was able to make his car affordable by cutting costs of production. For example, every car looked the same. The Model T came only in black for many years.

To decrease the time it took to make the cars, Ford also began using a **moving assembly line**. This system used conveyer belts to move parts and partly assembled cars from one group of workers to another. The workers stood in one place and did a specialized job.

The chassis, or frame, and the engine are assembled on separate lines. Workers on a third line then attach them.

The assembled chassis is then connected to the body of the car.

Workers use large amounts of leather to upholster the interiors of the carriages.

A foreman ensures that the line continues to run smoothly.

From the Collections of Henry Ford Museum and Greenfield Village

ANALYSIS SKILL **ANALYZING VISUALS**

How does the moving assembly line reduce the time it takes to build a car?

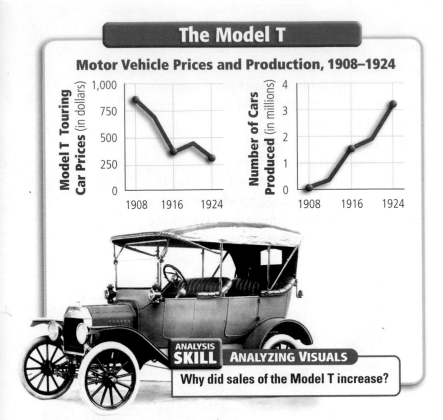

The Model T

Motor Vehicle Prices and Production, 1908–1924

Model T Touring Car Prices (in dollars): 1,000, 750, 500, 250, 0 — years 1908, 1916, 1924

Number of Cars Produced (in millions): 4, 3, 2, 1, 0 — years 1908, 1916, 1924

ANALYSIS SKILL — **ANALYZING VISUALS**

Why did sales of the Model T increase?

FOCUS ON NEW YORK

Though the country was experiencing unprecedented prosperity, not all groups benefited equally. There was high unemployment among African Americans, and many people were poor. Another drawback was the effect of industry on the environment—air pollution was becoming a problem in the 1920s and 1930s.

FOCUS ON READING

How is this paragraph an example of synthesized information?

In 1914 Ford raised the wages for his factory workers to $5 a day. This was good pay, compared with the $2 or $3 per day offered by many other factories. Ford believed the wage increase would keep his employees from quitting. He also lowered the workday to eight hours and employed people that other factories would not hire, such as African Americans and people with disabilities.

Even with the good wages, many workers had a hard time adjusting to the fast-paced and repetitive work on Ford's assembly line. One wife of an autoworker wrote to Ford saying, "My husband has come home and thrown himself down and won't eat his supper—so done out [tired]!...That $5 a day is a blessing—a bigger one than you know, but oh they earn it."

To help make his cars more affordable, Ford allowed customers to buy cars using an installment plan. Most people were used to saving up for years to buy items. Installment plans let people pay a small amount of the cost every month until the entire car was paid for. Ford's competitors also allowed customers to pay with installment plans. For a slightly higher price than the Model T, companies such as General Motors offered cars in a variety of colors and with more power.

The automobile changed the way Americans lived. They could now go on long drives or take jobs farther away from where they lived, leading to the growth of suburbs. Cars gave people a sense of freedom and adventure. As *Motor Car* magazine told drivers, "You are your master, the road is ahead . . . your freedom is complete."

Growing Industries

The rise of the automobile affected the entire American economy. Millions of Americans found work making steel for car bodies, rubber for tires, or glass for windows. To improve road safety, the government spent millions of dollars paving highways and building new bridges. People opened roadside businesses to serve travelers, such as gas stations, restaurants, and motels. The rising number of cars also created a demand for car repair shops and car insurance.

Following Ford's example, other manufacturers began using assembly lines and allowing customers to pay on installment plans. Many companies also took advantage of the increasing number of homes with electricity. By 1929 about 85 percent of all Americans living in towns or cities had electricity. Companies responded by building new electrical appliances designed to make household chores easier, such as washing machines, vacuum cleaners, and refrigerators.

As companies competed to sell these new goods, the advertising industry boomed. Companies advertised in magazines and on the radio to convince people that their lives would be improved if they owned a certain product. Many advertisers targeted women, hoping to convince them that they needed the newest labor-saving products. For example, one advertisement for an electric dishwasher called its product "the greatest gift of electricity to the modern housewife."

READING CHECK **Identifying Cause and Effect**
How did the automobile change society?

Hoover Elected

With the economy booming, public support for the Republican Party remained strong. When President Coolidge decided not to run for reelection in 1928, the party chose his secretary of commerce, **Herbert Hoover**, as its nominee. Hoover had gained national attention during World War I as head of the U.S. Food Administration. He organized the nation's food supply so more food could be sent to soldiers overseas. After the war, he headed the American Relief Administration, which sent food and supplies to the war-torn countries of Europe. The Democrats nominated New York governor Alfred E. Smith.

Hoover told voters that he was the right choice to maintain economic prosperity. Hoover boldly claimed that "we in America today are nearer to the final triumph over poverty than ever before in the history of any land."

Smith's campaign focused mainly on issues facing city dwellers. This concerned some rural voters. Smith's religious faith also became an issue. He was the first Catholic to run for president. His opponents stirred up fears that

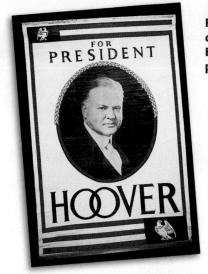

Republican Herbert Hoover defeated Democrat Alfred E. Smith in the 1928 presidential election.

Smith would be controlled by the pope and other church officials. In the end, Hoover won easily, gaining 58 percent of the popular vote.

READING CHECK Drawing Conclusions What helped Herbert Hoover win the presidency in 1928?

SUMMARY AND PREVIEW In this section you learned about politics and the economy in the 1920s. In the next section you will learn more about how society changed during the decade.

FOCUS ON NEW YORK CITY

After losing to Herbert Hoover in the 1928 presidential election, Al Smith became the president of Empire State, Inc., which built and operated the Empire State Building in New York City. Smith was also involved with the 1934 modernization of the Central Park Zoo.

go.hrw.com
Online Quiz

Section 1 Assessment

Reviewing Ideas, Terms, and People

1. **a. Describe** What was the result of the 1920 presidential election, and why?
   b. Summarize What did the **Teapot Dome scandal** reveal about **Warren G. Harding**'s administration?
2. **a. Identify** Who succeeded Harding as president, and what were his main policies?
   b. Analyze What was the main weakness of the **Kellogg-Briand Pact**?
3. **a. Recall** Why did American businesses grow during the 1920s?
   b. Explain Why were Model T prices low?
4. **a. Recall** Why was **Herbert Hoover** elected?
   b. Elaborate Who would you have voted for in the 1928 election? Explain your answer.

Critical Thinking

5. **Summarizing** Review your notes on the presidents from the 1920s. Then copy the graphic organizer below and expand on your notes by summarizing the main ideas or achievements of each president.

President	Ideas/Achievements

FOCUS ON WRITING

6. **Taking Notes on Consumer Goods** Make a list of new products people had access to in this decade, including cheaper automobiles and appliances for the home. Be sure to note how these products improved the lives of Americans. Use the information about advertising in this section to help you with ideas for your radio advertisement.

Life during the 1920s

What You Will Learn...

Main Ideas

1. In the 1920s many young people found new independence in a changing society.
2. Postwar tensions occasionally led to fear and violence.
3. Competing ideals caused conflict between Americans with traditional beliefs and those with modern views.
4. Following the war, minority groups organized to demand their civil rights.

The Big Idea

Americans faced new opportunities, challenges, and fears as major changes swept the country in the 1920s.

Key Terms and People

flappers, *p. 179*
Red Scare, *p. 180*
Twenty-first Amendment, *p. 181*
fundamentalism, *p. 182*
Scopes trial, *p. 182*
Great Migration, *p. 183*
Marcus Garvey, *p. 183*

TAKING NOTES As you read, look for changes that affected American life in the 1920s. Record your notes in a diagram like this one.

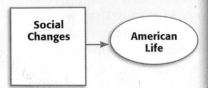

If **YOU** were there...

The year is 1925. You have just finished school and you are visiting a big city for the first time. You and your friends go to a club and watch young people dancing energetically to popular music. The women have short hair and wear makeup, trying to copy the glamorous style of movie stars. Some of your friends start talking about finding an apartment and looking for jobs in the city.

Would you want to move to a big city in 1925? Why?

BUILDING BACKGROUND The United States enjoyed nearly a decade of economic expansion during the 1920s. American society changed rapidly during this period. Although many people welcomed the new opportunities, others felt their traditional beliefs were being challenged. Conflicts between competing ideals and different groups of people ruffled the surface of America's peace and prosperity.

A Changing Society

The experience of living through World War I changed the way many young people saw the world around them. Young men returning from Europe had visited far-off countries and learned about other cultures. Many of them came home with a desire to continue expanding their horizons. The title of one popular song in 1919 asked, "How 'Ya Gonna Keep 'em Down on the Farm after They've Seen Paree [Paris]"? With labor saving devices available to more people, more nuclear families could afford to live apart from their extended families. The middle-class grew in size and importance, and spread their values to other Americans.

Many young people moved away from farms and small towns to cities, where many of them acquired new white-collar jobs in business offices. By 1920, for the first time in American history, more than half of the country's population lived in urban areas. Young people took advantage of the economic opportunities of the 1920s to gain independence. In the past most young people had lived and worked at home until they got married. Now more young adults were experiencing a time of freedom before settling down. A new youth culture developed, which included going to parties and dance clubs, listening to popular music, and driving fast cars.

For many young Americans, access to education was an important part of this new independence. High school attendance doubled during the decade. The percentage of students going on to college was higher in the United States than in any other country. This included women, who were attending college in higher numbers than ever before.

The number of women in the workforce continued to grow as well. Women with college degrees worked as nurses, teachers, librarians, and social workers. Women were also finding new opportunities in politics. In 1925 Nellie Tayloe Ross (Wyoming) and Miriam "Ma" Ferguson (Texas) became the first women to serve as governors in the United States. Three years later, there were 145 women serving in state legislatures. Five women had won terms in the U.S. House of Representatives.

Women were still discouraged from pursuing fields such as medicine, law, and architecture, however. By the end of the 1920s, less than 5 percent of the country's doctors, lawyers, and architects were women. The percentage was small—but it was beginning to rise.

Some young women found other ways to express their freedom. Young women known as **flappers** cut their hair short and wore makeup and short dresses, openly challenging traditional ideas of how women were supposed to behave. Many older Americans considered this behavior scandalous. One 1920s writer expressed her admiration for flappers, saying:

" I want my girl to do what she pleases, be what she pleases … I want [my daughter] to be a flapper, because flappers are brave. "
—Zelda Fitzgerald, quoted in *Zelda*, by Nancy Milford

Fashion magazines, Hollywood movies, and advertising helped promote these new images and ideas of youthful freedom.

READING CHECK **Generalizing** How did women in the 1920s express their independence?

Focus on Women

In 1923 suffrage leader Alice Paul introduced the Equal Rights Amendment to Congress, calling for equality of rights regardless of a person's gender. The U.S. Senate passed the amendment 49 years later, but it was never ratified by the states.

Bryn Mawr and other colleges provided education to women in new fields.

Bessie Coleman became the first African American woman to obtain her international pilot's license. She traveled the United States, performing stunts under the name "Brave Bessie."

Flappers challenged many of society's ideas about womanhood. They established new rules of speech, dress, and behavior.

ANALYSIS SKILL **ANALYZING VISUALS**

How do these images reflect new roles for women during the 1920s?

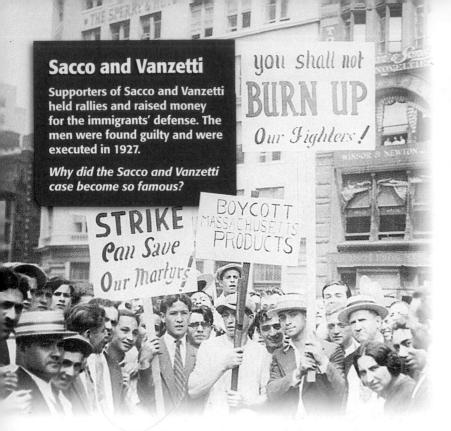

Sacco and Vanzetti

Supporters of Sacco and Vanzetti held rallies and raised money for the immigrants' defense. The men were found guilty and were executed in 1927.

Why did the Sacco and Vanzetti case become so famous?

Fear and Violence

Not all social changes during the 1920s were peaceful. You have read about the hard times that hit the U.S. economy after World War I—unemployment, inflation, and labor disputes that resulted in large strikes. These troubles worried many Americans. In this atmosphere, suspicion of foreigners and radicals, or people who believe in an extreme change in government, sometimes led to violence.

The Red Scare

After the Communists took power in Russia in 1917, many Americans began to fear Communist ideas. They worried that Communists would soon try to gain power in the United States. This fear increased when millions of American workers went on strike in 1919. Many Americans blamed Communists and radicals for the upheaval.

These attitudes led to a **Red Scare**, a time of fear of Communists, or Reds. The Red Scare began in April 1919, when U.S. postal workers found bombs hidden in several packages addressed to famous Americans. Officials never found out who sent the bombs, but they suspected members of the Communist Party.

In June a bomb exploded outside the home of Attorney General A. Mitchell Palmer. Palmer responded by organizing police raids to break up Communist and other groups. In what became known as the Palmer raids, government agents arrested thousands of suspected radicals, often without evidence. Palmer frightened the public by warning that radicals were planning a revolution.

The Red Scare led to one of the best-known criminal cases in American history. In 1920 police arrested Italian-born anarchists Nicola Sacco and Bartolomeo Vanzetti for the robbery and murder of a factory paymaster and his guard. (Anarchists are people opposed to organized government.) Though both men declared themselves innocent of the crime, Sacco and Vanzetti were found guilty. The American Civil Liberties Union (ACLU), founded in 1920 to defend people's civil rights, tried unsuccessfully to get the verdict overturned. Sacco and Vanzetti were convicted. They were executed in 1927.

Restricting Immigration

Some people thought the Sacco and Vanzetti case was influenced by a general fear of foreigners. Many recent immigrants were poor and did not speak English. Some Americans saw them as a threat to their jobs and culture. Immigrants "fill places that belong to the loyal wage-earning citizens of America," said Alabama senator James Thomas Heflin.

The government responded to these concerns with new laws. The Emergency Quota Act of 1921 limited the total number of immigrants allowed into the country. It also favored immigrants from western Europe. The Quota Act of the National Origins Act of 1924 banned immigration from East Asia entirely and further reduced the number of immigrants allowed to enter the country. These laws caused a dramatic drop in immigration to the United States.

READING CHECK **Drawing Conclusions** Why were new immigration laws passed in the 1920s?

Competing Ideals

Fear of radical ideas and foreigners was part of a larger clash over ideals and values in America. Differences were growing between older, rural traditions and the beliefs and practices of modern urban society. Americans had very different ideas about what was best for the country's future.

Prohibition

An issue that highlighted this conflict was prohibition. The Eighteenth Amendment—which outlawed the manufacture, sale, and transportation of alcoholic beverages—went into effect in 1920. Support for prohibition was strongest in rural areas, while opposition was strongest in cities.

Government officials found it nearly impossible to enforce prohibition. Congress passed the Volstead Act, which set fines and punishments for disobeying prohibition. Even respectable citizens, however, broke the law. Many people found ways to make alcohol at home using household products. Others bought alcohol at speakeasies, or illegal bars.

Organized criminals called bootleggers quickly seized control of the illegal alcohol business. They made their own alcohol or smuggled it in from Canada or Mexico. Gangsters were able to avoid arrest by bribing local police and politicians. Competition between gangs often led to violent fighting. In Chicago gangster Al "Scarface" Capone gained control of the alcohol trade by murdering his rivals. By 1927 Capone was earning more than $60 million a year from his illegal businesses.

By the end of the decade, the nation was weary of the effects of prohibition. The law had reduced alcohol consumption but had not stopped Americans from drinking. Prohibition had also created new ways for criminals to grow rich. Without government supervision of alcohol production, much of the alcohol consumed in speakeasies was more dangerous than what had been produced before prohibition. Many people came to believe that it would be better to have a legal alcohol trade that could be monitored by the government. In 1933 state and federal governments responded with the **Twenty-first Amendment**, which ended prohibition.

THE IMPACT TODAY

The Twenty-first Amendment made the manufacture and sale of alcohol legal again, but laws today still regulate drinking. The National Minimum Drinking Age Act of 1984 raised the minimum drinking age from 18 to 21 in every state.

Primary Source

PHOTOGRAPH
Prohibition

Agents of federal and state governments tried to enforce the Eighteenth Amendment against great odds. They usually destroyed any liquor that they found. This photograph shows an illegal barrel of beer being broken with an axe. More illegal beer and liquor would soon turn up, however. Faced with a lack of public support and an impossible task of enforcing the ban on alcohol, prohibition was repealed with the Twenty-first Amendment in 1933.

ANALYSIS SKILL **ANALYZING PRIMARY SOURCES**

Why was enforcing prohibition such a hard task?

Religious Ideals

ACADEMIC
VOCABULARY
traditional
customary, time-
honored

Youth culture of the 1920s and prohibition's failure concerned many religious leaders. They saw these changes as movements away from **traditional** values. This led to a Protestant religious movement known as **fundamentalism**—characterized by the belief in a literal, or word-for-word, interpretation of the Bible. Popular preachers like Aimee Semple McPherson used the radio and modern marketing tools to draw followers. Fundamentalism was especially strong in rural areas and small towns, where people often blamed society's problems on the culture of urban areas.

Many fundamentalists believed that modern scientific theories, such as Charles Darwin's theory of evolution, conflicted with the teachings of the Bible. Darwin's theory states that species evolve over time by adapting to their environment. To fundamentalists, this contradicted the biblical account of how the world was made. They opposed the teaching of evolution in public schools. Many cities and states passed laws to prevent the teaching of evolution.

In May 1925 a Dayton, Tennessee, high school science teacher named John T. Scopes was put on trial for teaching evolution in what became known as the **Scopes trial**. National interest in the event was heightened by the fact that famous Americans represented each side. Criminal attorney Clarence Darrow led the ACLU defense team. Three-time presidential candidate William Jennings Bryan assisted the prosecution.

Over live radio, Darrow and Bryan attacked each other's ideas. After more than a week on trial, Scopes was convicted and fined $100 for breaking the law. The state supreme court later overturned his conviction, but the debate over evolution continued.

READING CHECK **Evaluating** What cultural conflict did the Scopes trial represent?

Primary Source

POINTS OF VIEW
The Scopes Trial

Although the focus of the Scopes trial was whether or not John Scopes had broken the law, prosecution witness William Jennings Bryan saw the conflict as one between science and faith.

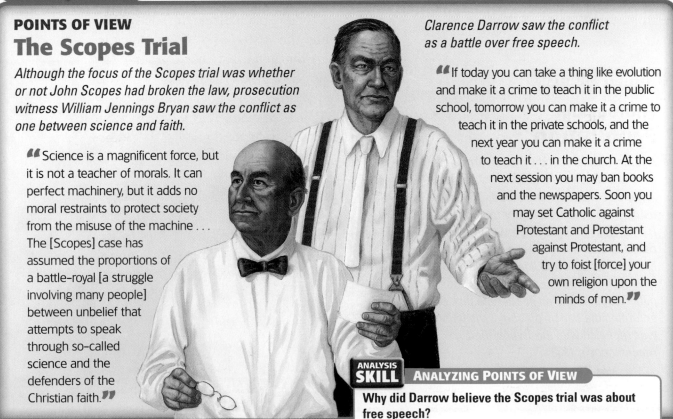

❝Science is a magnificent force, but it is not a teacher of morals. It can perfect machinery, but it adds no moral restraints to protect society from the misuse of the machine . . . The [Scopes] case has assumed the proportions of a battle-royal [a struggle involving many people] between unbelief that attempts to speak through so-called science and the defenders of the Christian faith.❞

Clarence Darrow saw the conflict as a battle over free speech.

❝If today you can take a thing like evolution and make it a crime to teach it in the public school, tomorrow you can make it a crime to teach it in the private schools, and the next year you can make it a crime to teach it . . . in the church. At the next session you may ban books and the newspapers. Soon you may set Catholic against Protestant and Protestant against Protestant, and try to foist [force] your own religion upon the minds of men.❞

ANALYSIS SKILL **ANALYZING POINTS OF VIEW**

Why did Darrow believe the Scopes trial was about free speech?

The Great Migration

CONNECT TO THE ARTS

From 1940 to 1941 artist Jacob Lawrence created a series of paintings that told the story of African Americans moving from the South to northern cities in search of jobs and equality. This is one of 60 paintings in the Migration Series. It shows African Americans about to begin their journey.

Where are the people in the painting going?

Minority Rights

During World War I large numbers of African Americans began leaving the South to take jobs in northern factories. This movement, called the **Great Migration**, continued during the economic boom of the 1920s. While African Americans found jobs in the North, they did not escape racism.

Racial Tensions

The economic recession that followed the war led to increased racial tensions. Many white laborers feared the competition for jobs. Several race riots broke out in 1919, including one in Chicago that left 38 dead.

Racial tensions and fear of foreigners helped give rise to a new form of the Ku Klux Klan, the racist group that had terrorized African Americans during Reconstruction. The new Klan harassed Catholics, Jews, and immigrants, as well as African Americans. It also worked against urbanization, women's rights, and modern technology. By the mid-1920s the Klan had become an influential force in American politics, with more than 5 million members. Its influence then began to decline as news of financial corruption became public.

Protecting Rights

People who were the targets of the Klan's hatred found new ways to protect their rights. In 1922, the NAACP began placing advertisements in newspapers that presented the harsh facts about the large number of lynchings taking place across the South.

During the 1910s and 1920s, **Marcus Garvey** encouraged black people around the world to express pride in their culture. Garvey argued that black people should establish economic independence by building their own businesses and communities. These ideas were the basis of a movement known as black nationalism.

Other groups also organized to fight prejudice. In 1929 Mexican American leaders met in Corpus Christi, Texas, to form the League of United Latin American Citizens (LULAC). The LULAC worked to end unfair treatment such as segregation in schools and voting restrictions.

Jews founded the Anti-Defamation League in 1913 to fight anti-Semitism. Hostility toward Jews, especially immigrants from Eastern Europe, became even stronger after World War I. Henry Ford, known for

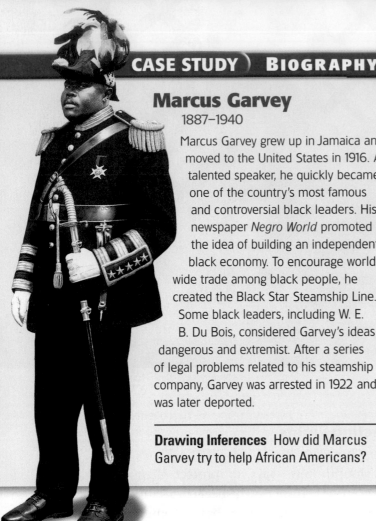

Marcus Garvey
1887–1940

Marcus Garvey grew up in Jamaica and moved to the United States in 1916. A talented speaker, he quickly became one of the country's most famous and controversial black leaders. His newspaper *Negro World* promoted the idea of building an independent black economy. To encourage world-wide trade among black people, he created the Black Star Steamship Line. Some black leaders, including W. E. B. Du Bois, considered Garvey's ideas dangerous and extremist. After a series of legal problems related to his steamship company, Garvey was arrested in 1922 and was later deported.

Drawing Inferences How did Marcus Garvey try to help African Americans?

his Model T, was also well known for his hatred of Jews. He blamed many of the world's problems on Jewish bankers.

Most Native Americans were not citizens of the United States. The fact that thousands of Native Americans had performed military service in World War I helped bring about change. In 1924 Congress passed the Indian Citizenship Act, granting citizenship to all Native Americans. However, the federal government also tried to buy or take back some reservation lands. Native Americans successfully organized to stop these attempts, which were part of a larger effort to encourage Indians to adopt the culture of white Americans.

READING CHECK **Finding Main Ideas** How did minorities react to discrimination in the 1920s?

SUMMARY AND PREVIEW Americans saw many conflicts as their culture changed. In the next section you will learn about entertainment and the arts in the 1920s.

go.hrw.com
Online Quiz

Section 2 Assessment

Reviewing Ideas, Terms, and People

1. **a. Recall** How did **flappers** express their freedom?
   b. Elaborate How were young people of the 1920s more independent than their parents?
2. **a. Identify** What caused the **Red Scare**? What was its result?
   b. Explain Describe the results of the immigration laws of the 1920s.
3. **a. Recall** What kinds of social conflicts developed during the 1920s?
   b. Describe What did the **Twenty-first Amendment** accomplish?
   c. Analyze How did **fundamentalism** influence the **Scopes trial**?
4. **a. Identify** How did minorities fight for their rights in the 1920s?
   b. Define What was the **Great Migration**?
   c. Draw Conclusions Why did **Marcus Garvey** call for black people to build their own businesses?

Critical Thinking

5. **Identifying Cause and Effect** Review your notes on social changes that took place in the 1920s. Then copy the graphic organizer below and use it to identify the causes and effects of several changes in American society.

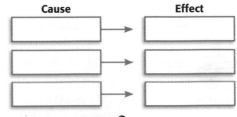

Cause		Effect
	→	
	→	
	→	

FOCUS ON WRITING

6. **Taking Notes on New Fashions** In the 1920s many women wore fashions that reflected their new independence. Look back at the example of flapper fashion on page 179. Think of how a radio advertisement could describe clothing like this to an audience that cannot see it.

The Jazz Age

If YOU were there...

The year is 1924, and the New York Giants are playing the Washington Senators in the World Series. You just bought your first radio, and you are listening to an announcer describe the tense action as the seventh and deciding game goes into extra innings. You used to have to wait to read about the games in the newspaper. Now you can follow your favorite team pitch by pitch!

What other forms of entertainment could the radio bring to you?

> **BUILDING BACKGROUND** You read earlier about the rise of mass culture in the United States in the late 1800s. Newspapers, department stores, and world's fairs allowed millions of Americans to share the same cultural activities. In the 1920s technologies such as radio broadcasts and movies helped the rise of mass culture continue.

A National Culture

On November 2, 1920, KDKA, the first commercial radio station, announced that Warren Harding had won the presidential election held that day. Just one year later, stations broadcast the action from the 1921 World Series. One newspaper writer predicted, "It might not be too long before farmers at the four corners of the Union may sit in their own houses and hear the president of the United States." Such an event seemed amazing to Americans in the early 1900s. But it quickly became a reality, as hundreds of radio stations began broadcasting all over the United States.

National radio networks, such as the National Broadcasting Company (NBC) and Columbia Broadcasting System (CBS), allowed people all over the country to listen to the same programs. People suddenly had access to music, news, weather reports, children's bedtime stories, sports broadcasts, and political speeches without leaving their homes. Business owners loved this technology because it allowed their advertisements to reach millions of listeners. Radio helped build a new national culture by allowing Americans everywhere to share common experiences.

What You Will Learn...

Main Ideas

1. Radio and movies linked the country in a national culture.
2. Jazz and blues music became popular nationwide.
3. Writers and artists introduced new styles and artistic ideas.

The Big Idea

Musicians, artists, actors, and writers contributed to American popular culture in the 1920s.

Key Terms and People

talkie, p. 186
Jazz Age, p. 187
Harlem Renaissance, p. 188
Langston Hughes, p. 188
Lost Generation, p. 188
expatriates, p. 188
Georgia O'Keeffe, p. 189

TAKING NOTES As you read, look for examples of popular culture in the 1920s. Record your notes in a diagram like this.

> **1920s Popular Culture**
> 1.
> 2.
> 3.
> 4.

THE IMPACT
TODAY

The Academy of Motion Picture Arts and Sciences has held the Oscar ceremony every year since 1929. It was first broadcast over the radio in 1930, and in 1953 the Academy Awards were first televised.

Movies also became a major national passion in the 1920s. Though early motion pictures had no sound, they opened a new world of exciting adventures for audiences. People packed theaters to see Westerns, romances, and stories about bootlegging gangsters. Movie fans were even more thrilled by the 1927 movie *The Jazz Singer*, in which actor Al Jolson shouted the line "You ain't heard nothin' yet!" This was the first **talkie**, or motion picture with sound.

The movies quickly became big business. By the end of the decade, Americans were buying 95 million movie tickets each week, an amazing figure considering that the U.S. population was only 123 million. Young movie fans copied hair and clothing styles of movie stars. Fans felt a personal connection to stars like Douglas Fairbanks, Charlie Chaplin, and Mary Pickford, who was known as America's Sweetheart. Few fans at the time realized that Pickford was also a smart businessperson. She was one of the highest paid actors in Hollywood and a founder of United Artists, one of the nation's most successful film companies.

Movie stars were not the only national heroes. Fans packed baseball stadiums to watch the great players of the 1920s, especially George Herman "Babe" Ruth. Ruth shattered home-run records, drawing thousands of new fans to the sport. Because baseball was segregated, African American players and business leaders started their own league. Negro League stars such as Satchel Paige and Josh Gibson are considered to be among the best baseball players in history.

Fans always loved to see athletes break records. In 1926 American swimmer Gertrude Ederle became the first woman to swim the English Channel between England and France, beating the men's world record by almost two hours.

Pilots also became national heroes in the 1920s. Charles Lindbergh dominated the national news in 1927 when he completed the first nonstop solo flight across the Atlantic Ocean, traveling from New York to Paris. A few years later, Amelia Earhart became the first woman to fly solo across the Atlantic.

New ideas like psychoanalysis became more popular. Developed by psychologist Sigmund Freud, psychoanalysis is a method for examining human behavior to find out why people behave the way they do.

READING CHECK **Summarizing** How did American culture change during the 1920s?

Time Line

Popular Culture of the 1920s

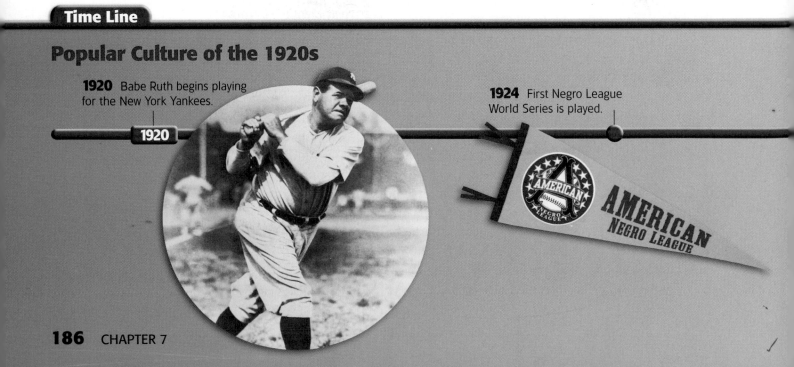

1920 Babe Ruth begins playing for the New York Yankees.

1920

1924 First Negro League World Series is played.

AMERICAN NEGRO LEAGUE

Popular Music

With a booming economy and exciting forms of entertainment, the 1920s became known as the Roaring Twenties. An explosion in the popularity of jazz music gave the decade another nickname—the **Jazz Age**.

Jazz developed in New Orleans, where African American musicians blended spirituals with European harmonies and West African rhythms. When blacks moved north during the Great Migration, they brought their music with them.

As with many new forms of popular culture, jazz sparked arguments between older and younger generations. "When my grandmother found out that I was playing jazz music . . . she told me that I had disgraced the family," remembered "Jelly Roll" Morton, an early jazz composer. But young Americans loved the music and the wild, fast-paced dances that went along with it. Dance crazes sweeping the nation included the Charleston, the Toddle, and the Shimmy. New magazines arose that taught dance steps to subscribers.

Jazz musicians such as Louis Armstrong experimented with various sounds and rhythms to create a new kind of music. Armstrong, who played the trumpet, was known for his solo numbers. His method of stepping out from the band to perform a solo was an **innovation** that is still copied by musicians today. Another major figure of the Jazz Age was conductor and composer Edward "Duke" Ellington. His "big band" sound blended many instruments together in songs such as "Take the A Train." Ellington described the exciting life of Jazz Age musicians in New York City:

> " A lot of guys liked to play so much that in spite of being on a regular job, they'd still hire out to work matinees, or breakfast dances . . . Nobody went to bed at nights and round three or four in the mornings you'd find everyone making the rounds bringing their horns with them. "
>
> — Duke Ellington, quoted in *Reminiscing in Tempo*, by Stuart Nicholson

Blues music, which came from the rural South of the Mississippi Delta, also gained national popularity in the 1920s. Blues began as an expression of the suffering of African Americans during slavery. One of the leading blues singers of the 1920s was Bessie Smith, nicknamed the Empress of the Blues. "She had music in her soul," said Louis Armstrong.

READING CHECK **Finding Main Ideas** Where did jazz originate? What musical styles influenced it?

ACADEMIC VOCABULARY

innovation a new idea or way of doing something

1925 F. Scott Fitzgerald's *The Great Gatsby* is published.

1925 Louis Armstrong begins recording with his band, the Hot Five.

1926 Gertrude Ederle becomes the first woman to swim across the English Channel.

1926 NBC, the first national radio network, begins broadcasting.

1927 Charles Lindbergh completes the first non-stop solo flight across the Atlantic Ocean.

1927 *The Jazz Singer*, the first full-length talkie, is released.

1928

ANALYSIS SKILL **READING TIME LINES**

Which events reflected people's interest in breaking records?

Writers and Artists

While musicians were creating new forms of music, writers and artists were also reshaping American culture. Many creative works of the 1920s are still admired today.

The Harlem Renaissance

Many of the African Americans who came north in the Great Migration built a thriving community in the Harlem neighborhood of New York City. This community became the center of the **Harlem Renaissance**, a period of African American artistic accomplishment.

Primary Source

POEM
"I, Too"

In one of his most celebrated poems, Langston Hughes expressed both pride in being African American and faith in the American dream.

"I, Too

    I, too, sing America.
    I am the darker brother.
    They send me to eat in the kitchen
    When company comes,
    But I laugh,
    And eat well,
    And grow strong.

    Tomorrow,
    I'll be at the table
    When company comes.
    Nobody'll dare
    Say to me,
    'Eat in the kitchen,'
    Then.

    Besides,
    They'll see how beautiful I am
    And be ashamed—
    I, too, am America."

ANALYSIS SKILL **ANALYZING PRIMARY SOURCES**

Analyzing Who do you think Hughes is referring to when he speaks of "they"?

Harlem Renaissance writers included **Langston Hughes** and Claude McKay. Hughes produced poems, plays, and novels about African American life. His works often incorporated African American slang and jazz rhythms. McKay was a poet and activist who spoke out against racial discrimination and called on African Americans to stand up against lynchings and other violence.

Another important writer of the Harlem Renaissance was Zora Neale Hurston. Her novels, such as *Their Eyes Were Watching God*, reflected the experiences of African American women.

The Lost Generation

Other Americans also wrote of their experiences living in the United States and in places around the world. Soon after he graduated from high school in Illinois, Ernest Hemingway volunteered as an ambulance driver in World War I. Hemingway called the war "the most colossal, murderous, mismanaged butchery that had ever taken place on earth." He began writing short stories and novels, and soon he gained fame for his powerful and direct writing style. Hemingway was among a group of young American writers who expressed feelings of disillusionment in the American society that they felt denied them a voice in their own futures. Author Gertrude Stein called these writers "a lost generation." Writers who criticized American society in the 1920s thus became known as the **Lost Generation**.

Many members of the Lost Generation moved to Paris in the 1920s and formed a community of **expatriates**—people who leave their home country to live elsewhere. Hemingway wrote about the expatriate community in his best-selling novel *The Sun Also Rises*. Another Lost Generation writer was F. Scott Fitzgerald. His novel *The Great Gatsby* focused on what he saw as the loss of morality behind the seemingly fun and free-spirited times of the Jazz Age. Criticizing a glamorous couple, Fitzgerald wrote:

> *"They were careless people ...they smashed up things and creatures and then retreated back into their money or their vast carelessness or whatever it was that kept them together, and let other people clean up the mess they had made."*
>
> —F. Scott Fitzgerald, *The Great Gatsby*

Another writer of the time, Sinclair Lewis, became the first American to receive the Nobel Prize in literature.

New Directions in Art

Painters were also experimenting with new artistic styles in the 1920s. Edward Hopper painted images of the loneliness of modern urban life. **Georgia O'Keeffe** was well known for her detailed paintings of flowers and of the Southwest.

Architects of the 1920s embraced a style they called art deco. Buildings constructed in this style had clean, sharp lines that resembled machines. Today art deco skyscrapers still stand out in American city skylines.

READING CHECK **Comparing and Contrasting** Compare the artists of the Harlem Renaissance and the Lost Generation.

CASE STUDY) BIOGRAPHY

Georgia O'Keeffe
1887–1986

Georgia O'Keeffe grew up in Wisconsin and studied art in Chicago and New York. While teaching art at a college in Canyon, Texas, she would sometimes hike in Palo Duro Canyon, where she sketched scenes of amazing colors and rock formations. This was the start of a lifelong fascination with the beauty of the desert landscape. O'Keeffe lived much of her life in rural New Mexico, where many of her paintings were created. Animal bones, rocks, and desert flowers fill her works. She would often paint these objects in close-up view, showing tiny details. O'Keeffe said, "Most people in the city rush around so, they have no time to look at a flower. I want them to see it whether they want to or not."

Finding Main Ideas How did Georgia O'Keeffe's life influence her painting?

SUMMARY AND PREVIEW Americans became interested in new forms of entertainment and art in the 1920s. In the next chapter you will learn about how life changed in the 1930s.

Section 3 Assessment

Reviewing Ideas, Terms, and People

1. **a. Recall** What new forms of entertainment dominated American society during the 1920s?
   b. Identify What was the first **talkie**?
2. **a. Explain** Why were the 1920s called the **Jazz Age**?
   b. Make Inferences Why do you think jazz music became so popular?
3. **a. Recall** How did writers and artists express new ideas during the 1920s?
   b. Describe What did the **Lost Generation** writers express in their works?
   c. Predict How might the artists of the **Harlem Renaissance** influence African American artists of later generations?

Critical Thinking

4. **Categorizing** Review your notes on examples of popular culture in the 1920s. Then copy the graphic organizer below. Use it to categorize examples of popular culture in the 1920s.

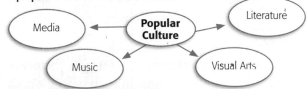

FOCUS ON WRITING

5. **Taking Notes on Entertainment** Make a list of popular forms of entertainment in the 1920s. How would you persuade people to attend a sports event, a talkie, or a jazz club? Begin to think about which product or form of entertainment you will choose for your radio advertisement.

Social Studies Skills

Comparing Graphs

Define the Skill

Graphs are often a very useful way to organize historical information. They can present a large amount of detailed information clearly. Graphs can be an especially good way of showing how something like population or average income changed over time.

When information is organized in a graph, it is often easy to see patterns. Looking at two related graphs, you can compare patterns and make conclusions. For example, you can ask yourself, "Do the numbers in the graphs go up or down for the same reasons? What are the causes behind the changes shown by these graphs?"

Learn the Skill

These guidelines will help you to compare information in two or more graphs.

1. Use your basic graph-interpreting skills. Identify each graph's subject, purpose, and type. Study its parts and categories.

2. Analyze the data in each graph. Then compare any increases, decreases, changes, or patterns you find.

3. Finally, draw conclusions about the relationship between the information in each graph. Think about what could cause such relationships. It will probably help you to review what you know about related events at the same time.

Practice the Skill

Compare the graphs below to answer the following questions.

1. What are the topics of these graphs?

2. What percentage of American households had electricity in 1922? What was the first year when more than half of American households had electricity?

3. Based on the information in the graphs, draw a conclusion about how electricity changed American households.

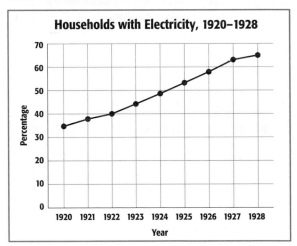

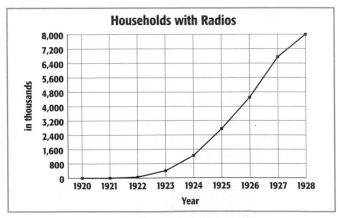

Source: *Historical Atlas of the United States*

Chapter Review

HOLT
History's Impact
▶ video series
Review the video to answer the closing question:
How did the post–World War I economy have an impact on film, literature, and music?

Visual Summary

Use the visual summary below to help you review the main ideas of the chapter.

Political leaders tried to create economic prosperity during the 1920s.

Women found new freedom and opportunity in post–World War I America.

People enjoyed new forms of entertainment during the 1920s.

Reviewing Vocabulary, Terms, and People

Identify the descriptions below with the correct term or person from the chapter.

1. Harlem Renaissance writer who wrote poems, plays, and novels about African American life

2. Agreement signed by the United States and other nations that outlawed war

3. Trial in which Clarence Darrow defended a high school teacher for teaching evolution

4. Repealed prohibition

5. Writers who criticized American culture during the 1920s

6. The movement of African Americans to the north for jobs.

Comprehension and Critical Thinking

SECTION 1 *(Pages 172–177)*

7. **a. Describe** What was President Warren Harding's plan for strengthening the U.S. economy?

   b. Explain What methods did Henry Ford's competitors use to attract customers?

   c. Elaborate How do you think the Kellogg-Briand Pact might have been more effective?

SECTION 2 *(Pages 178–184)*

8. **a. Recall** What was the Red Scare?

   b. Analyze What are some reasons women had more opportunities in the 1920s?

   c. Evaluate Would you have become involved in the youth culture if you had lived during the 1920s? Why or why not?

9. a. Identify What were talkies?

b. Explain How did African Americans play an important role in Jazz Age culture?

c. Predict How do you think new aspects of American culture affected life after the 1920s?

Reviewing Themes

10. Society and Culture How did the prosperity of the 1920s change American culture?

11. Science and Technology What new forms of technology emerged in the 1920s?

Social Studies Skills

Comparing Graphs *Use the Social Studies Skills taught in this chapter to answer the question below.*

12. Look at the line graphs on page 190. Why would a graph showing the number of radio stations in the United States during the 1920s look similar to or different from these graphs? Explain your answer.

Using the Internet go.hrw.com

13. Activity: Experiencing the Jazz Age The arts flourished in America during the 1920s. There were amazing developments in the literary and visual arts, and new forms of performing arts, like blues and jazz, became popular. Enter the activity keyword. Use the Internet links provided to research some of the most influential writers, artists, and musicians of the 1920s. Choose one and conduct an imaginary interview with that person about his or her work and impact on American culture. Document your conversation by creating an audio recording or by writing a transcript.

Reading Skills

Synthesizing Information *Use the Reading Skills taught in this chapter to answer the question below.*

> The number of women in the workforce continued to grow as well. Women with college degrees worked as nurses, teachers, librarians, and social workers . . . Women were still discouraged from pursuing fields such as medicine, law, and architecture, however. By the end of the 1920s, less than 5 percent of the country's doctors, lawyers, and architects were women. The percentage was small—but it was beginning to rise. *(p. 179)*

14. Which of the following sources might have been used to synthesize the information above?

a. a history of architecture

b. an instructional manual for nurses

c. a history of working women in the 1920s

d. the list of graduates from a women's college in 1910

FOCUS ON WRITING

15. Writing Your Radio Advertisement Look over your notes and choose one product that was popular in the 1920s. Think about these questions as you design your radio ad: Who is your audience? How will this product improve people's lives? What words or sounds will best describe your product? Write the dialogue for your ad, including directions for the actors. Also, include information about music or sound effects you want to use.

Grade 8 Intermediate-Level Test Preparation

Directions (1–7): For each statement or question, write on the separate answer sheet the *number* of the word or expression that, of those given, best completes the statement or answers the question.

1 President Warren Harding's secretary of the interior was convicted and jailed for his participation in the

(1) Scopes trial.

(2) Teapot Dome scandal.

(3) Red Scare.

(4) Kellogg-Briand Pact.

2 Marcus Garvey was a leader in which of the following movements?

(1) black nationalism

(2) fundamentalism

(3) socialism

(4) communism

3 Which of the following is a reason why consumers bought more manufactured products in the 1920s?

(1) More Americans had electricity in their homes, so thcy could use new electric appliances.

(2) Radio and print advertising made it easier to buy products.

(3) Immigrants came to the United States in record numbers and bought new goods.

(4) The Lost Generation felt separated from American culture.

4 Which of the following was a famous jazz musician and composer?

(1) Zora Neale Hurston

(2) Mary Pickford

(3) Charles Lindbergh

(4) Edward "Duke" Ellington

5 One effect of the Red Scare was

(1) the election of Herbert Hoover in 1928.

(2) the trial and execution of Nicola Sacco and Bartolomeo Vanzetti.

(3) new opportunities for women, immigrants, and minorities.

(4) the Scopes trail.

6 Which of the following quotes reflects the beliefs of Calvin Coolidge?

(1) "The business of America is business."

(2) "I will build a motor car for the great multitude."

(3) "I want my girl to be a flapper, because flappers are brave."

(4) "America's present need is not heroics, but healing; not nostrums but normalcy."

7 What was the Harlem Renaissance?

(1) A period of Latino musical accomplishment

(2) A period of African American artistic accomplishment

(3) A period of extensive construction

(4) A period of increased racial discrimination

Base your answer to question 8 on the text below and on your knowledge of social studies.

*"*We in America today are nearer to the final triumph over poverty than ever before in the history of any land . . . We have not yet reached the goal, but given a chance to go forward with the policies of the last eight years, we shall soon with the help of God be in sight of the day when poverty will be banished from this nation.*"*

— Herbert Hoover, 1928 inaugural speech

8 **Constructed-Response Question** What did Hoover believe about poverty in the United States?

CHAPTER **8** 1929–1939

The Great Depression

FOCUS ON WRITING

Journal Entry We know a lot about life during the Great Depression because many Americans described their experiences in journals and letters. In this chapter you will read about how people struggled through hard times in the 1930s. Read the chapter and then write a one-page journal entry as if you were a person living during the Depression. You may choose to write from the point of view of a student, artist, farmer, or other individual. As you read, think about how the events in the 1930s may have affected this person.

UNITED STATES

1929 The U.S. stock market crashes on Black Tuesday.

1930

WORLD

1930 Mahatma Gandhi and a group of followers begin the Salt March.

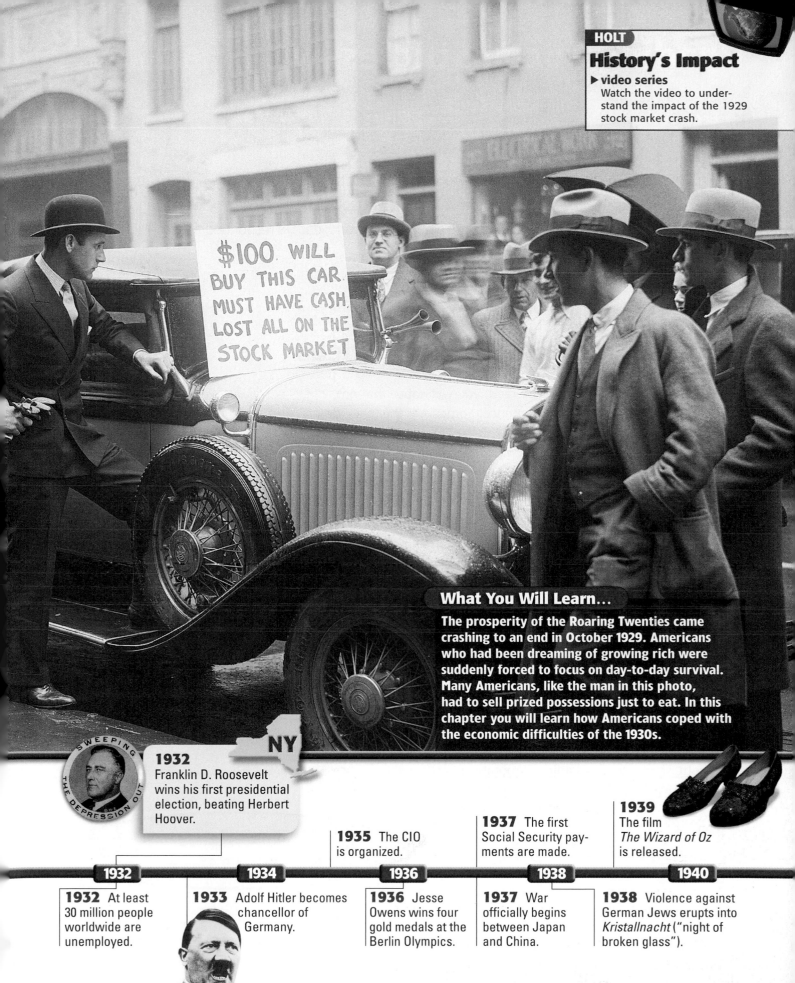

HOLT

History's Impact
▶ video series
Watch the video to understand the impact of the 1929 stock market crash.

$100. WILL BUY THIS CAR. MUST HAVE CASH. LOST ALL ON THE STOCK MARKET

What You Will Learn...

The prosperity of the Roaring Twenties came crashing to an end in October 1929. Americans who had been dreaming of growing rich were suddenly forced to focus on day-to-day survival. Many Americans, like the man in this photo, had to sell prized possessions just to eat. In this chapter you will learn how Americans coped with the economic difficulties of the 1930s.

1932 Franklin D. Roosevelt wins his first presidential election, beating Herbert Hoover.

1935 The CIO is organized.

1937 The first Social Security payments are made.

1939 The film *The Wizard of Oz* is released.

1932 At least 30 million people worldwide are unemployed.

1933 Adolf Hitler becomes chancellor of Germany.

1936 Jesse Owens wins four gold medals at the Berlin Olympics.

1937 War officially begins between Japan and China.

1938 Violence against German Jews erupts into *Kristallnacht* ("night of broken glass").

1932   1934   1936   1938   1940

Reading Social Studies

by Kylene Beers

| Economics | Geography | Politics | Society and Culture | Science and Technology |

Focus on Themes In this chapter, you will learn about the Great Depression, one of the most serious **economic** crises in America's history. You will also learn about the **politics** that arose to try to deal with this crisis. Finally, you will read about how the Depression affected the global economy and how world leaders responded to it.

Recognizing Implied Main Ideas

Focus on Reading When you read, you will notice that not every paragraph has a main idea sentence. Sometimes the main idea is implied.

Implied Main Ideas While main ideas give a basic structure to a paragraph, supporting details help convince the reader of the author's point. Main ideas can be presented in a sentence, or simply implied. Usually, a paragraph without a main idea sentence will still have an implied main idea that ties the sentences together.

Notice how one reader found the main idea of the following paragraph.

During the boom years of the 1920s, one General Motors executive boldly declared: "Anyone not only can be rich, but ought to be rich." For almost all of the Roaring Twenties, the stock market was a bull market, or one with rising stock values. It seemed easy to make money by investing in stocks. For example, you could have bought shares in the Radio Corporation of America for $85 each at the beginning of 1928. You could have sold them a year later for $549 each. *(p. 198)*

> This quote is about making money and being rich. Maybe the main idea is about money or economics.

> This sentence is about making money through the stock market. I guess the main idea has to do with investing.

> Here is a great example of how easy it was to make money in the late 1920s. I think the main idea is something like "The stock market provided an easy way for many to become rich in the 1920s."

196 CHAPTER 8

You Try It!

Read the following paragraph and then answer the questions below.

> The action began when Roosevelt called Congress into a special session. Known as the Hundred Days, the session started just after the inauguration and lasted until the middle of June. During the Hundred Days, Roosevelt and Congress worked together to create new programs to battle the Depression and aid economic recovery. These programs became known as the New Deal.
>
> *From Chapter 8, p. 204*

1. List two ideas that this paragraph discusses.

2. How are these two ideas related to each other?

3. Write an example of the main idea of this paragraph.

4. Which details support your main idea?

As you read **Chapter 8,** think of a main idea for any paragraph that does not have a main idea sentence.

Key Terms and People

Academic Vocabulary

In this chapter you will learn the following academic words:
implement *(p. 201)*
authority *(p. 206)*

The End of Prosperity

What You Will Learn...

Main Ideas

1. The U.S. stock market crashed in 1929.
2. The economy collapsed after the stock market crash.
3. Many Americans were dissatisfied with Hoover's reaction to economic conditions.
4. Roosevelt defeated Hoover in the election of 1932.

The Big Idea

The collapse of the stock market in 1929 helped lead to the start of the Great Depression.

Key Terms and People

buying on margin, *p. 198*
Black Tuesday, *p. 199*
business cycle, *p. 200*
Great Depression, *p. 200*
Bonus Army, *p. 201*
Franklin D. Roosevelt, *p. 202*

TAKING NOTES As you read, look for information about the American economy in the 1920s and 1930s. Take notes about your findings in a diagram like the one shown.

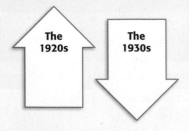

The 1920s   The 1930s

If YOU were there...

For almost a year you've been working part-time at a neighborhood store. You earn money for your family and still have time to go to school. But when you arrive at work today, your boss says business has been so bad that he can't afford to pay you anymore. With your father out of work, your family had been counting on your income from this job.

How can you continue earning money to help your family?

BUILDING BACKGROUND By the late 1920s many Americans were used to year after year of economic expansion. It was easy to believe that the prosperity of the 1920s would last forever. But the U.S. economy historically has experienced periods of prosperity followed by periods of economic downturn. This cycle would continue in a way that shocked Americans in the 1930s, leading to the worst economic depression in the nation's history.

The Stock Market Crashes

During the boom years of the 1920s, one General Motors executive boldly declared: "Anyone not only can be rich, but ought to be rich." For almost all of the Roaring Twenties, the stock market was a bull market, or one with rising stock values. It seemed easy to make money by investing in stocks. For example, you could have bought shares in the Radio Corporation of America for $85 each at the beginning of 1928. You could have sold them a year later for $549 each.

The chance to make huge profits from small investments encouraged many people to buy stocks. Some who could not afford the stocks' full price began **buying on margin**—purchasing stocks on credit, or with borrowed money. These stockholders planned to sell the stocks at a higher price, pay back the loan, and keep what remained as profit. But this plan only worked if stock values went up. Few considered what would happen if the bull market turned into a bear market, or one with declining stock prices.

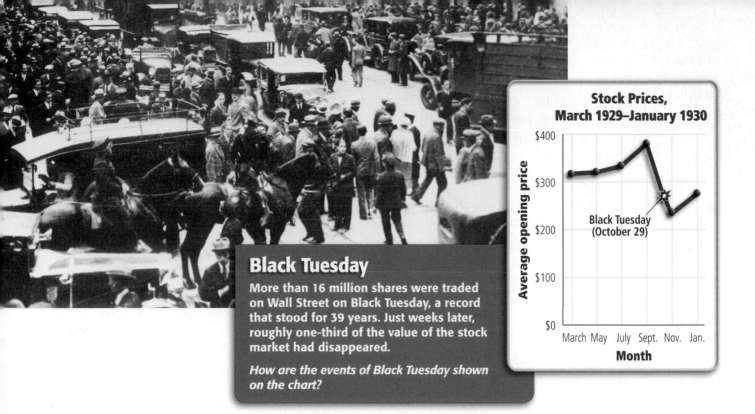

Black Tuesday

More than 16 million shares were traded on Wall Street on Black Tuesday, a record that stood for 39 years. Just weeks later, roughly one-third of the value of the stock market had disappeared.

How are the events of Black Tuesday shown on the chart?

Stock Prices, March 1929–January 1930

Black Tuesday (October 29)

Stock prices peaked in the late summer of 1929. Then prices started to drop. Frightened investors who had bought stocks on margin rushed to sell their stocks in order to pay off their loans. On Thursday, October 24, panic hit the stock market. Within three hours the market had lost $11 billion in value. The following Monday, prices dropped again. On Tuesday, October 29—a day that became known as **Black Tuesday**—the stock market crashed. So many people wanted to sell their stocks, and so few wanted to buy, that stock prices collapsed. One journalist described the nightmare:

"The wires to other cities were jammed with frantic orders to sell [stock]. So were the cables, radio, and telephones to Europe and the rest of the world. Buyers were few, sometimes wholly absent ... This was real panic ... When the closing bell rang, the great bull market was dead and buried."

—Jonathan Norton Leonard, from *Three Years Down*

In September 1929 the total value of all stocks was $87 billion. Less than two months later, more than $30 billion in stock value had disappeared.

READING CHECK **Analyzing Information** Why was buying on margin risky?

The Economy Collapses

President Herbert Hoover tried to calm public fears by assuring Americans that the economy was still strong. "The fundamental business of the country . . . is on a sound and prosperous basis," he said. But this was just the beginning of more than 10 years of economic hard times.

The Banking Crisis

One immediate effect of the stock market crash was a banking crisis. Banks had invested heavily in the stock market, so they lost heavily when the market crashed. Banks had also lent their customers money to buy stocks on margin. Now those customers were unable to pay back their loans. Some banks went out of business. People who had deposited their life savings in those banks lost everything.

This created a panic all over the country, as customers rushed to their banks to withdraw their money. But since banks usually do not keep enough cash on hand to cover all deposits, the banks soon ran out of money. Many had to close their doors. In 1931 alone, more than 2,200 banks closed. The banking crisis contributed to a business crisis. Some businesses lost their savings in failed banks and had to close. Others were forced to cut back production, which meant they needed fewer workers. In the last three months of 1929, U.S. unemployment soared from under half a million workers to more than 4 million.

The Causes

Throughout the history of the United States, the economy has followed a pattern of ups and downs. When businesses produce more than they can sell, unsold goods pile up. Businesses then cut back on their production and lay off workers. People who have lost their jobs, and others who are afraid they might soon lose their jobs, buy fewer goods. This causes more businesses to fail. This economic event is called a recession. Deep and long-lasting recessions are known as depressions.

As time passes, an economy will tend to bounce back. Consumers buy surplus goods, and companies increase production to meet the demand. Soon, more workers are hired and unemployment drops. This up-and-down pattern is known as the **business cycle**.

The United States had experienced recessions and depressions before 1929. Each time, the economy followed the business cycle and recovered. But the economy did not recover quickly from the downturn that began in 1929. Because of its severity and length, it was called the **Great Depression**.

Historians and economists still debate the exact causes of the Great Depression. Some believe that the government's monetary policy was a cause. Most agree that a major factor was the overproduction of goods at a time when the market for those goods was shrinking. Companies built millions of cars and appliances during the 1920s. By the late 1920s, however, most people who could afford these products already had them. That meant that American businesses were producing far more goods than people were consuming.

Uneven distribution of wealth made this problem worse. In 1929 the wealthiest 5 percent of Americans earned one-third of all income, while the bottom 40 percent earned only one-eighth of all income. Millions of Americans simply did not earn enough money to buy expensive new products.

Declining world trade also hurt American manufacturers. Europeans were still recovering from World War I and could not afford many American goods. At the same time, high tariffs made it difficult for European nations to sell products to the United States. As a result, Europeans had even less money to buy American goods.

READING CHECK **Making Predictions** Do you think the Great Depression could have been avoided? How?

Unemployment during the Depression

CONNECT TO ECONOMICS

People are considered unemployed if they are trying to find work but do not have a job. High rates of unemployment hurt the economy because unemployed people cannot buy many goods and services. This causes businesses to lose money.

During what year was unemployment the highest?

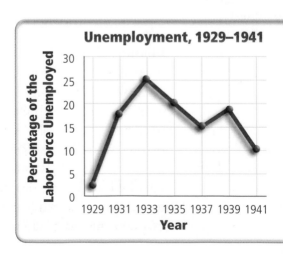

Unemployment, 1929–1941

WORK-IS-WHAT-I WANT-AND-NOT-CHARITY WHO-WILL-HELP-ME- GET-A-JOB-7 Years- IN-DETROIT. NO-MONEY SENT-AWAY-FURNISH- BEST-OF-REFERENCES PHONE RANDOLPH 8381 Room #59.

POLITICAL CARTOON
"Blame It on Hoover"

Presidents can affect the economy to some degree through their policies. During the Great Depression, President Hoover was blamed for the financial crisis. Political cartoons like this one gave voice to those Americans who thought Hoover could have prevented the crisis or could have brought it to an end quickly through government programs.

> How does the cartoonist show Hoover reacting to the crisis?

> What kind of people are blaming Hoover?

ANALYSIS SKILL **ANALYZING PRIMARY SOURCES**

Why is this cartoon useful for showing the feelings of the American public during the Great Depression?

A Most Vicious Circle
—Costello in the Albany "News."

Hoover's Reaction

As unemployment skyrocketed, more and more Americans struggled just to feed themselves and their families. Hungry people searched city dumps for scraps of food. One woman remembered taking off her glasses when she cooked so she could not see the maggots in the meat her family was about to eat. Private charities, as well as state and local governments, set up soup kitchens and breadlines. But the need far exceeded the available resources. Many people turned to President Herbert Hoover and the federal government to lead the relief effort.

Hoover knew that many Americans needed help. He did not believe, however, that it was the federal government's role to provide direct relief to Americans. Hoover felt it was up to private individuals and institutions, not the government, to offer relief. Despite this belief, Hoover did **implement** some new government programs. In 1932 he created the Reconstruction Finance Corporation (RFC). That year, the RFC loaned $1.2 billion to 5,000 different financial institutions, including banks and farm mortgage companies. Hoover continued to resist giving direct assistance to individuals.

This angered Americans who believed the president should do more to fix the economy. People bitterly referred to empty pockets turned inside out as Hoover flags. Groups of tin and cardboard shacks built by homeless families were nicknamed Hoovervilles.

In 1932 a new Hooverville was built in Washington, D.C. Its more than 17,000 residents were World War I veterans, some with their families. Called the **Bonus Army**, they had come to the capital to demand early payment of a military bonus. After the government denied the payment, most of the veterans returned home. About 2,000, however, stayed in their shantytown.

President Hoover authorized General Douglas MacArthur to use U.S. troops to evict the Bonus Army. MacArthur used force, including tear gas and tanks, to scatter the veterans. Several veterans were killed. The public reacted with outrage to the government's treatment of war veterans. Americans would have a chance to express this frustration in the upcoming election.

READING CHECK **Making Generalizations**
How would you describe President Hoover's response to the Depression?

FOCUS ON NEW YORK

Even people who were able to find work in New York and elsewhere felt the effects of the Great Depression— losing their jobs was always a possibility during this economic crisis.

ACADEMIC VOCABULARY

implement put in place

Election of 1932

THE IMPACT TODAY

Before 1932, candidates did not attend their party's nominating convention. Roosevelt broke with this tradition, setting a new precedent. Today presidential candidates give televised speeches at party conventions.

The Republican Party nominated Herbert Hoover again for president in 1932, but few people believed he could win. Regarding his chances of re-election, even Hoover realized that "the prospects are dark." Still, he began campaigning hard for a second term.

He called the election "a contest between two philosophies of government." He warned that the government aid programs Democrats were promising would weaken Americans' spirit of self-reliance.

By 1932, however, much of the public had lost confidence in Hoover. Many even blamed him for the Depression. In contrast, as governor of New York during the first years of the Depression, **Franklin D. Roosevelt** had taken active steps to provide aid. He directed the state government to provide relief for the state's citizens, especially farmers. He also helped establish the Temporary Emergency Relief Administration, which gave unemployment assistance to many out-of-work New Yorkers.

Roosevelt's confident and optimistic personality appealed to many voters. At the Democratic Party convention, Roosevelt declared to Americans: "I pledge you, I pledge myself, to a new deal for the American people." Voters responded overwhelmingly to this message of hope. Roosevelt won the 1932 election in a landslide. In addition, the Democrats won strong majorities in both houses of Congress.

READING CHECK **Analyzing Information** How did Franklin D. Roosevelt win the 1932 presidential election?

SUMMARY AND PREVIEW After the stock market crash and the start of the Great Depression, Franklin Roosevelt offered hope for the future. In the next section you will learn about his programs for relief.

Section 1 Assessment

go.hrw.com
Online Quiz

Reviewing Ideas, Terms, and People

1. **a. Recall** Why did the stock market crash in 1929?
   b. Compare How is **buying on margin** similar to buying on an installment plan?
2. **a. Recall** What happened to the economy as a result of the stock market crash?
   b. Explain Why did many banks close in the late 1920s and early 1930s?
   c. Draw Conclusions What do you think was the goal of U.S. tariffs?
3. **a. Make Inferences** Why did many Americans blame President Hoover for the Depression?
   b. Describe What did the **Bonus Army** want?
   c. Elaborate Do you think Americans were justified in blaming Hoover for the hard times?
4. **a. Identify** Which party was more successful in the 1932 elections?
   b. Make Inferences Why do you think voters did not listen to Hoover's ideas about government?
   c. Elaborate How do you think **Franklin D. Roosevelt**'s experiences as governor of New York helped him appeal to voters?

Critical Thinking

5. **Identifying Cause and Effect** Review your notes on the American economy in the 1920s and 1930s. Then copy the graphic organizer below and use it to identify the economic causes of the Depression and their effects.

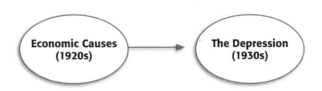

Economic Causes (1920s) → The Depression (1930s)

FOCUS ON WRITING

6. **Taking Notes on the End of Prosperity** To begin thinking about creating a character for your journal entry, answer the question at the end of the "If YOU were there" on page 198. Then make some notes on the stock market crash, the banking crisis, and rising unemployment. Decide how your character would feel about these developments.

Franklin Delano Roosevelt

How would you try to lead your country through times of national crisis?

When did he live? 1882–1945

Where did he live? Roosevelt lived much of his life in New York State, where he served in the state senate and as governor. He also lived in Washington, D.C., while he was serving as assistant secretary of the navy and later as president. He had a second home in Warm Springs, Georgia.

What did he do? He began the New Deal, a set of government programs designed to help the country survive and recover from the Great Depression. He gave many Americans hope for the future when he spoke to them in his fireside chats. Roosevelt also led the country through World War II. His support for strong ties between the Allied countries helped the Allies achieve victory.

Why is he so important? Roosevelt led the United States during two of the most serious crises that our country has ever faced: the Great Depression and World War II. He served as president for 12 years, longer than any other. Many of the programs he began in the 1930s expanded the role of government in American life.

Making Predictions How do you think Franklin Roosevelt's experience as president during the Depression might have helped him lead the country during World War II?

KEY EVENTS

1905
Marries Eleanor Roosevelt

1921
Stricken with polio; unable to walk without leg braces and canes for the rest of his life

1928
Elected governor of New York

1932
Elected president; re-elected in 1936, 1940, and 1944

1941
U.S. entry into World War II

1945
Dies at his home in Warm Springs, Georgia

"*The only thing we have to fear is fear itself, nameless, unreasoning, unjustified terror.*"

Franklin Roosevelt, 1933 inaugural address

Roosevelt's New Deal

What You Will Learn...

Main Ideas

1. Congress approved many new programs during the Hundred Days.
2. Critics expressed concerns about the New Deal.
3. New Deal programs continued through Roosevelt's first term in what became known as the Second New Deal.
4. Roosevelt clashed with the Supreme Court over the New Deal.

The Big Idea

Franklin Roosevelt's New Deal included government programs designed to relieve unemployment and help the economy recover.

Key Terms and People

New Deal, *p. 204*
fireside chats, *p. 205*
Tennessee Valley Authority, *p. 205*
Frances Perkins, *p. 205*
Eleanor Roosevelt, *p. 207*
Social Security Act, *p. 207*
Congress of Industrial Organizations, *p. 208*
sit-down strike, *p. 208*

TAKING NOTES As you read, take notes on the challenges the nation and President Roosevelt faced during the Great Depression in a chart like the one below.

The Nation	President Roosevelt

If YOU were there...

It has been five months since you lost your job. One of your friends has found work in a new government program that is hiring young people to work in national parks and forests. The pay is low, and you would have to leave home, but you would have enough food, a place to live, and a little money to send back to your family every month.

Would you take a job with the Civilian Conservation Corps? Why or why not?

BUILDING BACKGROUND When he ran for president in 1932, Franklin D. Roosevelt promised to provide relief to people suffering from the Depression. Even before he took office, Roosevelt began making plans with his Brain Trust, a group of expert advisers. People endured the harsh winter of 1932–1933, looking forward to Roosevelt's inauguration.

The Hundred Days

Immediately after taking the oath of office in March 1933, President Franklin Roosevelt spoke to the nation. In his first inaugural address, Roosevelt told nervous Americans that economic recovery was possible. "The only thing we have to fear is fear itself," he said, "nameless, unreasoning, unjustified terror." It was only fear of the future, he argued, that could keep America from moving forward. Roosevelt spoke openly of the severe problems facing the American people—unemployment, failing banks, and products with no markets. He promised that the government would help. "This nation asks for action," he said, "and action now."

The action began when Roosevelt called Congress into a special session. Known as the Hundred Days, the session started just after the inauguration and lasted until the middle of June. During the Hundred Days, Roosevelt and Congress worked together to create new programs to battle the Depression and aid economic recovery. These programs became known as the **New Deal**.

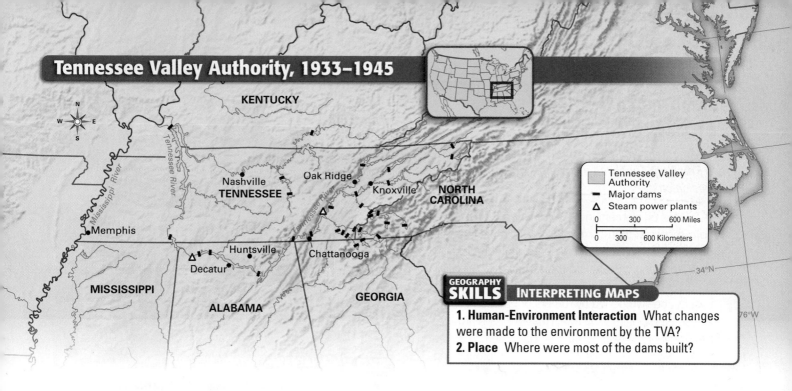

Tennessee Valley Authority, 1933–1945

KENTUCKY

Tennessee River

Mississippi River

Nashville • Oak Ridge
TENNESSEE • Knoxville

Memphis •

Decatur
Huntsville • Chattanooga

MISSISSIPPI

ALABAMA

GEORGIA

NORTH
CAROLINA

Tennessee Valley Authority
■ Major dams
△ Steam power plants

0   300   600 Miles
0   300   600 Kilometers

34°N

76°W

GEOGRAPHY SKILLS INTERPRETING MAPS

1. **Human-Environment Interaction** What changes were made to the environment by the TVA?
2. **Place** Where were most of the dams built?

Restoring Confidence

One of Roosevelt's first goals was to restore confidence in American banks. The day after his inauguration, Roosevelt announced a "bank holiday," ordering all banks to close temporarily. Congress quickly passed the Emergency Banking Relief Act, and President Roosevelt signed it into law.

That Sunday, President Roosevelt gave the first of his **fireside chats**—radio addresses in which he spoke directly to the American people. He explained the new law. The government would inspect the finances of every bank and allow only healthy banks to reopen. The law also created the Federal Deposit Insurance Corporation (FDIC), which insured individual deposits up to $5,000. The new bank law and the fireside chats helped Americans trust banks again. As banks reopened, there was no rush to withdraw money. In fact, over the next month, Americans deposited almost $1 billion.

Relief and Recovery

Roosevelt next turned his attention to other serious problems. In 1933 some 13 million Americans—about 25 percent of the nation's workforce—were unemployed. Although many workers still held jobs, they worked reduced hours and received lower wages than

previously. New Deal programs helped to get Americans back to work. The Civil Works Administration (CWA) employed more than 4 million Americans, building roads and airports. One grateful CWA worker expressed the feelings of many when he said, "I was working, and I could again hold my head up when I met people." The Civilian Conservation Corps (CCC) provided jobs for hundreds of thousands of people through projects such as planting trees and improving national parks.

Another federal project, the **Tennessee Valley Authority** (TVA), hired people to build dams and generators, bringing electricity and jobs to communities in the Tennessee River valley. The New Deal also included programs to help farmers. The Farm Credit Administration (FCA) helped farmers refinance their mortgages so they could keep their farms. The Agricultural Adjustment Act (AAA) helped stabilize agricultural prices.

The National Industrial Recovery Act (NIRA) addressed business concerns by eliminating unfair competition among companies. This law was passed with support from Secretary of Labor **Frances Perkins**, the nation's first woman cabinet member.

FOCUS ON READING
What is the main idea of this paragraph?

READING CHECK Categorizing Which New Deal programs employed people to build public projects?

RADIO BROADCAST
Fireside Chats

An American family sits around the radio listening to President Roosevelt answer his critics in his first fireside chat.

❝There is an element in . . . our financial system more important than currency [money], more important than gold, and that is the confidence of the people. Confidence and courage are the essentials of success in carrying out our plan. You people must have faith; you must not be stampeded by rumors or guesses. Let us unite in banishing [driving away] fear. We have provided the machinery to restore our financial system; it is up to you to support and make it work. It is your problem no less than it is mine. Together we cannot fail.**❞**

ANALYSIS SKILL   **ANALYZING PRIMARY SOURCES**

According to Roosevelt, how should the American people help the government deal with the banking crisis?

New Deal Critics

While many Americans approved of the New Deal, others criticized President Roosevelt's programs. New Deal critics fell into two main groups—those who believed the New Deal went too far, and those who believed it did not go far enough.

Those who felt the New Deal went too far criticized the enormous expansion of the federal government. For example, members of the American Liberty League said that New Deal laws gave the president too much **authority**. Many business leaders were concerned that the high cost of new government programs would lead to new taxes.

One critic who thought the New Deal did not go far enough was Dr. Francis E. Townsend. He proposed a plan aimed at helping poor elderly Americans through the Depression. The Townsend Plan called for the government to make payments of $200 a month to people over sixty. Huey Long, a U.S. Senator from Louisiana, proposed a program called Share Our Wealth. This plan would tax rich Americans and use the money to help the poor. Every family would be guaranteed an annual income of $5,000. As Long prepared to challenge Roosevelt in the 1936 election, he announced his goal "to break up the swollen fortunes of America and to spread the wealth among all our people." Long's White House dreams ended when an assassin shot him in 1935.

Another fierce critic of the New Deal was Father Charles Coughlin. Coughlin was a Roman Catholic priest in Detroit who developed a large following by broadcasting sermons on the radio. Coughlin was openly anti-Semitic and blamed the depression on a so-called international conspiracy of bankers. Although he supported Roosevelt at first, he decided that the New Deal helped only business interests. Coughlin wanted the government to nationalize, or take over, all of the country's wealth and natural resources. The most extreme New Deal critics wanted to see the nation's capitalist system replaced with socialism or communism.

READING CHECK   **Supporting a Point of View**
Do you agree with any of the New Deal critics? Why or why not?

ACADEMIC VOCABULARY

authority power, right to rule

The New Deal Continues

Despite criticism of the New Deal, Democrats increased their majorities in both houses of Congress in the 1934 election. With this show of support from the American people, Roosevelt continued to introduce additional New Deal legislation. These later laws were known as the Second New Deal.

The Second New Deal

After the Civil Works Administration ended in 1934, Congress formed a new agency to provide jobs for unemployed Americans. Between 1935 and 1943, the Works Progress Administration (WPA) employed some 8.5 million people on tens of thousands of projects all over the country. WPA employees built more than 650,000 miles of roads; 75,000 bridges; 8,000 parks; and 800 airports. WPA workers also built the Grand Coulee Dam in Washington and New York City's Lincoln Tunnel, as well as prisons, swimming pools, hospitals, and courthouses nationwide.

First Lady **Eleanor Roosevelt** was an active supporter of New Deal programs. She was concerned, however, that the WPA was not solving the problem of unemployment among young Americans in their teens and early twenties. "I live in real terror when I think we may be losing this generation," she said. "We have got to bring these young people into the active life of the community and make them feel that they are necessary." The first lady helped convince the president to create the National Youth Administration (NYA). The NYA gave part-time jobs to many students. These jobs allowed young workers to stay in school and help their families. One NYA worker said, "I tell you, the first time I walked through the front door with my paycheck, I was somebody!"

President Roosevelt also wanted to help those who were "unable . . . to maintain themselves independently . . . through no fault of their own." The **Social Security Act**, passed in 1935, provided some financial security for the elderly, the disabled, children, and the unemployed. To help pay for these programs, the law placed a new tax on workers and employers. The passage of the Social Security Act marked the first time the federal government took direct responsibility

THE IMPACT TODAY

Social Security today is a matter of great debate. Some Americans support the continuation of the program, while others believe that the government spends too much on the program and it should be privatized.

Selected New Deal Programs — QUICK FACTS

Program	Purpose
Emergency Banking Relief Act	Gave the executive branch the right to regulate banks
Farm Credit Act (FCA)	Refinanced loans to keep farmers from losing their land
Civilian Conservation Corps (CCC)	Created jobs for single, unemployed young men
Agricultural Adjustment Act (AAA)	Paid farmers to grow less (declared unconstitutional)
Tennessee Valley Authority (TVA)	Built dams and power plants in the Tennessee Valley
Federal Deposit Insurance Corporation (FDIC)	Guaranteed deposits in individual bank accounts
National Industrial Recovery Act (NIRA)	Established fair competition laws (declared unconstitutional)
Civil Works Administration (CWA)	Provided jobs for the unemployed
Works Progress Administration (WPA)	Created jobs in construction, research, and the arts
National Youth Administration (NYA)	Provided part-time jobs to students
National Labor Relations Act (Wagner Act)	Recognized unions' right to bargain collectively
Social Security Act	Provided government aid to the retired and unemployed

Robert F. Wagner arrived in New York City with his parents, immigrants from Germany, at age eight. After studying law and becoming involved in city politics, Wagner served in the New York State Assembly and the state Senate, as well as on the New York Supreme Court. As a U.S. senator, he made numerous proposed legislation to address social problems, but it was not until the New Deal that many of his proposals became law.

for many citizens' economic well-being. The growing number of American workers who were retiring without a pension now had a source of income. In a national radio address, Secretary of Labor Perkins told Americans she believed Social Security was "a most significant step in our national development, a milestone in our progress toward the better-ordered society."

New Deal Labor Programs

The National Industrial Recovery Act of 1933 helped regulate business by requiring minimum wage and allowing collective bargaining. In 1935, however, the Supreme Court declared the NIRA unconstitutional.

In response to this setback, Congress passed the National Labor Relations Act (NLRA). This law is sometimes called the Wagner Act after its sponsor, Senator Robert F. Wagner of New York. This law allowed workers to join labor unions and take part in collective bargaining. It also established the National Labor Relations Board to oversee union activities. Union membership grew after the passage of the Wagner Act. Organized labor became a powerful political force.

At the start of the Depression, many skilled workers belonged to craft unions. Such unions were often associated with the American Federation of Labor, which had existed since the 1880s. Unskilled workers, however, such as those who worked on assembly lines, did not qualify to belong to AFL unions. In 1935 a new union called the **Congress of Industrial Organizations** (CIO) organized workers into unions based on industry, not skill level. For example, all workers in the automobile industry would belong to the same union. The CIO also welcomed African American and Hispanic members, as well as women and immigrants.

Unions led a number of major strikes during the Depression. On New Year's Eve 1936, the CIO went on strike against General Motors for 44 days. Instead of leaving the buildings as strikers usually did, workers stayed in the factories so they could not be replaced by new workers. This strategy became known as the **sit-down strike**. The success of the General Motors strike attracted more workers to CIO unions.

READING CHECK Comparing and Contrasting
How were the WPA and the Social Security Act similar? How were they different?

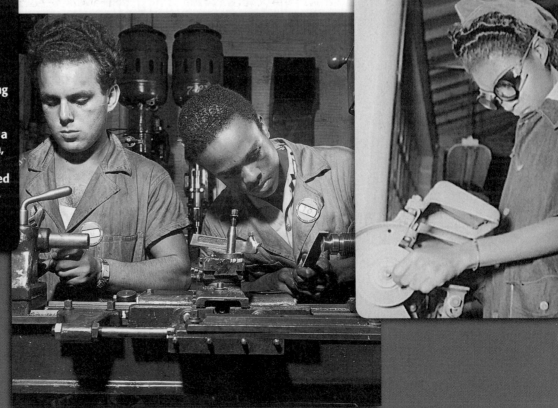

National Youth Administration

A New Deal program called the National Youth Administration (NYA) helped thousands of young people continue their education while working to support their families. Eleanor Roosevelt was a strong supporter of the program, which aimed to teach young people the skills they would need to remain part of the workforce.

How did the NYA demonstrate the ideals of the New Deal?

Clashes with the Court

Roosevelt won re-election by a huge margin in 1936, carrying every state but Maine and Vermont. Democrats expanded their dominant control of Congress. But Roosevelt and the Democrats in Congress could not control the Supreme Court.

In 1935 the Supreme Court issued a series of rulings declaring several New Deal programs, including the AAA, unconstitutional. Roosevelt and his advisers felt that the entire New Deal was in danger. "Mr. President, they mean to destroy us," said Attorney General Homer Cummings.

Roosevelt decided to propose a plan for reorganizing the federal judiciary that was soon to be labeled the "court-packing" bill. This bill would allow the president to appoint a new Supreme Court justice for every justice who was 70 years old or older. Roosevelt would be able to appoint six new justices immediately.

Roosevelt's judiciary plan drew harsh criticism from Congress and the public. Critics charged that Roosevelt was trying to change the balance of power so carefully defined in the U.S. Constitution. After a heated debate, Congress rejected the bill. The Supreme Court, however, did not overturn any more New Deal legislation. Roosevelt eventually had the opportunity to nominate nine new Supreme Court justices to replace those who had retired or died.

READING CHECK **Analyzing Information** Why did Roosevelt try to alter the Supreme Court?

SUMMARY AND PREVIEW Roosevelt's New Deal programs brought economic relief to many Americans. In the next section you will read about how the country continued to suffer the effects of the Depression.

go.hrw.com
Online Quiz

Section 2 Assessment

Reviewing Ideas, Terms, and People

1. **a. Recall** What were the Hundred Days?
   b. Make Inferences What was the purpose of the bank holiday Roosevelt declared?
   c. Evaluate Which of the **New Deal** programs that passed during the Hundred Days was most effective? Why?
2. **a. Describe** Who were some of the critics of the New Deal?
   b. Contrast How were the ideas of Huey Long and the American Liberty League different?
   c. Elaborate Why do you think people supported New Deal critics such as Huey Long and Father Coughlin?
3. **a. Identify** What programs were part of the Second New Deal?
   b. Make Inferences Why did the Wagner Act encourage people to join unions?
4. **a. Recall** What happened to some of the New Deal programs when they were challenged in court?
   b. Make Inferences What was the purpose of Roosevelt's judiciary reorganization bill?

Critical Thinking

5. **Problem Solving** Review your notes on the challenges faced by the nation and the president during the Depression. Then copy the graphic organizer below and use it to identify Depression problems and New Deal solutions.

Problems	New Deal solutions

FOCUS ON WRITING

6. **Thinking about New Deal Programs** Take notes on the New Deal programs. Think about how your character might be affected by one or more of the programs. For example, how do you think he or she would feel about getting a construction job with the Works Progress Administration?

Americans Face Hard Times

What You Will Learn...

Main Ideas

1. Parts of the Great Plains came to be known as the Dust Bowl as severe drought destroyed farms there.
2. Families all over the United States faced hard times.
3. Depression-era culture helped lift people's spirits.
4. The New Deal had lasting effects on American society.

The Big Idea

All over the country, Americans struggled to survive the Great Depression.

Key Terms and People

Dust Bowl, *p. 210*
Mary McLeod Bethune, *p. 212*
John Steinbeck, *p. 213*
Woody Guthrie, *p. 213*

TAKING NOTES As you read, take notes on people's lives during the Depression. In each circle of a diagram like the one below, fill in details about their challenges, struggles, and culture.

Life during the Depression

If YOU were there...

You own a wheat farm on the Great Plains, where you and your family live and work. Wheat prices have been low for years, and you have managed to get by only by borrowing thousands of dollars. Now the region is suffering through a terrible drought. Without water, you have been unable to grow any wheat at all. But if you do not start paying your debts, you will lose your farm.

Would you stay on your farm or leave and start a new life somewhere else?

BUILDING BACKGROUND The New Deal provided jobs and relieved suffering for many Americans, but it did not end the Great Depression. Unemployment fell to about 14 percent in 1937 but then rose again to about 17 percent in 1939. All over the country, people still struggled to survive.

The Dust Bowl

For American farmers, hard times began well before the start of the Great Depression. Despite the widespread prosperity of the 1920s, prices for farm products remained low. The Depression worsened this already bad situation. Conditions worsened again when a severe drought hit the Great Plains in the early 1930s and lasted most of the decade. From North Dakota to Texas, crops withered away. With no roots to hold it in place, topsoil began to blow away.

Massive dust storms swept the region, turning parts of the Great Plains into the **Dust Bowl**. "These storms were like rolling black smoke," recalled one Texas schoolboy. "We had to keep the lights on all day. We went to school with the headlights on, and with dust masks on." A woman from Kansas remembered dust storms "covering everything—including ourselves—in a thick, brownish gray blanket . . . Our faces were as dirty as if we had rolled in the dirt; our hair was gray and stiff and we ground dirt between our teeth."

Unable to raise crops, farmers in the Dust Bowl region could not pay their mortgages. Many lost their farms. Several New Deal programs tried to assist farmers by offering loans and by working to stabilize prices for farm products. Scientists also began thinking of ways to prevent dust storms during future droughts. Soil conservation experts encouraged farmers to adopt new farming methods to protect the soil. Grass was planted to hold soil in place, and rows of trees were planted to help break the wind. These changes have helped prevent another Dust Bowl in the years since the Great Depression.

For many farmers in the 1930s, however, the new programs came too late. After losing their crops and livestock to dust storms, about 2.5 million people left the area. Many packed up whatever they could fit in the family car or truck and drove to California to look for any kind of work they could find. These migrants were called "Okies" because so many were from Oklahoma. Once there, they often found that there were already more workers than available jobs.

READING CHECK Identifying Cause and **Effect** How did the Dust Bowl affect farmers?

Hard Times

The Great Depression took a heavy toll on families all over the United States. Many families were forced to split up, as individual members roamed the country in search of work. To help their families buy food, children often had to drop out of school and take very low-paying jobs. Others left home

Primary Source

PERSONAL ACCOUNT
The Dust Bowl

Lawrence Svobida was a Kansas wheat farmer who saw his life's work destroyed in the 1930s.

"When I knew that my crop was irrevocably [forever] gone I experienced a deathly feeling which, I hope, can affect a man only once in a lifetime. My dreams and ambitions . . . and my shattered ideals seemed gone forever. The very desire to make a success of my life was gone, the spirit and urge to strive were dead within me. Fate had dealt me a cruel blow above which I felt utterly unable to rise."

ANALYSIS SKILL **ANALYZING PRIMARY SOURCES**
How did Svobida feel after his crop was destroyed?

Interactive Map
The Dust Bowl

Severe drought during the 1930s destroyed the livelihood of many Great Plains farmers. Here, a black cloud of dust rages toward the outbuildings of a farm.

CANADA

MT ND
SD
WY
NV NE
CA IL Chicago
CO Liberal KS MO
Pueblo Dodge City 66 St. Louis
Boise City OK
Los Angeles 66 Oklahoma City ATLANTIC OCEAN
AZ Amarillo 30°N
NM
TX
120°W
PACIFIC OCEAN MEXICO Gulf of Mexico
90°W 80°W

Great Plains

Dust Bowl
Other areas with severe wind erosion
Migration routes

0 300 600 Miles
0 300 600 Kilometers

ANALYSIS SKILL **ANALYZING VISUALS**
Which part of the United States was affected by wind erosion?

to fend for themselves. One boy wrote this diary entry in 1932:

"Slept in paper box. Bummed swell breakfast three eggs and four pieces meat …Rode freight [train] to Roessville. Small burg [town], but got dinner. Walked Bronson …Couple a houses. Rode to Sidell …Hit homes for meals and turned down. Had to buy supper 20 cents. Raining."

—Anonymous, quoted in *The Great Depression*, by Thomas Minehan

Besides splitting families apart, the Great Depression took a psychological toll on men who equated success at work with success as a provider for their families. As white families moved west in search of jobs, Mexican Americans found it harder to get work. In California local leaders and unions convinced the government to deport many Mexican-born workers. Some of the workers' children were American-born, which made them U.S. citizens, but they were deported anyway.

African Americans also faced discrimination. Many lost jobs to unemployed white workers. One man recalled traveling around Michigan in search of work. He went into a factory that was hiring workers:

"They didn't hire me because I didn't belong to the right kind of race. Another time I went into Saginaw, it was two white fellas and myself made three. The fella there hired the two men and didn't hire me. I was back out on the streets. That hurt me pretty bad, the race part."

—Louis Banks, quoted in *Hard Times: An Oral History of the Great Depression*, by Studs Terkel

In spite of this type of discrimination, hundreds of thousands of African Americans were able to find work though relief programs such as the CCC and WPA. President Roosevelt also consulted with African American leaders, including educator **Mary McLeod Bethune**. Bethune was one of several African Americans who Roosevelt appointed to his administration. Other members included Walter White and William Henry Hastie. These advisers became known as the Black Cabinet. Their role was to advance the concerns of African Americans in the Roosevelt White House.

First Lady Eleanor Roosevelt was a strong supporter of equal rights. She encouraged the president to include African Americans in his recovery programs. In 1939 the Daughters of the American Revolution (DAR) refused to rent their auditorium to the African American singer Marian Anderson. In protest, Eleanor Roosevelt resigned her membership in the DAR. She then helped Anderson arrange a concert at the base of the Lincoln Memorial. Some 75,000 people attended.

READING CHECK **Drawing Inferences** What weakened families during the Depression?

Primary Source

PHOTOGRAPH
Migrant Mother

Photographer Dorothea Lange gained fame in the 1930s for documenting the conditions of the poor during the Depression. Lange took this famous photograph of a widowed migrant worker and two of her seven children. The woman worked in the pea fields of Nipomo, California. Her family survived by eating frozen peas and birds the children caught. The woman had just sold her car's tires for money to buy food.

ANALYSIS SKILL **ANALYZING PRIMARY SOURCES**

How would you describe the expression on the face of the woman in the photograph?

Depression-Era Culture

Starting in 1935, new Works Progress Administration projects began to put the country's painters, sculptors, writers, and actors to work. When he was criticized for hiring artists, WPA director Henry Hopkins said, "They've got to eat just like other people."

Some of the work done by WPA artists has become an important part of American culture. For example, WPA musicians went into the nation's rural areas to record cowboy ballads, folk songs, and African American spirituals. This music might have been lost without these recordings. Artists employed by the WPA made more than 2,500 murals and 17,000 pieces of sculpture for public spaces. WPA writers created a permanent record of American life by interviewing Americans of many different backgrounds about their lives and memories.

Like many people at the time, author **John Steinbeck** was deeply affected by the Great Depression. Depression life became a main theme of Steinbeck's most famous novel, *The Grapes of Wrath*. The novel tells the story of the Joads, a family of farmers who are forced to move to California for work.

Some of the music of the day expressed themes similar to Steinbeck's. Oklahoma-born folk singer **Woody Guthrie** crisscrossed the country singing his songs of loss and struggle. One contained the line, "All along your green valley I'll work till I die"—a grim reality for some Americans.

Swing music, meanwhile, became popular for a different reason. Instead of focusing on the sadness of the Depression, swing helped people forget their troubles. Big band leaders such as Duke Ellington, Benny Goodman, and Count Basie helped make swing wildly popular in the 1930s. People tuned into swing music shows on inexpensive radios and danced to the fast-paced rhythms. Radios provided people with other forms of entertainment as well. Every week millions of Americans put aside their

Escape to the Movies

Weekly Movie Attendance, 1929–1939

ANALYSIS SKILL **ANALYZING INFORMATION**

How many Americans attended movies in 1930?

worries to listen to radio shows such as *Little Orphan Annie* and *The Lone Ranger*.

Movies and fiction offered Americans another welcome escape from reality. One boy remembered how he and his friends would save their pennies for movie tickets. "[It] was two for a nickel," he said. "You'd come to the movie in the summer like 8:30 in the mornin' and you'd see about 200 kids." For 25 cents or less, adults, too, could forget their troubles as they watched historical dramas, gangster films, comedies, and musicals.

READING CHECK **Evaluating** How was the work of writers and musicians affected by the Great Depression?

THE IMPACT TODAY

Today many of the thousands of interviews conducted by WPA writers are available on the Internet. You can read the stories of former slaves, pioneers, Native American leaders, and others in their own words.

Causes and Effects of the New Deal

Causes
- Stock market crash
- Banking crisis
- Soaring unemployment
- Farmers' troubles
- Widespread poverty

Effects
- Expanded role of federal government
- Created major programs such as Social Security and the FDIC
- Provided hope and relief to many Americans but did not end the Great Depression

Effects of the New Deal

People are still debating the effects of the New Deal today. New Deal critics point out that Roosevelt's programs did not end the Great Depression. Full recovery occurred in the early 1940s, after the United States entered World War II. Roosevelt's supporters, however, believe that the New Deal gave Americans help and hope in a time of severe economic crisis.

People today do agree that the New Deal greatly expanded the role of the federal government. Some of the programs and agencies created as part of the New Deal, such as Social Security and the Federal Deposit Insurance Corporation (FDIC), remain part of our lives. Social Security still provides economic relief to the elderly, children, and those with disabilities. The FDIC protects the savings of bank customers.

READING CHECK **Finding the Main Idea** What are some current government programs that began during the New Deal?

SUMMARY AND PREVIEW The New Deal helped Americans but did not end the Great Depression. The Depression finally ended after the United States entered World War II, which you will learn about in the next chapter.

Section 3 Assessment

go.hrw.com
Online Quiz

Reviewing Ideas, Terms, and People

1. a. Identify What was the **Dust Bowl**?
   b. Explain What factors contributed to farmers' difficulties in the 1920s and 1930s?
2. a. Recall What were some of the problems people faced during the Depression?
   b. Compare How was the experience of African Americans and Mexican Americans in the Depression similar?
   c. Evaluate Do you think President Roosevelt did enough to help African Americans? Explain your answer.
3. a. Draw Conclusions Why do you think swing music, radio shows, and movies were popular during the Great Depression?
   b. Identify How did the WPA help the arts?
4. a. Recall What are the different viewpoints on the success of the New Deal?
   b. Elaborate How are Social Security and the FDIC still important today?

Critical Thinking

5. Categorizing Review your notes on life during the Great Depression. Then copy the graphic organizer below and use it to identify challenges people faced during the Depression and the ways they coped.

Challenges people faced	Ways people coped with challenges

FOCUS ON WRITING

6. Taking Notes on the Hard Times As you read this section, add notes about the Dust Bowl, family life, and Depression-era culture. What would it have been like to be a farmer at this time? How would you describe your experiences?

Depression-Era Literature

from *The Grapes of Wrath*

by John Steinbeck (1902–1968)

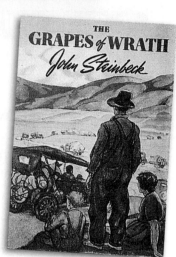

About the Reading *Published in 1939,* The Grapes of Wrath *described the impact of the Great Depression on the nation. In this passage, Steinbeck describes a journey of Dust Bowl families to California.*

AS YOU READ Look for details that appeal to the five senses.

Highway 66 is the main migrant road. 66—the long, concrete path across the country, waving gently up and down the map, from the Mississippi [River] to Bakersfield [California]—over the red lands and the gray lands, twisting up into the mountains, crossing the Divide and down into the bright and terrible desert to the mountains again, and into the rich California valleys.

66 is the path of people in flight,❶ refugees from dust and shrinking land, from the thunder of tractors and shrinking ownership, from the desert's slow northward invasion, from the twisting winds that howl up out of Texas, from the floods that bring no richness to the land and steal what little richness is there.❷ From all of these the people are in flight, and they come into 66 from the tributary side roads, from the wagon tracks and the rutted country roads. 66 is the mother road, the road of flight.

GUIDED READING

WORD HELP

migrant a person who moves regularly

Divide The Continental Divide separates rivers that flow east from those that flow west.

tributary stream that feeds into a larger river or lake (Steinbeck applies the word to the road system.)

❶ *From what are people on Highway 66 fleeing?*

❷ *How does Steinbeck describe what people are running from?*

CONNECTING LITERATURE TO HISTORY

1. **Steinbeck describes in vivid detail the fear that people on the road felt.** According to this passage, why might driving between towns be a terror? What does this tell you about the migrants?

2. ***The Grapes of Wrath* became a favorite among readers for its honest portrayal of the realities of the Depression.** Based on Steinbeck's description and on what you already know, how might people traveling on Route 66 have felt? Why?

Social Studies Skills

Having a Debate

Define the Skill

The First Amendment to the U.S. Constitution guarantees freedom of speech, assembly, and the press. These freedoms have become a key part of American democracy. They guarantee that both government officials and citizens can express their opinions. People also have the right to express disagreement with leaders or the government.

The ability to discuss opposing points of views is key to a democratic society. In the United States, citizens vote for their leaders. Having access to different points of view helps people decide which candidates to support in elections.

One way to express opposing points of view is to have a debate. Debates are organized to present two sides of an issue. Debate rules make sure that both sides are treated fairly. By learning about the strengths and weaknesses of two positions on an issue, people can decide which position is more convincing.

Learn the Skill

Think about the opposition President Franklin D. Roosevelt faced when he tried to begin new programs during the Great Depression. He had to convince people to support his ideas. Roosevelt and members of his administration used radio programs and newspaper articles to promote their point of view and answer questions from their critics.

In a debate, it is important to make your point of view clear. Explain why you support a certain position or give specific reasons why you oppose it. The more detailed the argument, the more persuasive it will be. When you are in a debate, make sure

to prepare plenty of evidence and examples to support your case.

Debaters have the chance not only to present a case but also to argue against the opposite point of view. One way to get ready for this is to think of possible arguments against your position. Prepare responses to each of these arguments in advance. Having good answers to criticism makes your position stronger.

In a debate, it is important to follow any rules that have been set up. Not all debates have the same rules. They do share some basic guidelines, however. Only one person is allowed to speak at once, and speaking time is limited. The two sides take turns presenting their arguments. Debates may have additional rules as well.

Practice the Skill

Suppose that your class is the Senate in 1933. President Roosevelt has already begun several new government programs. Now he is asking you to pass more new laws, which he believes will help the economy. Follow the guidelines above to have a debate about the New Deal. One group should support expanding the New Deal, and one group should oppose it. When the debate is over, answer the following questions.

1. Did your group make its point of view clear? Did it explain the reasons for taking that position? What do you think was your group's most persuasive supporting detail or example?

2. Did your group prepare arguments against the other side in advance? Were any of these arguments particularly effective?

HOLT

History's Impact
▶ video series
Review the video to answer
the closing question:

*How did some of Roosevelt's
programs lessen the damage
caused by the recessions of
1987 and the early 2000s?*

Visual Summary

*Use the visual summary below to help you review
the main ideas of the chapter.*

Stock Prices Plunge

**The economy began to decline
when the stock market crashed
in 1929.**

**Many farmers from the Great
Plains moved elsewhere to escape
the devastation of the Dust Bowl.**

**President Roosevelt and
Congress tried to end the
financial crisis.**

Reviewing Vocabulary, Terms, and People

Read each question and write the letter of the best response.

1. Which of the following refers to a severe economic downturn that lasted for more than 10 years?

a. the Bonus Army   **c.** the bull market

b. the Great Depression   **d.** the business cycle

2. Who was Franklin Roosevelt's secretary of labor and the first woman cabinet member?

a. Frances Perkins   **c.** Eleanor Roosevelt

b. Mary McLeod Bethune   **d.** Dorothea Lange

3. Parts of the Great Plains where a severe drought struck were known as the

a. Tennessee Valley.   **c.** Dust Bowl.

b. New Deal.   **d.** Hoovervilles.

4. Which of the following means purchasing stocks on credit with a loan?

a. the installment plan   **c.** the banking crisis

b. buying on margin   **d.** bear market

Comprehension and Critical Thinking

SECTION 1 *(Pages 198–202)*

5. a. Describe What happened on Black Tuesday—October 29, 1929?

b. Summarize How did President Hoover respond to the Depression?

c. Elaborate Why do you think Americans were so unprepared for difficult times?

SECTION 2 *(Pages 204–209)*

6. a. Recall What New Deal programs did lawmakers create during the Hundred Days?

b. Explain How did the Works Progress Administration help Americans?

c. Evaluate Do you think the New Deal was successful? Explain your answer.

7. a. Recall How did the Great Depression affect Mexican Americans?

b. Contrast How did Depression-era culture show both hope and the difficulties of everyday life?

c. Draw Conclusions Why do you think many African Americans supported President Roosevelt, even though they continued to face discrimination and segregation?

Reviewing Themes

8. Economics How did the economy of the country change during the Great Depression?

9. Politics What role did politics play in easing the Great Depression?

Reading Skills

Recognizing Implied Main Ideas *Use the Reading Skills taught in this chapter to answer the question about the reading selection below.*

> Banks had invested heavily in the stock market, so they lost heavily when the market crashed. Banks had also lent their customers money to buy stocks on margin. Now those customers were unable to pay back their loans. Some banks went out of business. People who had deposited their life savings in those banks lost everything. *(p.199)*

10. Write a main idea for the paragraph above.

Using the Internet go.hrw.com

11. Activity: Writing an Article During the 1930s, part of the Great Plains region of the United States became known as the Dust Bowl. The troubled region earned its nickname from the dust storms that swept through the dry, drought-stricken area. Enter the activity keyword. Research accounts of the Dust Bowl and write a magazine feature article about it. Your article should include references to your research and quotations from accounts of the Depression, and it should have correct spelling, punctuation, and grammar.

Social Studies Skills

Having a Debate *Use the Social Studies Skills taught in this chapter to answer the question below.*

12. Suppose you have been invited to participate in a debate on Franklin Roosevelt's plan to "pack" the Supreme Court by adding extra justices. First decide on your position. Then prepare several supporting arguments. Summarize the main points of your argument in a paragraph.

FOCUS ON WRITING

13. Writing Your Journal Entry Review your notes. Then decide on a fictional character and a set of circumstances for your character. Choose one or more events from the Great Depression for your character to talk about. Write a one-page journal entry about the life of this person. Begin by placing a date from the 1930s at the top of the page. Think about what life would have been like for this person. Remember to describe how the character feels about his or her experiences. What are your character's hopes and fears for the future?

Grade 8 Intermediate-Level Test Preparation

Directions (1–6): For each statement or question, write on the separate answer sheet the *number* of the word or expression that, of those given, best completes the statement or answers the question.

1 The day the stock market crashed in 1929, bringing on the great Depression, became known as

(1) Black Tuesday.

(2) Red Friday.

(3) Dark Monday.

(4) D-Day

2 President Roosevelt successfully used his fireside chats to

(1) promote the American movie industry.

(2) hold negotiations between labor unions and business owners.

(3) persuade many Americans to vote for him in the election of 1932.

(4) convince people that it was safe to keep their money in reopened banks.

3 Dorothea Lange contributed to our understanding of Depression life by

(1) writing novels about Dust Bowl farmers.

(2) singing songs about loss and hardship.

(3) photographing migrant workers.

(4) making movies that helped people forget their troubles.

4 How did the National Labor Relations Act affect organized labor?

(1) It increased the power of labor unions and helped them grow.

(2) It banned all strikes and increased the power of big business.

(3) It created new government jobs but did not affect labor unions.

(4) It gave relief money directly to labor unions to help unemployed workers.

5 What part of the business cycle contributes to a depression?

(1) Consumers begin buying more and companies increase production.

(2) Businesses produce more than they can sell and manufacturing slows.

(3) The stock market is a bull market and investors make large profits.

(4) People are buying products with cash.

6 Which of the following was a part of the New Deal?

(1) nationalizing businesses

(2) relieving unemployment

(3) guaranteeing every family an income of at least $5,000

(4) discouraging negotiations between labor unions and business owners

Base your answer to question 7 on the text below and on your knowledge of social studies.

> "66 is the path of people in flight, refugees from dust and shrinking land, from the thunder of tractors and shrinking ownership, from the desert's slow northward invasion, from the twisting winds that howl up out of Texas, from the floods that bring no richness to the land and steal what little richness is there."
>
> —John Steinbeck, *The Grapes of Wrath*

7 Constructed-Response Question Why did people travel on Highway 66, according to Steinbeck?

World War II

FOCUS QUESTION

How do competing views of power and morality lead to global conflict?

FOCUS ON WRITING

A Radio News Broadcast During World War II, millions of Americans had relatives fighting overseas. They relied on radio broadcasts for up-to-date news from the battlefronts around the world. In this chapter, you will read about American involvement in World War II. Then you will write a radio news broadcast about an event from the war.

UNITED STATES

1938 Orson Welles broadcasts "War of the Worlds."

1938

WORLD

What You Will Learn...

In this chapter, you will learn how the United States prepared for and fought in World War II. Life changed at home, as U.S. industries worked around the clock to supply the Allied armies. Life also changed for the 16 million Americans who served in the military around the world, like these soldiers who took part in the D-Day invasion of Normandy, France.

1943
A race riot in Harlem leaves five dead and 500 arrested.

1941 On December 7, the Japanese attack the U.S. fleet at Pearl Harbor, Hawaii.

1942 German submarines begin attacking the United States.

1944 U.S. forces participate in the D-Day invasion.

1945 The United States drops atomic bombs on Hiroshima and Nagasaki, Japan.

1940

1942

1944

1946

1940 Alan Turing devises a way to break the code of the German Enigma machine.

1943 Mussolini is overthrown and executed in Italy.

1944 The Allies enter Paris.

1945 Hideki Tojo, prime minister of Japan, attempts suicide after atomic bombs are dropped on Japan.

WORLD WAR II **221**

Reading Social Studies

by Kylene Beers

Economics   Geography   Politics   Society and Culture   Science and Technology

Focus on Themes In this chapter, you will read about the causes and consequences of World War II. You will learn about how **geography** played an important role in the fighting of the war. You will also read about how **society and culture** reacted to the Second World War.

Categorizing

Focus on Reading Have you ever read a schoolbook and been overwhelmed by the amount of information it contained? Categorizing events, people, and ideas can help you make sense of the facts you learn in this book.

Understanding Categorizing Ideas, people, events, and things can all be categorized in many different ways. For the study of history, some of the most useful ways are by time period and by similarity between events. Categorizing events by the people involved can also be helpful. Within a category, you can make subcategories to further organize the information.

People involved in WWII	Events of WWII
• Winston Churchill • Franklin D. Roosevelt • Adolf Hitler • Benito Mussolini • Hideki Tojo • Soldiers • Civilians	• Key battles • Treaties • Invasions

Invasions
• China • Rhineland • Czechoslovakia • Poland • Dunkirk • French Indochina • D-Day

You Try It!

The following passage is from the chapter you are getting ready to read. As you read the passage, look for ways to organize the information.

Japan Advances

American and Filipino forces under the command of American general Douglas MacArthur could not stop Japan's advance in the Philippines. MacArthur left the islands in March 1942, vowing to return. More than 70,000 American and Filipino soldiers surrendered to the Japanese. The exhausted soldiers were forced to march 63 miles up the Bataan Peninsula to prison camps. Many prisoners were starved and beaten by Japanese soldiers. More than 600 Americans and about 10,000 Filipinos died in the Bataan Death March.

From Chapter 9, p. 240

After you read the passage, answer the following questions.

1. What are two categories you could use to organize the information in this passage?

2. How many different kinds of people are mentioned in this passage?

3. What different places are mentioned in this passage?

4. Complete the chart below using the information from the passage above.

People involved	Countries involved	Places mentioned

As you read Chapter 9, remember to look for categories that can help you organize the information you read.

The War Begins

If YOU were there...

The year is 1933, and your family is struggling through the Great Depression along with millions of others. Sometimes your parents wonder if they should have left Italy to come to the United States. But conditions in Italy are far from ideal. A dictator rules the country, and the people have little personal freedom.

What would you say to your parents?

BUILDING BACKGROUND The Great Depression had a devastating impact on Europe. Nations there experienced the same credit problems, business failures, decreasing money supply, less demand and production of goods, and widespread unemployment that the United States experienced. Since European economies were tied together by trade and loans, effects of the Depression spread quickly across the continent. War debt and the huge costs of rebuilding made economic recovery even more difficult.

The Rise of Totalitarianism

Desperate to end the hard times, many people were willing to give up individual rights for the promise of prosperity and national glory. As a result, in the 1920s and 1930s, several European countries moved toward **totalitarianism**, a political system in which the government controls every aspect of citizens' lives.

Italy

The people of Italy suffered through economic depression, unemployment, strikes, and riots. Many Italians looked for a strong leader who offered stability. They found such a leader in **Benito Mussolini**, who gained complete control of Italy in 1922. Mussolini's rule was based on **fascism**, a political system in which the "state "—or government— is seen as more important than individuals. Fascist systems are typically militaristic and headed by a strong leader.

The fascist government violently crushed all opposition, destroying basic individual rights such as freedom of speech. In 1935 Mussolini tried to expand Italy's territory by attacking the nation of Ethiopia, making it a colony. Mussolini then turned his attention to Albania and other European territories that he viewed as constituting "a new Roman Empire."

Germany

Germany was also suffering the effects of the global depression. In addition, many Germans were furious about the crippling reparation

What You Will Learn...

Main Ideas

1. During the 1930s, totalitarian governments rose to power in Europe and Japan.
2. German expansion led to the start of World War II in Europe in 1939.
3. The United States joined the war after Japan attacked Pearl Harbor in 1941.

The Big Idea

The rise of aggressive totalitarian governments led to the start of World War II.

Key Terms and People

totalitarianism, p. 224
Benito Mussolini, p. 224
fascism, p. 224
Adolf Hitler, p. 225
Nazis, p. 225
Joseph Stalin, p. 225
Axis Powers, p. 226
appeasement, p. 226
Winston Churchill, p. 226
Allied Powers, p. 226
Lend-Lease Act, p. 228
Pearl Harbor, p. 228

TAKING NOTES As you read, take notes on the countries in which totalitarian governments gained power before World War II. Use a graphic organizer like the one below.

Totalitarianism before WW II	
Country	Leader

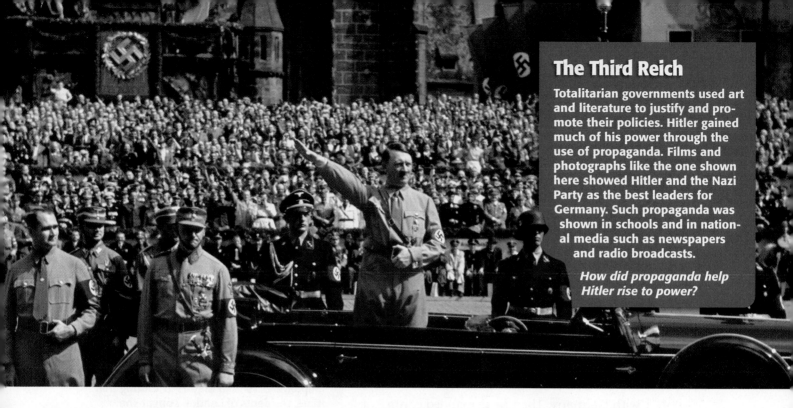

The Third Reich

Totalitarian governments used art and literature to justify and promote their policies. Hitler gained much of his power through the use of propaganda. Films and photographs like the one shown here showed Hitler and the Nazi Party as the best leaders for Germany. Such propaganda was shown in schools and in national media such as newspapers and radio broadcasts.

How did propaganda help Hitler rise to power?

payments for its role in World War I. **Adolf Hitler** used this public anger to gain power.

Hitler offered Germans a scapegoat, or someone to blame for their problems. He accused intellectuals, Communists, and Jews of causing defeat in World War I and economic problems after the war. Only by ridding itself of Jews, Hitler declared, would Germany again be great. Hitler 's National Socialist Party, or **Nazis**, gained a large following. Hitler became chancellor in 1933 and quickly seized all government power.

The Soviet Union

By 1928 **Joseph Stalin** had become dictator of the Soviet Union. In the 1930s Stalin terrorized those he saw as political enemies, killing or imprisoning millions of Soviet citizens.

Japan

In Japan a group of military leaders had gained control during the early 1900s. They wanted to build a large empire in East Asia. In 1931 Japan conquered a region in northern China. In 1937–1938, Japan invaded China proper. At least 360,000 Chinese were killed, and as many as 100,000 civilians and prisoners of war were massacred in Nanking.

Spain

In Spain, many political parties struggled for control of the government. The defenders of the government received military aid from the Soviet Union, Mexico, and the United States. Their opponents, led by General Francisco Franco, received military aid from Nazi Germany and Fascist Italy. The battle against Franco and his troops was viewed by many as the most important front against the spread of fascism. By 1939 Franco's forces had won the war, and he was declared dictator.

Despite the fight against Franco, the international community had little success in stopping the spread of fascism. The League of Nations failed to halt the expansion of Germany and other totalitarian nations. Although the World Court heard cases against fascist countries, it could only condemn their actions with strong words.

READING CHECK **Comparing** What did the leaders of totalitarian governments have in common?

Germany Expands

Hitler dreamed of avenging Germany's defeat in World War I. "The lost land will never be won back by solemn appeals to God," he told Germans, "nor by hopes in any League of Nations, but only by force of arms." Hitler wanted to build an empire, uniting all German-speaking people in Europe. He also wanted "living space" for the growing German population.

In violation of the Treaty of Versailles, Hitler began to rebuild the German military. In 1936 Nazi troops invaded the Rhineland, a former German territory lost during World War I. That year he also signed an alliance with Mussolini, forming the **Axis Powers**. Japan later joined this pact. In 1938 Hitler forced Austria to unite with Germany. Then he demanded control of the Sudetenland, a region in Czechoslovakia where many Germans lived. When the Czechs refused, Hitler threatened war.

Nazi planes bombed London from September 1940 to May 1941. During that time, residents of London sought shelter wherever they could, including subway stations. Here, a relief effort passes out food to Londoners who have lost their homes.

Appeasement Fails

Czech leaders looked to their allies in France and Great Britain for help. But neither country wanted to be pulled into an armed conflict. British prime minister Neville Chamberlain organized a meeting with Hitler to work out a peaceful solution. At the 1938 Munich Conference, Germany was given control over the Sudetenland in return for a promise not to demand more land. This approach was known as **appeasement**—a policy of avoiding war with an aggressive nation by giving in to its demands. British admiral **Winston Churchill** was convinced that this strategy would not stop Hitler. "The government had to choose between shame and war," Churchill warned. "They have chosen shame. They will get war."

Churchill was right. In March 1939, German troops seized the rest of Czechoslovakia and began demanding territory from Poland. Great Britain and France pledged to defend Poland if Hitler attacked. To keep the Soviets out of the conflict, Hitler signed a nonaggression pact with Joseph Stalin in August 1939. In addition to promising not to attack each other, the two countries secretly agreed to divide Poland between them.

On September 1, 1939, Hitler's troops and tanks rushed into Poland. This was the start of World War II. Two days later, Britain and France, known as the **Allied Powers**, declared war on Germany. Neville Chamberlain spoke bitterly of the failure of appeasement, saying, "Everything that I believed in during my public life has crashed into ruins."

Hitler Moves West

The Allied Powers had little time to organize their forces to protect Poland. Using a strategy called *blitzkrieg*, or "lightning war," German tanks and airplanes broke through Polish defenses. As German forces drove into Poland from the west, the Soviets attacked from the east. Within a month, the two powers had taken control of Poland.

With Poland secure, Hitler turned toward western Europe. In the spring of 1940, Germany quickly conquered Denmark, Norway,

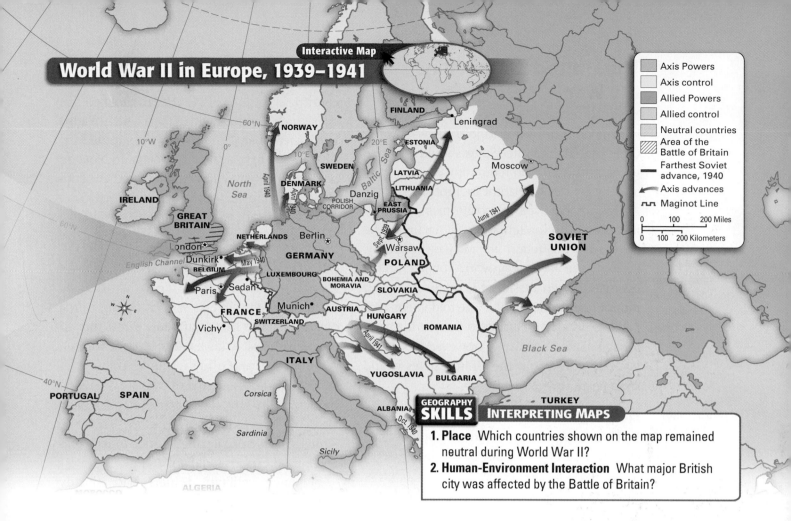

World War II in Europe, 1939–1941

Interactive Map

Legend:
- Axis Powers
- Axis control
- Allied Powers
- Allied control
- Neutral countries
- Area of the Battle of Britain
- Farthest Soviet advance, 1940
- Axis advances
- Maginot Line

0   100   200 Miles
0   100   200 Kilometers

GEOGRAPHY SKILLS INTERPRETING MAPS

1. **Place** Which countries shown on the map remained neutral during World War II?
2. **Human-Environment Interaction** What major British city was affected by the Battle of Britain?

Belgium, Luxembourg, and the Netherlands. German troops then invaded France, trapping hundreds of thousands of Belgian, British, and French soldiers in the French port city of Dunkirk. British ships raced to Dunkirk and carried the soldiers across the English Channel to safety in Britain.

German forces, meanwhile, continued their march through France. As the Germans approached the French capital of Paris, Italy declared war on the Allied powers. France surrendered to Germany on June 22, 1940. Many of the French soldiers who had escaped at Dunkirk, however, continued to resist Germany's occupation of France. In London, French general Charles de Gaulle organized a "Free French" army to fight alongside the Allies. "France has lost a battle," de Gaulle declared. "But France has not lost the war!"

The Battle of Britain

Great Britain now stood alone against Hitler's war machine. "The final German victory over England is now only a question of time," said German general Alfred Jodl. Hitler prepared to invade Britain. To safely move troops and equipment across the English Channel, Germany first had to defeat the British Royal Air Force (RAF). In July 1940 the Luftwaffe, or German air force, began attacking British planes and airfields in what became known as the Battle of Britain.

In August Hitler ordered the Luftwaffe to begin bombing British cities in the hope of crushing British morale. But Winston Churchill, the new prime minister, refused to give in. "We shall fight on the beaches," he vowed. "We shall fight in the fields and in the streets, we shall never surrender." Using the new technology of radar, the RAF was able to detect and destroy some 2,300 of the Luftwaffe's aircraft. Hitler canceled the invasion of Britain.

READING CHECK Sequencing What event sparked World War II?

The United States Joins the War

Most Americans opposed Hitler's actions, but they did not want to join the war. Many thought that the United States should continue to focus its efforts on rebuilding the economy and correcting other domestic problems. These Americans believed in isolationism, or non-involvment in foreign affairs. They urged the government to retain its policy of neutrality, even in the face of growing totalitarianism overseas. When President Franklin Roosevelt ran for re-election in 1940, he told voters that "your boys are not going to be sent into any foreign wars." Privately, however, Roosevelt was convinced that the United States would soon be at war.

THE IMPACT TODAY

Pearl Harbor is still the headquarters of the U.S. Pacific Fleet today. The sunken USS *Arizona*, still visible beneath the harbor waters, is a national memorial to the victims of the Pearl Harbor attack.

Helping the Allies

In 1941 Roosevelt proposed new programs to assist the Allies. "We must be the great arsenal [arms supply] of democracy," he told Congress. In March 1941 Congress passed the **Lend-Lease Act**, allowing the president to aid any nation believed vital to U.S. defense. Under Lend-Lease, the United States sent billions of dollars' worth of aid in the form of weapons, tanks, airplanes, and food to Great Britain, the Nationalists in China, and other Allied countries. In June 1941 Hitler violated his nonaggression pact with Stalin and invaded the Soviet Union. The Soviets then joined the Allies in the fight against Germany. In November the United States extended the Lend-Lease program to the Soviet Union, though many Americans worried about giving aid to a Communist country.

Japan Attacks Pearl Harbor

Like Germany and Italy, Japan was quickly building an empire. After conquering much of China in the 1930s, Japanese forces moved into Southeast Asia. Japan's leaders wanted control of oil and other resources there.

When Japanese forces captured French Indochina in July 1941, Roosevelt protested. He demanded that Japan withdraw. Then the United States froze Japanese funds in its banks and cut off exports to Japan.

Japanese military leaders had already begun planning a large-scale attack to destroy the U.S. naval fleet stationed at **Pearl Harbor**, in Hawaii. This would give Japan time to secure control of East Asia before the U.S. military could respond.

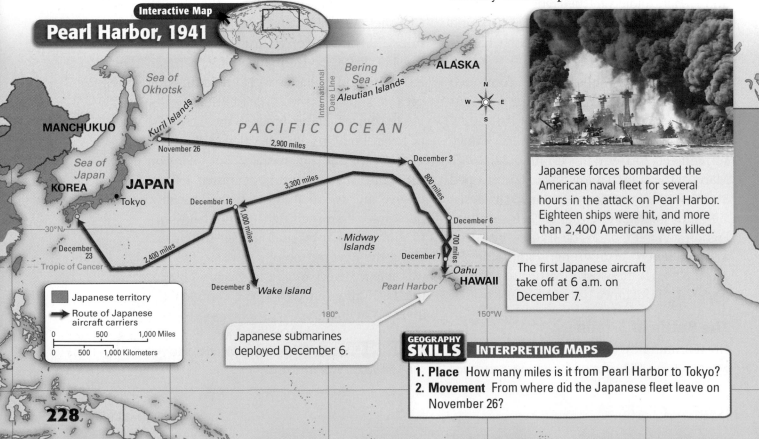

Pearl Harbor, 1941

Interactive Map

Japanese forces bombarded the American naval fleet for several hours in the attack on Pearl Harbor. Eighteen ships were hit, and more than 2,400 Americans were killed.

The first Japanese aircraft take off at 6 a.m. on December 7.

Japanese submarines deployed December 6.

Japanese territory

Route of Japanese aircraft carriers

0   500   1,000 Miles
0   500   1,000 Kilometers

GEOGRAPHY SKILLS ▶ **INTERPRETING MAPS**

1. **Place** How many miles is it from Pearl Harbor to Tokyo?
2. **Movement** From where did the Japanese fleet leave on November 26?

At 7:55 a.m. on Sunday, December 7, 1941, Japanese airplanes dove from the sky and attacked Pearl Harbor. An American sailor aboard the USS *Arizona* remembered how quickly his battleship was hit and destroyed:

"I began to realize there were dead men all around me . . . it was obvious the ship was doomed. I made my way to the side of the ship, which by this time was sinking fast, and jumped off."

—George D. Phraner, quoted in *World War II,* by H. P. Willmott

In just a few hours, the Japanese sank or damaged all of the battleships anchored at Pearl Harbor. More than 2,400 Americans were killed. Almost 200 airplanes were destroyed.

Speaking to Congress the next day, President Roosevelt called December 7, 1941, "a date which will live in infamy [disgrace]." Congress voted to declare war on Japan. Germany then declared war on the United States. Less than 25 years after entering World War I, the United States joined the Allies in another global war. This one would be even more devastating.

CASE STUDY BIOGRAPHY

Daniel Inouye
1924–

Daniel Inouye was born in Honolulu, Hawaii, to Japanese parents. When the Japanese attacked Pearl Harbor, the 17-year-old Inouye used his medical aid training to help treat victims. He joined the army the next year, winning several medals for bravery in combat. In an attack in Italy, Inouye was shot three times, and his right arm had to be amputated. After the war, Inouye studied law and entered politics. In 1959 he became Hawaii's first representative in Congress, as well as the first Japanese American to serve in Congress. He was elected to the U.S. Senate in 1962 and became an important figure in U.S. politics.

Drawing Conclusions Why do you think Inouye went into politics?

READING CHECK **Identifying Cause and Effect** What did Japan hope to gain by attacking Pearl Harbor?

SUMMARY AND PREVIEW Military aggression in Europe and Asia drew the United States into war. In the next section you will learn how the war affected the home front.

Section 1 Assessment

go.hrw.com
Online Quiz

Reviewing Ideas, Terms, and People

1. **a. Identify** What types of leaders came to power in Italy, Germany, and the Soviet Union before World War II?
   b. Explain Why did some Europeans have faith in these leaders?
2. **a. Summarize** What did **Adolf Hitler** promise the German people? How did he act on this promise?
   b. Recall Which countries formed the **Axis Powers** and the **Allied Powers**?
   c. Elaborate Do you think **Winston Churchill** was a good choice for Britain's prime minister? Explain your answer.
3. **a. Explain** What event brought the United States into World War II?
   b. Describe How did the **Lend-Lease Act** help the Allies?

Critical Thinking

4. **Identifying Cause and Effect** Review your notes on totalitarian countries and their leaders prior to World War II. Then copy the graphic organizer below and use it to give details on the causes of World War II.

FOCUS ON WRITING

5. **Taking Notes on Pearl Harbor** Look back at what you have read about the attack on Pearl Harbor. Take notes on who attacked Pearl Harbor, where the attack took place, and when. What were the results of the attack?

The Home Front

What You Will Learn...

Main Ideas

1. Businesses, soldiers, and citizens worked to prepare the United States for war.
2. The war brought new opportunities for many women and minorities.
3. Japanese Americans faced internment during the war.

The Big Idea

American involvement in World War II helped the U.S. economy and changed the lives of many Americans.

Key Terms and People

War Production Board, *p. 230*
A. Philip Randolph, *p. 232*
Tuskegee Airmen, *p. 232*
Benjamin O. Davis, Jr., *p. 232*
zoot-suit riots, *p. 233*
internment, *p. 233*

TAKING NOTES As you read, look for information about how the war brought both opportunities and challenges to minorities. Record your notes in a graphic organizer like the one below.

Opportunities   Challenges

If **YOU** were there...

Shopping for food has become a whole new experience since the United States entered World War II. When your mother sends you to the grocery store these days, she gives you government-issued ration stamps. These stamps limit the amount of sugar, butter, and meat each family can buy. The sacrifice is difficult, but you know it will help the soldiers fighting overseas.

In what other ways can you help the war effort?

BUILDING BACKGROUND As World War II raged in 1940 and 1941, the Allies relied on war supplies and food from the United States. President Roosevelt and Congress also increased defense spending at home, believing that the United States would soon join the fighting. The increased spending boosted the U.S. economy.

Preparing for War

The United States was still experiencing the effects of the Great Depression when the Japanese attacked Pearl Harbor in December 1941. The enormous effort of mobilizing for war finally brought the Depression to an end. Factories ran 24 hours a day, producing ships, tanks, jeeps, guns, and ammunition. Americans turned their knowledge of mass production toward the production of war supplies. One remarkable example was the building of Liberty ships— transport vessels for troops and supplies. Workers could build an entire 441-foot-long Liberty ship in as little as four days.

American workers were soon doubling the war production of Germany, Japan, and all other Axis Power countries combined. Unemployment fell to 1 percent in 1944. Agricultural production increased as well, as farmers sent food overseas to feed Allied soldiers. To organize the war effort, the government created the **War Production Board** (WPB) to oversee the conversion of factories to war production. In 1942, for example, the WPB banned the production of cars so that auto plants could produce military equipment.

The United States also needed millions of soldiers. Congress had begun to prepare for war by passing the Selective Training and Service Act in 1940. This was the first peacetime draft in the country's history.

Men from the ages of 21 to 35 (later 18 to 38) were required to register for the draft. More than 16 million Americans served during the war.

To finance the war effort, the government increased taxes and sold war bonds. War bonds were essentially loans that people made to the government. People who bought war bonds in 1942, for example, would get their money back 10 years later, with interest.

Americans also contributed to the war effort by collecting scrap metal that could be used in weapons factories. People learned to adjust to government rations limiting the supply of gasoline, rubber, shoes, and some foods. Posters urged Americans to "Use it up, wear it out, make it do, or do without."

READING CHECK **Identifying Cause and Effect** How did the war affect the U.S. economy?

Wartime Opportunities

You read that wartime production during World War I created new opportunities for many women and minorities. The same thing happened on an even larger scale during World War II.

New Roles for Women

With so many men leaving home to fight in World War II, factories badly needed new workers. The government urged women to fill these positions. Women found themselves doing work that had traditionally been considered "unladylike." One female riveter (a person who fastens parts on a machine) recalled her experiences building airplanes:

" [I] learned to use an electric drill . . . and I soon became an outstanding riveter . . . The war really created opportunities for women. It was the first time we got a chance to show that we could do a lot of things that only men had done before. "
—Winona Espinosa, quoted in *Ordinary Americans*, edited by Linda Monk

Women also filled new roles in military service. About 300,000 women served in the armed forces through special divisions such as the Women's Auxiliary Army Corps (WAAC) and Women's Airforce Service Pilots (WASP). WASP pilots flew test flights and ferried planes between factories and air bases. Army and navy nurses served in combat areas.

Primary Source

POSTERS
Supporting the War

Posters like these encouraged Americans to support their troops in a variety of ways. Building weaponry, growing food, saving scrap metal, and rationing all helped the war effort and allowed soldiers to have necessary supplies.

"Rosie the Riveter" became a symbol of women's work to support the war.

Victory gardens planted at home allowed more commercially produced food to be sent from farms to troops overseas.

We Can Do It

WAR GARDENS FOR VICTORY

GROW VITAMINS AT YOUR KITCHEN DOOR

ANALYSIS SKILL **ANALYZING PRIMARY SOURCES**

How did posters like these aim to help troops overseas?

African Americans

The Great Migration that began during World War I continued as African Americans moved to northern cities to find factory jobs. In most cases, however, black workers received lower pay than did white workers. They also were restricted in what kinds of jobs they were hired to perform.

To protest this unfair treatment, African American labor leader **A. Philip Randolph** began to organize a march to Washington, D.C., in 1941. "If freedom and equality are not [granted for] the peoples of color, the war for democracy will not be won," he argued. President Roosevelt issued Executive Order 8802, which prohibited racial discrimination in the government and in companies producing war goods.

AUTOBIOGRAPHY
Tuskegee Airmen

Benjamin O. Davis was a graduate of West Point who became the first African American Air Force officer to achieve the rank of general. During World War II he led the first African American flying unit, the 99th Fighter Squadron. These men had been trained at the Tuskegee Institute in Alabama.

❝While no AAF [American Air Force] unit had gone into combat better trained or better equipped than the 99th Fighter Squadron, we lacked actual combat experience. So as we approached our first missions, my own inexperience and that of my flight commanders was a major source of concern. On the other hand, we had averaged about 250 hours per man in a P-40 (quite a lot for pilots who had not yet flown their first missions), and we possessed an unusually strong sense of purpose and solidarity.**❞**

—Benjamin O. Davis,
*Benjamin O. Davis,
American: An Autobiography*

ANALYSIS SKILL **ANALYZING PRIMARY SOURCES**

What advantages did the Tuskegee Airmen bring to battle?

Although members of every race participated in the war as American soldiers, life for minorities at home changed very little. African Americans were still subject to segregation, and Mexican Americans continued to have very little economic opportunity. After the attack on Pearl Harbor, Japanese Americans were removed from their communities and ordered into internment camps far away from the West Coast.

About 1 million African Americans served in the armed forces during the war, mostly in segregated units. In the Navy, African Americans were assigned only to support positions and denied the right to participate in combat. Despite this, many black soldiers became national heroes during the war, including Dorie Miller. Leaving his post as ship's cook, Miller manned a machine gun on the deck of the USS *West Virginia* until he was ordered to abandon the ship because it was sinking.

The **Tuskegee Airmen** were African American pilots who trained at the Tuskegee Army Air Field in Alabama. **Benjamin O. Davis, Jr.,** who later became the first African American general in the U.S. Air Force, led the group. Davis and his pilots had to overcome prejudice in the military as well as the hazards of war. He later described the pilots as "outstanding Americans who served their country unselfishly. Despite treatment that would have demoralized men of lesser strength and character, they persisted through humiliations and dangers to earn the respect of their fellows." The Tuskegee Airmen flew thousands of successful combat missions in North Africa and Italy.

Japanese American Internment

- Not interned — 6%
- Japanese citizens living in America interned — 37%
- American citizens of Japanese descent interned — 57%

Mexican Americans

About 300,000 Mexican Americans served in the military during the war. Many Mexican Americans also found wartime jobs on the West Coast and in the Midwest. Because of a shortage of farm workers, the federal government asked Mexico to provide agricultural workers. The workers, called *braceros*, were guaranteed a minimum wage, food, shelter, and clean living conditions. About 200,000 Mexicans worked in the *bracero* program.

Young Mexican Americans of the time created their own culture by blending different music styles and clothing styles. Some men wore zoot suits—fancy, loose-fitting outfits with oversized hats. Despite their aiding of the war effort, many faced discrimination. In Los Angeles in June 1943, groups of sailors attacked Mexican Americans wearing zoot suits, beginning the **zoot-suit riots**. During the 10-day period, white mobs attacked many Mexican Americans.

READING CHECK **Evaluating** How did the war create both opportunities and challenges for minorities?

Japanese American Internment

Japanese Americans faced a different form of prejudice during World War II. After the Japanese attack on Pearl Harbor, some Americans began to look at Americans of Japanese descent with fear and suspicion. Most Japanese Americans lived on the West Coast at this time. It was feared that they would serve as secret agents for Japan and help Japan prepare an invasion of the West Coast or try to sabotage U.S. war efforts.

The U.S. government had no evidence to support these fears. In spite of this fact, President Roosevelt issued Executive Order 9066. This order allowed the government to begin the process of **internment**, or forced relocation and imprisonment, of Japanese Americans. About 115,000 Japanese Americans were evacuated from their homes and held in isolated internment camps. Half of those held in the camps were children. A smaller number of Americans of German and Italian ancestry were also held in internment camps during the war.

THE IMPACT TODAY

Congress passed the Civil Liberties Act of 1988 to compensate victims of internment. Each living Japanese American who had been interned—60,000 in all—received $20,000 and a formal apology signed by President Ronald Reagan.

After the Japanese Americans were released from internment, many chose to move to New York City in an effort to restart their lives. The West Coast, because of its proximity to Japan, had always been home to many more Japanese Americans than the East Coast. Anti-Japanese sentiment was so strong in California, however, that many released internees looked elsewhere to open businesses and find jobs. The influx of internees more than doubled the Japanese American population in New York City.

At this time, some Japanese Americans were *Issei*, or immigrants born in Japan. But most were *Nisei*, American citizens born in the United States to Japanese immigrant parents. Whether they were U.S. citizens or not, Japanese Americans lost their jobs, homes, and belongings when they were forced to move to internment camps. A farm owner named Yuri Tateishi spoke of feeling betrayed by his government. "You hurt," he said. "You give up everything that you worked for that far, and I think everybody was at the point of just having gotten out of the Depression and was just getting on his feet. And then all that happens! You have to throw everything away."

After the Pearl Harbor attack, the government banned young Japanese American men from serving in the military. But Roosevelt reversed this policy in 1943. Daniel Inouye remembered the excitement he and his fellow Japanese Americans in Hawaii felt when they heard that the government was going to form an all-*Nisei* combat team. An army recruiter had prepared a pep talk for the young Japanese Americans, but this proved to be unnecessary:

" As soon as he said that we were now eligible to volunteer, that room exploded into a fury of yells and motion. We went bursting out of there and ran—ran!—the three miles to the draft board …jostling for position, like a bunch of marathoners gone berserk. "

—Daniel Inouye, quoted in *Only What We Could Carry*, edited by Lawson Fusao Inada

Inouye was one of about 33,000 *Nisei* who served in World War II. The Japanese American 100th/442nd Regimental Combat Team received more than 18,000 decorations for bravery—more than any other unit of its size in U.S. military history. Many of the soldiers of the 100th/442nd served while their families were held in internment camps back home.

READING CHECK **Evaluating** Why were Japanese Americans interned?

SUMMARY AND PREVIEW The war effort changed life on the home front. In the next section you will learn about the fighting in Europe and North Africa.

**go.hrw.com
Online Quiz**

Section 2 Assessment

Reviewing Ideas, Terms, and People

1. **a. Describe** How did people on the home front support the war effort?
   b. Identify What government agency oversaw factory production during the war?
2. **a. Recall** What were the WAAC and the WASP?
   b. Explain Why did **A. Philip Randolph** organize a march on Washington and then cancel it?
   c. Elaborate How did the *bracero* program benefit both Mexicans and Americans?
3. **a. Define** What was the **internment** program?
   b. Contrast How did the U.S. government change its policy toward Japanese Americans serving in the military? How did many respond?

Critical Thinking

4. **Categorizing** Review your notes on challenges and opportunities for different groups of people in America during World War II. Then copy the graphic organizer below and use it to list opportunities that women, African Americans, and Mexican Americans found during the war.

Wartime Opportunities

Women	African Americans	Mexican Americans

FOCUS ON WRITING

5. **Taking Notes on the Home Front** Radio broadcasts often reminded Americans to "do your part" in winning World War II. Take notes on the ways ordinary citizens helped the troops by supporting the war effort on the home front. How might you convince someone to support the effort?

War in Europe and North Africa

SECTION 3

If YOU were there...

The year is 1943, and you are a senior in high school. You know that you will be drafted into the armed forces as soon as you graduate. Every day after school you listen to radio reports about the battles being fought around the world. Your future, and the future of the whole world, seems so uncertain.

How do you feel about fighting in this war?

> **BUILDING BACKGROUND** By the time the United States entered the war, the Allies were in trouble. The Axis Powers controlled much of western Europe and were advancing in North Africa and the Soviet Union. German submarine attacks on Allied ships were making it difficult to get American supplies to the British.

The Allies Fight Back

In December 1941, soon after the United States entered the war, President Roosevelt met with British prime minister Winston Churchill to work out a plan to defeat the Axis Powers. Roosevelt agreed that the United States would place "Europe first" in its plans to defeat the Axis, while still aiding China in the fight against Japan in the Pacific. In addition, Roosevelt and Churchill agreed on two initial strategies: a buildup of troops in Great Britain to be used to invade France, and an assault on German forces in North Africa.

Meanwhile, the Soviets had been demanding Allied help on the eastern front, where they had borne the brunt of the European war for months after Hitler's invasion. Stalin wanted the Allies to attack

The Allies began using sonar to destroy German U-boats, shown here in a German harbor.

What You Will Learn...

Main Ideas
1. The Allies fought back against the Axis Powers in North Africa and Europe.
2. Key Allied victories halted the German advance.
3. In the D-Day invasion, Allied forces attacked German-controlled France.

The Big Idea

After fierce fighting in North Africa and Europe, the Allies stopped the German advance and slowly began driving back German forces.

Key Terms and People
Battle of El Alamein, *p. 236*
Dwight D. Eisenhower, *p. 236*
Battle of Stalingrad, *p. 237*
D-Day, *p. 239*

TAKING NOTES As you read, make a list of the major battles and campaigns in different areas of the world. You may want to organize your list in a table like this one.

North Africa	Italy	Eastern Europe	Western Europe

in Europe immediately, to take some of the pressure off of the Soviet forces in the east. In July 1942, however, the Allies decided to put a European invasion on hold and launch an initial offensive in North Africa. Stalin was angry. The Soviets would have to continue to fight the war on the eastern front without a western European assault to distract the Germans.

As they prepared their battle plans, the Allies faced many obstacles. One major threat the Allies had to combat was U-boat attacks. In 1942 alone German U-boats sank more than 6,000,000 tons of Allied materials. To prevent further damage, the Allies used the convoy system of multiple ships traveling at once, along with new sonar technology. Sonar, which uses sound waves to detect objects underwater, helped Allied ships find and destroy German U-boats. In addition, new long-range Allied planes protected the convoys from the air. Long-range planes could also fly into German territory to drop bombs on factories, railroads, and cities, inflicting tremendous damage on German targets.

FOCUS ON READING
What categories could you use to organize the information in this paragraph?

READING CHECK Explaining What battle plan did the Allies agree to pursue after American entry into the war?

CASE STUDY **BIOGRAPHY**

Dwight D. Eisenhower
1890–1969

Dwight D. Eisenhower was born in Denison, Texas. "Ike," as his friends called him, attended the U.S. Military Academy at West Point and trained soldiers for tank warfare during World War I. With a strong ability to organize and plan strategies, as well as a persuasive and optimistic personality, Eisenhower rose to the rank of general during World War II. He was named supreme commander of Allied forces in western Europe in 1943. His standing as a war hero helped him win the presidential elections of 1952 and 1956.

Drawing Inferences What were some of Eisenhower's strengths?

Halting the German Advance

Churchill predicted that the road to victory would be long and difficult. By winning several key battles, however, Allied forces finally stopped the German advance.

North Africa and Italy

As you have read, a main focus for the Allies when the United States entered the war was North Africa. The Germans and British were battling for control there because Axis leaders wanted to grab control of the Suez Canal, a crucial supply route in Egypt. Germany's Afrika Korps was led by General Erwin Rommel, nicknamed the Desert Fox for his bold, surprise attacks.

In the summer of 1942, Rommel began an offensive to take Egypt. General Bernard Montgomery led the British forces to stop the Germans. The British stopped the Afrika Korps in July at the **Battle of El Alamein**. At the same time, U.S. and British troops, led by American general **Dwight D. Eisenhower**, came ashore in Morocco and Algeria, west of Egypt. Caught between two Allied forces, the Afrika Korps surrendered in May 1943.

With North Africa under their control, the Allies prepared to attack the Axis Powers in Europe. Churchill identified Italy as the "soft underbelly" of the Axis. Allied forces invaded the island of Sicily in July 1943 and moved from there to the Italian mainland. Italian leaders overthrew Mussolini and surrendered to the Allies. But Hitler refused to recognize the Axis defeat. He sent German troops to Italy to block the Allied advance.

In January 1944, Allied forces tried to get behind the Germans with a surprise attack at Anzio, on the western coast of Italy. American and British troops landed at Anzio but were pinned down on the beach for several months. The "soft underbelly" proved to be much tougher than expected. Finally, the Allied forces in southern Italy battled north to Anzio. The combined forces captured Rome, the capital of Italy, in June

Winston Churchill
Prime Minister of
Great Britain

Franklin Roosevelt
President of
the United States

Joseph Stalin
Premier of
the Soviet Union

Adolf Hitler
Chancellor of
Germany

Benito Mussolini
Prime Minister
of Italy

1944. Early in 1945, German forces were driven out of Italy. Italian freedom fighters executed Mussolini.

The Battle of Stalingrad

Meanwhile, massive German and Soviet armies were battling on the eastern front. By the middle of 1942, Axis armies had driven deep into Soviet territory. Millions of Soviet soldiers had been killed or captured.

German forces then advanced to the key industrial city of Stalingrad. German firebombs set much of the city on fire. But Soviet leader Joseph Stalin was determined to hold on to Stalingrad at all costs. Savage street fighting dragged on for months. Soviet snipers used the ruined buildings to their advantage, firing at German soldiers from behind piles of stone and brick.

German supplies began to run desperately low as the harsh Russian winter began. Hitler remained obsessed with capturing Stalingrad, however. He ordered his troops to keep fighting, though he did not send enough new supplies or soldiers. Thousands of Germans froze or starved to death. In late January 1943 the German commander at Stalingrad defied Hitler and surrendered to save his remaining troops. The **Battle of Stalingrad** thus became a key turning point of the war.

The Soviet victory came at an enormous cost—more than 1 million Soviet soldiers died at Stalingrad. About 800,000 Axis soldiers were killed. After Stalingrad, the Soviets won another victory in the city of Kursk, in the biggest tank battle ever fought. The Axis Powers now began to retreat from the Soviet Union. The tide of the war in the east had turned.

READING CHECK **Sequencing** What events led to the Allied victories in Italy and Russia?

The D-Day Invasion

After hard-fought victories in North Africa and Italy, the Allies were ready for an even tougher task—the invasion of German-occupied France. This was the first step toward the goal of liberating Europe and forcing Hitler to surrender.

Interactive Map

World War II in Europe, 1942–1945

Axis controlled, June 1944
Allied controlled, June 1944
Neutral country
Farthest Axis advance, 1942
Allied advance
Major battle
Allied air attack

0   150   300 Miles
0   150   300 Kilometers

Tanks thundered across Europe, destroying much of what lay in their paths.

Airplanes dropped millions of bombs on opposing forces. They were also used for moving troops and for spying on the enemy.

NORWAY
FINLAND
Leningrad
SWEDEN
DENMARK
North Sea
Baltic Sea
GREAT BRITAIN
London
Antwerp
English Channel
NETHERLANDS
BELGIUM
Berlin Apr.–May 1945
Elbe River
Oder River
Vistula River
SOVIET UNION
Stalingrad Nov. 1942–Feb. 1943
D-Day June 1944
Battle of the Bulge Dec. 1944
Paris
GERMANY
SLOVAKIA
HUNGARY
ATLANTIC OCEAN
FRANCE
Rhine River
Danube River
SWITZERLAND
AUSTRIA
ROMANIA
VICHY FRANCE
AUG. 1944
CROATIA
SERBIA
PORTUGAL
SPAIN
Corsica
Rome
Anzio Jan. 1944
ITALY
Adriatic Sea
MONTENEGRO
ALBANIA
BULGARIA
GIBRALTAR (BR)
NOV. 1942
Sardinia
40°N
Aegean Sea
GREECE
SPANISH MOROCCO
NOV. 1942
NOV. 1942
SEPT. 1943
Sicily
Malta
Crete
MOROCCO
ALGERIA
TUNISIA
JULY 1943
Mediterranean Sea
LIBYA
El Alamein Oct.–Nov. 1942
EGYPT

60°N
10°E
20°E
0°

November 1942
Allies win the Battle of El Alamein.

May 1943
Axis forces in North Africa surrender.

1942

February 1943
Final German troops surrender at Stalingrad.

July 1943
Allies begin an invasion of Sicily.

Dwight Eisenhower was in charge of planning what would be the largest sea-to-land invasion ever attempted. Eisenhower knew that German forces were expecting an invasion of France. The Germans had planted mines and stretched barbed wire along the French coastline. Heavily armed German soldiers waited on the beaches in bombproof bunkers. Eisenhower warned his troops of the danger but expressed confidence in their ability to succeed. "The hopes and prayers of liberty-loving people everywhere march with you," he told them.

American, British, and Canadian troops invaded France on June 6, 1944—known as **D-Day**, or "designated day." They crossed the choppy waters of the English Channel and landed on five beaches in Normandy. More than 6,000 ships, 11,000 planes, and 156,000 men were part of the invasion. Soldiers jumped from boats and waded ashore, often under heavy fire.

The Americans landed on two beaches, code named Utah and Omaha. Fighting was especially fierce on Omaha Beach, where almost 3,000 men were killed or wounded. "The entire beach was strewn with mines," wrote one U.S. soldier to his wife. "With a stream of lead coming towards us, we were at the mercy of the Germans."

By the end of D-Day, all five beaches were secured. The Allies then began driving east through French villages and countryside toward Germany.

READING CHECK **Summarizing** What was the goal of the D-Day invasion?

SUMMARY AND PREVIEW Allied victories led to the D-Day invasion. In the next section you will read about the Pacific war.

June 5, 1944
Allies capture Rome.

June 6, 1944
Allied forces invade France on D–Day.

1945

American soldiers landed on the beaches of Normandy during the D-Day invasion.

go.hrw.com
Online Quiz

Section 3 Assessment

Reviewing Ideas, Terms, and People

1. **a. Describe** What new strategies did the Allies use in the fight in Europe and North Africa?
   b. Draw Conclusions Why was it important for no individual Allied Power to make peace with the Axis countries?
2. **a. Recall** What role did **Dwight D. Eisenhower** play in the North Africa campaign?
   b. Analyze Why did the Allies decide to invade North Africa and Italy?
   c. Evaluate Why do you think people call the **Battle of Stalingrad** a turning point in the war?
3. **a. Define** What was **D-Day**?
   b. Elaborate What did Eisenhower mean when he said, "The hopes and prayers of liberty-loving people everywhere march with you"?

Critical Thinking

4. **Categorizing** Review your list of the major battles and campaigns in different areas of the world. Then copy the graphic organizer below and use it to explain the significance of each event shown.

Event	Significance
Battle of El Alamein	
Capture of Rome	
Battle of Stalingrad	
D-Day invasion	

FOCUS ON WRITING

5. **Taking Notes on the Progress of the War** Take notes on the major battles involving American soldiers. How did American leaders, strategies, and individual soldiers contribute to victories in Europe and North Africa?

War in the Pacific

Main Ideas

1. The Japanese continued advancing across the Pacific in 1942.
2. The Allies stopped Japan's advance with key victories over the Japanese navy.
3. The Allies began battling toward Japan.

The Big Idea

Allied forces reversed Japan's expansion in the Pacific and battled toward the main Japanese islands.

Key Terms and People

Douglas MacArthur, *p. 240*
Bataan Death March, *p. 240*
Chester Nimitz, *p. 241*
Battle of the Coral Sea, *p. 241*
Battle of Midway, *p. 241*
island hopping, *p. 242*
Battle of Leyte Gulf, *p. 242*
kamikaze, *p. 242*

TAKING NOTES As you read, take notes on the main events of the war in the Pacific. You may want to organize your list in a chart like this one.

Pacific War
1.
2.
3.
4.

If YOU were there...

It is spring 1945, and your older brother is fighting the Japanese in the Pacific. You've been following the news reports closely, and you know that fighting in the Pacific is terribly fierce. You hear that the Japanese soldiers often refuse to surrender, fighting to the death instead. Your brother reveals in his letters that he is lonely and suffering many hardships. Now you are writing to him.

What would you say to encourage him?

BUILDING BACKGROUND Japan attacked China in the early 1930s, leading to all-out war between Japan and China in 1937. Japanese forces captured key Chinese cities, including Nanjing, where they killed up to 300,000 civilians. Under the command of General Hideki Tojo, Japanese forces continued to expand the Japanese empire in Asia.

Japan Advances

Japan's attack on Pearl Harbor left the U.S. Pacific Fleet so weakened that it could not immediately respond to the Japanese advance. While the United States recovered from Pearl Harbor, Japan conquered Thailand, Burma, the British colonies of Hong Kong and Singapore, and the U.S. territories of Guam and Wake Island. The same day as the attack on Pearl Harbor, Japan invaded Hong Kong. British, Canadian, and Indian forces attempting to stop the invasion were outnumbered. Japan attacked the American-controlled Philippines the same day.

American and Filipino forces under the command of American general **Douglas MacArthur** could not stop Japan's advance in the Philippines. MacArthur left the islands in March 1942, vowing to return. More than 70,000 American and Filipino soldiers surrendered to the Japanese. The exhausted soldiers were forced to march 63 miles up the Bataan Peninsula to prison camps. Many prisoners were starved and beaten by Japanese soldiers. More than 600 Americans and about 10,000 Filipinos died in the **Bataan Death March**.

READING CHECK **Identifying Cause and Effect** Why could the U.S. Pacific Fleet not immediately stop the Japanese advance?

Code Talkers

More than 40,000 Native Americans served in the U.S. armed forces during the war. About 400 Navajo Native Americans served as "Code Talkers," relaying coded messages based on the complex Navajo language. Japan's expert code breakers were never able to crack the Navajo code.

Why might the Japanese have been unable to break the Navajo code?

Key Allied Victories

The Allies feared the Japanese might next attack India, Australia, or even the United States mainland. Admiral **Chester Nimitz** led the U.S. Pacific Fleet. Nimitz was determined to stop the Japanese advance, and he had an important advantage—the ability to crack secret Japanese codes.

American code breakers helped the Allies in two key naval battles in the Pacific. Nimitz learned that the Japanese were planning an attack on Port Moresby, New Guinea, an island just north of Australia. If the Japanese took New Guinea, they would have a base from which to invade Australia. In May 1942 Nimitz sent Allied forces to stop the Japanese fleet. American and Japanese aircraft carriers and fighter planes clashed in the **Battle of the Coral Sea**. Neither side won a clear victory, but the Japanese assault on Port Moresby was stopped.

Allied leaders then learned that the Japanese planned a surprise attack on the Midway Islands. Nimitz was prepared. The **Battle of Midway** began on June 4, 1942, when Japan started bombing the islands.

American aircraft carriers launched their planes, catching the Japanese aircraft carriers while many of their planes were refueling on deck. American dive bombers destroyed four of Japan's aircraft carriers, severely weakening Japanese naval power. "Pearl Harbor has now been partially avenged," said Nimitz.

The Allies then began the enormous and difficult task of recapturing territory from Japan. In August 1942 American marines invaded Guadalcanal, one of the Solomon Islands northeast of Australia. Intense fighting raged for nearly six months. Marine Louis Ortega remembered that enemy bombs and bullets were only part of the danger in the hot, rainy jungles of Guadalcanal. Soldiers also suffered from diseases, such as malaria, and from hunger due to lack of supplies. "I had gone to Guadalcanal weighing about 150," Ortega said. "I left weighing about 110." American forces finally took control of the island in February 1943.

READING CHECK Drawing Conclusions How did the Allied victory at Midway change the course of the war in the Pacific?

Battling toward Japan

Allied victories at Midway and Guadalcanal helped change the course of the war in the Pacific. The Allies now saw their chance to go on the offensive, with the goal of reaching Japan itself.

Island Hopping

To fight their way toward Japan, Allied war planners developed a strategy called **island hopping**, where Allied forces took only the most strategically important islands, instead of each Japanese-held island. They could use each captured island as a base for the next attack, while isolating the Japanese forces on the bypassed islands.

Island hopping proved to be a successful strategy, though very costly to **execute**. Japanese forces fortified key islands and fought fiercely to hold on to them. In November 1943, U.S. Marines leapt off their boats and waded toward Tarawa, one of the Gilbert Islands. They advanced into ferocious fire from Japanese machine guns. "The water seemed never clear of . . . men," one marine said. "They kept falling, falling, falling." Both sides sustained heavy casualties at Tarawa, but the marines captured the island. The Allies won similar victories in the Marshall, Mariana, Volcano, and Bonin islands.

In October 1944 General MacArthur led a mission to retake the Philippines. The Japanese navy confronted the Allies at the **Battle of Leyte Gulf**, the largest naval battle in history. The Allies crushed the Japanese fleet, crippling Japan's naval power for the remainder of the war. It also gave the Allies a base from which to attack the main shipping routes that supplied Japan. After splashing ashore on Leyte, MacArthur proudly declared: "People of the Philippines: I have returned." Securing the Philippines took many more months of fighting. Allied forces and Filipino guerrillas finally drove out or captured all of the Japanese defenders by the summer of 1945.

ACADEMIC VOCABULARY

execute perform, carry out

FOCUS ON NEW YORK CITY

The U.S. Navy aircraft carrier USS *Intrepid* was launched in 1943 and sent to the Pacific to assist in the island-hopping strategy. The carrier participated in several key battles, including the Battle of Leyte Gulf. After being retrofitted several times, the *Intrepid* was used to retrieve the first astronauts from their landings at sea. After more than 30 years of service, the *Intrepid* was decommissioned. Today it is docked on the Hudson River in New York City, where it has been converted to a museum.

Final Battles

With key islands close to Japan secured, Allied planes began bombing targets in Japan in November 1944. American B-29 bombers, able to carry 20,000 pounds of explosives each, led bombing raids on more than 60 major Japanese cities. A March 1945 raid set Japan's capital city of Tokyo on fire, leaving 1 million people homeless. Japanese factories were destroyed, and food became so scarce that many people neared starvation. Still, Japan refused to surrender.

Two of the war's fiercest battles occurred on Japan's outer islands early in 1945. In February U.S. Marines stormed the beaches of Iwo Jima, now known as Iwo To. Japanese defenders were dug into caves, with orders to fight to the death. "On Iwo, we hardly ever saw the enemy," recalled one marine. After the marines raised the American flag on Iwo Jima, a month of bloody fighting followed. Of more than 20,000 Japanese defenders on Iwo Jima, about a thousand were taken prisoner—the rest were killed or wounded in battle. About 6,800 Americans had died.

Beginning in April an even deadlier battle was fought for the island of Okinawa. There were an estimated 100,000 Japanese soldiers on the island when U.S. forces began their attack. One U.S. Marine officer described the hard fighting at the Battle of Okinawa:

> "We poured a tremendous amount of metal in on those positions . . . It seemed nothing could possibly be living in that churning mass where the shells were falling and roaring but when we next advanced, [Japanese troops] would still be there and madder than ever."
>
> —Colonel Wilburt S. Brown, quoted in *The Final Campaign: Marines in the Victory on Okinawa* by Colonel Joseph H. Alexander

In the waters near the island, Japanese planes struck U.S. ships with the tactic of **kamikaze**—purposely crashing piloted planes into enemy ships. In wave after wave, kamikaze pilots flew planes loaded with explosives straight down onto the decks of Allied ships. An American sailor who was on the deck of an aircraft carrier when a kamikaze attacked the ship described the scene.

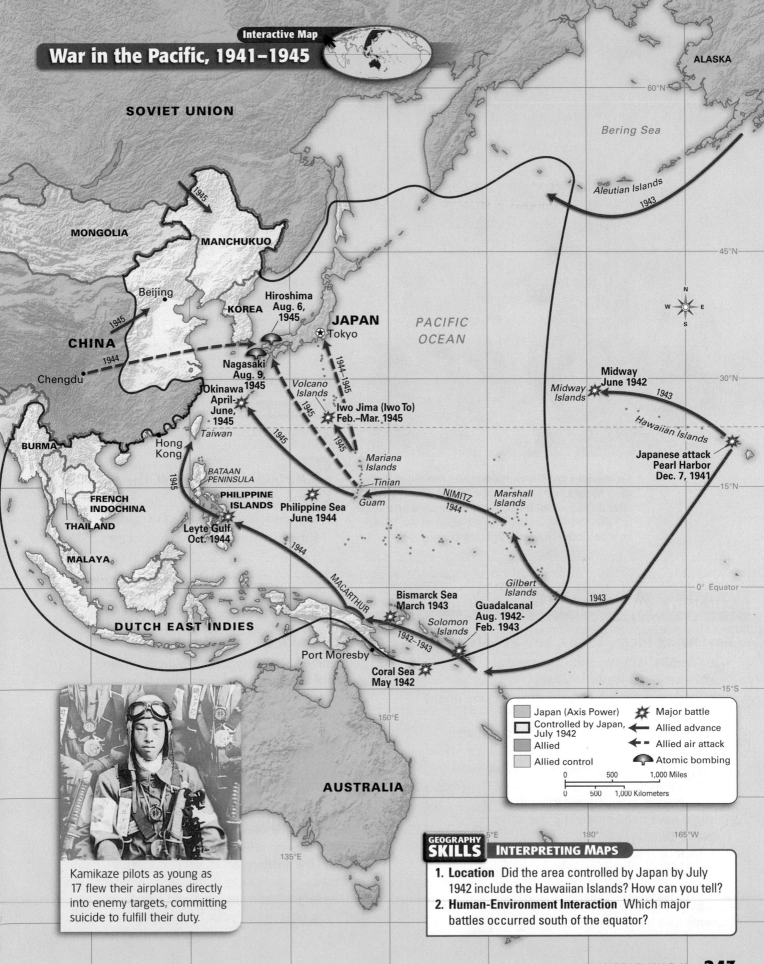

War in the Pacific, 1941–1945

Interactive Map

SOVIET UNION

Bering Sea

ALASKA

60°N

MONGOLIA

MANCHUKUO

1945

45°N

Beijing

KOREA

Hiroshima
Aug. 6,
1945

JAPAN

*PACIFIC
OCEAN*

★ Tokyo

Aleutian Islands

1943

CHINA

1945

1944

Chengdu

Nagasaki
Aug. 9,
1945

*Volcano
Islands*

1944–1945

1945

30°N

Midway
June 1942

*Midway
Islands*

1943

Okinawa
April–
June,
1945

1945

Iwo Jima (Iwo To)
Feb.–Mar. 1945

Hawaiian Islands

Taiwan

1945

BURMA

Hong
Kong

*Mariana
Islands*

Japanese attack
Pearl Harbor
Dec. 7, 1941

15°N

*BATAAN
PENINSULA*

1945

PHILIPPINE
ISLANDS

Philippine Sea
June 1944

Tinian

Guam

NIMITZ
1944

*Marshall
Islands*

FRENCH
INDOCHINA

THAILAND

Leyte Gulf
Oct. 1944

MALAYA

1944

MACARTHUR

*Gilbert
Islands*

0° Equator

1943

DUTCH EAST INDIES

Bismarck Sea
March 1943

Guadalcanal
Aug. 1942–
Feb. 1943

*Solomon
Islands*

1942–1943

Port Moresby

Coral Sea
May 1942

15°S

150°E

Legend:

- Japan (Axis Power)
- Controlled by Japan, July 1942
- Allied
- Allied control
- ✸ Major battle
- ← Allied advance
- ◄-- Allied air attack
- ⛨ Atomic bombing

0   500   1,000 Miles
0   500   1,000 Kilometers

AUSTRALIA

135°E

5°E

180°

165°W

Kamikaze pilots as young as
17 flew their airplanes directly
into enemy targets, committing
suicide to fulfill their duty.

GEOGRAPHY SKILLS   INTERPRETING MAPS

1. **Location** Did the area controlled by Japan by July 1942 include the Hawaiian Islands? How can you tell?
2. **Human-Environment Interaction** Which major battles occurred south of the equator?

Six marines are shown raising the American flag atop Mount Suribachi on the island of Iwo Jima after an important battle there. They were instructed to raise the flag on the highest point of the island so that all the men still fighting could see it.

The plane "cartwheeled the length of the carrier and plowed into the planes we had on the [flight deck]. We were burning bow to stern . . . All the guys manning the guns were dead. Standing up. Pointing their guns. They never left their posts."

More than 2,500 kamikaze missions were flown, killing more than 4,000 Allied sailors. The fighting on Okinawa lasted nearly three months and led to terrible casualties. By the time the island was secure, some 12,000 Allied troops were dead and 36,000 wounded. The Japanese losses were staggering—some 110,000 troops and 80,000 civilians had been killed.

After their victories at Iwo Jima and Okinawa, the Allies were one step closer to final victory. Allied leaders began to plan for an all-out assault on the main Japanese islands.

READING CHECK Analyzing How did the Allied strategy in the Pacific change starting in 1943?

SUMMARY AND PREVIEW The Allies made major gains in the Pacific war, moving closer to Japan. In the next section, you will learn how the Allies achieved full victory.

Section 4 Assessment

go.hrw.com
Online Quiz

Reviewing Ideas, Terms, and People

1. **a. Identify** Why were the Japanese able to advance in the Pacific in 1942?
   b. Explain Why did so many prisoners die on the **Bataan Death March**?
2. **a. Recall** What Allied victories halted Japan's advance?
   b. Analyze Why was the **Battle of the Coral Sea** important?
   c. Elaborate How do you think the war might have been different if the Allies had lost at Midway?
3. **a. Define** What was **island hopping**?
   b. Sequence What event led to the retaking of the Philippines?
   c. Evaluate Why do you think someone would serve as a **kamikaze** pilot?

Critical Thinking

4. **Sequencing** Review your notes on the main events of the Pacific war. Then copy the graphic organizer below and use it to put the events in the correct sequence.

1942	→	1943	→	1944	→	1945

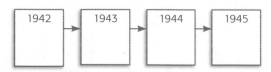
FOCUS ON WRITING

5. **Taking Notes on Military Achievements** Take notes on the challenges U.S. soldiers faced in the Pacific. How was fighting in the Pacific different from and similar to fighting in Africa and Europe? How might you describe a Pacific battle to someone?

Victory and Consequences

If YOU were there...

It is August 1944. You are an American soldier in France. You have seen the horrors of battle up close, but today is a day to rejoice. You and other Allied soldiers are marching through the streets of Paris, celebrating its liberation from Nazi control. It seems as if the whole city has come out to greet the Americans. People rush up to shake your hand. Children cheer and hand you flowers.

How does it feel to be part of this moment in history?

> **BUILDING BACKGROUND** By late 1944 Allied forces were advancing in Europe and Asia. But Germany and Japan were both resisting, showing no signs of being willing to surrender. Allied leaders knew there was much more fighting still to be done.

Germany Surrenders

In the weeks after the successful D-Day invasion, hundreds of thousands of Allied troops landed in France. Led by American general Omar Bradley, Allied forces began fighting their way across France toward Germany. At the same time, the Soviets were closing in on Germany from the east. Although Germany's defeat seemed certain to the Allies, Hitler refused to surrender.

In July 1944 Allied tank forces led by American general George Patton broke through German lines on the western front. While Patton drove forward, more Allied forces invaded southern France. Both groups of Allied forces fought their way toward Paris. Encouraged by the Allies' success, the citizens of Paris rebelled against the German occupying force. By the end of August, General Bradley was leading Allied troops through the streets of the freed city. "All Paris surged out to meet the Allied columns and welcome their liberators," remembered one witness. After securing Paris, the Allies continued driving through Belgium and Luxembourg, making their way toward Germany. Hitler drafted every able-bodied German man from the age of 16 to 60 and planned one last desperate attack.

What You Will Learn...

Main Ideas

1. The Allies gained victory in Europe with Germany's surrender.
2. Nazis murdered millions of Jews and other people in the Holocaust.
3. Victory in the Pacific came after the United States dropped atomic bombs on Japan.

The Big Idea

The Allies won World War II, the most devastating war in world history.

Key Terms and People

Battle of the Bulge, *p. 246*
Harry S. Truman, *p. 246*
Holocaust, *p. 247*
genocide, *p. 247*
Manhattan Project, *p. 248*
atomic bomb, *p. 248*

TAKING NOTES As you read, take notes on the final days of the war in both Europe and the Pacific. You may want to use a graphic organizer like the one below.

Europe	Pacific

Hitler's goal was for German forces to drive through a weak spot in the Allied lines and capture the city of Antwerp, Belgium. On December 16 the Germans seized a moment when Allied planes were grounded due to bad weather. In heavy snow some 25 German divisions attacked the Ardennes (ahr-DEN), a densely forested region defended by just a few American divisions. The Germans quickly pushed the Allied forces back about 65 miles, creating a huge bulge in the Allied lines. This gave the battle its name—the **Battle of the Bulge**.

Allied forces recovered rapidly and stopped the German advance. When the skies cleared in late December, Allied planes began pounding German troops. In early January 1945 the Germans began to retreat. American losses were heavy—between 70,000 and 81,000 casualties. Germany's losses were even greater, and Hitler's ability to wage offensive war was now completely crushed.

In the final months of the war, Allied bombing raids devastated major German cities such as Berlin and Hamburg. Both sides in World War II had used these kinds of bombing raids against the enemy's cities. German raids,

for example, killed about 30,000 civilians in the British capital of London. In February 1945 Allied bombers attacked the German city of Dresden, igniting a firestorm that destroyed the city and killed more than 35,000 civilians. "Dresden was an inferno," recalled one U.S. soldier. "I have nightmares, even today."

As Allied forces surrounded Berlin, Hitler retreated to an underground bunker in the heart of the ruined city. On April 30, as Soviet troops entered Berlin, Hitler committed suicide. A week later, the Germans surrendered. The surrender was an unconditional surrender, which meant Germany would have no voice in the postwar peace decisions. The war in Europe had finally come to an end. The Allies celebrated May 8, 1945, as V-E (Victory in Europe) Day.

President Franklin Roosevelt, who had led the United States throughout World War II, did not live to see V-E Day. He died of a stroke on April 12. **Harry S. Truman** became president and immediately faced the challenge of winning the war in the Pacific.

READING CHECK **Sequencing** What events led to Germany's surrender?

Primary Source

INTERVIEW TRANSCRIPT
Battle of the Bulge

In the Battle of the Bulge, American soldiers faced a strong German attack in snowy forests during the coldest winter northern Europe had seen in 40 years. Private Dave Nutt described the long, tense nights on the front lines:

❝The cold, the snow, and the darkness were enough to set young nerves on edge. The thud of something as innocuous [harmless] as snow plopping to the ground from a tree branch could be terrifying. Was it snow? Was it maybe a German patrol? Should you fire at the sound and risk giving away your position, or worse, hitting one of your own men? But did the Germans have us surrounded?❞

—Dave Nutt, quoted in *Citizen Soldiers*, by Stephen Ambrose

ANALYSIS SKILL **ANALYZING PRIMARY SOURCES**

What factors made the Battle of the Bulge especially hard on soldiers?

Buchenwald

Jews, Gypsies, and other victims of Hitler and the Nazis were sent to concentration camps. Many were killed immediately upon arrival at the camps, while others were executed later. Families were forced apart, and prisoners were poorly fed and clothed. Some were used as subjects for medical experiments. This photo shows survivors of the Buchenwald concentration camp after their liberation.

How did Hitler use the concentration camps to fulfill part of his goals for Germany?

Horrors of the Holocaust

When Allied forces liberated Europe, they uncovered evidence of horrifying Nazi crimes against humanity. In a program of mass murder that became known as the **Holocaust**, Hitler and the Nazis had attempted to exterminate the entire Jewish population of Europe in the name of Aryan supremacy.

The Final Solution

Soon after gaining power in Germany, Hitler began his campaign of terror against the Jews. The Nazis stripped German Jews of their citizenship and seized their property. On the "night of broken glass," or *Kristallnacht*, many Jewish homes and businesses were destroyed. Many Jews who did not escape the country were imprisoned in concentration camps such as Dachau (DAH-kow), near Munich.

When Germany conquered huge sections of Europe and the Soviet Union early in World War II, nearly 10 million Jews came under Hitler's control. The Nazis forced many Jews into urban centers called ghettos. Others were sent to concentration camps and used as slave labor where many died from hunger or disease. The Nazis also formed special killing squads that rounded up groups of Jews, shot them, and buried them in mass graves. When the Germans invaded the Soviet Union, these squads murdered more than 33,000 Soviet Jews near Kiev in three days. By the end of 1941, the death squads had executed nearly 1 million people.

The Death Camps

In January 1942 senior Nazi officials met to plan what they called "a final solution to the Jewish question." Hitler's "final solution" was **genocide**, or the extermination of an entire group of people. The Nazi plan was to kill the Jews in specially built death camps, mainly in German-occupied Poland. The camps were equipped with gas chambers designed to kill large numbers of people, and furnaces were used to cremate the bodies of victims.

By mid-1942 the Nazis had begun to ship Jews from throughout German-occupied Europe to the camps. Several hundred thousand Jews, for example, were transported by train from the ghetto in the Polish capital of Warsaw to a death camp called Treblinka. In April 1943 Jews in the Warsaw ghetto staged a violent uprising, attacking the Germans with guns and homemade bombs. It took German troops nearly a month to crush the revolt. Survivors were sent to Treblinka.

THE IMPACT TODAY

There are more than 50 museums in the world that honor victims of the Holocaust. The United States Holocaust Memorial Museum in Washington, D.C., displays historical film footage and artifacts from the Holocaust.

At the death camps most children, the elderly, and the sick were immediately executed. Those strong enough to work were used as laborers. When they became too weak to work, they too were sent to the gas chambers. Moritz Vegh was 13 when his family was sent from Czechoslovakia to Auschwitz, one of the most notorious of the death camps. He later described what happened to his mother and sister:

"When we got off the cattle truck, they ordered, 'Men, right; women, left.' … I went with my father. My little sister, Esther, she went with my mother. Esther was only eleven. She was holding my mother's hand. When they made a selection of the women, Esther clung to my mother. My mother wouldn't give her up … They went straight to the gas chamber."

—Moritz Vegh, quoted in *The Boys: Triumph over Adversity*

FOCUS ON NEW YORK

Fort Ontario in Oswego, New York, was used as an emergency refugee center for victims of the Holocaust between 1944–1946.

Moritz survived the war, working as a laborer at Auschwitz.

The Allied soldiers who liberated the death camps were horrified by what they found. About 6 million Jews—some two-thirds of Europe's prewar Jewish population—had been killed in the Holocaust. The Nazis had also murdered millions of others, including Gypsies, Slavs, political opponents, and people with physical or mental disabilities.

READING CHECK Summarizing What was the purpose of the Nazis' "final solution"?

Victory in the Pacific

In the Pacific Allied war planners prepared for an invasion of Japan. They estimated that the invasion could result in more than 1 million Allied casualties.

The Allies had another option. Since 1942 Allied scientists had been working on a secret program known as the **Manhattan Project**. The goal was to develop an **atomic bomb**, a weapon that produces tremendous power by splitting atoms. On July 16, 1945, the Allies successfully tested the first atomic bomb in the New Mexico desert. The massive explosion melted the desert sand into glass for 800 yards in all directions.

When Japanese leaders refused the Allies' demand for an unconditional surrender, President Truman gave the order to use the atomic bomb. On August 6, 1945, the B-29 bomber *Enola Gay* dropped an atomic bomb above the city of Hiroshima. "When I saw a very strong light, a flash, I put my arms over my face unconsciously," said one Japanese survivor. "Almost instantly I felt my face was inflating … I saw people looking for water and they died soon after they drank it … The whole city was destroyed and burning. There was no place to go." The explosion killed almost 80,000 people instantly. Thousands more died later from burns and radiation poisoning.

The atomic blast over Hiroshima destroyed the city. Over 80,000 people were killed instantly, and thousands more died later from the effects of radiation.

Japanese leaders still refused to surrender. On August 9 U.S. forces dropped a second atomic bomb on the city of Nagasaki. About one-third of the city was destroyed, and approximately 22,000 people died immediately. The Japanese announced their unconditional surrender on August 15, 1945.

After six years, World War II was finally over. More than 50 million people had been killed—more than half of them civilians. National economies in Europe and Asia were devastated, and millions of people were left without food, water, or shelter. Since the war had been fought far from American soil, the United States escaped this level of destruction. As the strongest power left in the world, much of the responsibility for postwar rebuilding fell to the United States.

READING CHECK **Drawing Conclusions** Why did Japan surrender?

SUMMARY AND PREVIEW In this section you learned how World War II ended. In the next chapter you will learn how the world recovered from the war and worked to prevent such wars in the future.

Causes and Effects of World War II

Causes
- Global and local economic problems
- Totalitarian governments
- Germany's aggression in Europe
- Japanese aggression in Asia and the Pacific

Effects
- Millions of deaths worldwide
- Widespread destruction of cities and industries
- The Holocaust
- Rise of the United States as the leading world power
- Rise of nationalism in Asia and Africa leads to growing independence movements in many nations under European colonial control.

Section 5 Assessment

go.hrw.com
Online Quiz

Reviewing Ideas, Terms, and People

1. **a. Identify** What was the last major battle of the war in Europe?
   b. Evaluate What was the biggest task facing **Harry S. Truman** when he became president?
2. **a. Define** What was the **Holocaust**?
   b. Elaborate How did the oppression of Jews increase during the war?
3. **a. Recall** What was the purpose of the **Manhattan Project**? How did it result in the end of the war against Japan?
   b. Explain What was the status of the United States after the war?
   c. Predict How do you think the invention of the **atomic bomb** changed people's views of war?

Critical Thinking

4. **Identifying Causes** Review your notes on the final days of the war in both Europe and the Pacific. Then copy the graphic organizer below and use it to show the short-term causes of Germany's and Japan's surrenders.

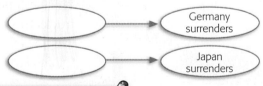

FOCUS ON WRITING

5. **Taking Notes on the Impact of the War** Take notes on the last days of World War II. How did the Allies finally win the war? What impact did the war have on people and countries around the world?

Literature of the
Holocaust

from *Diary of Anne Frank*
by Anne Frank (1929–1945)

About the Reading *Anne Frank was a Jewish teenager in Amsterdam who experienced the Nazi occupation of the Netherlands firsthand. Frank and her family hid for more than two years in the sealed-off back room of an office. The family was betrayed to the Gestapo in 1944. Frank and her family members were sent to concentration camps in Germany. Frank died in 1945 at the Bergen-Belsen concentration camp.*

AS YOU READ Notice how Frank describes the oppression of Jews.

19th November, 1942

Mr. Dussel has told us much about the outside world we've missed for so long. He had sad news. Countless friends and acquaintances have been taken off to a dreadful fate. ❶ Night after night, green and grey military vehicles cruise the streets. They knock on every door, asking whether any Jews live there. If so, the whole family is immediately taken away. If not, they proceed to the next house. It's impossible to escape their clutches unless you go into hiding. They often go around with lists, knocking only on those doors where they know there's a big haul to be made... In the evenings when it's dark, I often see long lines of good, innocent people, accompanied by crying children, walking on and on, ordered about by a handful of men who bully and beat them until they nearly drop. No one is spared. The sick, the elderly, children, babies and pregnant women—all are marched to their death. ❷

9th October, 1942

Our many Jewish friends and acquaintances are being taken away in droves. The Gestapo is treating them very roughly and transporting them in cattle-trucks to Westerbork, the big camp in Drenthe to which they're sending all the Jews. ❸

GUIDED READING

WORD HELP

Mr. Dussel a friend of Anne's father

droves large numbers

Gestapo German military police

Westerbork a concentration camp on the Dutch-German border

Drenthe a province of the Netherlands

❶ *Jews in hiding knew that they would be sent to concentration camps if discovered.*

❷ *Anne cannot hide her feelings at seeing innocent victims of the Germans being treated poorly.*

❸ *Jews suffered harsh treatment before and after arrest.*

from *Night*

by Elie Wiesel (1928–), translated by Stella Rodway

About the Reading *Elie Wiesel was taken to Auschwitz when he was age 15. Though he survived the camp, not all of his family did. Years after the war, Wiesel wrote about his time spent imprisoned at Auschwitz.*

AS YOU READ Look for ways that Wiesel describes the trauma of being taken away.

By eight o'clock in the morning, a weariness like molten lead began to settle in the veins, the limbs, the brain. I was in the midst of my prayers when suddenly there were shouts in the street. I tore myself from my phylacteries and ran to the window. Hungarian police had entered the ghetto and were shouting in the neighboring street:

"All Jews outside! Hurry!"

Some Jewish police went into the houses, saying in broken voices:

"The time's come now . . . you've got to leave all this . . . "

The Hungarian police struck out with truncheons and rifle butts, to right and left, without reason, indiscriminately, their blows falling upon old men and women, children and invalids alike. ❶

One by one the houses emptied, and the street filled with people and bundles. By ten o'clock, all the condemned were outside. The police took a roll call, once, twice, twenty times. The heat was intense. Sweat streamed from faces and bodies.

Children cried for water.

Water? There was plenty, close at hand, in the houses, in the yards, but they were forbidden to break the ranks. "Water! Mummy! Water!"

The Jewish police from the ghetto were able to go and fill a few jugs secretly. Since my sisters and I were destined for the last convoy and we were still allowed to move about, we helped them as well as we could.

GUIDED READING

WORD HELP

molten melted

phylacteries wooden prayer devices

ghetto neighborhood set aside for Jews

truncheons sticks

indiscriminately without care

invalids people who are ill

convoy military escort

❶ *The Hungarian police used physical force to gather people together.*

CONNECTING LITERATURE TO HISTORY

1. **The Nazi oppression of Jews eventually led to the Gestapo taking Jews from their homes.** How does Frank describe the job that the Gestapo did?

2. **The oppression soon changed to removal.** How does Wiesel describe the removal of the Jews from his hometown?

3. **Jews were treated with physical violence by Nazi supporters.** Give two examples of violence against Jews found in these passages.

251

Social Studies Skills

Constructing Time Lines

Define the Skill

Time lines are a good way to organize historical information. Time lines clearly show a sequence of historical events over a certain period of time. Many time lines focus on a specific theme within a time period.

When you construct a time line, it often makes the sequence of events easier to follow. Time lines show events in the order they happened and the amount of time between events. Constructing a time line can therefore help you better understand events' context. For example, organizing events on a time line can help you determine their causes and effects.

Learn the Skill

When you construct a time line, you need to make some basic decisions. First, the time line needs a topic. This topic can be general or specific. One example of a general topic is the 1940s. A more specific topic might be major battles of World War II. The time line should cover a time period that includes the main events related to the topic. For example, it would make sense for a time line on American battles in World War II to cover the period 1941 to 1945.

The next step in constructing a time line is gathering information. This includes taking notes on events from the chosen time period related to the topic. It is important to write down the date when each event happened. Putting the events in order

before making the time line is often helpful. If there are too many events, it is a good idea to include only the most important ones.

The first step in actually constructing the time line is to draw a straight line using a ruler. The next step is to mark even intervals on the line. Intervals are dates that divide the time line into smaller, equal time periods. For example, a time line of the 1940s might include two-year intervals: 1940, 1942, 1944, and so on. Then add events in the correct places on the time line. The beginning and end of the time line, each interval, and each event should be labeled with dates. The finished time line should include at least six events. As a final touch, the time line needs a title. The title tells what the entries in the time line are about and may include the dates the time line covers.

Practice the Skill

Follow these instructions to construct a time line.

1. Using your textbook, choose a topic related to World War II for your time line. Decide on the dates your time line will need to cover.

2. Use your textbook to take notes on events to include in your time line and their dates. Put the events in order.

3. Following the steps described above, construct your time line. The finished time line should include clearly labeled dates, at least six events, and a title.

Chapter Review

HOLT
History's Impact
▶ video series
Review the video to answer the closing question:
Why do you think the United States made the GI Bill of Rights a permanent policy?

Visual Summary

QUICK FACTS

Use the visual summary below to help you review the main ideas of the chapter.

The bombing of Pearl Harbor drew the United States into World War II.

To help supply the troops, women worked in jobs usually held by men.

American soldiers helped defeat the Axis Powers in Europe and the Pacific.

Reviewing Vocabulary, Terms, and People

Identify the term or person from the chapter that best fits each of the following descriptions.

1. The first African American flying unit in the U.S. military

2. American general who retreated from and then retook the Philippines

3. The dictator of the Soviet Union

4. A weapon that produces a massive explosion by splitting atoms

5. Battle at which British troops stopped the German Afrika Korps

6. Policy of avoiding war with an aggressive nation by giving in to its demands

7. Extermination of an entire group of people

Comprehension and Critical Thinking

SECTION 1 *(Pages 224–229)*

8. **a. Define** What is fascism?

   b. Make Inferences Before Pearl Harbor, what U.S. policies suggested that the United States would join the Allies?

   c. Evaluate How well did the policy of appeasement work? Explain your answer.

SECTION 2 *(Pages 230–234)*

9. **a. Recall** What happened during the zoot-suit riots?

   b. Analyze Why was the War Production Board important to the war effort?

   c. Elaborate How do you think Japanese Americans felt about internment?

SECTION 3 *(Pages 235–239)*

10. a. Identify What led the Axis powers to retreat from the Soviet Union?

b. Summarize In which regions and countries did the Allies win major victories against Germany?

c. Draw Conclusions Why do you think D-Day succeeded?

SECTION 4 *(Pages 240–244)*

11. a. Describe What did kamikaze pilots do?

b. Explain How did cracking Japanese codes help the Allies in the Pacific?

c. Draw Conclusions Why do you think Japan was determined to continue fighting?

SECTION 5 *(Pages 245–249)*

12. a. Recall What were the effects of the atomic bombs on Hiroshima and Nagasaki?

b. Contrast How was the Holocaust different from other wartime tragedies?

c. Evaluate Do you think the strategy of bombing civilian centers was fair? Why or why not?

Reviewing Themes

13. Geography How did geography affect the course of World War II?

14. Society and Culture What changes in society did World War II bring about?

Using the Internet `go.hrw.com`

15. Activity: Understanding Code Talkers Guns and bombs were not the only weapons of World War II. Cryptography, or the use of secret codes, was also an important tool for the Allied forces. Some Native Americans in the U.S. military used their own language as a form of cryptography. They spoke Navajo, a complex language, and adapted it for battlefield communications and to transmit secret information by radio and telephone. Soldiers who could speak it became known as code talkers. Enter the activity keyword. Research the Navajo code talkers of World War II and then create a poster to present your findings.

Reading Skills

Categorizing *Use the Reading Skills taught in this chapter to answer the question from the reading selection below.*

> American, British, and Canadian troops invaded France on June 6, 1944—known as D-Day or "designated day." They crossed the choppy waters of the English Channel and landed on five beaches in Normandy. More than 6,000 ships, 11,000 planes, and 156,000 men were part of the invasion. Soldiers jumped from boats and waded ashore, often under heavy fire. *(p. 239)*

16. Which of the following general categories could help you organize this information?

a. generals of the American forces

b. types of ammunition used

c. resources of invading forces

d. leaders of Allied nations

Social Studies Skills

Constructing Time Lines *Use the Social Studies Skills taught in this chapter to answer the question below.*

17. Make a time line about the end of World War II, covering the events of 1945.

FOCUS ON WRITING

18. Writing Your Radio News Broadcast Review your notes. Choose one event or story from World War II as the focus of your radio broadcast. You can include quotes from soldiers or national leaders. Remember that people cannot see your broadcast, so use descriptive language. Be sure to answer the following questions: Who? What? Where? When? Why? and How?

Grade 8 Intermediate-Level Test Preparation

Directions (1–7): For each statement or question, write on the separate answer sheet the *number* of the word or expression that, of those given, best completes the statement or answers the question.

Base your answer to question 1 on the map below and on your knowledge of social studies.

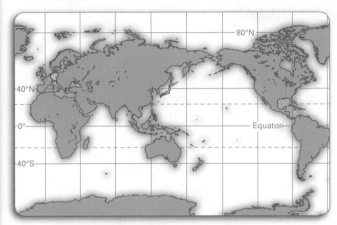

1 The yellow countries above represent the

(1) Central Powers.

(2) Allied Powers.

(3) Axis Powers.

(4) Big Three.

2 The forced relocation and imprisonment of Japanese Americans during World War II was known as

(1) dislocation.

(2) retaliation.

(3) reparations.

(4) internment.

3 During the war, many American women

(1) did work that traditionally had been done by men.

(2) served in battlefront combat positions in the military.

(3) worked as *braceros*.

(4) participated in labor strikes.

4 The Allies' successful 1944 invasion of France is known as

(1) D-Day.

(2) the Desert Fox.

(3) sonar.

(4) the Battle of Britain.

5 Who became president when Franklin D. Roosevelt died in 1945?

(1) Eleanor Roosevelt

(2) Harry S. Truman

(3) Winston Churchill

(4) Douglas MacArthur

6 The majority of Holocaust victims were

(1) Slavs.   (3) disabled people.

(2) Japanese.   (4) Jews.

7 An example of a segregated unit in the United States military during World War II was the

(1) Tuskegee Airmen.

(2) Mobile U-boaters.

(3) Pensicola Divers.

(4) Flying Lions.

Base your answer to question 8 on the text below and on your knowledge of social studies.

July 15, 1944

"It's a wonder I haven't abandoned all my ideals, they seem so absurd and impractical. Yet I cling to them because I still believe, in spite of everything, that people are truly good at heart."

—Anne Frank, *The Diary of Anne Frank*

8 **Constructed-Response Question** Why does Frank call her ideals "absurd and impractical"?

Conflict and Crisis

Part A: Short-Answer Questions

Directions: Read and examine the following documents. Then, on a separate sheet of paper, answer the questions using complete sentences.

DOCUMENT 1

In the early 1900s, Clarence Darrow was one of the best-known lawyers in the country. During the Scopes trial, he used the bold strategy of putting the trial's other famous figure, William Jennings Bryan, who was helping the prosecution, on the witness stand. Teaching evolution was against state law in Tennessee until 1967.

> If today you can take a thing like evolution and make it a crime to teach it in the public school, tomorrow you can make it a crime to teach it in the private schools, and the next year you can make it a crime to teach it . . . in the church. At the next session you may ban books and the newspapers. Soon you may set Catholic against Protestant and Protestant against Protestant, and try to foist [force] your own religion upon the minds of men.
>
> —**Clarence Darrow,** defending John Scopes

1a. What does Darrow say could be banned in addition to teaching evolution?

_____

1b. Do you agree with Darrow's statement? Why or why not?

_____

DOCUMENT 2

Dorothea Lange's pictures brought the Depression to life for people outside of the worst affected areas. Published in magazines and newspapers, her pictures helped spur the government to create relief programs. In 1939 Lange published many of her Depression-era photos in her book *An American Exodus: A Record of Human Erosion.*

2a. What has Lange chosen not to show in this picture?

_____

2b. What do you think this woman was thinking when Lange took her picture?

_____

DOCUMENT 3

War posters expressed a great deal with a powerful image and a few words. This poster, created by the artist J. Howard Miller to inspire women to work in factories, uses only four carefully chosen words. Copies of the poster are still available today. Rosie the Riveter's image also appears on T-shirts, magnets, mugs, and even mouse pads.

3a. What visual elements does the poster use to show women in the new role demanded of them by the war?

_____

3b. What do the words on the poster mean?

_____

DOCUMENT 4

When Japanese Americans were finally permitted to fight for their country in World War II, many rushed to enlist. One of them was Daniel Inouye, who rose from a private to a captain. He fought in Italy and France and won several medals. After Hawaii became a state, he served in Congress, representing Hawaii.

> As soon as he said that we were now eligible to volunteer, that room exploded into a fury of yells and motion. We went bursting out of there and ran—ran!—the three miles to the draft board . . . jostling for position, like a bunch of marathoners gone berserk.
>
> —**Daniel Inouye,** quoted in *Only What We Could Carry*, edited by Lawson Fusao Inada

4a. What words does Inouye use to give the reader a sense of how these young men reacted to being allowed to enlist?

_____

4b. To what does Inouye compare the attitude toward enlisting? What does this say about these men?

_____

Part B: Essay

Historical Context: The documents on these two pages are from the 1920s, 1930s, and 1940s. They reflect some of the conflicts and crises Americans experienced during these decades.

TASK: Using information from the four documents and your knowledge of U.S. history, write an essay in which you:

- discuss the events of the 1920s and 1930s as they relate to our country today.
- describe solutions to problems that the United States encountered during these years.

Postwar America

After the end of World War II, Americans became concerned with the global spread of communism. The government began taking steps to defend the nation against possible aggression from Communist nations. At home, many Americans enjoyed the economic prosperity of 1950s society. Not everyone benefited, however. Some Americans spoke out against American society and a government that did not guarantee equality to all citizens.

During the civil rights movement many Americans demanded equal rights for minority groups. Despite sometimes violent opposition, many successes were achieved. Differing viewpoints within society were further exposed, however, by reactions to the Vietnam War, a war fought in Southeast Asia over Communist expansion.

Explore the Art

The movies of the 1950s often portrayed American life as prosperous and content, although this was not true for everyone. What does this image suggest about the prosperity of postwar America?

Early Years of the Cold War

How has America reacted to the challenges of the modern world?

FOCUS ON WRITING

Song Lyrics The end of World War II brought economic prosperity to the United States, along with new fears and challenges. Americans adjusted to changes in their everyday lives and the new threat of nuclear war. In this chapter you will read about life at the beginning of the Cold War. Then you will write the words to a song that reflects some aspect of American life in the 1950s.

UNITED STATES

1945
After Roosevelt's death, Harry S. Truman becomes president.

1945

WORLD

1946 Winston Churchill declares an "iron curtain" between Western powers and the Soviet Union.

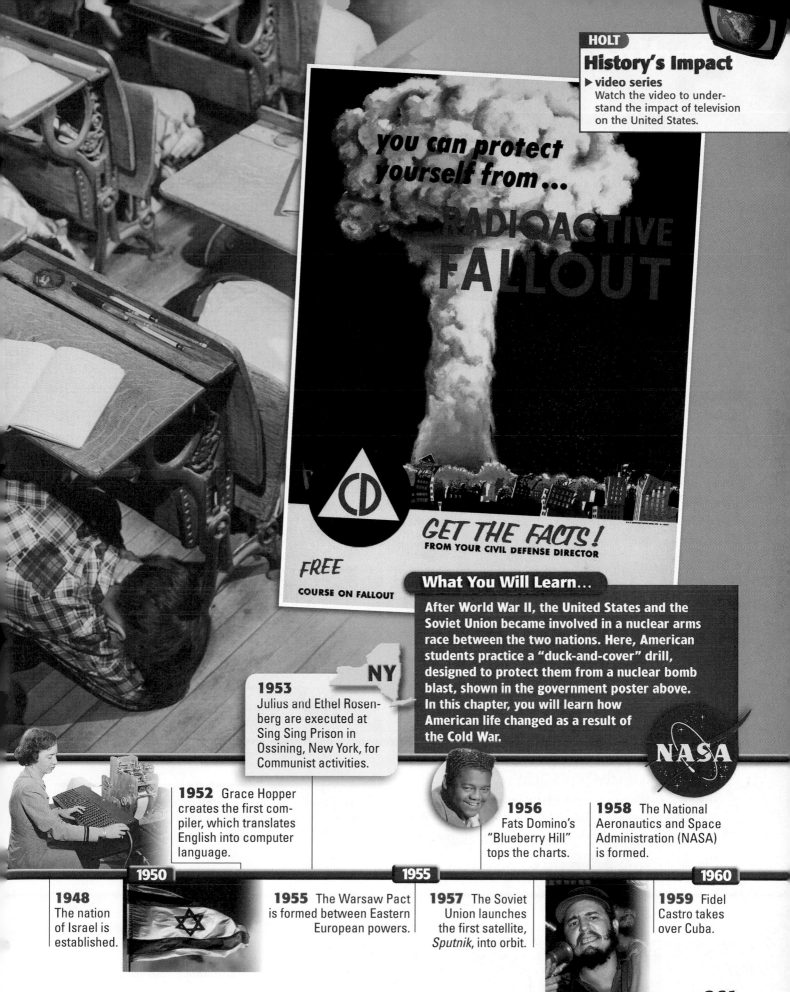

you can protect yourself from...

RADIOACTIVE FALLOUT

GET THE FACTS!
FROM YOUR CIVIL DEFENSE DIRECTOR

FREE

COURSE ON FALLOUT

What You Will Learn...

After World War II, the United States and the Soviet Union became involved in a nuclear arms race between the two nations. Here, American students practice a "duck-and-cover" drill, designed to protect them from a nuclear bomb blast, shown in the government poster above. In this chapter, you will learn how American life changed as a result of the Cold War.

NY

1953 Julius and Ethel Rosenberg are executed at Sing Sing Prison in Ossining, New York, for Communist activities.

1952 Grace Hopper creates the first compiler, which translates English into computer language.

1956 Fats Domino's "Blueberry Hill" tops the charts.

1958 The National Aeronautics and Space Administration (NASA) is formed.

1950

1955

1960

1948 The nation of Israel is established.

1955 The Warsaw Pact is formed between Eastern European powers.

1957 The Soviet Union launches the first satellite, *Sputnik*, into orbit.

1959 Fidel Castro takes over Cuba.

Reading Social Studies

by Kylene Beers

Economics | Geography | **Politics** | Society and Culture | Science and Technology

Focus on Themes In this chapter, you will learn about the Cold War between the United States and the Soviet Union. This war was unlike other wars in that it was often fought between **politicians** instead of soldiers. Each country used developments in **science and technology** to declare itself superior. You will also read about U.S. society and its reaction to the Cold War.

Visualizing

Focus on Reading Visualizing how your life might have been different if you had been alive during a period in history can help you understand life at that time.

Understanding Visualizing Using clues about everyday life that you find in a history book like this one can help you imagine what life was like in the past. You can imagine yourself and your life, and how life would have been different if you had lived in the past. Or, you can try to imagine what life was like for the people alive then.

Notice the clues in this passage that give you an idea of the feelings of people living during the Cold War.

All the time, in the homely [plain], cluttered rooms of our private lives the television displayed the continuing spectacle of public life— <u>all of it still going on in the windless places on the other side of the screen.</u> Presidents and First Secretaries trod [climbed] down the metal staircases from the bellies of great aircraft to shake hands on the tarmac [runway] and climb into big black cars. <u>Tanks wheeled down blind streets and across muddy fields. Rolls of heavy wire netting were unwound and veered [turned] upwards against a dawn sky.</u>

— From *The Cruel Peace,* by Fred Inglis

The author is using description to inform the reader about the feeling of watching the Cold War unfold on television.

Here the author uses frightening images to help the reader understand the fear of the Cold War.

You Try It!

The following passage is from the chapter you are getting ready to read. As you read the passage, look for details that help you visualize the past.

> In 1946 Winston Churchill described how Soviet control cut these countries off from the Western world. "An iron curtain has descended [fallen] across the [European] Continent," he said. The term *iron curtain* thus came to be used to describe this division. Presidential adviser Bernard Baruch warned of the seriousness of the Soviet threat, saying, "Let us not be deceived—we are today in the midst of a cold war." The phrase *Cold War* came to be used to describe the struggle for global power between the United States and the Soviet Union.
>
> *From Chapter 10, p. 266*

After you read the passage, answer the following questions.

1. Which details help you understand the attitude existing between the United States and the Soviet Union?

2. How does the quote by Winston Churchill help you visualize the political atmosphere of the time?

3. How does the phrase *Cold War* help you visualize the political atmosphere of the time?

Key Terms and People

Chapter 10

Section 1

Yalta Conference *(p. 264)*
Nuremberg trials *(p. 265)*
United Nations *(p. 266)*
Cold War *(p. 266)*
containment *(p. 267)*
Truman Doctrine *(p. 267)*
Marshall Plan *(p. 267)*
North Atlantic Treaty Organization *(p. 268)*
GI Bill of Rights *(p. 268)*
Fair Deal *(p. 270)*

Section 2

Mao Zedong *(p. 272)*
38th parallel *(p. 272)*
Joseph McCarthy *(p. 275)*
hydrogen bomb *(p. 276)*
arms race *(p. 276)*
Sputnik (p. 276)
brinkmanship *(p. 276)*

Section 3

baby boom *(p. 278)*
Sun Belt *(p. 278)*
urban renewal *(p. 279)*
beats *(p. 281)*

Academic Vocabulary

In this chapter, you will learn the following academic words:
concrete *(p. 275)*

As you read Chapter 10, look for details that help you visualize the past.

Adjusting to Peace

What You Will Learn...

Main Ideas

1. As World War II ended, leaders began planning the future of the postwar world.
2. The United States and the Soviet Union went from being allies to enemies after World War II.
3. Americans adjusted to postwar life.

The Big Idea

After World War II, Americans adjusted to new challenges both at home and around the world.

Key Terms and People

Yalta Conference, *p. 264*
Nuremberg trials, *p. 265*
United Nations, *p. 266*
Cold War, *p. 266*
containment, *p. 267*
Truman Doctrine, *p. 267*
Marshall Plan, *p. 267*
North Atlantic Treaty Organization, *p. 268*
GI Bill of Rights, *p. 268*
Fair Deal, *p. 270*

TAKING NOTES As you read, take notes on the results of the end of World War II. Organize your notes in a diagram like this one.

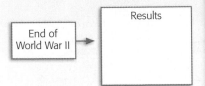

If **YOU** were there...

You are an adviser to President Harry S. Truman in July 1945. You have traveled with him to Potsdam, outside the ruined city of Berlin, where Allied leaders are discussing postwar plans. Everyone agrees that steps must be taken to prevent another world war. But you are worried that Soviet leader Joseph Stalin cannot be trusted.

What advice would you give to President Truman?

BUILDING BACKGROUND U.S. leaders had mistrusted the Soviet government before World War II. The goals of the totalitarian, Communist Soviet state conflicted with American democratic, capitalistic ideals. In addition, Soviet dictator Joseph Stalin used brutal tactics, including murder, to maintain power and control political opposition. During the war, the rivals put aside their differences to defeat Germany. After the war, however, old tensions resurfaced.

The Future of the Postwar World

As 1945 began, it was becoming clear that the Allies were going to win World War II. In February Allied leaders known as the Big Three—Franklin D. Roosevelt of the United States, Winston Churchill of Great Britain, and Joseph Stalin of the Soviet Union—met in the Soviet city of Yalta to discuss plans for peace.

At the **Yalta Conference**, the three leaders made important decisions about the future of European governments. They expressed support for the creation of an international peacekeeping organization. They also agreed that nations freed from Germany should have the right "to create democratic institutions of their own choice." Stalin promised to allow free elections in the Soviet-occupied countries in Eastern Europe. However, after driving German troops out of Poland, Soviet forces set up a pro–Soviet Communist government.

In July 1945 President Truman met with British and Soviet leaders near Berlin, Germany, at the Potsdam Conference. The Allied leaders divided conquered Germany into four zones. Britain, France, the United States, and the Soviet Union would each occupy one zone. The capital city of Berlin—located deep inside the Soviet zone—was also divided into four zones.

War Crimes Trials

After World War II, Allied leaders formed a special court, called the International Military Tribunal, to try Axis leaders accused of war crimes. In November 1945 the tribunal put high-ranking Nazis on trial in the German city of Nuremberg in what became known as the **Nuremberg trials**. U.S. Supreme Court justice Robert H. Jackson served as the chief American attorney. In his opening statement, Jackson explained the importance of the trials:

" The wrongs which we seek to condemn and punish have been so calculated [well planned], so malignant [evil] and devastating, that civilization cannot tolerate their being ignored because it cannot survive their being repeated. "

—Robert H. Jackson, quoted in *The Nuremberg Trial*, edited by Mitchell Bard

The court charged Nazi officials with "crimes against humanity." One defendant was Hermann Goering, a key planner of Hitler's "final solution." Another was Hans Frank, Poland's wartime governor, who had organized the killing of hundreds of thousands of Poles and Polish Jews. The tribunal found 19 Nazi leaders guilty. Of these, 12, including Goering and Frank, were sentenced to death.

The International Military Tribunal for the Far East held trials in Japan. Japan's wartime leader Hideki Tojo was convicted and executed. Seven other Japanese leaders were also sentenced to death. The trials in Germany and Japan helped establish the principle that individuals must be held responsible for committing war crimes, even when acting on behalf of a government.

The United Nations

During the war, President Roosevelt had spoken of the need for a new international organization to promote world peace. Roosevelt did not believe the United States alone could bring peace to the whole world. "The structure of world peace," he said, "must be a peace which rests on the cooperative effort of the whole world."

FOCUS ON READING

How does the quote from Robert H. Jackson help you visualize the atmosphere of the Nuremberg trials?

QUICK FACTS

Yalta Conference, February 1945

Who attended?
- Franklin Roosevelt, United States
- Winston Churchill, Great Britain
- Joseph Stalin, Soviet Union

What was the outcome?
- Free elections for countries liberated from German control
- Strong support for creation of an international peacekeeping organization

Winston Churchill, Franklin Roosevelt, and Joseph Stalin (seated left to right) met at Yalta in 1945.

QUICK FACTS

Potsdam Conference, July 1945

Who attended?
- Harry S. Truman, United States
- Winston Churchill and Clement Attlee, Great Britain
- Joseph Stalin, Soviet Union

What was the outcome?
- Germany and the city of Berlin would be divided into four zones. Britain, France, the United States, and the Soviet Union would each control one zone.

Clement Attlee, Harry Truman, and Joseph Stalin (seated left to right) met at Potsdam in 1945.

The United Nations

Written in 1945, the United Nations Charter declared the organization's commitment "to unite our strength to maintain international peace and security." Since 1945 the UN has grown from 51 member nations to more than 190. In addition to working to prevent war, the United Nations today works to provide disaster relief, prevent hunger and disease, and combat international terrorism.

ANALYSIS SKILL **ANALYZING INFORMATION**

How have the goals of the United Nations expanded since 1945?

In 1944 American, British, Soviet, and Chinese representatives met to draft a plan for the **United Nations** (UN)—an organization dedicated to resolving international conflicts. In 1945, representatives from 50 countries met to write the UN Charter. President Truman appointed Eleanor Roosevelt as one of the first U.S. delegates to the UN.

One of the UN's first actions concerned Palestine, occupied by the British after World War I. The UN General Assembly voted to divide the area into separate Arab and Jewish states. Jews had begun moving to Palestine, an area important to the Jewish, Christian, and Islamic religions, after World War I. Many more moved there before and during World War II. On May 14, 1948, Jewish leaders announced the creation of the nation of Israel.

The United States quickly recognized the new Jewish state. Arab leaders refused to do so and claimed the land as their own. Armies from five Arab states attacked Israel. Israeli forces drove them back, and the two sides reached a truce in 1949. Israel then joined the UN. But tensions remained high.

READING CHECK **Finding Main Ideas** What steps did world leaders take to establish peace?

From Allies to Enemies

During World War II, the United States and the Soviet Union cooperated to win the war. Afterward, the differences between the two nations led to new hostility. The Soviet Union hoped to spread communism around the world. Americans remained committed to capitalism and democracy.

The Iron Curtain

After Stalin created a Communist government in Poland, the Soviet Union expanded its control over Eastern Europe by creating "satellite states"—countries under complete Soviet control. In 1946 Winston Churchill described how Soviet control cut these countries off from the Western world. "An iron curtain has descended [fallen] across the [European] Continent," he said. The term *iron curtain* thus came to be used to describe this division. Presidential adviser Bernard Baruch warned of the seriousness of the Soviet threat, saying, "Let us not be deceived—we are today in the midst of a cold war." The phrase **Cold War** came to be used to describe the struggle for global power between the United States and the Soviet Union.

Cold War Policies

The United States quickly developed a new foreign policy to deal with the Cold War. It was based on the goal of **containment**, or preventing the Soviet Union from expanding its influence around the world.

In 1945 the Soviet Union began demanding control over areas in the Mediterranean Sea that were under Turkish authority. In 1946 Communist rebels in Greece threatened to topple the Greek monarchy. At Truman's request, Congress passed an aid package worth millions of dollars for Greece and Turkey. The money, the president said, would "support free peoples who are resisting attempted subjugation [conquest] by armed minorities or outside pressures." U.S. aid helped the Greek army defeat the Communist rebels and protected Turkey from Soviet expansion. This policy of providing aid to help foreign countries fight communism became known as the **Truman Doctrine**.

The nations of Europe, meanwhile, were still devastated from World War II. American secretary of state George C. Marshall saw this as a threat both to stability in Europe and to the U.S. economy, which depended on trade with Europe. Marshall called on European leaders to develop plans for economic recovery, which the United States would help fund. Under the **Marshall Plan**, Western Europe received more than $13 billion in U.S. loans and grants for European economic recovery between 1948 and 1952. Soviet leaders rejected Marshall Plan aid. They also kept Eastern European nations from participating.

Cold War tensions rose further in 1948 when France, Britain, and the United States

This cartoon shows Czechoslovakia's freedom being crushed by the Soviet Union.

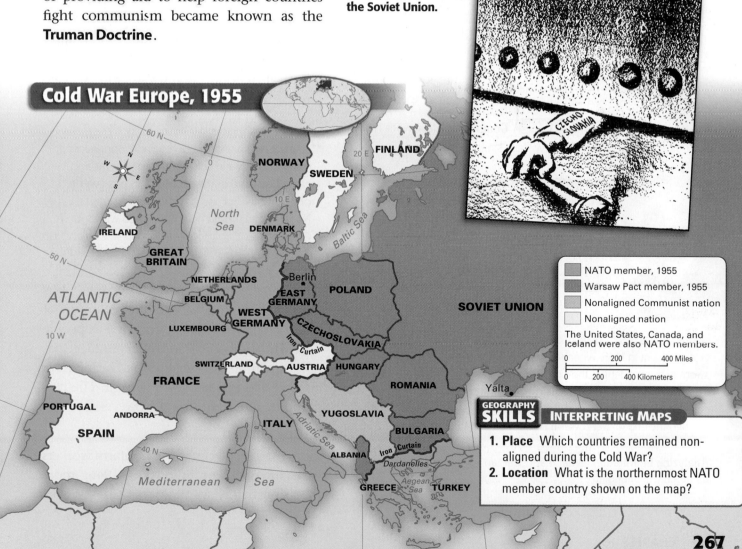

Cold War Europe, 1955

NATO member, 1955
Warsaw Pact member, 1955
Nonaligned Communist nation
Nonaligned nation

The United States, Canada, and Iceland were also NATO members.

0   200   400 Miles
0   200   400 Kilometers

GEOGRAPHY SKILLS   INTERPRETING MAPS

1. **Place** Which countries remained nonaligned during the Cold War?
2. **Location** What is the northernmost NATO member country shown on the map?

decided to join their occupation zones of Germany into one unit. The Soviet Union had good reason to fear the creation of a strong West German state. On June 24, the Soviet Union suddenly blocked all rail, highway, and water traffic between western Germany and the city of Berlin. West Berlin's 2 million residents were trapped behind the iron curtain.

To respond to this crisis without using military force, U.S. and British planes began airlifting supplies into West Berlin. For more than a year, planes delivered lifesaving food, fuel, and machinery to West Berliners. The Soviet Union made no determined effort to stop the airlift, fearing a war. It then lifted the blockade in May 1949.

THE IMPACT TODAY

When the Cold War ended, many former Warsaw Pact nations joined NATO. Today NATO has 26 member nations.

That same year, the United States joined nine Western European countries, along with Iceland and Canada, to form the **North Atlantic Treaty Organization** (NATO). NATO members promised to defend each other if attacked. In 1955 the Soviet Union created the Warsaw Pact, which provided a unified system of military command between the Soviet Union and its Eastern European satellite countries for their mutual defense.

READING CHECK **Comparing** How were NATO and the Warsaw Pact similar?

CASE STUDY) BIOGRAPHY

Harry S. Truman
1884–1972

Harry S. Truman grew up in Independence, Missouri. He was an artillery officer in France during World War I, then he returned to Missouri and later became active in politics. He was elected to the U.S. Senate in 1934, where he served until becoming vice president in 1945. When President Roosevelt died, Truman was sworn in as president of the United States. "I felt like the moon, the stars, and all the planets had fallen on me," he said. Truman later called his first year in office a "year of decisions," as he led the country through the end of World War II and the start of the Cold War.

Analyzing Information What made Truman's first year as president especially challenging?

Postwar America

You have read about the economic depression that followed the end of World War I. As World War II ended, President Truman was worried about a similar downturn. More than 16 million Americans had served in the armed forces during the war. Now they were coming home, and most would be looking for work.

The Postwar Economy

To provide jobs for returning veterans, the government urged the millions of women who had gone to work during the war to give up their jobs. New laws also eased the transition for returning soldiers. The Servicemen's Readjustment Act, or **GI Bill of Rights**, offered veterans money for school as well as loans for houses, farms, and businesses. The GI Bill's home loans enabled veterans to buy about 20 percent of the new houses built right after the war. Some 8 million veterans used the GI Bill's educational benefits to attend colleges and technical schools. Bob Dole, former U.S. senator from Kansas, described how the GI Bill changed his life:

❝In my case, I went from a couple of nondescript [ordinary] years in college before the war, and came back and made excellent grades. I went on to law school and got involved in politics. None of that would have happened without the GI Bill.❞

—Bob Dole, quoted in *GI Bill: The Law That Changed America*, by Milton Greenberg

Another major postwar change was Truman's decision to end the rationing of scarce products. Prices skyrocketed as people rushed to buy gasoline and other products that had been limited during the war. The inflation rate in 1946 rose above 18 percent. The U.S. economy remained strong, however.

Labor Unrest

More than 35 percent of all nonfarm workers were members of unions in 1946, more than ever before. With prices rising quickly,

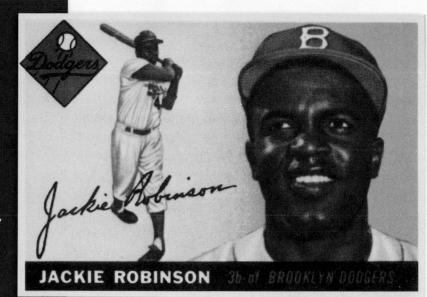

Jackie Robinson

On April 15, 1947, Jackie Robinson played his first game for the Brooklyn Dodgers. Robinson became a hero to millions by ending segregation in major league baseball. He went on to be a Hall of Fame player—and an outspoken supporter of equal rights. "The right of every American to first-class citizenship is the most important issue of our time," Robinson said.

How did Robinson show his support for equal rights for all Americans?

JACKIE ROBINSON *3b-of BROOKLYN DODGERS*

workers went on strike to demand higher wages. In 1946 alone, 4.5 million workers participated in nearly 5,000 strikes.

The strikes became a major political problem for President Truman. Many people began to wonder if he could handle the presidency. In April 1946 the 400,000-member United Mine Workers Union went on strike. When Truman was unable to negotiate a settlement, he placed the mines under government control. In May Truman ended a railroad strike by threatening to draft all the striking workers into the army.

To reduce the power of labor unions, Congress passed the Taft-Hartley Act in 1947. This act outlawed closed shops—businesses that could hire only union members. It also allowed the president to order an 80-day "cooling-off" period before a strike began. In addition, union leaders had to swear they were not Communists. In spite of his clashes with unions, Truman thought this bill went too far to weaken unions. He vetoed the bill, but Congress overrode his veto.

Civil Rights

After serving their country in World War II, many African Americans faced prejudice and segregation at home. "Black servicemen were overseas dying for this country," said civil rights lawyer Constance Baker Motley. "And . . . they would be coming home to a situation that said, in effect, You're a second-class citizen." African American veterans helped lead a major effort to gain equal rights.

Truman responded in 1946 by appointing the Committee on Civil Rights to investigate discrimination and suggest solutions. As a result of the committee's report, Truman recommended that Congress pass anti-lynching laws, outlaw segregation, and protect civil rights. Congress failed to act on Truman's ideas. But in 1948, under pressure from African American groups, Truman issued an executive order ending segregation in the armed forces. He also banned discrimination in the hiring of federal employees.

The Election of 1948

As the election of 1948 drew near, President Truman's chances of re-election looked bleak. The Republicans had gained control of Congress in 1946. They felt confident that their presidential candidate, New York governor Thomas Dewey, could beat Truman.

Truman faced challenges from within the Democratic Party as well. Some southern Democrats protested Truman's support for civil rights laws by walking out of the 1948 Democratic National Convention. Many joined the States' Rights Party, or Dixiecrats, which favored racial segregation. The Dixiecrats nominated their own presidential candidate—South Carolina governor Strom Thurmond.

Truman took his case for re-election directly to the American people. He traveled more than 30,000 miles by train and delivered hundreds of speeches. He attacked what he called the "do-nothing, good-for-nothing" Congress for refusing to pass his legislation. "I spoke I believe altogether to between fifteen and twenty million people," he later said. "I met them face to face, and I convinced them, and they voted for me." Truman won a surprise victory. The Democratic Party also regained control of both houses of Congress.

In his 1949 State of the Union Address, Truman urged Congress to support his plans for the nation. Truman's domestic program, called the **Fair Deal**, included a higher minimum wage, the creation of a national health insurance plan for all Americans, and expanded Social Security benefits for the elderly. It also asked for federal protection of civil rights and an end to racial discrimination in hiring.

Congress approved some parts of the Fair Deal, such as a higher minimum wage and expanded Social Security benefits. Congress rejected other Fair Deal proposals. These included civil rights legislation that would have created a permanent Fair Employment Practices Committee.

READING CHECK **Analyzing** How did the GI Bill help returning soldiers?

SUMMARY AND PREVIEW The United States faced a series of new challenges after World War II. In the next section you will learn how the fear of communism grew in the 1950s.

QUICK FACTS

The Fair Deal

The Fair Deal included
- National health insurance
- Expanded social security
- Higher minimum wage
- Public housing
- Civil rights legislation
- Federal aid to education

Section 1 Assessment

go.hrw.com
Online Quiz

Reviewing Ideas, Terms, and People

1. **a. Describe** How did the Allies divide Germany at the Potsdam Conference?
   b. Explain Why were the **Nuremberg trials** important?
   c. Predict Based on its founding and early years, do you think the **United Nations** would be an effective organization?

2. **a. Define** What was the **Truman Doctrine**?
   b. Analyze How did the **Marshall Plan** help stabilize Western Europe?
   c. Elaborate Why do you think the United States and Western European countries were concerned about Soviet expansion?

3. **a. Recall** What kinds of programs were included in President Truman's **Fair Deal**?
   b. Explain What was the purpose of the Taft-Hartley Act?
   c. Evaluate Do you think President Truman did enough to promote civil rights? Why or why not?

Critical Thinking

4. **Categorizing** Review your notes on the results of World War II. Then copy the graphic organizer below and use it to identify the effects of the war's end on the United States and the world.

Effects of World War II	
In the United States	In the World

FOCUS ON WRITING

5. **The Postwar World** Take notes on postwar developments in the United States and the world. Which events might have given Americans hope? Which might have made them concerned? If you had lived during the 1950s, which issue would have been of the most interest to you?

Eleanor Roosevelt

How would you work for human rights for all?

When did she live? 1884–1962

Where did she live? She lived much of her life in New York, where she married Franklin D. Roosevelt in 1905. She also lived in Washington, D.C., when her husband was assistant secretary of the navy and, later, president.

What did she do? During the Great Depression, Eleanor Roosevelt acted as President Roosevelt's "eyes and ears" by traveling around the United States to study conditions among the people. She investigated New Deal programs and reported on their effectiveness. She also worked for equal rights for African Americans. Serving on the UN Commission on Human Rights from 1946 to 1951, she helped write the Universal Declaration of Human Rights, which the UN adopted in 1948. In 1961 President John F. Kennedy chose her to chair his Commission on the Status of Women.

Why is she so important? She changed the role of First Lady by acting as a public figure. She held her own press conferences, made speeches, and wrote newspaper columns. She was a leading figure in the movements to promote human rights, children's welfare, and equal rights for women and minorities.

Making Inferences How did Eleanor Roosevelt's different jobs and activities reflect her values and beliefs?

KEY EVENTS

1905
Marries Franklin D. Roosevelt

1921
Becomes active in politics

1936
Begins writing daily newspaper columns; holds press conferences for women correspondents

1945
Appointed delegate to the UN

1946
Becomes chair of the UN Commission on Human Rights

1961
Appointed chair of the Commission on the Status of Women

1962
Dies in New York City

War in Korea and a New Red Scare

What You Will Learn...

Main Ideas

1. The United States fought Communist North Korea in the Korean War.
2. Fear of Communists led to a new Red Scare at home.
3. President Eisenhower faced Cold War crises around the world.

The Big Idea

During the Cold War, the U.S. government confronted communism globally and within the United States.

Key Terms and People

Mao Zedong, *p. 272*
38th parallel, *p. 272*
Joseph McCarthy, *p. 275*
hydrogen bomb, *p. 276*
arms race, *p. 276*
Sputnik, *p. 276*
brinkmanship, *p. 276*

TAKING NOTES As you read, take notes on Cold War conflicts and crises. In each circle of a diagram like the one below, describe one conflict or crisis. You may need to add more circles.

Cold War Conflicts and Crises

If YOU were there...

A radio broadcast on June 26, 1950, delivers a shocking announcement. Communist forces from North Korea have just invaded South Korea. President Truman has demanded that the North Koreans halt their invasion, but they seem to be ignoring this demand. Now Truman has to decide whether to use American military force to stop the North Koreans.

Do you think the United States should send troops to Korea? Why or why not?

BUILDING BACKGROUND The earliest Cold War conflicts were in Central and Eastern Europe, where countries were divided by the Iron Curtain. But the Truman Doctrine committed the United States to containing communism on a wider scale. The Communist takeover of China in 1949 soon focused Cold War fears on Asia.

The Korean War

The Cold War began in Europe but quickly spread to the Asian nations of China and Korea. In China, the Communist Party and the Nationalist Party had been struggling for control of the country since the early 1900s. The two rivals joined forces against Japan during World War II but then resumed their civil war after Japan's defeat. The United States, as part of its commitment to stop the spread of communism, backed the Nationalists. The Nationalists were defeated, however, and were forced to flee to the island of Taiwan. Led by **Mao Zedong**, the Communists officially established the People's Republic of China on October 1, 1949. Many Americans saw this as a disastrous failure of U.S. foreign policy. They feared that all of Asia might soon fall to communism.

These fears were heightened by a crisis in Korea. Japan had controlled Korea from 1910 to the end of World War II. After the war, the Allies divided Korea at the **38th parallel**. The Soviet Union

The Korean War

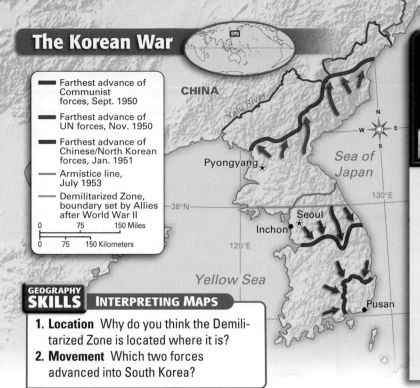

Farthest advance of Communist forces, Sept. 1950

Farthest advance of UN forces, Nov. 1950

Farthest advance of Chinese/North Korean forces, Jan. 1951

Armistice line, July 1953

Demilitarized Zone, boundary set by Allies after World War II

0   75   150 Miles
0   75   150 Kilometers

CHINA

Yalu River

Pyongyang

Sea of Japan

130°E

38°N

Seoul
Inchon

125°E

Yellow Sea

Pusan

GEOGRAPHY SKILLS **INTERPRETING MAPS**

1. **Location** Why do you think the Demilitarized Zone is located where it is?
2. **Movement** Which two forces advanced into South Korea?

CASE STUDY BIOGRAPHY

Douglas MacArthur
1880–1964

Douglas MacArthur grew up on a series of military bases, where his father served in the U.S. Army. "It was here I learned to ride and shoot even before I could read or write," he later said. After graduating first in his class at West Point, MacArthur began an army career that would last more than 50 years. He reached the rank of general in 1918 and commanded troops in World War I, World War II, and the Korean War. "When I joined the Army," he told Congress in 1951, "it was the fulfillment of all my boyhood hopes and dreams."

Drawing Inferences How can you tell how MacArthur felt about the U.S. Army?

---

controlled the northern part of Korea, and the United States occupied the south. Both sides set up governments, neither of which recognized the other as legitimate.

Fighting in Korea

On June 25, 1950, North Korea's Soviet-trained and equipped army stormed across the 38th parallel and invaded South Korea. The United Nations called for a cease-fire. But the North Koreans continued their attack.

President Truman had to make an immediate decision: Should the United States use force to try to stop the North Korean invasion? On June 27 Truman announced: "I have ordered United States air and sea forces to give the [South] Korean government troops cover and support." That same day, the UN decided to help South Korea "to repel the armed attack." American general Douglas MacArthur was put in command of the UN forces, which included troops from the United States and 15 other countries. The majority of the troops were from the United States and South Korea.

In the early battles, MacArthur's forces were driven back to the southeastern tip of the Korean Peninsula, near the city of Pusan. Fierce fighting raged for six weeks before the UN troops turned the tide of the war with a surprise attack. Landing at the port city of Inchon on September 15, UN forces attacked the North Koreans from behind. About a month later, MacArthur's troops captured Pyongyang, North Korea's capital. They then advanced north to the Yalu River, the border between North Korea and China. MacArthur told Truman he would "have the boys home by Christmas."

Then China suddenly sent hundreds of thousands of soldiers across the border to join the North Koreans. They drove UN forces south again, back below the 38th parallel. MacArthur suggested air strikes on Chinese cities and an attack on mainland China. Truman refused permission. He was determined to contain the war in Korea.

When MacArthur publicly criticized the president's strategy, Truman relieved the general of command. "I fired General MacArthur because he wouldn't respect the authority of the president," Truman said. This was a very unpopular decision with the American public. MacArthur came home to a hero's welcome.

FOCUS ON NEW YORK

The almost 500,000 New Yorkers who served in the Korean War are honored by the New York State Korean War Veterans Memorial in Albany. The site features a pool, bronze flags, and a wall of information about the war.

The War Ends

By the spring of 1951 the fighting in Korea settled into a violent stalemate. The UN forces had driven the North Koreans and Chinese back across the 38th parallel. But neither side seemed able to win the war.

Primary Source

POLITICAL CARTOON
Fear of Communism

In the 1950s the fear of communism caused some government leaders to ignore the civil liberties of suspected Communists. Some critics, like this cartoonist, believed these tactics threatened the freedom of all Americans. Here, a frightened man climbs the arm of the Statue of Liberty to put out her torch.

"FIRE!"

The Statue of Liberty's burning torch symbolizes freedom.

Hysteria means "senseless excitement."

The frightened man carries water to put out the fire.

"FIRE!" from *Herblock: A Cartoonist's Life* (Times Books 1998)

ANALYSIS SKILL **ANALYZING PRIMARY SOURCES**

Why is the man shown to be putting out Liberty's torch?

Americans' frustration with the war dominated the 1952 presidential election. The Republicans nominated war hero Dwight D. Eisenhower. He promised to end the increasingly unpopular conflict, saying, "The first task of a new administration will be to . . . bring the Korean War to an early and honorable end."

This promise helped Eisenhower win the election. Eisenhower visited Korea, but the conflict dragged on. A cease-fire finally ended the fighting on July 27, 1953. After three years of fighting, North and South Korea were again divided near the 38th parallel. More than 130,000 Americans had been killed or wounded. Korean and Chinese casualties topped 2 million.

READING CHECK **Summarizing** What were the effects of the Korean War?

A New Red Scare

The first Red Scare swept America after the Russian Revolution in 1917. Cold War fears led to another Red Scare in the late 1940s and 1950s. Attorney General J. Howard McGrath summed up these fears when he said, "There are today many Communists in America. They are everywhere—in factories, offices, butcher shops, on street corners."

Fear of Communists

A congressional committee called the House Un-American Activities Committee (HUAC) investigated Communist influence in America. In 1947 HUAC launched a series of hearings to expose what it believed was Communist influence in the Hollywood movie industry. The committee branded as "red," or Communist, actors and writers who would not answer questions or who refused to reveal the names of suspected Communists. People suspected of Communist sympathies were often blacklisted, or denied work. Some of these people never worked in movies again.

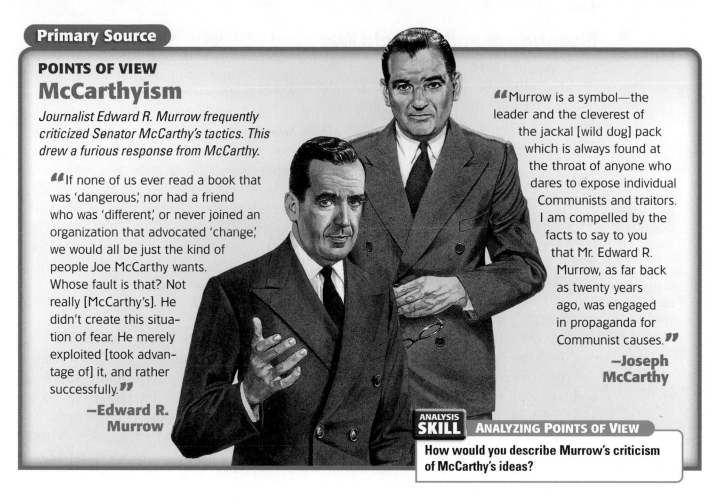

Primary Source

POINTS OF VIEW
McCarthyism

Journalist Edward R. Murrow frequently criticized Senator McCarthy's tactics. This drew a furious response from McCarthy.

❝If none of us ever read a book that was 'dangerous,' nor had a friend who was 'different,' or never joined an organization that advocated 'change,' we would all be just the kind of people Joe McCarthy wants. Whose fault is that? Not really [McCarthy's]. He didn't create this situation of fear. He merely exploited [took advantage of] it, and rather successfully.❞

—Edward R. Murrow

❝Murrow is a symbol—the leader and the cleverest of the jackal [wild dog] pack which is always found at the throat of anyone who dares to expose individual Communists and traitors. I am compelled by the facts to say to you that Mr. Edward R. Murrow, as far back as twenty years ago, was engaged in propaganda for Communist causes.❞

—Joseph McCarthy

ANALYSIS SKILL   ANALYZING POINTS OF VIEW

How would you describe Murrow's criticism of McCarthy's ideas?

Explosive spy cases also fed the fears that Communists were at work in the United States. In 1950 a German-born physicist was convicted of providing the Soviets information about the atomic bomb project at Los Alamos, New Mexico, that allowed them to develop an atomic bomb at least one year earlier than they would have. In 1951 Julius and Ethel Rosenberg also were tried for providing Soviet spies with secret details about atomic bomb design. The Rosenbergs denied the charges but were found guilty and executed in 1953.

The Rise of McCarthy

Wisconsin senator **Joseph McCarthy** contributed to fears in the early 1950s by charging that Communists were working inside the State Department. He claimed to have the names of 57 people who were "either card-carrying members or certainly loyal to the Communist Party."

McCarthy produced no **concrete** proof of crimes. When challenged, he made up new charges, labeling those who questioned him as "soft on communism." This method of making aggressive accusations without proof became known as McCarthyism.

McCarthy finally went too far in 1954. In televised Senate hearings, he charged that there were Communists in the U.S. Army. For five weeks, Americans watched McCarthy's bullying tactics. At one point, McCarthy tried to discredit Joseph Welch, the army's attorney, by attacking a young assistant in Welch's law firm. This shocked Welch—and the nation. "Let us not assassinate this lad further, Senator," Welsh said. "Have you left no sense of decency?" A later Senate vote condemned McCarthy's actions, but it came too late for those whose careers had been ruined by his attacks.

READING CHECK **Comparing** How were HUAC's and McCarthy's actions similar?

ACADEMIC VOCABULARY

concrete
specific, real

Eisenhower and the Cold War

Cold War tensions increased around the world during the presidency of Dwight Eisenhower. In this hostile atmosphere, Americans adjusted to the reality of living with the constant threat of nuclear war.

The Arms Race

THE IMPACT TODAY

Today Americans, Russians, and astronauts from other countries work side by side on the International Space Station, which has been in orbit since 1998.

In 1950 President Truman approved work on the **hydrogen bomb**, a weapon far more powerful than the atomic bombs used in World War II. American scientists tested the first hydrogen bomb in the South Pacific in 1952. "The fireball expanded to three miles in diameter," said a test observer. He soon saw that the entire island on which the bomb exploded "had vanished, vaporized."

The Soviet Union tested its first atomic bomb in 1949 and its first hydrogen bomb in 1953. In what became a nuclear **arms race**, both the United States and the Soviet Union rushed to build more and more weapons. American school children practiced "duck-and-cover" drills, in which they were taught to crouch under their desks in case of nuclear attack. Some families built under ground bomb shelters in their backyards.

In October 1957 the Soviets launched **Sputnik**, the world's first artificial satellite. Americans feared that if the Soviet Union could launch a satellite, it could launch missiles to attack the United States. In January 1958 the United States responded by launching its own satellite. Later that year, the U.S. government established the National Aeronautics and Space Administration (NASA) to conduct space research.

Cold War Crises

President Eisenhower modified Truman's policy of containment. He and Secretary of State John Foster Dulles supported **brinkmanship**—a willingness to go to the brink of war to oppose communism. "The ability to get to the verge [edge] without getting into war is the necessary art," Dulles explained. The president and Dulles also

History Close-up

Inside a Bomb Shelter

Many families built personal bomb shelters for use in a nuclear emergency. The shelters were stocked with essentials like food and water and were often located in the family's backyard.

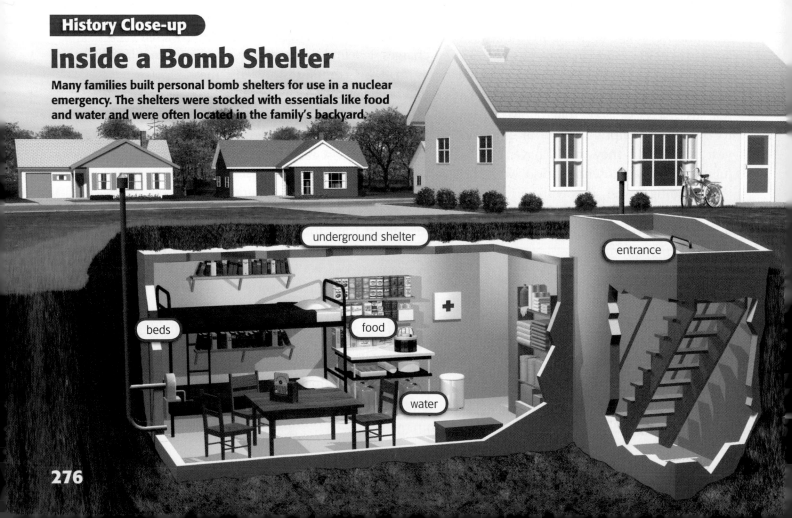

underground shelter

entrance

beds

food

water

threatened the Soviet Union with "massive retaliation" against Soviet advances.

As part of his effort, Eisenhower used covert, or secret, operations around the world. In 1953, for example, the Central Intelligence Agency (CIA) helped overthrow the premier of Iran. American officials had feared he was a Communist. In 1954 the CIA helped organize the removal of the Guatemalan president for similar reasons.

In 1956 a crisis in Egypt seemed to push the world to the brink of a third world war. Egyptian leader Gamal Abdel Nasser nationalized the Suez Canal, a vital waterway connecting the Mediterranean and Red seas, in an attempt to collect tolls from the canal to finance a major dam project. Britain and France, which relied on the canal for trade, allied with Israel, a longtime enemy of Egypt, and invaded the area around the canal. The Soviet Union, an ally of Egypt, threatened to crush the invaders. This would force the United States to defend its allies. Finally, the Americans and the Soviet Union agreed to condemn the invasion, and the Suez crisis ended. After the brief moment of cooperation, the Cold War continued.

READING CHECK **Analyzing** How was the arms race a display of brinkmanship?

Families practiced getting into their shelters as quickly as possible. Some families spent free time in the shelters to adjust to spending weeks or months there.

ANALYSIS SKILL **ANALYZING INFORMATION**

Which essentials did families keep in their bomb shelters?

SUMMARY AND PREVIEW After World War II, Americans responded to Communist threats at home and abroad. In the next section you will read about how America prospered during these challenging times.

Section 2 Assessment

go.hrw.com
Online Quiz

Reviewing Ideas, Terms, and People

1. **a. Identify** What is the **38th parallel**? Why was it important in the Korean War?
   b. Analyze How did the outcome of China's civil war affect the U.S. response to North Korea's attack?
   c. Evaluate Do you think President Truman should have fired MacArthur? Explain your answer.

2. **a. Describe** Why did a second Red Scare occur in the late 1940s and 1950s?
   b. Explain How did television affect **Joseph McCarthy**'s power?
   c. Elaborate Why do you think the Red Scare lasted so long?

3. **a. Recall** How did Eisenhower deal with Cold War crises during his administration?
   b. Make Inferences How can you tell that the U.S. government took the launch of *Sputnik* seriously?
   c. Elaborate Why do you think the United States and the Soviet Union were able to cooperate during the Suez crisis?

Critical Thinking

4. **Categorizing** Review your notes on Cold War conflicts and crises. Then copy the graphic organizer below and use it to list each event under its appropriate location.

Asia	Soviet Union	United States	Other

FOCUS ON WRITING

5. **Taking Notes on Challenges at Home and Abroad** Take notes on the challenges and fears Americans faced during the Korean War, McCarthy era, and Eisenhower presidency. How did the government and individuals respond to these challenges and fears?

The Nation Prospers

What You Will Learn...

Main Ideas

1. America's economy boomed in the 1950s.
2. Americans enjoyed new forms of popular culture.
3. Social critics found fault with 1950s society.

The Big Idea

An expanding economy led to new ways of life for many Americans in the 1950s.

Key Terms and People

baby boom, *p. 278*
Sun Belt, *p. 278*
urban renewal, *p. 279*
beats, *p. 281*

TAKING NOTES As you read, take notes on the suburban lifestyle and culture of the 1950s. You can organize your notes in a table like this one.

Suburban Life and Culture

If YOU were there...

You live with your parents in an apartment building in 1954. You have grown up in the city, and you are used to walking or taking the subway everywhere you need to go. But your parents are talking about moving out to the suburbs. They like the idea of having a house of their own, with a driveway and a backyard. They ask what you think about moving to the suburbs.

How would you respond?

BUILDING BACKGROUND Americans enjoyed a long economic boom in the years after World War II. Improving technology helped boost the productivity of American industries, creating new products and new jobs. Americans' incomes rose rapidly, and unemployment declined. By the mid-1950s nearly 60 percent of the U.S. population qualified as middle class. This prosperity brought many changes to American life.

America's Economy in the 1950s

The American economy boomed during the 1950s. Millions of Americans earned more money than ever before and, therefore, had more money to spend on homes, cars, vacations, and large appliances. Feeling better off than they had during the Depression and World War II, many young Americans were getting married and starting families. This led to a **baby boom**, or a significant increase in the number of babies born.

A Nation on the Move

Americans were also on the move in the 1950s, as people relocated to new parts of the country to take jobs and improve the quality of their lives. Many businesses and workers moved to the **Sun Belt**—southern and western states that offered a warm climate year-round and low tax rates. As a result, the region's population doubled in the 30 years after World War II.

The 1956 Highway Act also encouraged travel. This new law provided billions of dollars for the construction of a 41,000-mile

New Housing Construction

Amount Spent (in billions): $0, $10, $20, $30, $40
1945 — 1960

Live Births

Births (in millions): 20, 30, 40, 50
1945 — 1960

Personal Income

Total (in billions): $50, $150, $250, $350, $450
1945 — 1960

ANALYSIS SKILL ANALYZING VISUALS

How did rising wealth affect families in the 1950s?

Many American families used their newfound wealth to buy consumer products like houses, automobiles, and appliances. Advertisements like this one used an idealized version of an American family to sell products.

interstate highway system. New highways helped to greatly increase both business and personal travel between cities throughout the country. The roads also made it easier for people to move to suburbs and commute to jobs in cities.

Suburbs and Cities

The rising demand for homes in the suburbs encouraged developers to build new suburban neighborhoods. On Long Island, New York, William Levitt created Levittown, one of the nation's first preplanned suburbs. Between 1946 and 1951, Levitt built more than 17,000 low-priced, mass-produced houses. Like Henry Ford's Model T, Levitt's homes were designed to be simple and affordable. By the mid-1950s, builders were constructing similar suburban homes all over the country. By 1970 more Americans lived in suburbs than in cities.

Many families welcomed the comfort and convenience of suburban living. Suburban homes usually had driveways, large lawns, and labor-saving appliances. Suburban children could participate in a wide variety of sports and other activities. Many mothers spent so much

time driving their children from one activity to another that one commentator referred to the task as "motherhood on wheels."

Some critics of suburbs complained that suburban life was too heavily based on consumer culture. They also criticized the suburbs for encouraging conformity, or sameness. Most of the people living in the suburbs were white and middle class. In fact, some communities—including Levittown—refused to sell homes to black families.

As middle-class families moved to the suburbs, cities collected fewer tax dollars. This led to a decline in city services. Those who were unable to afford a move to the suburbs lived in increasingly decaying urban areas. As conditions worsened, the federal government began an **urban renewal** program—a plan to improve life in cities. Urban renewal projects focused on improving city services and urban housing. In reality, however, the programs sometimes led to more problems for urban residents.

READING CHECK Contrasting How was life different in suburbs and cities?

FOCUS ON NEW YORK CITY

Levittown, New York, was built in 1947–51 as a suburb of New York City. Although nicknamed "America's First Suburb," Levittown was not in fact the first. It was, however, one of the earliest preplanned suburbs to be built in the nation. Levitt and Sons built a second Levittown near Philadelphia.

Life in the 1950s

Life for the average citizen in the United States changed dramatically in the prosperous years after World War II. More money was available to buy a wider variety of products, and technological advances made life safer and easier for many.

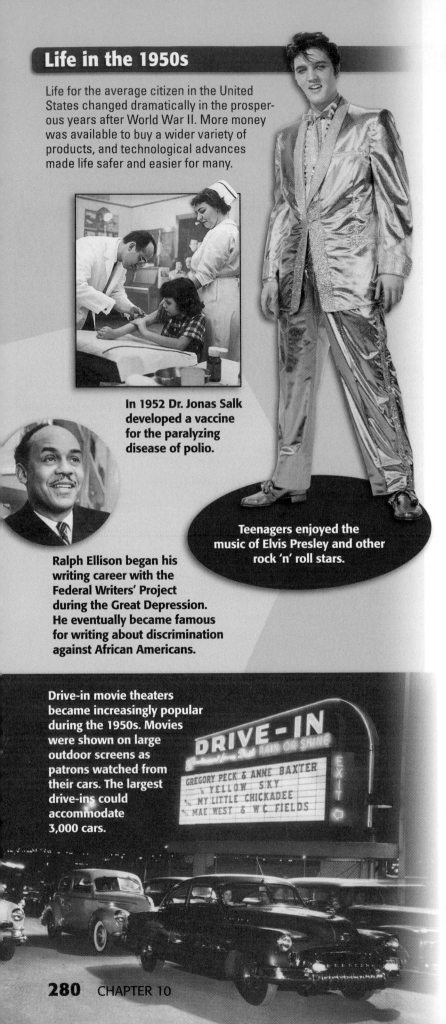

In 1952 Dr. Jonas Salk developed a vaccine for the paralyzing disease of polio.

Ralph Ellison began his writing career with the Federal Writers' Project during the Great Depression. He eventually became famous for writing about discrimination against African Americans.

Teenagers enjoyed the music of Elvis Presley and other rock 'n' roll stars.

Drive-in movie theaters became increasingly popular during the 1950s. Movies were shown on large outdoor screens as patrons watched from their cars. The largest drive-ins could accommodate 3,000 cars.

DRIVE-IN
GREGORY PECK & ANNE BAXTER
YELLOW SKY
MY LITTLE CHICKADEE
MAE WEST & W C FIELDS
EXIT

American Pop Culture

American life was changing quickly in the 1950s as new technology developed. Many people began shopping in malls and eating at new fast-food restaurants. By the end of the decade, nearly 90 percent of all American families owned at least one television set. On average, American families watched about six hours of television a day.

Americans all over the country shared the experience of watching the same news, comedies, and sports programs. Many shows, such as *The Lone Ranger*, were versions of shows that began on the radio. Early hits included Milton Berle's variety show *Texaco Star Theater* and the Western drama *Gunsmoke*. But the most popular show was *I Love Lucy*, a situation comedy (or sitcom) starring Lucille Ball and her real-life husband, Cuban American bandleader Desi Arnaz. About 44 million Americans tuned in to one episode of *I Love Lucy* in 1953 to see the birth of their son—twice the number that watched President Eisenhower's inauguration the next day.

New styles of music also helped reshape American culture in the 1950s. African American jazz greats Charlie Parker and Dizzy Gillespie became known as the "Fathers" of Bebop, a complex jazz style often played at a rapid pace. Meanwhile, musicians like Elvis Presley, Buddy Holly, Chuck Berry, and Little Richard helped rock 'n' roll sweep the nation. Teenage music fans powered the rock 'n' roll revolution, buying more than 70 percent of all records sold in the late 1950s. Just like jazz in the 1920s, rock music drew criticism from some adults. One journalist even labeled rock 'n' roll "a menace to morals." An Arizona teenager responded to this type of criticism by saying, "Man, I believe the older generation just doesn't want the younger generation to have any fun."

READING CHECK Finding Main Ideas What changes took place in American pop culture during the 1950s?

Social Critics

Though the postwar years were happy and productive for many Americans, not everyone was happy with American society in the 1950s. Some women, for instance, were frustrated that they could only find work in a limited number of fields such as teaching, nursing, or office work. Others were discouraged by the expectation that they would give up their jobs when they got married. One woman recalled,

"There was always the assumption, even when I was getting my graduate degree in education, that any work I did was temporary, something to do until I assumed [began] my principal role in life which was to be the perfect wife and mother, supported by my husband."

—Sally Ann Carter, quoted in *The Fifties: A Women's Oral History*, by Brett Harvey

Many writers commented on 1950s society in their work. In 1951 J. D. Salinger published *The Catcher in the Rye*. The novel's teenage narrator, Holden Caulfield, criticizes the "phoniness" of the adults around him, who he believed loved only money and wanted everyone to be the same. In his 1952 novel *Invisible Man*, Ralph Ellison wrote about how African Americans felt left out by American society. "I am an invisible man," Ellison wrote. "I am invisible, understand, simply because people refuse to see me."

Young people known as beatniks, or **beats**, criticized society with unusual writing styles and rebellious behavior. The works of beat poet Allen Ginsberg and novelist Jack Kerouac inspired many young people to question the rules of mainstream American society. Many young people also identified with rebellious characters in popular movies of the 1950s. In the 1953 film *The Wild One*, actor Marlon Brando plays Johnny, a wild biker who challenges the rules of society. When asked, "Hey Johnny, what are you rebelling against?" Johnny replies, "Whadda ya got?"

READING CHECK **Finding Main Ideas** Why did people criticize 1950s society?

SUMMARY AND PREVIEW In the 1950s, suburban life, television, and pop culture changed American society. In the next chapter you will learn how the civil rights movement affected the United States.

---

go.hrw.com
Online Quiz

Section 3 Assessment

Reviewing Ideas, Terms, and People

1. **a. Recall** How did a booming economy affect life in the United States in the 1950s?
   b. Explain How did the growth of suburbs affect cities?
   c. Elaborate How do you think the **baby boom** affected 1950s society?
2. **a. Identify** How did American pop culture change in the 1950s?
   b. Make Inferences Based on what you have read, how was teenage culture in the 1950s different from adult culture?
3. **a. Describe** What was *Invisible Man* about?
   b. Compare What did J. D. Salinger and Jack Kerouac have in common?
   c. Predict How do you think some women in the 1950s might have wanted to change their lives?

Critical Thinking

4. **Analyzing Information** Review your notes on 1950s suburban life and culture. Then copy the graphic organizer below and use it to list the benefits and challenges of suburban life and culture.

Benefits   Challenges

FOCUS ON WRITING

5. **Taking Notes on Daily Life and Culture** Take notes on daily life and pop culture during the 1950s. What did Americans want, and what was important to them? What kind of music would be appropriate for a song about the 1950s?

Social Studies Skills

Interpreting Battle Maps

Define the Skill

Battle maps show events during a battle or war. They may show army movements or locations of battles. A single battle map often shows events that occurred at different times. Reading the map key is very important when you interpret battle maps. Battle maps usually include many different symbols. The map key explains the symbols used on the map.

Learn the Skill

Follow these steps to interpret battle maps.

1 Read the title to determine what the map is about.

2 Study the map key to understand what the symbols on the map mean. Locate the symbols from the key on the map.

3 Look for labels and other information on the map. Use what you already know about the time period to determine the importance of these features.

4 Use the map to make a generalization about a battle or war, such as which side won.

Practice the Skill

1. What is this map about?

2. What does the solid blue line on this map represent? What does the dotted red line represent?

3. What does the green line on the 38th parallel show? Why is this important?

Based on this map, make a generalization about the Korean War.

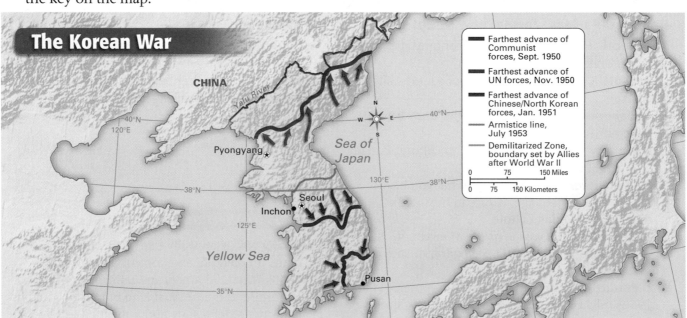

The Korean War

Key:
- Farthest advance of Communist forces, Sept. 1950
- Farthest advance of UN forces, Nov. 1950
- Farthest advance of Chinese/North Korean forces, Jan. 1951
- Armistice line, July 1953
- Demilitarized Zone, boundary set by Allies after World War II

0 — 75 — 150 Miles
0 — 75 — 150 Kilometers

CHINA
Yalu River
Pyongyang
Sea of Japan
Seoul
Inchon
Yellow Sea
Pusan

Chapter Review

HOLT
History's Impact
▸ video series
Review the video to answer the closing question:
How might Americans' awareness of world events have changed once television became popular?

Visual Summary

QUICK FACTS

Use the visual summary below to help you review the main ideas of the chapter.

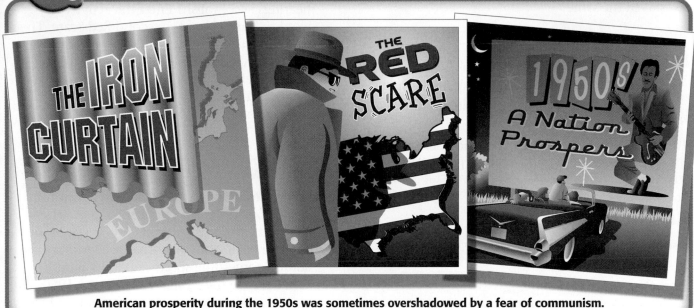

American prosperity during the 1950s was sometimes overshadowed by a fear of communism.

Reviewing Vocabulary, Terms, and People

Match the numbered person or term with the correct lettered definition.

1. GI Bill of Rights
2. Yalta Conference
3. Truman Doctrine
4. Joseph McCarthy
5. Fair Deal

a. U.S. senator who unfairly accused many citizens of being Communists

b. meeting at which Franklin Roosevelt, Winston Churchill, and Joseph Stalin discussed strategy for postwar peace

c. package of domestic reforms proposed by President Truman

d. U.S. policy of containing communism through economic aid

e. program that offered veterans money for school after World War II

Comprehension and Critical Thinking

SECTION 1 *(Pages 264–270)*

6. **a. Recall** What is the United Nations?

b. Explain Why did Franklin Roosevelt support the formation of the UN?

c. Elaborate Would you have supported the policy of containment? Why or why not?

SECTION 2 *(Pages 272–277)*

7. **a. Identify** How did the United States battle communism in Asia in the 1950s?

b. Explain What effect did the launch of *Sputnik* have on the United States?

c. Evaluate What were some risks and advantages of the strategy of brinkmanship?

8. a. Describe How did life in the United States change in the 1950s?

b. Summarize Why were some women frustrated with 1950s society?

c. Elaborate How has American popular culture changed since the 1950s? How has it stayed the same?

Reviewing Themes

9. Politics How did the Cold War affect political relations between the United States and the Soviet Union?

10. Science and Technology How did science and technology advance during the 1950s?

Reading Skills

Visualizing *Use the Reading Skills taught in this chapter to answer the question below.*

> Wisconsin senator Joseph McCarthy contributed to fears in the early 1950s by charging that Communists were working inside the State Department. He claimed to have the names of 57 people who were "either card-carrying members or certainly loyal to the Communist Party." *(p. 275)*

11. What elements of the selection above help you visualize the feelings created by the Red Scare?

Social Studies Skills

Interpreting Battle Maps *Use the Social Studies Skills taught in this chapter to answer the question below.*

12. Look back at the battle map on page 273. In what year did North Korean forces make their farthest advance?

Using the Internet go.hrw.com

13. Activity: Researching the Second Red Scare Fear of communism and spies grew during the late 1940s and 1950s. What were Americans' fears? How did Senator Joseph McCarthy and congressional hearings affect the lives of those accused of Communist activities? What did the hearings accomplish? Enter the activity keyword to learn about the second Red Scare. Then write a journal entry from the point of view of Senator McCarthy, a blacklisted writer, or Joseph Welch, attorney for the U.S. Army. Your journal entry should include direct references to your research.

FOCUS ON WRITING

14. Writing Your Song Lyrics Review your notes. Decide on a theme for your song about the 1950s. It can focus either on one event or idea or on several. Remember that the lyrics should address something specific about what it was like to live in the United States in the 1950s. You may even want to write from the point of view of a young person living in the 1950s. What would that person think about? What would be his or her hopes and fears?

Grade 8 Intermediate-Level Test Preparation

Directions (1–7): **For each statement or question, write on the separate answer sheet the *number* of the word or expression that, of those given, best completes the statement or answers the question.**

1 **At the Yalta Conference, Joseph Stalin promised**

(1) to allow free elections in the Soviet Union.

(2) to allow free elections in Eastern Europe.

(3) to prosecute Soviet war criminals.

(4) that the Soviet Union would join the United Nations.

2 **The United Nations was formed to**

(1) promote world peace.

(2) deal with problems in Palestine.

(3) bring Nazi leaders responsible for the Holocaust to justice.

(4) plan how to divide Germany among the Allies.

3 **What is McCarthyism?**

(1) denying people work

(2) a type of communism

(3) going to the brink of nuclear war

(4) making accusations of Communist activity without proof

4 **Which president decided to use U.S. troops to help defend South Korea in 1950?**

(1) Franklin Roosevelt

(2) Dwight Eisenhower

(3) Harry Truman

(4) Herbert Hoover

5 **The Nuremberg trials were established for the following purpose:**

(1) to reward Germans who fought for the allies

(2) to try Axis leaders for war crimes

(3) to punish post-was looters

(4) to try Allied soldiers for desertion

6 **Which country sent hundreds of thousands of troops to fight alongside North Korean forces in the Korean War?**

(1) Japan

(2) China

(3) the United States

(4) the Soviet Union

7 **What does the term Cold War describe?**

(1) the struggle for land among the former Allies

(2) the long battle fought in the winter of 1948

(3) the struggle for global power between the United States and the Soviet Union

(4) the fight for global economic control in the Far East

Base your answer to question 8 on the text below and on your knowledge of social studies.

> "Every gun that is made, every warship launched, every rocket fired signifies, in the final sense, a theft from those who hunger and are not fed, those who are cold and not clothed. This world in arms is not spending money alone. It is spending the sweat of its laborers, the genius of its scientists, the hopes of its children."
>
> —Dwight D. Eisenhower, April 16, 1953

8 **Constructed-Response Question What desire do you think Eisenhower was expressing in this passage?**

The Civil Rights Movement

FOCUS QUESTION

How has America reacted to the challenges of the modern world?

WRITING JOURNAL

A Civil Rights Bill In the 1950s and 1960s, African Americans began successfully to challenge the discrimination they had faced for so many years. In this chapter, you will read about the civil rights movement and about the passage of new civil rights laws. Imagine that you are a member of Congress at this time. You will write a new civil rights bill to help people gain fair treatment under the law.

UNITED STATES

1945

1954 Thurgood Marshall argues against segregation in the Supreme Court case *Brown* v. *Board of Education.*

1953 Soviet leader Joseph Stalin dies.

WORLD

HOLT

History's Impact
▶ **video series**
Watch the video to under-
stand the impact of equal
rights and justice for all
Americans.

AMERICAN
NEWSPAPER
GUILD
(AFL-CIO-CLC)

AMERICAN
NEWSPAPER
GUILD
AFL-CIO-CLC

WE
DEMAND
AN FEPC
LAW
NOW!

CHICAGO
TEACHERS
FOR
INTEGRATED
SCHOOLS

WE
DEMAND
EQUAL
RIGHTS
NOW!

WE
MARCH
FOR
EFFECTIVE

What You Will Learn...

African Americans launched a major civil rights
movement in the years following World War II.
Members of the movement organized demonstrations to protest unfair treatment, like the
March on Washington shown here. In this chapter,
you will learn about the efforts of
African Americans and others to gain
civil rights protections in the 1950s,
1960s, and 1970s.

1968
Columbia University
student protesters take
over five university
buildings and clash with
police.

NY

1963 Lee Harvey
Oswald assas-
sinates President
John F. Kennedy.

1966 The Nation-
al Organization for
Women is formed.

1969 La Raza Unida
is organized to support
the rights of Mexican
Americans.

1973 The
American Indian
Movement protests
at Wounded Knee.

1960

1970

1957 The Soviets
launch *Sputnik*, the
first human made
satellite.

1961 The
Berlin Wall di-
vides East and
West Berlin.

1966 Indira Gandhi
becomes prime
minister of India.

287

Reading Social Studies

by Kylene Beers

Economics   Geography   **Politics**   **Society and Culture**   Science and Technology

Focus on Themes In this chapter, you will read about the important changes in American **society** during the period called the civil rights era. You will learn about how many people came to see **politics** as a way to correct social inequalities that existed for minority groups in the United States, such as African Americans, women, Mexican Americans, Native Americans, and people with disabilities. You will also read about life in the 1960s.

Using Context Clues: Synonyms

Focus on Reading Some words mean almost the same thing. Understanding the similarities can help you understand words whose meaning you may not know.

Understanding Synonyms Words that have similar meanings are called synonyms. Often, a synonym is given as a definition. The synonym will probably be a word you already understand. This will help you learn the new word through context clues.

Notice how one reader uses synonyms to understand words she does not understand.

An AIM leader described the group's goals, saying, "We don't want civil rights in the white man's society—we want our own *sovereign [self-governing]* rights."

From Chapter 11, pp. 304–08

This is a word I don't know the meaning of.

These brackets mean that the word inside is a synonym of the word or phrase that comes before. The word inside is a synonym of *sovereign*.

The word *sovereign* must mean to govern on one's own.

You Try It!

The following passage is from the chapter you are getting ready to read. As you read the passage, look for synonyms in the definitions of unfamiliar words.

> On February 1, 1960, the students went into Woolworth and staged a sit-in—a demonstration in which protesters sit down and refuse to leave. They sat in the "whites-only" section of the lunch counter and ordered coffee. They were not served, but they stayed until the store closed. The next day, they returned with dozens more students to continue the sit-in. Soon, another sit-in began at the lunch counter of a nearby store.
>
> *From Chapter 11, p. 294*

After you read the passage, answer the following questions.

1. What word is a synonym of sit-in that is given in that word's definition?

2. What clue is given that helps you find the synonym in the above passage?

3. Can you think of another synonym for sit-in that might have been used?

As you read Chapter 11, look for synonyms that can help you define words you don't know.

Key Terms and People

Chapter 11

Section 1
Thurgood Marshall *(p. 291)*
Brown v. *Board of Education (p. 291)*
Little Rock Nine *(p. 291)*
Rosa Parks *(p. 292)*
Montgomery bus boycott *(p. 293)*
Martin Luther King Jr. *(p. 293)*
sit-in *(p. 294)*
Student Nonviolent Coordinating Committee *(p. 294)*

Section 2
John F. Kennedy *(p. 296)*
Freedom Rides *(p. 297)*
March on Washington *(p. 298)*
Lyndon B. Johnson *(p. 299)*
Civil Rights Act of 1964 *(p. 299)*
Voting Rights Act of 1965 *(p. 299)*
Great Society *(p. 300)*
Black Power *(p. 300)*
Malcolm X *(p. 300)*

Section 3
Cesar Chavez *(p. 302)*
United Farm Workers *(p. 302)*
Betty Friedan *(p. 303)*
National Organization for Women *(p. 303)*
Shirley Chisholm *(p. 303)*
Equal Rights Amendment *(p. 303)*
Phyllis Schlafly *(p. 303)*
American Indian Movement *(p. 305)*
Disabled in Action *(p. 305)*

Academic Vocabulary
In this chapter, you will learn the following academic words:
implement *(p. 291)*
consequences *(p. 303)*

The Civil Rights Movement Takes Shape

What You Will Learn...

Main Ideas

1. Civil rights leaders battled school segregation in court.
2. The Montgomery bus boycott helped end segregation on buses.
3. Students organized sit-ins to protest segregation.

The Big Idea

Civil rights activists used legal challenges and public protests to confront segregation.

Key Terms and People

Thurgood Marshall, *p. 291*
Brown v. *Board of Education*, p. 291
Little Rock Nine, *p. 291*
Rosa Parks, *p. 292*
Montgomery bus boycott, *p. 293*
Martin Luther King Jr., *p. 293*
sit-in, *p. 294*
Student Nonviolent
    Coordinating Committee, *p. 294*

TAKING NOTES As you read, take notes on key events in the fight against segregation in a web diagram like the one below. In each outer circle of the web, describe one event. You may need to add more circles.

Challenges to Segregation

If YOU were there...

You are an African American student in the 1950s. You get up early every day and take a long bus ride across the city to an African American public school. There is another school just three blocks from your home, but only white students are welcome there. You have heard, however, that this school will soon be opening its doors to black students as well.

Would you want to be one of the first African Americans to attend this school? Why or why not?

BUILDING BACKGROUND African Americans continued to face segregation and discrimination after World War II. Early victories in the civil rights movement included the end of segregation in baseball in 1947 and President Truman's ban on segregation in the military in 1948. These successes were the beginning of a national movement for civil rights.

Battling School Segregation

The 1896 Supreme Court case *Plessy* v. *Ferguson* established the "separate-but-equal" doctrine. This doctrine stated that federal, state, and local governments could allow segregation as long as separate facilities were equal. One result of this ruling was that states in both the North and South maintained separate schools for white and black students. Government officials often insisted that though these schools were separate, they were equal in quality.

In fact, however, schools for black children typically received far less funding. Early civil rights leaders, led by members of the National Association for the Advancement of Colored People (NAACP), focused on ending segregation in America's public schools.

Brown v. Board of Education

The NAACP's strategy was to show that separate schools were unequal. The NAACP attorneys **Thurgood Marshall**, who went on to become Supreme Court Justice, and Jack Greenberg led the courtroom battles against segregation. In the early 1950s, five school segregation cases from Delaware, Kansas, South Carolina, Virginia, and Washington, D.C., came together under the title of *Brown v. Board of Education*. The "Brown" in the case title was a seven-year-old African American girl from Topeka, Kansas, named Linda Brown. Though she lived near a school for white children, Linda Brown had to travel across town to a school for black children. Linda's father and the NAACP sued to allow Linda to attend the school closer to her home.

On May 17, 1954, the Supreme Court issued a unanimous ruling on *Brown* v. *Board of Education*. The Court ruled that segregation in public schools was illegal.

The next year, the Court ordered public schools to desegregate, or integrate, "with all deliberate speed." These rulings would prove difficult to enforce.

Little Rock Nine

In the entire South, only three school districts began desegregating in 1954. Most others **implemented** gradual integration plans. In Little Rock, Arkansas, the school board started by integrating one high school. It allowed nine outstanding black students to attend Central High School. These students became known as the **Little Rock Nine**. Arkansas governor Orval Faubus was determined to prevent desegregation at Central High School, however. He used National Guard troops to block the Little Rock Nine from entering the school.

On the morning of September 4, 1957, eight of the nine students arrived at the school together and were turned away by the National Guard. Then the ninth student, 15-year-old Elizabeth Eckford, arrived at the school by herself. She found the entrance blocked by the National Guard. Turning around, she faced a screaming mob. Someone began yelling, *"Lynch her! Lynch her!"* Finally, a white man and woman guided Eckford to safety.

Elizabeth Eckford and the rest of the Little

ACADEMIC VOCABULARY

implement
put in place

FOCUS ON READING

What is a synonym for *desegregrate*?

THE IMPACT TODAY

In 1967 Thurgood Marshall became the first African American Supreme Court justice. Clarence Thomas became the second African American justice in 1991.

SUPREME COURT DECISIONS

Brown v. Board of Education (1954)

Background of the Case In 1896 the Supreme Court had ruled in *Plessy* v. *Ferguson* that "separate-but-equal" facilities were constitutional. In 1951 the NAACP sued the Board of Education of Topeka, Kansas. It argued that segregated schools did not give equal opportunities to black and white children. After hearing many arguments, the Court made its ruling in 1954.

The Court's Ruling
The Supreme Court overturned the *Plessy* doctrine of "separate-but-equal." It ruled that racially segregated schools were not equal and were therefore unconstitutional. All of the justices agreed to the ruling, making it unanimous.

The Court's Reasoning
The Supreme Court decided that segregation violated the Fourteenth Amendment's guarantee of "equal protection of the laws." Its opinion stated, "We conclude that, in the field of public education, the doctrine of 'separate-but-equal' has no place. Separate educational facilities are inherently [naturally] unequal."

Why It Matters
The ruling in *Brown* v. *Board of Education* led to integrated public schools. It also opened the door to other successful challenges to segregation in public places.

Linda Brown, age 9

ANALYSIS SKILL **ANALYZING INFORMATION**

1. How did the ruling in *Brown* v. *Board of Education* overturn the 1896 Supreme Court ruling in *Plessy* v. *Ferguson*?
2. How might parents of both black and white children at the time have reacted to the ruling in *Brown* v. *Board of Education*?

An Apology

The famous photograph to the right shows Elizabeth Eckford walking to Little Rock's Central High School on September 4, 1957. The young woman shouting at Eckford is Hazel Massery. Massery was later sorry for what she had done. She decided that she did not want to be, she said, the "poster child of the hate generation, trapped in the image captured in the photograph." In 1963 Massery apologized to Eckford. The two women, shown below, have since become friends and have spoken publicly together about their experiences.

FOCUS ON NEW YORK CITY

Like Rosa Parks, the baseball player Jackie Robinson was an important figure in African American history. He became the first black player in Major League Baseball in the modern era when he joined the Brooklyn Dodgers in 1947. He was inducted into the National Baseball Hall of Fame in 1968.

Rock Nine went home. For weeks, Governor Faubus refused to allow them to attend the school. The tense situation lasted until President Eisenhower sent federal troops to escort the students into the school.

The Little Rock Nine began attending classes, but resistance to integration continued. Some white students insulted, harassed, and attacked the black students. In spite of these obstacles, eight of the nine remained at the school. In May 1958 Ernest Green became the first African American student to graduate from Central High. When Green's name was called at the graduation ceremony, no one clapped. "But I figured they didn't have to," he later said. "After I got that diploma, that was it. I had accomplished what I had come there for."

READING CHECK Summarizing What obstacles faced supporters of desegregation?

Montgomery Bus Boycott

The victory in *Brown* v. *Board of Education* was part of a larger struggle against segregation. Most facilities in the South, including public transportation, remained segregated.

The NAACP decided to continue the battle against segregation in Montgomery, Alabama. Black passengers there were required to sit in the back of city buses. If the whites-only front section filled up, black passengers had to give up their seats.

On December 1, 1955, a seamstress and NAACP worker named **Rosa Parks** boarded a bus and sat in the front row of the section reserved for black passengers. When the bus became full, the driver told Parks and three others to give their seats to white passengers. Parks refused. The bus driver called the police, and Parks was taken to jail.

ANALYSIS
SKILL **FINDING THE MAIN IDEA**

Why did Hazel Massery apologize to Elizabeth Eckford?

To protest Parks's arrest, African American professor Jo Ann Robinson organized a boycott of Montgomery buses. Local leaders formed the Montgomery Improvement Association (MIA) to help strengthen the boycott. In the **Montgomery bus boycott**, thousands of African Americans stopped riding the buses. Some white residents supported the boycott as well. Bus ridership fell by 70 percent.

To lead the MIA, African American leaders turned to **Martin Luther King Jr.**, a young Baptist minister. The 26-year-old King already had a reputation as a powerful speaker whose words could motivate and inspire listeners.

As the boycott continued, bus drivers guided nearly empty buses down the city streets. Leaders planned a carpool system that helped people find rides at more than 40 locations throughout Montgomery. For 381 days, boycotters carpooled, took taxis, rode bicycles, and walked. Still, Montgomery's leaders refused to integrate the bus system.

As in Little Rock during the school segregation fight, many white residents were angry about the attempt to end segregation. Some people resorted to violence. King's home was bombed, and he received hate mail and phone calls threatening him and his family. The police also harassed and arrested carpool drivers. In spite of this intimidation, the boycott gained national attention, sparking similar protests in other cities.

Finally, in November 1956 the Supreme Court ruled that segregation on public transportation was illegal. The next month, King joined other black and white ministers to ride the first integrated bus in Montgomery. "It . . . makes you feel that America is a great country and we're going to do more to make it greater," remembered Jo Ann Robinson.

The Montgomery bus boycott helped make Martin Luther King Jr. a nationally known civil rights leader. He formed the Southern Christian Leadership Conference (SCLC), which led campaigns for civil rights throughout the South.

READING CHECK **Identifying Cause and Effect**
What event sparked the Montgomery bus boycott?

THE IMPACT TODAY

When Rosa Parks died in 2005, she became the first woman to lie in honor at the capitol building rotunda.

CASE STUDY **BIOGRAPHY**

Rosa Parks
1913–2005

Rosa Parks was born in Tuskegee, Alabama, and spent most of her childhood in Montgomery. While working as a seamstress, Parks became an active member of the NAACP.

She was fired from her seamstress job for her leading role in the Montgomery bus boycott. After the boycott succeeded, she and her husband moved to Detroit, Michigan. She continued working for fair treatment for all Americans and started a program to teach children about the Underground Railroad and the civil rights movement.

Finding the Main Idea How did Rosa Parks work for equal rights?

Sit-ins and the SNCC

Like public schools and buses, many private businesses in the South were segregated. In Greensboro, North Carolina, four students decided to challenge this form of segregation. They targeted a lunch counter at Woolworth, a popular department store. Black customers were supposed to eat standing up at one end of the counter. White customers sat down to eat at the other end.

On February 1, 1960, the students went into Woolworth and staged a **sit-in**—a demonstration in which protesters sit down and refuse to leave. They sat in the whites-only section of the lunch counter and ordered coffee. They were not served, but they stayed until the store closed. The next day, they returned with dozens more students to continue the sit-in. Soon, another sit-in began at the lunch counter of a nearby store.

People across the country read newspaper stories about the Greensboro sit-ins. Other black students in the South began to hold similar protests. The student protesters practiced the strategy of nonviolent resistance.

No matter how much they were insulted or threatened, they refused to respond with violence. They were inspired by Martin Luther King Jr., who was a strong supporter of nonviolent action.

Over time, some restaurants and businesses, including Woolworth, began the process of integration. To continue the struggle for civil rights, the leaders of the student protests formed the **Student Nonviolent Coordinating Committee** (SNCC) in the spring of 1960. The SNCC activists trained protesters and organized civil rights demonstrations. Bob Moses, a leader of the SNCC, helped organize sit-ins and voter registration drives.

READING CHECK **Comparing** How were sit-ins similar to other civil rights protests?

SUMMARY AND PREVIEW In the 1950s court rulings and protests challenged segregation. In the next section you will learn how the civil rights movement continued the fight against inequality.

THE IMPACT TODAY

Today Bob Moses runs the Algebra Project. Its goals include helping students in poor communities become skilled in math, get into college, and compete for jobs.

---

go.hrw.com
Online Quiz

Section 1 Assessment

Reviewing Ideas, Terms, and People

1. **a. Summarize** How did the Supreme Court impact the desegregation of public schools?
   b. Identify Who were the **Little Rock Nine**?
2. **a. Recall** What was the purpose of the **Montgomery bus boycott**?
   b. Analyze Why was the arrest of **Rosa Parks** a turning point in the civil rights movement?
   c. Elaborate Why do you think the bus boycott lasted so long?
3. **a. Identify** What means did the **Student Nonviolent Coordinating Committee** use to protest segregation?
   b. Make Inferences What might have inspired the Greensboro students to stage a **sit-in**?
   c. Evaluate Do you think nonviolent resistance is an effective form of protest? Why or why not?

Critical Thinking

4. **Sequencing** Review your notes on events that challenged segregation. Then copy the graphic organizer below and use it to show the sequence of major events in the civil rights movement described in this section.

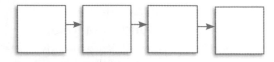

FOCUS ON WRITING

5. **Explaining Major Issues** Take notes on the major issues behind the civil rights movement. What were these issues? Why were they important to African Americans? What changes did the movement try to make?

Martin Luther King Jr.

How would you help lead a national movement?

When did he live? 1929–1968

Where did he live? King grew up in Atlanta, Georgia, where his father was a pastor. He studied to become a minister in Pennsylvania. He received his doctorate in Massachusetts, then became pastor of a church in Alabama. He traveled throughout the country as a civil rights leader.

What did he do? As a powerful and moving speaker, King became one of the leading voices of the civil rights movement. He was committed to achieving equality through nonviolent protest. He led a series of successful marches and protests, including the 1955 Montgomery bus boycott and the 1963 March on Washington.

Why is he so important? His leadership helped make the civil rights movement a success. His belief in and passion for nonviolence led to the boycotts, sit-ins, and marches that helped African Americans gain equal treatment. King's work helped bring an end to legal segregation and led to new laws guaranteeing equal rights for all Americans.

Evaluating Which of Martin Luther King Jr.'s contributions to the civil rights movement was most important? Why?

KEY EVENTS

- **1953** Marries Coretta Scott
- **1955** Becomes leader of the Montgomery Improvement Association
- **1957** Forms the Southern Christian Leadership Conference
- **1963** Writes "Letter from Birmingham Jail"; gives the "I Have a Dream" speech at the March on Washington
- **1964** Wins the Nobel Peace Prize; Civil Rights Act of 1964 is passed
- **1968** Shot and killed in Memphis, Tennessee
- **1986** Martin Luther King Jr. Day becomes a national holiday.

" I have a dream that my four children will one day live in a nation where they will not be judged by the color of their skin but by the content of their character. "

—Martin Luther King Jr., speech at March on Washington

Kennedy, Johnson, and Civil Rights

What You Will Learn...

Main Ideas

1. John F. Kennedy was elected president in 1960.
2. Civil rights leaders continued to fight for equality.
3. Lyndon B. Johnson became president when Kennedy was assassinated.
4. Changes occurred in the civil rights movement in the late 1960s.

The Big Idea

The civil rights movement made major advances during the presidencies of John F. Kennedy and Lyndon B. Johnson.

Key Terms and People

John F. Kennedy, *p. 296*
Freedom Rides, *p. 297*
March on Washington, *p. 298*
Lyndon B. Johnson, *p. 299*
Civil Rights Act of 1964, *p. 299*
Voting Rights Act of 1965, *p. 299*
Great Society, *p. 300*
Black Power, *p. 300*
Malcolm X, *p. 300*

TAKING NOTES As you read, take notes on the names of leaders who supported civil rights. Use a chart like this one for your notes on these leaders and their goals.

Leaders	Goals

If YOU were there...

You are a civil rights activist living and working in the South. It is 1960, a presidential election year. The battle for fair treatment has been difficult, and you hope that the next president will support civil rights. Both major presidential candidates will be visiting your area soon, and you might have a chance to meet them and ask some questions.

What questions would you ask the candidates?

BUILDING BACKGROUND In the 1960 presidential election Republican Richard M. Nixon, who had served as Eisenhower's vice president, ran against Democrat John F. Kennedy, a senator from Massachusetts. For the first time, presidential candidates debated each other on television. Kennedy's performance in the televised debates helped him win a very close election.

Kennedy Elected

When **John F. Kennedy** won the election of 1960, he became the youngest person ever elected president of the United States. For many Americans, Kennedy and his wife, Jacqueline, brought a sense of style and excitement to the White House. Kennedy was also the first Roman Catholic to become president.

In his inaugural address, Kennedy spoke of the opportunities and dangers facing Americans. "Man holds in his mortal hands the power to abolish all forms of human poverty and all forms of human life," he said. He encouraged all Americans to support freedom throughout the world, saying, "And so, my fellow Americans, ask not what your country can do for you—ask what you can do for your country."

As president, Kennedy pursued a set of proposals he called the New Frontier. His plan included a higher minimum wage and tax cuts to help stimulate economic growth. It called for new spending on the military and on the space program, and new programs to help

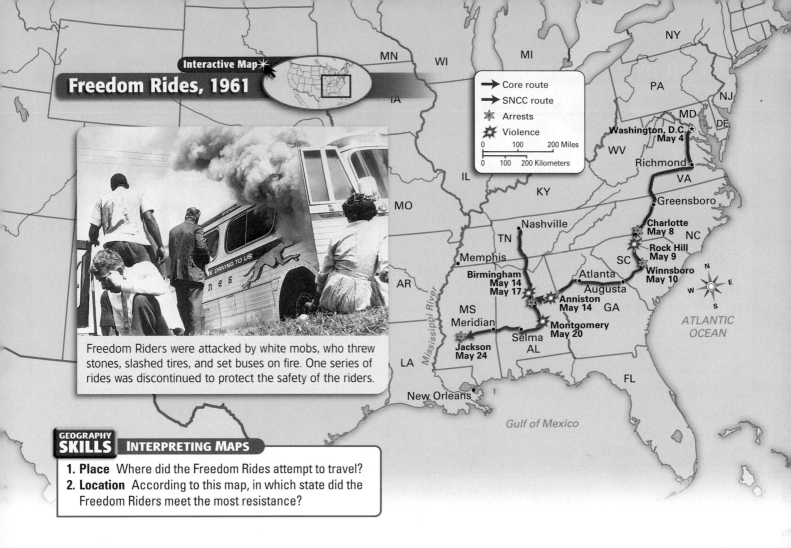

Interactive Map

Freedom Rides, 1961

Core route
SNCC route
✳ Arrests
✴ Violence

0   100   200 Miles
0 100 200 Kilometers

Washington, D.C.
May 4

Richmond

Greensboro

Charlotte
May 8

Rock Hill
May 9

Winnsboro
May 10

Nashville

Memphis

Atlanta

Augusta

Birmingham
May 14
May 17

Anniston
May 14

Meridian

Montgomery
May 20

Selma

Jackson
May 24

New Orleans

Gulf of Mexico

ATLANTIC OCEAN

Freedom Riders were attacked by white mobs, who threw stones, slashed tires, and set buses on fire. One series of rides was discontinued to protect the safety of the riders.

GEOGRAPHY SKILLS **INTERPRETING MAPS**

1. **Place** Where did the Freedom Rides attempt to travel?
2. **Location** According to this map, in which state did the Freedom Riders meet the most resistance?

---

poor and unemployed Americans. Kennedy also proposed providing greater financial help to public schools. Fearing a budget imbalance, Republicans and conservative southern Democrats blocked much of the legislation Kennedy introduced.

Kennedy also spoke of his support for the goals of the civil rights movement. This had helped convince many African Americans to vote for him in the election of 1960. As president, however, Kennedy moved slowly on civil rights legislation. He was reluctant to anger Republicans and conservative southern Democrats in Congress, whose support he needed to pass other items on his agenda. Kennedy was also busy dealing with foreign policy crises, as you will read in the next chapter.

READING CHECK **Drawing Inferences** What do you think African American voters hoped for from the new president?

The Fight for Rights Continues

Public schools and some businesses had begun to desegregate. But other facilities remained strictly segregated.

Freedom Rides

In 1947 a civil rights group called the Congress for Racial Equality (CORE) began protests in which African Americans rode in the whites-only section of interstate buses. In 1960 the Court ruled that segregation of bus stations was illegal. CORE decided to put pressure on President Kennedy to enforce this ruling.

To accomplish this, CORE organized a series of protests called the **Freedom Rides,** in which black and white bus riders traveled together to segregated bus stations in the South. White riders planned to use facilities set aside for African Americans in bus stations. Black riders would use whites-only facilities.

FOCUS ON NEW YORK CITY

While the majority of violent confrontations in the civil rights movement occurred in the South, African Americans struggled in the North as well. New York City's Harlem neighborhood, an important center of the movement, was home to leaders such as Marcus Garvey, A. Philip Randolph, Adam Clayton Powell Jr., and Malcolm X. Organizations such as the NAACP and the National Urban League were first located there.

THE CIVIL RIGHTS MOVEMENT **297**

John F. Kennedy
1917–1963

John F. Kennedy was born to a politically powerful and wealthy family in Massachusetts. He graduated from Harvard University, then joined the U.S. Navy. He commanded a patrol boat in the South Pacific during World War II and was wounded in a sea battle. Kennedy was elected to the House of Representatives at the age of 29 and to the Senate six years later. He was elected president in 1960, bringing a youthful energy to the White House. He had served for fewer than three years when he was assassinated.

Lyndon B. Johnson
1908–1973

Lyndon B. Johnson grew up in rural Texas. After working his way through college, Johnson taught school for a year. In 1937, at the age of 29, he was elected to the House of Representatives. He was elected to the Senate in 1948. Johnson was known for his ability to guide bills through Congress by convincing members from both political parties to support them. As one fellow member of Congress said, "Lyndon got me by the lapels [jacket collar] and put his face on top of mine and he talked and talked." Johnson was elected vice president in 1960 and became president in 1963.

Contrasting How were Kennedy's and Johnson's careers similar, and how were they different?

The Freedom Rides began in May 1961, when 13 riders boarded a bus travel-ing from Washington, D.C., to New Orleans, Louisiana. In one Alabama town, the riders were viciously attacked by a white mob. After more attacks, CORE leaders decided to stop the protest to protect the riders' lives.

The leaders of the SNCC decided to contin-ue the Freedom Rides. The SNCC activists faced the same violence as the CORE riders. Arriving in Montgomery, Alabama, in late May, they were attacked by a furious mob. Many free-dom riders were jailed in Jackson, Mississippi. That same month, President Kennedy ordered the Interstate Commerce Commission to en-force strict bans on segregation in interstate bus terminals.

King in Birmingham

In 1963 Martin Luther King Jr. organized marches in Birmingham, Alabama. King was arrested and jailed for marching without a permit. While jailed, he wrote a "Letter from Birmingham Jail," explaining his commitment to nonviolence. "We will reach the goal of freedom in Birmingham and all over the nation, because the goal of America is freedom."

King was released from prison and led a new round of marches. In May 1963, some 2,500 demonstrators marched through downtown Birmingham. Police commissioner Eugene "Bull" Connor ordered his officers to unleash their attack dogs and blast the marchers with high-pressure water hoses. Televised images of their tactics shocked Americans.

The March on Washington

Pressure for civil rights legislation continued to grow. President Kennedy called racial discrimina-tion "a moral crisis." In June 1963 he announced support for a sweeping civil rights bill to end racial discrimination completely.

To demonstrate support for the civil rights bill, African American leaders held the **March on Washington**—a massive demonstration for civil rights. On August 28, 1963, Martin Luther King Jr. stood at the Lincoln Memorial before a diverse crowd of more than 200,000 people. In his famous "I Have a Dream" speech, King expressed his hope for a future in which all Americans would enjoy equal rights and opportunities.

READING CHECK **Summarizing** How did the Birmingham marches affect public opinion?

Johnson and Civil Rights

After he became president, Lyndon Johnson promised to continue Kennedy's plans for civil rights legislation. Johnson worked with Congress and African American leaders to create and pass laws that would help ensure equality for all Americans. Here, Johnson is shown signing the Civil Rights Act of 1964 as Martin Luther King Jr. and other leaders look on.

How did Johnson work to continue Kennedy's campaign promises?

Johnson Becomes President

In the months following the March on Washington, Congress debated Kennedy's civil rights legislation. In November 1963 Kennedy began a quick tour of Texas cities.

Kennedy Assassinated

On November 22, 1963, Kennedy rode through Dallas in a convertible, waving to supporters in the streets. Suddenly, gunshots rang out. Kennedy had been shot twice, and he died soon afterward in a Dallas hospital. Vice President **Lyndon B. Johnson** was quickly sworn in as president. Dallas police arrested an alleged assassin, Lee Harvey Oswald.

The assassination stunned Americans, who grieved the young president's death. Many of Kennedy's goals, including passing a major civil rights law, were left unfinished. Vowing to continue Kennedy's work, President Johnson urged Congress to pass a civil rights bill.

Civil Rights Laws

On July 2, 1964, President Johnson signed the **Civil Rights Act of 1964**. The act banned segregation in public places. It also outlawed discrimination in the workplace on the basis of color, gender, religion, or national origin.

That summer, activists began to push for equal voting rights for African Americans in the South. Legally, of course, African Americans had the right to vote. But in much of the South, threats and unfair election rules often kept them from the polls. During the "Freedom Summer" of 1964, hundreds of volunteers, including many white college students, came to Mississippi. Their goal was to help African Americans register to vote.

Volunteers were threatened and attacked. On June 21 three civil rights workers— James Chaney, a young black Mississippian plasterer's apprentice; Andrew Goodman, a Jewish Queen's College student; and Michael Schwerner, a Jewish social worker from New York City—were murdered by members of the Ku Klux Klan. Martin Luther King Jr. organized a voting rights march from Selma, Alabama, to Montgomery, during which many marchers were beaten and jailed. Violence against civil rights workers convinced many people to support voter registration efforts.

Congress approved the **Voting Rights Act of 1965**, which Johnson signed into law in August. This law gave the federal government new powers to protect African Americans' voting rights. Within three years, more than half of all qualified African Americans in the South registered to vote.

THE IMPACT TODAY

In June 2005 a judge in Mississippi sentenced Edgar Ray Killen to 60 years in prison for his role in the murder of the three civil rights workers. The 1967 case had ended in a deadlocked jury.

The Great Society

- Civil Rights Act of 1964
- Voting Rights Act of 1965
- Elementary and Secondary Education Act of 1965
- Medicare and Medicaid Bill, 1965
- Department of Housing and Urban Development Act of 1965

The Great Society

President Johnson won the election of 1964 by a huge margin. He saw this as a vote of approval for his program of domestic reforms that he called the **Great Society**. "The Great Society rests on abundance and liberty for all," Johnson said.

Congress quickly passed most of Johnson's Great Society legislation. Great Society programs included Medicare and Medicaid, which help senior citizens and low-income citizens afford health care. Another act gave local schools more than $1 billion to help students with special needs. The Department of Housing and Urban Development (HUD) was created to help low-income families get better housing. Robert Weaver served as HUD's secretary, becoming the first African American appointed to a presidential cabinet.

READING CHECK **Summarizing** How did President Johnson support civil rights?

Changes in the Civil Rights Movement

Many young civil rights reformers found the pace of change too slow. Others entirely rejected the goal of racial integration.

New Directions

One such activist was Stokely Carmichael, who had participated in the Freedom Rides and many marches. But in the mid-1960s, he broke with the goal of nonviolence. Carmichael was a founder of the **Black Power** movement, which called for African American independence. Black Power activists believed that blacks should reject integration, focusing instead on controlling their own communities.

Malcolm X helped inspire the Black Power movement. He was a leader of the Nation of Islam, an organization that combined ideas about African American independence with the teachings of Islam. Malcolm X argued that African Americans should work for social and political independence. He believed that African Americans had the right to defend themselves, using violence if necessary.

Time Line

Civil Rights Movement, Key Events

1955 An African American tailor's assistant named Rosa Parks refused to give up her seat on a Montgomery, Alabama, bus, sparking a citywide bus boycott that would last more than a year.

1950

1960 The first sit-in at a lunch counter occurs in Greensboro, North Carolina. During these sit-ins, young African Americans sat at segregated lunch counters along with their white counterparts and asked to be served.

In 1964 Malcolm X traveled to the Muslim holy city of Mecca, where he met Muslims of many races. He began to hope that different races could coexist in peace, although he still supported freedom "by any means necessary." But in 1965 Malcolm X broke with the Nation of Islam and was killed by three of its members.

Violence in the Streets

Slow progress in the civil rights movement frustrated many members of the black community. In some U.S. cities, tensions exploded into violent, sometimes deadly, riots. One such riot occurred in August 1965 in the Watts section of Los Angeles. Twenty-four people were killed, and much of Watts was destroyed.

In April 1968 Martin Luther King Jr. was shot and killed in Memphis, Tennessee. As televised reports spread the news of King's assassination, furious rioters took to the streets in more than 100 American cities. The movement had lost its most visible leader.

1963 Four young girls die in the racially motivated bombing of a Birmingham, Alabama, church. The deaths lead to riots and civil unrest during which police attack African Americans. Televised images of the events shocked many people.

1965

1964 Civil rights leader Martin Luther King Jr. receives the Nobel Peace Prize for his work in nonviolent demonstrations against segregation.

READING CHECK Contrasting How did Malcolm X's goals differ from Martin Luther King Jr.'s?

SUMMARY AND PREVIEW Under Kennedy and Johnson, major civil rights legislation was passed. In the next section, you will learn how more groups began to push for equal rights.

go.hrw.com
Online Quiz

Section 2 Assessment

Reviewing Ideas, Terms, and People

1. a. Describe How was **John F. Kennedy** different from previous presidents?
b. Analyze Why did many African Americans vote for Kennedy?

2. a. Identify What were the **Freedom Rides**?
b. Explain How did television influence public opinion about the civil rights movement?

3. a. Recall What happened in Dallas, Texas, on November 22, 1963?
b. Draw Conclusions Based on Johnson's plans for the **Great Society**, what do you think he believed was the purpose of government?

4. a. Recall What challenges did the civil rights movement face in the late 1960s?
b. Elaborate Why did **Malcolm X** reject the goal of racial integration?

Critical Thinking

5. Evaluating Review your notes on the goals and achievements of leaders who supported civil rights. Then copy the graphic organizer below and use it to evaluate the leaders discussed in the section. Tell whether or not you think the leaders' actions were effective.

Leader	Evaluation

FOCUS ON WRITING

6. Listing Laws List new civil rights laws passed in the 1960s. What were the goals of these laws? What problems or events did they respond to? As a member of Congress, would you have approved of these laws? Why or why not?

Rights for Other Americans

What You Will Learn...

Main Ideas

1. Hispanic Americans organized for civil rights and economic opportunities.
2. The women's movement worked for equal rights.
3. Other Americans also fought for change.

The Big Idea

Encouraged by the success of the civil rights movement, many groups worked for equal rights in the 1960s.

Key Terms and People

Cesar Chavez, *p. 302*
United Farm Workers, *p. 302*
Betty Friedan, *p. 303*
National Organization for Women, *p. 303*
Shirley Chisholm, *p. 303*
Equal Rights Amendment, *p. 303*
Phyllis Schlafly, *p. 303*
American Indian Movement, *p. 305*
Disabled in Action, *p. 305*

TAKING NOTES As you read, make a list of major events that occurred as various groups worked for equal rights. You may want to organize your list in a table like this one.

Social Movements in the 1960s

If YOU were there...

Your parents came to the United States from Mexico, and you were born in California in the 1950s. You and your family work year-round picking crops—the work is hard, and the pay is low. You're trying to put aside some money for school, but your family barely makes enough to get by. Some farmworkers are talking about going on strike for better wages.

Would you join the strike? Why or why not?

BUILDING BACKGROUND Many Americans faced unfair treatment in the 1960s. Women were paid lower wages and had fewer job opportunities than men. Hispanic Americans had long faced discrimination as well. The victories of the civil rights movement inspired many groups to struggle for equal rights.

Hispanic Americans Organize for Change

The Hispanic population of the United States grew to 4 million by 1960, and to more than 10 million by 1970. Though people of Mexican descent made up the majority of this population, Hispanic Americans were a diverse group. Many people from Puerto Rico, Cuba, and other Latin American countries also lived in the United States.

The success of African Americans encouraged Hispanic Americans to fight for their own rights. **Cesar Chavez** was one of many Hispanic Americans who worked to improve conditions. In 1962 Chavez formed a union that would later become the **United Farm Workers** (UFW). This union was committed to the goal of better pay and working conditions for migrant farmworkers—those who move seasonally from farm to farm for work. Chavez led the UFW in a five-year strike and boycott against California grape growers. The workers finally won better wages and benefits in 1970.

Chavez shared the commitment to nonviolent protest. To those who complained about the slow pace of change, he replied:

" Nonviolence takes time … I despise exploitation [unfair gain] and I want change, but I'm willing to pay the price in terms of time. There's a Mexican saying, 'Hay más tiempo que vida'—there's more time than life. We've got all the time in the world. "

—Cesar Chavez, quoted in *Chávez, César: Autobiography of La Causa*

Chavez helped inspire young leaders in what became known as the Chicano movement. To fight discrimination and gain greater political influence, Chicano activists formed a political party called *La Raza Unida*, or the United Race. The Hispanic civil rights movement had important **consequences**. A 1968 amendment to the Elementary and Secondary Education Act required schools to teach students whose first language was not English in both languages until they learned English. The Voting Rights Act of 1975 required communities with large immigrant populations to print ballots in the voters' preferred language.

READING CHECK Sequencing What group helped inspire the Chicano movement?

The Women's Movement

Activists also brought public attention to women's position in society. In 1963 a government commission reported that women had fewer job opportunities than men and were often paid less for the same work. President Kennedy responded by ordering an end to discrimination based on gender in civil service jobs. That same year Congress passed the Equal Pay Act, which required many employers to pay men and women equal salaries for the same work. The Civil Rights Act of 1964 banned discrimination based on both gender and race.

Some women also began to question their traditional roles in society. In her 1963 book *The Feminine Mystique*, **Betty Friedan** described the dissatisfaction some women felt with their traditional roles of wife, mother, and homemaker.

CASE STUDY **BIOGRAPHY**

Cesar Chavez
1927–1993

Cesar Chavez was born on a small family ranch in Arizona. After losing their land during the Great Depression, Chavez and his family began working as migrant farmworkers. Moving from town to town in search of work, Chavez went to more than 30 different schools. He served in the U.S. Navy during World War II, then returned to the fields to help migrant workers fight for better pay and working conditions. The soft-spoken Chavez seemed to many an unlikely leader of a protest movement. But Chavez quickly became an influential leader, continuing to lead the struggle for farmworkers' rights into the 1990s. Before his death, Chavez insisted, "It's not me who counts, it's the Movement."

Making Inferences Why do you think Chavez began the farmworkers' movement?

Friedan became a leader of the modern women's rights movement. In 1966 she helped found the **National Organization for Women** (NOW) to fight for equal educational and career opportunities for women. Other women worked for change by running for public office. In 1968 **Shirley Chisholm** was elected to represent a New York City district in the House of Representatives. She was the first African American woman elected to the U.S. Congress.

In the early 1970s, NOW and other women's rights activists supported an amendment to the Constitution. The **Equal Rights Amendment** (ERA) would outlaw all discrimination based on sex. The ERA was approved by Congress in 1972.

For an amendment to go into effect, it must be ratified by three-fourths of the states—or 38 out of 50 states. The ERA was ratified by 30 state legislatures by the end of 1973. But many opponents came forward to block the ERA. **Phyllis Schlafly**, a conservative activist, founded the group STOP ERA to prevent its ratification. Schlafly and her supporters argued that the ERA would hurt

ACADEMIC VOCABULARY

consequences the effects of a particular event or events

THE IMPACT TODAY

Ninety women served in the 110th Congress, the highest total in history. In 2007, Nancy Pelosi was elected the first female Speaker of the House.

In the 1960s, women began to organize to demand equal rights. The movement became known as women's liberation. Many activists supported a woman's right to equal pay and equal protection under the law. Some opposing activists worked to maintain what they saw as women's protected status under the law.

Shirley Chisholm became the first African American woman elected to Congress in 1968.

Betty Friedan authored *The Feminine Mystique*, a book declaring that many women wanted achievements beyond those of becoming a wife and mother.

Phyllis Schlafly argued against the Equal Rights Amendment, saying it would reduce the legal rights of wives and mothers.

families by encouraging women to focus on careers rather than on motherhood. Such opposition weakened support for the ERA. In June 1982 the amendment fell three states short of ratification.

Despite this failure, the women's movement achieved many of its goals. Women found new opportunities in education and the workplace. For example, women began attending many formerly all-male universities. Increasing numbers of women pursued careers in traditionally all-male fields such as law and medicine. Many women also won political office at all levels of government.

READING CHECK **Finding Main Ideas**
What were some achievements of the women's movement of the 1960s?

Other Voices for Change

Other Americans also began to demand change in laws and other discriminating practices during the 1960s and 1970s. In 1974 the Asian American Legal Defense and Education Fund was founded with the purpose of building an "informed and active Asian America." The National Italian American Foundation (1975) advocates for Italian Americans. League of United Latin American Citizens, which was founded much earlier, played an important activist role for Hispanic Americans during this period as well and continues to do so today. Native Americans and people with disabilities were among those who were inspired by the civil rights movement.

Native Americans

One major issue for Native Americans was their lack of control over tribal lands. Many worked through the National Congress of American Indians (NCAI) to gain more control over reservation lands from the federal government. They helped win passage of the Indian Civil Rights Act of 1968.

Other activists thought that groups like the NCAI worked too slowly. In November 1969 a group of young Native Americans occupied Alcatraz Island in San Francisco

Bay to protest the government's takeover of Native American lands.

One of the groups that participated in the Alcatraz protest was the **American Indian Movement** (AIM), founded in 1968 to fight for Native Americans' rights. In February 1973 AIM activists seized a trading post and church at Wounded Knee, South Dakota—the site of the U.S. Army's massacre of Sioux Indians in 1890. Federal marshals surrounded Wounded Knee, and the standoff ended with a gun battle killing two protesters and wounding one federal agent.

Such protests brought attention to issues facing Native Americans. In the early 1970s Congress began passing laws granting Native Americans greater self-government on tribal lands.

The Disability Rights Movement

In 1970 Judy Heumann and other activists created **Disabled in Action** (DIA) to make people aware of challenges facing people with disabilities. People with disabilities often lacked access to both job opportunities and to public places. The DIA's work led to the passage of new laws. The Rehabilitation

Disabled in Action

Judy Heumann and other activists formed Disabled in Action in 1970. The group promotes legislation and access to independent living for people with disabilities.

What kind of rights might people with disabilities seek?

Act of 1973 banned federal agencies from discriminating against people with disabilities. The Education of Handicapped Children Act of 1975 required public schools to provide a quality education to children with disabilities. In 1990 the Americans with Disabilities Act (ADA) outlawed all discrimination against people with disabilities.

READING CHECK **Contrasting** How were the tactics of AIM and DIA different?

SUMMARY AND PREVIEW The fight for equal rights had far-reaching effects on American society. In the next chapter you will learn about world conflicts that also affected Americans.

go.hrw.com
Online Quiz

Section 3 Assessment

Reviewing Ideas, Terms, and People

1. **a. Evaluate** How did Hispanic Americans fight for civil rights?
   b. Describe Who benefited from laws like the Elementary and Secondary Education Act of 1968 and the Voting Rights Act of 1975?
2. **a. Recall** What were the goals of the women's movement?
   b. Explain What happened during the ratification process of the **Equal Rights Amendment**?
   c. Elaborate Do you think we need the ERA today? Explain your answer.
3. **a. Compare** In what way was the **American Indian Movement** similar to the Black Power movement?
   b. Identify What laws banned discrimination against people with disabilities?

Critical Thinking

4. **Categorizing** Review your notes on the achievements of groups that worked for equal rights. Then copy the graphic organizer below and use it to identify the achievements of each group.

Hispanic Americans	Women	Native Americans	People with Disabilities

FOCUS ON WRITING

5. **Describing New Movements** Describe new rights movements inspired by the success of the African American civil rights movement. What groups did these movements represent? What were their goals? What did they accomplish?

Social Studies Skills

Making Speeches

Define the Skill

In a democracy, activists, government leaders, and candidates for public office often need to address people directly. Speeches allow public figures to deliver a message to many people at once. People can use speeches to make their views known. They can use speeches to try to persuade people to support their ideas or programs.

Learn the Skill

Think about the role of speeches in the civil rights movement. Speakers increased awareness of and support for the movement's goals. Civil rights leader Martin Luther King Jr. is remembered as a powerful and effective speaker. His words moved and inspired many listeners—and continue to do so today. Here is a brief excerpt from King's famous "I Have a Dream" speech, delivered during the March on Washington on August 28, 1963:

"I have a dream that one day on the red hills of Georgia the sons of former slaves and the sons of former slaveowners will be able to sit down together at the table of brotherhood."

"I have a dream that my four little children will one day live in a nation where they will not be judged by the color of their skin but by the content of their character."

"I have a dream today."

In his speech, King followed one basic idea. He used the same words over and over to emphasize his hopes for racial equality. Every time he said "I have a dream," however, King gave a different example of equality. With these different examples on the same topic, King laid out a powerful vision for the future.

The words of the "I Have a Dream" speech are powerful, but King's delivery made the speech even stronger. King spoke with confidence in a loud, clear voice. He also looked at his audience and connected with them.

Following these steps can help you make a persuasive speech.

1 **Write the speech.** Make sure it includes a clear main idea, good examples, and convincing language.

2 **Practice.** Practice reading your speech out loud to a friend. You can also practice at home in front of a mirror.

3 **Give the speech.** Remember to speak loudly and clearly and to look at your audience.

Practice the Skill

Suppose that you are a civil rights leader in the 1960s. Following the steps above, write a short speech in favor of equal rights for African Americans, Hispanic Americans, women, Native Americans, or Americans with disabilities. After you have written and practiced your speech, give the speech to the class.

Chapter Review

HOLT
History's Impact
▶video series
Review the video to answer the closing question:
How did the Civil Rights Act of 1964 inspire a push for equality among other minority groups?

Visual Summary

QUICK FACTS

Use the visual summary below to help you review the main ideas of the chapter.

Many groups of Americans organized to demand their civil rights during the 1960s and 1970s.

Reviewing Vocabulary, Terms, and People

Identify the descriptions below with the correct term or person from the chapter.

1. African American civil rights leader and minister who believed in nonviolent, direct action

2. Event staged by black students at a Woolworth lunch counter in Greensboro, North Carolina

3. Organized by the Congress of Racial Equality to protest segregation in bus stations throughout the South

4. Act that protected the voting rights of African Americans

5. Organization that worked to get better pay and working conditions for migrant farmworkers

6. First African American woman elected to the U.S. Congress

Comprehension and Critical Thinking

SECTION 1 *(Pages 290–294)*

7. **a. Describe** What was the Court's ruling in the *Brown* v. *Board of Education* case?

b. Explain What did the Student Nonviolent Coordinating Committee do to fight segregation?

c. Draw Conclusions Why do you think Martin Luther King Jr. was chosen to lead the MIA?

SECTION 2 *(Pages 296–301)*

8. **a. Recall** What was the New Frontier?

b. Contrast What roles did leaders from CORE and SNCC play in the Freedom Rides?

c. Contrast How did Malcolm X's ideas about integration differ from those of Martin Luther King Jr.?

9. **a. Identify** What is the National Organization for Women?

   b. Summarize How did Cesar Chavez help migrant farmworkers?

   c. Elaborate How did the Americans with Disabilities Act help disabled Americans?

Reviewing Themes

10. **Politics** How did political changes help minorities achieve their goals?

11. **Society and Culture** How did society change during the civil rights era?

Reading Skills

Using Context Clues: Synonyms *Use the Reading Skills taught in this chapter to answer the question below.*

> The Little Rock Nine began attending classes, but resistance to integration continued. Some white students insulted, harassed, and attacked the black students. In spite of these obstacles, eight of the nine remained at the school. *(p. 292)*

12. Which of the following would be a good synonym for the word *harassed*?

    a. comforted

    b. assisted

    c. helped

    d. insulted

Social Studies Skills

Making Speeches *Use the Social Studies Skills taught in this chapter to answer the question below.*

13. What steps should you follow to make a persuasive speech?

Using the Internet   **go.hrw.com**

14. **Activity: Creating a Newspaper** Even after the ruling in *Brown* v. *Board of Education*, integration was slow to take effect. Many districts began gradual integration plans, as in Little Rock, Arkansas, where local leaders chose the Little Rock Nine to start the process. Enter the activity keyword. Research the Little Rock Nine and then create a two pages of a newspaper. Make sure your newspaper articles include direct references to your research. Include quotations from the historical figures that were involved in the integration of Central High School.

FOCUS ON WRITING

15. **Writing Your Bill** Review your notes. Then start writing your civil rights bill. What is its goal? Explain how it will expand civil rights. Is it designed to help a certain group of people? Discuss the reasons you believe it is important to expand civil rights in this way. You may refer to problems or events the bill responds to as well as to earlier civil rights laws and legal decisions.

Grade 8 Intermediate-Level Test Preparation

Directions (1–5): **For each statement or question, write on the separate answer sheet the *number* of the word or expression that, of those given, best completes the statement or answers the question.**

Base your answer to question 1 on the graph below and on your knowledge of social studies.

Women in the Labor Force

1 **By about how much did the percentage of women in the workforce increase between 1960 and 1980?**

(1) 5 percent   (3) 15 percent

(2) 25 percent   (4) 50 percent

2 **The Supreme Court case that led to the integration of public schools was called**

(1) *Plessy* v. *Ferguson.*

(2) *Brown* v. *Board of Education.*

(3) *Chisholm* v. *Marshall.*

(4) *King* v. *Alabama.*

3 **Leaders of the MIA organized the Montgomery Bus Boycott after**

(1) black students staged a sit-in at a Woolworth lunch counter.

(2) Martin Luther King Jr. founded the Southern Christian Leadership Conference.

(3) Rosa Parks was arrested for sitting in the whites-only section of a public bus.

(4) the Little Rock Nine began attending Central High School.

4 **In the 1960s Cesar Chavez became**

(1) the first Hispanic American to serve in the U.S. Congress.

(2) a nationally recognized Hispanic rights leader.

(3) a member of President Johnson's cabinet.

(4) a leader of the Native American rights movement.

5 **In 1969 a group of activists seized Alcatraz Island to**

(1) demand better wages and conditions for migrant farmworkers.

(2) protest the government's takeover of Native American lands.

(3) demonstrate in favor of the Equal Rights Amendment.

(4) call attention to the needs of Americans with disabilities.

Base your answer to question 6 on the text below and on your knowledge of social studies.

*"*When we allow freedom to ring, when we let it ring from every village and every hamlet [community], from every state and every city, we will be able to speed up that day when all of God's children, black men and white men, Jews and Gentiles [non-Jews], Protestants and Catholics, will be able to join hands and sing in the words of the old Negro spiritual, 'Free at last! Free at last! Thank God Almighty, we are free at last!'*"*

—Martin Luther King Jr.,
speech at the March on Washington

6 **Constructed-Response Question What is the main idea King is expressing in this passage?**

CHAPTER 12 1960–1975

The Vietnam War Years

FOCUS QUESTION

How has America reacted to the challenges of the modern world?

FOCUS ON WRITING

Newscast Writing in the 1960s, Michael Arlen called the Vietnam War the first American "living room war." For the first time, Americans could sit in their homes and watch scenes from the war on TV newscasts. In this chapter, you will read about American involvement in Cold War conflicts, such as the Cuban missile crisis and the Vietnam War. Then you will present a newscast on major events of the Cold War.

UNITED STATES

1961 Kennedy sends military advisers to Vietnam.

1960

WORLD

1960 Cuba and the Soviet Union sign a trade agreement and establish diplomatic relations.

What You Will Learn...

Tensions between the United States and the Soviet Union continued to cause conflicts in the 1960s. In this chapter you will read about the major Cold War crises of the 1960s. You will also learn how the commitment to stop the spread of communism worldwide led the United States into a long and costly war in Vietnam. Here, soldiers in the U.S. 173 Airborne are shown taking part in the Iron Triangle assault.

NY

1968 Martin Luther King Jr. and Robert Kennedy are assassinated.

1969 Joan Baez, The Who, and Jimi Hendrix headline the Woodstock Music Festival.

1971 Prisoners at Attica State Prison riot and take control of the prison.

1973 Last U.S. ground troops leave Vietnam.

1965

1970

1975

1965 North Vietnamese leader Ho Chi Minh refuses peace talks with President Lyndon Johnson.

1969 Ho Chi Minh dies in Hanoi.

1975 North Vietnamese troops capture Saigon.

311

Reading Social Studies

by Kylene Beers

Economics

Geography

Politics

Society and Culture

Science and Technology

Focus on Themes In this chapter, you will learn about the Vietnam War years. American soldiers faced many obstacles in Vietnam, including the country's **geography**. Jungles and mountains prevented Americans from gaining an easy victory. You will read about how the long, drawn-out conflict caused divisions between the nation's leaders and many Americans.

Setting a Purpose

Focus on Reading Setting a purpose for your reading can help you to understand the things that you read. Understanding the author's goal is often an important part of this task.

Setting a Purpose When you open this book to a page you have been assigned to read, there will be clues about what you will be learning. The information in this book is organized under headings that help explain the text. When you read a section like the one below, try to determine how the text explains the heading.

Notice how one reader used the headings to determine his purpose for reading the passage below.

Society in the 1960s

As the Vietnam War continued, growing numbers of Americans began to criticize the war . . .

From Chapter 12, p. 328

Antiwar Protests

College students often took the lead in organizing antiwar protests . . .

This large heading lets me know that the text below will be about everyday life during the 1960s.

The text below this heading might answer questions about what antiwar protests are and who took part in them.

I guess protests were frequent during the 1960s. I should read to find out what they were and why they took place.

You Try It!

The following passage is from the chapter you are getting ready to read. As you read the passage, look for information in the headings that tell you what to look for.

The Vietnam War Ends

While Nixon was running for re-election in 1972, Henry Kissinger continued peace negotiations with the North Vietnamese . . .

From Chapter 12, pp. 331–332

The Impact in Southeast Asia

The war ended when North Vietnamese forces captured Saigon in April 1975 . . .

The Impact at Home

The Vietnam War carried heavy costs for the United States as well . . .

After you read the passage, answer the following questions.

1. After reading the headings, what do you think this section is going to be about?

2. What are some questions you might ask before reading this section?

3. What information do you think you will learn from the section?

As you read Chapter 12, set a purpose before you read each section.

Kennedy and Foreign Policy

What You Will Learn...

Main Ideas

1. President Kennedy confronted Communist threats around the world.
2. The United States and the Soviet Union raced to send a person to the moon.
3. The Cold War conflict in Vietnam led the United States into war.

The Big Idea

The United States confronted Communist nations in Cold War conflicts around the world.

Key Terms and People

Peace Corps, *p. 314*
Fidel Castro, *p. 315*
Berlin Wall, *p. 316*
Cuban missile crisis, *p. 316*
Neil Armstrong, *p. 318*
Edwin "Buzz" Aldrin, *p. 318*
Ho Chi Minh, *p. 318*
domino theory, *p. 318*
Vietcong, *p. 319*

TAKING NOTES As you read, take notes on Cold War crises that took place during the Kennedy administration. You may want to use a graphic organizer like this one.

Bay of Pigs	Berlin Wall	Cuban Missile Crisis

If YOU were there...

You are a student in 1960. Whenever you discuss current events in class, students talk nervously about the ongoing nuclear arms race between the United States and the Soviet Union. If Cold War tensions ever spark an all-out nuclear war, entire cities and populations could be destroyed in just a matter of minutes.

Do you think Cold War tensions will lead to a nuclear war?

MEXICO

PACIFIC OCE

BUILDING BACKGROUND In the 1950s some Americans feared that the United States was falling behind the Soviet Union in missile production. The United States began using U-2 spy planes to gather information about Soviet military technology. On May 1, 1960, a U-2 plane was shot down over Soviet territory. Soviet leaders reacted angrily. Cold War tensions were running high as the Kennedy presidency began in 1961.

Kennedy Confronts Communism

As president, John F. Kennedy was committed to the Cold War policy of stopping the spread of communism worldwide. He maintained strong military forces and expanded the nation's supply of nuclear weapons. He also sought nonmilitary ways to defeat communism. For example, in a program called the Alliance for Progress, the United States pledged $20 billion in aid to countries in Latin America. This assistance did little to improve conditions in Latin America or U.S.–Latin American relations. Another nonmilitary program was more successful. Beginning in 1961, the **Peace Corps** sent volunteers to developing countries to help with projects such as digging wells and building schools.

Bay of Pigs

Much of Kennedy's attention, in his early days as president, involved confronting communism with U.S. military forces. The first Cold

Crises in Cuba

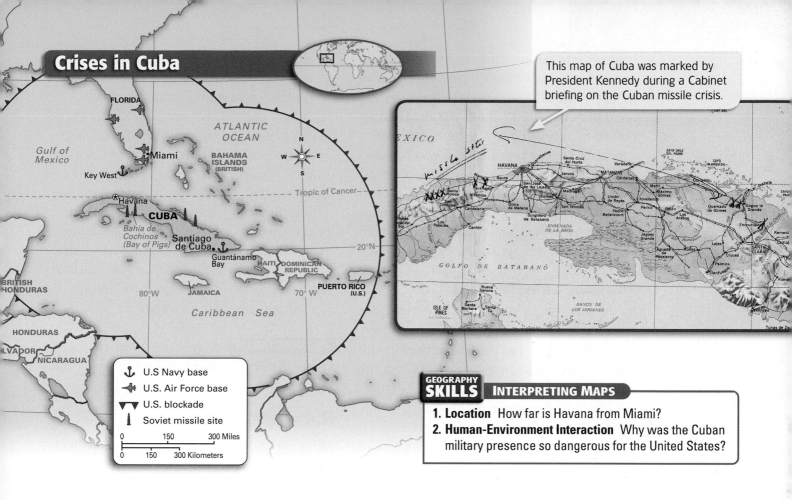

This map of Cuba was marked by President Kennedy during a Cabinet briefing on the Cuban missile crisis.

Legend:
- ⚓ U.S Navy base
- ✈ U.S. Air Force base
- ▼ U.S. blockade
- | Soviet missile site

0   150   300 Miles
0   150   300 Kilometers

GEOGRAPHY SKILLS **INTERPRETING MAPS**

1. **Location** How far is Havana from Miami?
2. **Human-Environment Interaction** Why was the Cuban military presence so dangerous for the United States?

War crisis during his administration took place in Cuba. In the late 1950s Cuban rebel **Fidel Castro** had led a revolution against an unpopular dictator. In 1959 he overthrew the dictator and soon established a Communist government allied to the Soviet Union. Many Cubans who had opposed Castro fled to the United States.

Castro's close ties with the Soviet Union worried Kennedy, especially since Cuba is only about 90 miles from Florida. Soviet leaders could use Cuba as a base from which to attack the United States.

While president, Dwight Eisenhower had developed a plan to remove Castro from power. The Central Intelligence Agency began training Cuban exiles to invade the island and overthrow Castro. Kennedy learned of the plan when he became president. He approved the operation.

On April 17, 1961, about 1,500 Cuban exiles landed by boat at Cuba's Bay of Pigs. Castro's forces quickly responded, killing about 300 of the invaders and capturing the rest. Many Americans criticized Kennedy for the disastrous invasion attempt. His administration was off to a shaky start.

The Berlin Wall

Located behind the Iron Curtain in East Germany, the city of Berlin was the site of Kennedy's second crisis. East Berlin was part of Communist East Germany. West Berlin remained a part of democratic West Germany and stood as a model of prosperity and freedom. Desperate for freedom and better economic opportunities, about 2.5 million East Germans fled to West Berlin between 1949 and 1961. The steady loss of skilled workers alarmed Communist officials. Calling the open border between East and West Berlin a "handy escape route," Soviet premier Nikita Khrushchev demanded that the border be closed.

Khrushchev threatened to take over West Berlin. President Kennedy responded by vowing to defend the free city. "We cannot and will not permit the Communists to drive us out of Berlin," he warned. Then, on the night of August 12–13, 1961, the East German government began building the **Berlin Wall**, a barrier of concrete and barbed wire between East and West Berlin. Kennedy rushed American troops to West Berlin. But he was unwilling to go to war with the Soviet Union over the Berlin Wall. The wall stood as a symbol of the Cold War for nearly three decades.

The Cuban Missile Crisis

In October 1962 Kennedy faced yet another problem in Cuba when American U-2 spy planes discovered that the Soviets were installing nuclear missiles in Cuba. If launched, the missiles could reach, and possibly destroy, American cities within minutes.

At a press conference on October 22, Kennedy demanded that the Soviet Union remove the missiles. During the **Cuban missile crisis**, the U.S. Navy formed a blockade around Cuba to prevent Soviet ships from bringing in more weapons. As Soviet ships approached

ACADEMIC
VOCABULARY
aspect
part

the blockade, terrified Americans waited tensely for news updates. Then came some welcome news—the Soviet ships had turned back.

After the crisis ended, Khrushchev agreed to remove the nuclear missiles from Cuba. In return, Kennedy promised not to invade Cuba. He also agreed to remove some missiles in Italy and Turkey. To improve future communication, Kennedy and Khrushchev set up a telephone "hotline" so the leaders could talk directly to each other at a moment's notice. They also signed the Limited Nuclear Test Ban Treaty, which banned the testing of new nuclear weapons aboveground.

READING CHECK **Sequencing** When did Kennedy's three Cold War crises occur?

Race to the Moon

Although Kennedy and Khrushchev had taken some steps to prevent conflicts, the Cold War continued. One **aspect** of the Cold War that heated up in the 1960s was the space race—the competition between the United

Primary Source

BOOK
Thirteen Days

During the Cuban missile crisis, President Kennedy considered several options: blockade Cuba, invade the island, or bomb missile sites by air. After choosing the blockade, Kennedy and his advisers could only wait to see how Khrushchev would respond. The president's brother, Attorney General Robert F. Kennedy, later described these tense moments in the White House.

Robert Kennedy describes the doubts he and others in the room felt.

I think these few minutes were the time of gravest concern for the President. Was the world on the brink of a holocaust? Was it our error? A mistake? Was there something further that should have been done? Or not done?. . . The minutes in the Cabinet Room ticked slowly by. What could we say now—what could we do?

Then it was 10:25—a messenger brought in a note . . . 'Mr. President . . . some of the Russian ships have stopped dead in the water . . . Six ships . . . have stopped or have turned back toward the Soviet Union' . . .

Then we were back to the details. The meeting droned on. But everyone looked like a different person. For a moment the world had stood still, and now it was going around again.

—Robert F. Kennedy, from *Thirteen Days: A Memoir of the Cuban Missile Crisis*

ANALYSIS
SKILL **ANALYZING PRIMARY SOURCES**

What details from the passage show that the moment was tense?

States and the Soviet Union to explore space. The Soviet Union pulled ahead in April 1961 when Soviet cosmonaut Yuri Gagarin became the first person to travel into space, orbiting Earth once.

The United States was determined to catch up to and surpass the Soviet Union in the space race. Kennedy outlined a bold plan in a 1961 speech to Congress:

"I believe that this nation should commit itself to achieving the goal, before this decade is out, of landing a man on the moon and returning him safely to the earth."

—John F. Kennedy, speech to Congress, May 25, 1961

It is difficult for us to imagine what it was like for Kennedy's audience to hear these words. Space travel seems normal to us today. But to people in the early 1960s, the idea of humans landing on the moon seemed like something out of a science fiction novel. Still, Americans supported the project. Congress provided NASA with billions of dollars to fund the development of new technology.

In May 1961 astronaut Alan Shepard Jr. became the first U.S. astronaut in space. The next year, John Glenn became the first American to orbit Earth. Then NASA pushed ahead with Project Apollo, with the goal of landing an astronaut on the moon. Even with careful planning, Apollo astronauts faced great danger. Three astronauts died in a fire during a prelaunch test in 1967.

Mission to the Moon

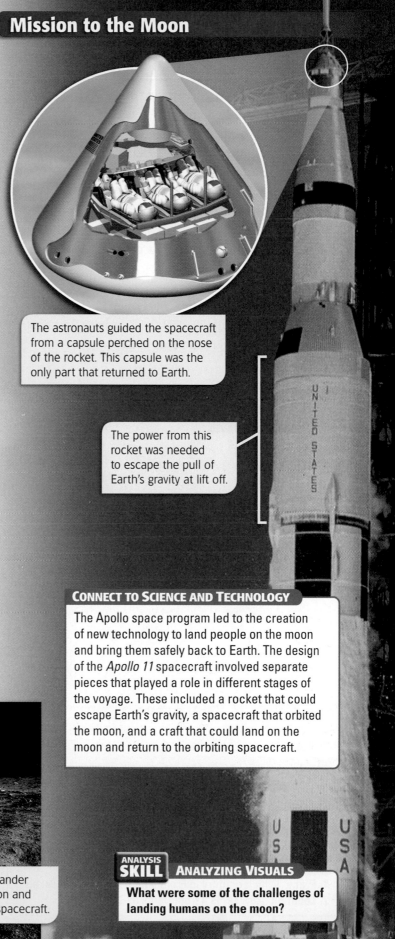

The astronauts guided the spacecraft from a capsule perched on the nose of the rocket. This capsule was the only part that returned to Earth.

The power from this rocket was needed to escape the pull of Earth's gravity at lift off.

CONNECT TO SCIENCE AND TECHNOLOGY

The Apollo space program led to the creation of new technology to land people on the moon and bring them safely back to Earth. The design of the *Apollo 11* spacecraft involved separate pieces that played a role in different stages of the voyage. These included a rocket that could escape Earth's gravity, a spacecraft that orbited the moon, and a craft that could land on the moon and return to the orbiting spacecraft.

A vehicle known as the moon lander took two astronauts to the moon and returned them to the orbiting spacecraft.

ANALYSIS SKILL **ANALYZING VISUALS**

What were some of the challenges of landing humans on the moon?

On July 20, 1969, while millions of people around the world watched on television, the lunar module *Eagle* landed on the surface of the moon. American astronauts **Neil Armstrong** and **Edwin "Buzz" Aldrin** climbed out and became the first people to walk on the moon. "That's one small step for [a] man, one giant leap for mankind," said Armstrong as he touched the lunar surface. Armstrong and Aldrin planted the American flag on the moon's surface and collected samples of moon rocks. The Apollo program continued, achieving five more successful moon landings by 1972.

READING CHECK **Analyzing** How did the events of July 20, 1969, fulfill the hope President Kennedy had expressed in 1961?

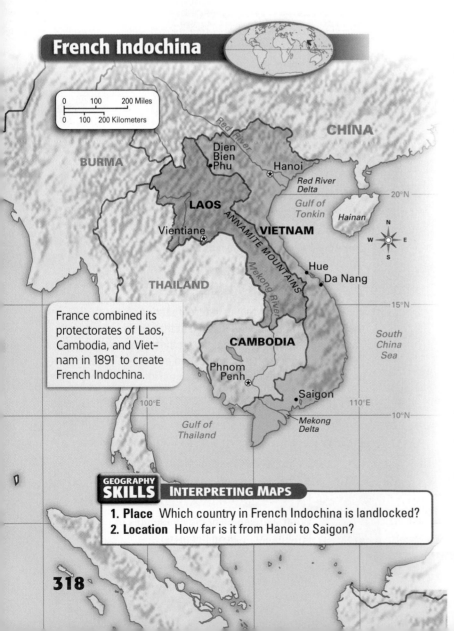

French Indochina

France combined its protectorates of Laos, Cambodia, and Vietnam in 1891 to create French Indochina.

0   100   200 Miles
0   100   200 Kilometers

BURMA
CHINA
Dien Bien Phu
Hanoi
Red River
Red River Delta
20°N
LAOS
Gulf of Tonkin
Hainan
Vientiane
ANNAMITE MOUNTAINS
VIETNAM
THAILAND
Hue
Da Nang
Mekong River
15°N
CAMBODIA
South China Sea
Phnom Penh
100°E
Saigon
110°E
10°N
Gulf of Thailand
Mekong Delta

GEOGRAPHY SKILLS **INTERPRETING MAPS**

1. **Place** Which country in French Indochina is landlocked?
2. **Location** How far is it from Hanoi to Saigon?

Conflict in Vietnam

The most serious and deadly event of the Cold War took place in Vietnam, a country in Southeast Asia. The Vietnamese struggled against the domination of China for centuries. By the early 1880s all of Vietnam was conquered by France. The French combined Vietnam with neighboring Laos and Cambodia to create a colony called French Indochina. French leaders imposed harsh taxes and put limits on political freedoms. Vietnamese nationalists began a struggle for independence in the early 1900s.

France and Vietnam

One of the leading Vietnamese nationalists was **Ho Chi Minh**. Inspired by the Russian Revolution, Ho came to believe that only a Communist revolution could free the Vietnamese people.

During World War II, Japan drove the French out of Indochina. Ho Chi Minh did not want Vietnam to be controlled by yet another foreign power. He organized a group called the Vietminh to resist Japanese occupation. When Japan was defeated by the Allies in 1945, Ho declared Vietnamese independence. Using words echoing those of the American Declaration of Independence, he said, "All men are born equal: the Creator has given us inviolable rights, life, liberty, and happiness." In reality, Ho did not believe in the democratic principles outlined in the American document.

Vietnam was still not free of foreign rule, however. France insisted that Vietnam was a French colony. French forces moved to regain control of Vietnam, leading to new fighting between the two sides.

Presidents Truman and Eisenhower both supported France with military aid. They were concerned that a Vietminh victory would lead to the spread of communism in Asia. American leaders feared that if one country became Communist, nearby countries would also fall to communism. This was called the **domino theory**. Americans had already watched Communist victories in China and North Korea. They did not want Vietnam to be next.

The Vietminh had fewer weapons and supplies than the French, but they used hit-and-run guerrilla tactics to gradually weaken French forces. In May 1954 the Vietminh trapped a French army at Dien Bien Phu, where the French surrendered. In July French and Vietnamese leaders worked out an agreement called the Geneva Accords. This compromise temporarily divided Vietnam into North and South. It also called for democratic elections in July 1956 that would unite the two countries under one government.

North and South Vietnam

North Vietnam became a Communist dictatorship led by Ho Chi Minh. South Vietnam had a Western-style government led by Ngo Dinh Diem (en-GOH DIN de-EM) and supported by the United States. U.S. officials hoped Diem would win control of the country in the 1956 elections.

Diem, however, quickly proved to be a disappointing leader. He put his own family members in top government positions and used his security forces to imprison and torture his political enemies. President Eisenhower was concerned, but he and his advisers saw Diem as the only realistic alternative to a Communist Vietnam.

In North Vietnam, meanwhile, Ho Chi Minh introduced land redistribution plans. Like Diem, Ho and the Vietminh violently persecuted their opponents. During the land redistribution process, they imprisoned and killed thousands of landowners.

As the 1956 reunification elections approached, however, a growing number of South Vietnamese supported Ho and the Vietminh. Diem refused to allow South Vietnam to participate in the elections. The United States backed this decision. Diem also arrested thousands of people who supported Ho.

In 1960 members of the North Vietnamese government formed the National Liberation Front (NLF). The NLF recruited South Vietnamese who were opposed to Diem to fight against the South Vietnamese

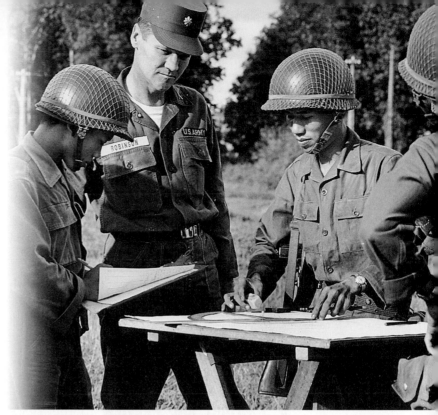

South Vietnamese soldiers plot a firing pattern under the guidance of American military personnel.

government. The NLF relied on Communist guerrilla forces called the **Vietcong** as its army, which was supplied and funded by the North Vietnamese Communists.

American Involvement

President Eisenhower sent aid, weapons, and military advisers to South Vietnam to aid Diem. Soon after taking office in 1961, President Kennedy sent more advisers and special forces. Although they were not official combat troops, the U.S. military advisers often accompanied the South Vietnamese army on combat missions. Some were killed in action. By late 1963 about 16,000 U.S. military personnel were serving in Vietnam.

The increased U.S. support did not help Diem, who was becoming less and less popular in South Vietnam. Several attempts were made to overthrow his government, all of which failed. Diem would not hold elections, and his opponents began to consider violence as their only option. He lost more support when he ordered his troops to fire on Buddhist demonstrators.

FOCUS ON NEW YORK CITY

Almost as soon as U.S. troops were sent to Vietnam, Americans began protesting the war there. The earliest organized protests against the war in Vietnam occurred in New York City and Philadelphia in 1963. Student groups coordinated peaceful protests in New York City for several years, and Martin Luther King Jr.'s first speech against the war was at Riverside Church in 1967.

Some Buddhist monks protested by setting themselves on fire. Horrifying images of these protests helped turn U.S. public opinion against Diem.

In November 1963 a group of South Vietnamese army officers seized power and killed Diem and his brother. Only weeks later, Kennedy was assassinated, and Vice President Lyndon Johnson became president. Johnson immediately faced tough decisions about how to handle an increasingly unstable South Vietnam.

READING CHECK **Evaluating** Why did the United States see the Vietnam conflict as a Cold War struggle?

SUMMARY AND PREVIEW In the 1950s and early 1960s, Cold War tensions caused conflicts around the world. In the next section you will read about increased U.S. involvement in Vietnam.

The Beginning of the Vietnam War — QUICK FACTS

Causes
- French lose control of Vietnam
- Cold War tensions
- Civil war in Vietnam
- Assassination of President Diem

Effects
- Eisenhower and Kennedy send military advisers
- Gulf of Tonkin Resolution

---

go.hrw.com
Online Quiz

Section 1 Assessment

Reviewing Ideas, Terms, and People

1. **a. Describe** What nonmilitary tactics did President Kennedy use to confront communism?
   b. Explain How was the **Cuban missile crisis** resolved?
   c. Evaluate In which Cold War crisis do you think President Kennedy showed the strongest leadership? Explain your answer.
2. **a. Recall** How did the Soviet Union take the lead in the space race in 1961?
   b. Predict How do you think the Soviet Union responded to the successful U.S. landing of a man on the moon?
3. **a. Identify** Who was **Ho Chi Minh**?
   b. Describe According to the **domino theory**, what did U.S. leaders think might happen if Vietnam became a Communist country?
   c. Analyze Do you think the United States was justified in supporting Ngo Dinh Diem? Why or why not?

Critical Thinking

4. **Identifying Cause and Effect** Review your notes on Cold War crises during the Kennedy administration. Then copy the graphic organizer below and use it to list the causes and effects of each crisis.

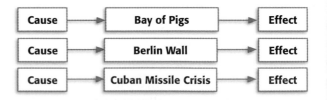

Cause	→	Bay of Pigs	→	Effect
Cause	→	Berlin Wall	→	Effect
Cause	→	Cuban Missile Crisis	→	Effect

FOCUS ON WRITING

5. **Listing Cold War Conflicts** List Cold War conflicts the United States faced during the 1960s. Who was involved in each conflict? How could you explain each conflict to a television audience? What could you show in your newscast to illustrate the conflicts?

Escalation in Vietnam

If **YOU** were there...

It is 1965, and you have just been elected to Congress. You know voters are concerned about events in Vietnam, and you are carefully following the progress of the war. No one knows what will happen if the United States gets more deeply involved in the conflict. It might turn back the tide of communism. On the other hand, thousands of young soldiers might die.

Would you support sending U.S. troops to Vietnam? Why or why not?

BUILDING BACKGROUND Lyndon Johnson had spent most of his political career focused on domestic issues. After becoming president, he dedicated himself to civil rights legislation and his Great Society programs. But Johnson also had the same goal as presidents before him—to stop the spread of communism around the world.

Johnson Commits to Victory

Lyndon Johnson was determined to prevent Communists from taking over in South Vietnam. "We have the resources and the will to follow this course as long as it may take," Johnson said. He waited for a spark that might allow him to take action.

The Tonkin Gulf Resolution

In the summer of 1964, a naval skirmish led to a rapid expansion of U.S. involvement in Vietnam. On August 2, 1964, the USS *Maddox* reportedly exchanged gunfire with North Vietnamese torpedo boats in the Gulf of Tonkin, off the North Vietnamese coast. Two days later, during a night of thunderstorms, U.S. ships reported a second attack. The captain of the *Maddox* was not sure his ship had actually been attacked, but the USS *Turner Joy* claimed to have picked up high-speed vessels on its radar. Despite the conflicting stories, President Johnson declared the incident an act of war.

What You Will Learn...

Main Ideas
1. President Johnson committed the United States to victory in Vietnam by expanding U.S. involvement.
2. American soldiers faced new challenges fighting the Vietnam War.
3. The Tet Offensive was an important turning point in the war.

The Big Idea
Johnson quickly expanded U.S. involvement in Vietnam, but American soldiers faced a determined enemy.

Key Terms and People
Tonkin Gulf Resolution, *p. 322*
Ho Chi Minh Trail, *p. 322*
escalation, *p. 322*
William Westmoreland, *p. 323*
search-and-destroy missions, *p. 323*
Tet Offensive, *p. 324*
doves, *p. 324*
hawks, *p. 324*

TAKING NOTES As you read, list the events that led to the escalation of U.S. involvement in the Vietnam War. Write your notes in a table like this one.

Events that led to escalation:
1.
2.
3.
4.

Johnson asked Congress to give him the authority to take military action. Congress passed the **Tonkin Gulf Resolution**, giving the president the authority "to take all necessary measures to repel any armed attack against the forces of the United States." Johnson used the Tonkin Gulf Resolution to greatly expand the U.S. role in Vietnam.

Air Strikes Begin

Johnson sent the first U.S. combat troops to South Vietnam in March 1965. At the same time, he ordered Operation Rolling Thunder, a series of air strikes on war industries in North Vietnam. The air strikes were also designed to disrupt the **Ho Chi Minh Trail**, a supply route used by the North Vietnamese. The trail was a network of paths and tunnels that led from North Vietnam, through Laos and Cambodia, and into South Vietnam.

Because some of the Ho Chi Minh Trail was located in neutral countries, U.S. soldiers could not surround it on the ground. Instead, U.S. airplanes bombed the route, sometimes with napalm, or jellied gasoline, to kill troops and destroy supplies. Planes also released chemicals such as Agent Orange to kill the dense forests on the trail and to increase visibility from the air. American veterans and Vietnamese civilians later suffered serious health problems from exposure to these chemicals.

By late 1968 more than a million tons of explosives had been dropped on North and South Vietnam. Many Vietnamese soldiers and civilians were killed. The Communists' ability to wage war, however, was not destroyed.

READING CHECK Summarizing What authority did the Tonkin Gulf Resolution give to President Johnson?

U.S. Soldiers in Vietnam

From 1965 to 1968, President Johnson pursued a policy of **escalation**, or increased involvement, in the war. By 1968 more than 500,000 U.S. troops were serving in Vietnam. Backed by superior military technology, U.S. generals expected to win a quick victory. But the Vietnam War proved to be different from previous wars.

Strategies and Tactics

In Vietnam, there was rarely a front line where armies met face to face. Much of the war was

CASE STUDY **BIOGRAPHY**

John McCain
1936–

John McCain's father and grandfather were both U.S. Navy admirals. The younger McCain also attended the Naval Academy and served in Vietnam as a combat pilot. On a bombing mission over Hanoi in 1967, his plane was shot down. McCain was held as a prisoner of war (POW) for more than five years and was often tortured and kept in solitary confinement. McCain entered politics after the war. In 2004 he was elected to his fourth term as U.S. senator from Arizona. One of his priorities as a senator was to help repair and strengthen U.S. relations with Vietnam. McCain was the Republican nominee for president in 2008.

Drawing Inferences If you were John McCain, would you want to establish good relations with Vietnam? Why or why not?

As a lieutenant, John McCain served as a flight instructor.

fought in the jungles and villages of South Vietnam. General **William Westmoreland** commanded the U.S. ground forces involved in Vietnam. He developed a strategy based on **search-and-destroy missions**, where U.S. patrols searched for hidden enemy camps, then destroyed them with massive firepower and air raids.

To make up for their disadvantage in firepower, Vietcong and North Vietnamese Army (NVA) troops used guerrilla warfare tactics. Moving quickly, they set deadly traps and land mines. They also knew the local geography, which allowed them to make quick surprise assaults on small groups of U.S. soldiers. Though the Vietcong and NVA suffered high casualty rates, they were able to match U.S. escalation by continuing to send new troops into combat. They also received supplies and weapons from Communist China and the Soviet Union.

The civilians of South Vietnam were often caught in the middle of the fighting. Vietcong forces entered villages at night and killed people they believed were cooperating with the South Vietnamese government. South Vietnamese and American troops attacked villages they suspected of assisting the Vietcong. About 4 million South Vietnamese were driven from their homes. This undermined the crucial U.S. goal of winning the support and loyalty of South Vietnamese civilians.

Soldiers' Stories

More than 2 million American soldiers served in the Vietnam War. Their average age was 18–21, several years younger than in previous American wars. About one-quarter of the soldiers were drafted, many from minority groups and poor families. College students—most of whom were white and from wealthier families—were able to get draft releases called deferments.

American troops patrolled jungles and rice paddies, carrying 75–90 pounds of equipment through 100-degree heat and rainstorms that

Primary Source

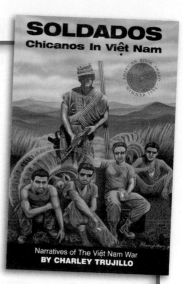
SOLDADOS
Chicanos In Việt Nam

Narratives of The Việt Nam War
BY CHARLEY TRUJILLO

ORAL HISTORY
Vietnam War

Charley Trujillo was a soldier in the Vietnam War. He later became a writer and filmmaker, focusing on the experiences of Latinos and Chicanos in the Vietnam War. Below he describes a day in Vietnam.

" Throughout the day we received mortar and sniper fire. By that evening we had suffered more casualties. The one I remember most was a guy we called the yippie. He was totally against the war and usually tried to avoid any violence. He was even thinking, for a while, of not carrying a rifle. It didn't help him much because the dude lost his leg that afternoon. **"**

—Charley Trujillo, quoted in *Soldados: Chicanos In Việt Nam*

ANALYZING PRIMARY SOURCES

Why might Trujillo have remembered this casualty the most?

could last for days. They never knew when they might run into enemy fire. Soldiers also faced the constant danger of land mines and booby traps. "We required this kind of instant hair-trigger alertness," said marine Philip Caputo. "You simply trusted absolutely no one. I mean, from a 5-year-old kid to a 75-year-old woman."

While American troops were often able to win individual battles, they were rarely able to control the territory they had won for long. "You were just constantly walking out over the same ground," Caputo explained. "The enemy you were supposed to be defeating statistically kept coming back for more."

READING CHECK Comparing and Contrasting How was Vietnam different from previous wars for U.S. soldiers?

Turning Points in Vietnam

By the end of 1967, U.S. military leaders argued that they were nearing victory in Vietnam. General Westmoreland said that he saw "a light at the end of the tunnel." But events in 1968 weakened the American public's confidence in this claim.

The Tet Offensive

On January 30, 1968, the Vietnamese celebrated their New Year, called Tet. In previous years, a cease-fire had halted fighting on this holiday. In 1968, however, Vietcong and North Vietnamese forces launched the **Tet Offensive** —surprise attacks all over South Vietnam, including an attack on the U.S. Embassy in Saigon, South Vietnam's capital.

South Vietnamese and U.S. forces successfully fought off the enemy strikes. Still, the massive size of the Tet Offensive shocked Americans. They had been told that the war would soon be over. Now they saw that the enemy was still strong and determined. Many began to wonder if government officials were being honest about the war. One poll taken after the Tet Offensive showed that only 33 percent of Americans believed that the United States was winning the war in Vietnam. About 49 percent said that the United States should never have become involved in the war.

In February 1968 Westmoreland asked for some 200,000 more troops. Many Americans questioned the wisdom of further escalation in Vietnam. President Johnson denied the general's request.

Hawks and Doves

Television reports had an important impact on public opinion about the war. Americans could watch action from the battlefield and see real images of the war's brutality on nightly news broadcasts. Many were dismayed by what they saw.

Gradually, some Americans who had been supporters of the Vietnam War began to call for an end to U.S. involvement. Opponents of the war were called **doves**—named after the birds that symbolize peace. Many doves believed that the war was draining money that should be spent on social programs at home. Supporters of the war were called **hawks**. Hawks called for increased military spending, based on the belief that winning the Cold War took priority over domestic programs.

The bitter divisions between hawks and doves deepened as the Vietnam War continued. On March 16, 1968, a company of U.S. soldiers under the command of

The Vietnam War, 1968

Interactive Map

Legend:
- Major U.S. air strikes
- Major U.S. bases
- Areas under attack in Tet Offensive,1968
- Base areas/war zone
- Areas of prolonged fighting

0   100   200 Miles
0   100   200 Kilometers

BURMA

NORTH VIETNAM

Dien Bien Phu
Xam Nua
Hanoi
Red River Delta
Lach Chao Estuary
Gulf of Tonkin
LAOS
Muang Ngat
Vientiane
U.S. Seventh Fleet
Demilitarized Zone (DMZ)
Ho Chi Minh Trail
Mekong River
THAILAND
My Lai
South China Sea
CAMBODIA
SOUTH VIETNAM
Gulf of Thailand
Phnom Penh
Da Lat
Cam Rahn Bay
U.S. Seventh Fleet
Saigon
Ben Tre
Mekong Delta

20°N
15°N
10°N
100°E
105°E
110°E

GEOGRAPHY SKILLS | **INTERPRETING MAPS**

1. **Place** In which countries did major U.S. air strikes occur?
2. **Human-Environment Interaction** Which country experienced most of the fighting in the Vietnam War?

Lieutenant William Calley entered the South Vietnamese village of My Lai. Calley and his men expected to find Vietcong forces in My Lai. Their search-and-destroy mission turned into a massacre when American soldiers opened fire, killing about 500 unarmed villagers, including women and children.

At first, U.S. military officials tried to cover up news of the massacre. But former soldiers eventually made details of the events public. Lieutenant Calley was tried by the military and convicted of murder. As with the Tet Offensive, the My Lai massacre caused many Americans to question U.S. involvement in Vietnam.

READING CHECK **Summarizing** What events made some Americans oppose the war?

SUMMARY AND PREVIEW The Vietnam War escalated steadily under President Johnson. In the next section, you will learn about the final years of the war.

A Reporter in the Field

Millions of Americans watched correspondent Walter Cronkite report the Vietnam War from the field. When Cronkite called the war a stalemate, or tie, President Johnson said "I've lost middle America."

How did Cronkite affect American's view of the war?

go.hrw.com
Online Quiz

Section 2 Assessment

Reviewing Ideas, Terms, and People

1. **a. Recall** What events led Johnson to ask Congress for authority to take military action in Vietnam?
   b. Explain Why was the **Ho Chi Minh Trail** the target of U.S. air strikes?
   c. Predict What problems might arise from giving a president powers such as those defined in the **Tonkin Gulf Resolution**?
2. **a. Define** What was **escalation**?
   b. Contrast How did strategies and tactics of U.S. troops differ from those of the NVA and Vietcong?
3. **a. Describe** What were the goals of the **doves** and the **hawks** during the Vietnam War?
   b. Analyze How did television influence public opinion during the Vietnam War?
   c. Elaborate Why was the Tet Offensive such a surprise to U.S. forces?

Critical Thinking

4. **Sequencing** Review your notes on events that led to increased U.S. involvement in the Vietnam War. Then copy the graphic organizer below and use it to put these events in the correct order.

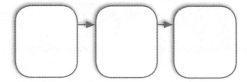

FOCUS ON WRITING

5. **Comparing Points of View** Take notes on different people's points of view on the war. What different points of view should you present in your newscast to give a complete picture of the war in Vietnam? What kinds of people might you want to interview?

CASE STUDY **History and Geography**

The Vietcong Tunnels

Besides knowing the geography and terrain much better than U.S. forces, the Vietcong had the advantage of an underground system of tunnels. One large system of tunnels was installed some 47 miles north of Saigon in the Cu Chi district of South Vietnam. The picture on these pages is a re-created representation of these tunnels. The tunnels provided a place from which to fight that the Americans could not attack. A tunnel complex included special rooms in which to sleep, eat, plan, store weapons and supplies, and tend wounded soldiers.

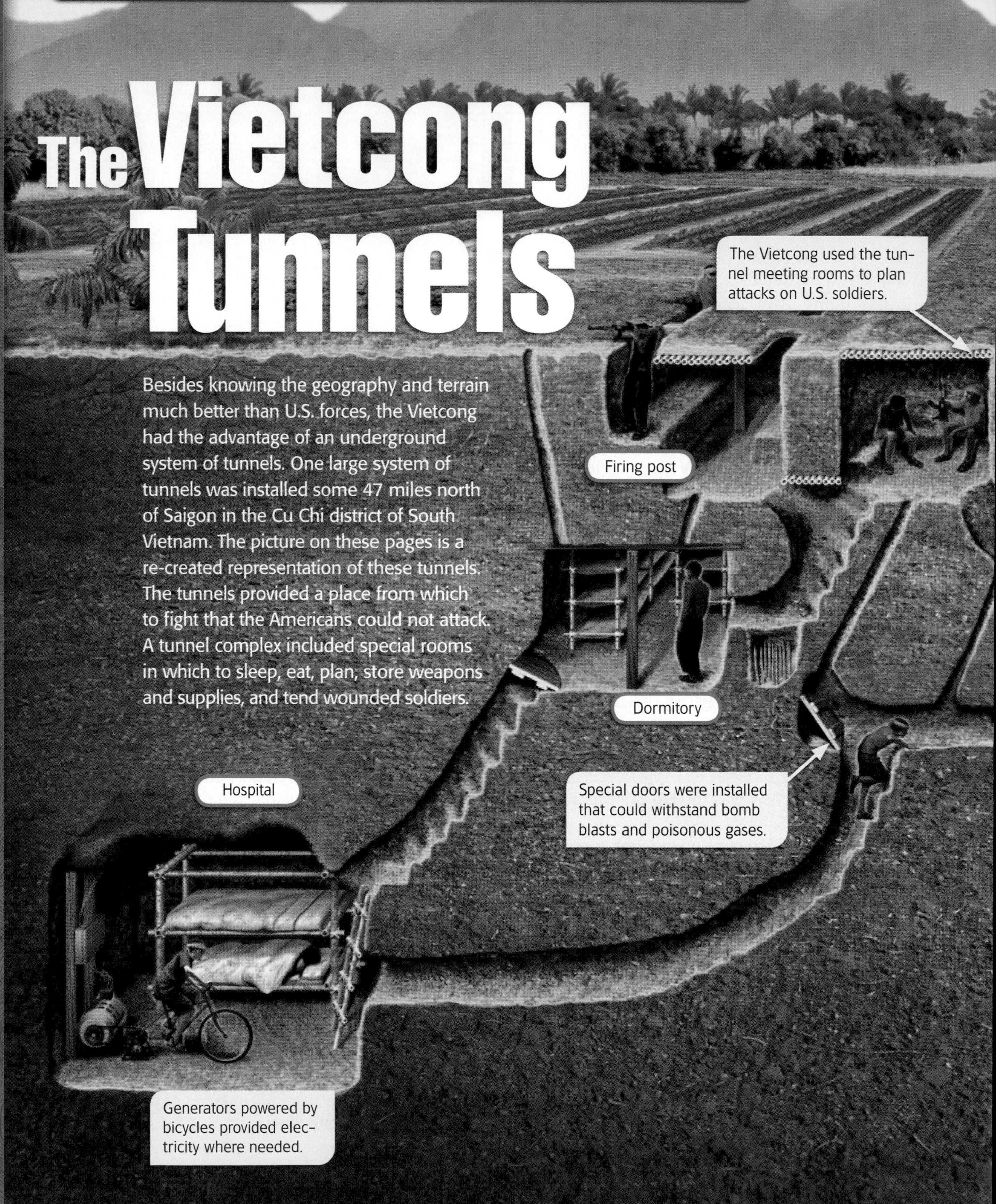

The Vietcong used the tunnel meeting rooms to plan attacks on U.S. soldiers.
Firing post
Dormitory
Hospital
Special doors were installed that could withstand bomb blasts and poisonous gases.
Generators powered by bicycles provided electricity where needed.

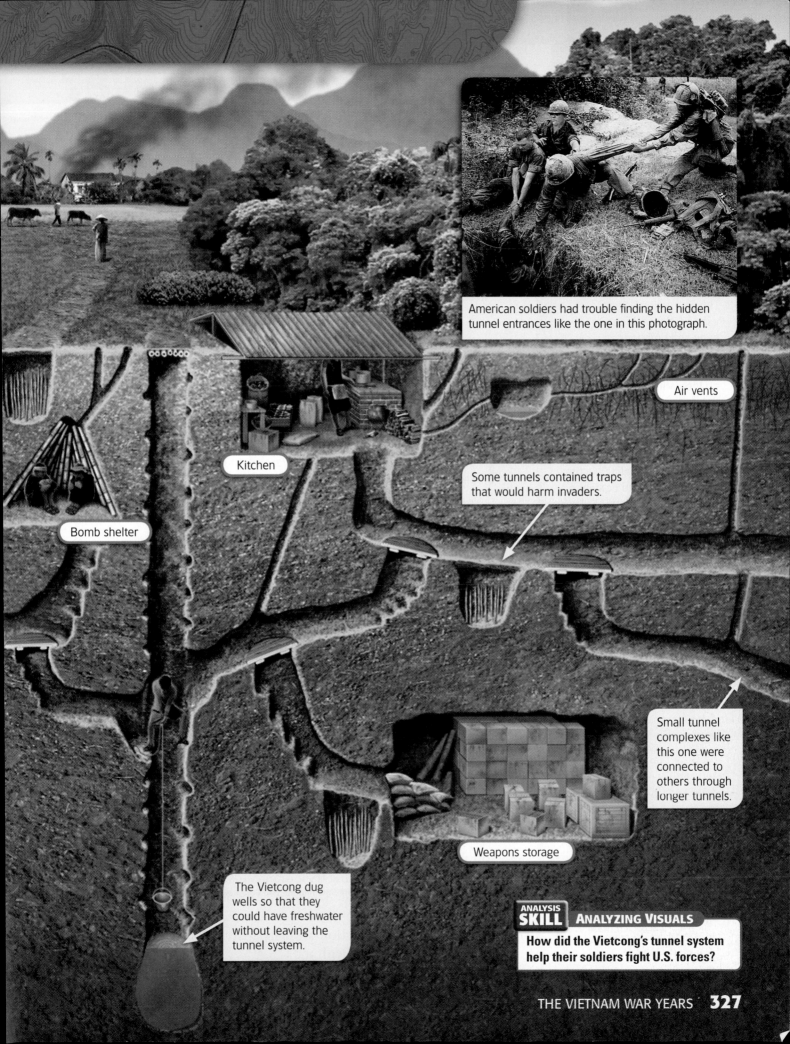

American soldiers had trouble finding the hidden tunnel entrances like the one in this photograph.

Air vents

Some tunnels contained traps that would harm invaders.

Kitchen

Bomb shelter

Small tunnel complexes like this one were connected to others through longer tunnels.

Weapons storage

The Vietcong dug wells so that they could have freshwater without leaving the tunnel system.

ANALYSIS SKILL **ANALYZING VISUALS**

How did the Vietcong's tunnel system help their soldiers fight U.S. forces?

The End of the War

If **YOU** were there...

You are a high school student in 1969. You follow events in Vietnam very closely and often talk about the war with your friends. Some of your friends are active in the antiwar movement, but you also have friends who support the war. You think each group makes good points, but you are having a hard time deciding which position you support.

Would you join the antiwar protests? Why or why not?

What You Will Learn...

Main Ideas

1. Opinions about the Vietnam War divided American society in the 1960s.
2. The war under Nixon expanded from Vietnam to Laos and Cambodia.
3. The Vietnam War ended in 1973, but it had lasting effects on Vietnam and the United States.

The Big Idea

Growing antiwar feelings in the United States helped convince the government to end U.S. involvement in the Vietnam War.

Key Terms and People

Students for a Democratic Society, *p. 328*
hippies, *p. 329*
Richard M. Nixon, *p. 330*
Henry Kissinger, *p. 330*
Vietnamization, *p. 330*
Twenty-sixth Amendment, *p. 331*
War Powers Act, *p. 333*
Vietnam Veterans Memorial, *p. 333*

TAKING NOTES As you read, take notes on the causes of the end of the Vietnam War. Organize your notes in a graphic organizer like the one below.

Causes → End of Vietnam War

BUILDING BACKGROUND Should the United States continue fighting in Vietnam? The debate over this question caused deep divisions in American society in the late 1960s. Antiwar demonstrators marched in cities and on college campuses. Others demonstrated in support of the war.

Society in the 1960s

As the Vietnam War continued, growing numbers of Americans began to criticize the war. "The peaceniks [war protesters] these days are legion [many]," said Charlotte Keyes, who helped organize a group called Women Strike for Peace. "They are ninety-years-old and fifteen, heads of families and housewives with babies, students, [and] young people."

Antiwar Protests

College students often took the lead in organizing antiwar protests. One of the most active protest groups was **Students for a Democratic Society** (SDS). Members of SDS protested the draft, as well as companies that made weapons used in Vietnam.

By the end of 1968, students had held antiwar demonstrations on nearly 75 percent of college campuses. Some young men protested by publicly burning their draft cards. Others avoided military service by moving to Canada. Many Americans, however, criticized the antiwar movement as anti-American. In 1970, for example, thousands of construction workers marched in New York City, shouting, "All the way with the U.S.A."

A Society Divided

Some young Americans supported the war in Vietnam. Many saw it as the only way to stop the spread of communism.

Other young Americans protested the war. They believed the United States should not be involved in a violent conflict far from home.

ANALYSIS
SKILL **ANALYZING INFORMATION**

What differing views did young Americans have about the Vietnam War?

For some Americans, the antiwar movement was part of a rejection of traditional **values** and government authority. Some young people chose to "drop out" of mainstream society and built a counterculture—a culture with its own values and ways of behaving. Members of this counterculture, called **hippies**, emphasized individual freedom, nonviolence, and communal sharing. Hippies expressed their rejection of traditional society by growing their hair long and wearing unusual clothes. The views of hippies and war protesters upset many Americans. Commentators described a "generation gap," or division between older and younger Americans. "I know of no time in our history when the gap between the generations has been wider," said one university professor.

The Election of 1968

News of the Tet Offensive led to a sharp drop in the popularity of President Johnson. In early 1968 the percentage of Americans who approved of Johnson's performance as president fell from 48 to 36. The number of Americans who approved of the way Johnson was handling the war was even lower. As the 1968 presidential election approached, Johnson was even losing support within his own Democratic Party. On March 31 he went on live television and told Americans: "I shall not seek, and I will not accept, the nomination of my party for another term as president."

Several other candidates campaigned for the Democratic nomination. Johnson backed his vice president, Hubert Humphrey. Eugene McCarthy, a senator from Minnesota, ran as an outspoken antiwar candidate. Senator Robert F. Kennedy of New York argued that the United States should do everything possible to negotiate a quick and peaceful end to the war.

Kennedy won the California primary on June 5, 1968—an important step before the upcoming Democratic National Convention in Chicago. After giving his victory speech that night, he was assassinated by a man named Sirhan Sirhan.

The Democrats were badly divided going into their party's convention in Chicago.

ACADEMIC VOCABULARY
values ideas that people hold dear and try to live by

FOCUS ON NEW YORK

The Woodstock Music and Art Festival, held on a farm in Bethel, New York, in 1969, became a symbol of 1960s counterculture. Hundreds of thousands of people attended the festival, which featured famous musicians such as Joan Baez, Jimi Hendrix, and Janis Joplin.

Vice President Humphrey seemed certain to win the nomination. But many delegates disliked his close ties with President Johnson and the Vietnam War. Angry debates inside the convention hall were matched by anti-war protests on the streets. When police officers moved in to stop the demonstrations, a riot broke out. Television cameras broadcast live images of the violent chaos in Chicago. More than 100 police and 100 demonstrators were injured.

Humphrey won the Democratic nomination for president, but the events in Chicago damaged his chances of victory. Republican nominee **Richard M. Nixon** promised to restore order to American society and bring "peace with honor" to Vietnam. Nixon won the election, receiving 301 electoral votes to Humphrey's 191. Southern voters gave 46 electoral votes to George Wallace, a segregationist candidate of the American Independent Party.

READING CHECK **Summarizing** Who were the candidates in the 1968 election? What was the outcome of the election?

The War under Nixon

President Nixon wanted to get U.S. troops out of Vietnam without creating the appearance of an American defeat. "I will not be the first president of the United States to lose a war," he told his fellow Republicans. With his national security adviser, **Henry Kissinger**, Nixon created a plan to pull U.S. troops from Vietnam and have the South Vietnamese Army take over all the fighting. This strategy was called **Vietnamization**.

Nixon began slowly withdrawing American troops from Vietnam. Without the knowledge of Congress or the American public, however, he approved bombing raids on Cambodia and Laos. The goal of these raids was to disrupt Vietcong supply lines. On April 30, 1970, Nixon announced that he had sent U.S. troops into Cambodia to attack Communist bases. "If, when the chips are down," he said, "the United States of America acts like a pitiful helpless giant, the forces of totalitarian anarchy will threaten free nations." Many Americans were furious. Rather than seeking peace, Nixon seemed to be expanding the war.

LINKING TO TODAY

The United States and Vietnam Today

Since the end of the Vietnam War, relations between the United States and Vietnam have slowly improved. In 1994 the United States lifted its long-standing trade embargo against Vietnam. In 1995 the former enemies officially established diplomatic relations. It became more common for American veterans and tourists to visit Vietnam.

According to the 2000 census, more than a million Vietnamese immigrants now live in the United States. Vietnamese, Laotian, and Cambodian immigrants to the United States have made significant contributions to the communities they join, many of which are along the West and Gulf coasts.

GEOGRAPHY SKILLS **ANALYZING INFORMATION**

How did the relationship between Vietnam and the United States change from the end of the war to today?

330 CHAPTER 12

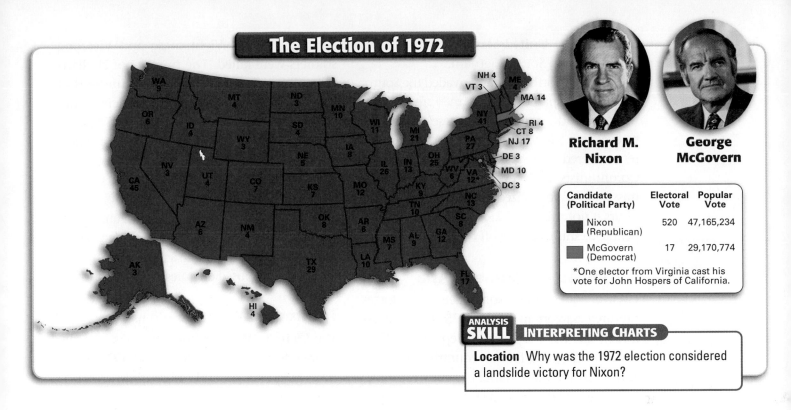

The Election of 1972

Richard M. Nixon

George McGovern

Candidate (Political Party)	Electoral Vote	Popular Vote
Nixon (Republican)	520	47,165,234
McGovern (Democrat)	17	29,170,774

*One elector from Virginia cast his vote for John Hospers of California.

ANALYSIS SKILL **INTERPRETING CHARTS**

Location Why was the 1972 election considered a landslide victory for Nixon?

Student protests erupted on hundreds of college campuses. On May 4, at Kent State University in Ohio, the National Guard was called in to break up a demonstration. When the students refused to leave, guard troops used tear gas. Some students began throwing rocks at the National Guard. Several guard troops then opened fire into the crowd. Four students were killed. Horrified by the killings, antiwar activists expanded their protests all over the nation.

Antiwar feelings grew in June 1971 when the *New York Times* published secret government documents known as the Pentagon Papers. These documents revealed that U.S. officials had been lying to the American public about the progress of the war for years.

Public opinion was hardening against the war as the 1972 presidential race began. Democratic candidate George McGovern was an outspoken opponent of the war who promised voters an immediate U.S. troop withdrawal from Vietnam. "The doors of government will be opened, and that brutal war will be closed," he said.

McGovern hoped to appeal to young voters, many of whom would be voting for the first time. The **Twenty-sixth Amendment**, which was ratified in 1971, lowered the federal voting age from 21 to 18. McGovern did win a majority of these younger voters in 1972, but a majority of voters over 21 from both parties supported Nixon. Many of these voters feared that a McGovern victory would lead to greater disorder and protests. Nixon won by a landslide, receiving 520 electoral votes to McGovern's 17.

READING CHECK **Drawing Conclusions** Why did McGovern lose in a landslide?

The Vietnam War Ends

While Nixon was running for re-election in 1972, Henry Kissinger continued peace negotiations with the North Vietnamese. On January 27, 1973, the United States signed a cease-fire called the Paris Peace Accords with representatives of North Vietnam, South Vietnam, and the Vietcong. The United States agreed to withdraw all its troops from Vietnam. North Vietnam agreed to return all American prisoners of war. Despite the peace agreement, fighting broke out between North and South Vietnam

FOCUS ON READING

What is a purpose you can set for reading this section?

in 1974. The United States refused to send troops back to South Vietnam.

In 1975 North Vietnam invaded the South. Thousands of panic-stricken American Embassy workers and South Vietnamese scrambled to evacuate Saigon. "The city was in flames," remembered one American worker. "And the Communists had the city surrounded with missiles . . . We realized that we were down to hours if not minutes." Helicopters lifted many people to ships waiting off the coast.

THE IMPACT TODAY

Today the U.S. government is more prepared to meet the needs of veterans with post-traumatic stress disorder. It offers counseling and information to vets and their families on how to deal with symptoms of trauma.

The Impact in Southeast Asia

The war ended when North Vietnamese forces captured Saigon in April 1975. Communist leaders created the Socialist Republic of Vietnam, uniting the former countries of North and South Vietnam. Hanoi became the capital, and Saigon was renamed Ho Chi Minh City.

Life remained extremely difficult in Vietnam. Cities, villages, forests, and farms had been destroyed. Some 250,000 South Vietnamese soldiers died in the war. About 1 million North Vietnamese and Vietcong soldiers were killed. The number of civilians killed is estimated at 2 million. Hundreds of thousands of former soldiers, officials, and other professionals were forced to live in "re-education camps." Another 1.5 million Vietnamese fled the country—about half of them settling in the United States.

Communist dictators took over Laos and Cambodia in 1975. The Cambodian Communist army, the Khmer Rouge, killed about 1.5 million people in a massive campaign to destroy supposed enemies of communism.

The Impact at Home

The Vietnam War carried heavy costs for the United States as well. Some 58,000 Americans were killed, and more than 300,000 were wounded.

Returning American soldiers were not always welcomed home as heroes as other war veterans had been. Some were insulted by antiwar protesters. As veterans struggled

CASE STUDY **BIOGRAPHY**

Maya Ying Lin
1959–

Ohio-born Maya Lin was a 21-year-old architecture student when she designed the Vietnam Veterans Memorial. Her design was chosen from more than 1,400 proposed memorial designs. The memorial is a V-shaped black granite wall that lists the names of more than 58,000 dead and missing Americans. Explaining the design, Lin said, "It was important to me to be extremely honest; not be concerned with the politics of war, but the results. I wanted to bring the visitor a concrete realization of the great loss." The memorial is now one of the most-visited spots in Washington, D.C. Many visitors leave letters, flowers, or other objects at the memorial to honor loved ones.

Drawing Conclusions How does Lin's design achieve the goal she describes?

to readjust to civilian life, many suffered from post-traumatic stress disorder. This condition includes symptoms such as nightmares and flashbacks to traumatic experiences.

Another effect of the war was that Americans had less trust in government officials, including the president. This led to passage in 1973 of the **War Powers Act**, which requires the president to get congressional approval before committing U.S. troops to an armed struggle.

Americans took a step toward healing the wounds of the war with the 1982 dedication of the **Vietnam Veterans Memorial**. Designed by Maya Ying Lin, the black granite memorial lists the names of dead or missing American soldiers.

READING CHECK **Summarizing** What were the long-term effects of the Vietnam War?

SUMMARY AND PREVIEW American society was deeply divided by the Vietnam War. In the next chapter, you will read about how American life changed in the 1970s and 1980s.

Causes and Effects of the Vietnam War — QUICK FACTS

Long-Term Causes
- Fear of Communist expansion
- U.S. support of South Vietnam's government

Immediate Causes
- Gulf of Tonkin incident
- Communist attacks against South Vietnam

Vietnam War

Effects
- Many thousands of Americans and millions of Vietnamese killed and injured
- Vietnam united as a Communist nation
- Political divisions created in the United States
- Increased Vietnamese immigration to the United States

go.hrw.com
Online Quiz

Section 3 Assessment

Reviewing Ideas, Terms, and People

1. **a. Identify** What was **Students for a Democratic Society**?
   b. Elaborate How did **hippies** express their disapproval of traditional culture?
   c. Evaluate How did the Republicans win the presidential election of 1968?
2. **a. Explain** What was **Vietnamization**?
   b. Summarize Why did the Pentagon Papers fuel antiwar feelings?
   c. Elaborate How did the **Twenty-sixth Amendment** affect the 1972 presidential election?
3. **a. Recall** How did the Vietnam War end?
   b. Describe What was the experience of veterans returning home from Vietnam?
   c. Analyze Do you think U.S. leaders made the right decision in signing the Paris Peace Accords? Why or why not?

Critical Thinking

4. **Identifying Effects** Review your notes on the causes of the end of the Vietnam War. Then copy the graphic organizer below and use it to list the effects of the end of the war.

FOCUS ON WRITING

5. **Taking Notes on the Effects of the War** Take notes on the effects of the Vietnam War. How did it affect American politics? How did it affect American culture? How did it affect the American and Vietnamese people? How will you explain these effects to television viewers?

Social Studies Skills

Analysis   Critical Thinking   Civic Participation   Study

Using Primary Sources: Oral Histories

Define the Skill

An important part of history is understanding the lives and experiences of people in the past. Oral histories and personal memoirs are primary sources that help historians understand how people in the past acted and felt.

Oral histories are interviews in which people talk about events they participated in or witnessed. In personal memoirs, people write about their memories of such events. Both oral histories and personal memoirs are different from other kinds of primary sources because they can be written long after an event takes place. However, they both include descriptions of firsthand experiences.

Learn the Skill

Follow these guidelines to analyze oral histories and personal memoirs.

❶ Identify the situation that the oral history or memoir describes.

❷ Find the emotions or events that stand out in the description.

❸ Make a generalization about how the individual's experience helps us understand the time period or event. Do you think other people might have had similar experiences?

In the following quotation, Diana Dwan Poole describes her experience serving in the Army Nurse Corps in Vietnam.

"One of my rules was that nurses were not allowed to cry. The wounded and dying men in our care need our strength, I told them. We couldn't indulge in the luxury of our own feelings ... I was always straight with the soldiers. I would never say, 'Oh, you're going to be just fine,' if they were on their way out. I didn't lie."

Poole was a nurse in Vietnam. In this quotation, she describes working with other nurses and with wounded and dying patients. Her strength in the face of sadness and her honesty stand out.

Other nurses might have had experiences similar to Poole's. The nurses' situation—treating the wounded and the dying—also suggests the dangers soldiers faced.

Practice the Skill

Harold Bryant was a combat engineer in Vietnam. Read the primary source quotation from Bryant below.

"Today I'm constantly thinking about the war. I walk down streets different. I look at places where individuals could hide. Maybe assault me or rob me or just harass me. I hear things that other people can't hear. My wife, she had a habit at one time of buying cheap watches and leaving them on top of the dresser. I could hear it ticking, so she would put it in a drawer. I could still hear it ticking."

1. What situation does Bryant describe?
2. Based on this description, how do you think Bryant felt at the time?
3. How can Bryant's experience help us better understand soldiers serving in Vietnam?

HOLT

History's Impact
▶ **video series**
Review the video to answer
the closing question:
*How was the passing of the
War Powers Act a reaction to
the Vietnam War?*

Visual Summary

QUICK FACTS

*Use the visual summary below to help you review
the main ideas of the chapter.*

The spread of communism encouraged the United States to escalate the Vietnam War.

The Vietcong's superior knowledge of the geography helped them win the war.

Richard Nixon won the 1968 presidential election and pulled troops out of Vietnam.

Reviewing Vocabulary, Terms, and People

*Identify the descriptions below with the correct term or
person from the chapter.*

1. The Cuban rebel who overthrew an unpopular dictator and established a Communist government

2. A barrier made of concrete and barbed wire that separated East Berlin and West Berlin

3. The commander of U.S. ground forces in Vietnam who developed the strategy of search-and-destroy missions

4. Supporters of the Vietnam War who believed winning the Cold War took priority over domestic reform

5. The Republican nominee who won the 1968 election for president of the United States

6. The amendment that lowered the voting age from 21 to 18

Comprehension and Critical Thinking

SECTION 1 *(Pages 314–320)*

7. a. Recall What is the Peace Corps?

b. Sequence Describe the sequence of events that led to American astronauts landing on the moon in 1969.

c. Evaluate How do you think the Cuban missile crisis would have ended had the United States pursued air strikes or an invasion of Cuba?

SECTION 2 *(Pages 321–325)*

8. a. Define What is guerrilla warfare?

b. Describe How did the American military try to disrupt the Ho Chi Minh Trail?

c. Predict Do you think Americans' opinions about the war would have been different had there been no television reporting? Explain your answer.

9. a. Identify What was the War Powers Act?

b. Explain What was Henry Kissinger's role in the Vietnam War?

c. Summarize What long-term effects did the Vietnam War have on the United States?

Reviewing Themes

10. Geography How did the geography of Vietnam help the Vietcong?

11. Geography How did the geography of Vietnam affect American forces?

Reading Skills

Setting a Purpose *Use the Reading Skills taught in this chapter to answer the question about the reading selection below.*

Johnson Commits to Victory

Lyndon B. Johnson was determined to prevent Communists from taking over in South Vietnam. "We have the resources and the will to follow this course as long as it may take," Johnson said . . . .

The Tonkin Gulf Resolution

In the summer of 1964, a naval skirmish led to a rapid expansion of U.S. involvement in Vietnam. On August 2, 1964, the USS *Maddox* reportedly exchanged gunfire with North Vietnamese torpedo boats in the Gulf of Tonkin, off the North Vietnamese coast . . . . *(p. 321)*

12. Which of the following is an example of a purpose you could set for the passage above?

a. Find out why the Vietnam War was fought.

b. Find out Johnson's view of the Vietnam War.

c. Find out when the Vietnam War ended.

d. Find out what the Vietnam Veterans Memorial is.

Social Studies Skills

Using Primary Sources: Oral Histories *Read this passage from marine officer Philip Caputo. Then use the Social Studies Skills taught in this chapter to answer the question below.*

> "You simply trusted absolutely no one. I mean, from a 5-year-old kid to a 75-year-old woman." *(p. 323)*

13. How do you think Caputo felt about not being able to trust anyone? Do you think he felt safe? Why or why not?

Using the Internet go.hrw.com

14. Activity: Mapping the Terrain Geography played a very important role in the Vietnam War. American soldiers struggled to fight against enemy soldiers who knew the land and were able to use that knowledge to their advantage. Enter the activity keyword and find information about the geography of Southeast Asia. Then create a map showing the area's various geographic features. Include notes on the map that describe some of the geographical challenges American soldiers faced.

FOCUS ON WRITING

15. Presenting Your Newscast Review your notes and prepare your newscast. You will have about five minutes for your newscast. Include several segments on different topics from the chapter. One could be an interview with a friend in the role of a soldier back from Vietnam, a government official, or an antiwar protester. You can also use pictures to illustrate the events you are reporting. Write your script and practice reading it before your presentation.

Grade 8 Intermediate-Level Test Preparation

Directions (1–7): **For each statement or question, write on the separate answer sheet the *number* of the word or expression that, of those given, best completes the statement or answers the question.**

1 The Berlin Wall separated

(1) Eastern Europe and Western Europe.

(2) East Berlin and West Berlin.

(3) West Germany and the Soviet Union.

(4) East Germany and the Soviet Union.

2 Upon walking in the moon for the first time, which astronaut said, "That's on small step for [a] man, one giant leap for mankind."?

(1) Alan Shepard, Jr.

(2) Buzz Aldrin

(3) Neil Armstrong

(4) John Glenn

3 President Johnson's policy of escalation called for

(1) a gradual withdrawal of U.S. troops from Vietnam.

(2) an immediate withdrawal of U.S. troops from Vietnam.

(3) a rapid buildup of U.S. forces in Vietnam.

(4) expanding the war into Laos and Cambodia.

4 What was a major influence that turned public opinion against the war in Vietnam?

(1) television reports from the battlefield

(2) trouble with the economy

(3) radio stories about battles

(4) antiwar protestors

5 The Pentagon Papers revealed that

(1) the Bay of Pigs invasion was a disaster.

(2) U.S. officials had been lying about the progress of the war.

(3) the USS *Maddox* was attacked by North Vietnamese torpedo boats.

(4) the War Powers Act was ineffective.

6 Which of the following contributed to Richard Nixon's victory in the 1972 presidential election?

(1) success of the Vietnamization strategy

(2) the Tonkin Gulf resolution

(3) passage of the Twenty-sixth Amendment lowering the federal voting age to 18

(4) violence at the Democratic convention in Chicago, which weakened McGovern

7 What was the main purpose of the War Powers Act?

(1) It allowed President Kennedy to blockade Cuba.

(2) It allowed President Johnson to expand the U.S. role in Vietnam.

(3) It repealed the Tonkin Gulf Resolution.

(4) It limited the right of any president to commit troops to an armed struggle.

Base your answer to question 8 on the text below and on your knowledge of social studies.

> "On Tuesday morning, October 16, 1962, shortly after 9:00, President Kennedy called and asked me to come to the White House. He said only that we were facing great trouble. Shortly afterward, in his office, he told me that a U-2 had just finished a photographic mission and that the Intelligence Community had become convinced that Russia was placing missiles and atomic weapons in Cuba."
>
> —Robert F. Kennedy, *Thirteen Days: A Memoir of the Cuban Missile Crisis*

8 Constructed-Response Question What clues can you read that tell you how frightening the Cuban missile crisis was for Americans?

The Nation in the 20th Century

Part A: Short-Answer Questions

Directions: Read and examine the following documents. Then, on a separate sheet of paper, answer the questions using complete sentences.

DOCUMENT 1

From 1945 to 1949, there were a total of 12 Nuremberg trials. The first trial focused on Nazis of high rank or status. Later trials focused on doctors who performed medical experiments on prisoners. When chief American attorney Robert H. Jackson gave his opening statement at the first trial, he included powerful reasons why the hearings were important.

> The wrongs which we seek to condemn and punish have been so calculated [well planned], so malignant [evil] and devastating, that civilization cannot tolerate their being ignored because it cannot survive their being repeated.
>
> —**Robert H. Jackson,** quoted in *The Nuremberg Trial*, edited by Mitchell Bard

1a. According to Jackson, why is it important that the world pay attention to the crimes the Nazi officials were accused of?

_____

1b. Why does Jackson point out that these crimes were "so calculated" and "so malignant"?

_____

DOCUMENT 2

Herbert Block (1909–2001) was one of the most well-known American political cartoonists of the 20th century. He signed his cartoons "Herblock," a combination of his first and last names. He started working at the Washington Post in 1946. His work appeared in that newspaper and in many others for more than 50 years. The Washington Post published this cartoon on June 17, 1949.

2a. What does the man believe he will accomplish by putting out the fire?

_____

2b. Why do you think Block called this drawing "Fire!"? How does the title help Block make his point?

_____

In the 1950s, many people believed that women should stay home to take care of their husbands and families rather than get a job outside the house. However, some women wanted to do other things with their lives. In 1993, a writer published a book of interviews with women about what it was like to live during this time.

> There was always the assumption, even when I was getting my graduate degree in education, that any work I did was temporary, something to do until I assumed [began] my principal role in life which was to be the perfect wife and mother, supported by my husband.
>
> —**Sally Ann Carter,** quoted in *The Fifties: A Women's Oral History*, by Brett Harvey

3a. What was this woman's main role in life supposed to be?

_____

3b. Are women treated the same or differently today? In what ways?

_____

The Cuban missile crisis brought the world perilously close to nuclear war. As Soviet ships steamed toward Cuba, Americans were glued to televisions and radios, waiting to see what would happen. This statement by Robert F. Kennedy, describing what it was like to be in the White House as decisions were being made, shows that even the nation's leaders were unsure of how the crisis would end.

> I think these few minutes were the time of gravest concern for the President. Was the world on the brink of a holocaust? Was it our error? A mistake? Was there something further that should have been done? Or not done?. . . The minutes in the Cabinet Room ticked slowly by. What could we say now—what could we do? Then it was 10:25—a messenger brought in a note . . . Mr. President . . . some of the Russian ships have stopped dead in the water . . . Six ships . . . have stopped or have turned back toward the Soviet Union' . . . Then we were back to the details. The meeting droned on. But everyone looked like a different person. For a moment the world had stood still, and now it was going around again.
>
> —**Robert F. Kennedy,** from *Thirteen Days: A Memoir of the Cuban Missile Crisis*

4a. What is the mood of the first paragraph?

_____

4b. What is Kennedy trying to express in his last sentence?

_____

Part B: Essay

Historical Context: The documents on these two pages reflect the political and social issues affecting the United States in the middle of the 20th century.

TASK: Using information from the four documents and your knowledge of U.S. history, write an essay in which you:

- discuss one of the issues affecting the United States in the middle of the 20th century.
- describe how this issue affect life in the United States today.

Modern America

What You Will Learn…

By the end of the Vietnam War, Americans were living in a society very different from previous eras. Economic and political changes continue today. People are choosing new kinds of jobs in new industries, and the role of the United States in international affairs is increasing. Rapid advances in technology will also affect the future of American society. As the population becomes larger and more diverse, new solutions are needed to provide all Americans with equality and opportunity.

Explore the Art
Millennium Park in Chicago was designed to be an exciting public place for the people of the large city to enjoy. How might the people of Chicago use the park?

CHAPTER **13** 1968–1988

Searching for Order

FOCUS QUESTION

How has America reacted to the challenges of the modern world?

FOCUS ON WRITING

Writing an Autobiographical Sketch When you read about history, it can be difficult to imagine how the events you read about affected ordinary people. In this chapter you will read about the important people, events, and conflicts of the 1970s and 1980s. Then you will write an autobiography of a fictional character, telling how these events affected him or her. Your fictional character can live in any part of the United States and have any job. He or she might be an immigrant from the Middle East, the owner of a gas station, or an environmental activist.

UNITED STATES

1968 Richard Nixon is elected president.

1969

1969 Golda Meir becomes prime minister of Israel.

WORLD

The Washington Star

What You Will Learn...

Americans celebrated their nation's 200th birthday on July 4, 1976, with celebrations across the country. As you will read in the chapter, this celebration was a welcome distraction from difficult times. A major political scandal had weakened Americans' trust in government. Economic troubles, soaring oil prices, and international crises shook many Americans' confidence in the future.

NY

1979
A government report sites toxic waste in Love Canal as a cause of local residents' poor health.

1970
America celebrates its first Earth Day.

1974
Nixon resigns the presidency. Gerald Ford is sworn in.

1976 Jimmy Carter is elected president.

1979 The Three Mile Island accident creates doubts about nuclear energy.

1985
Ronald Reagan is sworn in to his second term as president.

1970

1973 Egypt and Syria attack Israel.

1975

1975 South Vietnam surrenders to North Vietnam.

1979 The Soviet Union invades Afghanistan.

1980

1985

Focus on Themes In this chapter, you will learn about issues faced by several modern presidents. You will also read about crises in the **economy** and in **politics** that changed the way Americans viewed their role as a nation. Finally, you will learn about American society in the 1970s.

Summarizing

Focus on Reading After reading a large amount of information, you can summarize it into a shorter amount that is easier for you to understand.

Understanding Summarizing Using the ideas and information presented in a book can be easier if you summarize what the author is saying. When you summarize, you can use some of the key ideas and words to write your own sentences that explain the information. When you write a summary, some details can be left out.

Read the following passage and its summary. Notice which details the author chose to include and which to leave out.

The American population was changing in the 1970s. Throughout American history, most immigrants to the United States had come from Europe. Beginning in the 1970s, however, a majority of new immigrants came from the Americas and Asia. This pattern continues today.

From Chapter 13, p. 352

Summary:

The population immigrating to the United States began changing during the 1970s. Now the majority of immigrants come from Latin America and Asia.

This passage contains most of the same information but is shorter. Not all of the information is included.

You Try It!

The following passage is from the chapter you are getting ready to read. As you read the passage, look for information that is important enough to go in a summary.

"Are you better off than you were four years ago?" That was the question Republican candidate Ronald Reagan asked voters during the 1980 presidential campaign. Millions of voters answered "No," giving Reagan an easy victory over President Carter. Reagan won 489 electoral votes to Carter's 49. On January 20, 1981—the day of Reagan's inauguration—Iran finally released the American hostages after 444 days in captivity.

From Chapter 13, p. 357

After you read the passage, answer the following questions.

1. Do you think the campaign slogan from the passage above is essential information for a summary of the election?

2. Do you think the number of electoral votes should be included in your summary?

3. Write a two-sentence summary of the passage above.

Key Terms and People

Chapter 13

Section 1
stagflation *(p. 347)*
Organization of Petroleum Exporting Countries *(p. 347)*
realpolitik *(p. 348)*
Strategic Arms Limitation Talks *(p. 348)*
détente *(p. 348)*
Watergate *(p. 349)*
Gerald Ford *(p. 350)*
pardon *(p. 351)*

Section 2
affirmative action *(p. 353)*
Rachel Carson *(p. 353)*
Jimmy Carter *(p. 354)*
human rights *(p. 355)*
apartheid *(p. 355)*
sanctions *(p. 355)*
Camp David Accords *(p. 355)*
Iran hostage crisis *(p. 356)*

Section 3
Ronald Reagan *(p. 357)*
supply-side economics *(p. 358)*
deficit *(p. 358)*
Iran-Contra affair *(p. 359)*
Mikhail Gorbachev *(p. 360)*

Academic Vocabulary

In this chapter, you will learn the following academic words:
consequences *(p. 350)*
implications *(p. 358)*

As you read Chapter 13, practice summarizing the information from several paragraphs.

Nixon's Presidency and Watergate

TAKING NOTES Create a concept web like the one below. Fill in the outer ovals with facts about Nixon's domestic policy, foreign policy, and the Watergate scandal.

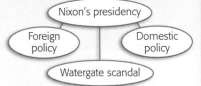

If YOU were there...

You experienced a decade of conflict and change in the 1960s. You were a witness to major events in the civil rights movement, and you lived through frightening Cold War crises. You saw leaders assassinated and astronauts walk on the moon. You have some friends who fought in Vietnam and others who led antiwar protests.

Do you think the United States is now headed in the right direction? Why or why not?

BUILDING BACKGROUND Protests over the Vietnam War led to bitter divisions among Americans in the 1960s. When Republican Richard Nixon ran for president in 1968, he said he would work to restore law and order to American society. Nixon won a close election over Democratic candidate Hubert Humphrey.

Domestic Challenges

As president, Richard Nixon promised to work on behalf of Americans who opposed protests and supported his plan for ending the war. Nixon called these Americans the Silent Majority. He criticized student protesters and called on them to stop their activities. He did not believe Americans should leave Vietnam quickly.

New Federalism

Nixon also had a new plan for government. Nixon knew that his supporters blamed the federal government for setting high taxes and interfering in citizens' lives. He proposed a plan called the New Federalism, which would limit the power of the federal government. His policies represented a major shift in direction from Lyndon Johnson's Great Society ideas. Under Nixon's plan, grants of money from the federal government went directly to state and local governments, who decided how to spend the money. This plan reflected Nixon's conservatism, or a belief in limiting the involvement of government in citizens' lives.

CONNECT TO ECONOMICS

Rising oil prices in the early 1970s had a major impact on the U.S. economy. Because oil was more expensive, the cost of everything made from oil—gasoline, heating oil, electricity, and other key products—also shot up. These higher prices led to rising inflation.

U.S. Inflation Rates, 1970–1985

Percent change from previous year

World Oil Prices, 1970–1985

Dollars per barrel

ANALYSIS SKILL ANALYZING GRAPHS

Comparing How were trends in oil prices and inflation similar during the 1970s?

President Nixon promised to reduce welfare spending and to restore law and order. He supported policies that gave more power to police and to the courts.

His political philosophy affected the Supreme Court as well. As president, he appointed four new justices. Many Court decisions soon began to reflect a more conservative point of view.

Nixon did not push for new civil rights legislation. He believed that the government had done enough in the 1960s, saying, "The laws have caught up with our consciences."

Economic Troubles

Nixon faced the difficult economic challenge of so-called **stagflation**—the economic condition of combined stagnant economic growth and high inflation. From 1967 to 1974, rising prices reduced the purchasing power of the U.S. dollar by more than 30 percent.

One cause of inflation was the rising cost of oil. By the early 1970s, the United States was importing about one-third of its oil. Much of this oil was purchased from Middle Eastern nations that were members of the **Organization of Petroleum Exporting Countries**, or OPEC. This group worked to control the production and sale of oil to keep prices high.

Most OPEC countries were Arab countries that had been opposed to the creation of the Jewish state of Israel. On October 6, 1973, the Jewish holy day of Yom Kippur, Egypt and Syria attacked Israel in what would become known as the Yom Kippur War. The United States sent military supplies to help Israel.

OPEC members responded angrily to support for Israel by declaring an embargo, or ban, on oil sales to the United States. The oil embargo and soaring oil prices caused an energy crisis. This worsened an already weak U.S. economy.

THE IMPACT TODAY

Today about half of U.S. oil imports comes from OPEC countries.

READING CHECK Identifying Cause and Effect
What was one cause of inflation?

Nixon's Foreign Policy

As the energy crisis demonstrated, international events could have a serious impact on life in the United States. Henry Kissinger, a German American professor who became Nixon's senior foreign policy adviser, helped Nixon develop a new approach to foreign policy. Nixon's foreign policy decisions would be based on practical American interests, not on moral or political ideals. This approach was known as **realpolitik**, the German term meaning "actual politics." Nixon credited his realpolitik strategies with bringing an end to the Vietnam War by using political pressure from the Soviet Union and China to convince the North Vietnamese to negotiate.

Realpolitik was controversial. In several Latin American countries, for example, the United States backed harsh military governments because they were friendly to U.S. interests.

In the ongoing Cold War rivalries with China and the Soviet Union, the realpolitik approach led to important changes. American officials had long feared China and the Soviet Union would work together to spread communism. But by 1970, it was clear that these two Communist powers had become bitter rivals. Nixon believed it was in America's interest to widen this split and to improve U.S. relations with both Communist powers.

Nixon first turned his attention to China. He lifted restrictions on trade and travel and opened negotiations with its leaders. In 1972 Nixon became the first U.S. president to make an official visit to China. Newscasts showed Nixon and Chinese leader Mao Zedong shaking hands and trading jokes.

Nixon's trip led to improved U.S.–China relations. It also caught the attention of Soviet leaders, who became more open to talks with the United States. In May 1972 Nixon flew to Moscow, where he and Soviet leader Leonid Brezhnev participated in the **Strategic Arms Limitation Talks** (SALT). These talks led to a treaty limiting each country's nuclear weapons. The SALT agreement opened a period of **détente** (day-TAHNT), or less hostile relations, between the United States and the Soviet Union. Détente brought economic benefits, as the Soviets began buying millions of tons of grain from American farmers.

READING CHECK Supporting a Point of View
Do you think realpolitik was a good strategy? Why or why not?

The Watergate Scandal

On June 17, 1972, five men were arrested while breaking in to the Democratic National Committee's offices at the Watergate Hotel in Washington, D.C. The burglars were carrying camera equipment and secret recording devices. Police soon discovered that some of them had ties to the Nixon administration. One had worked for the Committee to Reelect the President (CRP).

Nixon denied that anyone in his administration was involved in the Watergate break-in. He went on to win the 1972 election in a landslide. But early in Nixon's second term,

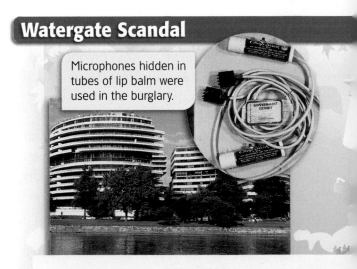

Watergate Scandal

Microphones hidden in tubes of lip balm were used in the burglary.

On May 28, 1972, five men burglarized the Democratic National Committee headquarters in the Watergate Hotel, shown here. They took pictures of files and bugged telephones. The burglars returned for more information on June 17 and were arrested.

the seemingly minor break-in exploded into a massive political scandal that became known as **Watergate**.

Investigating the Break-in

Did Nixon administration officials have anything to do with the Watergate break-in? Reporters Bob Woodward and Carl Bernstein investigated that question in a series of articles in the *Washington Post*. Key figures in the Nixon administration refused to talk to the reporters. Then Woodward was contacted by a government official who had inside information on the Watergate investigation. To protect the identity of their source, Woodward called him by a secret codename. With the informant's information, Woodward and Bernstein began publishing stories about illegal activities by Nixon administration officials. The stories revealed that the CRP had hidden illegal campaign contributions and spread false rumors about Democratic candidates. They also presented evidence that officials in the Nixon White House were trying to cover-up the facts of the Watergate break-in.

Americans watched the Watergate drama unfold through the intense media coverage of the scandal.

A Senate committee led by Senator Sam Ervin launched its own investigation of Watergate. When the committee began televised hearings in May 1973, millions of Americans tuned in. The most damaging witness was former White House attorney John Dean, who testified that Nixon was personally involved in the Watergate cover-up. Dean could not prove this, however. Then another witness revealed that Nixon had tape-recorded almost all of his Oval Office conversations.

THE IMPACT TODAY

The identity of the *Post's* informant remained confidential for more than 30 years. In 2005 W. Mark Felt, second-in-command at the FBI during Watergate, revealed that he was the inside source for information.

Washington Post reporters soon linked the break-in to the presidential re-election campaign. A White House cover-up began.

The Senate formed a committee to investigate the break-in and possible cover-up. Its hearings (shown above) were televised.

Faced with impeachment for an illegal cover-up of the break-in, Nixon resigned. He was later pardoned by President Gerald Ford.

ANALYSIS SKILL **ANALYZING INFORMATION**

Why was Nixon threatened with impeachment by the House?

SUPREME COURT DECISIONS

United States v. Nixon (1974)

Background of the Case During the Watergate investigation, a special prosecutor asked for the tapes of President Nixon's Oval Office conversations. Nixon claimed that he did not have to obey court orders to turn over the tapes because of executive privilege. On July 8, 1974, the case went before the Supreme Court.

The Court's Ruling

The Supreme Court announced its unanimous decision on July 24. It stated, "the legitimate [lawful] needs of the judicial process may outweigh presidential privilege." Nixon could not use executive privilege to avoid the subpoenas.

The Court's Reasoning

The Court decided to hear the case more quickly than most cases because of its importance to the functioning of government and the interest of the American public. The Supreme Court ruled that to claim executive privilege a president would have to show a compelling national security reason. Nixon had no such reason for refusing to hand over the tapes.

Why It Matters

The Supreme Court ruling showed that, despite their unique and important position, presidents do have to obey the law. It also showed that the government could use the powers defined in the Constitution to prevent one branch from becoming too powerful. Less than a week later, the House Judiciary Committee voted to impeach Nixon.

ANALYSIS SKILL · ANALYZING INFORMATION

1. How is this case an example of the checks and balances system?
2. What do you think was the most important impact of this Supreme Court decision?

ACADEMIC VOCABULARY
consequences
the effects of a particular event or events

Committee members asked Nixon to allow them to listen to the tapes. Nixon refused to hand the tapes over to a special prosecutor, claiming executive privilege—a president's right to keep information secret for reasons of national security. In July 1974 the Supreme Court ordered Nixon to turn over the tapes. The recordings proved that Nixon had directed the Watergate cover-up and lied about it to Congress and the public.

While this investigation was unfolding, Vice President Spiro Agnew resigned amid charges that he had taken bribes and failed to pay taxes. Nixon appointed Michigan senator **Gerald Ford** as vice president.

Nixon Resigns

After studying the case, the House Judiciary Committee recommended impeachment. Judiciary Committee member Barbara Jordan of Texas explained why she thought Nixon should be impeached:

" My faith in the Constitution is whole, it is complete, it is total. And I am not going to sit here and be an idle spectator to the ... destruction of the Constitution. "

—Barbara Jordan, in a speech before Congress, 1974

On July 27, 1974, the committee approved its first article of impeachment, charging Nixon with obstruction of justice. Within the next week, two more articles were approved by the committee, one for the abuse of power and one for contempt of Congress.

On August 8, 1974, Nixon appeared on national television and announced, "I shall resign the presidency effective at noon tomorrow." He became the first president in American history to resign from office. Gerald Ford was sworn in as president on August 9.

One of the **consequences** of Watergate was that many Americans lost faith in government officials. In a poll taken in 1974, just 36 percent of Americans said they trusted the government. Others, however, saw a more positive side of Watergate. Senator Sam Ervin viewed the hearings and Nixon's resignation as evidence that the government was able to rid itself of corruption. "Watergate . . . proved our Constitution works," he said.

READING CHECK Sequencing What events led to Nixon's impeachment?

Ford as President

Vice President Gerald Ford became the first modern president to hold the office without being elected to it. Ford lost some public support when he granted Richard Nixon a **pardon**, or freedom from punishment. He declared it was best for the nation that Nixon not be tried for his crimes because he would be "cruelly and excessively penalized" and "ugly passions would again be aroused [stirred]."

Adding to Ford's difficulties, oil prices and unemployment remained high, and stagflation continued. The United States also had an increasing trade deficit, an imbalance in which a country imports more than it exports.

Arguing that inflation was the main cause of the economic troubles, Ford began a campaign called Whip Inflation Now (WIN). WIN encouraged people to save money and businesses to hold down wages and prices. Ford's plan met with resistance from many members of Congress, who wanted to increase spending to help the poor and unemployed. In 1975

A U.S. Marine changes the official presidential photograph from one of Nixon to one of Ford.

Ford and Congress began to compromise. Still, inflation and unemployment remained high.

READING CHECK **Evaluating** Do you think President Ford was right to pardon Nixon?

SUMMARY AND PREVIEW Gerald Ford became president after the Watergate scandal ended Nixon's presidency. In the next section you will learn about life in the 1970s.

FOCUS ON NEW YORK CITY

In 1975 the government of New York City asked the federal government to provide funds for the city to cover its debts. President Gerald Ford refused, prompting the *New York Daily News* to run one of its most famous headlines: "Ford to City: Drop Dead." Although it eventually backed Ford for reelection the newspaper is sometimes blamed with Ford's defeat in the state.

---

go.hrw.com
Online Quiz

Section 1 Assessment

Reviewing Ideas, Terms, and People

1. **a. Describe** What challenges did the United States face during President Nixon's terms of office?
   b. Make Inferences Why do you think the **Organization of Petroleum Exporting Countries** objected to U.S. support for Israel?
2. **a. Identify** Who was Henry Kissinger?
   b. Contrast How was **realpolitik** different from other foreign policy approaches?
   c. Draw Conclusions Why do you think improved U.S.–China relations made the Soviets more open to talks with the United States?
3. **a. Recall** What was the **Watergate** scandal?
   b. Explain Why were President Nixon's tapes important?
   c. Elaborate Why do you think President Nixon decided to resign?
4. **a. Describe** How did **Gerald Ford** become president of the United States?
   b. Predict Do you think WIN was effective in helping the economy?

Critical Thinking

5. **Sequencing** Review your notes on Richard Nixon's presidency. Then copy the graphic organizer below and use it to list, in order, events in his presidency.

Event	Date

FOCUS ON WRITING

6. **Describing Major Events** Take notes on Nixon's domestic policy, Cold War strategy, and the Watergate scandal. What were the major events of this time period? Who were the major public figures involved, and what roles did they play? Which of these events and people would have had the greatest effect on your fictional character?

America in the 1970s

What You Will Learn...

Main Ideas

1. American society debated key social issues during the 1970s.
2. Jimmy Carter was elected president in 1976.
3. Carter had successes as well as failures in foreign policy during his administration.

The Big Idea

Americans faced major challenges both at home and around the world in the 1970s.

Key Terms and People

affirmative action, *p. 353*
Rachel Carson, *p. 353*
Jimmy Carter, *p. 354*
human rights, *p. 355*
apartheid, *p. 355*
sanctions, *p. 355*
Camp David Accords, *p. 355*
Iran hostage crisis, *p. 356*

TAKING NOTES As you read, take notes on new government policies in the 1970s. Write your notes in a chart like this one.

New Policies

If YOU were there...

It is July 4, 1976. Today the entire nation is celebrating the 200th anniversary of the signing of the Declaration of Independence. As you sit with your family watching a spectacular fireworks show, you think about the challenges this country has faced throughout its history. You think about the economic and foreign policy challenges facing Americans right now.

What are your hopes for the nation's future?

BUILDING BACKGROUND The celebration of the country's bicentennial, or 200th birthday, was a much-needed break from worries about political scandals, economic troubles, and Cold War dangers. This was a moment of renewal and hope—though many Americans still disagreed about how the country should move forward.

Social Issues of the 1970s

The American population was changing in the 1970s. Throughout American history, most immigrants to the United States had come from Europe. Beginning in the 1970s, however, a majority of new immigrants came from the Americas and Asia. This pattern continues today. Another change was that the birthrate, or number of births per 1,000 people, was declining. By 1970 Americans 65 and older became one of the fastest-growing population groups.

As the population grew and changed, American society faced the challenges of how to balance the views of all Americans. You read earlier that the Equal Rights Amendment caused nationwide debate in the 1970s. Although the ERA was not ratified, the women's movement did make important gains. A 1972 federal law known as Title IX banned discrimination on the basis of sex in educational programs that receive federal funds. The number of women admitted to medical and law schools climbed quickly. Title IX also opened the door for many more women to participate in college sports and earn athletic scholarships. In 1973 the Supreme Court legalized abortion in the case *Roe* v. *Wade*.

In the 1970s Americans also debated **affirmative action** , the practice of giving special consideration to nonwhites or women to make up for past discrimination. Supporters of affirmative action argued that it was needed to improve educational and job opportunities for minorities and women. Opponents insisted that any race- or gender-based preferences were unfair.

Many African Americans benefited from new opportunities in the 1970s. For example, the number of African Americans attending college in 1976 was four times higher than it had been a decade earlier. Many people credited affirmative action programs with this increase.

The environment also became a major issue in the 1970s. In her book *Silent Spring*, biologist **Rachel Carson** brought attention to the dangers of pollution. She explained how chemicals used to kills insects traveled through the food chain and affect people's health.

" Man, however much he may like to pretend the contrary, is part of nature. Can he escape a pollution that is now so thoroughly distributed throughout our world? *"*

—Rachel Carson, *Silent Spring*

First published in 1962, *Silent Spring* helped inspire a nationwide movement to improve the environment. Environmentalists in the United States celebrated the first Earth Day on April 22, 1970. "Earth Day is to remind each person of his [or her] . . . equal responsibility . . . to preserve and improve the Earth," explained activists.

Congress passed new laws to limit the release of pollutants. The Environmental Protection Agency (EPA) was established in 1970 to enforce these laws. As protections increased, debates sprung up about how to balance business interests with environmental concerns.

READING CHECK **Comparing and Contrasting** How are Title IX and affirmative action similar and different?

Issues of the 1970s

Environmental protection, women's rights, and affirmative action were among the major issues of the 1970s.

Activists brought the environment to the forefront of national debate, urging legislation and individual action to help protect the Earth.

Supporters of the Equal Rights Amendment urged states to ratify the amendment they believed would ensure equal protection to women under the Constitution.

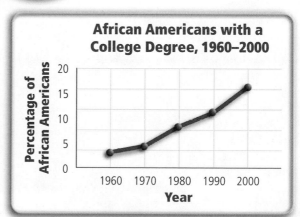

African Americans with a College Degree, 1960–2000

Affirmative action helped African Americans and other minorities gain access to universities and certain jobs but also created much debate.

**FOCUS ON
NEW YORK CITY**

The second oil
crisis of the 1970s
was triggered
when the U.S.-
backed regime in
Iran fell to funda-
mentalist Islamic
revolutionaries.
In the turmoil
surrounding Iran's
new government,
exports of oil to
the United States
declined. This
contributed to
gasoline short-
ages, such as
New Yorkers
experienced on
July 4, 1979, when
nine out of ten gas
stations closed
because they were
out of gas.

Carter Elected

To oppose Republican Gerald Ford in the 1976 presidential election Democrats nominated **Jimmy Carter**, a little-known former governor of Georgia. The Democrats purposely chose a candidate who was untouched by the recent scandals. Carter knew that the Vietnam War and Watergate had badly shaken American voters' trust in government. "I will never lie to you," he told voters.

Carter defeated Ford in a close election. As president, Carter wanted to show a new spirit of informality and openness at the White House. On inauguration day, he and his family broke with tradition by walking to the inauguration rather than riding in a limousine.

While Americans seemed to respond positively to his straightforward style, Carter faced serious challenges. High unemployment and inflation continued. The ongoing energy crisis also kept oil prices high. Many Americans became frustrated with the president's inability to solve these problems.

Although Democrats controlled Congress, Carter had a hard time convincing members to support his proposals. For example, Carter proposed a national energy plan that called for conservation and the use of alternative fuels such as solar energy. Congress demanded changes to the complex plan. The plan was never fully enacted.

One way Carter hoped to decrease the country's dependence on imported oil was by expanding the use of nuclear power. But an accident at the Three Mile Island nuclear power plant in Pennsylvania caused new worries about the safety of nuclear energy. On March 28, 1979, a reactor core at Three Mile Island overheated, and the plant released a small amount of radioactive gas into the air. This frightening incident damaged the nuclear power industry, and the federal government put in place a ban on building new reactors.

READING CHECK **Drawing Conclusions** How did the Three Mile Island incident affect Carter's energy plan?

Carter and Foreign Policy

President Carter rejected Nixon's realpolitik approach to foreign policy. He argued that "fairness, not force, should lie at the heart of our dealings with the nations of the world."

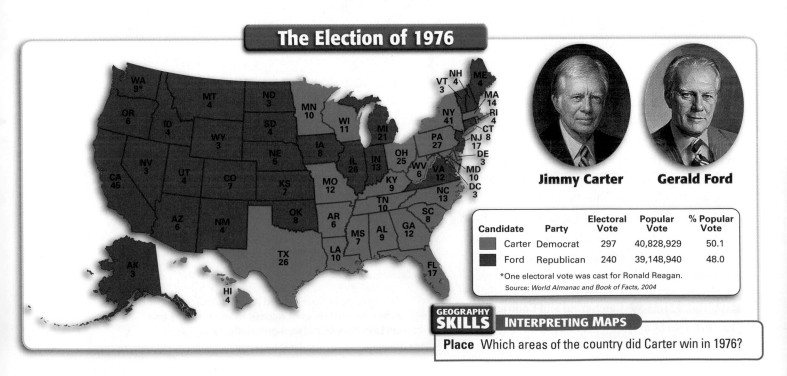

The Election of 1976

Candidate	Party	Electoral Vote	Popular Vote	% Popular Vote
Carter	Democrat	297	40,828,929	50.1
Ford	Republican	240	39,148,940	48.0

*One electoral vote was cast for Ronald Reagan.
Source: *World Almanac and Book of Facts, 2004*

Jimmy Carter   Gerald Ford

GEOGRAPHY SKILLS **INTERPRETING MAPS**

Place Which areas of the country did Carter win in 1976?

Primary Source

HISTORIC DOCUMENT
The Camp David Accords

During the long and often bitter Camp David negotiations, Carter worked hard to keep Israel's Menachem Begin and Egypt's Anwar el-Sadat from walking out. He later wrote about one moment when the talks nearly broke down.

"Within a few minutes Sadat announced angrily that a stalemate [standstill] had been reached. He saw no reason for the discussions to continue. As far as he was concerned, they were over . . . They [Sadat and Begin] were moving toward the door, but I got in front of them to partially block the way. I urged them not to break off their talks, to give me another chance to use my influence and analysis, to have confidence in me. Begin agreed readily. I looked straight at Sadat; finally, he nodded his head. They left without speaking to each other.**"**

Leaders Anwar el-Sadat (left), Jimmy Carter, and Menachem Begin reached a peace agreement for the Middle East in the Camp David Accords.

ANALYSIS SKILL **ANALYZING PRIMARY SOURCES**

Why do you think Begin and el-Sadat agreed to continue their negotiations?

Changing Policies

Carter favored policies that promoted **human rights**—the basic rights and freedoms of all people. He reduced U.S. aid to several former allies that committed human rights violations. In South Africa, Carter hoped to pressure the government into ending **apartheid**, a system of laws requiring racial segregation. He called for **sanctions**, or economic penalties, to encourage reform.

Carter's approach to foreign policy had effects in Latin America as well. Many Latin Americans resented previous U.S. interference in their countries. American control of the Panama Canal stood as a symbol of power in the region. In 1977 Carter signed treaties that would transfer control of the canal to Panama by the year 2000.

Carter had less success improving relations with the Soviet Union. Détente broke down when he criticized the Soviet Union for committing human rights abuses. Then in 1979 the Soviet Union invaded Afghanistan. Carter responded by breaking off arms-control talks and refusing to allow U.S. athletes to participate in the 1980 Summer Olympics in Moscow.

The Middle East

While Cold War tensions increased, Carter worked to ease tensions in the Middle East. Egypt and Israel had been at war for 30 years. In 1978 Carter invited Egyptian president Anwar el-Sadat and Israeli prime minister Menachem Begin (men-AHK-uhm BAY guhn) to the presidential retreat at Camp David, Maryland. After 13 days of meetings, the two leaders reached a peace agreement called the **Camp David Accords**, considered by many to be Carter's greatest achievement.

Carter also experienced disaster in the Middle East. Since the 1950s, the United States had supported the pro–American shah, or king, of Iran. Many Iranians resented the shah's reform efforts and the country's shift from a traditional and agricultural society to a more urban and industrial one. The government severely punished its opponents and controlled all political participation. Many members of the opposition supported the views of Islamic spiritual leader Ayatollah Ruhollah Khomeini, who had been forced to leave the country because of his criticisms of the shah's policies. In 1979 Khomeini's

Hostages Released

Approximately 52 Americans were held hostage by Iranian militants during the Iran hostage crisis. The men and women were kept blindfolded by their captors. After 444 days in captivity, the Americans were released.

How do these photographs show the experiences of the hostages?

supporters drove the shah out of Iran, and a month later, Khomeini took control of the government. On November 4, a group of Iranian students attacked the U.S. embassy in Tehran, the capital of Iran, seizing about 90 American hostages. The **Iran hostage crisis** lasted for more than a year.

In the early days of the crisis, some hostages were released. The remaining hostages were often blindfolded and beaten by their Iranian captors. Carter ended Iranian oil imports and froze Iranian assets in American banks. After a failed rescue attempt in April 1980, many Americans lost confidence in Carter's leadership.

READING CHECK **Making Generalizations**
Overall, do you think President Carter's foreign policy was effective? Why or why not?

SUMMARY AND PREVIEW President Carter's policies included both successes and failures. In the next section, you will learn about the policies of Ronald Reagan.

go.hrw.com
Online Quiz

Section 2 Assessment

Reviewing Ideas, Terms, and People

1. **a. Define** What social issues did Americans debate during the 1970s?
   b. Contrast How had immigration patterns changed by the 1970s?
   c. Draw Conclusions Why do you think *Silent Spring* remained important in the 1970s?
2. **a. Describe** How did **Jimmy Carter** break with tradition at his inauguration?
   b. Analyze Why did Carter's promise of honesty appeal to voters?
   c. Elaborate How did the Three Mile Island accident affect the energy crisis?
3. **a. Recall** Describe the successes and failures of President Carter's foreign policy.
   b. Explain What did the treaties Carter signed about the Panama Canal promise?
   c. Draw Conclusions Why do you think many people consider the **Camp David Accords** Carter's greatest achievement?

Critical Thinking

4. **Evaluating** Review your notes on new policies in the 1970s. Then copy the graphic organizer below and use it to show President Carter's successes and failures.

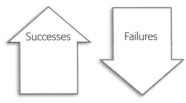

Successes   Failures

FOCUS ON WRITING

5. **Identifying Important Issues** Identify important issues and challenges facing Americans during the 1970s. Which of these issues or challenges would have most affected your fictional character? How might your fictional character have viewed these issues and challenges?

The Reagan Presidency

If YOU were there...

It is 1980, and you are a top adviser to the newly elected president, Ronald Reagan. You think about the challenges Reagan will face. High inflation and unemployment are plaguing the economy. Relations with the Soviet Union are falling apart. Also 52 Americans are still being held hostage in Iran.

What would be your first recommendation to the president?

BUILDING BACKGROUND Many Americans blamed President Carter for the nation's economic problems and the continuing hostage crisis in Iran. These became major issues in the presidential election of 1980. Republican candidate Ronald Reagan promised to take the country in a new direction.

Reagan and Conservative Ideas

"Are you better off than you were four years ago?" That was the question Republican candidate **Ronald Reagan** asked voters during the 1980 presidential campaign. Millions of voters answered "No," giving Reagan an easy victory over President Carter. Reagan won 489 electoral votes to Carter's 49. On January 20, 1981—the day of Reagan's inauguration—Iran finally released the American hostages after 444 days in captivity.

Reagan's approach to government was based on conservative ideas. He wanted to cut taxes and reduce regulations on businesses. He promised to scale back the size of government, arguing that government involvement in business and society harmed individual ambition. "Government is not the solution to our problem; government is the problem," Reagan declared in his inaugural address.

Just two months into his presidency, Reagan was shot and severely wounded in an assassination attempt by John Hinckley Jr. Reagan was released from the hospital within two weeks and returned to work.

What You Will Learn...

Main Ideas

1. President Reagan based his policies on conservative ideas.
2. Reagan took a tough stand against communism in his foreign policy.

The Big Idea

President Reagan enacted conservative policies at home and took a strong anti-Communist stance in the Cold War.

Key Terms and People

Ronald Reagan, *p. 357*
supply-side economics, *p. 358*
deficit, *p. 358*
Iran-Contra affair, *p. 359*
Mikhail Gorbachev, *p. 360*

TAKING NOTES As you read, take notes on President Reagan's domestic and foreign policies. Organize your notes in a diagram like this one.

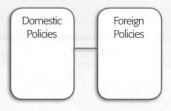

Sandra Day O'Connor
1930–

Sandra Day O'Connor grew up on a ranch in Arizona and entered Stanford University at age 16. She graduated third in her class from Stanford Law School in 1952. When she applied for jobs as a lawyer, however, she found that law firms were not willing to hire women. She turned instead to public service in Arizona, holding jobs including assistant attorney general, state senator, and judge. She was serving on the Arizona Court of Appeals when she was nominated to the Supreme Court by Ronald Reagan. The Senate confirmed O'Connor's appointment by a vote of 99–0. O'Connor retired from the bench in 2005.

Analyzing Information Why did Sandra Day O'Connor begin working in public service?

Reaganomics

Reagan's economic policies, which some called Reaganomics, were based on a theory called **supply-side economics**. This theory calls for sharp tax cuts with the goal of increasing the amount of money people and businesses have to invest. This investment would lead to economic growth and the creation of new jobs. Over time, the expanding economic activity would produce increased tax revenues for the government.

Though many Democrats opposed this theory, Congress approved most of Reagan's plan for large cuts in business and personal taxes. To help balance the budget, Reagan called for spending cuts as well. Congress agreed to cut rate of the growth of spending on social programs such as school lunches, low-income housing, and food stamps.

The economy experienced a brief recession early in Reagan's presidency. Then in 1983 the economy rebounded and began a long period of expansion. Business profits and tax revenues increased.

At the same time, spending on defense was increased dramatically, from $180 billion in 1981 to nearly $280 billion in 1985. The

ACADEMIC VOCABULARY
implications effects of a decision

new spending outpaced the new tax revenues. The result was a rapidly rising **deficit**—the amount by which a government's spending exceeds its revenues.

Conservative Goals

One of Reagan's conservative goals was to reduce government regulation of key industries. Reagan hoped fewer rules would encourage expansion in those industries, thereby improving the U.S. economy. Congress responded by reducing regulations on industries such as television, airlines, and banking.

Reagan was also able to move the Supreme Court in a more conservative direction by appointing politically conservative judges. In 1981 he appointed Sandra Day O'Connor to the Court. She became the first woman to serve as a Supreme Court justice. Reagan later appointed two more conservative justices: Antonin Scalia and Anthony M. Kennedy.

Election of 1984

President Reagan ran for re-election in 1984 against Democratic candidate Walter Mondale, who had served as Jimmy Carter's vice president. Mondale chose Geraldine Ferraro as his running mate. Ferraro was the first woman to run for vice president on a major-party ticket. She spoke of the **implications** of her nomination:

" By choosing an American woman to run for our nation's second-highest office, you send a powerful signal to all Americans …We will place no limits on achievement. If we can do this, we can do anything. "

—Geraldine Ferraro, *Ferraro: My Story*

The economy was booming as the election approached. Mondale argued that Reagan's economic policies unfairly favored the wealthy. Voters, however, gave Reagan a landslide victory. Reagan received 59 percent of the popular vote and captured 525 of the 538 electoral votes.

READING CHECK **Summarizing** What theories did Reaganomics include?

Reagan and Foreign Policy

President Reagan was an outspoken critic of communism and the Soviet Union, which he called an "evil empire." He saw the Cold War as a fight of "good versus evil, right versus wrong."

Conflicts in Central America

Civil wars raged in several Central American countries in the 1980s as communism spread in the area. Reagan supported anti-Communist governments in El Salvador and Guatemala with financial aid. Critics of this policy charged that the aid went to military governments that committed major human rights violations.

In Nicaragua, a revolutionary group called the Sandinistas overthrew the country's pro-American dictator in 1979. U.S. leaders became concerned when the Sandinistas formed closer ties with Communist Cuba.

Reagan cut all U.S. aid to Nicaragua and began supporting anti-Sandinista rebels known as the Contras. This led to fears that the United States could be drawn into war. In 1984 Congress passed a ban on further U.S. military aid to the Contras.

A group of Reagan administration officials secretly found a way to continue funding the Contras. One member of the group was Oliver North, a marine officer serving as a national security aide. North helped arrange the sale of U.S. missiles to Iran. In exchange, Iran released U.S. hostages that had been taken by Iranian terrorists. Profits from this secret deal were sent to the Contras, in violation of the congressional ban. The so-called **Iran-Contra affair** became a national controversy when it was exposed in 1986. Congressional hearings concluded that President Reagan was not guilty of illegal activity. Several White House officials, however, were convicted of crimes related to the affair.

The United States provide military aid to the Contras in Nicaragua.

Central American Conflicts in the 1980s

GEOGRAPHY SKILLS INTERPRETING MAPS

1. **Location** In which two countries did the United States intervene in 1983?
2. **Human-Environment Interaction** Why might the United States have intervened in the countries it did?

An Easing of Tensions

President Reagan and his wife Nancy developed a friendship with Mikhail Gorbachev and his wife Raisa that symbolized the easing of Cold War tensions between their countries. Gorbachev's policies helped greatly to bring about this change in foreign affairs.

How did the friendship between the Reagans and the Gorbachevs help unite the two countries?

Reagan and Gorbachev

During his first term, President Reagan took a tough stand against the Soviet Union. He halted arms negotiations and quickly expanded the U.S. military.

The Soviet Union tried to keep up with American spending in the arms race. This contributed to desperate economic times in the Soviet Union during the 1980s. In 1985

Mikhail Gorbachev became the new Soviet leader. To deal with his country's economic problems, he began a process of political and economic reforms called *perestroika*. He also adopted a new policy of political openness called *glasnost*. The newfound freedoms introduced by Gorbachev's policies threatened other leaders of the Soviet Union but were mostly supported by its citizens and by leaders in the West.

Reagan became convinced of Gorbachev's desire for change. In 1987 the two leaders signed the Intermediate-Range Nuclear Forces Treaty, eliminating all medium-range nuclear weapons in Europe. Cold War tensions were decreasing for the first time since the early 1970s.

READING CHECK **Identifying Cause and Effect** Why did President Reagan change his tough stand toward the Soviet Union?

SUMMARY AND PREVIEW Conservative ideas influenced many of Ronald Reagan's policies. In the next chapter, you will learn about the policies of presidents in the 1990s.

Section 3 Assessment

go.hrw.com
Online Quiz

Reviewing Ideas, Terms, and People

1. **a. Recall** What was **Ronald Reagan**'s view of government?
   b. Analyze Why did the federal budget deficit rise during Reagan's presidency?
   c. Draw Conclusions Why do you think so many Americans voted for Reagan in the 1984 election?
2. **a. Recall** What changes did **Mikhail Gorbachev** make in the Soviet Union?
   b. Explain How did Reagan administration officials violate the law in the **Iran-Contra affair**?
   c. Predict Do you think Reagan's policies were effective in fighting communism?

Critical Thinking

3. **Categorizing** Review your notes on Ronald Reagan's domestic and foreign policies. Then copy the graphic organizer below and use it to list each policy with its correct geographic focus.

United States	Central America	Soviet Union

FOCUS ON WRITING

4. **Describing Events** How would you describe the fall of the Soviet Union or other events during Reagan's presidency? How are the events of Reagan's presidency interrelated, and how did his decisions affect these events? Make notes on what you will use in your autobiographical sketch.

Ronald Reagan

How would you lead your country during the Cold War?

When did he live? 1911–2004

Where did he live? Ronald Reagan grew up in Illinois. In 1937 he moved to California, where he became a well-known movie actor. He later entered politics and was elected governor of California. After serving eight years as president, he retired to his California ranch.

What did he do? Reagan worked to reshape the American government and economy based on conservative principles. In foreign policy, he took an aggressive stand toward communism and the Soviet Union. In a famous speech at the Berlin Wall, he challenged the Soviet leader to allow freedom in Eastern Europe, saying, "Mr. Gorbachev, open this gate! Mr. Gorbachev, tear down this wall!" Reagan and Gorbachev later signed the Intermediate-Range Nuclear Forces (INF) Treaty, the first treaty reducing the number of nuclear weapons held by both countries.

Why is he so important? Nicknamed the Great Communicator, Reagan inspired many Americans with his sense of humor and his optimistic view of America's future. Many voters credited him with restoring their confidence after the difficulties of the 1970s. Reagan's buildup of the U.S. military is believed by many to have contributed to major changes in the Cold War and the eventual fall of Communist governments in the Soviet Union and Eastern Europe.

Finding Main Ideas What was Reagan's biggest foreign policy achievement? Use evidence from the reading to support your answer.

KEY EVENTS

1937
Becomes a movie actor

1952
Marries his second wife, Nancy Davis

1966
Elected governor of California

1980
Elected president

1981
Shot by John Hinckley Jr.

1984
Elected to second term

1987
Signs INF Treaty

2004
Dies in California

Ronald Reagan used his California ranch as a retreat during his years in the White House.

Social Studies Skills

Analysis · Critical Thinking · Civic Participation · Study

Determining the Strength of an Argument

Define the Skill

Studying history often involves learning about different opinions. In order to understand these opinions, it is important to recognize strong arguments. Strong arguments are based on convincing supporting evidence. Examples and points should be true and should make sense in the context of the argument. For example, supporting points should relate to the main idea of the argument. It is also important to consider any evidence against the argument.

Many people in the past have made decisions based on the strength of an argument. Determining the strength of an argument is important for the present as well. Your judgments can help you decide whether or not to support a policy, idea, or candidate.

During the 1970s, Americans had to determine the strength of arguments during the Watergate scandal. If Nixon had not resigned, for example, members of the House of Representatives would have had to decide whether or not to vote to impeach the president. They would have had to weigh the evidence and determine the strength of arguments for and against him.

Learn the Skill

In *Silent Spring,* Rachel Carson argued that environmental pollution was harmful and had to be stopped. Here is part of her argument:

"Man, however much he may like to pretend the contrary, is part of nature. Can he escape a pollution that is now so thoroughly distributed throughout our world?"

How strong is Carson's argument? In *Silent Spring,* she gives many examples of the harmful effects of pollutants and insect poisons. This makes her argument stronger. In the quotation above, Carson points out that humans rely upon nature. As nature becomes polluted, she argues, humans will not be able to avoid the harmful health effects of that pollution.

Carson's argument was strong enough to convince the American people and Congress to take action. The environmental movement grew, and new laws were passed to protect the nation's air and water.

Practice the Skill

Suppose that you are a member of Congress during the Watergate scandal. You have to decide whether or not to impeach President Nixon. Your decision will depend on the strength of the arguments in favor of impeachment. Review the chapter and answer the following questions to help determine the strength of those arguments.

1. What is the evidence against President Nixon? How does this evidence strengthen or weaken the case against him?

2. Is there any evidence that President Nixon is innocent? How strong is this evidence?

3. Would you vote to impeach the president? Explain your answer.

Chapter Review

HOLT
History's Impact
▶ video series
Review the video to answer the closing question:

How did the Supreme Court contribute to the series of checks and balances that eventually led to President Nixon's resignation?

Visual Summary

QUICK FACTS

Use the visual summary below to help you review the main ideas of the chapter.

Positives and Negatives of the Presidencies

Richard Nixon

Positive: Nixon brought China and the United States together diplomatically.

Negative: His administration ended because of the Watergate scandal.

Jimmy Carter

Positive: Carter helped create the Camp David Accords.

Negative: He also faced the Iran hostage crisis.

Ronald Reagan

Positive: Reagan signed a major arms treaty with several countries.

Negative: His administration was linked to the Iran-Contra affair.

Reviewing Vocabulary, Terms, and People

Read each question and write the letter of the best response.

1. Which of the following refers to a period of less hostile U.S.–Soviet relations in the 1970s?

   a. détente   **c.** realpolitik

   b. stagflation   **d.** *perestroika*

2. The South African government's system of official racial segregation was known as

   a. Title IX.   **c.** sanctions.

   b. the ERA.   **d.** apartheid.

3. Which of the following was a theory that influenced President Reagan's policies?

   a. Whip Inflation Now   **c.** SALT

   b. supply-side economics   **d.** *glasnost*

Comprehension and Critical Thinking

SECTION 1 *(Pages 346–351)*

4. **a. Identify** Who were the reporters who uncovered the Watergate scandal?

   b. Analyze What were some results of Nixon's visit to China?

   c. Elaborate Why do you think Nixon called his supporters the Silent Majority?

SECTION 2 *(Pages 352–356)*

5. **a. Recall** What happened at Three Mile Island?

   b. Contrast How were the foreign policies of Nixon and Carter different?

   c. Draw Conclusions Why do you think many Americans responded to *Silent Spring*?

6. a. Describe What happened in the election of 1980?

b. Summarize What were some results of Reagan's conservative policies?

c. Evaluate Do you think Congress was right to ban aid to the Contras in Nicaragua?

Reviewing Themes

7. Economics How did the energy crisis affect the economy of the United States?

8. Politics How did the politics of the presidents discussed in this chapter affect the foreign policy of the United States?

Reading Skills

Summarizing *Use the Reading Skills taught in this chapter to answer the question below.*

Carter also experienced disaster in the Middle East. Since the 1950s, the United States had supported the pro–American shah, or king, of Iran. Many Iranians resented the shah's reform efforts and the country's shift from a traditional and agricultural society to a more urban and industrial one. The government severely punished its opponents and controlled all political participation. Many members of the opposition supported the views of Islamic spiritual leader Ayatollah Ruhollah Khomeini, who had been forced to leave the country because of his criticisms of the shah's policies. In 1979 Khomeini's supporters drove the shah out of Iran, and a month later, Khomeini took control of the government. On November 4, a group of Iranian students attacked the U.S. embassy in Tehran, the capital of Iran, seizing about 90 American hostages. The Iran hostage crisis lasted for more than a year. *(pp. 355–356)*

9. Summarize the beginning of the Iran hostage crisis in three sentences.

Using the Internet `go.hrw.com`

10. Activity: Making Connections The cost of oil rose steadily in the early 1970s, and it reached a new high after OPEC nations placed an embargo on oil exports to the United States. Americans felt the impact as costs increased for all products that were made from oil, and the already weakened U.S. economy struggled to survive. Enter the activity keyword. Research the causes, effects, results, and connections between the Yom Kippur War and the OPEC oil embargo. Create a model or diagram to illustrate your research. You should label your model or diagram and be prepared to explain it to the class.

Social Studies Skills

Determining the Strength of an Argument *Use the Social Studies Skills taught in this chapter to answer the question about the selection below.*

In this chapter, you have read about the Supreme Court case *United States v. Nixon.* Nixon argued that executive privilege, a president's right to keep information secret for reasons of national security, protected him from having to give up tapes of his official conversations.

11. In your opinion, how strong was Nixon's argument?

FOCUS ON WRITING

12. Writing Your Autobiographical Sketch Review your notes. Then write your autobiography, being sure to mention each of the events from your notes. Tell how your character heard about each event, what he or she was doing at the time, how he or she felt about the event, and how it affected him or her. What are your character's hopes and fears for the future?

Grade 8 Intermediate-Level Test Preparation

Directions (1–8): **For each statement or question, write on the separate answer sheet the *number* of the word or expression that, of those given, best completes the statement or answers the question.**

1 **The Camp David Accords were**
(1) secret deals supplying Iran with weapons and the Nicaraguan Contras with money.
(2) the negotiations that ended the Iran hostage crisis.
(3) U.S.–Soviet nuclear arms reduction treaties.
(4) a set of peace agreements between Israel and Egypt.

2 **Which of the following was a result of Reagan's economic plan?**
(1) The deficit decreased.
(2 Tax rates were lowered.
(3) Military spending was cut.
(4) Unemployment and inflation rose.

3 **Which president participated in the 1972 Strategic Arms Limitation Talks?**
(1) Gerald Ford   (3) Ronald Reagan
(2) Richard Nixon   (4) Jimmy Carter

4 **The practice of giving special consideration to nonwhites or woman to make up for past discrimination is known as:**
(1) the Equal Rights Amendment.
(2) affirmative action.
(3) the Equal Protection Clause.
(4) the 21st Amendment.

5 **What was one aspect of Reagan's tough stance against communism?**
(1) He dramatically increased military spending.
(2) He made peace agreements in the Middle East.
(3) He visited and established diplomatic relations with China.
(4) He focused on human rights.

6 **How did the Watergate scandal begin?**
(1) Government officials were caught giving information to newspaper reporters.
(2) Five men were caught breaking in to the Democrats' headquarters.
(3) Richard Nixon refused to share his tapes with Congress.
(4) Gerald Ford pardoned Richard Nixon.

7 **How were Nixon's and Reagan's influences on the Supreme Court similar?**
(1) Both tried to give the Supreme Court more power.
(2) Both denied the authority of the Supreme Court to issue subpoenas.
(3) Both appointed women as Supreme Court justices.
(4) Both appointed conservative Supreme Court justices.

8 ***Stagflation* refers to the unusual economic condition of**
(1) high oil prices but low inflation.
(2) stagnant economic growth and high inflation.
(3) low unemployment and low inflation.
(4) stagnant deficits and falling exports.

Base your answer to question 9 on the text below and on your knowledge of social studies.

> *"*What the president has done threatens to destroy our system of law. It smacks of dictatorship. Unless Congress responds in the only way provided in the Constitution for resisting such a usurpation [stealing] of authority, we endanger our country's future.*"*
> —Senator Edmund S. Muskie, quoted in the *Washington Post*, October 21, 1973

9 **Constructed-Response Question Why did Muskie feel Nixon should be impeached?**

America Looks to the Future

FOCUS QUESTION

How has America reacted to the challenges of the modern world?

FOCUS ON WRITING

Web Site The popularity of the Internet dramatically increased in the 1990s, changing the way we communicate and share information. The attacks of September 11, 2001, made terrorism a major concern for Americans. In this chapter you will learn about these and other important events that have taken place in your lifetime. Then you will write the text for a Web site about late twentieth century and early twenty-first century America.

UNITED STATES

1988 George H. W. Bush is elected president.

1980

WORLD

1989 Most of the Berlin Wall is dismantled.

HOLT

History's Impact
▶ video series
Watch the video to understand the impact of government in our daily lives.

What You Will Learn...

Young people like those pictured here are helping to shape the future of the United States. In this chapter, you will read about the amazing events that have changed our world in recent years. From the end of the Cold War to the rising terrorist threat and the development of new technology, life in the United States has been changing quickly. Today Americans are working together to face new challenges and take advantage of new opportunities.

NY

1990 U.S. and UN forces liberate Kuwait from Iraqi control in the Persian Gulf War.

1995 Extremists bomb a federal building in Oklahoma.

2001 Terrorists attack the World Trade Center and the Pentagon on September 11.

2005 The Cassini-Huygens Mission photographs Saturn's moon Titan.

1990

2000

PRESENT

1991 Nelson Mandela is elected president of South Africa.

1997 Hong Kong returns to Chinese control.

2005 Pope John Paul II dies.

Economics

Geography

Politics

Society and Culture

Science and Technology

Focus on Themes In this chapter, you will read about the most recent presidents and their administrations. You will learn about the changing role the United States has gained in global **politics** and the global **economy.** You will also read about September 11, 2001, and learn how that tragedy helped shape the world you live in today.

Predicting

Focus on Reading Often when you are reading, predicting what might come next can help you understand what is happening in the story of history.

Understanding Summarizing Predicting what may come next in the logical progression of a story relies on understanding what has happened in the past. You have learned many different responses to crises that have occurred throughout U.S. history. You can use this knowledge to predict what may come in the future.

Notice how one reader uses information from the past to predict what may happen in the future.

In October 2001 the United States began air strikes in Afghanistan. By December U.S. forces had driven the Taliban from power and captured many of al Qaeda's members. Osama bin Laden remained at large. The United States began helping Afghanistan to rebuild and establish a democratic government.

Although most Americans supported the use of force in Afghanistan, disagreement arose, about how best to move forward in the war against terrorism.

From Chapter 14, p. 376

After reading this section, one reader thought:

I have read about other wars in which the American public was divided over the action the country should take. In the War of 1812, there was a convention of delegates opposed to the war. During the Civil War, President Lincoln silenced antiwar Democrats by imprisoning them. In the 1960s and 1970s, many citizens publicly protested the Vietnam War, while others supported the war. What happened in these past wars that might happen in the war against terrorism?

You Try It!

The following passage is from the chapter you are getting ready to read. As you read the passage, look for the facts that can help you predict what might happen in the future.

> The Internet was first developed in 1969 by scientists at the U.S. Department of Defense. Early computer networks were used mainly by government and university researchers. Then in the 1990s, computer programmers developed the World Wide Web, enabling people to access information from computers around the world.
>
> *From Chapter 14, p. 381*
>
> Internet use exploded in the 1990s. Computers and the Internet made it easier and faster for people at home, work, and school to access and share information. This important development was known as the Information Revolution.

After you read the passage, answer the following questions.

1. What other revolutions have you read about in the study of American history, and how have they affected American society?

2. Is the Information Revolution similar to any other revolution you have read about?

3. How might the Information Revolution affect American society in the future?

As you read Chapter 14, use the information given to predict what may happen in American society in the next 10 years.

Key Terms and People

Chapter 14

Section 1
George H. W. Bush *(p. 370)*
Saddam Hussein *(p. 371)*
Operation Desert Storm *(p. 371)*
Colin Powell *(p. 371)*
Bill Clinton *(p. 372)*
North American Free Trade Agreement *(p. 372)*
Madeleine Albright *(p. 373)*
terrorism *(p. 373)*

Section 2
Al Gore *(p. 374)*
George W. Bush *(p. 374)*
World Trade Center *(p. 376)*
Pentagon *(p. 376)*
al Qaeda *(p. 376)*
Osama bin Laden *(p. 376)*
weapons of mass destruction *(p. 376)*

Section 3
service economy *(p. 380)*
globalization *(p. 380)*
Internet *(p. 381)*
Information Revolution *(p. 381)*
AIDS *(p. 381)*
ozone layer *(p. 382)*
global warming *(p. 382)*

Academic Vocabulary

In this chapter, you will learn the following academic words:
facilitate *(p. 381)*
ideals *(p. 383)*

The End of the Twentieth Century

What You Will Learn...

Main Ideas

1. Major global changes took place during the presidency of George H. W. Bush.
2. During Bill Clinton's presidency, the nation experienced scandal, economic growth, and the rise of terrorist threats.

The Big Idea

The United States and the world faced many new challenges at the end of the 20th century.

Key Terms and People

George H. W. Bush, *p. 370*
Saddam Hussein, *p. 371*
Operation Desert Storm, *p. 371*
Colin Powell, *p. 371*
Bill Clinton, *p. 372*
North American Free Trade Agreement, *p. 372*
Madeleine Albright, *p. 373*
terrorism, *p. 373*

TAKING NOTES As you read, look for information about key events that happened during the presidencies of George H. W. Bush and Bill Clinton. Use a diagram like the one below to help you organize your notes.

Bush	Clinton

If YOU were there...

You are visiting the city of West Berlin in 1989. Just after midnight on November 9, you see huge crowds of people pouring into the streets to celebrate. You rush outside to find out what's going on. "The wall is falling!" people shout. You run toward the Berlin Wall, and there you see East and West Germans working together to rip down the hated wall.

What might the fall of the Berlin Wall mean for the future?

BUILDING BACKGROUND Mikhail Gorbachev began a process of political and economic reforms in the Soviet Union in the late 1980s. Encouraged by these changes, people from many Eastern European countries continued to demand change as well. They were eager to break free from Soviet domination and establish their own democratic governments.

George H. W. Bush

Ronald Reagan was popular with a majority of voters as his second term as president came to an end. Republicans hoped this would help Reagan's vice president, **George H. W. Bush**, win the election of 1988. Bush's Democratic opponent was Massachusetts governor Michael Dukakis. After a hard-fought campaign, Bush won the election with 426 electoral votes to Dukakis's 111.

The Cold War Ends

As Bush began his presidency, Mikhail Gorbachev continued his reform programs in the Soviet Union. In the Soviet-controlled states of Eastern Europe, people demanded even faster change and more freedom. Prodemocracy movements in Hungary, Poland, and other nations put increasing pressure on Communist governments. This pressure produced world-changing results in 1989, as pro-Soviet governments across Eastern Europe began to fall.

In October 1989 massive protests in East Germany lead to the resignation of Communist leader Erich Honecker. The new government agreed to open the borders of East Germany—including the border guarded by the Berlin Wall. At midnight on November 9, a wild celebration broke out as East and West Berliners jumped onto the Berlin Wall, shouting and dancing. Some smashed through parts of the wall with hammers and chisels. The wall, which had stood as a symbol of the Cold War since 1961, began crumbling to the ground. Within a year, the two Germanys reunited as one democratic country.

Several Soviet republics soon declared independence from the Soviet regime. In a desperate attempt to hold on to power, hard-line Communists took Gorbachev hostage and tried to seize the government. Thousands of Soviets took to the streets in protest. Ignoring orders to stop the protesters, many soldiers joined the crowds. Prodemocracy leader Boris Yeltsin encouraged the protesters to stand strong. The Soviet Union soon broke apart, confirming the end of the Cold War.

The Persian Gulf War

President Bush called for all countries to work together, especially during times of crisis. A major crisis soon developed in the Middle East. In August 1990 Iraq's dictator, **Saddam Hussein**, invaded neighboring oil-rich Kuwait.

Members of the United Nations called for the immediate withdrawal of Iraqi troops. President Bush, with strong public support, began assembling a coalition of nations to drive Iraq from Kuwait by force.

When Saddam refused to withdraw from Kuwait, a U.S.-led multinational coalition launched **Operation Desert Storm**. This air offensive was led by U.S. generals Norman Schwarzkopf and **Colin Powell**—chair of the joint chiefs of staff and the highest-ranking African American ever to serve in the U.S. military. After a six-week bombing campaign, ground forces entered Kuwait. Within days, Iraq agreed to a cease-fire.

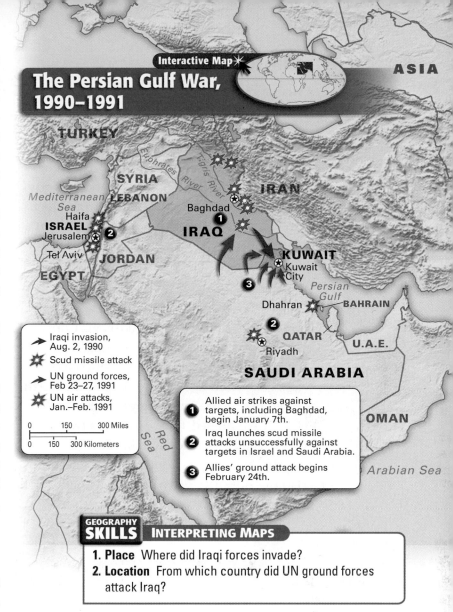

Interactive Map

The Persian Gulf War, 1990–1991

ASIA

- ➤ Iraqi invasion, Aug. 2, 1990
- ✳ Scud missile attack
- ➤ UN ground forces, Feb 23–27, 1991
- ✳ UN air attacks, Jan.–Feb. 1991

0   150   300 Miles
0   150   300 Kilometers

1 Allied air strikes against targets, including Baghdad, begin January 7th.

2 Iraq launches scud missile attacks unsuccessfully against targets in Israel and Saudi Arabia.

3 Allies' ground attack begins February 24th.

GEOGRAPHY SKILLS **INTERPRETING MAPS**

1. **Place** Where did Iraqi forces invade?
2. **Location** From which country did UN ground forces attack Iraq?

About 22,300 Iraqi soldiers and civilians were killed in the Persian Gulf War. The coalition forces lost around 223 soldiers, 148 of whom were American. More than 35,000 American women served in the war, though federal laws prevented them from serving in combat.

President Bush explained the importance of the war, telling Congress:

" Now, we can see a new world coming into view. A world in which there is the very real prospect of a new world order ... A world in which freedom and respect for human rights find a home among all nations. "

—George H. W. Bush, March 6, 1991

READING CHECK **Summarizing** How did the world change between 1989 and 1991?

Clinton's Presidency

An overwhelming majority of Americans supported President Bush's handling of the Gulf War. By the time of the 1992 election, however, the struggling U.S. economy had become a more important issue for most voters. The Democratic nominee, Arkansas governor **Bill Clinton**, told voters he would focus on improving the economy. Clinton won a three-way race against Bush and H. Ross Perot, who ran as an independent candidate.

THE IMPACT TODAY

In 2005 Congress approved a similar accord with the Central American countries of Costa Rica, El Salvador, Guatemala, Honduras, and Nicaragua. The treaty is known as CAFTA.

Clinton and Congress

Under President Clinton's leadership, Congress passed a budget designed to reduce the deficit by cutting spending and raising taxes. He also convinced Congress to support the **North American Free Trade Agreement** (NAFTA), which eliminated trade barriers between the United States, Canada, and Mexico.

In the 1994 congressional elections, House minority leader Newt Gingrich of Georgia helped lead Republicans to an important victory. Gingrich and other Republicans promoted a set of policies called the Contract with America, promising lower taxes and smaller government. Republicans gained control of both houses of Congress for the first time since 1952.

A growing economy helped Clinton win a second term in 1996 over Senator Bob Dole of Kansas. By 1998 the U.S. government was taking in more money than it was spending. Clinton's second term, however, was dominated by questions about his personal and official conduct. Government investigators charged that the president had conducted an improper relationship with a White House intern and then lied about it under oath. In 1998 the House of Representatives voted to impeach Clinton for obstruction of justice. The Senate acquitted him of the charges in 1999. The scandal damaged Clinton's public image, though his approval ratings remained high, due in part to the booming economy.

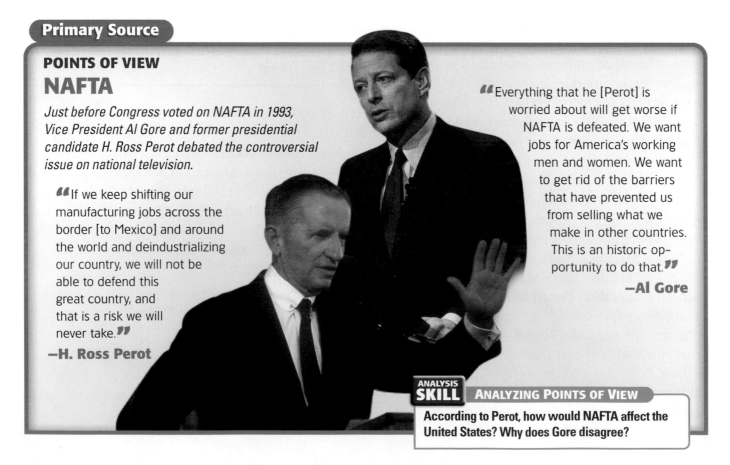

Primary Source

POINTS OF VIEW

NAFTA

Just before Congress voted on NAFTA in 1993, Vice President Al Gore and former presidential candidate H. Ross Perot debated the controversial issue on national television.

"If we keep shifting our manufacturing jobs across the border [to Mexico] and around the world and deindustrializing our country, we will not be able to defend this great country, and that is a risk we will never take."

—H. Ross Perot

"Everything that he [Perot] is worried about will get worse if NAFTA is defeated. We want jobs for America's working men and women. We want to get rid of the barriers that have prevented us from selling what we make in other countries. This is an historic opportunity to do that."

—Al Gore

ANALYSIS SKILL **ANALYZING POINTS OF VIEW**

According to Perot, how would NAFTA affect the United States? Why does Gore disagree?

A Dangerous World

The collapse of the Soviet Union left the United States as the world's only superpower. In 1997 President Clinton appointed **Madeleine Albright** as the first woman to be secretary of state. Albright had been born in Prague before her family moved to the United States, fleeing the Holocaust. She helped adapt U.S. foreign policy to this complex new world.

The United States worked to protect global peace and democracy. In the Balkan region of Europe, for example, the former nation of Yugoslavia broke apart. Different ethnic and religious groups fought for control of territory. U.S. diplomats helped negotiate an end to the bloody war. President Clinton then sent 20,000 U.S. troops to the region to help maintain peace.

In the 1990s **terrorism**—the use of violence by individuals or small groups to advance political goals—became a major issue. In April 1995 American terrorists bombed the Alfred P. Murrah Federal Building in Oklahoma City, killing 168 people. The United States also faced increasingly deadly attacks by extremist Islamic groups. Hundreds were killed in bomb attacks on U.S. embassies in Africa in 1998.

BIOGRAPHY

Bill Clinton
1946–

Bill Clinton was born in Hope, Arkansas. As a teenager he met and shook hands with President John Kennedy—an experience that heightened his interest in becoming a politician. He became a Rhodes scholar at Oxford after graduating from college. After graduating from Yale Law School, Clinton returned to Arkansas and was elected governor in 1978. He lost his bid for re-election in 1980 but ran again in 1982 and won, serving 10 more years as governor. Clinton was elected president in 1992 and re-elected in 1996. The country experienced the longest period of continued economic growth during his presidency. In 1998, however, Clinton became only the second president in U.S. history to be impeached.

Drawing Conclusions Why might meeting President Kennedy have influenced Clinton?

READING CHECK **Identifying Cause and Effect** How did the end of the Cold War change the U.S. role in the world?

SUMMARY AND PREVIEW The Cold War ended in 1990. In the next section you will learn about new world challenges.

go.hrw.com
Online Quiz

Section 1 Assessment

Reviewing Ideas, Terms, and People

1. **a. Summarize** What were some of the major world events during **George H. W. Bush**'s presidency?
   b. Identify What was the purpose of **Operation Desert Storm**?
   c. Evaluate How did the Persian Gulf War test President Bush's vision of a new world order?
2. **a. Recall** What were some of the high points and low points of **Bill Clinton**'s presidency?
   b. Contrast How is **terrorism** different from standard warfare?
   c. Elaborate Do you think Congress was right to pass the **North American Free Trade Agreement**? Explain your answer.

Critical Thinking

3. **Sequencing** Review your notes on the presidencies of George H. W. Bush and Bill Clinton. Then copy the graphic organizer below and use it to identify major events and the year they occurred.

Year	Event

FOCUS ON WRITING

4. **Identifying Important Figures** Take notes on the main people in the chapter. Identify why each of these people was important. In what major events was each person involved? How did he or she affect the United States?

George W. Bush in Office

What You Will Learn...

Main Ideas

1. George W. Bush won the disputed 2000 presidential election.
2. Americans debated the future of the War on Terror that began after terrorists attacked the United States.
3. The nation faced difficult challenges during President Bush's second term.

The Big Idea

George W. Bush led the country in response to terrorist attacks and through domestic challenges.

Key Terms and People

Al Gore, *p. 374*
George W. Bush, *p. 374*
World Trade Center, *p. 376*
Pentagon, *p. 376*
al Qaeda, *p. 376*
Osama bin Laden, *p. 376*
weapons of mass destruction, *p. 376*

TAKING NOTES As you read, take notes on the major policies of George W. Bush. Use a diagram like the one below. You may need to add more circles.

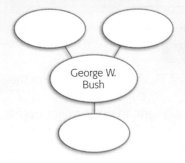

If YOU were there...

It is the December after the presidential election between George W. Bush and Al Gore. For weeks, people have been talking about whether the votes can be recounted by hand. The race was too close to call on election night, and now the candidates are involved in a court case that will decide who the next president will be.

How would you solve the problem of recounting votes?

BUILDING BACKGROUND In the 1990s extremist Islamic groups in the Middle East vowed to attack the United States. They carried out deadly attacks on U.S. embassies in Africa and against the ship the USS *Cole*. Terrorism was not a major issue in the 2000 presidential election, but it would soon begin to dominate American politics.

The 2000 Presidential Election

The United States was at peace and enjoying economic prosperity as the 2000 presidential election neared. The Democrats chose **Al Gore**, who had served as Bill Clinton's vice president, as their nominee. The Republican candidate was Texas governor **George W. Bush**, the son of former president George H. W. Bush.

Campaign Issues

One major campaign issue was how to use the federal budget surplus, which totaled nearly $100 billion in 1999. Gore said he would use the money for education and health care and to pay off a part of the national debt. Bush promised to return the money to taxpayers in the form of tax cuts. Bush and Gore also debated the role that the United States—now the world's only superpower—should play in global affairs. Campaign polls showed that the race was very close.

On election night, the voting in some states was so close that no winner could be declared. It soon became clear that Florida's 25 electoral votes would determine the outcome of the election.

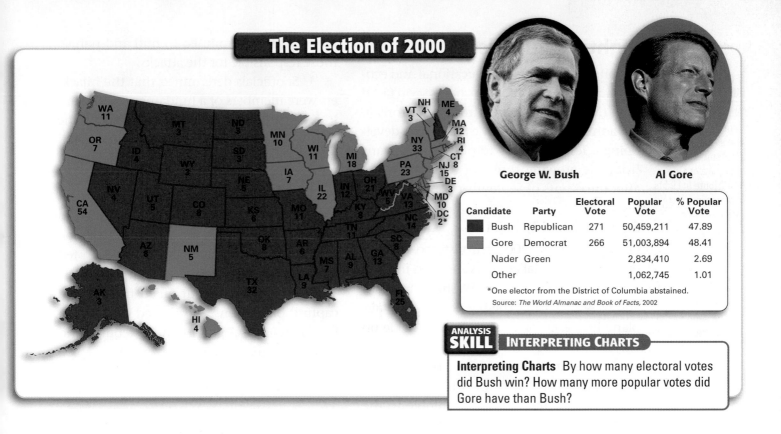

The Election of 2000

George W. Bush

Al Gore

Candidate	Party	Electoral Vote	Popular Vote	% Popular Vote
Bush	Republican	271	50,459,211	47.89
Gore	Democrat	266	51,003,894	48.41
Nader	Green		2,834,410	2.69
Other			1,062,745	1.01

*One elector from the District of Columbia abstained.
Source: *The World Almanac and Book of Facts*, 2002

ANALYSIS SKILL INTERPRETING CHARTS

Interpreting Charts By how many electoral votes did Bush win? How many more popular votes did Gore have than Bush?

The popular vote in Florida was so close that state law required the votes to be recounted. A machine recount found that Bush had received a few hundred more votes than Gore. But Gore supporters wanted the votes in four counties to be counted by hand, arguing that this would ensure all votes were counted. The Bush campaign challenged this manual recount in court.

After several weeks of suspense, the Supreme Court ruled that the manual recounts could not ensure that all votes would be counted the same way. They ordered the recount to stop. Florida's electoral votes went to Bush, making him the winner of the election. He was the first president in more than 100 years to win the electoral vote while receiving fewer popular votes than his opponent.

At his inauguration, President Bush urged Americans to come together.

❝This is my solemn pledge: I will work to build a single nation of justice and opportunity ... Today, we affirm a new commitment to live out our nation's promise through civility, courage, compassion, and character.❞
—George W. Bush, January 20, 2001

Bush's Early Days in Office

The disputed election, however, caused lingering bitterness between Democrats and Republicans. Republicans held a small majority in the House of Representatives, while the Senate was split 50–50. When votes in the Senate are tied, the vice president casts the tie-breaking vote. This gave Vice President Dick Cheney an important role in helping to pass Republican legislation.

Bush put together his cabinet, appointing Colin Powell to the key position of secretary of state. Powell became the first African American to hold this office. Bush carried through with his campaign promise to cut taxes. Six months after taking office, he signed into law a $1.35 trillion tax-cut plan. He also signed into law an education reform plan called No Child Left Behind. This act created a national set of standards for every student and every school to meet. It also raised funding for schools.

READING CHECK **Analyzing** What was unusual about the outcome of the 2000 presidential election?

FOCUS ON NEW YORK CITY

New York City remembers the events of September 11 in many ways. One is the Tribute in Lights, a temporary installation of searchlights in 2002 that created two vertical columns of light where the Twin Towers once stood. The display now can be seen every September 11.

Fighting Terrorism

Despite many plans for educational and economic reform, President Bush was soon faced with the challenge of confronting terrorism. His administration became focused on developing a foreign policy to protect Americans from the growing threat of terrorist attacks after the events of September 11, 2001.

September 11, 2001

On September 11, 2001, terrorists took control of four commercial airliners and used them as weapons to attack sites in Washington, D.C., and New York City. The hijackers flew an airplane into each of two towers that made up the **World Trade Center**, an important business center in New York City. The resulting fires caused the buildings, which had been the tallest in the nation, to crumble to the ground. About 2,500 people were killed in the collapsing buildings. Another airplane was flown into the **Pentagon**—the headquarters of the Department of Defense located outside of Washington, D.C. A fourth hijacked airplane crashed in a Pennsylvania field. The tragedy brought Americans together, and the nation received support from foreign leaders and citizens. One French newspaper's headline read, "WE ARE ALL AMERICANS."

President Bush promised to find and punish those responsible for the attacks.

U.S. officials determined that the hijackers were members of a fundamentalist Islamic terrorist group called **al Qaeda**, or "the Base." The group was led by a wealthy Saudi Arabian exile, **Osama bin Laden**. Bin Laden and his followers were based in Afghanistan. The Taliban, an extreme Islamic group, ruled the country. After Taliban leaders refused to turn over bin Laden, the United States took military action. In October 2001 the United States attacked Afghanistan and drove the Taliban from power but failed to find and capture bin Laden. The United States then began helping Afghanistan to rebuild and establish a democratic government.

War in Iraq

After the attack on Afghanistan, President Bush argued that Saddam Hussein, the dictator of Iraq, posed an immediate threat to U.S. security. When the Persian Gulf War ended in 1991, Saddam had agreed to give up Iraq's **weapons of mass destruction**—chemical, biological, or nuclear weapons that can kill thousands. However, Saddam failed to fully cooperate with UN weapons inspectors.

Leaders from France, Germany, and Russia argued that the UN inspectors should be

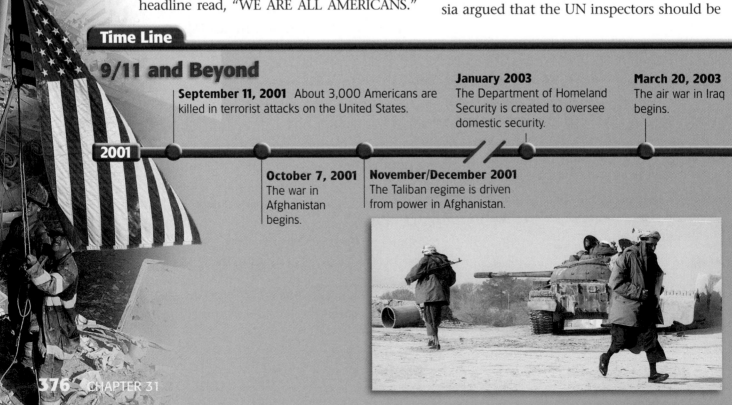

Time Line

9/11 and Beyond

September 11, 2001 About 3,000 Americans are killed in terrorist attacks on the United States.

January 2003 The Department of Homeland Security is created to oversee domestic security.

March 20, 2003 The air war in Iraq begins.

2001

October 7, 2001 The war in Afghanistan begins.

November/December 2001 The Taliban regime is driven from power in Afghanistan.

given more time to search for weapons. President Bush and British prime minister Tony Blair said force should be used to ensure Iraq was complying with the weapons ban. On March 20, 2003, the United States and a coalition of allies launched a ground attack on Iraq. Saddam's government collapsed, and Saddam was eventually captured.

As in Afghanistan, U.S. officials began working with Iraqis to establish a democratic government. Violence continued, however, with attacks on U.S. soldiers and Iraqis who were working to rebuild the country. Iraqi voters elected new government leaders and approved a new constitution in 2005. In 2006 an Iraqi court sentenced Saddam to death, and he was executed a short time later. Deep divisions among Iraqis remained an issue, however, threatening the stability of the new government.

Debates at Home

The war in Iraq caused fierce debate at home. After months of searching, no weapons of mass destruction were uncovered, and no concrete ties between Saddam and al Qaeda could be proven. Critics began to accuse the Bush administration of exaggerating the danger Saddam posed to the United States. The continuing violence between Iraqi insurgents and U.S. soldiers led many Americans to call for an end to the war. Meanwhile, growing concerns that Iraq's neighbor, Iran, was working to develop nuclear weapons caused additional tensions in the region. President Bush lost much of his support among voters, and during the elections of 2006 Democrats gained a majority in both houses of Congress. The new Congress elected Nancy Pelosi the first female speaker in the House of Representatives. In response to the outcome of the election, Secretary of Defense Donald Rumsfeld resigned and a new secretary, Robert Gates, was appointed. The newly elected Congress began calling for a plan to withdraw from Iraq.

READING CHECK **Summarizing** What led to the war in Iraq?

Domestic Issues

After the 2004 election, Secretary of State Colin Powell resigned. Bush appointed Condoleezza Rice as his replacement. She became the first African American woman to hold the office. Bush's other new cabinet appointees included Alberto Gonzales, the first Hispanic attorney general.

December 13, 2003 Saddam Hussein is captured.

October 9, 2004 Afghanistan holds elections for a new government.

2005

October 29, 2004 Osama bin Laden, still at large, releases a videotaped message criticizing and threatening the United States.

January 30, 2005 Iraqis choose new leaders in a democratic election. Violence continues.

July 2005 Suicide bombers attack the mass transit system in London.

Al-Jazeera
Exclusive

أسامة بن لادن
زعيم تنظيم القاعدة

ANALYSIS SKILL **READING TIME LINES**

How long did it take American forces to capture Saddam Hussein after the war in Iraq began?

AMERICA LOOKS TO THE FUTURE **377**

BIOGRAPHY

George W. Bush

1946–

George W. Bush was born in Connecticut and grew up mainly in Texas. His family has a long history of political success—his grandfather was a U.S. senator and his father served as president from 1989 to 1993. Bush was a member of the National Guard during the Vietnam War, then attended Harvard Business School. After running unsuccessfully for Congress in 1978, he started several oil businesses in Texas and became part owner of the Texas Rangers baseball team. He was elected governor of Texas in 1994 and re-elected in 1998. In 2000 he defeated Al Gore in one of the closest presidential races in American history.

Sequencing What did George W. Bush do before he was elected president?

In late 2005 Bush nominated two new Supreme Court justices, John Roberts and Samuel Alito. The Senate investigated each thoroughly before approving them. With the confirmation of Bush's nominees, the court began making more conservative rulings.

Bush's administration faced much criticism for its response to the natural disaster of Hurricanes Katrina and Rita. Rain associated with Hurricane Katrina flooded many parts of the Gulf Coast and the city of New Orleans. The director of the Federal Emergency Management Agency (FEMA) stepped down amid criticism that the local, state, and federal governments responded inadequately to the crisis. As victims tried to rebuild their towns and cities, Hurricane Rita struck a second blow to the region. Although alone not as serious as Hurricane Katrina, the combined effects of the two storms caused many residents to move permanently from their homes along the Gulf Coast.

READING CHECK **Analyzing** What issues did Bush face in his second term?

SUMMARY AND PREVIEW Terrorism became a major concern after September 11, 2001. In the next section you will learn about other debates in America today.

Section 2 Assessment

go.hrw.com
Online Quiz

Reviewing Ideas, Terms, and People

1. **a. Describe** What was the outcome of the 2000 presidential election?
   b. Explain How did **George W. Bush** promise to use the government surplus?
   c. Elaborate How do you think the election of 2000 shows the importance of voting?
2. **a. Identify** What is al Qaeda?
   b. Explain Why did the United States enter into the war with Iraq?
   c. Predict What do you think the future holds for the war on terror?
3. **a. Recall** Who is Condoleezza Rice?
   b. Interpret How might Hurricane Katrina have affected people's view of government?

Critical Thinking

4. **Categorizing** Review your notes on the major policies of George W. Bush. Then copy the graphic organizer below and use it to describe George W. Bush's approach to dealing with terrorism.

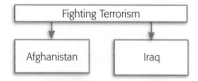

FOCUS ON WRITING

5. **Describing the Effects of September 11** Take notes on the effects of the September 11, 2001, terrorist attacks. What are your own memories of that day? How did Americans respond to the attacks? How did the attacks change the focus of the American people? How did they affect the presidency of George W. Bush?

The Road Ahead

If YOU were there...

You are a student studying American history. You have read about the dramatic impact that inventions, new industries, political changes, and wars have had on daily life over the years. In your own life, you have seen how much things can change in just a few years. Now picture yourself living in the United States 50 years from now.

What will be different about life in America?

BUILDING BACKGROUND Think of the challenges Americans have faced throughout our history. Consider how much the country has changed since it was founded and how much progress has been made. Today the United States continues to face challenges and to search for solutions.

America's Changing Economy

In public opinion polls taken in 2007, Americans listed terrorism and the continuing violence in Iraq among the most important challenges facing the United States. Other major concerns included the economy and the availability of jobs, health care costs, education, immigration, and the environment. The growing national debt was another key concern. After several years of surpluses, the government began running a deficit again in 2002. Slow economic growth, the cost of the war in Iraq, and tax cuts all contributed to the rising budget imbalance.

The American economy and job market have also experienced important ups and downs in recent years. During the 1990s the United States enjoyed the longest period of economic growth in its history. The stock market boomed, and unemployment fell to its lowest level in 30 years. Much of this economic growth was powered by Internet companies and other high-tech firms. When some high-tech firms failed to earn profits, however, their stocks lost value, and many went out of business. Unemployment began rising again.

Although high-tech industries have remained a key part of the U.S. economy, other industries have declined in importance. In recent years, for example, many textile companies have closed

What You Will Learn...

Main Ideas
1. The American economy and job market are changing.
2. Technological advances continue to solve everyday problems.
3. Americans are a diverse people united by shared ideals.

The Big Idea
The United States continues to grow and change as we move ahead in the twenty-first century.

Key Terms and People
service economy, *p. 380*
globalization, *p. 380*
Internet, *p. 381*
Information Revolution, *p. 381*
AIDS, *p. 381*
ozone layer, *p. 382*
global warming, *p. 382*

TAKING NOTES As you read, look for information about changes taking place in the United States. Use a diagram like the one below to help you organize your notes.

Changes		
Economy	Technology	Population

mills and shifted their operations to countries where labor is less expensive. This is part of a larger trend in which the percentage of Americans working in manufacturing has steadily fallen. The U.S. economy has moved toward becoming a **service economy**. This means that most people have jobs providing services, such as medical care or entertainment, rather than producing goods.

By the end of the 1900s, about 75 percent of American workers were employed in service jobs. Economists predict that service industries will continue to grow in the 2000s. Health care, computer engineering, and education are expected to be among the fastest-growing fields. Such predictions are based partly on population trends. As the number of older Americans increases, for example, so will the need for nurses and other health-care professionals.

Another ongoing change in our economy is the process of **globalization**—growing connections among economies and cultures all over the world. Multinational corporations—companies that do business in more than one country—play a large part in globalization. For example, you can find American fast-food restaurants in Russia and Japanese car factories in the United States. Increasing international trade has also contributed to

globalization. In 1995 more than 120 nations joined to form the World Trade Organization (WTO). The WTO's goal is to promote international trade by removing political and economic trade barriers between nations.

Increasing globalization contributed to a worldwide economic crisis. In the 2000s many U.S. lenders had made numerous risky loans to home buyers. These loans were then bundled and sold to other financial institutions, some based overseas. As many homeowners failed to repay their loans, money supplies began to shrink, reducing the amount available for credit. The U.S. economy began to contract dramatically, and unemployment rose. Other nations experienced similar effects. President Bush and the federal government began offering billions of dollars to financial companies in an attempt to bail out failing businesses. One of the first actions of President Barack Obama, elected in 2008, was to attempt to repair the American economy. In early 2009, Congress passed laws devoting nearly $800 billion toward spurring the struggling economy.

READING CHECK **Identifying Cause and Effect** What economic trend led to the creation of the World Trade Organization?

THE IMPACT TODAY

Today, many retired and disabled Americans rely on the government for their health care and general welfare. Some leaders want the government to provide health insurance for every citizen, but others debate the necessity of this.

Life in the Twenty-first Century
QUICK FACTS

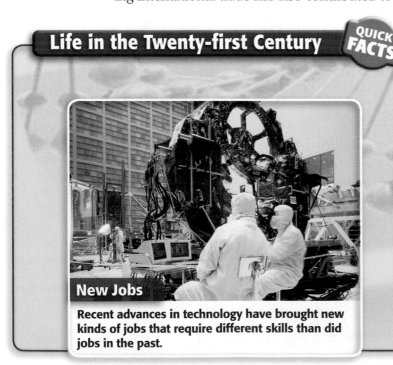

New Jobs

Recent advances in technology have brought new kinds of jobs that require different skills than did jobs in the past.

New Research

Medical research has improved the lives of millions, as new medicines combat old and new diseases.

Technology Moves Forward

As you have seen throughout this book, technological changes and new inventions have dramatic effects on life in the United States and around the world. This continues to be true of our lives today. Just think about all the ways you use technology every day.

One of the new technologies that has changed everyday life is the **Internet**—a global system of computer networks through which people anywhere in the world can communicate and share information. The Internet was first developed in 1969 by scientists at the U.S. Department of Defense. Early computer networks were used mainly by government and university researchers. Then in the 1990s, computer programmers developed the World Wide Web, enabling people to access information from computers around the world.

Internet use exploded in the 1990s. Computers and the Internet made it easier and faster for people at home, work, and school to access and share information. This important development was known as the **Information Revolution**. Bill Gates, a leader in the computer industry, described the exciting changes this revolution promised:

"We are watching something historic happening, and it will affect the world ...the same way the scientific method, the invention of printing, and the arrival of the Industrial Age did."

—Bill Gates, quoted in *Newsweek*

The Information Revolution and the growth of the Internet helped fuel the economic boom of the 1990s and they have changed the way we find information and communicate. Internet use continues to grow rapidly around the world. Use of the Internet to organize voters influenced the outcome of the 2008 election.

Technology is also helping to **facilitate** new medical research. For example, researchers have made important breakthroughs in understanding connections between genetics and illness. In 2003 scientists completed the Human Genome Project, a project to identify more than 30,000 genes in human DNA. Medical researchers hope to use this information to find treatments for a wide range of diseases.

Another ongoing challenge for medical reasearchers is fighting **AIDS**—acquired immune deficiency syndrome. Caused by the human immunodeficiency virus (HIV), AIDS shuts down the body's immune system.

FOCUS ON READING
Predict how the use of the Internet might change American society.

ACADEMIC VOCABULARY
facilitate
bring about

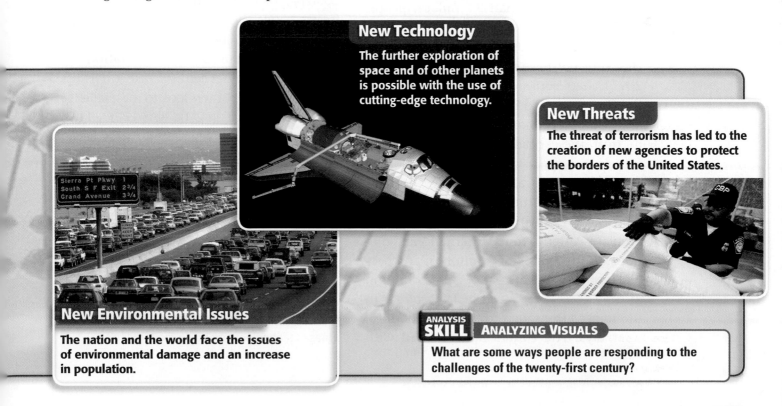

New Technology
The further exploration of space and of other planets is possible with the use of cutting-edge technology.

New Threats
The threat of terrorism has led to the creation of new agencies to protect the borders of the United States.

New Environmental Issues
The nation and the world face the issues of environmental damage and an increase in population.

ANALYSIS SKILL **ANALYZING VISUALS**
What are some ways people are responding to the challenges of the twenty-first century?

BIOGRAPHY

Barack Obama
1961–

Born in Honolulu, Hawaii, Barack Obama is the son of a Kenyan father and a white American mother. He was raised by his mother and maternal grandparents. After graduating from Columbia University and Harvard Law School (where he became the first African American president of the *Harvard Law Review*), he began a career as a civil rights attorney and law professor in Chicago, Illinois.

Obama launched his bid for the presidency after a rapid rise in politics. He began his political career in 1997 in the Illinois Senate. In 2004 he was elected to the U.S. Senate, and in February 2007 he announced his intention to seek the Democratic nomination for president, which he secured in 2008. Obama won the general election, becoming the first African American president of the United States. As president, Obama faced a long list of challenges, including a severe financial crisis and wars in Iraq and Afghanistan. One of his first actions was to work with Congress to pass a bill designed to repair the U.S. economy.

Finding Main Ideas What experience did Barack Obama bring to the presidential race?

This makes it more likely that people with AIDS will contract other illnesses and die. As of 2005, more than 23 million people worldwide had died from AIDS. Scientists have developed drugs that help control the HIV virus but have not yet found a cure. In 2002 leaders from around the world founded the Global Fund to Fight AIDS, Tuberculosis, and Malaria. The Global Fund provides money to treat these deadly diseases and search for cures.

Scientists are also searching for ways to help protect the environment. In our increasingly global society, environmental problems often require international solutions. In the 1980s, for example, many people became concerned about the condition of the **ozone layer** —a thin layer of gas in the upper atmosphere that blocks harmful solar rays. The United States joined with more than 100 other nations to ban the use of chemicals that were harming the ozone layer. By 2004 some scientists reported that damage to the ozone layer was slowly being repaired.

Another environmental issue facing the world is climate change, or **global warming**. The burning of fossil fuels such as gasoline and coal releases carbon dioxide into Earth's atmosphere. Many scientists warn that rising levels of carbon dioxide are causing a greenhouse effect that traps heat from the sun in Earth's atmosphere. This could cause temperatures to rise, which could cause rising sea levels and more severe weather patterns. A 2001 United Nations scientific report predicted that Earth's average temperature could rise between 2 and 10 degrees by 2100.

Concerns about global warming and high oil prices have encouraged development of new transportation technologies. In 2007 Americans bought record numbers of hybrid cars, which run partially on electricity. Scientists are also developing vehicles that will run entirely on hydrogen and release almost no pollution. In the 2008 presidential campaign, Barack Obama focused on the need for clean energy sources and independence from oil, most of which is produced in foreign nations.

Even as some scientists take on issues facing our planet, others look to the challenge of exploring space. In 2004 NASA landed two robotic vehicles on Mars. The rovers began exploring the Martian surface, sending back images that people could see on NASA's Web site. Human exploration of space continues on the International Space Station and with successful shuttle flights. NASA has faced challenges, however. In 2003 the *Columbia* shuttle broke apart, killing seven astronauts.

READING CHECK **Summarizing** In what key areas is technology changing modern life?

The American People

The American population will continue to grow and change in the twenty-first century. The U.S. Census Bureau reports that our population is more ethnically diverse than ever before. In 2005 the bureau reported that Hispanics made up 14 percent of the country's total population, making them the country's largest minority group. African Americans made up just over 13 percent of the American population, and Asian Americans about 5 percent.

These changes are greatly influenced by immigration patterns. Of the more than 32.5 million foreign-born residents, 52 percent were born in Latin America and 25 percent were born in Asia. Based on these trends, the Census Bureau predicts that the country's white and nonwhite populations will be about equal by the year 2050.

Increased diversity is reflected not only in American society but also in individual Americans. In the year 2000 the Census Bureau began allowing people to indicate in official surveys that they were of more than one race. In the 2000 census, more than 6.8 million Americans listed themselves as belonging to more than one race. In 2008, American voters chose a man of mixed race, Barack Obama, as president for the first time.

While the diversity of our population grows, Americans of all backgrounds share a belief in many basic **ideals**. Our shared commitment to the ideals of freedom, equality, and justice helps keep our nation strong. So does our shared dedication to the responsibilities of citizenship. Americans also share many of the same hopes and dreams for the future.

ACADEMIC VOCABULARY

ideals
ideas or goals that people try to live up to

READING CHECK **Predicting** How might the U.S. population change over the next 100 years?

SUMMARY The United States continues to create opportunities and face challenges. How would you like to contribute to your country's future?

go.hrw.com
Online Quiz

Section 3 Assessment

Reviewing Ideas, Terms, and People

1. **a. Recall** How has the American economy changed in the past several decades?
   b. Explain What caused government deficits to rise in the early 2000s?
   c. Draw Conclusions How do you think **globalization** has changed the U.S. economy?
2. **a. Identify** What are some of the world's most recent technological advances?
   b. Explain How did the **Internet** spark an **Information Revolution**?
   c. Predict Do you think **global warming** will affect your life in the future? Why or why not?
3. **a. Describe** Describe the U.S. population today.
   b. Make Inferences Why do you think the Census Bureau started allowing people to mark more than one race?
   c. Elaborate How do you think diversity and shared ideals affect America?

Critical Thinking

4. **Categorizing** Review your notes on changes taking place in the United States. Then copy the graphic organizer below and use it to describe major technological challenges for the future.

Computers — Technological Challenges — Medicine — The Environment

FOCUS ON WRITING

5. **Elaborating on Key Themes** Identify key elements of American life today. In your opinion, what are some great things about life in America? What do you think are the major challenges facing Americans today? What are some possible solutions? Which subjects would you like to read more about? Think about links you could include on your Web site that would provide readers with more information about these topics.

Immigration Today

Immigrants from Asia make up about 25 percent of all foreign-born U.S. residents. Although Chinese and Japanese immigrants have been coming to the United States for generations, Southeast Asians such as the Hmong, Laotians, Vietnamese, and Cambodians are groups that have only recently begun to arrive.

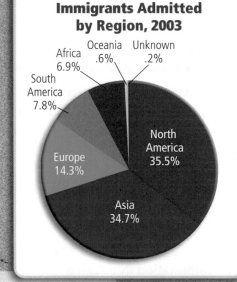

Immigrants Admitted by Region, 2003

- Africa 6.9%
- Oceania .6%
- Unknown .2%
- South America 7.8%
- Europe 14.3%
- North America 35.5%
- Asia 34.7%

America has always been a nation of immigrants. Today people from every country move to the United States. In 2005 approximately 13 percent of the U.S. population was foreign born. Many of these people will eventually choose to become naturalized citizens. With the threat of global terrorism, however, U.S. immigration policy is becoming more strict. People from certain countries are now required to register with the Department of Homeland Security.

Many immigrants from Eastern and Western Europe come to the United States seeking a better life. They accounted for about 16 percent of the immigrants admitted in 2002.

Immigrants from around the world often choose to become naturalized U.S. citizens. The day they take the oath of American citizenship is often a day of celebration, as it was for this mother and daughter from Uganda.

Immigrants arrive in the United States searching for economic, educational, and political opportunities. Immigrants from Mexico and Central America make up about 37 percent of the foreign-born population of the United States.

GEOGRAPHY SKILLS **INTERPRETING MAPS**

1. **Human-Environment Interaction** From which continent does the largest number of immigrants come?
2. **Movement** How do you think immigration affects U.S. society today?

Social Studies Skills

Analysis   Critical Thinking   Civic Participation   Study

Confronting Controversial Issues

Define the Skill

The United States and the world face many challenges in the twenty-first century. People often have different opinions on how to deal with these challenges, which can lead to controversy. Some of the issues discussed in this book remain controversial.

As citizens of a democracy, Americans have a responsibility to confront controversial issues. This includes learning about different issues and why they are controversial. It also involves discussing the issues and forming opinions about them. Part of the democratic system is listening to other people's ideas about how to solve controversial issues and presenting your own ideas in a helpful way. In this way, everyone's ideas can be heard and discussed so that the best course of action can be followed.

Learn the Skill

To confront controversial issues, it is important to understand them. You can start by identifying them. For example, one controversial issue in the twenty-first century is globalization—the process of economies and cultures becoming more closely connected. Some people think that globalization is a good way to improve the lives of all the world's citizens. Others think that globalization destroys what is unique about individual cultures.

Once the issue has been identified, you can learn more about it. Books, news reports, and articles are good sources of information on controversial issues. They can provide different points of view on an issue. Gathering different opinions about globalization, for example, can help you see why it is controversial. It can also help you determine your own point of view on the issue.

Follow these guidelines to confront other controversial issues.

1 Identify the issue.

2 Learn about the issue. Gather information on the subject from different sources. Determine why the issue is controversial.

3 Figure out your own point of view on the issue.

4 Discuss the issue with others. Because the issue is controversial and may lead to disagreements, it is important to be respectful of differences of opinion.

Practice the Skill

Follow these instructions to confront the controversial issue of how to deal with terrorism.

1. Find at least three articles showing different points of view about dealing with terrorism.

2. Read and take notes on the articles you have found. Based on what you have learned, determine your own point of view.

3. Have a class discussion about dealing with terrorism. Listen to opposing points of view. Share your own ideas and explain how you arrived at your point of view.

HOLT
History's Impact
▶ video series
Review the video to answer
the closing question:
*The National Park Service is
constantly challenged to find
a balance between wildlife
and visitors. Why is this?*

Visual Summary

QUICK FACTS

*Use the visual summary below to help you
review the main ideas of the chapter.*

The United States today acts as a member of
the global community as it faces the future.

Challenges
• Environmental issues
• Diseases
• Terrorism

Benefits
• Technology
• Political alliances

Reviewing Vocabulary, Terms, and People

*Match the numbered person or term with the correct
lettered definition.*

1. World Trade Center   **5.** Saddam Hussein

2. Colin Powell   **6.** Madeleine Albright

3. Al Gore   **7.** AIDS

4. global warming   **8.** terrorism

a. 2000 Democratic presidential candidate

b. the rise in average temperatures around the world

c. dictator of Iraq overthrown in 2003

d. buildings attacked on September 11, 2001

e. deadly disease that shuts down the body's
immune system

f. the use of violence by individuals or small
groups to achieve political goals

g. the first woman secretary of state

h. the first African American secretary of state

Comprehension and Critical Thinking

SECTION 1 *(Pages 370–373)*

9. a. Recall What important Cold War symbol was
destroyed in Germany in 1989?

b. Explain How did U.S. foreign policy change
in the Clinton administration?

c. Evaluate Do you think NAFTA helped the
U.S. economy? Why?

SECTION 2 *(Pages 374–378)*

10. a. Identify Who was responsible for the
September 11, 2001, terrorist attacks on the
United States?

b. Explain Why was the 2000 U.S. presidential
election controversial?

c. Evaluate Do you think the United States
was right to go to war with Iraq in 2003? Why?

11. a. Identify What trend is responsible for increasing diversity in the United States?

b. Analyze Why are some people concerned about globalization?

c. Predict What aspects of life do you think will be most affected by new technology in the future?

Reviewing Themes

12. Economics How have changes in the economy affected American society since the 1990s?

13. Politics How have international politics changed over the course of George W. Bush's presidency?

Reading Skills

Predicting *Use the Reading Skills taught in this chapter to answer the question below.*

14. What might you predict for the future of society in the United States? What about the U.S. economy? How might American politics stay the same or change? What ideas in the chapter lead you to these conclusions?

Using the Internet `go.hrw.com`

15. Activity: Ending the Cold War By the 1980s, the Cold War had been going on for decades. But times were changing—communism was falling apart, and the Soviet Union would never be the same again. Enter the activity keyword. Research the factors that led to the decline of the Soviet Union's political and economic power. Then create a brochure on the fall of communism in the Soviet Union, the factors that led to this decline, and the impact on Russian society.

Social Studies Skills

Confronting Controversial Issues *Use the Social Studies Skills taught in this chapter to answer the question below.*

16. Name one controversial issue today. What are two different points of view on the issue?

FOCUS ON WRITING

17. Designing Your Web Site Review your notes and plan your Web site. Decide whether it will be just one page or multiple linked pages. Remember to include information on significant people, events, and ideas. Include ideas for photos, audio, or video you would like to place on your site. You might also want to provide links to other Web sites where viewers can find more information. Make sure your links connect to reliable Web sites, such as government sites or those for newspapers or museums. Finally, choose the Web site address you would like to use.

Grade 8 Intermediate-Level Test Preparation

Directions (1–7): For each statement or question, write on the separate answer sheet the *number* of the word or expression that, of those given, best completes the statement or answers the question.

1 **Madeleine Albright and Colin Powell both**

   (1) conducted breakthrough medical research.

   (2) lost close presidential elections.

   (3) served as secretary of state.

   (4) commanded troops in Iraq.

2 **One way the U.S. economy is changing is that**

   (1) more people are working in service industries.

   (2) more people are working in manufacturing.

   (3) the health care and computer industries are shrinking.

   (4) textile mills are hiring thousands of new workers.

3 **Saddam Hussein was**

   (1) removed from power in Operation Desert Storm.

   (2) elected to the new Iraqi government in 2005.

   (3) killed in the September 11, 2001, attacks.

   (4) captured as a result of the 2003 U.S. invasion of Iraq.

4 **The Cold War came to an end after**

   (1) Communists lost power in East Germany.

   (2) prodemocracy movements began in Eastern Europe.

   (3) the Soviet Union dissolved in 1991.

   (4) Iraq invaded Kuwait in 1990.

5 **As a direct result of the terror attacks on the United States on September 11, 2001, the United States invaded which country?**

   (1) Afghanistan

   (2) Iran

   (3) Iraq

   (4) Saudi Arabia

6 **Which of the following was one of Bill Clinton's achievements as president?**

   (1) gaining the passage of the North American Free Trade Agreement

   (2) creating the Department of Homeland Security

   (3) allowing women in the military to serve in combat

   (4) setting new education standards in the No Child Left Behind act

7 **Which state's electoral votes were contested in the election of 2000?**

   (1) California

   (2) Florida

   (3) New York

   (4) Arkansas

Base your answer to question 8 on the text below and on your knowledge of social studies.

*"*We're a city of immigrants unlike any other city, within a nation of immigrants. Like the victims of the World Trade Center attack, we're of every race, we're of every religion, we're of every ethnicity . . . It's the thing that renews us and revives us in every generation, our openness to new people from all over the world.*"*

—Rudolph Giuliani, quote d in *The Washington Post*

8 **Constructed-Response Question What did Mayor Giuliani say was a unique strength of New York City? Why was this an important message to deliver after the attacks of September 11?**

The United States Looks to the Future

Part A: Short-Answer Questions

Directions: Read and examine the following documents. Then, on a separate sheet of paper, answer the questions using complete sentences.

DOCUMENT 1

Rachel Carson's 1962 book *Silent Spring* examined a situation that the general public was not aware of at the time. Chemicals that were used to kill insects were also killing birds. More and more birds were dying from these chemicals, and Carson warned that, if this continued, future generations would see far fewer birds. *Silent Spring* helped lead to new laws that protected the environment. In the following statement, taken from the book, Carson talks about people and nature.

> Man, however much he may like to pretend the contrary, is part of nature. Can he escape a pollution that is now so thoroughly distributed throughout our world?
>
> —**Rachel Carson,** *Silent Spring*

1a. According to Carson, what do people try to deny?

1b. Do you think the problem of pollution can be solved? Why or why not?

DOCUMENT 2

Jimmy Carter, Anwar el-Sadat, and Menachem Begin were at Camp David from September 5 to September 17, 1978, to reach an agreement on peace in the Middle East. Part of the agreement said, "The people of the Middle East yearn for peace [and hope that] this area can become a model for coexistence and cooperation among nations." The difficult talks proceeded slowly. In the following description, Carter recounts the experience.

> Within a few minutes Sadat announced angrily that a stalemate [standstill] had been reached. He saw no reason for the discussions to continue. As far as he was concerned, they were over . . . They [Sadat and Begin] were moving toward the door, but I got in front of them to partially block the way. I urged them not to break off their talks, to give me another chance to use my influence and analysis, to have confidence in me. Begin agreed readily. I looked straight at Sadat; finally, he nodded his head. They left without speaking to each other.
>
> —**Jimmy Carter,** *Keeping the Faith*

2a. What was the mood at the end of this meeting?

2b. What does Carter say the difference between Sadat and Begin was?

Geraldine Ferraro made history when she became the Democrats' candidate for vice president, paving the way for women to run for high office in the future. She made the following statement as part of her address to the Democratic National Convention in San Francisco, on July 19, 1984.

> By choosing an American woman to run for our nation's second-highest office, you send a powerful signal to all Americans . . . We will place no limits on achievement. If we can do this, we can do anything.
>
> —**Geraldine Ferraro,** *Ferraro: My Story*

3a. According to Ferraro, what message is being sent to Americans by choosing a woman to run for vice president?

_____

3b. What do you think Ferraro means when she says, "If we can do this, we can do anything"?

_____

Bill Gates, who is famous for his work in computer science, has also written books about computers. He has donated money from his books to organizations that work to encourage the use of computers and other technology in education. This statement by Gates was published in the magazine *Newsweek*.

> We are watching something historic happening, and it will affect the world . . . the same way the scientific method, the invention of printing, and the arrival of the Industrial Age did.
>
> —**Bill Gates,** quoted in *Newsweek*

4a. To what does Bill Gates compare the Information Revolution?

_____

4b. Why has the age of computers been called a "revolution"?

_____

Part B: Essay

Historical Context: The documents on these two pages relate to recent and current issues facing the United States and the world.

TASK: Using information from the four documents and your knowledge of U.S. history, write an essay in which you:

- discuss a current issue facing the United States and the world today.
- explain a solution to this issue.

References

The United States of America: Political

CANADA

PACIFIC OCEAN

WASHINGTON
Olympia ★
Seattle
Tacoma
Spokane
Puget Sound
Franklin D. Roosevelt Lake
Pend Oreille
Portland
Columbia River

OREGON
Salem ★
Eugene

IDAHO
Boise ★
Sun Valley
Snake River
Pocatello

MONTANA
Great Falls
Helena ★
Billings
Fort Peck Lake
Missouri River
Yellowstone River
Flathead Lake

NORTH DAKOTA
Bismarck ★
Lake Sakakawea

SOUTH DAKOTA
Pierre ★
Rapid City
Lake Oahe

WYOMING
Yellowstone Lake
Cheyenne ★

NEBRASKA
Platte River

Cape Mendocino
Goose Lake
Shasta Lake
Sacramento River
Pyramid Lake

NEVADA
Reno
Carson City ★
Lake Tahoe

UTAH
Ogden
Great Salt Lake
Salt Lake City ★
Provo
Utah Lake
Great River
Lake Powell

COLORADO
Boulder
Vail
Denver ★
Aspen
Colorado Springs
Pueblo
Arkansas River

KANSAS

Berkeley
Oakland
San Francisco
San Francisco Bay
San Jose
Sacramento
San Joaquin River
Monterey Bay
Fresno

CALIFORNIA
Las Vegas
Lake Mead
Colorado River

Santa Barbara
Ventura
Los Angeles
Long Beach
Riverside
Palm Springs
Anaheim
Santa Ana
San Diego
Channel Islands
Salton Sea

ARIZONA
Flagstaff
Phoenix ★
Casa Grande
Tucson
Gila River

NEW MEXICO
Taos
Santa Fe ★
Albuquerque
Las Cruces
El Paso

OKLAHOMA
Oklahoma City
Lawton
Canadian River
Amarillo
Lubbock
Brazos River

TEXAS
Abilene
Fort Worth
Midland
Odessa
Austin
San Antonio
Corpus Christi
Laredo
Pecos River
Colorado River
Amistad Reservoir
Rio Grande
Padre Island

Gulf of California

MEXICO

PACIFIC OCEAN

To understand the relative locations of Alaska and Hawaii, as well as the vast distances separating them from the rest of the United States, see the world map.

HAWAII
Kauai
Niihau
Oahu
Honolulu
Molokai
Lanai
Maui
Kahoolawe
Hilo
Hawaii
PACIFIC OCEAN
22°N
19°N
160°W
155°W
0   75   150 Miles
0   75   150 Kilometers
Projection: Mercator

ALASKA
ARCTIC OCEAN
Arctic Circle
RUSSIA
Bering Strait
Nome
Yukon River
Fairbanks
Anchorage
Valdez
Skagway
Juneau
CANADA
Gulf of Alaska
Kodiak Island
Alexander Archipelago
St. Lawrence Island
St. Matthew Island
Nunivak Island
Bering Sea
Attu Island
55°N
50°N
170°E
180°
170°W
160°W
150°W
140°W
0   250   500 Miles
0   250   500 Kilometers
Projection: Albers Equal Area
PACIFIC OCEAN

45°N
40°N
35°N
30°N
125°W
120°W

CANADA

MINNESOTA
Grand Forks
Red River
Fargo
Duluth
Superior
Marquette
Sault Ste. Marie

Lake Superior

WISCONSIN
Minneapolis
★ St. Paul
Green Bay
Madison
Milwaukee

MICHIGAN
Lake Michigan
Lake Huron

Grand Rapids
Saginaw
Lansing
Detroit
Ann Arbor

MAINE
Augusta ★
Burlington
Montpelier
Portland
VT
NH
Concord
Manchester
Boston
Worcester
Providence
Cape Cod
MA
Springfield
CT **RI**
Hartford
New Haven
Bridgeport
Long Island Sound
Long Island

Lake Champlain
Hudson R.
Connecticut R.
St. Lawrence River

Rochester
Syracuse
Albany
Buffalo
NEW YORK

Lake Ontario
Lake Erie
Erie
Cleveland
Youngstown
Akron
Toledo

Jersey City
Newark
New York City
Yonkers
Trenton
Allentown
PENNSYLVANIA
Harrisburg
Pittsburgh
Philadelphia
Camden
NJ
Atlantic City
Susquehanna River

IOWA
Sioux Falls
Sioux City
Cedar Rapids
Davenport
Des Moines
Rockford
Chicago
Gary
South Bend
Fort Wayne
Peoria
INDIANA
Springfield
Indianapolis ★
ILLINOIS

OHIO
Columbus
Dayton
Cincinnati

Illinois River
Mississippi River
Missouri River

Omaha
Lincoln
MISSOURI
Kansas City
Topeka
Kansas City
Jefferson City
St. Louis
East St. Louis
Louisville
Evansville
Frankfort ★
Lexington
KENTUCKY
Ohio River

Baltimore
Washington, D.C. ⊛
Annapolis ★
MD
DE
Dover
Delaware Bay
WEST VIRGINIA
Charleston ★
Chesapeake Bay
VIRGINIA
Richmond ★
Newport News
Norfolk
Virginia Beach

ATLANTIC OCEAN

Wichita
Lake of the Ozarks
Springfield
Lake Barkley
Kentucky Lake

Keystone Lake
Tulsa
Fayetteville
Nashville ★
Knoxville
Asheville
TENNESSEE
Chattanooga
Memphis
Greensboro
Winston-Salem
Durham
Raleigh ★
NORTH CAROLINA
Charlotte
Greenville

Cape Hatteras

Eufaula Lake
ARKANSAS
Little Rock ★
Pine Bluff
Huntsville
SOUTH CAROLINA
★ Columbia
Charleston

Lake Texoma
Mississippi River
Kentucky River
Savannah River
Sea Islands

Dallas
Waco
Shreveport
MISSISSIPPI
Vicksburg
Jackson ★
Meridian
ALABAMA
Birmingham
Montgomery ★
Atlanta ★
Columbus
GEORGIA
Macon
Savannah

Red River
Toledo Bend Reservoir
LOUISIANA
Beaumont
Houston
Galveston
Baton Rouge ★
Biloxi
New Orleans
Chandeleur Islands
Mobile
Pensacola
Tallahassee ★
Jacksonville
Gainesville
FLORIDA

Chattahoochee R.

Charleston

Gulf of Mexico

Cape Canaveral
Orlando
Tampa
St. Petersburg
Lake Okeechobee
Fort Myers
Fort Lauderdale
Miami
Cape Sable
Florida Keys
Straits of Florida

THE BAHAMAS

N W E S

Legend	
⊛	National capital
★	State capitals
•	Other cities

0 ——— 100 ——— 200 Miles
0 ——— 100 ——— 200 Kilometers
Projection: Albers Equal Area

40°N
70°W
35°N
30°N
80°W
25°N
95°W
90°W
85°W
75°W

The United States of America: Physical

CANADA

Mount Rainier
14,410 ft.
(4,392 m)

Puget Sound

COAST RANGES

CASCADE RANGE

Franklin D.
Roosevelt Lake

Pend
Oreille
Lake

Flathead River

Flathead Lake

Lewis Range

Milk River

Missouri River

Fort Peck
Lake

ROCKY

GREAT

Lake
Sakakawea

Clark Fork

Columbia River

Willamette River

Bitterroot Range

Salmon River

Salmon
River
Mts.

Sawtooth
Mts.

CONTINENTAL

Yellowstone
Lake

Yellowstone River

Bighorn Mts.

Bighorn River

Powder
River

Yellowstone
River

Black
Hills

Cheyenne
River

Lake
Oahe

White
River

James River

Klamath
River

Goose
Lake

Columbia Plateau

Snake
River

Grand
Tetons

Gannett Peak
13,804 ft.
(4,207 m)

Wind
River
Range

Niobrara - River

INTERIOR

Cape
Mendocino

Shasta
Lake

Pyramid
Lake

Great
Salt
Lake

Wasatch Range

Uinta
Mts.

MOUNTAINS

DIVIDE

Front Range

North Platte River

Platte River

San Francisco Bay

Lake Tahoe

Central Valley

Sacramento River

San Joaquin River

SIERRA NEVADA

Utah
Lake

Green River

Colorado River

Mount Elbert
14,433 ft.
(4,400 m)

Pikes Peak
14,110 ft.
(4,301 m)

South Platte River

Republican River

PLAINS

Monterey
Bay

Coast Ranges

Mount Whitney
14,494 ft.
(4,419 m)

Death Valley

GREAT

BASIN

COLORADO

Lake
Powell

San Juan River

Smoky Hill River

Mojave
Desert

Lake
Mead

Grand
Canyon

PLATEAU

Painted Desert

San Luis
Valley

Sangre De Cristo Mts.

PACIFIC

OCEAN

Channel
Islands

Colorado River

Salton
Sea

Imperial
Valley

DIVIDE

Rio Grande

Canadian River

Gila   River

Sonoran

Desert

CONTINENTAL

MEXICO

Gulf of
California

Pecos River

Amistad
Reservoir

Rio Grande

Colorado River

Nueces River

To understand the relative locations of Alaska and Hawaii,
as well as the vast distances separating them from the rest
of the United States, see the world map.

Kauai

Niihau

Oahu

HAWAII

Molokai

Maui

PACIFIC
OCEAN

Lanai

Kahoolawe

Mauna Kea
13,796 ft.
(4,206 m)

Hawaii

| 0 | 75 | 150 Miles |

| 0 | 75 | 150 Kilometers |

Projection: Mercator

ARCTIC OCEAN

RUSSIA

BROOKS RANGE

Arctic Circle

Bering
Strait

St. Lawrence
Island

St. Matthew
Island

Nunivak
Island

Kuskokwim River

Yukon River

Tanana River

ALASKA   RANGE

Mount McKinley
20,320 ft.
(6,194 m)

CANADA

Bering Sea

Attu Island

| 0 | 250 | 500 Miles |

| 0 | 250 | 500 Kilometers |

Projection: Albers Equal Area

PACIFIC
OCEAN

Gulf of Alaska

Kodiak Island

Alexander
Archipelago

Padre
Island

CANADA

Red River

Isle Royale

Mesabi Range

Lake Superior

Minnesota River

Mississippi River

Wisconsin River

Lake Michigan

Lake Huron

St. Lawrence River

St. Lawrence Seaway

St. John River

Penobscot River

Longfellow Mts.

White Mts.

Green Mts.

Lake Champlain

Adirondack Mts.

Hudson River

Connecticut River

Lake Ontario

Cape Cod

Long Island Sound

Long Island

Des Moines River

Illinois River

ALLEGHENY PLATEAU

Catskill Mts.

Allegheny R.

Susquehanna River

Delaware River

Lake Erie

40°N

Kansas R.

P L A I N S

Wabash River

Scioto River

Ohio River

Monongahela R.

Potomac River

Delaware Bay

Chesapeake Bay

70°W

ATLANTIC OCEAN

Lake of the Ozarks

OZARK PLATEAU

Kansas R.

Missouri River

O   R

Keystone Lake

Lake Barkley

Kentucky Lake

Cumberland River

Cumberland Plateau

Kanawha River

James River

Roanoke River

35°N

Pamlico Sound

Cape Hatteras

Eufaula Lake

White River

Arkansas River

Tennessee River

Great Smoky Mts.

BLUE RIDGE MOUNTAINS

A P P A L A C H I A N   M O U N T A I N S

Lake Texoma

Ouachita Mts.

Oconee River

Savannah River

P   I   E   D   M   O   N   T

Trinity River

Sabine River

Red River

Tombigbee River

Coosa River

Alabama R.

Chattahoochee River

Altamaha River

Sea Islands

Brazos River

Toledo Bend Reservoir

C O A S T A L

P L A I N

Pearl River

Mississippi River

Okefenokee Swamp

Cape Canaveral

ELEVATION

Feet	Meters
13,120	4,000
6,560	2,000
1,640	500
656	200
(Sea level) 0	0 (Sea level)
Below sea level	Below sea level

0   100   200 Miles

0   100   200 Kilometers

Projection: Albers Equal Area

G U L F

Chandeleur Islands

Mississippi Delta

N
W   E
S

Gulf of Mexico

FLORIDA PENINSULA

Cape Canaveral

THE BAHAMAS

80°W

Lake Okeechobee

The Everglades

Cape Sable

Florida Keys

Straits of Florida

25°N

95°W

90°W

85°W

25°N

75°W

ATLAS

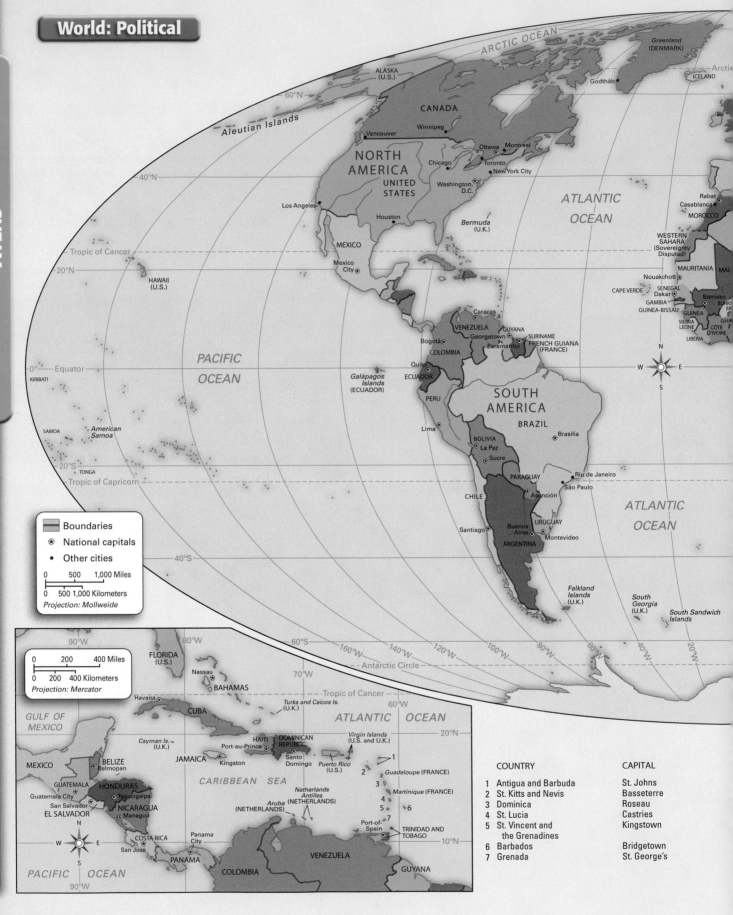

ATLAS

ARCTIC OCEAN

Greenland (DENMARK)

ALASKA (U.S.)

ICELAND

Godthåb

60°N

CANADA

Winnipeg

Aleutian Islands

Vancouver

NORTH AMERICA

Ottawa Montreal

Chicago

Toronto

New York City

40°N

UNITED STATES

Washington, D.C.

ATLANTIC OCEAN

Rabat

Casablanca

MOROCCO

Los Angeles

Houston

WESTERN SAHARA (Sovereignty Disputed)

Bermuda (U.K.)

Tropic of Cancer

MEXICO

MAURITANIA MAL

20°N

HAWAII (U.S.)

Mexico City

Nouakchott

CAPE VERDE

SENEGAL
Dakar

Bamako

BURK

GAMBIA

GUINEA-BISSAU

GUINEA

FA

GHA

Caracas

SIERRA
LEONE

CÔTE
D'IVOIRE

VENEZUELA GUYANA

LIBERIA

Bogotá

Georgetown

SURINAME

FRENCH GUIANA (FRANCE)

COLOMBIA

Paramaribo

PACIFIC OCEAN

0° Equator

Quito

ECUADOR

KIRIBATI

N

Galápagos
Islands
(ECUADOR)

W   E

PERU

SOUTH
AMERICA

S

BRAZIL

Lima

Brasília

American
Samoa

BOLIVIA

SAMOA

La Paz

Sucre

20°S

TONGA

Rio de Janeiro

Tropic of Capricorn

PARAGUAY

São Paulo

CHILE

Asunción

ATLANTIC
OCEAN

URUGUAY

Santiago

Buenos
Aires

Montevideo

ARGENTINA

Boundaries

National capitals

Other cities

0   500   1,000 Miles

0   500 1,000 Kilometers

Projection: Mollweide

40°S

Falkland
Islands
(U.K.)

South
Georgia
(U.K.)

South Sandwich
Islands

60°S

160°W

140°W

120°W

100°W

80°W

60°W

40°W

20°W

Antarctic Circle

0   200   400 Miles

0   200   400 Kilometers

Projection: Mercator

90°W

80°W

FLORIDA
(U.S.)

70°W

Tropic of Cancer

Nassau

60°W

Havana

BAHAMAS

20°N

GULF OF
MEXICO

CUBA

Turks and Caicos Is.
(U.K.)

ATLANTIC   OCEAN

Cayman Is.
(U.K.)

HAITI

DOMINICAN
REPUBLIC

Virgin Islands
(U.S. and U.K.)

MEXICO

BELIZE
Belmopan

JAMAICA

Port-au-Prince

Kingston

Santo
Domingo

Puerto Rico
(U.S.)

1

Guadeloupe (FRANCE)

2

GUATEMALA

CARIBBEAN   SEA

3

Martinique (FRANCE)

Guatemala City

HONDURAS

Tegucigalpa

Netherlands
Antilles
(NETHERLANDS)

4

San Salvador

NICARAGUA

Aruba
(NETHERLANDS)

5

6

EL SALVADOR

N

Managua

7

W   E

Port-of-
Spain

TRINIDAD AND
TOBAGO

S

COSTA RICA

Panama
City

10°N

San José

PANAMA

VENEZUELA

GUYANA

PACIFIC   OCEAN

COLOMBIA

90°W

COUNTRY	CAPITAL
1 Antigua and Barbuda	St. Johns
2 St. Kitts and Nevis	Basseterre
3 Dominica	Roseau
4 St. Lucia	Castries
5 St. Vincent and the Grenadines	Kingstown
6 Barbados	Bridgetown
7 Grenada	St. George's

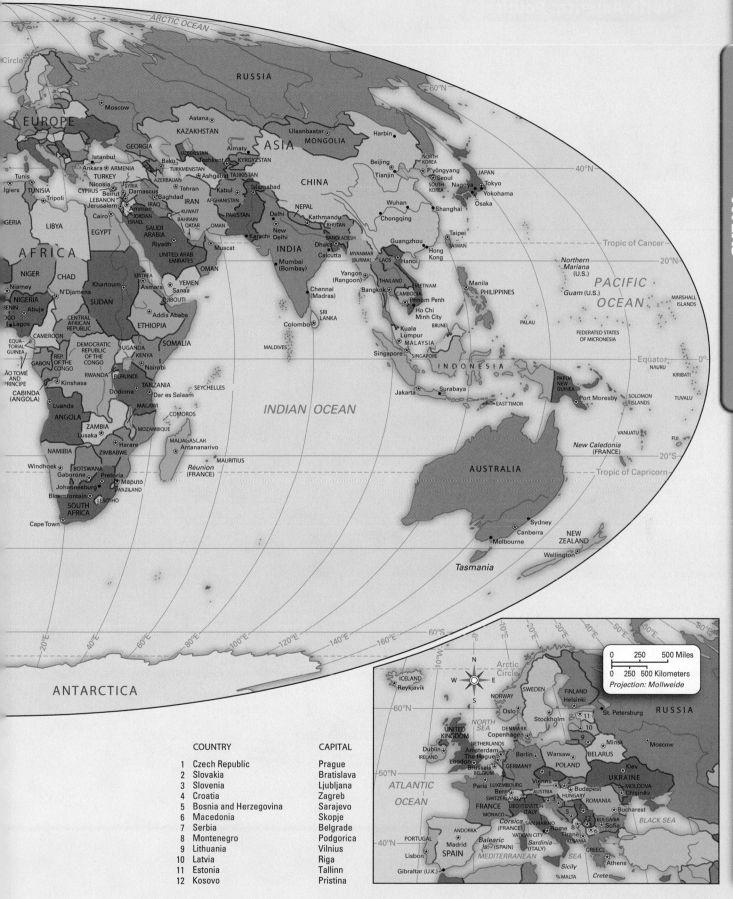

COUNTRY

1 Czech Republic
2 Slovakia
3 Slovenia
4 Croatia
5 Bosnia and Herzegovina
6 Macedonia
7 Serbia
8 Montenegro
9 Lithuania
10 Latvia
11 Estonia
12 Kosovo

CAPITAL

Prague
Bratislava
Ljubljana
Zagreb
Sarajevo
Skopje
Belgrade
Podgorica
Vilnius
Riga
Tallinn
Pristina

North America: Political

ARCTIC OCEAN

ASIA

EUROPE

+ North Pole

Nunivak Island
St. Lawrence Island
Bering Sea
Bering Strait
Point Barrow

ICELAND

Denmark Strait

Queen Elizabeth Islands

Ellesmere Island

Greenland (DENMARK)

Banks Island

Baffin Bay

ALASKA (U.S.)

Yukon River

Victoria Island

Baffin Island

Davis Strait

Anchorage

Great Bear Lake

Cape Farewell

Kodiak Island
Gulf of Alaska

Mackenzie River
Great Slave Lake

Southampton Island
Coats Island
Mansel Island

Hudson Strait

Labrador Sea

Juneau

Alexander Archipelago

Peace River

Hudson Bay

Queen Charlotte Islands

CANADA

Anticosti Island

Newfoundland

PACIFIC OCEAN

Vancouver Island

Edmonton

Lake Winnipeg

St. Pierre and Miquelon (FRANCE)

Vancouver

Calgary

Prince Edward Island
Gulf of St. Lawrence
Cape Breton Island

Seattle

Winnipeg

Quebec

Portland

Columbia River

Lake Superior

Lake Huron

Montreal

Cape Mendocino

Snake River

Missouri River

Minneapolis

Lake Michigan

Ottawa
Toronto

Lake Ontario
Lake Erie

Boston
Cape Cod
New York City

ATLANTIC OCEAN

San Francisco

Great Salt Lake

Salt Lake City

Milwaukee
Chicago

Detroit

Cleveland
Columbus

Philadelphia
Baltimore

San Jose

Platte River

Denver

Indianapolis

St. Louis

Washington, D.C.

Los Angeles
San Diego
Tijuana

Colorado River

Kansas City

Ohio River

Norfolk

UNITED STATES

Mississippi River

Cape Hatteras

Bermuda (U.K.)

Phoenix

Red River

Memphis

Atlanta
Birmingham

Rio Grande

Austin
San Antonio

Dallas

Houston

New Orleans

Jacksonville

Cape Canaveral

Tropic of Cancer

Gulf of California

Monterrey

Gulf of Mexico

Miami

THE BAHAMAS

Nassau

Turks and Caicos Islands (U.K.)

Puerto Rico (U.S.)

ST. KITTS & NEVIS
ANTIGUA & BARBUDA
Guadeloupe (FRANCE)

MEXICO

Florida Keys

Havana

CUBA

DOMINICAN REPUBLIC

San Juan

DOMINICA

Guadalajara
Mexico City

Mérida

HAITI

Santo Domingo

BARBADOS

Puebla

Cayman Is. (U.K.)

Kingston

Port-au-Prince

Santo Domingo
U.S. Virgin Is.
(U.S., U.K.)

Martinique (FRANCE)

ST. LUCIA
ST. VINCENT AND THE GRENADINES

Balsas R.

JAMAICA

Netherlands Antilles (NETHERLANDS)

GRENADA

Belmopan
BELIZE

Caribbean Sea

Aruba (NETHERLANDS)

TRINIDAD AND TOBAGO

GUATEMALA
Guatemala City
San Salvador
EL SALVADOR

HONDURAS
Tegucigalpa
NICARAGUA
Managua

Panama Canal

San José

Panama City

COSTA RICA

PANAMA

SOUTH AMERICA

Equator

Legend

	Boundaries
⊛	National capitals
•	Other cities

0   300   600 Miles
0   300   600 Kilometers

Projection: Azimuthal Equal Area

South America: Political

CENTRAL
AMERICA

Caribbean Sea

Barranquilla
Cartagena •
Caracas •
Lake
Maracaibo
VENEZUELA
Medellín •
Bogotá ⊛
Orinoco River
Georgetown ⊛
Paramaribo ⊛
GUYANA
Cayenne •
COLOMBIA
SURINAME FRENCH
GUIANA
(FRANCE)
Cali •

Malpelo
Island
(COLOMBIA)
Quito ⊛
ECUADOR
Guayaquil •
Río Negro
Amazon River
Belém •

0° Equator
Galápagos
Islands
(ECUADOR)
Amazon River
Equator 0°

Marañón River
PERU
BRAZIL
Trujillo •
Ucayali River
Recife •

Callao ⊛• Lima
10°S
Salvador •

PACIFIC
OCEAN
Arequipa •
Lake
Titicaca
⊛ La Paz
Lake
Poopó
BOLIVIA
Brasília ⊛
São Francisco River

Sucre ⊛
Belo Horizonte •

Paraguay River
20°S
Tropic of Capricorn
PARAGUAY
Campinas •
São Paulo •
Rio de Janeiro • Tropic of Capricorn
San Ambrosio
Island
(CHILE)
San Félix Island
(CHILE)
Asunción ⊛
Curitiba •

CHILE
Paraná River
Uruguay River
Pôrto Alegre •

Juan Fernández
Islands
(CHILE)
Córdoba •
Valparaíso •
Rosario •
URUGUAY
30°S
Santiago ⊛
Buenos Aires ⊛
Montevideo ⊛
Río de la Plata
ATLANTIC
OCEAN

ARGENTINA
40°S

Boundaries
⊛ National capitals
• Other cities
0   250   500 Miles
0   250   500 Kilometers
Projection: Azimuthal Equal Area

Strait of
Magellan
Falkland
Islands (U.K.)

Tierra del
Fuego
South Georgia
Island
(U.K.)
50°S

ATLANTIC
OCEAN

Europe: Political

ASIA

URAL MOUNTAINS

RUSSIA

Nizhny Novgorod

Moscow •

Ural River

Volga River

Caspian Sea

SOUTHWEST ASIA

Barents Sea

White Sea

North Cape

St. Petersburg

FINLAND

Helsinki ✪

Gulf of Bothnia

Tallinn ✪ ESTONIA

LATVIA Riga ✪

Minsk ✪

BELARUS

Dnieper River

Kiev ✪

UKRAINE

Chişinău ✪

MOLDOVA

Bucharest ✪

ROMANIA

Black Sea

Rhodes

Crete

Aegean Sea

ATLAS

ARCTIC OCEAN

SWEDEN

Stockholm ✪

Göteborg •

LITHUANIA

Vilnius ✪

RUSSIA

Baltic Sea

Warsaw ✪

POLAND

Krakow •

SLOVAKIA

Bratislava ✪

Budapest ✪

HUNGARY

Belgrade ✪

SERBIA

Sofia ✪

BULGARIA

Danube River

Skopje ✪

MACEDONIA

Tiranë ✪

ALBANIA

GREECE

Athens ✪

NORWAY

Oslo ✪

Bergen •

DENMARK

Copenhagen ✪

Hamburg •

Berlin ✪

Dresden •

GERMANY

Prague ✪

CZECH REPUBLIC

Vienna ✪

AUSTRIA

LIECHTENSTEIN

Zagreb ✪

CROATIA

SLOVENIA

Ljubljana ✪

BOSNIA AND HERZEGOVINA

Sarajevo ✪

MONTENEGRO

Podgorica ✪

KOSOVO

Priština ✪

Elbe River

Cologne •

Bonn •

Munich •

Bern ✪

Vaduz ✪

SWITZERLAND

Milan •

SAN MARINO

San Marino ✪

ITALY

Rome ✪

VATICAN CITY

Naples •

Adriatic Sea

Sea

MALTA

Valletta ✪

Sicily

North Sea

THE NETHERLANDS

Amsterdam ✪

The Hague ✪

BELGIUM

Brussels ✪

Luxembourg ✪

LUXEMBOURG

Paris ✪

FRANCE

Lyon •

MONACO

Monaco ✪

Corsica (FRANCE)

Sardinia (ITALY)

Mediterranean Sea

AFRICA

Shetland Islands

Faeroe Islands (DENMARK)

ICELAND

Reykjavík ✪

SCOTLAND

Edinburgh ✪

UNITED KINGDOM

Liverpool •

Belfast ✪

NORTHERN IRELAND

Dublin ✪

IRELAND

British Isles

WALES

ENGLAND

London ✪

English Channel

Channel Islands (U.K.)

Marseille •

PYRENEES

Andorra la Vella ✪

ANDORRA

Barcelona •

Balearic Islands (SPAIN)

Rhône River

Seine River

Bay of Biscay

ATLANTIC OCEAN

Madrid ✪

Seville •

SPAIN

Valencia •

Gibraltar (U.K.)

Strait of Gibraltar

PORTUGAL

Lisbon ✪

Tagus River

Arctic Circle

Gulf of Finland

70°N

60°N

50°N

40°N

50°E

40°E

30°E

20°E

10°E

0°

10°W

20°W

30°W

40°W

30°E

20°E

10°E

0°

10°E

20°E

30°E

Legend

Boundaries
✪ National capitals
• Other cities

0   150   300 Miles
0   150   300 Kilometers
Projection: Azimuthal Equal Area

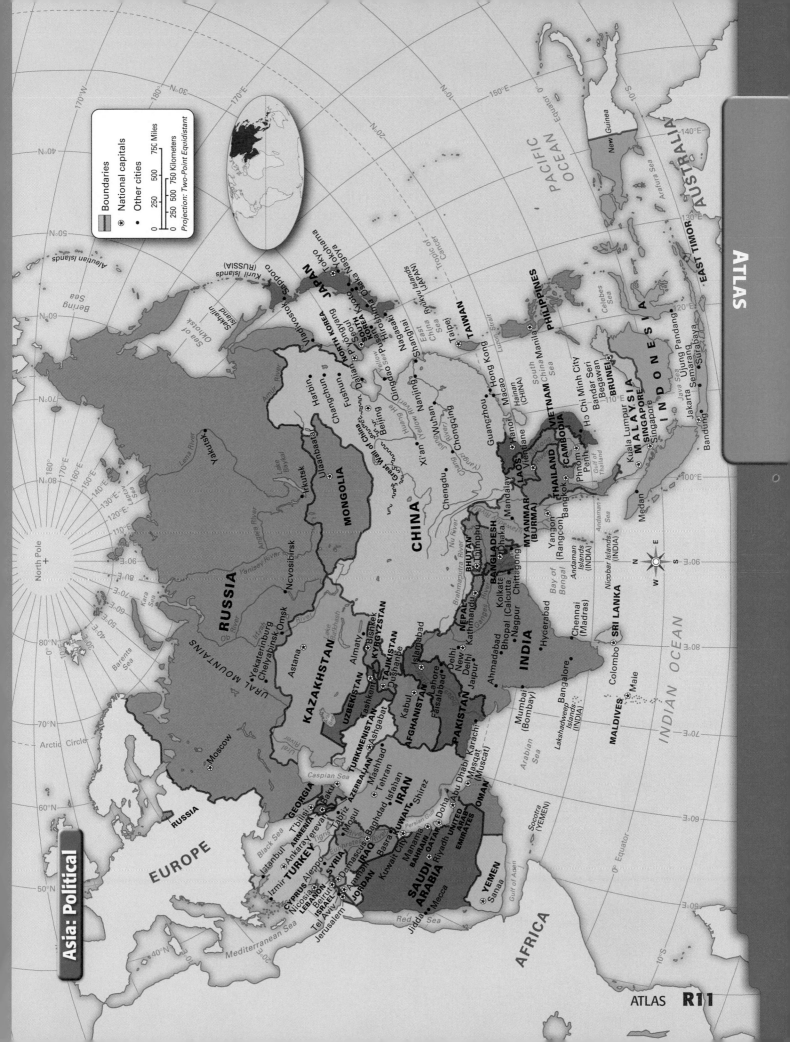

Asia: Political

Boundaries
⊛ National capitals
• Other cities

0 250 500 750 Miles
0 250 500 750 Kilometers
Projection: Two-Point Equidistant

EUROPE

AFRICA

AUSTRALIA

PACIFIC OCEAN

INDIAN OCEAN

RUSSIA

CHINA

MONGOLIA

KAZAKHSTAN

INDIA

IRAN

SAUDI ARABIA

TURKEY

JAPAN

NORTH KOREA

SOUTH KOREA

TAIWAN

PHILIPPINES

INDONESIA

MALAYSIA

THAILAND

MYANMAR (BURMA)

VIETNAM

LAOS

CAMBODIA

BANGLADESH

NEPAL

BHUTAN

PAKISTAN

AFGHANISTAN

UZBEKISTAN

TURKMENISTAN

TAJIKISTAN

KYRGYZSTAN

IRAQ

SYRIA

JORDAN

ISRAEL

LEBANON

CYPRUS

GEORGIA

ARMENIA

AZERBAIJAN

YEMEN

OMAN

UNITED ARAB EMIRATES

QATAR

BAHRAIN

KUWAIT

BRUNEI

SRI LANKA

MALDIVES

EAST TIMOR

Moscow

North Pole

Africa: Political

EUROPE

SOUTHWEST ASIA

Azores (PORTUGAL)

Mediterranean Sea

Madeira (PORTUGAL)

Strait of Gibraltar

Algiers Tunis

Casablanca Rabat

Tripoli

Alexandria

MOROCCO

TUNISIA

Giza Cairo

Suez Canal

Canary Islands (SPAIN)

ALGERIA

LIBYA

EGYPT

El Aaiún

Nile River

WESTERN SAHARA (Claimed by Morocco)

Lake Nasser

Tropic of Cancer

MAURITANIA

Nouakchott

MALI

NIGER

CHAD

Khartoum

ERITREA

Asmara

Red Sea

CAPE VERDE

Praia

SENEGAL

Dakar

GAMBIA

Banjul

Bissau

GUINEA-BISSAU

Niger River

Bamako

BURKINA FASO

Niamey

Lake Chad

N'Djamena

SUDAN

Gulf of Aden

DJIBOUTI

Djibouti

ETHIOPIA

Addis Ababa

GUINEA

Conakry

Freetown

Ouagadougou

NIGERIA

BENIN

TOGO

CÔTE D'IVOIRE

GHANA

Abuja

SIERRA LEONE

Yamoussoukro

Lomé

Monrovia

Abidjan Accra

Porto-Novo

Lagos

LIBERIA

Gulf of Guinea

Malabo

CAMEROON

CENTRAL AFRICAN REPUBLIC

Bangui

SOMALIA

Mogadishu

EQUATORIAL GUINEA

Yaoundé

SÃO TOMÉ AND PRÍNCIPE

São Tomé

UGANDA

Kampala

KENYA

Nairobi

Equator

REPUBLIC OF THE CONGO

Libreville

Congo River

Kisangani

GABON

DEMOCRATIC REPUBLIC OF THE CONGO

RWANDA

Kigali

Brazzaville

Bujumbura

BURUNDI

Lake Victoria

Mombasa

INDIAN OCEAN

Victoria

SEYCHELLES

CABINDA (ANGOLA)

Kinshasa

TANZANIA

Dodoma

Pemba

Zanzibar

Lake Tanganyika

Dar es Salaam

Luanda

ATLANTIC OCEAN

Lubumbashi

COMOROS

Moroni

MALAWI

Lilongwe

St. Helena (U.K.)

ANGOLA

ZAMBIA

Lusaka

Lake Malawi (Nyasa)

MOZAMBIQUE

Antananarivo

MAURITIUS

MADAGASCAR

Port Louis

Zambezi River

Harare

ZIMBABWE

Réunion (FRANCE)

NAMIBIA

Windhoek

BOTSWANA

Bulawayo

Tropic of Capricorn

Gaborone

Pretoria

Maputo

Johannesburg

Mbabane

SWAZILAND

Bloemfontein

Maseru

LESOTHO

Orange River

SOUTH AFRICA

Cape Town

Legend

Boundaries

⊛ National capitals

• Other cities

0   250   500 Miles

0 250 500 Kilometers

Projection: Azimuthal Equal Area

N S E W

Australia and New Zealand: Political

NORTH AMERICA

ASIA

NORTH PACIFIC OCEAN

SOUTH PACIFIC OCEAN

INDIAN OCEAN

Tropic of Cancer

Tropic of Capricorn

Equator

International Date Line

POLYNESIA

KIRIBATI

MICRONESIA

MELANESIA

Marquesas Islands (FRANCE)

Tuamotu Archipelago (FRANCE)

French Polynesia

Rapa Island (FRANCE)

Tubuai Islands (FRANCE)

Easter Island (CHILE)

Pitcairn (U.K.) Ducie Island

Pitcairn Island

Society Islands (FRANCE)

Tahiti (FRANCE)

Papeete

Starbuck Island

Manihiki Island

Cook Islands (NEW ZEALAND)

Rarotonga Island

Palmyra Island (U.S.)

Kingman Reef

Washington Island

Fanning Island

Jarvis I. (U.S.)

Baker I. (U.S.)

Howland I. (U.S.)

Phoenix Islands

McKean I.

Gardner Island

Tokelau (N.Z.)

American Samoa

Pago Pago

Niue (N.Z.)

SAMOA Apia

TONGA Nuku'alofa

Wallis & Futuna (FR.)

TUVALU Funafuti

FIJI Suva

Hawaiian Islands

Hawaii (U.S.)

Midway Island (U.S.)

Johnston Island (U.S.)

Wake Island (U.S.)

MARSHALL ISLANDS

Eniwetok I.

Kwajalein Island

Majuro

Tarawa

Gilbert Islands

NAURU Yaren

Palikir

FEDERATED STATES OF MICRONESIA

Truk Is.

Guam (U.S.) Agana

Northern Marianas (U.S.)

Bonin Islands (JAPAN)

Volcano Islands (JAPAN)

PALAU Koror

SOLOMON ISLANDS Honiara

Guadalcanal I.

PAPUA NEW GUINEA Port Moresby

New Guinea

Bismarck Archipelago

VANUATU Port-Vila

Espiritu Santo I.

Malekula I.

New Caledonia (FRANCE) Nouméa

Loyalty Islands (FRANCE)

Norfolk Island (AUSTRALIA)

Kermadec Islands (N.Z.)

Auckland

North Island

NEW ZEALAND

Wellington

Christchurch

South Island

Chatham Islands (N.Z.)

Bounty Islands (N.Z.)

Auckland Islands (NEW ZEALAND)

AUSTRALIA

Brisbane

Sydney

Canberra

Melbourne

Hobart

Adelaide

Perth

Darwin

Tasman Sea

Coral Sea

Arafura Sea

Timor Sea

Philippine Sea

South China Sea

Christmas Island (AUSTRALIA)

Flinders R.

Darling R.

Lachlan R.

Murray R.

N E W S

Legend

Boundaries
⊛ National capitals
• Other cities

1,000 Miles
500
0

1,000 Kilometers
500
0

Projection: Mercator

20°N, 30°N, 15°N, 0°, 15°S, 30°S, 45°S

135°E, 150°E, 165°E, 180°, 165°W, 150°W, 135°W, 120°W

ATLAS **R13**

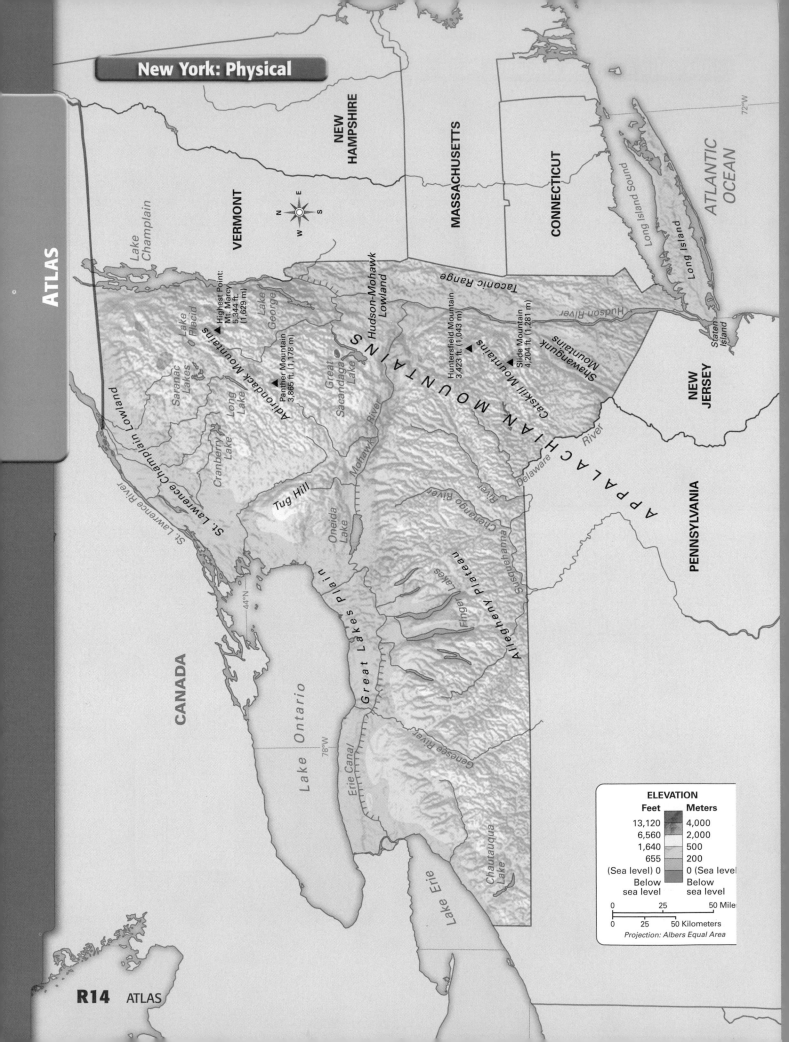

New York: Physical

CANADA

VERMONT

NEW
HAMPSHIRE

MASSACHUSETTS

CONNECTICUT

NEW
JERSEY

PENNSYLVANIA

ATLANTIC
OCEAN

Lake Champlain

Saranac Lakes

Lake Placid

Highest Point:
Mt. Marcy
5,344 ft.
(1,629 m)

Lake George

Adirondack Mountains

Panther Mountain
3,865 ft. (1,178 m)

Cranberry Lake

Long Lake

St. Lawrence River

St. Lawrence Champlain Lowland

Tug Hill

Great Sacandaga Lake

Mohawk River

Oneida Lake

Hudson-Mohawk Lowland

Huntersfield Mountain
3,423 ft. (1,043 m)

Slide Mountain
4,204 ft. (1,281 m)

Catskill Mountains

Shawangunk Mountains

Taconic Range

Hudson River

Staten Island

Long Island

Long Island Sound

APPALACHIAN MOUNTAINS

Delaware River

Susquehanna River

Chenango River

Finger Lakes

Allegheny Plateau

Genesee River

Great Lakes Plain

Erie Canal

Lake Ontario

Lake Erie

Chautauqua Lake

44°N

78°W

72°W

N E W S

ELEVATION

Feet		Meters
13,120		4,000
6,560		2,000
1,640		500
655		200
(Sea level) 0		0 (Sea level
Below sea level		Below sea level

0   25   50 Miles

0   25   50 Kilometers

Projection: Albers Equal Area

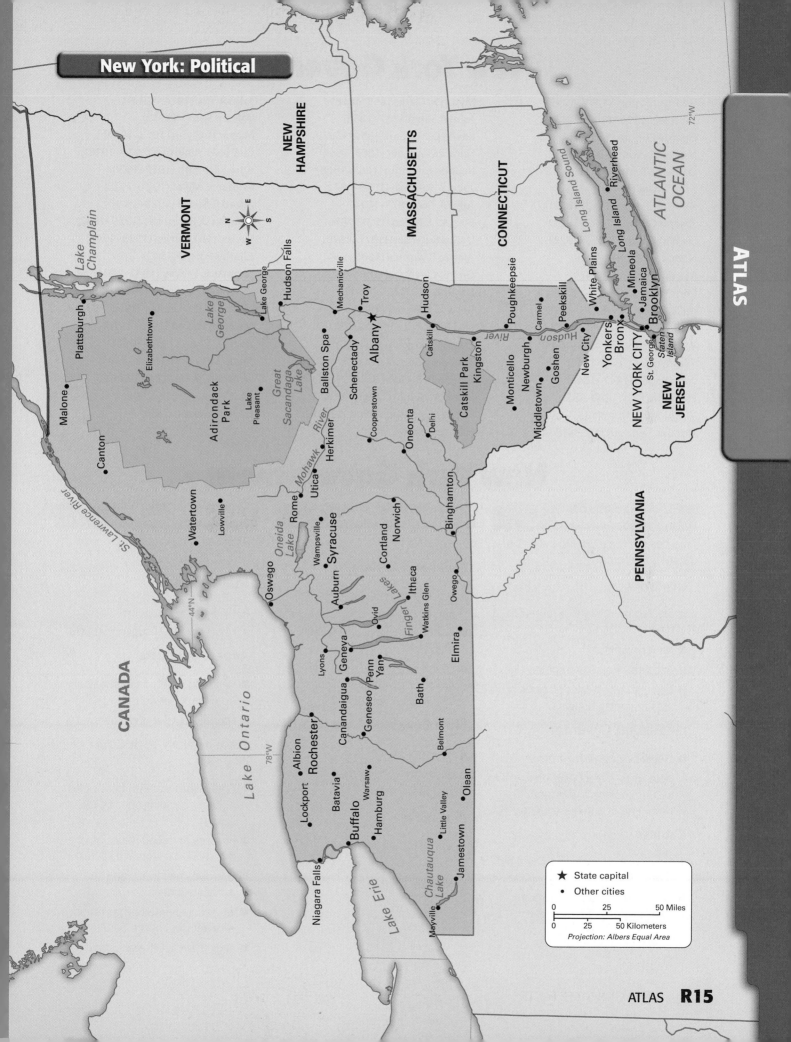

New York: Political

CANADA

VERMONT

NEW HAMPSHIRE

MASSACHUSETTS

CONNECTICUT

PENNSYLVANIA

NEW JERSEY

ATLANTIC OCEAN

St. Lawrence River

Lake Champlain

Lake George

Great Sacandaga Lake

Mohawk River

Hudson River

Lake Ontario

Lake Erie

Oneida Lake

Finger Lakes

Chautauqua Lake

Long Island Sound

Long Island

Adirondack Park

Catskill Park

Plattsburgh
Elizabethtown
Malone
Canton
Watertown
Lowville
Lake Pleasant
Hudson Falls
Lake George
Mechanicville
Troy
Ballston Spa
Schenectady
Albany
Cooperstown
Herkimer
Utica
Rome
Wampsville
Oswego
Syracuse
Auburn
Cortland
Norwich
Ithaca
Watkins Glen
Ovid
Oneonta
Delhi
Binghamton
Owego
Catskill
Hudson
Kingston
Monticello
Poughkeepsie
Newburgh
Middletown
Goshen
Carmel
Peekskill
New City
White Plains
Yonkers
Bronx
NEW YORK CITY
St. George
Staten Island
Brooklyn
Jamaica
Mineola
Riverhead
Elmira
Owego
Lyons
Geneva
Penn Yan
Canandaigua
Geneseo
Bath
Belmont
Rochester
Albion
Batavia
Warsaw
Lockport
Buffalo
Hamburg
Niagara Falls
Mayville
Jamestown
Little Valley
Olean

★ State capital
• Other cities

0   25   50 Miles
0   25   50 Kilometers
Projection: Albers Equal Area

44°N
78°W
72°W

N E W S

ATLAS

New York Governors

George Clinton (1777–1795)
John Jay (1795–1801)
George Clinton (1801–1804)
Morgan Lewis (1804–1807)
Daniel D. Tompkins (1807–1817)
John Tayler (1817)
De Witt Clinton (1817–1822)
Joseph C. Yates (1823–1824)
De Witt Clinton (1825–1828)
Nathaniel Pitcher (1828)
Martin Van Buren (1829)
Enos T. Throop (1829–1832)
William L. Marcy (1833–1838)
William H. Seward (1839–1842)
William C. Bouck (1843–1844)
Silas Wright (1845–1846)
John Young (1847–1848)
Hamilton Fish (1849–1850)
Washington Hunt (1851–1852)
Horatio Seymour (1853–1854)

Myron H. Clark (1855–1856)
John A. King (1857–1858)
Edwin D. Morgan (1859–1862)
Horatio Seymour (1863–1864)
Reuben E. Fenton (1865–1868)
John T. Hoffman (1869–1872)
John A. Dix (1873–1874)
Samuel J. Tilden (1875–1876)
Lucius Robinson (1877–1879)
Alonzo B. Cornell (1880–1882)
Grover Cleveland (1883–1884)
David B. Hill (1885–1891)
Roswell P. Flower (1892–1894)
Levi P. Morton (1895–1896)
Frank S. Black (1897–1898)
Theodore Roosevelt (1899–1900)
Benjamin B. Odell, Jr. (1901–1904)
Frank W. Higgins (1905–1906)
Charles E. Hughes (1907–1910)
Horace White (1910)

John A. Dix (1911–1912)
William Sulzer (1913)
Martin H. Glynn (1913–1914)
Charles S. Whitman (1915–1918)
Alfred E. Smith (1919–1920)
Nathan L. Miller (1921–1922)
Alfred E. Smith (1923–1928)
Franklin D. Roosevelt (1929–1932)
Herbert H. Lehman (1933–1942)
Charles Poletti (1942)
Thomas E. Dewey (1943–1954)
W. Averell Harriman (1955–1958)
Nelson A. Rockefeller (1959–1973)
Malcolm Wilson (1973–1974)
Hugh L. Carey (1975–1982)
Mario M. Cuomo (1983–1994)
George E. Pataki (1995–2006)
Eliot Spitzer (2007–2008)
David Paterson (2008–)

New York Government

Executive Branch

Carries out the laws and policies of state government

Governor

- Elected by voters to a four-year term
- No term limits
- Appoints officials and some judges
- Can veto whole laws or items of laws regarding budgets

Lieutenant Governor

- Elected along with governor
- Hold various responsibilities, include replacing governor should he or she leave office

Cabinet

- Consists of officials appointed by governor
- Offers advice to governor on specific areas of knowledge

Legislative Branch

Makes state laws

Bicameral System

- Has two houses—State Senate and Assembly
- Both houses take part in law-making
- Legislature can override the governor's veto with a two-thirds vote in both houses

State Senate

- 62 senators
- Serve two-year terms
- No term limits

Assembly

- 150 Assembly members
- Serve two-year terms
- No term limits

Judicial Branch

Decides conflicts and questions about the law

Trial Courts

- Hear civil and criminal cases
- Five divisions of superior courts

Appellate Courts

- Hear and determine appeals from the lower courts
- Four divisions of appellate courts

State of New York Court of Appeals

- Determines statewide principles of law in deciding specific lawsuits
- Focuses on broad issues of law, not individual factual disputes
- Has one chief judge and six associate judges
- Judges appointed by governor with approval of the Senate
- Judges serve 14-year terms

New York Facts

State tree	Sugar maple
State bird	Bluebird
State marine animal	Trout
State animal	Beaver
State insect	Ladybug
State fossil	Sea scorpion
State shell	Bay scallop
State flower	Rose
State fruit	Apple
Capital	Albany
Year of Statehood	1788 (11th state)
Nickname	The Empire State
Motto	Excelsior (Ever Upward)
Song	"I Love New York"
Highest Elevation	Mt. Marcy, 5,344 feet above sea level
Lowest Elevation	Sea level
Total Area	54,475 square miles
National Rank in Land Area	27
Total Coastline	1,850 miles (includes every bay and inlet on Long Island) 127 miles (Atlantic coastline only)
Largest City	New York City
Largest Lake	Lake Oneida
Number of Counties	62
Longest River	Hudson River
Population	19,190,115 (as of 2003)
National Rank in Population	3
Length (North to South)	310 miles
Width (East to West)	440 miles (including Long Island)

The rose is the New York State flower.

New York City Facts

Mayors Since 1898 Consolidation

Robert A. Van Wyck (1898–1901)

Seth Low (1902–1903)

George B. McClellan Jr. (1904–1909)

William Jay Gaynor (1910–1913)

Ardolph Loges Kline (1913–1913)

John Purroy Mitchel (1914–1917)

John F. Hylan (1918–1925)

James J. Walker (1926–1932)

Joseph V. McKee (1932–1932)

John P. O'Brien (1933)

Fiorello H. LaGuardia (1934–1945)

William O'Dwyer (1946–1950)

Vincent R. Impellitteri (1950–1953)

Robert F. Wagner Jr. (1954–1965)

John V. Lindsay (1966–1973)

Abraham D. Beame (1974–1977)

Edward I. Koch (1978–1989)

David N. Dinkins (1990–1993)

Rudolph W. Giuliani (1994–2001)

Michael R. Bloomberg (2002–)

City Nicknames

Gotham

The Big Apple

The Capital of The World
(Novum Caput Mundi)

The City So Nice,
They Named It Twice

The City That Never Sleeps

The Empire City

New York City Industry

New York City economy is based on its leading role in several industries, including financial services and banking, media, clothing manufacture, insurance, tourism, and the arts. The city has an enormous gross product figure of more than $1 trillion, second only to Tokyo. When compared to the gross product figures of entire countries, New York City ranks 17th, ahead of nations such as Australia, Ireland, Pakistan, and Chile.

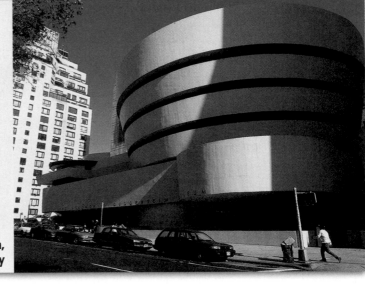

Solomon R. Guggenheim Museum, New York City

History of New York City, 1620–2020

1624 Established as trading post by Dutch (New Amsterdam)

1664 English take control from Dutch and rename the city New York

1792 New York Stock Exchange founded

1863 Civil War draft riots

1620 — 1780

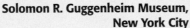

Brooklyn Bridge

1883 Brooklyn Bridge, then world's longest suspension bridge, opens

New York City Population

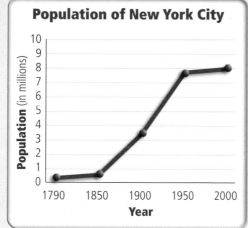

Population of New York City

Source: U.S. Census Bureau

New York City has been the largest city in the United States since the beginning of the nation. It is also the most densely populated city in the United States. The city was home to an estimated 8,250,567 people in 2007, making it the 13th most populous city in the world.

Ethnicity Of the more than 8 million people who live in New York City, more than a third were born outside of the United States. A 2005 survey found nearly 170 different languages spoken in the city. The city is home to the largest Jewish community outside of Israel, the largest Puerto Rican community outside of Puerto Rico, and the largest African American and Italian communities in the United States.

1926 First Macy's Thanksgiving Day Parade

1929 Stock market crash

2001 Terrorist attack destroys World Trade Center; killing about 2,800

1892 Ellis Island opens to receive immigrants

1931 Empire State Building opens, then world's tallest

2020

1904 First section of New York Subway opens

1886 Statue of Liberty dedicated

1898 New charter approves consolidation of five boroughs: The Bronx, Brooklyn, Manhattan, Queens, and Staten Island

The Statue of Liberty

This artist's sketch shows the new building that will stand where the World Trade Center once stood.

Gazetteer

A

Afghanistan Landlocked country in south central Asia. Capital: Kabul. (35°N 69°E) p. 355

Africa Second-largest continent. Lies in both the northern and the southern hemispheres. p. 236

Alabama (AL) State in the southern United States. Admitted as a state in 1819. Capital: Montgomery. (33°N 87°W) p. R3

Alaska (AK) U.S. state in northwestern North America. Purchased from Russia in 1867. Became a territory in 1912. Admitted as a state in 1959. Capital: Juneau. (64°N 150°W) p. 113

Algeria Country in northwest Africa along the Mediterranean Sea. Capital: Algiers. (37°N 03°E) p. 236

Appalachian Mountains Mountain system in eastern North America that extends from Canada to central Alabama. p. R5

Arizona (AZ) State in the southwestern United States. Organized into a territory in 1863. Admitted as a state in 1912. Capital: Phoenix. (34°N 113°W) p. R2

Arkansas (AR) State in the south-central United States. Admitted as a state in 1836. Capital: Little Rock. (35°N 93°W) p. R3

Asia Largest continent. Occupies the same land mass as Europe. p. 7

Atlantic Ocean Vast body of water separating North and South America from Europe and Africa. p. R3

Australia Independent country and smallest continent. Lies between the Indian and Pacific oceans. Capital: Canberra. (35°S 149°E) p. 241

Austria-Hungary Once a major European empire, Austria declined in power. A compromise in 1867 formed the dual monarchy of Austria-Hungary. p. 140

B

Baltimore Maryland city northeast of Washington, D.C., on the Chesapeake Bay. (39°N 76°W) p. 62

Balkan Peninsula Most southeastern extension of Europe, bounded by the Black Sea, Sea of Marmara, Aegean Sea, Mediterranean Sea, Ionian Sea, and Adriatic Sea. p. 141

Baltic Sea Sea in northern Europe. Arm of the Atlantic Ocean. p. 142

Bataan Peninsula and province between Manila Bay and South China Sea in the Philippines. Capital: Balanga. (15°N 120°E) p. 240

Belgium Country bordering the North Sea in northwestern Europe. Capital: Brussels. (51°N 04°E) p. 141

Berlin Capital of Germany both before city was divided into East and West and after it was reunited. (53°N 13°E) p. 315

Bosnia and Herzegovina Mountainous country located in southeastern Europe on the Balkan Peninsula. Formerly part of Yugoslavia. Capital: Sarajevo. (44°N 18°E) p. 141

Boston Capital of Massachusetts. (42°N 71°W) p. 62

Bulgaria Mountainous country in southeastern Europe on the Balkan Peninsula bordering the Black Sea. Capital: Sofia. (43°N 23°E) p. 141

Burma Renamed Myanmar, the largest nation in southeastern Asia. Capital: Yangon. (17°N 96°E) p. 240

California (CA) State in the western United States. Admitted as a state in 1850. Capital: Sacramento. (38°N 121°W) p. 6

Cambodia Country in southeastern Asia on the Indochina Peninsula and the Gulf of Thailand. Capital: Phnom Penh. (12°N 105°E) p. 318

Camp David Presidential retreat in the middle of Catoctin Mountain National Park in Maryland. p. 355

Canada Country in northern North America. Capital: Ottawa. (50°N 100°W) p. 9

Caribbean Sea Arm of the Atlantic Ocean between North and South America. p. 119

Central America Region of land connecting North and South America. p. 7

Chicago Large U.S. city in northeastern Illinois on Lake Michigan. Major port. (41°N 87°W) p. 35

China Country in East Asia with the world's largest population. Capital: Beijing. (Official name: People's Republic of China) p. 57

Colombia Country in northwest South America. Capital: Bogotá. (4°N 72°W) p. 125

Colorado (CO) State in the southwestern United States. Admitted as a state in 1876. Capital: Denver. (39°N 107°W) p. R2

Connecticut (CT) State in the northeastern United States. One of the original thirteen colonies. Admitted as a state in 1788. Capital: Hartford. (41°N 73°W) p. R3

Coral Sea Home to the Great Coral Reef. Arm of southwest Pacific Ocean. p. 241

Cuba Westernmost country of the West Indies, an island republic in the northern Caribbean Sea. Capital: Havana. (23°N 82°W) p. 117

Czechoslovakia Former name of the country in central Europe that included the current Czech and Slovak republics. Capital: Prague. (15°N 14°E) p. 226

Delaware (DE) State in the eastern United States. One of the original thirteen colonies. Capital: Dover. (38°N 75°W) p. R3

Denmark Southernmost Scandinavian country in northern Europe. Peninsula and island kingdom between the North and Baltic Seas. Capital: Copenhagen. (56°N 12°E) p. 226

Detroit Largest city in Michigan. (42°N 83°W) p. 62

Dominican Republic West Indies country that occupies approximately the eastern two-thirds of Hispaniola. Capital: Santo Domingo. (19°N 71°W) p. 127

Egypt Middle East country in northeast Africa along the Mediterranean and Red Sea coasts. Capital: Cairo. (30°N 31°E) p. 236

El Alamein Village in northwest Egypt where Germany's Africa Korps was defeated by the Allies during World War II. (31°N 29°E) p. 236

GAZETTEER

Ellis Island New York Bay island. Part of Statue of Liberty National Monument. U.S. immigration center. Entry point for millions of people from 1892–1954. (41°N 74°W) p. 57

Ethiopia Country, once known as Abyssinia, in northeastern Africa. Capital: Addis Ababa. (9°N 39°E) p. 224

Europe Continent occupying the same land mass as Asia. p. 7

Florida (FL) State in the southeastern United States. Organized as a territory in 1822. Admitted as a state in 1845. Capital: Tallahassee. (30°N 84°W) p. R3

France Country in Western Europe. Capital: Paris. (46°N 0°W) p. 115

Georgia (GA) State in the southeastern United States. Admitted as a state in 1788. One of the original thirteen colonies. Capital: Atlanta. (32°N 84°W) p. R3

Germany Country in Western Europe. Capital: Berlin. (51°N 8°E) p. 56

Great Britain Country in western Europe that includes England, Scotland, and Wales. Capital: London. p. 115

Great Plains Region of central North America that lies between the Mississippi River and the Rocky Mountains. p. 6

Greece Country in southern Europe with mountains, rugged coastlines, and scenic islands; the country is called the birthplace of democracy. Capital: Athens. p. 267

Guam Unincorporated U.S. territory that is the southernmost and largest of the Mariana Islands in the west Pacific Ocean. Capital: Agana. (13°N 145°E) p. 120

Gulf of Mexico Gulf on the southeastern coast of North America, bordered by the United States, Mexico, and Cuba. p. R3

Harlem A neighborhood in upper Manhattan in New York City that became a political and cultural hub for many African Americans in the early 1900s. (41°N 74°W) p. 198

Hawaii Largest of group of eight large and many smaller Hawaiian Islands in the Pacific Ocean admitted to the Union in 1959 as the 50th state. Capital: Honolulu. (21°N 158°W) p. 114

Herzegovina *See* Bosnia-Herzegovina

Hiroshima A city in Japan where the first atomic bomb was dropped. (34°N 132°E) p. 248

Ho Chi Minh Trail Network of trails of more than 12,000 miles through eastern Laos and Cambodia into South Vietnam used by the North Vietnamese during the Vietnam War. p. 322

Hong Kong City located on this south coast of China and a special administrative zone of China. Former British colony. Capital: Victoria. (22°N 114°E) p. 240

Hungary Central European nation. Capital: Budapest. (48°N 19°E) p. 37

Idaho (ID) State in the northwestern United States. Admitted as a state in 1890. Capital: Boise. (44°N 115°W) p. R2

Illinois (IL) State in the north-central United States. Admitted as a state in 1819. Capital: Springfield. (40°N 90°W) p. R3

India Large country in southern Asia. Capital: New Delhi. (28°N 77°E) p. 241

Indiana (IN) State in the north-central United States. Admitted as a state in 1816. Capital: Indianapolis. (40°N 86°W) p. R3

Iowa (IA) State in the north-central United States. Admitted as a state in 1846. Capital: Des Moines. (42°N 94°W) p. R3

Iran Islamic country in the Persian Gulf region. Formerly Persia. Capital: Tehran. (27°N 55°E) p. 356

Iraq Persian Gulf nation known in ancient times as Mesopotamia. Capital: Baghdad. (33°N 44°E) p. 371

Ireland Island in the British Isles. Divided into Northern Ireland (Capital: Belfast), and the Republic of Ireland (Capital: Dublin). (54°N 8°W) p. 56

Israel Modern Middle Eastern country on the Mediterranean Sea formed in 1948. Capital: Jerusalem. (32°N 35°E) p. 266

Italy Country in southern Europe. Capital: Rome. (44°N 11°E) p. 224

Japan Island chain nation of East Asia. Japan in Chinese means "Land of the rising sun." Capital: Tokyo. (36°N 140°E) p. 113

Kansas (KS) State in the central United States. Organized as a territory in 1854. Admitted as a state in 1861. Capital: Topeka. (38°N 99°W) p. R2

Kentucky (KY) State in the east-central United States. Admitted as a state in 1792. Capital: Frankfort. (37°N 87°W) p. R3

Korea See North Korea and South Korea

Kuwait Persian Gulf country on the Arabian Peninsula. Capital: Al-Kuwait, also known as Kuwait City. (29°N 48°E) p. 371

Latin America Spanish-speaking countries of North and South America that were once claimed by Spain and Portugal. p. 127

Laos Landlocked country in southeast Asia. Capital (Administrative): Vientiane (18°N 103°E) Capital (Historic royal): Luang Phabang. (18°N 108°E) p. 318

Leyte Gulf Large inlet of the Philippine Sea in the Pacific Ocean. (11°N 125°E) p. 242

Little Rock Capital city in central Arkansas on the Arkansas River. (35°N 92°W) p. 291

London Capital of the United Kingdom, in England. (52°N 0°W) p. 131

GAZETTEER

GAZETTEER

Louisiana (LA) State in the southeastern United States carved out of the Louisiana Territory. Admitted as a state in 1812. Capital: Baton Rouge. (31°N 92°W) p. R3

Luxembourg Also, Grand Duchy of Luxembourg. Small European country between France, Germany, and Belgium. Capital: Luxembourg City. (50°N 6°E) p. 227

M

Maine (ME) State in the northeastern United States. Admitted as a state in 1820. Capital: Augusta. (45°N 70°W) p. R3

Maryland (MD) State in the east-central United States. One of the original thirteen colonies. Admitted as a state in 1788. Capital: Annapolis. (39°N 76°W) p. R3

Massachusetts (MA) State in the northeastern United States. One of the original thirteen colonies. Admitted as a state in 1788. Capital: Boston. (42°N 72°W) p. R3

Mexico Country in southern North America. Capital: Mexico City. (23°N 104°W) p. 58

Michigan (MI) State in the north-central United States. Admitted as a state in 1837. Capital: Lansing. (46°N 87°W) p. R3

Midway Islands Coral atoll consisting of two islands in central Pacific Ocean west of the Hawaiian chain. Site of Battle of Midway, an Allied victory during World War II. p. 113

Minnesota (MN) State in the north-central United States. Admitted as a state in 1858. Capital: St. Paul. (46°N 90°W) p. R3

Mississippi (MS) State in the southeastern United States. Admitted as a state in 1817. Capital: Jackson. (32°N 89°W) p. R3

Mississippi River River that flows from Minnesota south to the Gulf of Mexico. p. R3

Missouri (MO) State in the central United States. Admitted as a state in 1821. Capital: Jefferson City. (38°N 93°W) p. R3

Montana (MT) State in the northwestern United States. Admitted as a state in 1889. Capital: Helena. (47°N 112°W) p. 16

Montgomery Capital of Alabama. (32°N 86°W) p. 293

Morocco Country in northwest Africa bounded by western Sahara, the Mediterranean Sea, and the Atlantic Ocean. Capital: Rabat. (34°N 07°W). p. 236

N

Nebraska (NE) State in the central United States. Admitted as a state in 1867. Capital: Lincoln. (41°N 101°W) p. 10

Netherlands Country in northwestern Europe. Capital: Amsterdam. (52°N 5°E) p. 227

Nevada (NV) State in the western United States. Organized as a territory in 1861. Admitted as a state in 1864. Capital: Carson City. (39°N 117°W) p. 7

New England Northeastern section of the United States. Made up of Connecticut, Maine, Massachusetts, New Hampshire, Rhode Island, and Vermont. p. 20

New Hampshire (NH) State in the northeastern United States. One of the original thirteen colonies. Admitted as a state in 1788. Capital: Concord. (44°N 71°W) p. R3

New Jersey (NJ) State in the northeastern United States. One of the original thirteen colonies. Admitted as a state in 1787. Capital: Trenton. (40°N 75°W) p. R3

New Mexico (NM) State in the southwestern United States. Admitted as a state in 1912. Capital: Santa Fe. (34°N 107°W) p. 17

New York (NY) State in the northeastern United States. One of the original thirteen colonies. Admitted as a state in 1788. Capital: Albany. (42°N 78°W) p. NY1

New York City Largest city in the United States. (41°N 74°W) p. NY2

Nicaragua Country between Caribbean Sea and Pacific Ocean in Central America. Capital: Managua. (12°N 86°W) p. 128

North Carolina (NC) State in the southeastern United States. One of the original thirteen colonies. Admitted as a state in 1789. Capital: Raleigh. p. R3

North Dakota (ND) State in north-central United States. Admitted as a state in 1889. Capital: Bismarck. (47°N 102°W) p. 210

North Korea Country in East Asia consisting of the northern half of Korean peninsula. Capital: P'yŏngyang. (39°N 126°E) p. 273

North Sea Arm of the Atlantic Ocean, between the east coast of Britain and the area northwest of the central European mainland. (Between 51°N and 62°N) p. 142

Norway Country on the northwestern part of Scandinavia in northern Europe. Capital: Oslo. (60°N 11°E) p. 226

Nuremberg Also, Nürnberg. City in southern Germany. Site of trials of German World War II war criminals. (49°N 11°E) p. 265

Ohio (OH) State in the north-central United States. Originally part of the Northwest Territory. Admitted as a state in 1803. Capital: Columbus. (40°N 83°W) p. R3

Oklahoma (OK) State in the south-central United States. Organized as a territory in 1890. Admitted as a state in 1907. Capital: Oklahoma City. (36°N 98°W) p. 14

Ottoman Empire Vast former Turkish empire that expanded to include much of southeastern Europe, the Middle East, and North Africa between the 1300s and 1900s. p. 141

Oregon (OR) State in the northwestern United States. Admitted as a state in 1859. Capital: Salem. (43°N 122°W) p. 17

Pacific Ocean Body of water extending from the Arctic Circle to Antarctica and from western North and South America to Australia, the Malay Archipelago, and East Asia. p. 6

Palestine Region between the Jordan River and the Mediterranean Sea containing modern-day Israel, the West Bank, and the Gaza Strip. Often called "The Holy Land." p. 266

Panama Country in southern Central America. Location of the Panama Canal. Capital: Panama City. (8°N 81°W) p. 125

Pearl Harbor An inlet on the Pacific island of Oahu, Hawaii. p. 228

Pennsylvania (PA) State in the eastern United States. One of the original thirteen colonies. Admitted as a state in 1787. Capital: Harrisburg. (41°N 78°W) p. R3

Persian Gulf Arm of the Arabian Sea in the Indian Ocean between the Arabian Peninsula and the Asian mainland. Called the Arabian Gulf by Arabs. p. 371

Philadelphia City in southeastern Pennsylvania. Capital of the United States from 1790 to 1800. (40°N 75°W) p. 62

GAZETTEER

Philippines Country in the western Pacific Ocean. Made up of about 7,100 islands. Capital: Manila. (14°N 125°E) p. 119

Pittsburgh Second largest city and major port in Pennsylvania. (40°N 80°W) p. 67

Poland Country in central Europe on the Baltic Sea. Capital: Warsaw. (52°N 21°E) p. 226

Puerto Rico Island east of Cuba and southeast of Florida. A U.S. territory acquired in the Spanish-American War. Capital: San Juan. (18°N 67°W) p. 120

Rhode Island (RI) State in the northeastern United States. One of the original thirteen colonies. Admitted as a state in 1790. Capital: Providence. (41°N 71°W) p. R3

Rome A city in Italy near the Mediterranean Sea; it was the capital of the Roman Empire. (42°N 13°E) p. 236

Russia Vast country that extends from Eastern Europe through northwestern Asia. Capital: Moscow. (61°N 60°E) p. 56

St. Louis City in Missouri on the Mississippi River. (39°N 90°W) p. 62

San Francisco City in western California on a peninsula between the Pacific Ocean and San Francisco Bay. (37°N 122°W) p. 57

San Juan Hill Hill close to the city of Santiago, Cuba. Site of a battle in the Spanish-American War. p. 119

Scandinavia Large peninsula in northern Europe. p. 56

Serbia Balkan republic. About 70 percent of former Yugoslavia. Capital: Belgrade. (45°N 21°E) p. 141

Singapore Island republic in southeast Asia. Capital: Singapore City. (1°N 104°E) p. 240

South America Continent in the southern Western Hemisphere. p. 7

South Carolina (SC) State in the southeastern United States. One of the original thirteen colonies. Admitted as a state in 1788. Capital: Columbia. (34°N 81°W) p. R3

South Dakota (SD) State in the north-central United States. Organized as part of the Dakota Territory in 1861. Admitted as a state in 1889. Capital: Pierre. (44°N 102°W) p. 17

South Korea Country in East Asia consisting of the southern half of Korean peninsula. Capital: Seoul. (38°N 127°E) p. 273

Soviet Union Former federation of republics succeeding the Russian empire. First Communist state. Full name: Union of Soviet Socialist Republics (USSR). p. 225

Stalingrad Russian city. Renamed Volgograd in 1961. (49°N 42°E) p. 237

Sun Belt Term given to the warmer climate region of southern U.S. states stretching between east and west coasts. p. 278

Switzerland Also known as Swiss Confederation. Alpine country in central Europe. Capital: Bern. (47°N 7°E) p. 142

Syria Ancient country and formerly larger region. Modern Middle East Arab country on the Mediterranean Sea. Capital: Damascus. (35°N 38°E) p. 347

Teapot Dome Rock formation rising above an oil field in Wyoming named for teapot-like shape. Known for a scandal during President Harding's administration. (43°N 116°W) p. 173

Tennessee (TN) State in the south-central United States. Admitted as a state in 1796. Capital: Nashville. (36°N 88°W) p. R3

Texas (TX) State in the south-central United States. Independent republic from 1836 to 1845. Admitted as a state in 1845. Capital: Austin. (31°N 101°W) p. R2

Thailand Country in central southeast Asia. Capital: Bangkok. (14°N 101°E) p. 240

Tonkin, Gulf of Arm of South China Sea between Vietnam and China. p. 321

Tuskegee City in Alabama. Home of Tuskegee Institute historic site. (32°N 86°W) p. 232

United States of America Country in central North America. Capital: Washington, D.C. (38°N 110°W) p. R2

Utah (UT) State in the western United States. Admitted as a state in 1896. Capital: Salt Lake City. (39°N 112°W) p. R2

Venezuela Country in South America. Capital: Caracas. (11°N 67°W) p. 127

Vermont (VT) State in the northeastern United States. Admitted as a state in 1791. Capital: Montpelier. (44°N 73°W) p. R3

Vietnam Country along east coast of Southeast Asian peninsula. North and South united in 1976 after Vietnam War ended. Capital: Hanoi. (21°N 106°E) p. 318

Virginia (VA) State in the eastern United States. One of the original thirteen colonies. Admitted as a state in 1788. Capital: Richmond. (37°N 80°W) p. R3

Washington (WA) State in the northwestern United States. Admitted as a state in 1889. Capital: Olympia. (47°N 121°W) p. R2

Washington, D.C. Capital of the United States. Located on the Potomac River between Virginia and Maryland. (39°N 77°W) p. R3

West Virginia (WV) State in the east-central United States. Part of Virginia until the area refused to join the Confederacy in 1861. Admitted as a state in 1863. Capital: Charleston. (39°N 81°W) p. R3

Western Hemisphere Term given to that half of the earth's sphere that contains the Americas. p. 127

Wisconsin (WI) State in the north-central United States. Became part of the Northwest Territory in 1787. Admitted as a state in 1848. Capital: Madison. (44°N 91°W) p. 87

Wyoming (WY) State in the northwestern United States. Admitted as a state in 1890. Capital: Cheyenne. (43°N 108°W) p. 22

GAZETTEER

Yalta Ukrainian city on south shore of the
Crimean peninsula by the Black Sea.
Meeting place of Churchill, Roosevelt, and
Stalin near end of World War II. (45°N 34°E)
p. 264

Yugoslavia Former country of the Balkan
peninsula in southeast Europe created in
1918 that crumbled during the late 1900s.
Capital: Belgrade. (45°N 21°E) p. 373

GAZETTEER

Presidents

1 GEORGE WASHINGTON
Born: 1732 Died: 1799
Years in Office: 1789–97
Political Party: None
Home State: Virginia
Vice President: John Adams

2 JOHN ADAMS
Born: 1735 Died: 1826
Years in Office: 1797–1801
Political Party: Federalist
Home State: Massachusetts
Vice President: Thomas Jefferson

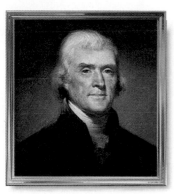

3 THOMAS JEFFERSON
Born: 1743 Died: 1826
Years in Office: 1801–09
Political Party: Republican*
Home State: Virginia
Vice Presidents: Aaron Burr,
George Clinton

4 JAMES MADISON
Born: 1751 Died: 1836
Years in Office: 1809–17
Political Party: Republican
Home State: Virginia
Vice Presidents: George Clinton,
Elbridge Gerry

5 JAMES MONROE
Born: 1758 Died: 1831
Years in Office: 1817–25
Political Party: Republican
Home State: Virginia
Vice President: Daniel D. Tompkins

6 JOHN QUINCY ADAMS
Born: 1767 Died: 1848
Years in Office: 1825–29
Political Party: Republican
Home State: Massachusetts
Vice President: John C. Calhoun

7 ANDREW JACKSON
Born: 1767 Died: 1845
Years in Office: 1829–37
Political Party: Democratic
Home State: Tennessee
Vice Presidents: John C. Calhoun,
Martin Van Buren

8 MARTIN VAN BUREN
Born: 1782 Died: 1862
Years in Office: 1837–41
Political Party: Democratic
Home State: New York
Vice President: Richard M. Johnson

* The Republican Party of the third through sixth presidents is not the party of Abraham Lincoln, which was founded in 1854.

9 WILLIAM HENRY HARRISON
Born: 1773   Died: 1841
Years in Office: 1841
Political Party: Whig
Home State: Ohio
Vice President: John Tyler

10 JOHN TYLER
Born: 1790   Died: 1862
Years in Office: 1841–45
Political Party: Whig
Home State: Virginia
Vice President: None

11 JAMES K. POLK
Born: 1795   Died: 1849
Years in Office: 1845–49
Political Party: Democratic
Home State: Tennessee
Vice President: George M. Dallas

12 ZACHARY TAYLOR
Born: 1784   Died: 1850
Years in Office: 1849–50
Political Party: Whig
Home State: Louisiana
Vice President: Millard Fillmore

13 MILLARD FILLMORE
Born: 1800   Died: 1874
Years in Office: 1850–53
Political Party: Whig
Home State: New York
Vice President: None

14 FRANKLIN PIERCE
Born: 1804   Died: 1869
Years in Office: 1853–57
Political Party: Democratic
Home State: New Hampshire
Vice President: William R. King

15 JAMES BUCHANAN
Born: 1791   Died: 1868
Years in Office: 1857–61
Political Party: Democratic
Home State: Pennsylvania
Vice President: John C. Breckinridge

16 ABRAHAM LINCOLN
Born: 1809   Died: 1865
Years in Office: 1861–65
Political Party: Republican
Home State: Illinois
Vice Presidents: Hannibal Hamlin,
Andrew Johnson

17 ANDREW JOHNSON
Born: 1808   Died: 1875
Years in Office: 1865–69
Political Party: Republican
Home State: Tennessee
Vice President: None

18 ULYSSES S. GRANT
Born: 1822   Died: 1885
Years in Office: 1869–77
Political Party: Republican
Home State: Illinois
Vice Presidents: Schuyler Colfax,
Henry Wilson

19 RUTHERFORD B. HAYES
Born: 1822   Died: 1893
Years in Office: 1877–81
Political Party: Republican
Home State: Ohio
Vice President: William A. Wheeler

20 JAMES A. GARFIELD
Born: 1831   Died: 1881
Years in Office: 1881
Political Party: Republican
Home State: Ohio
Vice President: Chester A. Arthur

21 CHESTER A. ARTHUR
Born: 1829   Died: 1886
Years in Office: 1881–85
Political Party: Republican
Home State: New York
Vice President: None

22 GROVER CLEVELAND
Born: 1837   Died: 1908
Years in Office: 1885–89
Political Party: Democratic
Home State: New York
Vice President: Thomas A. Hendricks

23 BENJAMIN HARRISON
Born: 1833   Died: 1901
Years in Office: 1889–93
Political Party: Republican
Home State: Indiana
Vice President: Levi P. Morton

24 GROVER CLEVELAND
Born: 1837   Died: 1908
Years in Office: 1893–97
Political Party: Democratic
Home State: New York
Vice President: Adlai E. Stevenson

25 WILLIAM MCKINLEY
Born: 1843   Died: 1901
Years in Office: 1897–1901
Political Party: Republican
Home State: Ohio
Vice Presidents: Garret A. Hobart,
Theodore Roosevelt

26 THEODORE ROOSEVELT
Born: 1858   Died: 1919
Years in Office: 1901–09
Political Party: Republican
Home State: New York
Vice President: Charles W. Fairbanks

27 WILLIAM HOWARD TAFT
Born: 1857 **Died:** 1930
Years in Office: 1909–13
Political Party: Republican
Home State: Ohio
Vice President: James S. Sherman

28 WOODROW WILSON
Born: 1856 **Died:** 1924
Years in Office: 1913–21
Political Party: Democratic
Home State: New Jersey
Vice President: Thomas R. Marshall

29 WARREN G. HARDING
Born: 1865 **Died:** 1923
Years in Office: 1921–23
Political Party: Republican
Home State: Ohio
Vice President: Calvin Coolidge

30 CALVIN COOLIDGE
Born: 1872 **Died:** 1933
Years in Office: 1923–29
Political Party: Republican
Home State: Massachusetts
Vice President: Charles G. Dawes

31 HERBERT HOOVER
Born: 1874 **Died:** 1964
Years in Office: 1929–33
Political Party: Republican
Home State: California
Vice President: Charles Curtis

32 FRANKLIN D. ROOSEVELT
Born: 1882 **Died:** 1945
Years in Office: 1933–45
Political Party: Democratic
Home State: New York
Vice Presidents: John Nance Garner, Henry Wallace, Harry S Truman

33 HARRY S. TRUMAN
Born: 1884 **Died:** 1972
Years in Office: 1945–53
Political Party: Democratic
Home State: Missouri
Vice President: Alben W. Barkley

34 DWIGHT D. EISENHOWER
Born: 1890 **Died:** 1969
Years in Office: 1953–61
Political Party: Republican
Home State: Kansas
Vice President: Richard M. Nixon

35 JOHN F. KENNEDY
Born: 1917 **Died:** 1963
Years in Office: 1961–63
Political Party: Democratic
Home State: Massachusetts
Vice President: Lyndon B. Johnson

36 LYNDON B. JOHNSON
Born: 1908 Died: 1973
Years in Office: 1963–69
Political Party: Democratic
Home State: Texas
Vice President: Hubert H. Humphrey

37 RICHARD M. NIXON
Born: 1913 Died: 1994
Years in Office: 1969–74
Political Party: Republican
Home State: California
Vice Presidents: Spiro T. Agnew,
Gerald R. Ford

38 GERALD R. FORD
Born: 1913 Died: 2006
Years in Office: 1974–77
Political Party: Republican
Home State: Michigan
Vice President: Nelson A. Rockefeller

39 JIMMY CARTER
Born: 1924
Years in Office: 1977–81
Political Party: Democratic
Home State: Georgia
Vice President: Walter F. Mondale

40 RONALD REAGAN
Born: 1911 Died: 2004
Years in Office: 1981–89
Political Party: Republican
Home State: California
Vice President: George Bush

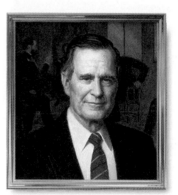

41 GEORGE BUSH
Born: 1924
Years in Office: 1989–93
Political Party: Republican
Home State: Texas
Vice President: J. Danforth Quayle

42 BILL CLINTON
Born: 1946
Years in Office: 1993–2001
Political Party: Democratic
Home State: Arkansas
Vice President: Albert Gore Jr.

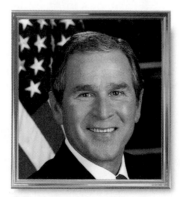

43 GEORGE W. BUSH
Born: 1946
Years in Office: 2001–2009
Political Party: Republican
Home State: Texas
Vice President: Richard B. Cheney

44 BARACK OBAMA
Born: 1961
Years in Office: 2009–
Political Party: Democratic
Home State: Illinois
Vice President: Joe Biden

Facts about the States

State	Year of Statehood	2006 Population	Area (Sq. Mi.)	Population Density (Sq. Mi.)	Capital
Alabama	1819	4,599,030	50,744	88.7	Montgomery
Alaska	1959	670,053	571,951	1.1	Juneau
Arizona	1912	6,166,318	113,635	49.1	Phoenix
Arkansas	1836	2,810,872	52,068	52.3	Little Rock
California	1850	36,457,549	155,959	227.5	Sacramento
Colorado	1876	4,753,377	103,718	43.9	Denver
Connecticut	1788	3,504,809	4,845	719.0	Hartford
Delaware	1787	853,476	1,954	418.4	Dover
District of Columbia	—	581,530	61	9,235.8	—
Florida	1845	18,089,888	53,927	315.6	Tallahassee
Georgia	1788	9,363,941	57,906	150.0	Atlanta
Hawaii	1959	1,285,498	6,423	195.8	Honolulu
Idaho	1890	1,466,465	82,747	16.5	Boise
Illinois	1818	12,831,970	55,584	227.6	Springfield
Indiana	1816	6,313,520	35,867	172.7	Indianapolis
Iowa	1846	2,982,085	55,869	52.7	Des Moines
Kansas	1861	2,764,075	81,815	33.3	Topeka
Kentucky	1792	4,206,074	39,728	103.7	Frankfort
Louisiana	1812	4,287,768	43,562	103.2	Baton Rouge
Maine	1820	1,321,574	30,862	42.3	Augusta
Maryland	1788	5,615,727	9,774	563.6	Annapolis
Massachusetts	1788	6,437,193	7,840	820.6	Boston
Michigan	1837	10,095,643	56,804	177.5	Lansing
Minnesota	1858	5,167,101	79,610	63.6	St. Paul

State	Year of Statehood	2006 Population	Area (Sq. Mi.)	Population Density (Sq. Mi.)	Capital
Mississippi	1817	2,910,540	46,907	61.4	Jackson
Missouri	1821	5,842,713	68,886	82.8	Jefferson City
Montana	1889	944,632	145,552	6.3	Helena
Nebraska	1867	1,768,331	76,872	22.6	Lincoln
Nevada	1864	2,495,529	109,826	20.4	Carson City
New Hampshire	1788	1,314,895	8,968	143.6	Concord
New Jersey	1787	8,724,560	7,417	1,164.7	Trenton
New Mexico	1912	1,954,599	121,356	15.4	Santa Fe
New York	1788	19,306,183	47,214	406.4	Albany
North Carolina	1789	8,856,505	48,711	172.6	Raleigh
North Dakota	1889	635,867	68,976	9.2	Bismarck
Ohio	1803	11,478,006	40,948	279.3	Columbus
Oklahoma	1907	3,579,212	68,667	51.1	Oklahoma City
Oregon	1859	3,700,758	95,997	37.1	Salem
Pennsylvania	1787	12,440,621	44,817	275.9	Harrisburg
Rhode Island	1790	1,067,610	1,045	1,029.8	Providence
South Carolina	1788	4,321,249	30,109	137.7	Columbia
South Dakota	1889	781,919	75,885	10.1	Pierre
Tennessee	1796	6,038,803	41,217	141.7	Nashville
Texas	1845	23,507,783	261,797	84.5	Austin
Utah	1896	2,550,063	82,144	28.6	Salt Lake City
Vermont	1791	623,908	9,250	66.9	Montpelier
Virginia	1788	7,642,884	39,594	186.6	Richmond
Washington	1889	6,395,798	66,544	92.1	Olympia
West Virginia	1863	1,818,470	24,078	75.2	Charleston
Wisconsin	1848	5,556,506	54,310	100.8	Madison
Wyoming	1890	515,004	97,100	5.2	Cheyenne

American Flag

The American flag is a symbol of the nation. It is recognized instantly, whether as a big banner waving in the wind or a tiny emblem worn on a lapel. The flag is so important that it is a major theme of the national anthem, "The Star-Spangled Banner." One of the most popular names for the flag is the Stars and Stripes. It is also known as Old Glory.

THE MEANING OF THE FLAG

The American flag has 13 stripes—7 red and 6 white. In the upper-left corner of the flag is the union—50 white five-pointed stars against a blue background.

The 13 stripes stand for the original 13 American states, and the 50 stars represent the states of the nation today. According to the U.S. Department of State, the colors of the flag also are symbolic:

Red stands for courage.

White symbolizes purity.

Blue is the color of vigilance, perseverance, and justice.

DISPLAYING THE FLAG

It is customary not to display the American flag in bad weather. It is also customary for the flag to be displayed outdoors only from sunrise to sunset, except on certain occasions. In a few special places, however, the flag is always flown day and night. When flown at night, the flag should be illuminated.

Near a speaker's platform, the flag should occupy the place of honor at the speaker's right. When carried in a parade with other flags, the American flag should be on the marching right or in front at the center. When flying with the flags of the 50 states, the national flag must be at the center and the highest point. In a group of national flags, all should be of equal size and all should be flown from staffs, or flagpoles, of equal height.

The flag should never touch the ground or the floor. It should not be marked with any insignia, pictures, or words. Nor should it be used in any disrespectful way—as an advertising decoration, for instance. The flag should never be dipped to honor any person or thing.

SALUTING THE FLAG

The United States, like other countries, has a flag code, or rules for displaying and honoring the flag. For example, all those present should stand at attention facing the flag and salute it when it is being raised or lowered or when it is carried past them in a parade or procession. A man wearing a hat should take it off and hold it with his right hand over his heart. All women and hatless men should stand with their right hands over their hearts to show their respect for the flag. The flag should also receive these honors during the playing of the national anthem and the reciting of the Pledge of Allegiance.

THE PLEDGE OF ALLEGIANCE

The Pledge of Allegiance was written in 1892 by Massachusetts magazine (*Youth's Companion*) editor Francis Bellamy. (Congress added the words "under God" in 1954.)

I pledge allegiance to the flag of the United States of America and to the republic for which it stands, one nation under God, indivisible, with liberty and justice for all.

Civilians should say the Pledge of Allegiance with their right hands placed over their hearts. People in the armed forces give the military salute. By saying the Pledge of Allegiance, we promise loyalty ("pledge allegiance") to the United States and its ideals.

"THE STAR-SPANGLED BANNER"

"The Star-Spangled Banner" is the national anthem of the United States. It was written by Francis Scott Key during the War of 1812. While being detained by the British aboard a ship on September 13–14, 1814, Key watched the British bombardment of Fort McHenry at Baltimore. The attack lasted 25 hours. The smoke was so thick that Key could not tell who had won. When the air cleared, Key saw the American flag that was still flying over the fort. "The Star-Spangled Banner" is sung to music written by British composer John Stafford Smith. In 1931 Congress designated "The Star-Spangled Banner" as the national anthem.

I

Oh, say, can you see, by the dawn's early light,
What so proudly we hailed at the twilight's last gleaming,
Whose broad stripes and bright stars through the perilous fight,
O'er the ramparts we watched were so gallantly streaming?
And the rockets' red glare, the bombs bursting in air,
Gave proof through the night that our flag was still there.
Oh, say, does that star-spangled banner yet wave
O'er the land of the free, and the home of the brave?

II

On the shore, dimly seen through the mists of the deep,
Where the foe's haughty host in dread silence reposes,
What is that which the breeze, o'er the towering steep,
As it fitfully blows, half conceals, half discloses?
Now it catches the gleam of the morning's first beam,
In full glory reflected, now shines on the stream.
'Tis the star-spangled banner; oh, long may it wave
O'er the land of the free, and the home of the brave!

III

And where is that band who so vauntingly swore
That the havoc of war and the battle's confusion
A home and a country should leave us no more?
Their blood has washed out their foul footsteps' pollution.
No refuge could save the hireling and slave
From the terror of flight, or the gloom of the grave:
And the star-spangled banner in triumph doth wave
O'er the land of the free, and the home of the brave!

IV

Oh! thus be it ever when freemen shall stand
Between their loved homes and the war's desolation!
Blest with victory and peace, may the heaven-rescued land
Praise the Power that hath made and preserved us a nation!
Then conquer we must, for our cause it is just,
And this be our motto: "In God is our trust!"
And the star-spangled banner in triumph shall wave,
O'er the land of the free, and the home of the brave!

THE NEW COLOSSUS

In 1883 Jewish American poet Emma Lazarus wrote the poem "The New Colossus" to help raise funds for the pedestal on which the Statue of Liberty would sit. The poem compares the United States to ancient societies. In 1903, after the poet's death, the poem was engraved on a plaque and placed in the pedestal as a memorial.

Not like the brazen giant of Greek fame,
With conquering limbs astride from land to land;
Here at our sea-washed, sunset gates shall stand
A mighty woman with a torch, whose flame
Is the imprisoned lightning, and her name
Mother of Exiles. From her beacon-hand
Glows world-wide welcome; her mild eyes command
The air-bridged harbor that twin cities frame.
"Keep, ancient lands, your storied pomp!" cries she
With silent lips. "Give me your tired, your poor,
Your huddled masses yearning to breathe free,
The wretched refuse of your teeming shore.
Send these, the homeless, tempest-tost to me,
I lift my lamp beside the golden door!"

"AMERICA, THE BEAUTIFUL"

One of the most beloved songs celebrating our nation is "America, the Beautiful." Katharine Lee Bates first wrote the lyrics to the song in 1893 after visiting Colorado. The version of the song we know today is set to music by Samuel A. Ward. The first and last stanzas of "America, the Beautiful" are shown below.

O beautiful for spacious skies,
For amber waves of grain,
For purple mountain majesties
Above the fruited plain!
America! America!
God shed his grace on thee
And crown thy good with brotherhood
From sea to shining sea!

O beautiful for patriot dream
That sees beyond the years
Thine alabaster cities gleam
Undimmed by human tears!
America! America!
God shed his grace on thee
And crown thy good with brotherhood
From sea to shining sea!

Supreme Court Decisions

Marbury v. Madison (1803)

Significance This ruling established the Supreme Court's power of judicial review, by which the Court decides whether laws passed by Congress are constitutional. This decision greatly increased the prestige of the Court and gave the judiciary branch a powerful check against the legislative and executive branches.

Background William Marbury and several others were commissioned as judges by Federalist president John Adams during his last days in office. This act angered the new Democratic-Republican president, Thomas Jefferson. Jefferson ordered his secretary of state, James Madison, not to deliver the commissions. Marbury took advantage of a section in the Judiciary Act of 1789 that allowed him to take his case directly to the Supreme Court. He sued Madison, demanding the commission and the judgeship.

Decision This case was decided on February 24, 1803, by a vote of 5 to 0. Chief Justice John Marshall spoke for the Court, which decided against Marbury. The court ruled that although Marbury's commission had been unfairly withheld, he could not lawfully take his case to the Supreme Court without first trying it in a lower court. Marshall said that the section of the Judiciary Act that Marbury had used was actually unconstitutional and that the Constitution must take priority over laws passed by Congress.

McCulloch v. Maryland (1819)

Significance This ruling established that Congress had the constitutional power to charter a national bank. The case also established the principle of national supremacy, which states that the Constitution and other laws of the federal government take priority over state laws. In addition, the ruling reinforced the loose-construction interpretation of the Constitution favored by many Federalists.

Background In 1816 the federal government set up the Second Bank of the United States to stabilize the economy following the War of 1812. Many states were opposed to the competition provided by the new national bank. Some of these states passed heavy taxes on the Bank. The national bank refused to pay the taxes. This led the state of Maryland to sue James McCulloch, the cashier of the Baltimore, Maryland, branch of the national bank.

Decision This case was decided on March 6, 1819, by a vote of 7 to 0. Chief Justice John Marshall spoke for the unanimous Court, which ruled that the national bank was constitutional because it helped the federal government carry out other powers granted to it by the Constitution. The Court declared that any attempt by the states to interfere with the duties of the federal government could not be permitted.

Gibbons v. Ogden (1824)

Significance This ruling was the first case to deal with the clause of the Constitution that allows Congress to regulate interstate and foreign commerce. This case was important because it reinforced both the authority of the federal government over the states and the division of powers between the federal government and the state governments.

Background Steamboat operators who wanted to travel on New York waters had to obtain a state license. Thomas Gibbons had a federal license to travel along the coast, but not a state license for New York. He wanted the freedom to compete with state-licensed Aaron Ogden for steam travel between New Jersey and the New York island of Manhattan.

Decision This case was decided on March 2, 1824, by a vote of 6 to 0. Chief Justice John Marshall spoke for the Court, which ruled in favor of Gibbons. The Court stated that the congressional statute (Gibbons's federal license) took priority over the state statute (Ogden's state-monopoly license). The ruling also defined commerce as more than simply the exchange of goods, broadening it to include the transportation of people and the use of new inventions (such as the steamboat).

Supreme Court Building, Washington, D.C.

Worcester v. *Georgia* (1832)

Significance This ruling made Georgia's removal of the Cherokee illegal. However, Georgia, with President Andrew Jackson's support, defied the Court's decision. By not enforcing the Court's ruling, Jackson violated his constitutional oath as president. As a result, the Cherokee and other American Indian tribes continued to be forced off of lands protected by treaties.

Background The state of Georgia wanted to remove Cherokee Indians from lands they held by treaty. Samuel Worcester, a missionary who worked with the Cherokee Nation, was arrested for failing to take an oath of allegiance to the state and to obey a Georgia militia order to leave the Cherokee's lands. Worcester sued, charging that Georgia had no legal authority on Cherokee lands.

Decision This case was decided on March 3, 1832, by a vote of 5 to 1 in favor of Worcester. Chief Justice John Marshall spoke for the Supreme Court, which ruled that the Cherokee were an independent political community. The Court decided that only the federal government, not the state of Georgia, had authority over legal matters involving the Cherokee people.

Dred Scott v. *Sandford* (1857)

Significance This ruling denied enslaved African Americans U.S. citizenship and the right to sue in federal court. The decision also invalidated the Missouri Compromise, which had prevented slavery in territories north of the 36° 30' line of latitude. The ruling increased the controversy over the expansion of slavery in new states and territories.

Background John Emerson, an army doctor, took his slave Dred Scott with him to live in Illinois and then Wisconsin Territory, both of which had banned slavery. In 1842 the two moved to Missouri, a slave state. Four years later, Scott sued for his freedom according to a Missouri legal principle of "once free, always free." The principle meant that a slave was entitled to freedom if he or she had once lived in a free state or territory.

Decision This case was decided March 6-7, 1857, by a vote of 7 to 2. Chief Justice Roger B. Taney spoke for the Court, which ruled that slaves did not have the right to sue in federal courts because they were considered property, not citizens. In addition, the Court ruled that Congress did not have the power to abolish slavery in territories because that power was not strictly defined in the Constitution. Furthermore, the Court overturned the once-free, always-free principle.

Civil Rights Cases (1883)

Significance This ruling struck down the Civil Rights Act of 1875. It allowed private businesses to discriminate based on race or color. The Court ruled that Congress could only make laws preventing states, not private individuals or companies, from discriminating.

Background Five separate cases were combined under this one decision. After the Civil Rights Act of 1875 was passed, individuals and private businesses continued to discriminate against former slaves and other African Americans. In the five separate cases, African Americans were denied the same accommodations that whites were provided.

Decision The case was decided on October 15, 1883, by a vote of 8 to 1. Justice Joseph P. Bradley wrote the opinion, which said of the 14th Amendment, "Individual invasion of individual rights is not the subject-matter of the amendment." Justice John Marshall Harlan was the lone dissenter, claiming that the 13th Amendment gave Congress the right to make the law. "The letter of the law is the body," he said. "[T]he sense and reason of the law is the soul."

Wabash, St. Louis & Pacific Railroad v. Illinois (1886)

Significance This ruling reversed an earlier decision in *Munn* v. *Illinois* and removed the power from the states to regulate railroad rates. It reasserted the authority of Congress over interstate commerce and led to the creation of the Interstate Commerce Commission.

Background The state of Illinois passed a law attempting to regulate the shipping rates of railroads that passed through the state, including the Wabash, St. Louis & Pacific line. In an attempt to operate without regulation, the railroad company sued the state.

Decision The Court struck down the Illinois law, saying that the state was able to regulate businesses that operated only within its boundaries. Businesses that operated between states were subject to regulation by the national government.

United States v. E. C. Knight Co. (1895)

Significance This ruling effectively put most monopolies out of the reach of the Sherman Antitrust Act of 1890. It declared that local manufacturing was out of the scope of the interstate-commerce regulatory power of Congress.

Background The E. C. Knight Company enjoyed a virtual monopoly of sugar refining within the United States. The federal government sued the company under the Sherman Antitrust Act in an attempt to break this monopoly and allow other companies to refine sugar.

Decision The court ruled that although the act was legal, it did not apply to manufacturing. Justice Melville Fuller said that manufacturing was not interstate commerce and could therefore not be regulated by Congress.

In Re Debs (1895)

Significance In this ruling the Court upheld the right of the federal government to halt strikes organized by union workers. After losing his case, Debs ran for president from his jail cell.

Background Railway union official Eugene V. Debs had organized a strike of union workers. The government petitioned him to halt the strike, and a court held him in contempt when he refused. Debs fought his conviction.

Decision In a unanimous decision, the Court declared that the federal government did have the power to order Debs to halt the strike. Justice David J. Brewer wrote the opinion of the Court, which stated the U.S. government "acts directly upon each citizen."

Plessy v. Ferguson (1896)

Significance This case upheld the constitutionality of racial segregation by ruling that separate facilities for different races were legal as long as those facilities were equal to one another. This case provided a legal justification for racial segregation for nearly 60 years until it was overturned by *Brown* v. *Board of Education* in 1954.

Background An 1890 Louisiana law required that all railway companies in the state use "separate-but-equal" railcars for white and African American passengers. A group of citizens in New Orleans banded together to challenge the law and chose Homer Plessy to test the law in 1892. Plessy took a seat in a whites-only coach, and when he refused to move, he was arrested. Plessy eventually sought review by the U.S. Supreme Court, claiming that the Louisiana law violated his Fourteenth Amendment right to equal protection.

Decision This case was decided on May 18, 1896, by a vote of 7 to 1. Justice Henry Billings Brown spoke for the Court, which upheld the constitutionality of the Louisiana law that segregated railcars. Justice John M. Harlan dissented, arguing that the Constitution should not be interpreted in ways that recognize class or racial distinctions.

Northern Securities Co. v. United States (1904)

Significance In this ruling the Court declared that the federal government had the right to break up companies if their formation was illegal, whether or not dissolving the company would have a harmful impact on the business community.

Background The Northern Securities Company held stock in several major railroads. Although President Theodore Roosevelt claimed the company was a trust and therefore illegal under the Sherman Antitrust Act, some disagreed that the idea of trusts extended into the realm of owning stocks.

Decision In a 5-to-4 decision, the Court ruled that the formation of the company was illegal, and that the federal government had the power to disband it. Writing for the majority, Justice John Marshall Harlan said, "every corporation created by a state is necessarily subject to the supreme law of the land," meaning the federal government.

Lochner v. New York (1905)

Significance This decision established the Supreme Court's role in overseeing state regulations. For more than 30 years, Lochner was often used as a precedent in striking down state laws such as minimum-wage laws, child labor laws, and regulations placed on the banking and transportation industries.

Background In 1895 the state of New York passed a labor law limiting bakers to working no more than 10 hours per day or 60 hours per week. The purpose of the law was to protect the health of bakers, who worked in hot and damp conditions and breathed in large quantities of flour dust. In 1902 Joseph Lochner, the owner of a small bakery in New York, claimed that the state law violated his Fourteenth Amendment rights by unfairly depriving him of the liberty to make contracts with employees. This case went to the U.S. Supreme Court.

Decision This case was decided on April 17, 1905, by a vote of 5 to 4 in favor of Lochner. The Supreme Court judged that the Fourteenth Amendment protected the right to sell and buy labor, and that any state law restricting that right was unconstitutional. The Court rejected the argument that the limited workday and workweek were necessary to protect the health of bakery workers.

Muller v. Oregon (1908)

Significance A landmark for cases involving social reform, this decision established the Court's recognition of social and economic conditions (in this case, women's health) as a factor in making laws.

Background In 1903 Oregon passed a law limiting workdays to 10 hours for female workers in laundries and factories. In 1905 Curt Muller's Grand Laundry was found guilty of breaking this law. Muller appealed, claiming that the state law violated his freedom of contract (the Supreme Court had upheld a similar claim that year in *Lochner* v. *New York*). When this case came to the Court, the National Consumers' League hired lawyer Louis D. Brandeis to present Oregon's argument. Brandeis argued that the Court had already defended the state's police power to protect its citizens' health, safety, and welfare.

Decision This case was decided on February 24, 1908, by a vote of 9 to 0 upholding the Oregon law. The Court agreed that women's well-being was in the state's public interest and that the 10-hour law was a valid way to protect their well-being.

Schechter Poultry Corporation v. United States (1935)

Significance This ruling declared that the United States could not regulate businesses that operated only within one state. It dealt a severe blow to President Franklin Roosevelt's New Deal.

Background In an attempt to lessen the effects of the Great Depression, Roosevelt encouraged Congress to pass a Recovery Act that set a minimum wage and restricted working hours. The Schechter Poultry Corporation, which operated only within New York City, maintained that the federal government did not have a constitutional right to regulate its businesses practices.

Decision In a unanimous decision, the Court upheld the Schechter Corporation's claim. Chief Justice Charles Evans Hughes wrote the opinion, which stated that the transactions in the case—wages, salaries, and working hours—were a local concern outside of the scope of federal regulation.

Korematsu v. United States (1944)

Significance This case addressed the question of whether government action that treats a racial group differently from other people violates the Equal Protection Clause of the Fourteenth Amendment. The ruling in the case held that distinctions based on race are "inherently suspect," and that laws and rules based on race must withstand "strict scrutiny" by the courts. The Court still applies the "strict scrutiny" standard today to cases involving race and other groups.

Background When the United States declared war on Japan in 1941, about 112,000 Japanese Americans lived on the West Coast. About 70,000 of these Japanese Americans were citizens. In 1942 the U.S. military was afraid that these people could not be trusted in wartime. They ordered most of the Japanese Americans to move to special camps far from their homes. Fred Korematsu, a Japanese American and an American citizen, did not go to the camps as ordered. He stayed in California and was arrested. He was sent to a camp in Utah. Korematsu then sued, claiming that the government acted illegally when it sent people of Japanese descent to camps.

Decision By a 6-to-3 margin, the Supreme Court said the orders moving the Japanese-Americans into the camps were constitutional. Justice Hugo Black wrote the opinion for the Court. He said that the unusual demands of wartime security justified the orders. However, he made it clear that distinctions based on race are "inherently suspect," and that laws based on race must withstand "strict scrutiny" by the courts. Justice Robert H. Jackson dissented; he wrote that Korematsu was "convicted of an act not commonly a crime … being present in the state [where] he is a citizen, near where he was born, and where all his life he has lived." Justice Frank Murphy, another dissenter, said the military order was based on racial prejudice.

Brown v. Board of Education (1954)

Significance This ruling reversed the Supreme Court's earlier position on segregation set by *Plessy v. Ferguson* (1896). The decision also inspired Congress and the federal courts to help carry out further civil rights reforms for African Americans.

Background Beginning in the 1930s, the National Association for the Advancement of Colored People (NAACP) began using the courts to challenge racial segregation in public education. In 1952 the NAACP took a number of school segregation cases to the Supreme Court. These included the Brown family's suit against the school board of Topeka, Kansas, over its "separate-but-equal" policy.

Decision This case was decided on May 17, 1954, by a vote of 9 to 0. Chief Justice Earl Warren spoke for the unanimous Court, which ruled that segregation in public education created inequality. The Court held that racial segregation in public schools was by nature unequal, even if the school facilities were equal. The Court noted that such segregation created feelings of inferiority that could not be undone. Therefore, enforced separation of the races in public education is unconstitutional.

Watkins v. United States (1957)

Significance The decision limited the inquiry powers of Congress. It was expected not to engage in law enforcement (an executive function), nor to act as a trial agency (a judicial function), but to inquire only as far as was necessary for the functioning of Congress.

Background Watkins was a labor union officer who appeared before the House Un-American Activities Committee during the 1950s Red Scare. Although he was willing to answer personal questions about himself and others whom he knew to be members of the Communist Party, he would not answer questions about past members of the Communist Party. He was therefore held in contempt of Congress.

Decision In a vote of 6 to 1 handed down on June 17, 1957, the Court threw out the charge of contempt against Watkins. Congress, it said, did not have the right to invade the private lives of individuals.

Mapp v. Ohio (1961)

Significance In this ruling the Court declared that evidence discovered in the process of an illegal search could not be used in state courts.

Background While searching for a bombing suspect, police found evidence of a separate crime in the house of Dollree Mapp. The police did not have permission to enter the home, nor did they have a search warrant. Upon conviction for the separate crime, Mapp appealed her case to the Supreme Court.

Decision In a 5-to-3 decision, the Court stated that convictions based on illegally obtained evidence must be overturned. Justice Tom Clark wrote for the majority, "all evidence obtained by searches and seizures in violation of the Constitution is ... inadmissible in a state court."

Baker v. Carr (1962)

Significance Through this decision, the Court ruled that the judiciary branch may involve itself in hearing cases about political matters.

Background Voters from Tennessee sued their state in federal court, arguing that the way the state drew the boundary lines between representative districts created unequal representation within the legislature, and therefore unequal protection under the laws of the state. Tennessee argued that the federal court did not have the jurisdiction to hear the case.

Decision By a 6-to-2 margin, the Court decided that the federal court did have the right to hear the case and that the voters had the right to sue over the issue. Writing for the majority, Justice William Brennan said that the voters "are entitled to a trial and a decision" on whether they were denied equal protection.

Engel v. Vitale (1962)

Significance This case deals with the specific issue of organized prayer in schools and the broader issue of the proper relationship between government and religion under the First Amendment. The question in the case was whether a state violates the First Amendment when it composes a prayer that students must say at the beginning of each school day.

Background The state of New York recommended that public schools in the state begin the day by having students recite a prayer written by the state government. A group of parents sued to stop the official prayer, saying that it was contrary to their beliefs and their children's beliefs. They believed the law was unconstitutional because it "established" (officially supported) religion. Though students were permitted to remain silent, the parents claimed that there would always be pressure on students to pray.

Decision By a 6-to-1 margin (two justices did not take part in the case), the Court agreed with the parents. It struck down the state law. Justice Hugo Black wrote for the decision for the majority. He pointed out that the prayer was clearly religious. He said that under the First Amendment, "it is no part of the business of government to compose official prayers for any group of American people to recite as part of a religious program carried on by government." Black, referring to Jefferson and Madison, said "These men knew that the First Amendment, which tried to put an end to governmental control of religion and prayer, was not written to destroy either."

Gideon v. Wainwright (1963)

Significance This ruling was one of several key Supreme Court decisions establishing free legal help for those who cannot otherwise afford representation in court.

Background Clarence Earl Gideon was accused of robbery in Florida. Gideon could not afford a lawyer for his trial, and the judge refused to supply him with one for free. Gideon tried to defend himself and was found guilty. He eventually appealed to the U.S. Supreme Court, claiming that the lower court's denial of a court-appointed lawyer violated his Sixth and Fourteenth Amendment rights.

Decision This case was decided on March 18, 1963, by a vote of 9 to 0 in favor of Gideon. The Court agreed that the Sixth Amendment (which protects a citizen's right to have a lawyer for his or her defense) applied to the states because it fell under the due process clause of the Fourteenth Amendment. Thus, the states are required to provide legal aid to those defendants in criminal cases who cannot afford to pay for legal representation.

Heart of Atlanta Motel v. United States (1964)

Significance This ruling upheld the public accommodations clause of the Civil Rights Act of 1964. It enforced the right of African Americans to receive access to the same accommodations as whites and gave Congress judicial backing for passing more civil rights legislation.

Background The owner of the Heart of Atlanta Motel routinely discriminated against African Americans. He claimed that his business was not an interstate business and therefore not subject to regulation by congressional acts.

Decision In a unanimous decision, the Court declared that as a business that served people from across state boundaries, the Heart of Atlanta Motel was in fact an interstate business and that, therefore, congressional acts did apply.

Miranda v. Arizona (1966)

Significance This decision ruled that an accused person's Fifth Amendment rights begin at the time of arrest. The ruling caused controversy because it made the questioning of suspects and collecting evidence more difficult for law enforcement officers.

Background In 1963 Ernesto Miranda was arrested in Arizona for a kidnapping. Miranda signed a confession and was later found guilty of the crime. The arresting police officers, however, admitted that they had not told Miranda of his right to talk with an attorney before his confession. Miranda appealed his conviction on the grounds that by not informing him of his legal rights the police had violated his Fifth Amendment right against self-incrimination.

Decision This case was decided on June 13, 1966, by a vote of 5 to 4. Chief Justice Earl Warren spoke for the Court, which ruled in Miranda's favor. The Court decided that an accused person must be given four warnings after being taken into police custody: (1) the suspect has the right to remain silent, (2) anything the suspect says can and will be used against him or her, (3) the suspect has the right to consult with an attorney and to have an attorney present during questioning, and (4) if the suspect cannot afford a lawyer, one will be provided before questioning begins.

Tinker v. Des Moines Independent Community School District (1969)

Significance This ruling established the extent to which American public school students can take part in political protests in their schools. The question the case raised is whether, under the First Amendment, school officials can prohibit students from wearing armbands to symbolize political protest.

Background Students in Des Moines, Iowa, decided to wear black armbands to protest the Vietnam War. Two days before the protest, the school board created a new policy. The policy stated that any student who wore an armband to school and refused to remove it would be suspended. Three students wore armbands and were suspended. They said that their First Amendment right to freedom of speech had been violated. In 1969 the United States Supreme Court decided their case.

The Decision By a 7-to-2 margin, the Court agreed with the students. Justice Abe Fortas wrote the decision for the majority. He said that students do not "shed their constitutional rights to freedom of speech ... at the schoolhouse gate." Fortas admitted that school officials had the right to set rules. However, their rules must be consistent with the First Amendment. In this case, Des Moines school officials thought their rule was justified. They feared that the protest would disrupt learning. Fortas's opinion held that wearing an armband symbolizing political protest was a form of speech called symbolic speech. Symbolic speech is conduct that expresses an idea. Symbolic speech is protected in the same manner as the spoken word. Fortas wrote that student symbolic speech could be punished only if it disrupts the learning process. Fortas also noted that school officials allowed other political symbols, such as campaign buttons, to be worn in school.

Reed v. Reed (1971)

Significance This ruling was the first in a century of Fourteenth Amendment decisions to say that gender discrimination violated the equal protection clause. This case was later used to strike down other statutes that discriminated against women.

Background Cecil and Sally Reed were separated. When their son died without a will, the law gave preference to Cecil to be appointed the administrator of the son's estate. Sally sued Cecil for the right to administer the estate, challenging the gender preference in the law.

Decision This case was decided on November 22, 1971, by a vote of 7 to 0. Chief Justice Warren Burger spoke for the unanimous Supreme Court. Although the Court had upheld laws based on gender preference in the past, in this case it reversed its position. The Court declared that gender discrimination violated the equal protection clause of the Fourteenth Amendment and therefore could not be the basis for a law.

New York Times v. United States (1971)

Significance In this ruling the Court dismissed the idea of "prior restraint," or attempting to stop an action before it happens, by the government as unconstitutional. The ruling allowed the *New York Times* to continue publishing documents that were critical of the government's handling of the Vietnam War.

Background The *New York Times* began publishing a series of papers called the Pentagon Papers that were critical of the government. The government attempted to stop publication of the papers with a court order, citing national security. Because of the national importance of the case, the Supreme Court agreed to hear the case quickly.

Decision In a 6-to-3 decision, the Court declared that the government could not stop publication of the Pentagon Papers. Although the government did have the right to stop publication if it could prove the danger to national security, the Court said that in this case the government had not met the burden of proof.

Roe v. Wade (1973)

Significance This ruling made abortions available to women during their first trimester of pregnancy, even when their health was not in danger.

Background The case was brought in the name of Jane Roe against the restrictive abortion laws of Texas. Until this case, states had widely varying laws about the availability of abortions, some restricting them altogether.

Decision With a 7 to 2 decision, the Court said that elective abortions must be available to any woman in her first three months of pregnancy. Because of the variety of moral opinions about when life begins, the court ruled that a fetus does not have the same rights as an infant.

United States v. Nixon (1974)

Significance This ruling forced President Nixon to turn over tapes of White House conversations to the congressional committee investigating his wrongdoing in the Watergate breakin. Nixon resigned shortly after.

Background Nixon had been secretly taping every conversation that took place in the Oval Office. After the president was implicated in the cover-up of the Watergate Hotel break in, Congress wanted to hear these tapes. Nixon refused to hand them over, claiming "executive privilege" to keep some information secret.

Decision In a unanimous decision, the Court ruled that Nixon must turn the tapes over to the prosecution as requested. Writing for the court, Chief Justice Warren Burger stated that finding the truth requires that courts have all the evidence they need, even if it includes presidential communication.

New Jersey v. TLO (1985)

Significance In this ruling, the Court declared that searches of juveniles on school grounds are not subject to the same standards of "reasonableness" and "probable cause" that protect other citizens.

Background T. L. O. was a fourteen year old who was caught smoking in the girls' bathroom of her school. A principal at the school questioned the girl and searched her purse, finding marijuana and other drug paraphernalia.

Decision In a 7 to 2 decision, the Court ruled that the suspension of the rules of "reasonable" search and seizure as defined by the Fourth Amendment and later court rulings applied only to school officials and not to law enforcement officers.

Texas v. Johnson (1989)

Significance This ruling answered the question of whether the First Amendment protects burning the U.S. flag as a form of symbolic speech. It deals with the limits of symbolic speech. This case is particularly important because it involves burning the flag, one of our national symbols.

Background At the 1984 Republican National Convention in Texas, Gregory Lee Johnson doused a U.S. flag with kerosene. He did this during a demonstration, as a form of protest. Johnson was convicted of violating a Texas law that made it a crime to desecrate [treat disrespectfully] the national flag. He was sentenced to one year in prison and fined $2,000. The Texas Court of Criminal Appeals reversed the conviction because, it said, Johnson's burning of the flag was a form of symbolic speech protected by the First Amendment. Texas then appealed to the U.S. Supreme Court.

Decision The Court ruled for Johnson, five to four. Justice William Brennan wrote for the majority. He said that Johnson was within his constitutional rights when he burned the U.S. flag in protest. As in Tinker v. Des Moines Independent Community School District (1969), the Court looked at the First Amendment and "symbolic speech." Brennan concluded that Johnson's burning the flag was a form of symbolic speech—like the students wearing armbands in Des Moines—is protected by the First Amendment. According to Brennan, "Government may not prohibit the expression of an idea [because it is] offensive." Chief Justice Rehnquist dissented. He said the flag is "the visible symbol embodying our Nation. It does not represent the views of any particular political party, and it does not represent any particular political philosophy. The flag is not simply another 'idea' or 'point of view' competing for recognition in the marketplace of ideas." Since this decision, several amendments banning flag burning have been proposed in Congress, but so far all have failed.

Cruzan v. Director, Missouri Department of Health (1990)

Significance This ruling helped define who may refuse medical treatment. Although the issue is still undecided, this case began a series of efforts to provide legislative and judicial guidelines for the "right to die."

Background The parents of comatose patient Nancy Cruzan wanted to remove her life support system. The Department of Health ruled that Cruzan had not previously made clear her desire to refuse medical treatment in the event of brain damage.

Decision By a 5-to-4 margin, the Court ruled that Cruzan's parents could not remove her from life support because she had not clearly expressed her desires previously. Writing for the majority, Chief Justice William Rehnquist stated that it was Nancy's demand to be removed from life support, not her parents' wishes, that the state must respect in such cases.

Planned Parenthood of Southeastern Pennsylvania, et al. v. Casey (1992)

Significance In this ruling the Court upheld its decision in *Roe* v. *Wade* of the right to elective abortion, but allowed the state of Pennsylvania to impose restrictions of notification and consent upon minors.

Background In 1988 and 1989, Pennsylvania revised its laws to require that, to receive an abortion, minors must receive consent from a parent, and married women must notify their husbands. The laws were challenged by several abortion clinics and physicians.

Decision In a 5-to-4 decision, the Court upheld its previous ruling of *Roe* v. *Wade* that women have the right to an abortion in the first trimester of pregnancy, but provided that a state may require that minors have the consent of one parent 24 hours before the procedure. The Court struck down the part of the Pennsylvania laws that required married women to notify their husbands, saying that it could be an "undue burden" upon women.

Vernonia School District v. Acton (1995)

Significance This ruling allowed random drug testing of minors on school property as a safety measure.

Background James Acton, a student athlete in the Vernonia School District, refused to participate in drug testing, stating that the policy invaded his right to privacy and was an illegal search and seizure.

Decision In a 6-to-3 decision, the Court ruled that while on school property, students are subject to greater control of personal rights than are free adults. Furthermore, concern over the safety of minors under governmental supervision outweighs the minimal intrusion into a student's privacy.

Bush v. *Gore* (2000)

Significance In this ruling, the question before the court was whether ballots that could not be read by voting machines should be recounted by hand. The broader issues were whether the Supreme Court can overrule state court decisions on state laws, and whether an appointed judiciary can affect the result of democratic elections.

Background The 2000 presidential election between Democrat Al Gore and Republican George Bush was very close. Ultimately, the outcome would be determined by votes in the state of Florida. People in Florida voted by punching a hole in a ballot card. The votes were counted by a machine that detected these holes. According to that count, Bush won the state of Florida by a few hundred votes. Florida's Election Commission declared that Bush had won Florida. However, about 60,000 ballots were not counted because the machines could not detect a hole in the ballot. Gore argued in the Florida Supreme Court that these votes should be recounted by hand. The Florida Supreme Court ordered counties to recount all those votes. Bush appealed to the United States Supreme Court, which issued an order to stop the recounts while it made a decision.

The Decision On December 12, 2000, the Supreme Court voted 5 to 4 to end the hand recount of votes ordered by the Florida Supreme Court. The majority said that the Florida Supreme Court had ordered a recount without setting standards for what was a valid vote. Different vote-counters might use different standards. The Court said that this inconsistency meant that votes were treated arbitrarily—based on a person's choice rather than on standards. This arbitrariness, said the Court, violated the due process clause and the equal protection clause of the Constitution. Also, the justices said that Florida law required the vote count to be finalized by December 12. The justices said that rules for recounts could not be made by that date, so they ordered election officials to stop recounting votes.

Gratz v. *Bollinger* and *Grutter* v. *Bollinger* (2003)

Significance These cases considered whether a university violates the Constitution by using race as a factor for admitting students to its undergraduate school and its law school. The ruling affects use of affirmative action programs in higher education. The decisions gave colleges guidelines as to what is permitted and what is not. The decisions were limited to higher education and may not apply to other affirmative action programs such as those for applying for a job or for a government contract.

Background Jennifer Gratz and Barbara Grutter are both white. They challenged the University of Michigan's affirmative action admissions policies. Gratz said that the university violated the Constitution by considering race as a factor in its undergraduate admissions programs. Grutter claimed that the University of Michigan Law School did so.

Decisions In Gratz, the Court ruled 6 to 3 that the undergraduate program—which gave each minority applicant an automatic 20 points toward admission—was unconstitutional. Chief Justice William Rehnquist's opinion held that the policy violated the equal protection clause because it did not consider each applicant individually. "The ... automatic distribution of 20 points has the effect of making 'the factor of race ... decisive' for virtually every minimally qualified underrepresented minority applicant." The result was different when the Court turned to the affirmative action policy of Michigan's Law School, however, which used race as one factor for admission. In Grutter, by a 5-to-4 margin, the Court held that this policy did not violate the equal protection clause. Justice Sandra Day O'Connor wrote for the majority. "Truly individualized consideration demands that race be used in a flexible, nonmechanical way ... Universities can ... consider race or ethnicity ... as a 'plus' factor [when individually considering] each and every applicant." Thus, the law school's policy was constitutional.

United States v. American Library Association (2003)

Significance This case deals with the constitutionality of a federal law called the Children's Internet Protection Act (CIPA). The law was designed to protect children from being exposed to pornographic Web sites while using computers in public libraries. The question before the court was this: Does a public library violate the First Amendment by installing Internet filtering software on its public computers?

Background CIPA applies to public libraries that accept federal money to help pay for Internet access. These libraries must install filtering software to block pornographic images. Some library associations sued to block these filtering requirements. They argued that by linking money and filters, the law required public libraries to violate the First Amendment's guarantees of free speech. The libraries argued that filters block some non-pornographic sites along with pornographic ones. That, they said, violates library patrons' First Amendment rights. CIPA does allow anyone to ask a librarian to unblock a specific Web site. It also allows adults to ask that the filter be turned off altogether. But, the libraries argued, people using the library would find these remedies embarrassing and impractical.

Decision In this case, Chief Justice William Rehnquist authored a plurality opinion. He explained that the law does not require any library to accept federal money. A library can choose to do without federal money. If the library makes that choice, it does not have to install Internet filters. And Rehnquist did not think that filtering software's tendency to overblock nonpornographic sites was a constitutional problem. Adult patrons could simply ask a librarian to unblock a blocked site or could have the filter disabled entirely.

The Dissents Justice John Paul Stevens viewed CIPA "as a blunt nationwide restraint on adult access to an enormous amount of valuable" and often constitutionally protected speech. Justice David Souter noted that he would have joined the plurality if the First Amendment interests raised in this case were those of children rather than those of adults.

Hamdi v. Rumsfeld and Rasul v. Bush (2004)

Significance These cases addressed the balance between the government's powers to fight terrorism and the Constitution's promise of due process. Each case raised a slightly different question:

1. Can the government hold American citizens for an indefinite period as "enemy combatants" and not permit them access to American courts, and

2. Do foreigners captured overseas and jailed at Guantánamo Bay, Cuba, have the right to take their cases to American courts to decide if they are being held legally?

Background In *Hamdi* v. *Rumsfeld*, Yaser Hamdi, an American citizen, was captured in Afghanistan in 2001. The U.S. military said Hamdi was an enemy combatant and claimed that "it has the authority to hold ... enemy combatants captured on the battlefield ... to prevent them from returning to the battle." Hamdi's attorney said that Hamdi deserved the due process rights that other Americans have, including a hearing in court to argue that he was not an enemy combatant.

The prisoners in *Rasul* v. *Bush* also claimed they were wrongly imprisoned. They wanted a court hearing, but Guantánamo Bay Naval Base is on Cuban soil. Cuba leases the base to the United States. In an earlier case, the Court had ruled that "if an alien is outside the country's sovereign territory, then ... the alien is not permitted access to the courts of the United States to enforce the Constitution."

Decision In *Hamdi*, the Court ruled 6 to 3 that Hamdi had a right to a hearing. Justice Sandra Day O'Connor wrote that the Court has "made clear that a state of war is not a blank check for the president when it comes to the rights of the nation's citizens." The government decided not to prosecute Hamdi. In *Rasul*, also decided 6 to 3, Justice John Paul Stevens wrote that the prisoners had been held for more than two years in territory under U.S. control. Thus, even though the prisoners are not on U.S. soil, they can ask U.S. courts if their detention is legal. The *Rasul* cases were still pending when this book was printed.

The Declaration of Independence

In Congress, July 4, 1776
The unanimous Declaration of the thirteen united States of America,

When in the Course of human events, it becomes necessary for one people to dissolve the political bands which have connected them with another, and to assume among the Powers of the earth, the separate and equal station to which the Laws of Nature and of Nature's God entitle them, a decent respect to the opinions of mankind requires that they should declare the causes which **impel** them to the separation.

We hold these truths to be self-evident, that all men are created equal, that they are **endowed** by their Creator with certain unalienable Rights, that among these are Life, Liberty, and the pursuit of Happiness. That to secure these rights, Governments are instituted among Men, deriving their just powers from the consent of the governed, That whenever any Form of Government becomes destructive of these ends, it is the Right of the People to alter or to abolish it, and to institute new Government, laying its foundation on such principles and organizing its powers in such form, as to them shall seem most likely to effect their Safety and Happiness. Prudence, indeed, will dictate that Governments long established should not be changed for light and transient causes; and accordingly all experience hath shown, that mankind are more disposed to suffer, while evils are sufferable, than to right themselves by abolishing the forms to which they are accustomed. But when a long train of abuses and **usurpations**, pursuing invariably the same Object **evinces** a design to reduce them under absolute **Despotism**, it is their right, it is their duty, to throw off such Government, and to provide new Guards for their future security.—Such has been the patient sufferance of these Colonies; and such is now the necessity which constrains them to alter their former Systems of Government. The history of the present King of Great Britain is a history of repeated injuries and usurpations, all having in direct object the establishment of an absolute **Tyranny** over these States. To prove this, let Facts be submitted to a **candid** world.

He has refused his Assent to Laws, the most wholesome and necessary for the public good.

He has forbidden his Governors to pass Laws of immediate and pressing importance, unless suspended in their operation till his Assent should be obtained; and when so suspended, he has utterly neglected to attend to them.

Vocabulary

impel force

endowed provided

usurpations wrongful seizures of power

evinces clearly displays

despotism unlimited power

tyranny oppressive power exerted by a government or ruler

candid fair

He has refused to pass other Laws for the accommodation of large districts of people, unless those people would **relinquish** the right of Representation in the Legislature, a right **inestimable** to them and **formidable** to tyrants only.

He has called together legislative bodies at places unusual, uncomfortable, and distant from the depository of their Public Records, for the sole purpose of fatiguing them into compliance with his measures.

He has dissolved Representative Houses repeatedly, for opposing with manly firmness his invasions on the rights of the people.

He has refused for a long time, after such dissolutions, to cause others to be elected; whereby the Legislative Powers, incapable of **Annihilation**, have returned to the People at large for their exercise; the State remaining in the mean time exposed to all the dangers of invasion from without, and **convulsions** within.

He has endeavored to prevent the population of these States; for that purpose obstructing the Laws of **Naturalization of Foreigners**; refusing to pass others to encourage their migration hither, and raising the conditions of new **Appropriations of Lands**.

He has obstructed the Administration of Justice, by refusing his Assent to Laws for establishing Judiciary Powers.

He has made Judges dependent on his Will alone, for the **tenure** of their offices, and the amount and payment of their salaries.

He has erected **a multitude of** New Offices, and sent hither swarms of Officers to harass our people, and eat out their substance.

He has kept among us, in times of peace, Standing Armies without the Consent of our legislature.

He has affected to render the Military independent of and superior to the Civil Power.

He has combined with others to subject us to a jurisdiction foreign to our constitution, and unacknowledged by our laws; giving his Assent to their Acts of pretended legislation:

For **quartering** large bodies of armed troops among us:

For protecting them, by a mock Trial, from Punishment for any Murders which they should commit on the Inhabitants of these States:

For cutting off our Trade with all parts of the world:

For imposing taxes on us without our Consent:

For depriving us in many cases, of the benefits of Trial by Jury:

Vocabulary

relinquish release, yield

inestimable priceless

formidable causing dread

annihilation destruction

convulsions violent disturbances

naturalization of foreigners the process by which foreign-born persons become citizens

appropriations of lands setting aside land for settlement

tenure term

a multitude of many

quartering lodging, housing

DECLARATION OF INDEPENDENCE

arbitrary not based on law

render make

abdicated given up

foreign mercenaries soldiers hired to fight for a country not their own

perfidy violation of trust

insurrections rebellions

petitioned for redress asked formally for a correction of wrongs

unwarrantable jurisdiction unjustified authority

magnanimity generous spirit

conjured urgently called upon

consanguinity common ancestry

acquiesce consent to

For transporting us beyond Seas to be tried for pretended offences:

For abolishing the free System of English Laws in a neighboring Province, establishing therein an **Arbitrary** government, and enlarging its Boundaries so as to **render** it at once an example and fit instrument for introducing the same absolute rule into these Colonies:

For taking away our Charters, abolishing our most valuable Laws, and altering fundamentally the Forms of our Governments:

For suspending our own Legislature, and declaring themselves invested with Power to legislate for us in all cases whatsoever.

He has **abdicated** Government here, by declaring us out of his Protection and waging War against us.

He has plundered our seas, ravaged our Coasts, burnt our towns, and destroyed the lives of our people.

He is at this time transporting large armies of **foreign mercenaries** to complete the works of death, desolation and tyranny, already begun with circumstances of Cruelty & **perfidy** scarcely paralleled in the most barbarous ages, and totally unworthy the Head of a civilized nation.

He has constrained our fellow Citizens taken Captive on the high Seas to bear Arms against their Country, to become the executioners of their friends and Brethren, or to fall themselves by their Hands.

He has excited domestic **insurrections** amongst us, and has endeavored to bring on the inhabitants of our frontiers, the merciless Indian Savages, whose known rule of warfare, is an undistinguished destruction of all ages, sexes and conditions.

In every stage of these Oppressions We have **Petitioned for Redress** in the most humble terms: Our repeated Petitions have been answered only by repeated injury. A Prince, whose character is thus marked by every act which may define a Tyrant, is unfit to be the ruler of a free People.

Nor have We been wanting in attention to our British brethren. We have warned them from time to time of attempts by their legislature to extend an **unwarrantable jurisdiction** over us. We have reminded them of the circumstances of our emigration and settlement here. We have appealed to their native justice and **magnanimity**, and we have **conjured** them by the ties of our common kindred to disavow these usurpations, which, would inevitably interrupt our connections and correspondence. They too have been deaf to the voice of justice and of **consanguinity**. We must, therefore, **acquiesce** in the necessity, which denounces our Separation, and hold them, as we hold the rest of mankind, Enemies in War, in Peace Friends.

We, therefore, the Representatives of the united States of America, in General Congress, Assembled, appealing to the Supreme Judge of the world for the **rectitude** of our intentions, do, in the Name, and by Authority of the good People of these Colonies, solemnly publish and declare, That these United Colonies are, and of Right ought to be Free and Independent States; that they are Absolved from all Allegiance to the British Crown, and that all political connection between them and the State of Great Britain, is and ought to be totally dissolved; and that as Free and Independent States, they have full Power to levy War, conclude Peace, contract Alliances, establish Commerce, and to do all other Acts and Things which Independent States may of right do. And for the support of this Declaration, with a firm reliance on the Protection of Divine Providence, we mutually pledge to each other our Lives, our Fortunes and our sacred Honor.

Vocabulary

rectitude rightness

John Hancock	Benjamin Harrison	Lewis Morris
Button Gwinnett	Thomas Nelson, Jr.	Richard Stockton
Lyman Hall	Francis Lightfoot Lee	John Witherspoon
George Walton	Carter Braxton	Francis Hopkinson
William Hooper	Robert Morris	John Hart
Joseph Hewes	Benjamin Rush	Abraham Clark
John Penn	Benjamin Franklin	Josiah Bartlett
Edward Rutledge	John Morton	William Whipple
Thomas Heyward, Jr.	George Clymer	Samuel Adams
Thomas Lynch, Jr.	James Smith	John Adams
Arthur Middleton	George Taylor	Robert Treat Paine
Samuel Chase	James Wilson	Elbridge Gerry
William Paca	George Ross	Stephen Hopkins
Thomas Stone	Caesar Rodney	William Ellery
Charles Carroll of Carrollton	George Read	Roger Sherman
George Wythe	Thomas McKean	Samuel Huntington
Richard Henry Lee	William Floyd	William Williams
Thomas Jefferson	Philip Livingston	Oliver Wolcott
	Francis Lewis	Matthew Thornton

The Constitution of the United States

Preamble

We the People of the United States, in Order to form a more perfect Union, establish Justice, insure domestic Tranquility, provide for the common defense, promote the general Welfare, and secure the Blessings of Liberty to ourselves and our Posterity, do ordain and establish this Constitution for the United States of America.

Article I — The Legislature

Section 1. — Congress

All legislative Powers herein granted shall be vested in a Congress of the United States, which shall consist of a Senate and House of Representatives.

Section 2. — The House of Representatives

1. Elections The House of Representatives shall be composed of Members chosen every second Year by the People of the several States, and the Electors in each State shall have the Qualifications requisite for Electors of the most numerous Branch of the State Legislature.

2. Qualifications No Person shall be a Representative who shall not have attained to the Age of twenty five Years, and been seven Years a Citizen of the United States, and who shall not, when elected, be an Inhabitant of that State in which he shall be chosen.

3. Number of Representatives Representatives and direct Taxes shall be apportioned among the several States which may be included within this Union, according to their respective Numbers, which shall be determined by adding to the whole Number of free Persons, including **those bound to Service**[1] for a Term of Years, and excluding Indians not taxed, three fifths of **all other Persons**.[2] The actual **Enumeration**[3] shall be made within three Years after the first Meeting of the Congress of the United States, and within every subsequent Term of ten Years, in such Manner as they shall by Law direct. The Number of Representatives shall not exceed one for every

Note: The parts of the Constitution that have been lined through are no longer in force or no longer apply because of later amendments. The titles of the sections and articles are added for easier reference.

Legislative Branch

Article I explains how the legislative branch, called Congress, is organized. The chief purpose of the legislative branch is to make laws. Congress is made up of the Senate and the House of Representatives.

The House of Representatives

The number of members each state has in the House is based on the population of the individual state. In 1929 Congress permanently fixed the size of the House at 435 members.

Vocabulary

[1] **those bound to Service** indentured servants

[2] **all other Persons** slaves

[3] **Enumeration** census or official population count

thirty Thousand, but each State shall have at Least one Representative; and until such enumeration shall be made, the State of New Hampshire shall be entitled to choose three, Massachoosetts eight, Rhode-Island and Providence Plantations one, Connecticut five, New-York six, New Jersey four, Pennsylvania eight, Delaware one, Maryland six, Virginia ten, North Carolina five, South Carolina five, and Georgia three.

4. Vacancies When vacancies happen in the Representation from any State, the Executive Authority thereof shall issue Writs of Election to fill such Vacancies.

5. Officers and Impeachment The House of Representatives shall choose their Speaker and other Officers; and shall have the sole Power of impeachment.

Section 3. The Senate

1. Number of Senators The Senate of the United States shall be composed of two Senators from each State, chosen by the Legislature thereof, for six Years; and each Senator shall have one Vote.

2. Classifying Terms Immediately after they shall be assembled in Consequence of the first Election, they shall be divided as equally as may be into three Classes. The Seats of the Senators of the first Class shall be vacated at the Expiration of the second Year, of the second Class at the Expiration of the fourth Year, and of the third Class at the Expiration of the sixth Year, so that one third may be chosen every second Year; and if Vacancies happen by Resignation, or otherwise, during the Recess of the Legislature of any State, the Executive thereof may make temporary Appointments until the next Meeting of the Legislature, which shall then fill such Vacancies.

3. Qualifications No Person shall be a Senator who shall not have attained to the Age of thirty Years, and been nine Years a Citizen of the United States, and who shall not, when elected, be an Inhabitant of that State for which he shall be chosen.

4. Role of Vice-President The Vice President of the United States shall be President of the Senate, but shall have no Vote, unless they be equally divided.

5. Officers The Senate shall choose their other Officers, and also a President **pro tempore**,[4] in the Absence of the Vice President, or when he shall exercise the Office of President of the United States.

6. Impeachment Trials The Senate shall have the sole Power to try all **Impeachments**.[5] When sitting for that Purpose, they shall be on Oath or Affirmation. When the President of the United States is tried, the Chief Justice shall preside: And no Person shall be convicted without the Concurrence of two thirds of the Members present.

7. Punishment for Impeachment Judgment in Cases of Impeachment shall not extend further than to removal from Office, and disqualification to hold

The Vice President

The only duty that the Constitution assigns to the vice president is to preside over meetings of the Senate. Modern presidents have usually given their vice presidents more responsibilities.

Vocabulary

[4] **pro tempore** temporarily

[5] **Impeachments** official accusations of federal wrongdoing

and enjoy any Office of honor, Trust or Profit under the United States: but the Party convicted shall nevertheless be liable and subject to Indictment, Trial, Judgment and Punishment, according to Law.

Section 4. Congressional Elections

1. Regulations The Times, Places and Manner of holding Elections for Senators and Representatives, shall be prescribed in each State by the Legislature thereof; but the Congress may at any time by Law make or alter such Regulations, except as to the Places of choosing Senators.

2. Sessions ~~The Congress shall assemble at least once in every Year, and such Meeting shall be on the first Monday in December, unless they shall by Law appoint a different Day.~~

Section 5. Rules/Procedures

1. Quorum Each House shall be the Judge of the Elections, Returns and Qualifications of its own Members, and a Majority of each shall constitute a **Quorum**[6] to do Business; but a smaller Number may **adjourn**[7] from day to day, and may be authorized to compel the Attendance of absent Members, in such Manner, and under such Penalties as each House may provide.

2. Rules and Conduct Each House may determine the Rules of its Proceedings, punish its Members for disorderly Behaviour, and, with the Concurrence of two thirds, expel a Member.

3. Records Each House shall keep a Journal of its Proceedings, and from time to time publish the same, excepting such Parts as may in their Judgment require Secrecy; and the Yeas and Nays of the Members of either House on any question shall, at the Desire of one fifth of those Present, be entered on the Journal.

4. Adjournment Neither House, during the Session of Congress, shall, without the Consent of the other, adjourn for more than three days, nor to any other Place than that in which the two Houses shall be sitting.

Section 6. Payment

1. Salary The Senators and Representatives shall receive a Compensation for their Services, to be ascertained by Law, and paid out of the Treasury of the United States. They shall in all Cases, except Treason, Felony and Breach of the Peace, be privileged from Arrest during their Attendance at the Session of their respective Houses, and in going to and returning from the same; and for any Speech or Debate in either House, they shall not be questioned in any other Place.

2. Restrictions No Senator or Representative shall, during the Time for which he was elected, be appointed to any civil Office under the Authority of the United States, which shall have been created, or the **Emoluments**[8]

Vocabulary

[6] **Quorum** the minimum number of people needed to conduct business

[7] **adjourn** to stop indefinitely

[8] **Emoluments** salary

whereof shall have been increased during such time; and no Person holding any Office under the United States, shall be a Member of either House during his **Continuance**[9] in Office.

Section 7. How a Bill Becomes a Law

1. Tax Bills All **Bills**[10] for raising Revenue shall originate in the House of Representatives; but the Senate may propose or concur with Amendments as on other Bills.

2. Lawmaking Every Bill which shall have passed the House of Representatives and the Senate, shall, before it become a Law, be presented to the President of the United States: If he approve he shall sign it, but if not he shall return it, with his Objections to that House in which it shall have originated, who shall enter the Objections at large on their Journal, and proceed to reconsider it. If after such Reconsideration two thirds of that House shall agree to pass the Bill, it shall be sent, together with the Objections, to the other House, by which it shall likewise be reconsidered, and if approved by two thirds of that House, it shall become a Law. But in all such Cases the Votes of both Houses shall be determined by yeas and Nays, and the Names of the Persons voting for and against the Bill shall be entered on the Journal of each House respectively. If any Bill shall not be returned by the President within ten Days (Sundays excepted) after it shall have been presented to him, the Same shall be a Law, in like Manner as if he had signed it, unless the Congress by their Adjournment prevent its Return, in which Case it shall not be a Law.

3. Role of the President Every Order, Resolution, or Vote to which the Concurrence of the Senate and House of Representatives may be necessary (except on a question of Adjournment) shall be presented to the President of the United States; and before the Same shall take Effect, shall be approved by him, or being disapproved by him, shall be repassed by two thirds of the Senate and House of Representatives, according to the Rules and Limitations prescribed in the Case of a Bill.

Section 8. Powers Granted to Congress

1. Taxation The Congress shall have Power To lay and collect Taxes, **Duties**,[11] **Imposts**[12] and **Excises**,[13] to pay the Debts and provide for the common Defense and general Welfare of the United States; but all Duties, Imposts and Excises shall be uniform throughout the United States;

2. Credit To borrow Money on the credit of the United States;

3. Commerce To regulate Commerce with foreign Nations, and among the several States, and with the Indian Tribes;

4. Naturalization and Bankruptcy To establish an uniform **Rule of Naturalization**,[14] and uniform Laws on the subject of Bankruptcies throughout the United States;

Vocabulary

[9] **Continuance** term

[10] **Bills** proposed laws

[11] **Duties** tariffs

[12] **Imposts** taxes

[13] **Excises** internal taxes on the manufacture, sale, or consumption of a commodity

[14] **Rule of Naturalization** a law by which a foreign-born person becomes a citizen

THE CONSTITUTION

Vocabulary

[15] **Securities** bonds

[16] **Letters of Marque and Reprisal** documents issued by governments allowing merchant ships to arm themselves and attack ships of an enemy nation

5. Money To coin Money, regulate the Value thereof, and of foreign Coin, and fix the Standard of Weights and Measures;

6. Counterfeiting To provide for the Punishment of counterfeiting the **Securities**[15] and current Coin of the United States;

7. Post Office To establish Post Offices and post Roads;

8. Patents and Copyrights To promote the Progress of Science and useful Arts, by securing for limited Times to Authors and Inventors the exclusive Right to their respective Writings and Discoveries;

9. Courts To constitute Tribunals inferior to the supreme Court;

10. International Law To define and punish Piracies and Felonies committed on the high Seas, and Offences against the Law of Nations;

11. War To declare War, grant **Letters of Marque and Reprisal**,[16] and make Rules concerning Captures on Land and Water;

12. Army To raise and support Armies, but no Appropriation of Money to that Use shall be for a longer Term than two Years;

13. Navy To provide and maintain a Navy;

14. Regulation of the Military To make Rules for the Government and Regulation of the land and naval Forces;

15. Militia To provide for calling forth the Militia to execute the Laws of the Union, suppress Insurrections and repel Invasions;

16. Regulation of the Militia To provide for organizing, arming, and disciplining, the Militia, and for governing such Part of them as may be employed in the Service of the United States, reserving to the States respectively, the Appointment of the Officers, and the Authority of training the Militia according to the discipline prescribed by Congress;

17. District of Columbia To exercise exclusive Legislation in all Cases whatsoever, over such District (not exceeding ten Miles square) as may, by Cession of particular States, and the Acceptance of Congress, become the Seat of the Government of the United States, and to exercise like Authority over all Places purchased by the Consent of the Legislature of the State in which the Same shall be, for the Erection of Forts, Magazines, Arsenals, dock-Yards, and other needful Buildings;—And

18. Necessary and Proper Clause To make all Laws which shall be necessary and proper for carrying into Execution the foregoing Powers, and all other Powers vested by this Constitution in the Government of the United States, or in any Department or Officer thereof.

Section 9. Powers Denied Congress

1. Slave Trade ~~The Migration or Importation of such Persons as any of the States now existing shall think proper to admit, shall not be prohibited~~

The Elastic Clause

The framers of the Constitution wanted a national government that was strong enough to be effective. This section lists the powers given to Congress. The last portion of Section 8 contains the so-called elastic clause.

~~by the Congress prior to the Year one thousand eight hundred and eight, but a Tax or duty may be imposed on such Importation, not exceeding ten dollars for each Person.~~

2. Habeas Corpus The Privilege of the **Writ of Habeas Corpus**[17] shall not be suspended, unless when in Cases of Rebellion or Invasion the public Safety may require it.

3. Illegal Punishment No **Bill of Attainder**[18] or **ex post facto Law**[19] shall be passed.

4. Direct Taxes No **Capitation**,[20] or other direct, Tax shall be laid, unless in Proportion to the Census or enumeration herein before directed to be taken.

5. Export Taxes No Tax or Duty shall be laid on Articles exported from any State.

6. No Favorites No Preference shall be given by any Regulation of Commerce or Revenue to the Ports of one State over those of another; nor shall Vessels bound to, or from, one State, be obliged to enter, clear, or pay Duties in another.

7. Public Money No Money shall be drawn from the Treasury, but in Consequence of Appropriations made by Law; and a regular Statement and Account of the Receipts and Expenditures of all public Money shall be published from time to time.

8. Titles of Nobility No Title of Nobility shall be granted by the United States: And no Person holding any Office of Profit or Trust under them, shall, without the Consent of the Congress, accept of any present, Emolument, Office, or Title, of any kind whatever, from any King, Prince, or foreign State.

Section 10. Powers Denied the States

1. Restrictions No State shall enter into any Treaty, Alliance, or Confederation; grant Letters of Marque and Reprisal; coin Money; emit Bills of Credit; make any Thing but gold and silver Coin a Tender in Payment of Debts; pass any Bill of Attainder, ex post facto Law, or Law impairing the Obligation of Contracts, or grant any Title of Nobility.

2. Import and Export Taxes No State shall, without the Consent of the Congress, lay any Imposts or Duties on Imports or Exports, except what may be absolutely necessary for executing it's inspection Laws: and the net Produce of all Duties and Imposts, laid by any State on Imports or Exports, shall be for the Use of the Treasury of the United States; and all such Laws shall be subject to the Revision and Control of the Congress.

3. Peacetime and War Restraints No State shall, without the Consent of Congress, lay any Duty of Tonnage, keep Troops, or Ships of War in time of Peace, enter into any Agreement or Compact with another State, or with a foreign Power, or engage in War, unless actually invaded, or in such imminent Danger as will not admit of delay.

[17] **Writ of Habeas Corpus** a court order that requires the government to bring a prisoner to court and explain why he or she is being held

[18] **Bill of Attainder** a law declaring that a person is guilty of a particular crime

[19] **ex post facto Law** a law that is made effective prior to the date that it was passed and therefore punishes people for acts that were not illegal at the time

[20] **Capitation** a direct uniform tax imposed on each head, or person

THE CONSTITUTION

Article II The Executive

Section 1. The Presidency

1. Terms of Office The executive Power shall be vested in a President of the United States of America. He shall hold his Office during the Term of four Years, and, together with the Vice President, chosen for the same Term, be elected, as follows:

2. Electoral College Each State shall appoint, in such Manner as the Legislature thereof may direct, a Number of Electors, equal to the whole Number of Senators and Representatives to which the State may be entitled in the Congress: but no Senator or Representative, or Person holding an Office of Trust or Profit under the United States, shall be appointed an Elector.

3. Former Method of Electing President The Electors shall meet in their respective States, and vote by Ballot for two Persons, of whom one at least shall not be an Inhabitant of the same State with themselves. And they shall make a List of all the Persons voted for, and of the Number of Votes for each; which List they shall sign and certify, and transmit sealed to the Seat of the Government of the United States, directed to the President of the Senate. The President of the Senate shall, in the Presence of the Senate and House of Representatives, open all the Certificates, and the Votes shall then be counted. The Person having the greatest Number of Votes shall be the President, if such Number be a Majority of the whole Number of Electors appointed; and if there be more than one who have such Majority, and have an equal Number of Votes, then the House of Representatives shall immediately choose by Ballot one of them for President; and if no Person have a Majority, then from the five highest on the List the said House shall in like Manner choose the President. But in choosing the President, the Votes shall be taken by States, the Representation from each State having one Vote; A quorum for this purpose shall consist of a Member or Members from two thirds of the States, and a Majority of all the States shall be necessary to a Choice. In every Case, after the Choice of the President, the Person having the greatest Number of Votes of the Electors shall be the Vice President. But if there should remain two or more who have equal Votes, the Senate shall choose from them by Ballot the Vice President.

4. Election Day The Congress may determine the Time of choosing the Electors, and the Day on which they shall give their Votes; which Day shall be the same throughout the United States.

5. Qualifications No Person except a natural born Citizen, or a Citizen of the United States, at the time of the Adoption of this Constitution, shall be eligible to the Office of President; neither shall any Person be eligible to

Executive Branch

The president is the chief of the executive branch. It is the job of the president to enforce the laws. The framers wanted the president's and vice president's terms of office and manner of selection to be different from those of members of Congress. They decided on four-year terms, but they had a difficult time agreeing on how to select the president and vice president. The framers finally set up an electoral system, which varies greatly from our electoral process today.

Presidential Elections

In 1845 Congress set the Tuesday following the first Monday in November of every fourth year as the general election date for selecting presidential electors.

THE CONSTITUTION

that Office who shall not have attained to the Age of thirty five Years, and been fourteen Years a Resident within the United States.

6. Succession In Case of the Removal of the President from Office, or of his Death, Resignation, or Inability to discharge the Powers and Duties of the said Office, the Same shall devolve on the Vice President, and the Congress may by Law provide for the Case of Removal, Death, Resignation or Inability, both of the President and Vice President, declaring what Officer shall then act as President, and such Officer shall act accordingly, until the Disability be removed, or a President shall be elected.

7. Salary The President shall, at stated Times, receive for his Services, a Compensation, which shall neither be increased nor diminished during the Period for which he shall have been elected, and he shall not receive within that Period any other Emolument from the United States, or any of them.

8. Oath of Office Before he enter on the Execution of his Office, he shall take the following Oath or Affirmation:—"I do solemnly swear (or affirm) that I will faithfully execute the Office of President of the United States, and will to the best of my Ability, preserve, protect and defend the Constitution of the United States."

Section 2. Powers of Presidency

1. Military Powers The President shall be Commander in Chief of the Army and Navy of the United States, and of the Militia of the several States, when called into the actual Service of the United States; he may require the Opinion, in writing, of the principal Officer in each of the executive Departments, upon any Subject relating to the Duties of their respective Offices, and he shall have Power to grant **Reprieves**[21] and **Pardons**[22] for Offences against the United States, except in Cases of Impeachment.

2. Treaties and Appointments He shall have Power, by and with the Advice and Consent of the Senate, to make Treaties, provided two thirds of the Senators present concur; and he shall nominate, and by and with the Advice and Consent of the Senate, shall appoint Ambassadors, other public Ministers and Consuls, Judges of the supreme Court, and all other Officers of the United States, whose Appointments are not herein otherwise provided for, and which shall be established by Law: but the Congress may by Law vest the Appointment of such inferior Officers, as they think proper, in the President alone, in the Courts of Law, or in the Heads of Departments.

3. Vacancies The President shall have Power to fill up all Vacancies that may happen during the Recess of the Senate, by granting Commissions which shall expire at the End of their next Session.

Presidential Salary

In 1999 Congress voted to set future presidents' salaries at $400,000 per year. The president also receives an annual expense account. The president must pay taxes only on the salary.

Commander in Chief

Today the president is in charge of the army, navy, air force, marines, and coast guard. Only Congress, however, can decide if the United States will declare war.

Appointments

Most of the president's appointments to office must be approved by the Senate.

Vocabulary

[21] **Reprieves** delays of punishment

[22] **Pardons** releases from the legal penalties associated with a crime

The State of the Union

Every year the president presents to Congress a State of the Union message. In this message, the president introduces and explains a legislative plan for the coming year.

Judicial Branch

The Articles of Confederation did not set up a federal court system. One of the first points that the framers of the Constitution agreed upon was to set up a national judiciary. In the Judiciary Act of 1789, Congress provided for the establishment of lower courts, such as district courts, circuit courts of appeals, and various other federal courts. The judicial system provides a check on the legislative branch: It can declare a law unconstitutional.

Section 3. Presidential Duties

He shall from time to time give to the Congress Information of the State of the Union, and recommend to their Consideration such Measures as he shall judge necessary and expedient; he may, on extraordinary Occasions, convene both Houses, or either of them, and in Case of Disagreement between them, with Respect to the Time of Adjournment, he may adjourn them to such Time as he shall think proper; he shall receive Ambassadors and other public Ministers; he shall take Care that the Laws be faithfully executed, and shall Commission all the Officers of the United States.

Section 4. Impeachment

The President, Vice President and all civil Officers of the United States, shall be removed from Office on Impeachment for, and Conviction of, Treason, Bribery, or other high Crimes and Misdemeanors.

Article III The Judiciary

Section 1. Federal Courts and Judges

The judicial Power of the United States shall be vested in one supreme Court, and in such inferior Courts as the Congress may from time to time ordain and establish. The Judges, both of the supreme and inferior Courts, shall hold their Offices during good Behavior, and shall, at stated Times, receive for their Services a Compensation, which shall not be diminished during their Continuance in Office.

Section 2. Authority of the Courts

1. General Authority The judicial Power shall extend to all Cases, in Law and Equity, arising under this Constitution, the Laws of the United States, and Treaties made, or which shall be made, under their Authority;—to all Cases affecting Ambassadors, other public Ministers and Consuls;—to all Cases of admiralty and maritime Jurisdiction;—to Controversies to which the United States shall be a Party;—to Controversies between two or more States —between a State and Citizens of another State; —between Citizens of different States;—between Citizens of the same State claiming Lands under Grants of different States, and between a State, or the Citizens thereof, and foreign States, Citizens or Subjects.

2. Supreme Authority In all Cases affecting Ambassadors, other public Ministers and Consuls, and those in which a State shall be Party, the supreme Court shall have original Jurisdiction. In all the other Cases before mentioned, the supreme Court shall have appellate Jurisdiction, both as to Law and Fact, with such Exceptions, and under such Regulations as the Congress shall make.

3. Trial by Jury The Trial of all Crimes, except in Cases of Impeachment, shall be by Jury; and such Trial shall be held in the State where the said Crimes shall have been committed; but when not committed within any State, the Trial shall be at such Place or Places as the Congress may by Law have directed.

Section 3. Treason

1. Definition Treason against the United States, shall consist only in levying War against them, or in adhering to their Enemies, giving them Aid and Comfort. No Person shall be convicted of Treason unless on the Testimony of two Witnesses to the same overt Act, or on Confession in open Court.

2. Punishment The Congress shall have Power to declare the Punishment of Treason, but no Attainder of Treason shall work **Corruption of Blood**,[23] or Forfeiture except during the Life of the Person attainted.

Vocabulary

[23] **Corruption of Blood** punishing the family of a person convicted of treason

Article IV Relations among States

Section 1. State Acts and Records

Full Faith and Credit shall be given in each State to the public Acts, Records, and judicial Proceedings of every other State. And the Congress may by general Laws prescribe the Manner in which such Acts, Records and Proceedings shall be proved, and the Effect thereof.

Section 2. Rights of Citizens

1. Citizenship The Citizens of each State shall be entitled to all Privileges and Immunities of Citizens in the several States.

2. Extradition A Person charged in any State with Treason, Felony, or other Crime, who shall flee from Justice, and be found in another State, shall on Demand of the executive Authority of the State from which he fled, be delivered up, to be removed to the State having Jurisdiction of the Crime.

3. Fugitive Slaves No Person held to Service or Labour in one State, under the Laws thereof, escaping into another, shall, in Consequence of any Law or Regulation therein, be discharged from such Service or Labour, but shall be delivered up on Claim of the Party to whom such Service or Labour may be due.

Section 3. New States

1. Admission New States may be admitted by the Congress into this Union; but no new State shall be formed or erected within the Jurisdiction of any other State; nor any State be formed by the Junction of two or more States, or Parts of States, without the Consent of the Legislatures of the States concerned as well as of the Congress.

The States

States must honor the laws, records, and court decisions of other states. A person cannot escape a legal obligation by moving from one state to another.

2. Congressional Authority The Congress shall have Power to dispose of and make all needful Rules and Regulations respecting the Territory or other Property belonging to the United States; and nothing in this Constitution shall be so construed as to Prejudice any Claims of the United States, or of any particular State.

Section 4. Guarantees to the States

The United States shall guarantee to every State in this Union a Republican Form of Government, and shall protect each of them against Invasion; and on Application of the Legislature, or of the Executive (when the Legislature cannot be convened), against domestic Violence.

Article V Amending the Constitution

The Congress, whenever two thirds of both Houses shall deem it necessary, shall propose Amendments to this Constitution, or, on the Application of the Legislatures of two thirds of the several States, shall call a Convention for proposing Amendments, which, in either Case, shall be valid to all Intents and Purposes, as Part of this Constitution, when ratified by the Legislatures of three fourths of the several States, or by Conventions in three fourths thereof, as the one or the other Mode of Ratification may be proposed by the Congress; Provided that ~~no Amendment which may be made prior to the Year One thousand eight hundred and eight shall in any Manner affect the first and fourth Clauses in the Ninth Section of the first Article; and~~ ~~that no State, without its Consent, shall be deprived of its equal Suffrage in the Senate.~~

Article VI Supremacy of National Government

All Debts contracted and Engagements entered into, before the Adoption of this Constitution, shall be as valid against the United States under this Constitution, as under the Confederation.

This Constitution, and the Laws of the United States which shall be made in Pursuance thereof; and all Treaties made, or which shall be made, under the Authority of the United States, shall be the supreme Law of the Land; and the Judges in every State shall be bound thereby, any Thing in the Constitution or Laws of any State to the Contrary notwithstanding.

The Senators and Representatives before mentioned, and the Members of the several State Legislatures, and all executive and judicial Officers, both of the United States and of the several States, shall be bound by Oath or Affirmation, to support this Constitution; but no religious Test shall ever be required as a Qualification to any Office or public Trust under the United States.

National Supremacy

One of the biggest problems facing the delegates to the Constitutional Convention was the question of what would happen if a state law and a federal law conflicted. Which law would be followed? Who would decide? The second clause of Article VI answers those questions. When a federal law and a state law disagree, the federal law overrides the state law. The Constitution and other federal laws are the "supreme Law of the Land." This clause is often called the supremacy clause.

Article VII Ratification

The Ratification of the Conventions of nine States, shall be sufficient for the Establishment of this Constitution between the States so ratifying the Same.

Done in Convention by the Unanimous Consent of the States present the Seventeenth Day of September in the Year of our Lord one thousand seven hundred and Eighty seven and of the Independence of the United States of America the Twelfth In witness whereof We have hereunto subscribed our Names,

George Washington—
President and deputy from Virginia

Delaware

George Read
Gunning Bedford Jr.
John Dickinson
Richard Bassett
Jacob Broom

Maryland

James McHenry
Daniel of
  St. Thomas Jenifer
Daniel Carroll

Virginia

John Blair
James Madison Jr.

North Carolina

William Blount
Richard Dobbs Spaight
Hugh Williamson

South Carolina

John Rutledge
Charles Cotesworth
  Pinckney
Charles Pinckney
Pierce Butler

Georgia

William Few
Abraham Baldwin

New Hampshire

John Langdon
Nicholas Gilman

Massachusetts

Nathaniel Gorham
Rufus King

Connecticut

William Samuel Johnson
Roger Sherman

New York

Alexander Hamilton

New Jersey

William Livingston
David Brearley
William Paterson
Jonathan Dayton

Pennsylvania

Benjamin Franklin
Thomas Mifflin
Robert Morris
George Clymer
Thomas FitzSimons
Jared Ingersoll
James Wilson
Gouverneur Morris

Attest:
William Jackson,
Secretary

Ratification

The Articles of Confederation called for all 13 states to approve any revision to the Articles. The Constitution required that 9 out of the 13 states would be needed to ratify the Constitution. The first state to ratify was Delaware, on December 7, 1787. Almost two-and-a-half years later, on May 29, 1790, Rhode Island became the last state to ratify the Constitution.

Bill of Rights

One of the conditions set by several states for ratifying the Constitution was the inclusion of a bill of rights. Many people feared that a stronger central government might take away basic rights of the people that had been guaranteed in state constitutions.

Vocabulary

[24] **quartered** housed

[25] **Warrants** written orders authorizing a person to make an arrest, a seizure, or a search

[26] **infamous** disgraceful

[27] **indictment** the act of charging with a crime

[28] **ascertained** found out

Rights of the Accused

The Fifth, Sixth, and Seventh Amendments describe the procedures that courts must follow when trying people accused of crimes.

Trials

The Sixth Amendment makes several guarantees, including a prompt trial and a trial by a jury chosen from the state and district in which the crime was committed.

Constitutional Amendments

Note: The first 10 amendments to the Constitution were ratified on December 15, 1791, and form what is known as the Bill of Rights.

Amendments 1–10. The Bill of Rights

Amendment I

Congress shall make no law respecting an establishment of religion, or prohibiting the free exercise thereof; or abridging the freedom of speech, or of the press; or the right of the people peaceably to assemble, and to petition the Government for a redress of grievances.

Amendment II

A well regulated Militia, being necessary to the security of a free State, the right of the people to keep and bear Arms, shall not be infringed.

Amendment III

No Soldier shall, in time of peace be **quartered**[24] in any house, without the consent of the Owner, nor in time of war, but in a manner to be prescribed by law.

Amendment IV

The right of the people to be secure in their persons, houses, papers, and effects, against unreasonable searches and seizures, shall not be violated, and no **Warrants**[25] shall issue, but upon probable cause, supported by Oath or affirmation, and particularly describing the place to be searched, and the persons or things to be seized.

Amendment V

No person shall be held to answer for a capital, or otherwise **infamous**[26] crime, unless on a presentment or **indictment**[27] of a Grand Jury, except in cases arising in the land or naval forces, or in the Militia, when in actual service in time of War or public danger; nor shall any person be subject for the same offence to be twice put in jeopardy of life or limb; nor shall be compelled in any criminal case to be a witness against himself, nor be deprived of life, liberty, or property, without due process of law; nor shall private property be taken for public use, without just compensation.

Amendment VI

In all criminal prosecutions, the accused shall enjoy the right to a speedy and public trial, by an impartial jury of the State and district wherein the crime shall have been committed, which district shall have been previously **ascertained**[28] by law, and to be informed of the nature and cause of the accusation; to be confronted with the witnesses against him; to have compulsory process for obtaining witnesses in his favor, and to have the Assistance of Counsel for his defence.

Amendment VII

In suits at common law, where the value in controversy shall exceed twenty dollars, the right of trial by jury shall be preserved, and no fact tried by a jury, shall be otherwise reexamined in any Court of the United States, than according to the rules of the common law.

Amendment VIII

Excessive bail shall not be required, nor excessive fines imposed, nor cruel and unusual punishments inflicted.

Amendment IX

The enumeration in the Constitution, of certain rights, shall not be construed to deny or disparage others retained by the people.

Amendment X

The powers not delegated to the United States by the Constitution, nor prohibited by it to the States, are reserved to the States respectively, or to the people.

Amendments 11–27

Amendment XI

Passed by Congress March 4, 1794. Ratified February 7, 1795.

The Judicial power of the United States shall not be **construed**[29] to extend to any suit in law or equity, commenced or prosecuted against one of the United States by Citizens of another State, or by Citizens or Subjects of any Foreign State.

Amendment XII

Passed by Congress December 9, 1803. Ratified June 15, 1804.

The Electors shall meet in their respective states and vote by ballot for President and Vice-President, one of whom, at least, shall not be an inhabitant of the same state with themselves; they shall name in their ballots the person voted for as President, and in distinct ballots the person voted for as Vice-President, and they shall make distinct lists of all persons voted for as President, and of all persons voted for as Vice-President, and of the number of votes for each, which lists they shall sign and certify, and transmit sealed to the seat of the government of the United States, directed to the President of the Senate;—the President of the Senate shall, in the presence of the Senate and House of Representatives, open all the certificates and the votes shall then be counted;—The person having the greatest number of votes for President, shall be the President, if such number be a majority of the whole number of Electors appointed; and if no person have such majority, then from the persons having the highest numbers not exceeding three on the list of those voted for as President, the House of Representatives shall choose immediately, by ballot, the President. But in choosing the

Vocabulary

[29] **construed** explained or interpreted

President and Vice President

The Twelfth Amendment changed the election procedure for president and vice president.

President, the votes shall be taken by states, the representation from each state having one vote; a quorum for this purpose shall consist of a member or members from two-thirds of the states, and a majority of all the states shall be necessary to a choice. ~~And if the House of Representatives shall not choose a President whenever the right of choice shall devolve upon them, before the fourth day of March next following, then the Vice-President shall act as President, as in case of the death or other constitutional disability of the President.~~—The person having the greatest number of votes as Vice-President, shall be the Vice-President, if such number be a majority of the whole number of Electors appointed, and if no person have a majority, then from the two highest numbers on the list, the Senate shall choose the Vice-President; a quorum for the purpose shall consist of two-thirds of the whole number of Senators, and a majority of the whole number shall be necessary to a choice. But no person constitutionally ineligible to the office of President shall be eligible to that of Vice-President of the United States.

Amendment XIII

Passed by Congress January 31, 1865. Ratified December 6, 1865.

1. Slavery Banned Neither slavery nor **involuntary servitude,**[30] except as a punishment for crime whereof the party shall have been duly convicted, shall exist within the United States, or any place subject to their jurisdiction.

2. Enforcement Congress shall have power to enforce this article by appropriate legislation.

Amendment XIV

Passed by Congress June 13, 1866. Ratified July 9, 1868.

1. Citizenship Defined All persons born or naturalized in the United States, and subject to the jurisdiction thereof, are citizens of the United States and of the State wherein they reside. No State shall make or enforce any law which shall abridge the privileges or immunities of citizens of the United States; nor shall any State deprive any person of life, liberty, or property, without due process of law; nor deny to any person within its jurisdiction the equal protection of the laws.

2. Voting Rights Representatives shall be apportioned among the several States according to their respective numbers, counting the whole number of persons in each State, ~~excluding Indians not taxed~~. But when the right to vote at any election for the choice of electors for President and Vice-President of the United States, Representatives in Congress, the Executive and Judicial officers of a State, or the members of the Legislature thereof, is denied to any of the ~~male~~ inhabitants of such State, ~~being twenty-one years of age~~, and citizens of the United States, or in any way abridged, except for participation in rebellion, or other crime, the basis of representation therein shall be reduced in the proportion which the number of such ~~male~~ citizens shall bear to the whole number of ~~male~~ citizens ~~twenty-one years of age~~ in such State.

Vocabulary

[30] **involuntary servitude** being forced to work against one's will

Abolishing Slavery

Although some slaves had been freed during the Civil War, slavery was not abolished until the Thirteenth Amendment took effect.

Protecting the Rights of Citizens

In 1833 the Supreme Court ruled that the Bill of Rights limited the federal government but not the state governments. This ruling was interpreted to mean that states were able to keep African Americans from becoming state citizens and keep the Bill of Rights from protecting them. The Fourteenth Amendment defines citizenship and prevents states from interfering in the rights of citizens of the United States.

3. Rebels Banned from Government No person shall be a Senator or Representative in Congress, or elector of President and Vice-President, or hold any office, civil or military, under the United States, or under any State, who, having previously taken an oath, as a member of Congress, or as an officer of the United States, or as a member of any State legislature, or as an executive or judicial officer of any State, to support the Constitution of the United States, shall have engaged in insurrection or rebellion against the same, or given aid or comfort to the enemies thereof. But Congress may by a vote of two-thirds of each House, remove such disability.

4. Payment of Debts The validity of the public debt of the United States, authorized by law, including debts incurred for payment of pensions and bounties for services in suppressing insurrection or rebellion, shall not be questioned. But neither the United States nor any State shall assume or pay any debt or obligation incurred in aid of insurrection or rebellion against the United States, or any claim for the loss or emancipation of any slave; but all such debts, obligations and claims shall be held illegal and void.

5. Enforcement The Congress shall have the power to enforce, by appropriate legislation, the provisions of this article.

Amendment XV

Passed by Congress February 26, 1869. Ratified February 3, 1870.

1. Voting Rights The right of citizens of the United States to vote shall not be denied or abridged by the United States or by any State on account of race, color, or previous condition of servitude.

2. Enforcement The Congress shall have the power to enforce this article by appropriate legislation.

Amendment XVI

Passed by Congress July 2, 1909. Ratified February 3, 1913.

The Congress shall have power to lay and collect taxes on incomes, from whatever source derived, without apportionment among the several States, and without regard to any census or enumeration.

Amendment XVII

Passed by Congress May 13, 1912. Ratified April 8, 1913.

1. Senators Elected by Citizens The Senate of the United States shall be composed of two Senators from each State, elected by the people thereof, for six years; and each Senator shall have one vote. The electors in each State shall have the qualifications requisite for electors of the most numerous branch of the State legislatures.

2. Vacancies When vacancies happen in the representation of any State in the Senate, the executive authority of such State shall issue writs of election to fill such vacancies: *Provided,* That the legislature of any State may empower the executive thereof to make temporary appointments until the people fill the vacancies by election as the legislature may direct.

3. Future Elections ~~This amendment shall not be so construed as to affect the election or term of any Senator chosen before it becomes valid as part of the Constitution.~~

Amendment XVIII

Passed by Congress December 18, 1917. Ratified January 16, 1919. Repealed by Amendment XXI.

1. Liquor Banned ~~After one year from the ratification of this article the manufacture, sale, or transportation of intoxicating liquors within, the importation thereof into, or the exportation thereof from the United States and all territory subject to the jurisdiction thereof for beverage purposes is hereby prohibited.~~

2. Enforcement ~~The Congress and the several States shall have concurrent power to enforce this article by appropriate legislation.~~

3. Ratification ~~This article shall be inoperative unless it shall have been ratified as an amendment to the Constitution by the legislatures of the several States, as provided in the Constitution, within seven years from the date of the submission hereof to the States by the Congress.~~

Amendment XIX

Passed by Congress June 4, 1919. Ratified August 18, 1920.

1. Voting Rights The right of citizens of the United States to vote shall not be denied or abridged by the United States or by any State on account of sex.

2. Enforcement Congress shall have power to enforce this article by appropriate legislation.

Amendment XX

Passed by Congress March 2, 1932. Ratified January 23, 1933.

1. Presidential Terms The terms of the President and the Vice President shall end at noon on the 20th day of January, and the terms of Senators and Representatives at noon on the 3d day of January, of the years in which such terms would have ended if this article had not been ratified; and the terms of their successors shall then begin.

2. Meeting of Congress The Congress shall assemble at least once in every year, and such meeting shall begin at noon on the 3d day of January, unless they shall by law appoint a different day.

3. Succession of Vice President If, at the time fixed for the beginning of the term of the President, the President elect shall have died, the Vice President elect shall become President. If a President shall not have been chosen before the time fixed for the beginning of his term, or if the President elect

Prohibition

Although many people believed that the Eighteenth Amendment was good for the health and welfare of the American people, it was repealed 14 years later.

Women's Suffrage

Abigail Adams and others were disappointed that the Declaration of Independence and the Constitution did not specifically include women. It took many years and much campaigning before suffrage for women was finally achieved.

Taking Office

In the original Constitution, a newly elected president and Congress did not take office until March 4, which was four months after the November election. The officials who were leaving office were called lame ducks because they had little influence during those four months. The Twentieth Amendment changed the date that the new president and Congress take office. Members of Congress now take office during the first week of January, and the president takes office on January 20.

shall have failed to qualify, then the Vice President elect shall act as President until a President shall have qualified; and the Congress may by law provide for the case wherein neither a President elect nor a Vice President shall have qualified, declaring who shall then act as President, or the manner in which one who is to act shall be selected, and such person shall act accordingly until a President or Vice President shall have qualified.

4. Succession by Vote of Congress The Congress may by law provide for the case of the death of any of the persons from whom the House of Representatives may choose a President whenever the right of choice shall have devolved upon them, and for the case of the death of any of the persons from whom the Senate may choose a Vice President whenever the right of choice shall have devolved upon them.

5. Ratification Sections 1 and 2 shall take effect on the 15th day of October following the ratification of this article.

6. Ratification This article shall be inoperative unless it shall have been ratified as an amendment to the Constitution by the legislatures of three-fourths of the several States within seven years from the date of its submission.

Amendment XXI

Passed by Congress February 20, 1933. Ratified December 5, 1933.

1. 18th Amendment Repealed The eighteenth article of amendment to the Constitution of the United States is hereby repealed.

2. Liquor Allowed by Law The transportation or importation into any State, Territory, or Possession of the United States for delivery or use therein of intoxicating liquors, in violation of the laws thereof, is hereby prohibited.

3. Ratification This article shall be inoperative unless it shall have been ratified as an amendment to the Constitution by conventions in the several States, as provided in the Constitution, within seven years from the date of the submission hereof to the States by the Congress.

Amendment XXII

Passed by Congress March 21, 1947. Ratified February 27, 1951.

1. Term Limits No person shall be elected to the office of the President more than twice, and no person who has held the office of President, or acted as President, for more than two years of a term to which some other person was elected President shall be elected to the office of President more than once. But this Article shall not apply to any person holding the office of President when this Article was proposed by Congress, and shall not prevent any person who may be holding the office of President, or acting as President, during the term within which this Article becomes operative from holding the office of President or acting as President during the remainder of such term.

2. Ratification ~~This article shall be inoperative unless it shall have been ratified as an amendment to the Constitution by the legislatures of three-fourths of the several States within seven years from the date of its submission to the States by the Congress.~~

Amendment XXIII

Passed by Congress June 16, 1960. Ratified March 29, 1961.

1. District of Columbia Represented The District constituting the seat of Government of the United States shall appoint in such manner as Congress may direct:

A number of electors of President and Vice President equal to the whole number of Senators and Representatives in Congress to which the District would be entitled if it were a State, but in no event more than the least populous State; they shall be in addition to those appointed by the States, but they shall be considered, for the purposes of the election of President and Vice President, to be electors appointed by a State; and they shall meet in the District and perform such duties as provided by the twelfth article of amendment.

2. Enforcement The Congress shall have power to enforce this article by appropriate legislation.

Amendment XXIV

Passed by Congress August 27, 1962. Ratified January 23, 1964.

1. Voting Rights The right of citizens of the United States to vote in any primary or other election for President or Vice President, for electors for President or Vice President, or for Senator or Representative in Congress, shall not be denied or abridged by the United States or any State by reason of failure to pay poll tax or other tax.

2. Enforcement The Congress shall have power to enforce this article by appropriate legislation.

Amendment XXV

Passed by Congress July 6, 1965. Ratified February 10, 1967.

1. Sucession of Vice President In case of the removal of the President from office or of his death or resignation, the Vice President shall become President.

2. Vacancy of Vice President Whenever there is a vacancy in the office of the Vice President, the President shall nominate a Vice President who shall take office upon confirmation by a majority vote of both Houses of Congress.

3. Written Declaration Whenever the President transmits to the President pro tempore of the Senate and the Speaker of the House of Representatives his written declaration that he is unable to discharge the powers and duties of his office, and until he transmits to them a written declara-

Voting Rights

Until the ratification of the Twenty-third Amendment, the people of Washington, D.C., could not vote in presidential elections.

Presidential Disability

The illness of President Eisenhower in the 1950s and the assassination of President Kennedy in 1963 were the events behind the Twenty-fifth Amendment. The Constitution did not provide a clear-cut method for a vice president to take over for a disabled president or upon the death of a president. This amendment provides for filling the office of the vice president if a vacancy occurs, and it provides a way for the vice president—or someone else in the line of succession—to take over if the president is unable to perform the duties of that office.

tion to the contrary, such powers and duties shall be discharged by the Vice President as Acting President.

4. Removing the President Whenever the Vice President and a majority of either the principal officers of the executive departments or of such other body as Congress may by law provide, transmit to the President pro tempore of the Senate and the Speaker of the House of Representatives their written declaration that the President is unable to discharge the powers and duties of his office, the Vice President shall immediately assume the powers and duties of the office as Acting President.

Thereafter, when the President transmits to the President pro tempore of the Senate and the Speaker of the House of Representatives his written declaration that no inability exists, he shall resume the powers and duties of his office unless the Vice President and a majority of either the principal officers of the executive department or of such other body as Congress may by law provide, transmit within four days to the President pro tempore of the Senate and the Speaker of the House of Representatives their written declaration that the President is unable to discharge the powers and duties of his office. Thereupon Congress shall decide the issue, assembling within forty-eight hours for that purpose if not in session. If the Congress, within twenty-one days after receipt of the latter written declaration, or, if Congress is not in session, within twenty-one days after Congress is required to assemble, determines by two-thirds vote of both Houses that the President is unable to discharge the powers and duties of his office, the Vice President shall continue to discharge the same as Acting President; otherwise, the President shall resume the powers and duties of his office.

Amendment XXVI

Passed by Congress March 23, 1971. Ratified July 1, 1971.

1. Voting Rights The right of citizens of the United States, who are eighteen years of age or older, to vote shall not be denied or abridged by the United States or by any State on account of age.

2. Enforcement The Congress shall have power to enforce this article by appropriate legislation.

Amendment XXVII

Originally proposed September 25, 1789. Ratified May 7, 1992.

No law, varying the compensation for the services of the Senators and Representatives, shall take effect, until an election of representatives shall have intervened.

Expanded Suffrage

The Voting Rights Act of 1970 tried to set the voting age at 18. However, the Supreme Court ruled that the act set the voting age for national elections only, not for state or local elections. The Twenty-sixth Amendment gave 18-year-old citizens the right to vote in all elections.

New York Constitution

The state of New York has had five different constitutions, the first of which was adopted in 1777. The current constitution was adopted in 1938. Like other state constitutions and the federal constitution, the document establishes the structure of the government and provides a framework for the passage and enforcement of specific laws. Below is an excerpt from the current New York state constitution.

The Constitution of New York

*[Preamble]

WE THE PEOPLE of the State of New York, grateful to Almighty God for our Freedom, in order to secure its blessings, DO ESTABLISH THIS CONSTITUTION.

ARTICLE I

BILL OF RIGHTS

[Rights, privileges and franchise secured; power of legislature to dispense with primary elections in certain cases]

Section 1. No member of this state shall be disfranchised, or deprived of any of the rights or privileges secured to any citizen thereof, unless by the law of the land, or the judgment of his or her peers, except that the legislature may provide that there shall be no primary election held to nominate candidates for public office or to elect persons to party positions for any political party or parties in any unit of representation of the state from which such candidates or persons are nominated or elected whenever there is no contest or contests for such nominations or election as may be prescribed by general law. (Amended by vote of the people November 3, 1959; November 7, 2001.)**

[Trial by jury; how waived]

§2. Trial by jury in all cases in which it has heretofore been guaranteed by constitutional provision shall remain inviolate forever; but a jury trial may be waived by the parties in all civil cases in the manner to be prescribed by law. The legislature may provide, however, by law, that a verdict may be rendered by not less than five-sixths of the jury in any civil case. A jury trial may be waived by the defendant in all criminal cases, except those in which the crime charged may be punishable by death, by a written instrument signed by the defendant in person in open court before and with the approval of a judge or justice of a court having jurisdiction to try the offense. The legislature may enact laws, not inconsistent herewith, governing the form, content, manner and time of presentation of the instrument effectuating such waiver. (Amended by Constitutional Convention of 1938 and approved by vote of the people November 8, 1938.)

[Freedom of worship; religious liberty]

§3. The free exercise and enjoyment of religious profession and worship, without discrimination or preference, shall forever be allowed in this state to all humankind;

(continued next page)

and no person shall be rendered incompetent to be a witness on account of his or her opinions on matters of religious belief; but the liberty of conscience hereby secured shall not be so construed as to excuse acts of licentiousness, or justify practices inconsistent with the peace or safety of this state. (Amended by vote of the people November 7, 2001.)

[Habeas corpus]

§4. The privilege of a writ or order of habeas corpus shall not be suspended, unless, in case of rebellion or invasion, the public safety requires it. (Amended by Constitutional Convention of 1938 and approved by vote of the people November 8, 1938.)

[Bail; fines; punishments; detention of witnesses]

§5. Excessive bail shall not be required nor excessive fines imposed, nor shall cruel and unusual punishments be inflicted, nor shall witnesses be unreasonably detained.

[Grand jury; protection of certain enumerated rights; duty of public officers to sign waiver of immunity and give testimony; penalty for refusal]

§6. No person shall be held to answer for a capital or otherwise infamous crime (except in cases of impeachment, and in cases of militia when in actual service, and the land, air and naval forces in time of war, or which this state may keep with the consent of congress in time of peace, and in cases of petit larceny under the regulation of the legislature), unless on indictment of a grand jury, except that a person held for the action of a grand jury upon a charge for such an offense, other than one punishable by death or life imprisonment, with the consent of the district attorney, may waive indictment by a grand jury and consent to be prosecuted on an information filed by the district attorney; such waiver shall be evidenced by written instrument signed by the defendant in open court in the presence of his or her counsel. In any trial in any court whatever the party accused shall be allowed to appear and defend in person and with counsel as in civil actions and shall be informed of the nature and cause of the accusation and be confronted with the witnesses against him or her. No person shall be subject to be twice put in jeopardy for the same offense; nor shall he or she be compelled in any criminal case to be a witness against himself or herself, providing, that any public officer who, upon being called before a grand jury to testify concerning the conduct of his or her present office or of any public office held by him or her within five years prior to such grand jury call to testify, or the performance of his or her official duties in any such present or prior offices, refuses to sign a waiver of immunity against subsequent criminal prosecution, or to answer any relevant question concerning such matters before such grand jury, shall by virtue of such refusal, be disqualified from holding any other public office or public employment for a period of five years from the date of such refusal to sign a waiver of immunity against subsequent prosecution, or to answer any relevant question concerning such matters before such grand jury, and shall be removed from his or her present office by the appropriate authority or shall forfeit his or her present office at the suit of the attorney-general. The power of grand juries to inquire into the wilful misconduct in office of public officers, and to find indictments or to direct the filing of informations in connection with such inquiries, shall never be suspended or impaired by law. No person shall be deprived of life, liberty or property without due process of law. (Amended by Constitutional Convention of 1938 and

(continued next page)

approved by vote of the people November 8, 1938; further amended by vote of the people November 8, 1949; November 3, 1959; November 6, 1973; November 7, 2001.)

[Compensation for taking private property; private roads; drainage of agricultural lands]

§7. (a) Private property shall not be taken for public use without just compensation. (c) Private roads may be opened in the manner to be prescribed by law; but in every case the necessity of the road and the amount of all damage to be sustained by the opening thereof shall be first determined by a jury of freeholders, and such amount, together with the expenses of the proceedings, shall be paid by the person to be benefitted. (d) The use of property for the drainage of swamp or agricultural lands is declared to be a public use, and general laws may be passed permitting the owners or occupants of swamp or agricultural lands to construct and maintain for the drainage thereof, necessary drains, ditches and dykes upon the lands of others, under proper restrictions, on making just compensation, and such compensation together with the cost of such drainage may be assessed, wholly or partly, against any property benefitted thereby; but no special laws shall be enacted for such purposes. (Amended by Constitutional Convention of 1938 and approved by vote of the people November 8, 1938. Subdivision (e) repealed by vote of the people November 5, 1963. Subdivision (b) repealed by vote of the people November 3, 1964.)

[Freedom of speech and press; criminal prosecutions for libel]

§8. Every citizen may freely speak, write and publish his or her sentiments on all subjects, being responsible for the abuse of that right; and no law shall be passed to restrain or abridge the liberty of speech or of the press. In all criminal prosecutions or indictments for libels, the truth may be given in evidence to the jury; and if it shall appear to the jury that the matter charged as libelous is true, and was published with good motives and for justifiable ends, the party shall be acquitted; and the jury shall have the right to determine the law and the fact. (Amended by vote of the people November 7, 2001.)

[Right to assemble and petition; divorce; lotteries; pool-selling and gambling; laws to prevent; pari-mutual betting on horse races permitted; games of chance, bingo or lotto authorized under certain restrictions]

§9. 1. No law shall be passed abridging the rights of the people peaceably to assemble and to petition the government, or any department thereof; nor shall any divorce be granted otherwise than by due judicial proceedings; except as hereinafter provided, no lottery or the sale of lottery tickets, pool-selling, book-making, or any other kind of gambling, except lotteries operated by the state and the sale of lottery tickets in connection therewith as may be authorized and prescribed by the legislature, the net proceeds of which shall be applied exclusively to or in aid or support of education in this state as the legislature may prescribe, and except pari-mutuel betting on horse races as may be prescribed by the legislature and from which the state shall derive a reasonable revenue for the support of government, shall hereafter be authorized or allowed within this state; and the legislature shall pass appropriate laws to prevent offenses against any of the provisions of this section.

2. Notwithstanding the foregoing provisions of this section, any city, town or village within the state may by an approving vote of the majority of the qualified electors in

(continued next page)

such municipality voting on a proposition therefor submitted at a general or special election authorize, subject to state legislative supervision and control, the conduct of one or both of the following categories of games of chance commonly known as: (a) bingo or lotto, in which prizes are awarded on the basis of designated numbers or symbols on a card conforming to numbers or symbols selected at random; (b) games in which prizes are awarded on the basis of a winning number or numbers, color or colors, or symbol or symbols determined by chance from among those previously selected or played, whether determined as the result of the spinning of a wheel, a drawing or otherwise by chance. If authorized, such games shall be subject to the following restrictions, among others which may be prescribed by the legislature: (1) only bona fide religious, charitable or non-profit organizations of veterans, volunteer firefighter and similar non-profit organizations shall be permitted to conduct such games; (2) the entire net proceeds of any game shall be exclusively devoted to the lawful purposes of such organizations; (3) no person except a bona fide member of any such organization shall participate in the management or operation of such game; and (4) no person shall receive any remuneration for participating in the management or operation of any such game. Unless otherwise provided by law, no single prize shall exceed two hundred fifty dollars, nor shall any series of prizes on one occasion aggregate more than one thousand dollars. The legislature shall pass appropriate laws to effectuate the purposes of this subdivision, ensure that such games are rigidly regulated to prevent commercialized gambling, prevent participation by criminal and other undesirable elements and the diversion of funds from the purposes authorized hereunder and establish a method by which a municipality which has authorized such games may rescind or revoke such authorization. Unless permitted by the legislature, no municipality shall have the power to pass local laws or ordinances relating to such games. Nothing in this section shall prevent the legislature from passing laws more restrictive than any of the provisions of this section. (Amendment approved by vote of the people November 7, 1939; further amended by vote of the people November 5, 1957; November 8, 1966; November 4, 1975; November 6, 1984; November 7, 2001.)

[Section 10 which dealt with ownership of lands, yellowtail tenures and escheat was repealed by amendment approved by vote of the people November 6, 1962]

[Equal protection of laws; discrimination in civil rights prohibited]

§11. No person shall be denied the equal protection of the laws of this state or any subdivision thereof. No person shall, because of race, color, creed or religion, be subjected to any discrimination in his or her civil rights by any other person or by any firm, corporation, or institution, or by the state or any agency or subdivision of the state. (New. Adopted by Constitutional Convention of 1938 and approved by vote of the people November 8, 1938; amended by vote of the people November 7, 2001.)

[Security against unreasonable searches, seizures and interceptions]

§12. The right of the people to be secure in their persons, houses, papers and effects, against unreasonable searches and seizures, shall not be violated, and no warrants shall issue, but upon probable cause, supported by oath or affirmation, and particularly describing the place to be searched, and the persons or things to be seized. The right of the people to be secure against unreasonable interception of telephone and telegraph communications shall not be violated, and ex parte orders or warrants shall issue only

(continued next page)

upon oath or affirmation that there is reasonable ground to believe that evidence of crime may be thus obtained, and identifying the particular means of communication, and particularly describing the person or persons whose communications are to be intercepted and the purpose thereof. (New. Adopted by Constitutional Convention of 1938 and approved by vote of the people November 8, 1938.)

[Section 13 which dealt with purchase of lands of Indians was repealed by amendment approved by vote of the people November 6, 1962]
[Common law and acts of the colonial and state legislatures]
§14. Such parts of the common law, and of the acts of the legislature of the colony of New York, as together did form the law of the said colony, on the nineteenth day of April, one thousand seven hundred seventy-five, and the resolutions of the congress of the said colony, and of the convention of the State of New York, in force on the twentieth day of April, one thousand seven hundred seventy-seven, which have not since expired, or been repealed or altered; and such acts of the legislature of this state as are now in force, shall be and continue the law of this state, subject to such alterations as the legislature shall make concerning the same. But all such parts of the common law, and such of the said acts, or parts thereof, as are repugnant to this constitution, are hereby abrogated.
(Formerly §16. Renumbered and amended by Constitutional Convention of 1938 and approved by vote of the people November 8, 1938.)

[Section 15 which dealt with certain grants of lands and of charters made by the king of Great Britain and the state and obligations and contracts not to be impaired was repealed by amendment approved by vote of the people November 6, 1962]

[Damages for injuries causing death]
§16. The right of action now existing to recover damages for injuries resulting in death, shall never be abrogated; and the amount recoverable shall not be subject to any statutory limitation. (Formerly §18. Renumbered by Constitutional Convention of 1938 and approved by vote of the people November 8, 1938.)

[Labor not a commodity; hours and wages in public work; right to organize and bargain collectively]
§17. Labor of human beings is not a commodity nor an article of commerce and shall never be so considered or construed. No laborer, worker or mechanic, in the employ of a contractor or subcontractor engaged in the performance of any public work, shall be permitted to work more than eight hours in any day or more than five days in any week, except in cases of extraordinary emergency; nor shall he or she be paid less than the rate of wages prevailing in the same trade or occupation in the locality within the state where such public work is to be situated, erected or used. Employees shall have the right to organize and to bargain collectively through representatives of their own choosing. (New. Adopted by Constitutional Convention of 1938 and approved by vote of the people November 8, 1938; amended by vote of the people November 7, 2001.)

[Workers' compensation]
§18. Nothing contained in this constitution shall be construed to limit the power of the legislature to enact laws for the protection of the lives, health, or safety of

(continued next page)

employees; or for the payment, either by employers, or by employers and employees or otherwise, either directly or through a state or other system of insurance or otherwise, of compensation for injuries to employees or for death of employees resulting from such injuries without regard to fault as a cause thereof, except where the injury is occasioned by the wilful intention of the injured employee to bring about the injury or death of himself or herself or of another, or where the injury results solely from the intoxication of the injured employee while on duty; or for the adjustment, determination and settlement, with or without trial by jury, of issues which may arise under such legislation; or to provide that the right of such compensation, and the remedy therefor shall be exclusive of all other rights and remedies for injuries to employees or for death resulting from such injuries; or to provide that the amount of such compensation for death shall not exceed a fixed or determinable sum; provided that all moneys paid by an employer to his or her employees or their legal representatives, by reason of the enactment of any of the laws herein authorized, shall be held to be a proper charge in the cost of operating the business of the employer. (Formerly §19. Renumbered by Constitutional Convention of 1938 and approved by vote of the people November 8, 1938; amended by vote of the people November 7, 2001.)

ARTICLE II

Suffrage

[Qualifications of voters]
Section 1. Every citizen shall be entitled to vote at every election for all officers elected by the people and upon all questions submitted to the vote of the people provided that such citizen is eighteen years of age or over and shall have been a resident of this state, and of the county, city, or village for thirty days next preceding an election. . . .

ARTICLE III

Legislature

[Legislative power]
Section 1. The legislative power of this state shall be vested in the senate and assembly.

[Number and terms of senators and assemblymen]
§2. The senate shall consist of fifty members, except as hereinafter provided. The senators elected in the year one thousand eight hundred and ninety-five shall hold their offices for three years, and their successors shall be chosen for two years. The assembly shall consist of one hundred and fifty members. The assembly members elected in the year one thousand nine hundred and thirty-eight, and their successors, shall be chosen for two years. (Amended by vote of the people November 2, 1937; November 7, 2001.)

*[Senate districts]
§3. The senate districts described in section three of article three of this constitution as adopted by the people on November sixth, eighteen hundred ninety-four are hereby continued for all of the purposes of future reapportionments of senate districts

(continued next page)

pursuant to section four of this article. (Formerly §3. Repealed and replaced by new §3 amended by vote of the people November 6, 1962.)

. . .

[Apportionment of assemblymen; creation of assembly districts]

§5. The members of the assembly shall be chosen by single districts and shall be apportioned by the legislature at each regular session at which the senate districts are readjusted or altered, and by the same law, among the several counties of the state, as nearly as may be according to the number of their respective inhabitants, excluding aliens. Every county heretofore established and separately organized, except the county of Hamilton, shall always be entitled to one member of assembly, and no county shall hereafter be erected unless its population shall entitle it to a member. The county of Hamilton shall elect with the county of Fulton, until the population of the county of Hamilton shall, according to the ratio, entitle it to a member. But the legislature may abolish the said county of Hamilton and annex the territory thereof to some other county or counties.

The quotient obtained by dividing the whole number of inhabitants of the state, excluding aliens, by the number of members of assembly, shall be the ratio for apportionment, which shall be made as follows: One member of assembly shall be apportioned to every county, including Fulton and Hamilton as one county, containing less than the ratio and one-half over. Two members shall be apportioned to every other county. The remaining members of assembly shall be apportioned to the counties having more than two ratios according to the number of inhabitants, excluding aliens. Members apportioned on remainders shall be apportioned to the counties having the highest remainders in the order thereof respectively. No county shall have more members of assembly than a county having a greater number of inhabitants, excluding aliens.

*The assembly districts, including the present ones, as existing immediately before the enactment of a law making an apportionment of members of assembly among the counties, shall continue to be the assembly districts of the state until the expiration of the terms of members then in office, except for the purpose of an election of members of assembly for full terms beginning at such expirations.

In any county entitled to more than one member, the board of supervisors, and in any city embracing an entire county and having no board of supervisors, the common council, or if there be none, the body exercising the powers of a common council, shall assemble at such times as the legislature making an apportionment shall prescribe, and divide such counties into assembly districts as nearly equal in number of inhabitants, excluding aliens, as may be, of convenient and contiguous territory in as compact form as practicable, each of which shall be wholly within a senate district formed under the same apportionment, equal to the number of members of assembly to which such county shall be entitled, and shall cause to be filed in the office of the secretary of state and of the clerk of such county, a description of such districts, specifying the number of each district and of the inhabitants thereof, excluding aliens, according to the census or enumeration used as the population basis for the formation of such districts; and such apportionment and districts shall remain unaltered until after the next reapportionment of members of assembly, except that the board of supervisors of any county containing a town having more than a ratio of apportionment and one-half over may alter the assembly districts in a senate district containing such town at any time on or before March first, nineteen hundred forty-six. In counties having more than one senate district, the

(continued next page)

same number of assembly districts shall be put in each senate district, unless the assembly districts cannot be evenly divided among the senate districts of any county, in which case one more assembly district shall be put in the senate district in such county having the largest, or one less assembly district shall be put in the senate district in such county having the smallest number of inhabitants, excluding aliens, as the case may require. No town, except a town having more than a ratio of apportionment and one-half over, and no block in a city inclosed by streets or public ways, shall be divided in the formation of assembly districts, nor shall any districts contain a greater excess in population over an adjoining district in the same senate district, than the population of a town or block therein adjoining such assembly district. Towns or blocks which, from their location may be included in either of two districts, shall be so placed as to make said districts most nearly equal in number of inhabitants, excluding aliens. Nothing in this section shall prevent the division, at any time, of counties and towns and the erection of new towns by the legislature. An apportionment by the legislature, or other body, shall be subject to review by the supreme court, at the suit of any citizen, under such reasonable regulations as the legislature may prescribe; and any court before which a cause may be pending involving an apportionment, shall give precedence thereto over all other causes and proceedings, and if said court be not in session it shall convene promptly for the disposition of the same. (Amended by vote of the people November 6, 1945.)

. . .

[Powers of each house]
§9. A majority of each house shall constitute a quorum to do business. Each house shall determine the rules of its own proceedings, and be the judge of the elections, returns and qualifications of its own members; shall choose its own officers; and the senate shall choose a temporary president and the assembly shall choose a speaker. (Formerly §10. Renumbered by Constitutional Convention of 1938 and approved by vote of the people November 8, 1938. Amended by vote of the people November 5, 1963.)

. . .

[Bills may originate in either house; may be amended by the other]
§12. Any bill may originate in either house of the legislature, and all bills passed by one house may be amended by the other. (Formerly §13. Renumbered by Constitutional Convention of 1938 and approved by vote of the people November 8, 1938.)

. . .

[Two-thirds bills]
§20. The assent of two-thirds of the members elected to each branch of the legislature shall be requisite to every bill appropriating the public moneys or property for local or private purposes.

. . .

[When yeas and nays necessary; three-fifths to constitute quorum]
§23. On the final passage, in either house of the legislature, of any act which imposes, continues or revives a tax, or creates a debt or charge, or makes, continues or revives any appropriation of public or trust money or property, or releases, discharges or commutes any claim or demand of the state, the question shall be taken by yeas and nays, which shall be duly entered upon the journals, and three-fifths of all the members elected to either house shall, in all such cases, be necessary to constitute a quo-

(continued next page)

rum therein. (Formerly §25. Renumbered by Constitutional Convention of 1938 and approved by vote of the people November 8, 1938.)

. . .

ARTICLE IV

EXECUTIVE

[Executive power; election and terms of governor and lieutenant-governor]

Section 1. The executive power shall be vested in the governor, who shall hold office for four years; the lieutenant-governor shall be chosen at the same time, and for the same term. The governor and lieutenant- governor shall be chosen at the general election held in the year nineteen hundred thirty-eight, and each fourth year thereafter. They shall be chosen jointly, by the casting by each voter of a single vote applicable to both offices, and the legislature by law shall provide for making such choice in such manner. The respective persons having the highest number of votes cast jointly for them for governor and lieutenant-governor respectively shall be elected. (Amended by Constitutional Convention of 1938 and approved by vote of the people November 8, 1938; further amended by vote of the people November 3, 1953; November 7, 2001.)

[Qualifications of governor and lieutenant-governor]

§2. No person shall be eligible to the office of governor or lieutenantgovernor, except a citizen of the United States, of the age of not less than thirty years, and who shall have been five years next preceding the election a resident of this state. (Amended by vote of the people November 7, 2001.)

[Powers and duties of governor; compensation]

§3. The governor shall be commander-in-chief of the military and naval forces of the state. The governor shall have power to convene the legislature, or the senate only, on extraordinary occasions. At extraordinary sessions convened pursuant to the provisions of this section no subject shall be acted upon, except such as the governor may recommend for consideration. The governor shall communicate by message to the legislature at every session the condition of the state, and recommend such matters to it as he or she shall judge expedient. The governor shall expedite all such measures as may be resolved upon by the legislature, and shall take care that the laws are faithfully executed. The governor shall receive for his or her services an annual salary to be fixed by joint resolution of the senate and assembly, and there shall be provided for his or her use a suitable and furnished executive residence. (Formerly §4. Renumbered and amended by Constitutional Convention of 1938 and approved by vote of the people November 8, 1938; further amended by vote of the people November 3, 1953; November 5, 1963; November 7, 2001.)

[Reprieves, commutations and pardons; powers and duties of governor relating to grants of]

§4. The governor shall have the power to grant reprieves, commutations and pardons after conviction, for all offenses except treason and cases of impeachment, upon such conditions and with such restrictions and limitations, as he or she may think proper,

(continued next page)

subject to such regulations as may be provided by law relative to the manner of applying for pardons. Upon conviction for treason, the governor shall have power to suspend the execution of the sentence, until the case shall be reported to the legislature at its next meeting, when the legislature shall either pardon, or commute the sentence, direct the execution of the sentence, or grant a further reprieve. The governor shall annually communicate to the legislature each case of reprieve, commutation or pardon granted, stating the name of the convict, the crime of which the convict was convicted, the sentence and its date, and the date of the commutation, pardon or reprieve. (Formerly §5. Renumbered by Constitutional Convention of 1938 and approved by vote of the people November 8, 1938; further amended by vote of the people November 7, 2001.)

[When lieutenant-governor to act as governor]
§5. In case of the removal of the governor from office or of his or her death or resignation, the lieutenant-governor shall become governor for the remainder of the term. In case the governor-elect shall decline to serve or shall die, the lieutenant-governor-elect shall become governor for the full term. In case the governor is impeached, is absent from the state or is otherwise unable to discharge the powers and duties of the office of governor, the lieutenant-governor shall act as governor until the inability shall cease or until the term of the governor shall expire. In case of the failure of the governor-elect to take the oath of office at the commencement of his or her term, the lieutenant-governor-elect shall act as governor until the governor shall take the oath. (Formerly §6. Renumbered and amended by Constitutional Convention of 1938 and approved by vote of the people November 8, 1938; further amended by vote of the people November 8, 1949; November 5, 1963; November 7, 2001.)

. . .

[Action by governor on legislative bills; reconsideration after veto]
§7. Every bill which shall have passed the senate and assembly shall, before it becomes a law, be presented to the governor; if the governor approve, he or she shall sign it; but if not, he or she shall return it with his or her objections to the house in which it shall have originated, which shall enter the objections at large on the journal, and proceed to reconsider it. If after such reconsideration, two-thirds of the members elected to that house shall agree to pass the bill, it shall be sent together reconsidered; and if approved by two-thirds of the members elected to that house, it shall become a law notwithstanding the objections of the governor. In all such cases the votes in both houses shall be determined by yeas and nays, and the names of the members voting shall be entered on the journal of each house respectively. If any bill shall not be returned by the governor within ten days (Sundays excepted) after it shall have been presented to him or her, the same shall be a law in like manner as if he or she had signed it, unless the legislature shall, by their adjournment, prevent its return, in which case it shall not become a law without the approval of the governor. No bill shall become a law after the final adjournment of the legislature, unless approved by the governor within thirty days after such adjournment. If any bill presented to the governor contain several items of appropriation of money, the governor may object to one or more of such items while approving of the other portion of the bill. In such case the governor shall append to the bill, at the time of signing it, a statement of the items to which he or

(continued next page)

she objects; and the appropriation so objected to shall not take effect. If the legislature be in session, he or she shall transmit to the house in which the bill originated a copy of such statement, and the items objected to shall be separately reconsidered. If on reconsideration one or more of such items be approved by two-thirds of the members elected to each house, the same shall be part of the law, notwithstanding the objections of the governor. All the provisions of this section, in relation to bills not approved by the governor, shall apply in cases in which he or she shall withhold approval from any item or items contained in a bill appropriating money. (Formerly §9. Renumbered by Constitutional Convention of 1938 and approved by vote of the people November 8, 1938; further amended by vote of the people November 7, 2001.)

. . .

ARTICLE V

OFFICERS AND CIVIL DEPARTMENTS

[Comptroller and attorney-general; payment of state moneys without audit void]

Section 1. The comptroller and attorney-general shall be chosen at the same general election as the governor and hold office for the same term, and shall possess the qualifications provided in section 2 of article IV. The legislature shall provide for filling vacancies in the office of comptroller and of attorney-general. No election of a comptroller or an attorney-general shall be had except at the time of electing a governor. The comptroller shall be required: (1) To audit all vouchers before payment and all official accounts; (2) to audit the accrual and collection of all revenues and receipts; and (3) to prescribe such methods of accounting as are necessary for the performance of the foregoing duties. The payment of any money of the state, or of any money under its control, or the refund of any money paid to the state, except upon audit by the comptroller, shall be void, and may be restrained upon the suit of any taxpayer with the consent of the supreme court in appellate division on notice to the attorney-general. In such respect the legislature shall define the powers and duties and may also assign to him or her: (1) supervision of the accounts of any political subdivision of the state; and (2) powers and duties pertaining to or connected with the assessment and taxation of real estate, including determination of ratios which the assessed valuation of taxable real property bears to the full valuation thereof, but not including any of those powers and duties reserved to officers of a county, city, town or village by virtue of sections seven and eight of article nine of this constitution. The legislature shall assign to him or her no administrative duties, excepting such as may be incidental to the performance of these functions, any other provision of this constitution to the contrary notwithstanding. (Amended by Constitutional Convention of 1938 and approved by vote of the people November 8, 1938; further amended by vote of the people November 3, 1953; November 8, 1955; November 7, 2001.)

[Civil departments in the state government]

§2. There shall be not more than twenty civil departments in the state government, including those referred to in this constitution. The legislature may by law change the names of the departments referred to in this constitution. (Amended by Constitutional

(continued next page)

Convention of 1938 and approved by vote of the people November 8, 1938; further amended by vote of the people November 2, 1943; November 3, 1959; November 7, 1961.)
. . .

ARTICLE VI*

JUDICIARY

[Unified court system; organization; process]

Section 1. a. There shall be a unified court system for the state. The state-wide courts shall consist of the court of appeals, the supreme court including the appellate divisions thereof, the court of claims, the county court, the surrogate's court and the family court, as hereinafter provided. The legislature shall establish in and for the city of New York, as part of the unified court system for the state, a single, city-wide court of civil jurisdiction and a single, city-wide court of criminal jurisdiction, as hereinafter provided, and may upon the request of the mayor and the local legislative body of the city of New York, merge the two courts into one city-wide court of both civil and criminal jurisdiction. The unified court system for the state shall also include the district, town, city and village courts outside the city of New York, as hereinafter provided.

b. The court of appeals, the supreme court including the appellate divisions thereof, the court of claims, the county court, the surrogate's court, the family court, the courts or court of civil and criminal jurisdiction of the city of New York, and such other courts as the legislature may determine shall be courts of record.

c. All processes, warrants and other mandates of the court of appeals, the supreme court including the appellate divisions thereof, the court of claims, the county court, the surrogate's court and the family court may be served and executed in any part of the state. All processes, warrants and other mandates of the courts or court of civil and criminal jurisdiction of the city of New York may, subject to such limitation as may be prescribed by the legislature, be served and executed in any part of the state. The legislature may provide that processes, warrants and other mandates of the district court may be served and executed in any part of the state and that processes, warrants and other mandates of town, village and city courts outside the city of New York may be served and executed in any part of the county in which such courts are located or in any part of any adjoining county.

. . .

[Judicial departments; appellate divisions, how constituted; governor to designate justices; temporary assignments; jurisdiction]

§4. a. The state shall be divided into four judicial departments. The first department shall consist of the counties within the first judicial district of the state. The second department shall consist of the counties within the second, ninth, tenth and eleventh judicial districts of the state. The third department shall consist of the counties within the third, fourth and sixth judicial districts of the state. The fourth department shall consist of the counties within the fifth, seventh and eighth judicial districts of the state. Each department shall be bounded by the lines of judicial districts. Once every ten years the legislature may alter the boundaries of the judicial departments, but without changing the number thereof.

(continued next page)

b. The appellate divisions of the supreme court are continued, and shall consist of seven justices of the supreme court in each of the first and second departments, and five justices in each of the other departments. In each appellate division, four justices shall constitute a quorum, and the concurrence of three shall be necessary to a decision. No more than five justices shall sit in any case.

c. The governor shall designate the presiding justice of each appellate division, who shall act as such during his or her term of office and shall be a resident of the department. The other justices of the appellate divisions shall be designated by the governor, from all the justices elected to the supreme court, for terms of five years or the unexpired portions of their respective terms of office, if less than five years.

d. The justices heretofore designated shall continue to sit in the appellate divisions until the terms of their respective designations shall expire. From time to time as the terms of the designations expire, or vacancies occur, the governor shall make new designations. The governor may also, on request of any appellate division, make temporary designations in case of the absence or inability to act of any justice in such appellate division, for service only during such absence or inability to act.

e. In case any appellate division shall certify to the governor that one or more additional justices are needed for the speedy disposition of the business before it, the governor may designate an additional justice or additional justices; but when the need for such additional justice or justices shall no longer exist, the appellate division shall so certify to the governor, and thereupon service under such designation or designations shall cease.

f. A majority of the justices designated to sit in any appellate division shall at all times be residents of the department.

g. Whenever the appellate division in any department shall be unable to dispose of its business within a reasonable time, a majority of the presiding justices of the several departments, at a meeting called by the presiding justice of the department in arrears, may transfer any pending appeals from such department to any other department for hearing and determination.

h. A justice of the appellate division of the supreme court in any department may be temporarily designated by the presiding justice of his or her department to the appellate division in another judicial department upon agreement by the presiding justices of the appellate division of the departments concerned.

i. In the event that the disqualification, absence or inability to act of justices in any appellate division prevents there being a quorum of justices qualified to hear an appeal, the justices qualified to hear the appeal may transfer it to the appellate division in another department for hearing and determination. In the event that the justices in any appellate division qualified to hear an appeal are equally divided, said justices may transfer the appeal to the appellate division in another department for hearing and determination. Each appellate division shall have power to appoint and remove its clerk.

j. No justice of the appellate division shall, within the department to which he or she may be designated to perform the duties of an appellate justice, exercise any of the powers of a justice of the supreme court, other than those of a justice out of court, and those pertaining to the appellate division, except that the justice may decide causes or proceedings theretofore submitted, or hear and decide motions submitted by consent of counsel, but any such justice, when not actually engaged in performing the duties

(continued next page)

of such appellate justice in the department to which he or she is designated, may hold any term of the supreme court and exercise any of the powers of a justice of the supreme court in any judicial district in any other department of the state.

k. The appellate divisions of the supreme court shall have all the jurisdiction possessed by them on the effective date of this article and such additional jurisdiction as may be prescribed by law, provided, however, that the right to appeal to the appellate divisions from a judgment or order which does not finally determine an action or special proceeding may be limited or conditioned by law. (Subdivision e amended by vote of the people November 8, 1977; further amended by vote of the people November 7, 2001.)

. . .

[Administrative supervision of court system]

§28. a. The chief judge of the court of appeals shall be the chief judge of the state of New York and shall be the chief judicial officer of the unified court system. There shall be an administrative board of the courts which shall consist of the chief judge of the court of appeals as chairperson and the presiding justice of the appellate division of the supreme court of each judicial department. The chief judge shall, with the advice and consent of the administrative board of the courts, appoint a chief administrator of the courts who shall serve at the pleasure of the chief judge. b. The chief administrator, on behalf of the chief judge, shall supervise the administration and operation of the unified court system. In the exercise of such responsibility, the chief administrator of the courts shall have such powers and duties as may be delegated to him or her by the chief judge and such additional powers and duties as may be provided by law. c. The chief judge, after consultation with the administrative board, shall establish standards and administrative policies for general application throughout the state, which shall be submitted by the chief judge to the court of appeals, together with the recommendations, if any, of the administrative board. Such standards and administrative policies shall be promulgated after approval by the court of appeals. (Formerly §28. Repealed and new §28 added by vote of the people November 8, 1977; amended by vote of the people November 7, 2001.)

. . .

ARTICLE VII

STATE FINANCES

[Estimates by departments, the legislature and the judiciary of needed appropriations; hearings]

Section 1. For the preparation of the budget, the head of each department of state government, except the legislature and judiciary, shall furnish the governor such estimates and information in such form and at such times as the governor may require, copies of which shall forthwith be furnished to the appropriate committees of the legislature. The governor shall hold hearings thereon at which the governor may require the attendance of heads of departments and their subordinates. Designated representatives of such committees shall be entitled to attend the hearings thereon and to make inquiry concerning any part thereof.

(continued next page)

Itemized estimates of the financial needs of the legislature, certified by the presiding officer of each house, and of the judiciary, approved by the court of appeals and certified by the chief judge of the court of appeals, shall be transmitted to the governor not later than the first day of December in each year for inclusion in the budget without revision but with such recommendations as the governor may deem proper. Copies of the itemized estimates of the financial needs of the judiciary also shall forthwith be transmitted to the appropriate committees of the legislature. (Amended by vote of the people November 8, 1977; November 7, 2001.)

[Executive budget]
§2. Annually, on or before the first day of February in each year following the year fixed by the constitution for the election of governor and lieutenant governor, and on or before the second Tuesday following the first day of the annual meeting of the legislature, in all other years, the governor shall submit to the legislature a budget containing a complete plan of expenditures proposed to be made before the close of the ensuing fiscal year and all moneys and revenues estimated to be available therefor, together with an explanation of the basis of such estimates and recommendations as to proposed legislation, if any, which the governor may deem necessary to provide moneys and revenues sufficient to meet such proposed expenditures. It shall also contain such other recommendations and information as the governor may deem proper and such additional information as may be required by law. (New. Derived in part from former §2 of Art. 4-a. Adopted by Constitutional Convention of 1938 and approved by vote of the people November 8, 1938; amended by vote of the people November 2, 1965; November 7, 2001.)

. . .

ARTICLE IX*

LOCAL GOVERNMENTS

Bill of rights for local governments.
Section 1. Effective local self-government and intergovernmental cooperation are purposes of the people of the state. In furtherance thereof, local governments shall have the following rights, powers, privileges and immunities in addition to those granted by other provisions of this constitution:
(a) Every local government, except a county wholly included within a city, shall have a legislative body elective by the people thereof. Every local government shall have power to adopt local laws as provided by this article.
(b) All officers of every local government whose election or appointment is not provided for by this constitution shall be elected by the people of the local government, or of some division thereof, or appointed by such officers of the local government as may be provided by law.
(c) Local governments shall have power to agree, as authorized by act of the legislature, with the federal government, a state or one or more other governments within or without the state, to provide cooperatively, jointly or by contract any facility, service, activity or undertaking which each participating local government has the power to provide separately. Each such local government shall have power to apportion its share of the

(continued next page)

cost thereof upon such portion of its area as may be authorized by act of the legislature.

(d) No local government or any part of the territory thereof shall be annexed to another until the people, if any, of the territory proposed to be annexed shall have consented thereto by majority vote on a referendum and until the governing board of each local government, the area of which is affected, shall have consented thereto upon the basis of a determination that the annexation is in the over-all public interest. The consent of the governing board of a county shall be required only where a boundary of the county is affected. On or before July first, nineteen hundred sixty-four, the legislature shall provide, where such consent of a governing board is not granted, for adjudication and determination, on the law and the facts, in a proceeding initiated in the supreme court, of the issue of whether the annexation is in the over-all public interest.

(e) Local governments shall have power to take by eminent domain private property within their boundaries for public use together with excess land or property but no more than is sufficient to provide for appropriate disposition or use of land or property which abuts on that necessary for such public use, and to sell or lease that not devoted to such use. The legislature may authorize and regulate the exercise of the power of eminent domain and excess condemnation by a local government outside its boundaries.

(f) No local government shall be prohibited by the legislature (1) from making a fair return on the value of the property used and useful in its operation of a gas, electric or water public utility service, over and above costs of operation and maintenance and necessary and proper reserves, in addition to an amount equivalent to taxes which such service, if privately owned, would pay to such local government, or (2) from using such profits for payment of refunds to consumers or for any other lawful purpose.

(g) A local government shall have power to apportion its cost of a governmental service or function upon any portion of its area, as authorized by act of the legislature.

(h) (1) Counties, other than those wholly included within a city, shall be empowered by general law, or by special law enacted upon county request pursuant to section two of this article, to adopt, amend or repeal alternative forms of county government provided by the legislature or to prepare, adopt, amend or repeal alternative forms of their own. Any such form of government or any amendment thereof, by act of the legislature or by local law, may transfer one or more functions or duties of the county or of the cities, towns, villages, districts or other units of government wholly contained in such county to each other or when authorized by the legislature to the state, or may abolish one or more offices, departments, agencies or units of government provided, however, that no such form or amendment, except as provided in paragraph (2) of this subdivision, shall become effective unless approved on a referendum by a majority of the votes cast thereon in the area of the county outside of cities, and in the cities of the county, if any, considered as one unit. Where an alternative form of county government or any amendment thereof, by act of the legislature or by local law, provides for the transfer of any function or duty to or from any village or the abolition of any office, department, agency or unit of government of a village wholly contained in such county, such form or amendment shall not become effective unless it shall also be approved on the referendum by a majority of the votes cast thereon in all the villages so affected considered as one unit. (2) After the adoption of an alternative form of county government by a county, any amendment thereof by act of the legislature or by local law which abolishes or creates an elective county office, changes the voting or

(continued next page)

veto power of or the method of removing an elective county officer during his or her term of office, abolishes, curtails or transfers to another county officer or agency any power of an elective county officer or changes the form or composition of the county legislative body shall be subject to a permissive referendum as provided by the legislature. (Amended by vote of the people November 7, 2001.)

. . .

ARTICLE X

CORPORATIONS

[Corporations; formation of]

Section 1. Corporations may be formed under general law; but shall not be created by special act, except for municipal purposes, and in cases where, in the judgment of the legislature, the objects of the corporation cannot be attained under general laws. All general laws and special acts passed pursuant to this section may be altered from time to time or repealed. (Formerly §1 of Art. 8. Renumbered by Constitutional Convention of 1938 and approved by vote of the people November 8, 1938.) [Dues of corporations] §2. Dues from corporations shall be secured by such individual liability of the corporators and other means as may be prescribed by law. (Formerly §2 of Art. 8. Renumbered by Constitutional Convention of 1938 and approved by vote of the people November 8, 1938.)

. . .

ARTICLE XI

EDUCATION

[Common schools]

Section 1. The legislature shall provide for the maintenance and support of a system of free common schools, wherein all the children of this state may be educated. (Formerly §1 of Art. 9. Renumbered by Constitutional Convention of 1938 and approved by vote of the people November 8, 1938.)

[Regents of the University]

§2. The corporation created in the year one thousand seven hundred eighty-four, under the name of The Regents of the University of the State of New York, is hereby continued under the name of The University of the State of New York. It shall be governed and its corporate powers, which may be increased, modified or diminished by the legislature, shall be exercised by not less than nine regents. (Formerly §2 of Art. 9. Renumbered and amended by Constitutional Convention of 1938 and approved by vote of the people November 8, 1938.)

(continued next page)

[Use of public property or money in aid of denominational schools prohibited; transportation of children authorized]

§3. Neither the state nor any subdivision thereof, shall use its property or credit or any public money, or authorize or permit either to be used, directly or indirectly, in aid or maintenance, other than for examination or inspection, of any school or institution of learning wholly or in part under the control or direction of any religious denomination, or in which any denominational tenet or doctrine is taught, but the legislature may provide for the transportation of children to and from any school or institution of learning. (Formerly §4 of Art. 9. Renumbered and amended by Constitutional Convention of 1938 and approved by vote of the people November 8, 1938. Formerly §4, renumbered §3 without change by amendment approved by vote of the people November 6, 1962; former § 4 repealed by same amendment.)

ARTICLE XII*

DEFENSE

[Defense; militia]

Section 1. The defense and protection of the state and of the United States is an obligation of all persons within the state. The legislature shall provide for the discharge of this obligation and for the maintenance and regulation of an organized militia.

. . .

ARTICLE XIII

PUBLIC OFFICERS

[Oath of office; no other test for public office]

Section 1. Members of the legislature, and all officers, executive and judicial, except such inferior officers as shall be by law exempted, shall, before they enter on the duties of their respective offices, take and subscribe the following oath or affirmation: "I do solemnly swear (or affirm) that I will support the constitution of the United States, and the constitution of the State of New York, and that I will faithfully discharge the duties of the office of ......, according to the best of my ability;" and no other oath, declaration or test shall be required as a qualification for any office of public trust, except that any committee of a political party may, by rule, provide for equal representation of the sexes on any such committee, and a state convention of a political party, at which candidates for public office are nominated, may, by rule, provide for equal representation of the sexes on any committee of such party. (Amended by Constitutional Convention of 1938 and approved by vote of the people November 8, 1938.)

. . .

ARTICLE XIV

. . .

[Forest and wild life conservation; use or disposition of certain lands authorized]

§3. 1. Forest and wild life conservation are hereby declared to be policies of the state. For the purpose of carrying out such policies the legislature may appropriate moneys for the acquisition by the state of land, outside of the Adirondack and Catskill parks as now fixed by law, for the practice of forest or wild life conservation. The prohibitions of section 1 of this article shall not apply to any lands heretofore or hereafter acquired or dedicated for such purposes within the forest preserve counties but outside of the Adirondack and Catskill parks as now fixed by law, except that such lands shall not be leased, sold or exchanged, or be taken by any corporation, public or private.

2. As to any other lands of the state, now owned or hereafter acquired, constituting the forest preserve referred to in section one of this article, but outside of the Adirondack and Catskill parks as now fixed by law, and consisting in any case of not more than one hundred contiguous acres entirely separated from any other portion of the forest preserve, the legislature may by appropriate legislation, notwithstanding the provisions of section one of this article, authorize: (a) the dedication thereof for the practice of forest or wild life conservation; or (b) the use thereof for public recreational or other state purposes or the sale, exchange or other disposition thereof; provided, however, that all moneys derived from the sale or other disposition of any of such lands shall be paid into a special fund of the treasury and be expended only for the acquisition of additional lands for such forest preserve within either such Adirondack or Catskill park. (Formerly §16 of Art. 7. Renumbered and amended by Constitutional Convention of 1938 and approved by vote of the people November 8, 1938; further amended by vote of the people November 5, 1957; November 6, 1973.)

[Protection of natural resources; development of agricultural lands]

§4. The policy of the state shall be to conserve and protect its natural resources and scenic beauty and encourage the development and improvement of its agricultural lands for the production of food and other agricultural products. The legislature, in implementing this policy, shall include adequate provision for the abatement of air and water pollution and of excessive and unnecessary noise, the protection of agricultural lands, wetlands and shorelines, and the development and regulation of water resources. The legislature shall further provide for the acquisition of lands and waters, including improvements thereon and any interest therein, outside the forest preserve counties, and the dedication of properties so acquired or now owned, which because of their natural beauty, wilderness character, or geological, ecological or historical significance, shall be preserved and administered for the use and enjoyment of the people. Properties so dedicated shall constitute the state nature and historical preserve and they shall not be taken or otherwise disposed of except by law enacted by two successive regular sessions of the legislature. (New. Added by vote of the people November 4, 1969.)

. . .

ARTICLE XV

CANALS

[Disposition of canals and canal properties prohibited]

Section 1. The legislature shall not sell, abandon or otherwise dispose of the now existing or future improved barge canal, the divisions of which are the Erie canal, the Oswego canal, the Champlain canal, and the Cayuga and Seneca canals, or of the terminals constructed as part of the barge canal system; nor shall it sell, abandon or otherwise dispose of any portion of the canal system existing prior to the barge canal improvement which portion forms a part of, or functions as a part of, the present barge canal system; but such canals and terminals shall remain the property of the state and under its management and control forever. This prohibition shall not prevent the legislature, by appropriate laws, from authorizing the granting of revocable permits or leases for periods of time as authorized by the legislature for the occupancy or use of such lands or structures. (Formerly §8 of Art. 7. Renumbered and amended by Constitutional Convention of 1938 and approved by vote of the people November 8, 1938; November 5, 1991.)

. . .

ARTICLE XVI*

TAXATION

[Power of taxation; exemptions from taxation]

Section 1. The power of taxation shall never be surrendered, suspended or contracted away, except as to securities issued for public purposes pursuant to law. Any laws which delegate the taxing power shall specify the types of taxes which may be imposed thereunder and provide for their review.

Exemptions from taxation may be granted only by general laws. Exemptions may be altered or repealed except those exempting real or personal property used exclusively for religious, educational or charitable purposes as defined by law and owned by any corporation or association organized or conducted exclusively for one or more of such purposes and not operating for profit.

. . .

ARTICLE XVII

SOCIAL WELFARE

[Public relief and care]

Section 1. The aid, care and support of the needy are public concerns and shall be provided by the state and by such of its subdivisions, and in such manner and by such means, as the legislature may from time to time determine. (New. Adopted by Constitutional Convention of 1938 and approved by vote of the people November 8, 1938.)

(continued next page)

[State board of social welfare; powers and duties]

§2. The state board of social welfare shall be continued. It shall visit and inspect, or cause to be visited and inspected by members of its staff, all public and private institutions, whether state, county, municipal, incorporated or not incorporated, which are in receipt of public funds and which are of a charitable, eleemosynary, correctional or reformatory character, including all reformatories for juveniles and institutions or agencies exercising custody of dependent, neglected or delinquent children, but excepting state institutions for the education and support of the blind, the deaf and the dumb, and excepting also such institutions as are hereinafter made subject to the visitation and inspection of the department of mental hygiene or the state commission of correction. As to institutions, whether incorporated or not incorporated, having inmates, but not in receipt of public funds, which are of a charitable, eleemosynary, correctional or reformatory character, and agencies, whether incorporated or not incorporated, not in receipt of public funds, which exercise custody of dependent, neglected or delinquent children, the state board of social welfare shall make inspections, or cause inspections to be made by members of its staff, but solely as to matters directly affecting the health, safety, treatment and training of their inmates, or of the children under their custody. Subject to the control of the legislature and pursuant to the procedure prescribed by general law, the state board of social welfare may make rules and regulations, not inconsistent with this constitution, with respect to all of the functions, powers and duties with which the department and the state board of social welfare are herein or shall be charged. (New. Derived in part from former §11 of Art. 8. Adopted by Constitutional Convention of 1938 and approved by vote of the people November 8, 1938.)

[Public health]

§3. The protection and promotion of the health of the inhabitants of the state are matters of public concern and provision therefor shall be made by the state and by such of its subdivisions and in such manner, and by such means as the legislature shall from time to time determine. (New. Adopted by Constitutional Convention of 1938 and approved by vote of the people November 8, 1938.)

[Care and treatment of persons suffering from mental disorder or defect; visitation of institutions for]

§4. The care and treatment of persons suffering from mental disorder or defect and the protection of the mental health of the inhabitants of the state may be provided by state and local authorities and in such manner as the legislature may from time to time determine. The head of the department of mental hygiene shall visit and inspect, or cause to be visited and inspected by members of his or her staff, all institutions either public or private used for the care and treatment of persons suffering from mental disorder or defect. (New. Adopted by Constitutional Convention of 1938 and approved by vote of the people November 8, 1938; amended by vote of the people November 7, 2001.)

[Institutions for detention of criminals; probation; parole; state commission of correction]

§5. The legislature may provide for the maintenance and support of institutions for the detention of persons charged with or convicted of crime and for systems of probation and parole of persons convicted of crime. There shall be a state commission of correction, which shall visit and inspect or cause to be visited and inspected by members of its staff, all institutions used for the detention of sane adults charged with or convicted of crime. (New. Derived in part from former §11 of Art. 8. Adopted by Constitutional Convention of 1938 and approved by vote of the people November 8, 1938. Amended by vote of the people November 6, 1973.)

[Visitation and inspection]
§6. Visitation and inspection as herein authorized, shall not be exclusive of other visitation and inspection now or hereafter authorized by law. (New. Derived from former §13 of Art. 8. Adopted by Constitutional Convention of 1938 and approved by vote of the people November 8, 1938.)

[Loans for hospital construction]
§7. Notwithstanding any other provision of this constitution, the legislature may authorize the state, a municipality or a public corporation acting as an instrumentality of the state or municipality to lend its money or credit to or in aid of any corporation or association, regulated by law as to its charges, profits, dividends, and disposition of its property or franchises, for the purpose of providing such hospital or other facilities for the prevention, diagnosis or treatment of human disease, pain, injury, disability, deformity or physical condition, and for facilities incidental or appurtenant thereto as may be prescribed by law. (New. Added by vote of the people November 4, 1969.)

ARTICLE XVIII*

Housing

[Housing and nursing home accommodations for persons of low income; slum clearance]
Section 1. Subject to the provisions of this article, the legislature may provide in such manner, by such means and upon such terms and conditions as it may prescribe for low rent housing and nursing home accommodations for persons of low income as defined by law, or for the clearance, replanning, reconstruction and rehabilitation of substandard and insanitary areas, or for both such purposes, and for recreational and other facilities incidental or appurtenant thereto. (Amended by vote of the people November 2, 1965.)

. . .

ARTICLE XIX

Amendments to Constitution

[Amendments to constitution; how proposed, voted upon and ratified; failure of attorney-general to render opinion not to affect validity]
Section 1. Any amendment or amendments to this constitution may be proposed in the senate and assembly whereupon such amendment or amendments shall be referred to the attorney-general whose duty it shall be within twenty days thereafter to render an opinion in writing to the senate and assembly as to the effect of such amendment

(continued next page)

or amendments upon other provisions of the constitution. Upon receiving such opinion, if the amendment or amendments as proposed or as amended shall be agreed to by a majority of the members elected to each of the two houses, such proposed amendment or amendments shall be entered on their journals, and the ayes and noes taken thereon, and referred to the next regular legislative session convening after the succeeding general election of members of the assembly, and shall be published for three months previous to the time of making such choice; and if in such legislative session, such proposed amendment or amendments shall be agreed to by a majority of all the members elected to each house, then it shall be the duty of the legislature to submit each proposed amendment or amendments to the people for approval in such manner and at such times as the legislature shall prescribe; and if the people shall approve and ratify such amendment or amendments by a majority of the electors voting thereon, such amendment or amendments shall become a part of the constitution on the first day of January next after such approval. Neither the failure of the attorney-general to render an opinion concerning such a proposed amendment nor his or her failure to do so timely shall affect the validity of such proposed amendment or legislative action thereon. (Formerly §1 of Art. 14. Renumbered and amended by Constitutional Convention of 1938 and approved by vote of the people November 8, 1938; further amended by vote of the people November 4, 1941; November 7, 2001.)

[Future constitutional conventions; how called; election of delegates; compensation; quorum; submission of amendments; officers; employees; rules; vacancies]

§2. At the general election to be held in the year nineteen hundred fifty-seven, and every twentieth year thereafter, and also at such times as the legislature may by law provide, the question "Shall there be a convention to revise the constitution and amend the same?" shall be submitted to and decided by the electors of the state; and in case a majority of the electors voting thereon shall decide in favor of a convention for such purpose, the electors of every senate district of the state, as then organized, shall elect three delegates at the next ensuing general election, and the electors of the state voting at the same election shall elect fifteen delegates-at-large. The delegates so elected shall convene at the capitol on the first Tuesday of April next ensuing after their election, and shall continue their session until the business of such convention shall have been completed. Every delegate shall receive for his or her services the same compensation as shall then be annually payable to the members of the assembly and be reimbursed for actual traveling expenses, while the convention is in session, to the extent that a member of the assembly would then be entitled thereto in the case of a session of the legislature. A majority of the convention shall constitute a quorum for the transaction of business, and no amendment to the constitution shall be submitted for approval to the electors as hereinafter provided, unless by the assent of a majority of all the delegates elected to the convention, the ayes and noes being entered on the journal to be kept. The convention shall have the power to appoint such officers, employees and assistants as it may deem necessary, and fix their compensation and to provide for the printing of its documents, journal, proceedings and other expenses of said convention. The convention shall determine the rules of its own proceedings, choose its own officers, and be the judge of the election, returns and qualifications of its members. In case of a vacancy, by death, resignation or other cause, of any district

(continued next page)

delegate elected to the convention, such vacancy shall be filled by a vote of the remaining delegates representing the district in which such vacancy occurs. If such vacancy occurs in the office of a delegate-at-large, such vacancy shall be filled by a vote of the remaining delegates-at-large. Any proposed constitution or constitutional amendment which shall have been adopted by such convention, shall be submitted to a vote of the electors of the state at the time and in the manner provided by such convention, at an election which shall be held not less than six weeks after the adjournment of such convention. Upon the approval of such constitution or constitutional amendments, in the manner provided in the last preceding section, such constitution or constitutional amendment, shall go into effect on the first day of January next after such approval. (Formerly §2 of Art. 14. Renumbered and amended by Constitutional Convention of 1938 and approved by vote of the people November 8, 1938; further amended by vote of the people November 7, 2001.)

[Amendments simultaneously submitted by convention and legislature]
§3. Any amendment proposed by a constitutional convention relating to the same subject as an amendment proposed by the legislature, coincidently submitted to the people for approval shall, if approved, be deemed to supersede the amendment so proposed by the legislature. (Formerly §3 of Art. 14. Renumbered and amended by Constitutional Convention of 1938 and approved by vote of the people November 8, 1938.)

ARTICLE XX

WHEN TO TAKE EFFECT

[Time of taking effect]
Section 1. This constitution shall be in force from and including the first day of January, one thousand nine hundred thirty-nine, except as herein otherwise provided. (Formerly §1 of Art. 15. Renumbered and amended by Constitutional Convention of 1938 and approved by vote of the people November 8, 1938.)

DONE *in Convention at the Capitol in the city of Albany, the twenty-fifth day of August, in the year one thousand nine hundred thirty- eight, and of the Independence of the United States of America the one hundred and sixty-third.*

IN WITNESS WHEREOF, we have hereunto subscribed our names.

FREDERICK E. CRANE,
President and Delegate-at-Large
U.H. Boyden, *Secretary*

Historic Documents

Magna Carta

England's King John angered many people with high taxes. In 1215 a group of English nobles joined the archbishop of Canterbury to force the king to agree to sign Magna Carta. This document stated that the king was subject to the rule of law, just as other citizens of England were. It also presented the ideas of a fair and speedy trial and due process of law. These principles are still a part of the U.S. Bill of Rights.

1. In the first place have granted to God, and by this our present charter confirmed for us and our heirs for ever that the English church shall be free, and shall have its rights undiminished and its liberties unimpaired . . . We have also granted to all free men of our kingdom, for ourselves and our heirs for ever, all the liberties written below, to be had and held by them and their heirs of us and our heirs.

2. If any of our earls or barons or others holding of us in chief by knight service dies, and at his death his heir be of full age and owe relief he shall have his inheritance on payment of the old relief, namely the heir or heirs of an earl 100 for a whole earl's barony, the heir or heirs of a baron 100 for a whole barony, the heir or heirs of a knight 100s, at most, for a whole knight's fee; and he who owes less shall give less according to the ancient usage of fiefs.

3. If, however, the heir of any such be under age and a ward, he shall have his inheritance when he comes of age without paying relief and without making fine.

40. To no one will we sell, to no one will we refuse or delay right or justice.

41. All merchants shall be able to go out of and come into England safely and securely and stay and travel throughout England, as well by land as by water, for buying and selling by the ancient and right customs free from all evil tolls, except in time of war and if they are of the land that is at war with us . . .

42. It shall be lawful in future for anyone, without prejudicing the allegiance due to us, to leave our kingdom and return safely and securely by land and water, save, in the public interest, for a short period in time of war—except for those imprisoned or outlawed in accordance with the law of the kingdom and natives of a land that is at war with us and merchants (who shall be treated as aforesaid).

62. And we have fully remitted and pardoned to everyone all the ill–will, indignation and rancour that have arisen between us and our men, clergy and laity, from the time of the quarrel. Furthermore, we have fully remitted to all, clergy and laity, and as far as pertains to us have completely forgiven, all trespasses occasioned by the same quarrel between Easter in the sixteenth year of our reign and the restoration of peace. And, besides, we have caused to be made for them letters testimonial patent of the lord Stephen archbishop of Canterbury, of the lord Henry archbishop of Dublin and of the aforementioned bishops and of master Pandulf about this security and the aforementioned concessions.

63. An oath, moreover, has been taken, as well on our part as on the part of the barons, that all these things aforesaid shall be observed in good faith and without evil disposition. Witness the above–mentioned and many others. Given by our hand in the meadow which is called Runnymede between Windsor and Staines on the fifteenth day of June, in the seventeenth year of our reign.

From "English Bill of Rights." Britannica Online. Vers. 99.1. 1994–1999. Copyright © 1994–1999 Encyclopaedia Britannica, Inc.

The Mayflower Compact

In November 1620, the Pilgrim leaders aboard the Mayflower *drafted the Mayflower Compact. This was the first document in the English colonies to establish guidelines for self-government. This excerpt from the Mayflower Compact describes the principles of the Pilgrim colony's government.*

The Mayflower Compact

  We whose names are underwritten, the loyal subjects of our dread Sovereign Lord King James, by the Grace of God of Great Britain, France and Ireland, King, Defender of the Faith, etc.

  Having undertaken, for the Glory of God and advancement of the Christian Faith and Honour of our King and Country, a Voyage to plant the First Colony in the Northern Parts of Virginia, do by these presents solemnly and mutually in the presence of God and one of another, Covenant and Combine ourselves together into a Civil Body Politic, for our better ordering and preservation and furtherance of the ends aforesaid; and by virtue hereof to enact, constitute and frame such just and equal Laws, Ordinances, Acts, Constitutions and Offices, from time to time, as shall be thought most meet and convenient for the general good of the Colony, unto which we promise all due submission and obedience. In witness whereof we have hereunder subscribed our names at Cape Cod, the 11th of November, in the year of the reign of our Sovereign Lord King James, of England, France and Ireland the eighteenth, and of Scotland the fifty-fourth. Anno Domini 1620.

From William Bradford, *Of Plymouth Plantation, 1620–1647* (Samuel Eliot Morison, ed., 1952), 75–76.

Fundamental Orders of Connecticut

In January 1639, settlers in Connecticut led by Thomas Hooker drew up the Fundamental Orders of Connecticut—America's first written constitution. It is essentially a compact among the settlers and a body of laws.

Forasmuch as it hath pleased the All-mighty God by the wise disposition of his divyne pruvidence so to Order and dispose of things that we the Inhabitants and Residents of Windsor, Harteford and Wethersfield are now cohabiting and dwelling in and uppon the River of Conectecotte and the Lands thereunto adioyneing; As also in our Civell Affaires to be guided and governed according to such Lawes, Rules, Orders and decrees as shall be made, ordered & decreed, as followeth:—

1. It is Ordered . . . that there shall be yerely two generall Assemblies or Courts, the one the second thursday in Aprill, the other the second thursday in September, following; the first shall be called the Courte of Election, wherein shall be yerely Chosen . . . soe many Magestrats and other publike Officers as shall be found requisitte: which choise shall be made by all that are admitted freemen and have taken the Oath of Fidelity, and doe cohabitte within this Jurisdiction, (having beene admitted Inhabitants by the major part of the Towne wherein they live,) or the major parte of such as shall be then present . . .

From F. N. Thorpe, ed., *Federal and State Constitutions,* vol. 1 (1909), 519.

The English Bill of Rights

In 1689, after the Glorious Revolution, Parliament passed the English Bill of Rights, which ensured that Parliament would have supreme power over the monarchy. The bill also protected the rights of English citizens.

Whereas the late King James the Second, by the assistance of divers evil counsellors, judges and ministers employed by him, did endeavour to subvert and extirpate the Protestant religion and the laws and liberties of this kingdom;

By assuming and exercising a power of dispensing with and suspending of laws and the execution of laws without consent of Parliament;

By committing and prosecuting divers worthy prelates for humbly petitioning to be excused from concurring to the said assumed power;

By issuing and causing to be executed a commission under the great seal for erecting a court called the Court of Commissioners for Ecclesiastical Causes;

By levying money for and to the use of the Crown by pretence of prerogative for other time and in other manner than the same was granted by Parliament;

By raising and keeping a standing army within this kingdom in time of peace without consent of Parliament, and quartering soldiers contrary to law; . . .

By violating the freedom of election of members to serve in Parliament;

By prosecutions in the Court of King's Bench for matters and causes cognizable only in Parliament, and by divers other arbitrary and illegal courses;

And whereas of late years partial corrupt and unqualified persons have been returned and served on juries in trials, and particularly divers jurors in trials for high treason which were not freeholders;

And excessive bail hath been required of persons committed in criminal cases to elude the benefit of the laws made for the liberty of the subjects;

And excessive fines have been imposed;

And illegal and cruel punishments inflicted;

And several grants and promises made of fines and forfeitures before any conviction or judgment against the persons upon whom the same were to be levied;

All which are utterly and directly contrary to the known laws and statutes and freedom of this realm; ...

That the pretended power of suspending of laws or the execution of laws by regal authority without consent of Parliament is illegal;

That the pretended power of dispensing with laws or the execution of laws by regal authority, as it hath been assumed and exercised of late, is illegal;

That the commission for erecting the late Court of Commissioners for Ecclesiastical Causes, and all other commissions and courts of like nature, are illegal and pernicious;

That levying money for or to the use of the Crown by pretence of prerogative, without grant of Parliament, for longer time, or in other manner than the same is or shall be granted, is illegal;

That it is the right of the subjects to petition the king, and all commitments and prosecutions for such petitioning are illegal;

That the raising or keeping a standing army within the kingdom in time of peace, unless it be with consent of Parliament, is against law;

That the subjects which are Protestants may have arms for their defence suitable to their conditions and as allowed by law;

That election of members of Parliament ought to be free;

That the freedom of speech and debates or proceedings in Parliament ought not to be impeached or questioned in any court or place out of Parliament;

(continued next page)

That excessive bail ought not to be required, nor excessive fines imposed, nor cruel and unusual punishments inflicted;

That jurors ought to be duly impanelled and returned, and jurors which pass upon men in trials for high treason ought to be freeholders;

That all grants and promises of fines and forfeitures of particular persons before conviction are illegal and void;

And that for redress of all grievances, and for the amending, strengthening and preserving of the laws, Parliaments ought to be held frequently.

From "English Bill of Rights." Britannica Online. Vers. 99.1. 1994–1999. Copyright © 1994–1999 Encyclopaedia Britannica, Inc.

Articles of Confederation

After winning the Revolutionary War in 1777, the newly formed United States of America created a government under the Articles of Confederation. This government allowed the states to have more power than the central government, a situation that would lead to problems later.

Articles of Confederation and perpetual Union between the states of New Hampshire, Massachusetts-bay Rhode Island and Providence Plantations, Connecticut, New York, New Jersey, Pennsylvania, Delaware, Maryland, Virginia, North Carolina, South Carolina and Georgia.

I.
The Stile of this Confederacy shall be
"The United States of America".

II.
Each state retains its sovereignty, freedom, and independence, and every power, jurisdiction, and right, which is not by this Confederation expressly delegated to the United States, in Congress assembled.

III.
The said States hereby severally enter into a firm league of friendship with each other, for their common defense, the security of their liberties, and their mutual and general welfare, binding themselves to assist each other, against all force offered to, or attacks made upon them, or any of them, on account of religion, sovereignty, trade, or any other pretense whatever.

VI.
No State, without the consent of the United States in Congress assembled, shall send any embassy to, or receive any embassy from, or enter into any conference, agreement, alliance or treaty with any King, Prince or State; nor shall any person holding any office of profit or trust under the United States, or any of them, accept any present, emolument, office or title of any kind whatever from any King, Prince or foreign State; nor shall the United States in Congress assembled, or any of them, grant any title of nobility.

VIII.
All charges of war, and all other expenses that shall be incurred for the common defense or general welfare, and allowed by the United States in Congress assembled, shall be defrayed out of a common treasury, which shall be supplied by the several States in proportion to the value of all land within each State, granted or surveyed for any person, as such land and the buildings and improvements thereon shall be estimated according to such mode as the United States in Congress assembled, shall from time to time direct and appoint.

The taxes for paying that proportion shall be laid and levied by the authority and direction of the legislatures of the several States within the time agreed upon by the United States in Congress assembled.

Federalist Paper No. 51

In 1788 the newly written Constitution faced opponents who believed it gave too much power to the federal government. James Madison, Alexander Hamilton, and John Jay wrote, anonymously, a collection of essays that became known as the Federalist Papers. The following essay, written by James Madison, outlines reasons why the division of power written into the Constitution would keep the government from harming citizens.

In order to lay a due foundation for that separate and distinct exercise of the different powers of government, which to a certain extent is admitted on all hands to be essential to the preservation of liberty, it is evident that each department should have a will of its own; and consequently should be so constituted that the members of each should have as little agency as possible in the appointment of the members of the others. Were this principle rigorously adhered to, it would require that all the appointments for the supreme executive, legislative, and judiciary magistracies should be drawn from the same fountain of authority, the people, through channels having no communication whatever with one another. Perhaps such a plan of constructing the several departments would be less difficult in practice than it may in contemplation appear. Some difficulties, however, and some additional expense would attend the execution of it. Some deviations, therefore, from the principle must be admitted. In the constitution of the judiciary department in particular, it might be inexpedient to insist rigorously on the principle: first, because peculiar qualifications being essential in the members, the primary consideration ought to be to select that mode of choice which best secures these qualifications; secondly, because the permanent tenure by which the appointments are held in that department, must soon destroy all sense of dependence on the authority conferring them.

Washington's Farewell Address

In 1796 at the end of his second term as president, George Washington wrote his farewell address with the help of Alexander Hamilton and James Madison. In it he spoke of the dangers facing the young nation. He warned against the dangers of political parties and sectionalism, and he advised the nation against permanent alliances with other nations.

In contemplating the causes, which may disturb our Union, it occurs as matter of serious concern, that any ground should have been furnished for characterizing parties by geographical discriminations-Northern and Southern-Atlantic and Western . . .

No alliances, however strict, between the parts can be an adequate substitute; they must inevitably experience the infractions and interruptions which all alliances in all times have experienced . . .

The great rule of conduct for us, in regard to foreign nations, is, in extending our commercial relations, to have with them as little political connexion as possible. So far as we have already formed engagements, let them be fulfilled with perfect good faith. Here let us stop.

From *Annals of Congress,* 4th Congress, pp. 2869–2880. American Memory. Library of Congress. 1999.

Monroe Doctrine

In 1823 President James Monroe proclaimed the Monroe Doctrine. Designed to end European influence in the Western Hemisphere, it became a cornerstone of U.S. foreign policy.

With the existing colonies or dependencies of any European power we have not interfered and shall not interfere. But with the governments who have declared their independence and maintained it, and whose independence we have, on great consideration and on just principles, acknowledged, we could not view any interposition for the purpose of oppressing them, or controlling in any other manner their destiny, by any European power in any other light than as the manifestation of an unfriendly disposition toward the United States. . . .

Our policy in regard to Europe, which was adopted at an early stage of the wars which have so long agitated that quarter of the globe, nevertheless remains the same, which is not to interfere in the internal concerns of any of its powers; to consider the government de facto as the legitimate government for us; to cultivate friendly relations with it, and to preserve those relations by a frank, firm, and manly policy, meeting in all instances the just claims of every power, submitting to injuries from none.

From "The Monroe Doctrine" by James Monroe. Reprinted in *The Annals of America: Volume 5, 1821–1832.* Copyright © 1976 by Encyclopaedia Britannica.

Seneca Falls Declaration of Sentiments

One of the first documents to express the desire for equal rights for women is the Declaration of Sentiments, issued in 1848 at the Seneca Falls Convention in Seneca Falls, New York. Led by Elizabeth Cady Stanton and Lucretia Mott, the delegates adopted a set of resolutions modeled on the Declaration of Independence.

When, in the course of human events, it becomes necessary for one portion of the family of man to assume among the people of the earth a position different from that which they have hitherto occupied, but one to which the laws of nature and of nature's God entitle them, a decent respect to the opinions of mankind requires that they should declare the causes that impel them to such a course.

We hold these truths to be self–evident: that all men and women are created equal; that they are endowed by their Creator with certain inalienable rights; that among these are life, liberty, and the pursuit of happiness; that to secure these rights governments are instituted, deriving their just powers from the consent of the governed. Whenever any form of government becomes destructive of these ends, it is the right of those who suffer from it to refuse allegiance to it, and to insist upon the institution of a new government, laying its foundation on such principles, and organizing its powers in such form, as to them shall seem most likely to effect their safety and happiness.

From "Seneca Falls Declaration on Women's Rights." Reprinted in *The Annals of America: Volume 7, 1841–1849.* Copyright © 1976 by Encyclopaedia Britannica.

The Emancipation Proclamation

When the Union army won the Battle of Antietam, President Abraham Lincoln decided to issue the Emancipation Proclamation, which freed all enslaved people in states under Confederate control. The proclamation, which went into effect on January 1, 1863, was a step toward the Thirteenth Amendment (1865), which ended slavery in all of the United States.

That on the 1st day of January, in the year of our Lord 1863, all persons held as slaves within any state or designated part of a state, the people whereof shall then be in rebellion against the United States, shall be then, thenceforward, and forever free; and the executive government of the United States, including the military and naval authority thereof, will recognize and maintain the freedom of such persons and will do no act or acts to repress such persons, or any of them, in any efforts they may make for their actual freedom. . . .

And I further declare and make known that such persons of suitable condition will be received into the armed service of the United States to garrison forts, positions, stations, and other places, and to man vessels of all sorts in said service.

And upon this act, sincerely believed to be an act of justice, warranted by the Constitution upon military necessity, I invoke the considerate judgment of mankind and the gracious favor of Almighty God.

From "Emancipation Proclamation" by Abraham Lincoln. Reprinted in *The Annals of America: Volume 9, 1858–1865*. Copyright © 1976 by Encyclopaedia Britannica, Inc.

Lincoln's Gettysburg Address

On November 19, 1863, Abraham Lincoln addressed a crowd gathered to dedicate a cemetery at the Gettysburg battlefield. His short speech, which is excerpted below, reminded Americans of the ideals on which the Republic was founded.

FOUR SCORE AND SEVEN YEARS ago our fathers brought forth on this continent a new nation, conceived in liberty and dedicated to the proposition that all men are created equal.

Now we are engaged in a great civil war, testing whether that nation or any nation so conceived and so dedicated can long endure. We are met on a great battlefield of that war. We have come to dedicate a portion of that field as a final resting–place for those who here gave their lives that that nation might live. It is altogether fitting and proper that we should do this.

But in a larger sense, we cannot dedicate—we cannot consecrate—we cannot hallow—this ground. The brave men, living and dead, who struggled here have consecrated it far above our poor power to add or detract. The world will little note nor long remember what we say here, but it can never forget what they did here. It is for us, the living, rather, to be dedicated here to the unfinished work which they who fought here have thus far so nobly advanced.

It is rather for us to be here dedicated to the great task remaining before us—that from these honored dead we take increased devotion to that cause for which they gave the last full measure of devotion; that we here highly resolve that these dead shall not have died in vain; that this nation, under God, shall have a new birth of freedom; and that government of the people, by the people, for the people shall not perish from the earth.

From "The Gettysburg Address" by Abraham Lincoln. Reprinted in *The Annals of America: Volume 9, 1858–1865*. Copyright © 1976 by Encyclopaedia Britannica, Inc.

"I Will Fight No More Forever"

In 1877 Chief Joseph and his group of Nez Percé surrendered to General Oliver Otis Howard. With this surrender, the Nez Percé were removed from their native lands in Idaho to a reservation in Oklahoma.

Tell General Howard I know his heart. What he told me before I have in my heart. I am tired of fighting. Our chiefs are killed. Looking Glass is dead. Toohoolhoolzote is dead. The old men are all killed. It is the young men who say yes or no. He who led the young men is dead. It is cold and we have no blankets. The little children are freezing to death. My people, some of them, have run away to the hills, and have no blankets, no food; no one knows where they are -- perhaps freezing to death. I want time to look for my children and see how many of them I can find. Maybe I shall find them among the dead. Hear me, my chiefs. I am tired; my heart is sick and sad. From where the sun now stands, I will fight no more forever.

Wilson's Fourteen Points

Even before the end of World War I, President Woodrow Wilson announced a 14-point plan to help maintain peace throughout Europe and the world. The goal of his plan was to provide "peace without victory."

Gentlemen of the Congress:

It will be our wish and purpose that the processes of peace, when they are begun, shall be absolutely open and that they shall involve and permit henceforth no secret understandings of any kind. The day of conquest and aggrandizement is gone by; so is also the day of secret covenants entered into in the interest of particular governments and likely at some unlooked-for moment to upset the peace of the world. It is this happy fact, now clear to the view of every public man whose thoughts do not still linger in an age that is dead and gone, which makes it possible for every nation whose purposes are consistent with justice and the peace of the world to avow now or at any other time the objects it has in view.

We entered this war because violations of right had occurred which touched us to the quick and made the life of our own people impossible unless they were corrected and the world secured once for all against their recurrence. What we demand in this war, therefore, is nothing peculiar to ourselves. It is that the world be made fit and safe to live in; and particularly that it be made safe for every peace-loving nation which, like our own, wishes to live its own life, determine its own institutions, be assured of justice and fair dealing by the other peoples of the world as against force and selfish aggression. All the peoples of the world are in effect partners in this interest, and for our own part we see very clearly that unless justice be done to others it will not be done to us. The program of the world's peace, therefore, is our program; and that program, the only possible program, as we see it, is this:

I. Open covenants of peace, openly arrived at, after which there shall be no private international understandings of any kind but diplomacy shall proceed always frankly and in the public view.

II. Absolute freedom of navigation upon the seas, outside territorial waters, alike in peace and in war, except as the seas may be closed in whole or in part by international action for the enforcement of international covenants.

III. The removal, so far as possible, of all economic barriers and the establishment of an equality of trade conditions among all the nations consenting to the peace and associating themselves for its maintenance.

(continued next page)

IV. Adequate guarantees given and taken that national armaments will be reduced to the lowest point consistent with domestic safety.

V. A free, open-minded, and absolutely impartial adjustment of all colonial claims, based upon a strict observance of the principle that in determining all such questions of sovereignty the interests of the populations concerned must have equal weight with the equitable claims of the government whose title is to be determined.

VI. The evacuation of all Russian territory and such a settlement of all questions affecting Russia as will secure the best and freest cooperation of the other nations of the world in obtaining for her an unhampered and unembarrassed opportunity for the independent determination of her own political development and national policy and assure her of a sincere welcome into the society of free nations under institutions of her won choosing; and, more than a welcome, assistance also of every kind that she may need and may herself desire. The treatment accorded Russia by her sister nations in the months to come will be the acid test of their good will, of their comprehension of her needs as distinguished from their own interests, and of their intelligent and unselfish sympathy.

VII. Belgium, the whole world will agree, must be evacuated and restored, without any attempt to limit the sovereignty which she enjoys in common with all other free nations. No other single act will serve as this will serve to restore confidence among the nations in the laws which they have themselves set and determined for the government of their relations with one another. Without this healing act the whole structure and validity of international law is forever impaired.

VIII. All French territory should be freed and the invaded portions restored, and the wrong done to France by Prussia in 1871 in the matter of Alsace-Lorraine, which has unsettled the peace of the world for nearly fifty years, should be righted, in order that peace may once more be made secure in the interest of all.

IX. A readjustment of the frontiers of Italy should be effected along clearly recognizable lines of nationality.

X. The peoples of Austria-Hungary, whose place among the nations we wish to see safeguarded and assured, should be accorded the freest opportunity of autonomous development.

XI. Rumania, Serbia and Montenegro should be evacuated; occupied territories restored; Serbia accorded free and secure access to the sea; and the relations of the several Balkan states to one another determined by friendly counsel along historically established lines of allegiance and nationality; and international guarantees of the political and economic independence and territorial integrity of the several Balkan states should be entered into.

XII. The Turkish portions of the present Ottoman Empire should be assured a secure sovereignty, but the other nationalities which are now under Turkish rule should be assured an undoubted security of life and an absolutely unmolested opportunity of autonomous development, and the Dardanelles should be permanently opened as a free passage to the ships and commerce of all nations under international guarantees.

XIII. An independent Polish state should be erected which should include the territories inhabited by indisputably Polish populations, which should be assured a free and secure access to the sea, and whose political and economic independence and territorial integrity should be guaranteed by international covenant.

XIV. A general association of nations must be formed under specific covenants for the purpose of affording mutual guarantees of political independence and territorial integrity to great and small states alike.

In regard to these essential rectifications of wrong and assertions of right we feel ourselves to be intimate partners of all the governments and peoples associated together against the Imperialists. We cannot be separated in interest or divided in purpose. We stand together until the end.

Brown v. Board of Education

In 1954 a collection of cases came before the Supreme Court under the name Brown v. Board of Education. *These cases challenged segregation in public schools based on the equal protection clause of the Fourteenth Amendment. Chief Justice Earl Warren wrote the majority opinion, which reversed the earlier decision in* Plessy v. Ferguson *that instituted the "separate but equal" doctrine."*

In the instant cases, that question is directly presented. Here, unlike Sweatt v. Painter, there are findings below that the Negro and white schools involved have been equalized, or are being equalized, with respect to buildings, curricula, qualifications and salaries of teachers, and other "tangible" factors. Our decision, therefore, cannot turn on merely a comparison of these tangible factors in the Negro and white schools involved in each of the cases. We must look instead to the effect of segregation itself on public education.

In approaching this problem, we cannot turn the clock back to 1868 when the Amendment was adopted, or even to 1896 when Plessy v. Ferguson was written. We must consider public education in the light of its full development and its present place in American life throughout the Nation. Only in this way can it be determined if segregation in public schools deprives these plaintiffs of the equal protection of the laws.

Today, education is perhaps the most important function of state and local governments. Compulsory school attendance laws and the great expenditures for education both demonstrate our recognition of the importance of education to our democratic society. It is required in the performance of our most basic public responsibilities, even service in the armed forces. It is the very foundation of good citizenship. Today it is a principal instrument in awakening the child to cultural values, in preparing him for later professional training, and in helping him to adjust normally to his environment. In these days, it is doubtful that any child may reasonably be expected to succeed in life if he is denied the opportunity of an education. Such an opportunity, where the state has undertaken to provide it, is a right which must be made available to all on equal terms.

We come then to the question presented: Does segregation of children in public schools solely on the basis of race, even though the physical facilities and other "tangible" factors may be equal, deprive the children of the minority group of equal educational opportunities? We believe that it does.

We conclude that in the field of public education the doctrine of "separate but equal" has no place. Separate educational facilities are inherently unequal. Therefore, we hold that the plaintiffs and others similarly situated for whom the actions have been brought are, by reason of the segregation complained of, deprived of the equal protection of the laws guaranteed by the Fourteenth Amendment.

John F. Kennedy's Inaugural Address

John F. Kennedy became president in 1961, during the middle of the Cold War. In his inaugural address, he spoke to citizens of the United States and the world, asking for peace to be restored for the good of humanity.

[W]e observe today not a victory of party, but a celebration of freedom—symbolizing an end, as well as a beginning—signifying renewal, as well as change. For I have sworn before you and Almighty God the same solemn oath our forebears prescribed nearly a century and three quarters ago.

The world is very different now. For man holds in his mortal hands the power to abolish all forms of human poverty and all forms of human life. And yet the same revolutionary beliefs for which our forebears fought are still at issue around the globe—the belief that the rights of man come not from the generosity of the state, but from the hand of God.

We dare not forget today that we are the heirs of that first revolution. Let the word go forth from this time and place, to friend and foe alike, that the torch has been passed to a new generation of Americans—born in this century, tempered by war, disciplined by a hard and bitter peace, proud of our ancient heritage—and unwilling to witness or permit the slow undoing of those human rights to which this Nation has always been committed, and to which we are committed today at home and around the world.

Let every nation know, whether it wishes us well or ill, that we shall pay any price, bear any burden, meet any hardship, support any friend, oppose any foe, in order to assure the survival and the success of liberty.

This much we pledge—and more.

So let us begin anew—remembering on both sides that civility is not a sign of weakness, and sincerity is always subject to proof. Let us never negotiate out of fear. But let us never fear to negotiate.

Let both sides explore what problems unite us instead of belaboring those problems which divide us.

Let both sides, for the first time, formulate serious and precise proposals for the inspection and control of arms—and bring the absolute power to destroy other nations under the absolute control of all nations.

Let both sides seek to invoke the wonders of science instead of its terrors. Together let us explore the stars, conquer the deserts, eradicate disease, tap the ocean depths, and encourage the arts and commerce.

Let both sides unite to heed in all corners of the earth the command of Isaiah—to "undo the heavy burdens ... and to let the oppressed go free."

And so, my fellow Americans: ask not what your country can do for you—ask what you can do for your country.

My fellow citizens of the world: ask not what America will do for you, but what together we can do for the freedom of man.

"I Have a Dream"

In 1963 civil rights leaders organized a march on Washington, D.C., that brought attention to the difference between the ideals of the United States and the reality faced by millions of African American citizens. Martin Luther King, Jr. gave the following speech in front of the more than 200,000 demonstrators at the Lincoln Memorial.

I say to you today, my friends, that in spite of the difficulties and frustrations of the moment, I still have a dream. It is a dream deeply rooted in the American dream.

I have a dream that one day this nation will rise up and live out the true meaning of its creed: "We hold these truths to be self-evident; that all men are created equal."

I have a dream that one day on the red hills of Georgia the sons of former slaves and the sons of former slaveowners will be able to sit down together at a table of brotherhood.

I have a dream that one day even the state of Mississippi, a desert state sweltering with the heat of injustice and oppression, will be transformed into an oasis of freedom and justice.

I have a dream that my four children will one day live in a nation where they will not be judged by the color of their skin but by the content of their character.

I have a dream today.

I have a dream that one day the state of Alabama, whose governor's lips are presently dripping with the words of interposition and nullification, will be transformed into a situation where little black boys and black girls will be able to join hands with little white boys and white girls and walk together as sisters and brothers.

I have a dream today.

I have a dream that one day every valley shall be exalted, every hill and mountain shall be made low, the rough places will be made plain, and the crooked places will be made straight, and the glory of the Lord shall be revealed, and all flesh shall see it together.

This is our hope. This is the faith with which I return to the South. With this faith we will be able to hew out of the mountain of despair a stone of hope. With this faith we will be able to transform the jangling discords of our nation into a beautiful symphony of brotherhood.

With this faith we will be able to work together, to pray together, to struggle together, to go to jail together, to stand up for freedom together, knowing that we will be free one day.

This will be the day when all of God's children will be able to sing with a new meaning, "My country, 'tis of thee, sweet land of liberty, of thee I sing. Land where my fathers died, land of the Pilgrim's pride, from every mountainside, let freedom ring."

Let freedom ring from every hill and every molehill of Mississippi. From every mountainside, let freedom ring.

When we let freedom ring, when we let it ring from every village and every hamlet, from every state and every city, we will be able to speed up that day when all of God's children, black men and white men, Jews and Gentiles, Protestants and Catholics, will be able to join hands and sing in the words of the old Negro spiritual, "Free at last! Free at last! Thank God Almighty, we are free at last!"

President Bush's Address to the Nation

On September 11, 2001, terrorists hijacked four passenger planes and used them to attack sites in the United States, including the World Trade Center in New York City. President George W. Bush addressed the country's citizens that evening.

Good evening. Today, our fellow citizens, our way of life, our very freedom came under attack in a series of deliberate and deadly terrorist acts. The victims were in airplanes, or in their offices; secretaries, businessmen and women, military and federal workers; moms and dads, friends and neighbors. Thousands of lives were suddenly ended by evil, despicable acts of terror.

The pictures of airplanes flying into buildings, fires burning, huge structures collapsing, have filled us with disbelief, terrible sadness, and a quiet, unyielding anger. These acts of mass murder were intended to frighten our nation into chaos and retreat. But they have failed; our country is strong.

A great people has been moved to defend a great nation. Terrorist attacks can shake the foundations of our biggest buildings, but they cannot touch the foundation of America. These acts shattered steel, but they cannot dent the steel of American resolve.

America was targeted for attack because we're the brightest beacon for freedom and opportunity in the world. And no one will keep that light from shining.

Today, our nation saw evil, the very worst of human nature. And we responded with the best of America—with the daring of our rescue workers, with the caring for strangers and neighbors who came to give blood and help in any way they could.

Immediately following the first attack, I implemented our government's emergency response plans. Our military is powerful, and it's prepared. Our emergency teams are working in New York City and Washington, D.C. to help with local rescue efforts.

Our first priority is to get help to those who have been injured, and to take every precaution to protect our citizens at home and around the world from further attacks.

The functions of our government continue without interruption. Federal agencies in Washington which had to be evacuated today are reopening for essential personnel tonight, and will be open for business tomorrow. Our financial institutions remain strong, and the American economy will be open for business, as well.

The search is underway for those who are behind these evil acts. I've directed the full resources of our intelligence and law enforcement communities to find those responsible and to bring them to justice. We will make no distinction between the terrorists who committed these acts and those who harbor them.

I appreciate so very much the members of Congress who have joined me in strongly condemning these attacks. And on behalf of the American people, I thank the many world leaders who have called to offer their condolences and assistance.

America and our friends and allies join with all those who want peace and security in the world, and we stand together to win the war against terrorism. Tonight, I ask for your prayers for all those who grieve, for the children whose worlds have been shattered, for all whose sense of safety and security has been threatened. And I pray they will be comforted by a power greater than any of us, spoken through the ages in Psalm 23: "Even though I walk through the valley of the shadow of death, I fear no evil, for You are with me."

This is a day when all Americans from every walk of life unite in our resolve for justice and peace. America has stood down enemies before, and we will do so this time. None of us will ever forget this day. Yet, we go forward to defend freedom and all that is good and just in our world.

Thank you. Good night, and God bless America.

Biographical Dictionary

A

Addams, Jane (1860–1935) American social worker and activist, she was the co–founder of Hull House, an organization that focused on the needs of immigrants. She helped found the American Civil Liberties Union and won the Nobel Peace Prize in 1931. (p. 68)

Aguinaldo (ahg-ee-NAHL-doh), Emilio (1869–1964) Filipino leader and commander of forces in rebellion against Spain, he led an insurrection against the authority of the United States. (p. 119)

Albright, Madeleine (1937–) First woman to serve as secretary of state, she was appointed by Bill Clinton and sworn into office in 1997. (p. 373)

Aldrin, Edwin "Buzz" (1930–) Copiloted the first lunar landing mission, he was the second man to walk on the moon. (p. 318)

Armstrong, Neil (1930–) Commander of the first lunar landing mission, he was also the first person to step on the surface of the moon. (p. 318)

B

Bell, Alexander Graham (1847–1922) American inventor and educator, his interest in electrical and mechanical devices to aid the hearing–impaired led to the development and patent of the telephone. (p. 37)

Bethune, Mary McLeod (1875–1955) An African American educator and leader who rose to national prominence during the presidency of Franklin Roosevelt, who appointed her director of the National Youth Administration's Division of Negro Affairs. (p. 212)

Bidwell, Annie (1839–1918) American pioneer activist, she worked for social and moral causes and for women's suffrage. (p. 22)

bin Laden, Osama (1957–) A Saudi millionaire and leader of al–Qaeda, the terrorist organization that claimed responsibility for the September 11 attacks on the United States. (p. 376)

Bryan, William Jennings (1860–1925) American lawyer and Populist politician, he favored free silver coinage, an economic policy expected to help farmers. He was a Democratic nominee for president in 1896 and was defeated by William McKinley. (p. 24)

Bush, George H. W. (1924–) The 41st president of the United States, also served as vice president to Ronald Reagan. He led the nation through the Persian Gulf War. (p. 370)

Bush, George W. (1946–) The 43rd president of the United States and son of George H. W. Bush, he was president during the September 11, 2001 terrorist attacks. (p. 374)

C

Carnegie, Andrew (1835–1919) American industrialist and humanitarian, he focused his attention on steelmaking and made a fortune through his vertical integration method. (p. 40)

Carson, Rachel (1907–1964) Author of *Silent Spring* and one of the founders of the modern environmental conservation movement. (p. 353)

Carter, Jimmy (1924–) The 39th president of the United States, his presidency saw a dramatic energy crisis. (p. 354)

Castro, Fidel (1926–) Communist leader of Cuba, came to power through a revolution in 1959. (p. 315)

Chavez, Cesar (1927–1993) Social activist and founder of the United Farm Workers, a leader in the movement for Hispanic Americans' civil rights. (p. 302)

BIOGRAPHICAL DICTIONARY

Chisholm, Shirley (1924–2005) First African American woman to be elected to Congress, as a Representative from New York. (p. 303)

Churchill, Winston (1874–1965) The prime minister of Britain during much of World War II, he is well–remembered for many speeches made in support of the Allies. (p. 226)

Clinton, Bill (1946–) The 42nd president of the United States, he became the second president impeached by the House of Representatives but found not guilty of the charges. (p. 372)

Coolidge, Calvin (1872–1933) The 30th president of the United States, his presidency helped restore faith in government leaders after the scandals of the Harding administration. (p. 172)

Crazy Horse (1842?–1877) Native American chief of Oglala Sioux, he took part in the Battle of the Little Bighorn, in which General Custer was surrounded and killed. He was killed after surrendering and resisting imprisonment. (p. 15)

Custer, George Armstrong (1839–1876) American army officer in the Civil War, he became a Native American fighter in the West and was killed with his troops in the Battle of the Little Bighorn. (p. 16)

Davis, Benjamin O., Jr. (1912–2002) The first African American general in the United States Air Force, he led the Tuskegee Airmen through World War II. (p. 232)

Du Bois, W. E. B. (1868–1963) African American educator, editor, and writer, he led the Niagara Movement, calling for economic and educational equality for African Americans. He helped found the National Association for the Advancement of Colored People (NAACP). (p. 98)

Edison, Thomas Alva (1847–1931) American inventor of over 1,000 patents, he invented the lightbulb and established a power plant that supplied electricity to parts of New York City. (p. 36)

Eisenhower, Dwight D. (1890–1969) The 34th president of the United States, he used his popularity as a war hero of World War II to become president, in which position he led the nation through the Korean War. (p. 236)

Ford, Gerald (1913– 2006) The 38th president of the United States, he became president upon Richard Nixon's resignation. Ford later pardoned Nixon for his involvement in the Watergate scandal. (p. 350)

Ford, Henry (1863–1947) Founder of Ford Motor Company, he created the moving assembly line and is often credited with helping to create a middle class in American culture. (p. 37)

Francis Ferdinand (Archduke) (1863–1914) Heir apparent to the Austrian emperor, the assassination of him and his wife led to the beginning of World War I. (p. 141)

Friedan, Betty (1921–2006) Author of *The Feminine Mystique,* she pointed out women's dissatisfaction with traditional roles and became a leader of the women's rights movement of the 1960s and 1970s. (p. 303)

Garvey, Marcus (1887–1940) African American leader of the black nationalism movement. (p. 183)

Geronimo (1829–1909) Chiricahua Apache leader, he evaded capture for years and led an extraordinary opposition struggle against white settlements in the American Southwest until his eventual surrender. (p. 17)

Gompers, Samuel (1850–1924) American labor leader, he helped found the American Federation of Labor to campaign for workers' rights, such as the right to organize boycotts. (p. 45)

Gorbachev, Mikhail (1931–) Leader of the Soviet Union who introduced perestroika and oversaw the dismantling of the Communist government there. (p. 360)

Gore, Al (1948–) Vice president of the United States and Democratic presidential nominee in 2000. (p. 374)

Guthrie, Woody (1912–1967) Folksinger who expressed the desperation felt by millions of Americans during the Great Depression, especially those rural residents hit by the Dust Bowl. (p. 213)

H

Harding, Warren G. (1865–1923) The 29th president of the United States, his administration was full of scandals. He died during his presidency while in California. (p. 172)

Haywood, William "Big Bill" (1869–1928) One of the leaders of the International Workers of the World, a Socialist labor union active in the early 1900s. (p. 94)

Hearst, William Randolph (1863–1951) American journalist, he was famed for sensational news stories, known as yellow journalism, that stirred feelings of nationalism and formed public opinion for the Spanish–American War. (p. 65)

Hitler, Adolf (1889–1845) Leader of Nazi Germany during World War II, he rose to power on a platform of intolerance and nationalism. (p. 225)

Ho Chi Minh (1890–1969) Communist leader of North Vietnam during the Vietnam War, his government aided the Vietcong. (p. 318)

Hoover, Herbert (1874–1964) The 31st president of the United States, he was president during the stock market crashes that helped lead to the Great Depression. (p. 177)

Hughes, Langston (1902–1967) African American writer who achieved fame during the Harlem Renaissance for his poetry, which discussed the alienation of African Americans from white American society. (p. 188)

Hussein, Saddam (1937– 2006) Socialist president of the Iraqi Republic until captured as a prisoner of war by U.S. forces in 2003. (p. 371)

I

Inouye, Daniel (1924–) Japanese American who served as Hawaii's first United States senator. He also served in the U.S. Army during World War II. (p. 229)

J

Johnson, Lyndon (1908–1973) The 36th president of the United States, became president after the assassination of John Kennedy. Johnson led the nation through the civil rights movement, signing many antidiscrimination bills into law. (p. 299)

Joseph (1840–1904) Native American chief of the Nez Percé group, he became involved in a war with the U.S. Army when his people were removed to a reservation in Idaho. (p. 19)

K

Kelley, Florence (1859–1932) American reformer, she was active in the settlement house movement and led progressive reforms in labor conditions for women and children. (p. 68)

Kennedy, John F. (1917–1963) The 35th president of the United States, led the country through several cold war crises, but was assassinated in 1963. (p. 296)

BIOGRAPHICAL DICTIONARY

Key, Francis Scott (1749–1843) American lawyer who was imprisoned on a British ship during the War of 1812. His poem written about the battle he witnessed has become the national anthem of the United States. (p. R37)

King, Martin Luther, Jr. (1929–1968) Civil rights leader who was committed to a nonviolent approach in bringing about the dramatic change of racial integration. He was assassinated in 1968. (p. 293)

Kissinger, Henry (1923–) Served as secretary of state under President Nixon and helped form the policy of realpolitik. (p. 330)

La Follette, Robert M. (1855–1925) Progressive American politician, he was active in local Wisconsin issues and challenged party bosses. As governor, he began the reform program called the Wisconsin Idea to make state government more professional. (p. 87)

Liliuokalani (li-lee-uh-who-kuh-LAHN-ee) (1838–1917) Queen of the Hawaiian Islands, she opposed annexation by the United States but lost power in a U.S.–supported revolt by planters that led to a new government. (p. 114)

Lin, Maya Ying (1959–) Chinese American sculptor and architect, designed the Vietnam Veterans' Memorial in Washington, D.C. (p. 332)

Lodge, Henry Cabot (1850–1924) A U.S. senator from Massachusetts, he was opposed to President Wilson's plan for the League of Nations, fearing it would draw the United States into wars not in the nation's interest. (p. 158)

MacArthur, Douglas (1880–1964) A U.S. general who achieved fame for his actions in the Pacific during World War II and the Korean War. (p. 240)

Malcolm X (1925–1965) African American civil rights leader who advocated using violence if necessary to secure equal rights. Originally a leader of the Nation of Islam, when he broke with the organization, three of its members assassinated him. (p. 300)

Mao Zedong (1893–1976) Communist leader of China, he defeated a nationalist army for control of china. (p. 272)

Marshall, Thurgood (1908–1993) First African American U.S. Supreme Court Justice, he represented as a lawyer the National Association for the Advancement of Colored People and fought racial segregation. (p. 291)

McCain, John (1936–) American who served as Arizona's United States senator beginning in 1987. He also served in the U.S. Army during the Vietnam War. (p. 322)

McCarthy, Joseph (1908–1957) A U.S. senator from Wisconsin, he led investigations into the spread of communism in American society and within the government itself. He was eventually discredited when he could produce no evidence. (p. 275)

Mussolini, Benito (1883–1945) Fascist leader of Italy during World War II. (p. 224)

Nimitz, Chester (1885–1966) Commander of the U.S. fleet in the Pacific during World War II, his strategy helped defeat Japan. (p. 241)

Nixon, Richard M. (1913–1994) The 37th president of the United States, he withdrew troops from Vietnam, ending the hugely unpopular war. He became the first president to resign, after the Watergate scandal affected his credibility. (p. 330)

O'Keeffe, Georgia (1887–1986) American artist whose works of flowers and cow skulls became famous. (p. 189)

Olmsted, Frederick Law (1822–1903) American landscape architect who promoted the idea of recreational parks across the nation and helped design Central Park in New York City. (p. 645)

P

Parks, Rosa (1913–2005) African American seamstress and civil rights activist who began the Montgomery bus boycott by refusing to give up her seat on a segregated city bus. (p. 292)

Paul, Alice (1885–1977) American social reformer, suffragist, and activist, she was the founder of the organization that became the National Woman's Party (NWP) that worked to obtain women's suffrage. (p. 97)

Perkins, Frances (1882–1962) Secretary of Labor under Franklin Roosevelt, she helped draft New Deal legislation and was the first female Cabinet member. (p. 205)

Pershing, John J. (1860–1948) American army commander, he commanded the expeditionary force sent into Mexico to find Pancho Villa. He was the major general and commander in chief of the American Expeditionary Forces in World War I. (p. 129)

Powderly, Terence V. (1849–1924) American labor leader for the Knights of Labor, he removed the secrecy originally surrounding the organization, leading to its becoming the first truly national American labor union. (p. 45)

Powell, Colin (1937–) Appointed the first African American secretary of state by George W. Bush in 2000, he resigned his position over the handling of the Iraq war. (p. 371)

Pulitzer, Joseph (1847–1911) American journalist and newspaper publisher, he established the Pulitzer Prize for public service and advancement of education. (p. 65)

R

Randolph, A. Philip (1889–1979) African American labor leader who proposed a March on Washington during Franklin Roosevelt's presidency. It was called off when Roosevelt barred discrimination in defense industries. (p. 232)

Reagan, Ronald (1911–2004) The 40th president of the United States, his presidency was the result of a rise in conservatism after the dramatic changes of the 1960s and 1970s. (p. 357)

Riis, Jacob (1849–1914) Photographer and journalist who took shocking pictures of the lives of poverty–stricken immigrants, sweatshop workers, and tenement dwellers. These photos were published in *How the Other Half Lives.* (p. 66)

Rockefeller, John D. (1839 –1937) American industrialist and philanthropist, he made a fortune in the oil business and used vertical and horizontal integration to establish a monopoly on the steel business. (p. 40)

Roosevelt, Eleanor (1884–1962) Author, diplomat, humanitarian, and First Lady of Franklin D. Roosevelt, she supported much New Deal legislation aimed at young people and minorities. (p. 207)

BIOGRAPHICAL DICTIONARY

BIOGRAPHICAL DICTIONARY

Roosevelt, Franklin D. (1882–1945) The 32nd president of the United States, he led the country through the Great Depression and World War II. He served four terms, more than any other president. (p. 202)

Roosevelt, Theodore (1858–1919) Twenty–sixth president of the United States after William McKinley was assassinated, he organized the first volunteer cavalry regiment known as the Rough Riders who fought in Cuba during the Spanish–American War. As President, he acquired the Panama Canal Zone, and announced the Roosevelt Corollary, making the United States the defender of the Western Hemisphere. (p. 100)

S

Schafly, Phyllis (1924–) A leader of the conservative movement against the Equal Rights Amendment, she spoke out against the forces of feminism that emerged in the 1970s. (p. 303)

Seward, William H. (1801–1872) Secretary of state under Abraham Lincoln, he also was responsible for the purchase of Alaska from Russia. (p. 113)

Sitting Bull (c.1831–1890) American Indian leader who became the head chief of the entire Sioux nation, he encouraged other Sioux leaders to resist government demands to buy lands on the Black Hills reservations. (p. 16)

Stalin, Joseph (1879–1953) Communist dictator of the Soviet Union, led that nation through World War II and greatly affected the postwar decisions made about Europe at the Yalta and Potsdam conferences. (p. 225)

Stanford, Leland (1824–1893) American railroad builder and politician, he established the California Central Pacific Railroad and founded Stanford University. (p. 41)

Steinbeck, John (1902–1968) Writer who captured the desperation of Americans struggling through the Great Depression, especially those affected by the Dust Bowl. (p. 213)

T

Taft, William Howard (1857–1930) Twenty–seventh president of the United States, he angered progressives by moving cautiously toward reforms and by supporting the Payne–Aldrich Tariff, which did not lower tariffs very much. He lost Roosevelt's support and was defeated for a second term. (p. 102)

Taylor, Frederick W. (1856–1915) American efficiency engineer, he introduced the manufacturing system known as scientific management that viewed workers as mechanical parts of the production process, not as human beings. (p. 44)

Truman, Harry S. (1884–1972) The 33rd president of the United States, he became president after the death of Franklin Roosevelt. Truman ended World War II after dropping atomic bombs on Japan. (p. 246)

Tweed, William Marcy (1823–1878) New York city politician known for his control of the corrupt political machine called the Tammany Ring. (p. 83)

V

Villa, Francisco "Pancho" (1878–1923) Mexican bandit and revolutionary leader, he led revolts against Carranza and Huerta. He was pursued by the U.S. but evaded General Pershing. (p. 129)

Washington, Booker T. (1856–1915) African American educator and civil rights leader, he was born into slavery and later became head of the Tuskegee Institute for career training for African Americans. He was an advocate for conservative social change. (p. 97)

Wells, Ida B. (1862–1931) African American journalist and anti–lynching activist, she was part owner and editor of the Memphis Free Speech. (p. 97)

Westmoreland, William (1914–2005) Commander of all U.S. forces in Vietnam during the Vietnam War, he began the strategy of search–and–destroy missions. (p. 323)

Willard, Frances(1839–1898) American reformer who helped found the Women's Christian Temperance Union and was also active in the Women's suffrage movement. (p. 96)

Wilson, Woodrow (1856–1924) Twenty–eighth president of the United States, his reform legislation was given the name New Freedom, and it included three constitutional amendments: direct election of senators, prohibition, and women's suffrage. He created the Federal Reserve System, the Federal Trade Commission, and he enacted child labor laws. (p. 102)

Winnemucca, Sarah (1844–1891) Paiute Indian reformer, she was an activist for Indian rights and lectured specifically about the problems of the reservation system. (p. 18)

Wright, Orville (1871–1948) and **Wilbur** (1867–1912) American pioneers of aviation, they went from experiments with kites and gliders to piloting the first successful gas–powered airplane flight and later founded the American Wright Company to manufacture airplanes. (p. 38)

BIOGRAPHICAL DICTIONARY

English and Spanish Glossary

TIME LINE:
Hispanic Immigration to New York State

1900
Total immigration to New York state from all of Latin America is under 10,000 people.

1960
Migrants from Puerto Rico and immigrants from the West Indies and Cuba make up the three largest Spanish-speaking groups in the state.

1980s
Immigrants from the Dominican Republic outnumber those from Cuba nationwide and become the largest Caribbean immigrant group.

2000
About 650,000 Dominicans live in New York state, accounting for about half of the Hispanic population.

2000
Almost 3 million Hispanics live in New York State, about 15 percent of the population.

1900 ———— **1950** ———— **2000**

1917
U.S. Congress passes the Jones Act granting U.S. citizenship to all Puerto Ricans.

1930
Hispanic immigration to the state reaches 35,000.

1970
More than 250,000 foreign-born Spanish speakers live in the state, nearly 20 percent of the Spanish-speaking population.

1970
More than 52,000 immigrants arrive in New York state from the Dominican Republic.

1990
Eighteen percent of immigrants to the state are of Hispanic origin.

A

affirmative action an active effort to improve the employment or educational opportunities of members of minority groups and women (p. 353)
acción afirmativa iniciativas para mejorar las oportunidades laborales o educativas de las minorías y de las mujeres (pág. 353)

AIDS Acquired Immunodeficincy Syndrome, a disease that affects the immune system, making patients vulnerable to infections (p. 381)
SIDA síndrome de inmunodeficiencia adquirida; enfermedad que afecta al sistema inmunológico y hace que los pacientes sean vulnerables a infecciones (pág. 381)

Allied Powers a group of nations that allied to fight the Central Powers in World War I, and those countries in opposition to the Axis Powers in World War II (pp. 141, 226)
fuerzas aliadas grupo de naciones que se aliaron para luchar contra las potencias centrales en la Primera Guerra Mundial y los países que se oponían a las fuerzas del Eje en la Segunda Guerra Mundial (págs. 141, 226)

al-Qaeda the name of the terrorist organization headed by Osama bin Laden and responsible for the September 11, 2001, attacks (p. 376)
al-Qaeda nombre de la organización terrorista encabezada por Osama bin Laden, responsable de los ataques del 11 de septiembre de 2001 (pág. 376)

American Expeditionary Force the U.S. military forces sent to Europe during World War I and led by General John J. Pershing (p. 150)
Fuerza Expedicionaria Estadounidense fuerzas armadas de Estados Unidos bajo el mando del general John J. Pershing que fueron enviadas a Europa en la Primera Guerra Mundial (pág. 150)

American Federation of Labor (AFL) an organization that united skilled workers into national unions for specific industries (p. 45)
Federación Americana del Trabajo organización que unió a obreros especializados en sindicatos nacionales para industrias específicas (pág. 45)

American Indian Movement (AIM) a civil rights group organized to promote the interests of Native Americans (p. 305)
Movimiento de los Indígenas Americanos (AIM) agrupación a favor de los derechos civiles que promueve los intereses de los indígenas norteamericanos (pág. 305)

Anti-Imperialist League a group of citizens opposed to imperialism, and, specifically, to the peace treaty that gave the United States control of Cuba, Guam, Puerto Rico, and the Philippines (p. 120)
Liga Antiimperialista grupo de ciudadanos que se oponían al imperialismo y, más específicamente, al tratado de paz que daba a Estados Unidos el control de Cuba, Guam, Puerto Rico y Filipinas (pág. 120)

apartheid a system of segregation practiced in South Africa (p. 355)
apartheid sistema de segregación practicado en Sudáfrica (pág. 355)

appeasement the policy of giving into the demands of a nation in order to avoid war (p. 226)
apaciguamiento ó contemporización política de ceder ante las exigencias de una nación para evitar la guerra (pág. 226)

armistice a truce or cease-fire agreement between warring nations (p. 154)
armisticio tregua o acuerdo de cese del fuego entre dos naciones en guerra (pág. 154)

arms race a growth in weapons based on the number of weapons an enemy country has (p. 276)
carrera armamentística aumento de armamentos según la cantidad de armas que tiene un país enemigo (pág. 276)

atomic bomb a weapon that receives its explosive power from the splitting of atoms (p. 248)
bomba atómica arma cuyo poder exploivo es generado por la división de átomos (pág. 248)

Axis Powers the coalition of nations in World War II that included Germany, Italy, and Japan (p. 226)
fuerzas del Eje coalición de naciones de la Segunda Guerra Mundial formada por Alemania, Italia y Japón (pág. 226)

B

baby boom a sharp increase in the number of American births during the 1950s and 1960s (p. 278)
boom de la natalidad gran aumento en la cantidad de nacimientos en Estados Unidos durante las décadas de 1950 y 1960 (pág. 278)

Bataan Death March a forced march of American and Filipino soldiers captured by the Japanese along the Bataan Penninsula (p. 240)
marcha de la muerte de Bataán marcha forzada en la península de Bataán de soldados estadounidenses y filipinos capturados por los japoneses (pág. 240)

Battle of El Alamein (1942) a turning point in World War II, in which Allied forces defeated the Afrika Korps of Germany (p. 236)
batalla del El-Alamein (1942) momento decisivo en la Segunda Guerra Mundial, en el que las fuerzas aliadas derrotaron al *Afrika Korps* de Alemania (pág. 236)

Battle of Leyte Gulf (1944) the largest naval battle in history, during which the American fleet destroyed most of the Japanese fleet (p. 242)
batalla del golfo de Leyte (1944) la mayor batalla naval de la historia, durante la cual la flota estadounidense destruyó la mayor parte de la flota japonesa (pág. 242)

Battle of Midway (1942) battle of World War II that ended the Japanese advance in the Pacific (p. 241)
batalla de Midway (1942) batalla de la Segunda Guerra Mundial que puso fin al avance de los japoneses en el Pacífico (pág. 241)

Battle of Stalingrad (1942–1943) a major turning point in World War II; Soviet forces defeated Nazi forces after which the Nazis never recovered (p. 237)
batalla de Stalingrado (1942–1943) momento decisivo de la Segunda Guerra Mundial; las fuerzas soviéticas vencieron a las fuerzas nazis, que nunca más se recuperaron (pág. 237)

Battle of the Bulge (1944–1945) the last German advance of World War II, which was stopped by Allied forces (p. 246)
batalla del Bulge (1944–1945) último avance alemán de la Segunda Guerra Mundial, que fue detenido por las fuerzas aliadas (pág. 246)

Battle of the Coral Sea (1942) the first strategic defeat of the Japanese Imperial Navy by American forces during World War II (p. 241)
batalla del mar del Coral (1942) primera derrota estratégica de la armada imperial japonesa ante las fuerzas estadounidenses en la Segunda Guerra Mundial (pág. 241)

Battle of the Little Big Horn (1876) "Custer's Last Stand"; battle between U.S. soldiers, led by George Armstrong Custer, and Sioux warriors, led by Crazy Horse and Sitting Bull, that resulted in the worst defeat for the U.S. Army in the West (p. 16)
batalla de Little Big Horn (1876) última batalla del general Custer; esta batalla entre las tropas de George Armstrong Custer y los guerreros siux al mando de Caballo Loco y Toro Sentado produjo la mayor derrota del ejército estadounidense en el Oeste (pág. 16)

beats young people, many of whom were writers and artists, who discussed their dissatisfaction with the American society of the 1950s (p. 281)
beatniks jóvenes, en su mayoría escritores y artistas, que debatían acerca de su descontento con la sociedad estadounidense de la década de 1950 (pág. 281)

benevolent society an aid organization formed by immigrant communities (p. 59)
sociedad de beneficencia organización de ayuda formada por comunidades de inmigrantes (pág. 59)

Berlin Wall a barrier of concrete and barbed wire between Communist East Berlin and West Berlin (p. 316)
Muro de Berlín barrera de concreto y alambre de púas que separaba la Berlín oriental comunista de la Berlín occidental (pág. 316)

Bessemer process a process developed in the 1850s that led to faster, cheaper steel production (p. 35)
proceso de Bessemer proceso de producción de acero más económico y rápido, desarrollado en la década de 1850 (pág. 35)

Black Power a social movement that called for African American power and independence (p. 300)
Poder Negro movimiento social que exigía el poder y la independencia de los afroamericanos (pág. 300)

Black Tuesday October 29, 1929, one of the largest U.S. stock market drops (p. 199)
martes negro 29 de octubre de 1929, una de las mayores caídas de la bolsa de valores de Estados Unidos (pág. 199)

Bonus Army a group of World War I veterans that demanded their bonus payments early (p. 201)
Ejército bono grupo de veteranos de la Primera Guerra Mundial que exigía el pago de sus bonos por adelantado (pág. 201)

boomtown a Western community that grew quickly because of the mining boom and often disappeared when the boom ended (p. 8)
pueblo de rápido crecimiento comunidad del Oeste que se desarrolló con gran rapidez debido a la fiebre del oro, pero que desapareció cuando la fiebre terminó (pág. 8)

Boxer Rebellion (1900) a siege of a foreign settlement in Beijing by Chinese nationalists who were angry at foreign involvement in China (p. 115)
rebelión de los boxers (1900) asedio a un asentamiento extranjero en Beijing por parte de un grupo de nacionalistas chinos que estaban enojados por la participación extranjera en China (pág. 115)

brinkmanship the Cold War foreign policy designed to "get to the verge without getting into the war" (p. 276)
política arriesgada política exterior durante la Guerra Fría diseñada para "llegar al borde de la guerra sin llegar a la guerra" (pág. 276)

Brown v. Board of Education (1954) Supreme Court decision that ended segregation in public schools (p. 291)
Brown contra la Junta de Educación (1954) decisión de la Corte Suprema que puso fin a la segregación en las escuelas públicas (pág. 291)

buffalo soldiers African American soldiers who served in the cavalry during the wars for the west (p. 16)
soldados búfalo soldados afroamericanos que sirvieron en la caballería durante las guerras del oeste (pág. 16)

business cycle the rhythm in which an economy expands and contracts its production (p. 200)
ciclo económico ritmo al que la producción de una economía se expande y se contrae (pág. 200)

buying on margin the process of purchasing stock with credit, hoping to sell at a high enough price to pay the loan and make a profit (p. 198)
compra a crédito proceso de comprar acciones con préstamos, con la esperanza de venderlas a un precio suficientemente alto para pagar el préstamo y obtener una ganancia (pág. 198)

C

Camp David Accords (1978) an agreement between the heads of Israel and Egypt that began a process for peace in the Middle East (p. 355)
Acuerdos de Camp David (1978) acuerdo entre los líderes de Israel y Egipto que dio inicio a un proceso de paz en el Medio Oriente (pág. 355)

capitalism an economic system in which private businesses run most industries (p. 94)
capitalismo sistema económico en el que las empresas privadas controlan la mayoría de las industrias (pág. 94)

cattle drive a long journey on which cowboys herded cattle to northern markets or better grazing lands (p. 9)
arreo de ganado viaje largo en el que los vaqueros arreaban ganado para llevarlo a los mercados del Norte o a mejores pastos (pág. 9)

Cattle Kingdom an area of the Great Plains on which many ranchers raised cattle in the late 1800s (p. 9)
Reino del Ganado área de las Grandes Planicies en la que muchos rancheros criaban ganado a finales de siglo XIX (pág. 9)

Central Powers the coalition of nations in World War I that included the German, Austrio-Hungary, and Ottoman empires (p. 141)
Potencias Centrales coalición de naciones de la Primera Guerra Mundial formada por los imperios alemán, austrohúngaro y otomano (pág. 141)

Chinese Exclusion Act (1882) a law passed by Congress that banned Chinese from immigrating to the United States for 10 years (p. 61)
Ley de Exclusión de Chinos (1882) ley aprobada por el Congreso que prohibió la inmigración de chinos a Estados Unidos por 10 años (pág. 61)

Chisholm Trail a trail that ran from San Antonio, Texas, to Abilene, Kansas, established by Jesse Chisholm in the late 1860s for cattle drives (p. 9)
Camino de Chisholm camino creado por Jesse Chisholm a finales de la década de 1860 que iba desde San Antonio, Texas hasta Abilene, Kansas, para arreos de ganado (pág. 9)

Civil Rights Act of 1964 a law that ended discrimination based on race or gender (p. 879)
Ley de Derechos Civiles de 1964 ley que puso fin a la discriminación en base a la raza o al sexo (pág. 879)

Cold War a period of hostility between Western powers and Communist powers (p. 266)
Guerra Fría período de hostilidades entre las potencias de Occidente y las potencias comunistas (pág. 266)

collective bargaining a technique used by labor unions in which workers act collectively to change working conditions or wages (p. 40)
negociación colectiva método empleado por los sindicatos en el que los trabajadores actúan colectivamente para cambiar las condiciones laborales o los salarios (pág. 40)

Communists people who believe in communism, or the political system in which all resources are shared equally (p. 151)
comunistas personas que creen en el comunismo, es decir, el sistema político en el que los recursos se distribuyen a todos por igual (pág. 151)

Comstock Lode Nevada gold and silver mine discovered by Henry Comstock in 1859 (p. 7)
veta de Comstock mina de oro y plata descubierto en Nevada por Henry Comstock en 1859 (pág. 7)

Congress of Industrial Organizations (CIO) a union that organized workers according to industry, not by skill (p. 208)
Congreso de las organizaciones industriales (CIO) una unión que ordenó a trabajadores según industria, no por la habilidad (pag. 208)

conservation the planned management of natural resources to prevent their destruction (p. 101)
conservación administración planificada de los recursos naturales para evitar su destrucción (pág. 101)

containment a foreign policy that attempts to stop the spread of communism without ending it in the countries in which it already exists (p. 267)
contención política exterior que intenta detener el avance del comunismo sin eliminarlo en los países en los que ya existe (pág. 267)

corporation a business that sells portions of ownership called stock shares (p. 39)
corporación compañía que vende algunas partes en forma de acciones (pág. 39)

Cuban missile crisis a threat to national security that occurred when the Soviet Union placed nuclear missiles in Cuba (p. 316)
crisis de los misiles cubanos amenaza a la seguridad nacional que ocurrió cuando la Unión Soviética colocó misiles nucleares en Cuba (pág. 316)

D

Dawes General Allotment Act (1887) legislation passed by Congress that split up Indian reservation lands among individual Indians and promised them citizenship (p. 18)
Ley de Adjudicación General de Dawes (1887) ley aprobada por el Congreso que dividía el terreno de las reservas indígenas entre sus habitantes y les prometía la ciudadanía (pág. 18)

D-Day (1944) an invasion of Nazi-occupied France by Allied forces (p. 239)
día D (1944) invasión de las fuerzas aliadas en Francia, ocupada por los nazis (pág. 239)

deficit the amount by which a government's spending exceeds its revenue (p. 358)
déficit cantidad en la que los gastos del gobierno superan sus ingresos (pág. 358)

deflation a decrease in money supply and overall lower prices (p. 24)
deflación reducción de la disponibilidad del dinero y baja general en los precios (pág. 24)

department store giant retail shop (p. 65)
tiendas por departamentos grandes comercios de venta al público (pág. 65)

détente a period of closer diplomatic relations between the United States and the Communist powers of China and the Soviet Union (p. 348)
distensión período de relaciones diplomáticas más estrechas entre Estados Unidos y las potencias comunistas de China y la Unión Soviética (pág. 348)

Disabled in Action (DIA) a group organized to promote the interests of people with disabilities (p. 305)
Discapacitados en Acción (DIA) grupo organizado para promover los intereses de personas con discapacidades (pág. 305)

domino theory the idea that Communism would spread rapidly throughout Southeast Asia (p. 318)
teoría del dominó idea de que el comunismo se extendería rápidamente por el sureste de Asia (pág. 318)

doves opponents of the Vietnam War (p. 324)
palomas opositores a la guerra de Vietnam (pág. 324)

ENGLISH AND SPANISH GLOSSARY

dry farming a method of farming used by Plains farmers in the 1890s that shifted focus from water-dependent crops to more hardy crops (p. 21)
agricultura sin irrigación método de cultivo que usaban los agricultores de las Planicies en la década de 1890 que provocó un cambio de los cultivos que dependían del agua a otros más resistentes (pág. 21)

Dust Bowl an area of the United States that suffered a severe drought during the 1930s (p. 210)
Dust Bowl área de Estados Unidos que sufrió una grave sequía en la década de 1930 (pág. 210)

E

Eighteenth Amendment (1919) a constitutional amendment that outlawed the production and sale of alcoholic beverages in the United States; repealed in 1933 (p. 96)
Decimoctava Enmienda (1919) enmienda constitucional que prohibió la producción y venta de bebidas alcohólicas en Estados Unidos; revocada en 1933 (pág. 96)

Equal Rights Amendment (ERA) a proposed amendment to the Constitution that would provide equal rights to women (p. 303)
Enmienda por la Igualdad de Derechos (ERA) enmienda constitucional propuesta que otorgaría la igualdad de derechos a la mujer (p. 303)

escalation increased involvment in the Vietnam War (p. 322)
escalada mayor participación en la guerra de Vietnam (pág. 322)

Exodusters African Americans who settled western lands in the late 1800s (p. 21)
Exodusters afroamericanos que se establecieron en el Oeste a finales del siglo XIX (pág. 21)

expatriates citizens who leave their country to live elsewhere (p. 188)
expatriados ciudadanos que abandonan su país para vivir en otro lugar (pág. 188)

F

fascism a political system in which the state or government is seen as more important than the individual (p. 224)
fascismo sistema político en el que se considera que el estado o gobierno es más importante que las personas (pág. 224)

Fair Deal President Truman's legislative plan for the nation that included antilynching laws (p. 270)
Fair Deal plan legislativo para la nación propuesto por el presidente Truman que incluía leyes en contra de los linchamientos (pág. 270)

fireside chats radio programs in which Franklin Roosevelt explained his plan for recovery from the Great Depression (p. 205)
charlas junto a la chimenea programas de radio en los cuales Franklin Roosevelt explicaba su plan para que el país se recuperara de la Gran Depresión (pág. 205)

flappers young women who challenged traditional ideas of womanhood in the 1920s (p. 179)
chicas a la moda mujeres jóvenes que desafiaron las ideas tradicionales sobre la condición de la mujer en la década de 1920 (pág. 179)

Freedom Rides a series of integrated bus rides through the South (p. 297)
Viajes de la Libertad serie de viajes en autobús por el Sur en los que se integraban las razas (pág. 297)

frontier an undeveloped area (p. 6)
frontera área que no está siendo utilizada por el ser humano (pág. 6)

fundamentalism a religious belief characterized by a literal interpretation of the Bible (p. 182)
fundamentalismo creencia religiosa caracterizada por una interpretación literal de la Biblia (pág. 182)

G

genocide the complete destruction of a racial or ethnic minority (p. 247)
genocidio destrucción total de una minoría racial o étnica (pág. 247)

Ghost Dance a religious movement among Native Americans that spread across the Plains in the 1880s (p. 18)
Danza de los Espíritus movimiento religioso de los indígenas norteamericanos que se extendió por la región de las Planicies en la década de 1880 (pág. 18)

GI Bill of Rights (1944) a law that offered veterans money for school, houses, farms, and businesses (p. 268)
Declaración de Derechos de los Soldados (1944) ley que ofrecía a los veteranos de guerra dinero para su educación, vivienda, granjas y negocios (pág. 268)

globalization the process in which the United States is becoming more interdependent with other nations (p. 380)
globalización proceso por el cual Estados Unidos empieza a tener más interdependencia con otras naciones (pág. 380)

global warming an environmental crisis in which the average temperature of the Earth is rising due to pollution (p. 382)
calentamiento global crisis del medio ambiente por la cual está aumentando la temperatura promedio de la Tierra debido a la contaminación (pág. 382)

Great Depression a severe economic crisis that lasted for the entire decade of the 1930s (p. 200)
Gran Depresión grave crisis económica que duró toda la década de 1930 (pág. 200)

Great Migration a period of African American movement from the South to cities in the North (p. 183)
Gran Migración período en que los afroamericanos del Sur se fueron a ciudades del Norte (pág. 183)

Great Society President Lyndon Johnson's legislative plan that included civil rights laws (p. 300)
Gran Sociedad plan legislativo del presidente Lyndon Johnson que incluía leyes a favor de los derechos civiles (pág. 300)

Harlem Renaissance a period of artistic achievement during the 1920s (p. 188)
Renacimiento de Harlem período de logros artísticos durante la década de 1920 (pág. 188)

hawks supporters of the Vietnam War (p. 324)
halcones partidarios de la guerra de Vietnam (pág. 324)

Haymarket Riot a riot that broke out at Haymarket Square in Chicago over the deaths of two strikers (p. 46)
Revuelta de Haymarket revuelta que se originó en la Plaza Haym arket de Chicago por la muerte de dos huelguistas (pág. 46)

hippies young people who rebelled against the mainstream culture of the 1960s (p. 329)
hippies jóvenes que se rebelaron contra la cultura convencional en la década de 1960 (pág. 329)

Ho Chi Minh Trail a series of jungle paths that allowed Communist forces to travel from North Vietnam to South Vietnam (p. 322)
Camino de Ho Chi Minh serie de caminos por la selva que permitía a las fuerzas comunistas ir desde Vietnam del Norte hacia Vietnam del Sur (pág. 322)

Holocaust a program of mass murder in which the Nazis tried to kill all Jews (p. 247)
Holocausto programa de asesinato en masa ideado por los nazis para exterminar a todos los judíos (pág. 247)

Homestead Act (1862) a law passed by Congress to encourage settlement in the West by giving government-owned land to small farmers (p. 20)
Ley de Colonización de Tierras (1862) ley aprobada por el Congreso para fomentar la colonización del Oeste mediante la cesión de tierras del gobierno a pequeños agricultores (pág. 20)

Homestead strike (1892) a labor-union strike at Andrew Carnegie's Homestead Steel factory in Pennsylvania that erupted in violence between strikers and private detectives (p. 47)
huelga de Homestead (1892) huelga sindical en la fábrica de acero Homestead de Andrew Carnegie en Pensilvania, que produjo violencia entre huelguistas y detectives privados (pág. 47)

horizontal integration owning all the businesses in a certain field (p. 41)
integración horizontal posesión de todas las empresas en un campo específico (pág. 41)

Hull House a settlement house founded by Jane Addams and Ellen Gates Starr in 1889 (p. 68)
Casa Hull casa de asistencia a la comunidad fundada por Jane Addams y Ellen Gates Starr en 1889 (pág. 68)

human rights the basic rights of all people (p. 355)
derechos humanos derechos fundamentales de todas las personas (pág. 355)

hydrogen bomb a thermonuclear weapon that gets its power from splitting a hydrogen atom (p. 276)
bomba de hidrógeno arma termonuclear cuya potencia es generada por la división de un átomo de hidrógeno (pág. 276)

imperialism the practice of extending a nation's power by gaining territories for a colonial empire (p. 112)
imperialismo práctica en la que una nación amplía su poder mediante adquiriendo territorios para un imperio colonial (pág. 112)

Industrial Workers of the World (IWW) a union founded in 1905 by socialists and union leaders that included workers not welcomed in the AFL (p. 94)
Trabajadores Industriales del Mundo (IWW) por sus siglas en inglés) sindicato fundado en 1905 por socialistas y líderes sindicales que incluía a los trabajadores que no admitía la Federación Americana del Trabajo (pág. 94)

Information Revolution an increase in the ability to share information between people and locations brought about by the Internet (p. 381)
Revolución de la información aumento de la capacidad de compartir información entre personas y lugares producido por Internet (pág. 381)

ENGLISH AND SPANISH GLOSSARY

initiative a method of allowing voters to propose a new law if enough signatures are collected on a petition (p. 86)
iniciativa método que permite a los votantes proponer una nueva ley si consiguen suficientes firmas para una petición (pág. 86)

Internet a global system of computers that allows people across the world to communicate (p. 381)
Internet sistema global de computadoras que permite la comunicación entre personas de todo el mundo (pág. 381)

internment the imprisonment of Japanese Americans in special camps during World War II (p. 233)
internamiento encarcelamiento de japoneses-americanos en campos especiales durante la Segunda Guerra Mundial (pág. 233)

Iran-Contra affair a scandal during the Reagan administration in which government officials were accused of selling weapons to Iran and passing the profits to a revolutionary group known as the Contras (p. 359)
escándalo Irán-contras escándalo durante el gobierno de Reagan en el cual funcionarios del gobierno fueron acusados de vender armas a Irán y de entregar las ganancias a un grupo revolucionario conocido como los contras (pág. 359)

Iran hostage crisis a crisis in which Americans were taken hostage by militants in Iran and held for over a year (p. 356)
crisis de los rehenes de Irán crisis en la cual varios estadounidenses fueron tomados como rehenes por militantes iraníes durante más de un año (pág. 356)

island-hopping the strategy used by U.S. forces in the Pacific during World War II that involved taking only strategically important islands (p. 242)
saltos de isla en isla estrategia de las fuerzas de Estados Unidos en el Pacífico durante la Segunda Guerra Mundial que consistía en tomar sólo las islas importantes desde el punto de vista estratégico (pág. 242)

isolationism a national policy of avoiding involvement in other countries' affairs (p. 113)
aislacionismo política nacional de evitar involucrarse en los asuntos de otras naciones (pág. 113)

Jazz Age a name for the decade of the 1920s based on the popularity of jazz music (p. 187)
Era del Jazz nombre que se le dio a la década de 1920 por la popularidad de la música de jazz (pág. 187)

kamikaze Japanese pilots who flew suicide missions during World War II (p. 242)
kamikaze piloto japonés que volaba en misiones suicidas durante la Segunda Guerra Mundial (pág. 242)

Kellogg-Briand Pact an agreement between nations proposing peaceful solutions to conflicts, signed after World War I (p. 174)
Pacto Kellogg-Briand acuerdo firmado entre naciones luego de la Primera Guerra Mundial que proponía soluciones pacíficas a los conflictos (pág. 174)

Knights of Labor secret society that became the first truly national labor union in the United States (p. 45)
Caballeros del Trabajo sociedad secreta que se convirtió en el primer sindicato verdaderamente nacional en Estados Unidos (pág. 45)

Laissez-faire the theory that the economy works best with as few regulations as possible (p. 26)
liberalismo económico teoría de que la economía funciona mejor si tiene los mímimos reglamentos posibles (pág. 26)

League of Nations a coalition of governments designed to find peaceful solutions to disagreements, proposed by Woodrow Wilson (p. 157)
Liga de las Naciones coalición de gobiernos propuesta por Woodrow Wilson y diseñada para buscar soluciones pacíficas a los desacuerdos (pág. 157)

Lend-Lease Act (1941) a law giving Franklin Roosevelt the power to sell, transfer, exchange, or lease military equipment to any country to help it defend itself against the Axis powers (p. 228)
Ley de Préstamo y Arriendo (1941) ley que dio a Franklin Roosevelt el poder de vender, transferir, intercambiar o arrendar equipo militar a cualquier país para la defensa contra las fuerzas del Eje (pág. 228)

Liberty bonds loans to the government that aided its ability to prepare for World War I (p. 147)
bonos de la Libertad préstamos hechos al gobierno que le permitieron prepararse para la Primera Guerra Mundial (pág. 147)

Little Rock Nine a group of nine African American students who began the integration of the Little Rock, Arkansas, public school system (p. 291)
los nueve de Little Rock grupo de nueve estudiantes afroamericanos que empezaron la integración del sistema de escuelas públicas de Little Rock, Arkansas (pág. 291)

Long Walk (1864) a 300-mile march made by Navajo captives to a reservation in Bosque Redondo, New Mexico, that led to the deaths of hundreds of Navajo (p. 17)
　La Larga Marcha (1864) caminata de 300 millas que hizo un grupo de prisioneros navajos hasta una reserva indígena en Bosque Redondo, Nuevo México, en la que murieron cientos de ellos (pág. 17)

Lost Generation the generation of young people who fought in World War I and eventually became disillusioned with the promise of American society (p. 188)
　generación perdida generación de jóvenes que lucharon en la Primera Guerra Mundial y terminaron desilusionados con las promesas de la sociedad estadounidense (pág. 188)

Lusitania a passenger ship bombed by Germany (p. 146)
Lusitania barco de pasajeros bombardeado por Alemania (pág. 146)

M

Manhattan Project the U.S. effort to build an atomic bomb (p. 248)
　Proyecto Manhattan plan de Estados Unidos de fabricar una bomba atómica (pág. 248)

March on Washington a huge demonstration organized by Martin Luther King Jr. to protest racial discrimination (p. 298)
　Marcha en Washington manifestación enorme organizada por Martin Luther King, Jr. en protesta por la discriminación racial (p. 298)

Marshall Plan the idea that the U.S. could help rebuild wartorn Europe with loans and other economic aid (p. 267)
　Plan Marshall idea de que Estados Unidos podía contribuir con préstamos y otros tipos de ayuda económica a la reconstrucción de la Europa devastada por la guerra (pág. 267)

Massacre at Wounded Knee (1890) the U.S. Army's killing of approximately 150 Sioux at Wounded Knee Creek in South Dakota; ended U.S-Indian wars on the Plains (p. 17)
　masacre de Wounded Knee (1890) matanza de aproximadamente 150 indios siux en Wounded Knee Creek, Dakota del Sur; dio por terminadas las guerras entre estadounidenses e indígenas en las Planicies (pág. 17)

mass culture leisure and cultural activities shared by many people (p. 64)
　cultura de masas actividades culturales y del tiempo libre que les gustan a muchas personas (pág. 64)

mass transit public transportation (p. 64)
　transporte colectivo transporte público (pág. 64)

Mexican Revolution a revolution led by Francisco Madero in 1910 that eventually forced the Mexican dictator Díaz to resign (p. 128)
　Revolución mexicana revolución iniciada en 1910 por Francisco Madero, que finalmente obligó al dictador mexicano Díaz a renunciar (pág. 128)

militarism an increase in the importance of the military of a country (p. 141)
　militarismo aumento de la importancia del ejército de un país (pág. 141)

mobilize to prepare for war (p. 141)
　mobilizarse prepararse para la guerra (pág. 141)

Model T Henry Ford's automobile designed with the average American in mind (p. 175)
　modelo T automóvil de Henry Ford diseñado para el estadounidense promedio (pág. 175)

monopoly a complete control over the entire supply of goods or a service in a particular market (p. 42)
　monopolio control absoluto de toda la oferta de bienes o de un servicio en un mercado en particular (pág. 42)

Montgomery bus boycott a boycott of the Montgomery, Alabama, public bus system to protest its policy of segregation (p. 293)
　boicot a los autobuses de Montgomery boicot al sistema público de autobuses de Montgomery, Alabama, en protesta por su política de segregación (pág. 293)

Morrill Act (1862) a federal law passed by Congress that gave land to western states to encourage them to build colleges (p. 20)
　Ley de Morrill (1862) ley federal aprobada por el Congreso que otorgaba tierras a los estados del Oeste para fomentar la construcción de universidades (pág. 20)

moving assembly line an innovation of Henry Ford's that dramatically reduced the cost of production (p. 175)
　cadena de montaje móvil innovación de Henry Ford que redujo significativamente el costo de producción (pág. 175)

muckrakers a term coined for journalists who "raked up" and exposed corruption and problems of society (p. 84)
　muckrakers término acuñado para nombrar a los periodistas que se dedicaban a investigar y exponer la corrupción y los problemas de la sociedad (pág. 84)

ENGLISH AND SPANISH GLOSSARY

National American Woman Suffrage Association
(NAWSA) an organization founded by Elizabeth Cady
Stanton and Susan B. Anthony in 1890 to obtain
women's right to vote (p. 96)
**Asociación Nacional Americana para el Sufragio
Femenino** (NAWSA) por sus siglas en inglés
organización fundada en 1890 por Elizabeth Cady
Stanton y Susan B. Anthony para obtener el derecho
al voto de las mujeres (pág. 96)

**National Association for the Advancement of Colored
People (NAACP)** an organization founded in 1909
by W. E. B. Du Bois and other reformers to bring
attention to racial inequality (p. 98)
**Asociación Nacional para el Progreso de la Gente de
Color (NAACP, por sus siglas en inglés)** organización
fundada en 1909 por W. E. B. Du Bois y otros
reformadores para llamar la atención sobre la
desigualdad racial (pág. 98)

National Grange a social and educational organization
for farmers (p. 23)
National Grange organización social y educativa para
los agricultores (pág. 23)

National Organization for Women (NOW) a group that
organized to promote the interests of women (p. 303)
Organización Nacional de la Mujer (NOW, por sus
siglas en inglés) grupo organizado para promover los
intereses de la mujer (pág. 303)

National War Labor Board a government agency
organized to help settle disputes between workers
and employers in war industries (p. 149)
Junta nacional del trabajo en Tiempos de Guerra
agencia de gobierno destinada a resolver disputas
entre trabajadores y empleadores en las industrias
relacionadas con la guerra (pág. 149)

Nazis the National Socialist Party of Germany, headed
by Adolf Hitler (p. 225)
nazi Partido Nacional Socialista de Alemania,
liderado por Adolf Hitler (pág. 225)

New Deal Franklin Roosevelt's legislative plan to end
the Great Depression that included dramatic reforms
of government agencies and powers (p. 204)
New Deal **(Nuevo Trato)** plan legislativo de Franklin
Roosevelt para poner fin a la Gran Depresión; incluía
profundas reformas en las agencias y poderes del
gobierno (pág. 204)

new immigrant a term often used for an immigrant who
arrived in the United States beginning in the 1880s
(p. 56)
nuevo inmigrante término empleado a menudo para
referirse a los inmigrantes que llegaron a Estados
Unidos a partir de la década de 1880 (pág. 56)

Nineteenth Amendment (1920) a constitutional
amendment that gave women the vote (p. 97)
Decimonovena Enmienda (1920) enmienda
constitucional que dio a la mujer el derecho al voto
(pág. 97)

North American Free Trade Agreement (NAFTA) a treaty
that eliminated trade barriers between Canada, the
United States, and Mexico (p. 372)
Tratado de Libre Comercio de América del Norte
(TLCAN o NAFTA) tratado que eliminó las barreras
comerciales entre Canadá, Estados Unidos y México
(pág. 372)

North Atlantic Treaty Organization (NATO) an alliance of
Western powers (p. 268)
Organización del Tratado del Atlántico Norte (OTAN)
alianza de potencias occidentales (pág. 268)

Nuremberg trials the war crimes trials of Nazi leaders
(p. 265)
Ensayos de Nuremberg los ensayos de los crímenes
de guerra de arranques de cinta nazis (pág. 265)

old immigrant a term often used for an immigrant who
arrived in the United States before the 1880s (p. 56)
antiguo inmigrante término empleado con frecuencia
para referirse a los inmigrantes que llegaron a Estados
Unidos antes de la década de 1880 (pág. 56)

Open Door Policy a policy established by the United
States in 1899 to promote equal access for all nations
to trade in China (p. 115)
política de puertas abiertas política establecida por
Estados Unidos en 1899 para promover el acceso
igualitario de todas las naciones al comercio con
China (pág. 115)

Operation Desert Storm the military effort to free
Kuwait from Saddam Hussein's invasion (p. 371)
Operación Tormenta del Desierto acción militar para
liberar a Kuwait de la invasión de Saddam Hussein
(pág. 371)

Organization of Petroleum Exporting Countries (OPEC)
an alliance of oil rich countries that coordinates oil
policies (p. 347)
Organización de Países Exportadores de Petróleo
(OPEP) alianza de países ricos en petróleo que
coordina las políticas petroleras (pág. 347)

ozone layer a level of the Earth's atmosphere that is
being depleted by pollution (p. 382)
capa de ozono nivel de la atmósfera de la Tierra
que se está reduciendo debido a la contaminación
(pág. 382)

Panama Canal an artificial waterway across the Isthmus of Panama; completed by the United States in 1914 (p. 125)
canal de Panamá canal artificial que atraviesa el istmo de Panamá; Estados Unidos completó su construcción en 1914 (pág. 125)

pardon freedom from punishment (pp. 351)
indulto (perdón) liberación de un castigo (págs. 351)

patent an exclusive right to make or sell an invention (p. 36)
patente derecho exclusivo para fabricar o vender un invento (pág. 36)

Peace Corps a nonmilitary aid program introduced by John Kennedy (p. 314)
Cuerpos de Paz programa de ayuda no militar introducido por John Kennedy (pág. 314)

Pearl Harbor a harbor in Hawaii that serves as the base of the U.S. Pacific fleet and was bombed in 1941 by Japan (p. 228)
Pearl Harbor puerto de Hawai que es la base de la flota del Pacífico de Estados Unidos; fue bombardeado por Japón en 1941 (pág. 228)

Pendleton Civil Service Act (1883) a law applying a merit system controlled by the Civil Service Commission to federal government jobs (p. 84)
Ley Pendleton de Administración Pública (1883) ley que estableció un sistema de méritos controlado por la Comisión de Administración Pública para dar empleos en el gobierno federal (pág. 84)

Pentagon the headquarters of the U.S. military, located outside of Washington, D.C. (p. 376)
Pentágono sede central del ejército de Estados Unidos, ubicada en las afueras de Washington D.C. (pág. 376)

Platt Amendment a part of the Cuban constitution drafted under the supervision of the United States that limited Cuba's right to make treaties, gave the U.S. the right to intervene in Cuban affairs, and required Cuba to sell or lease land to the U.S (p. 221)
Enmienda Platt parte de la constitución cubana redactado bajo la supervisión de Estados Unidos que limitaba el derecho de Cuba a firmar tratados, le daba a Estados Unidos el derecho de intervenir en los asuntos cubanos y le exigía a Cuba vender o arrendar tierras a Estados Unidos (pág. 221)

political machine a powerful organization that influenced city and county politics in the late 1800s (p. 82)
maquinaria política organización poderosa que influía en la política municipal y del condado a finales del siglo XIX (pág. 82)

Pony Express a system of messengers that carried mail between relay stations on a route 2,000-miles long in 1860 and 1861 (p. 10)
Pony Express sistema de mensajeros que llevaban el correo entre estaciones de relevo a lo largo de una ruta de 2,000 millas en 1860 y 1861 (pág. 10)

Populist Party a political party formed in 1892 that supported free coinage of silver, work reforms, immigration restrictions, and government ownership of railroads and telegraph and telephone systems (p. 24)
Partido Populista partido político formado en 1892 que apoyaba la libre producción de monedas de plata, reformas laborales y restricciones de la inmigración, además de asignar al gobierno la propiedad de los sistemas ferroviario, telegráfico y telefónico (pág. 24)

Progressives a group of reformers who worked to improve social and political problems in the late 1800s (p. 84)
progresistas grupo de reformistas que trabajaron para resolver problemas sociales y políticos a finales del siglo XIX (pág. 84)

Progressive Party a short-lived political party that attempted to institute social reforms (p. 102)
partido Progresista partido político de poca duración que intentó establecer reformas sociales (pág. 102)

Pullman strike (1894) a railroad strike that ended when President Grover Cleveland sent in federal troops (p. 47)
huelga de Pullman (1894) huelga del ferrocarril que terminó cuando el presidente Grover Cleveland envió a tropas federales (pág. 47)

Pure Food and Drug Act (1906) a law that set regulatory standards for industries involved in preparing food (p. 101)
Ley de Alimentos y Drogas Puros (1906) ley que estableció normas regulatorias para las industrias de fabricación de productos alimenticios (pág. 101)

realpolitik a foreign policy in which U.S. interests are put over ethical or principled concerns (p. 348)
realpolitik política exterior según la cual los intereses de Estados Unidos están por encima de los asuntos éticos o de principios (pág. 348)

recall a vote to remove an official from office (p. 86)
destitución votación para sacar a un funcionario de su cargo (pág. 86)

ENGLISH AND SPANISH GLOSSARY

ENGLISH AND SPANISH GLOSSARY

Red Scare a widespread fear of communism and Communists (p. 180)
Terror rojo miedo ampliamente difundido al comunismo y los comunistas (pág. 180)

referendum a procedure that allows voters to approve or reject a law already proposed or passed by government (p. 86)
referéndum proceso que permite a los ciudadanos votar para aprobar o rechazar una ley previamente propuesta o aprobada por el gobierno (pág. 86)

reparations financial payments by the loser of a war (p. 157)
indemnizaciones compensación económica pagada por el bando que es vencido en la guerra (pág. 157)

reservations federal lands set aside for American Indians (p. 15)
reservas territorios federales reservados para los indígenas norteamericanos (pág. 15)

Roosevelt Corollary (1904) Theodore Roosevelt's addition to the Monroe Doctrine warning nations in the Americas that if they didn't pay their debts, the United States would get involved (p. 127)
Corolario de Roosevelt (1904) agregado del presidente Theodore Roosevelt a la Doctrina Monroe advirtiendo a las naciones de América que si no pagaban sus deudas, el gobierno de Estados Unidos intervendría (pág. 127)

sanctions economic restrictions placed on a country in an attempt to change its policy decisions (p. 355)
sanciones restricciones económicas aplicadas a un país en un intento de cambiar sus políticas (pág. 355)

Scopes trial a trial in which John Scopes was accused of teaching evolution illegally (p. 182)
juicio de Scopes juicio en el cual John Scopes fue acusado de enseñar ilegalmente la teoría de la evolución (pág. 182)

search-and-destroy missions the strategy used in the Vietnam War in which enemy targets were located and attacked (p. 323)
misiones de búsqueda y destrucción estrategia de localización y ataque de objetivos enemigos usada en la guerra de Vietnam (pág. 323)

Second Industrial Revolution a period of rapid growth in manufacturing and industry in the late 1800s (p. 35)
segunda revolución industrial período de gran crecimiento en la manufactura y en la industria, a finales del siglo XIX (pág. 35)

Selective Service Act (1917) a law that allowed the president to draft soldiers in times of war (p. 147)
Ley de Servicio Selectivo (1917) ley que permitía al Presidente reclutar soldados en épocas de guerra (pág. 147)

service economy an economy in which most jobs involve providing services instead of producing goods (p. 380)
economía de servicios economía en la cual la mayoría de los trabajos consisten en ofrecer un servicio en lugar de producir bienes (pág. 380)

settlement houses neighborhood centers staffed by professionals and volunteers for education, recreation, and social activities in poor areas (p. 68)
organizaciones de servicio a la comunidad centros comunitarios atendidos por profesionales y voluntarios para ofrecer educación, recreación y actividades sociales en zonas pobres (pág. 68)

Seventeenth Amendment (1913) a constitutional amendment allowing American voters to directly elect U.S. senators (p. 86)
Decimoséptima Enmienda (1913) enmienda constitucional que permite a los votantes estadounidenses elegir directamente a los senadores de Estados Unidos (pág. 86)

Sherman Antitrust Act (1890) a law that made it illegal to create monopolies or trusts that restrained free trade (p. 42)
Ley Antimonopolio de Sherman (1890) ley que prohibía la creación de monopolios o consorcios que restringieran el libre comercio (pág. 42)

sit-down strike a strike in which workers stay at their work stations so that strikebreakers cannot replace them (p. 208)
huelga de brazos caídos huelga en la cual los trabajadores permanecen en el lugar de trabajo para que los rompehuelgas no los puedan reemplazar (pág. 208)

sit-in a form of protest in which African Americans sat at segregated lunch counters and requested service (p. 294)
sentada forma de protesta de los afroamericanos; se sentaban en los comedores que practicaban la segregación racial y pedían servicio (pág. 294)

Sixteenth Amendment (1913) an amendment to the Constitution that allows personal income to be taxed (p. 103)
Decimosexta Enmienda (1913) enmienda constitucional que permite los impuestos sobre los ingresos personales (pág. 103)

social Darwinism a view of society based on Charles Darwin's scientific theory of natural selection (p. 41)
darwinismo social visión de la sociedad basada en la teoría científica de la selección natural de Charles Darwin (pág. 41)

socialism economic system in which the government owns and operates a country's means of production (p. 94)
socialismo sistema económico en el que el gobierno controla y maneja los medios de producción de un país (pág. 94)

sodbusters the name given to Plains farmers who worked hard to break up the region's tough sod (p. 21)
sodbusters nombre dado a los agricultores de las Planicies que se esforzaron mucho para trabajar el duro terreno de la región (pág. 21)

Social Security Act (1935) a law that instituted the pension plan Social Security (p. 207)
Ley del Seguro Social (1935) ley que estableció el plan de pensiones del Seguro Social (pág. 207)

sphere of influence an area where foreign countries control trade or natural resources of another nation or area (p. 115)
esfera de influencia nación o lugar cuyos recursos naturales y comercio son controlados por otro país (pág. 115)

Sputnik the first artificial satellite, launched by the Soviet Union in 1957 (p. 276)
Sputnik primer satélite artificial, lanzado por la Unión Soviética en 1957 (pág. 276)

stagflation a term describing a slowing economy mixed with high unemployment (p. 347)
estagflación término que describe una economía que disminuye su ritmo, acompañado de un desempleo alto (pág. 347)

stalemate a situation in which neither side can win a victory (p. 143)
punto muerto situación en la cual ninguna de las partes puede alcanzar la victoria (pág. 143)

steerage the area on a ship in the lower levels where the steering mechanisms were located and where cramped quarters were provided for people who could only afford cheap passage (p. 57)
tercera clase nivel inferior un barco en el que se encontraban los mecanismos del timón y se ofrecían habitaciones reducidas para las personas que sólo podían comprar un pasaje barato (pág. 57)

Strategic Arms Limitation Talks (SALT) negotiations between the United States and the Soviet Union designed to limit nuclear weapons (p. 348)
Tratados de Limitación de Armas Estratégicas (SALT) negociaciones entre Estados Unidos y la Unión Soviética diseñadas para limitar el número de armas nucleares (pág. 348)

Student Nonviolent Coordinating Committee (SNCC) a group organized to promote civil rights for African Americans through nonviolent protests (p. 294)
Comité Coordinador Estudiantil No Violento (SNCC) grupo organizado para promover los derechos civiles de los afroamericanos con protestas no violentas (pág. 294)

Students for a Democratic Society (SDS) a group organized to protest U.S. involvement in the Vietnam War (p. 328)
Estudiantes por una Sociedad Democrática (SDS) grupo organizado para protestar por la participación de Estados Unidos en la guerra de Vietnam (pág. 328)

suburb a neighborhood outside of a downtown area (p. 64)
suburbio vecindario en las afueras de una ciudad (pág. 64)

Sun Belt the southern area of the United States from Florida to California that experienced an increase in population during the 1970s (p. 278)
Sun Belt área del sur de Estados Unidos, desde Florida hasta California, en la que hubo un aumento de la población durante la década de 1970 (pág. 278)

supply-side economics economic theory that focuses on influencing the supply of labor and goods; it usually involves sharp tax cuts (p. 358)
economía de la oferta teoría económica que pretende influenciar la oferta de mano de obra y de bienes; por lo general, implica grandes reducciones de impuestos (pág. 358)

sweatshops hot, stuffy workshops in which workers prepare materials for low wages (p. 60)
fábricas explotadoras talleres calurosos y con el aire cargado en los cuales los trabajadores preparan materiales por salarios reducidos (pág. 60)

talkie a film that includes sound (p. 186)
película sonora película que incluye sonido (pág. 186)

Teapot Dome scandal a scandal under the Harding adminstration in which government officials were accused of taking bribes to allow oil to be mined from federal lands (p. 173)
escándalo de Teapot Dome escándalo durante el gobierno de Harding en el que se acusó a funcionarios del gobierno de aceptar sobornos para permitir que se usaran tierras federales para extraer petróleo (pág. 173)

ENGLISH AND SPANISH GLOSSARY

Teller Amendment (1898) a congressional resolution stating that the U.S. had no interest in taking control of Cuba (p. 118)
Enmienda Teller (1898) resolución del Congreso en la que Estados Unidos declaró que no tenía intención de tomar el control de Cuba (pág. 118)

Tennessee Valley Authority (TVA) a governmental agency designed to bring jobs and electricity to rural areas of the Tennessee River valley (p. 205)
Autoridad del valle del Tennessee (TVA) agencia del gobierno destinada a proveer empleos y energía eléctrica a las áreas rurales del valle del río Tennessee (pág. 205)

terrorism the systematic use of fear or terror to gain goals (p. 373)
terrorismo uso sistemático del miedo o el terror para alcanzar objetivos (pág. 373)

Tet Offensive (1968) a series of attacks by Vietcong forces that proved to many Americans the Vietnam War was not being won (p. 324)
ofensiva del Tet (1968) serie de ataques de las fuerzas del Vietcong que demostró a muchos estadounidenses que no estaban ganando la guerra de Vietnam (pág. 324)

38th Parallel the boundary between North and South Korea before the Korean War (p. 272)
paralelo 38 límite entre Corea del Sur y Corea del Norte antes de la Guerra de Corea (pág. 272)

Tonkin Gulf Resolution (1964) gave President Johnson the power to send combat troops to Vietnam (p. 322)
Resolución del golfo de Tonkin (1964) otorgó al presidente Johnson la autoridad de enviar tropas de combate a Vietnam (pág. 322)

totalitarianism a form of government in which every aspect of citizen's lives are controlled by the government (p. 224)
totalitarismo forma de gobierno en la cual todos los aspectos de la vida de los ciudadanos están bajo el control del gobierno (pág. 224)

transcontinental railroad a railroad system that crossed the continental United States; construction began in 1863 (p. 10)
tren transcontinental línea ferroviaria que cruzaba Estados Unidos de un extremo a otro; su construcción se inició en 1863 (pág. 10)

Treaty of Fort Laramie (1851) a treaty signed in Wyoming by the United States and northern Plains nations (p. 14)
Tratado del fuerte Laramie (1851) tratado firmado en Wyoming por Estados Unidos y las naciones indígenas de las Planicies del norte (pág. 14)

Treaty of Medicine Lodge (1867) an agreement between the U.S. government and southern Plains Indians in which the Indians agreed to move onto reservations (p. 15)
Tratado de Medicine Lodge (1867) acuerdo entre el gobierno de Estados Unidos y los indígenas de las Planicies del sur en el que los indígenas aceptaron irse a las reservas (pág. 15)

Treaty of Versailles (1919) brought an end to World War I, but was never ratified by the United States (p. 158)
Tratado de Versalles (1919) puso fin a la Primera Guerra Mundial, pero Estados Unidos nunca lo ratificó (pág. 158)

trench warfare a new kind of warfare in World War I that involved troops digging and fighting from deep trenches (p. 144)
guerra de trincheras nuevo tipo de guerra utilizado en la Primera Guerra Mundial en el cual las tropas cavaban trincheras profundas y luchaban desde ellas (pág. 144)

Triangle Shirtwaist Fire a factory fire that killed 146 workers trapped in the building; led to new safety standard laws (p. 93)
incendio de Triangle Shirtwaist incendio de una fábrica en la que murieron 146 trabajadores atrapados en el edificio; este suceso obligó a crear nuevas leyes de seguridad (pág. 93)

Truman Doctrine a policy attempting to contain the spread of communism, beginning with military aid to the monarchies of Turkey and Greece (p. 267)
Doctrina Truman política que intentaba contener el avance del comunismo, ofreciendo inicialmente ayuda militar a las monarquías de Turquía y Grecia (pág. 267)

trust a number of companies legally grouped under a single board of directors (p. 41)
consorcio varias compañías agrupadas legalmente bajo el mando de una sola junta directiva (pág. 41)

Tuskegee Airmen a group of African American pilots who flew missions in World War I; they were the first African American military pilots (p. 232)
Aviadores de Tuskegee grupo de pilotos afroamericanos que volaron en misiones de la Primera Guerra Mundial; fueron los primeros pilotos afroamericanos del ejército (pág. 232)

Twenty-first Amendment (1933) an amendment to the Constitution that ended Prohibition (p. 181)
Vigésimoprimera Enmienda (1933) enmienda constitucional que puso fin a la Ley seca (pág. 181)

Twenty-sixth Amendment (1971) an amendment to the Constitution that lowered the voting age to 18 (p. 331)
Vigésimosexta Enmienda (1971) enmienda constitucional que redujo la edad mínima para votar a 18 años (pág. 331)

U-boats German submarines or "untersee boats" (p. 144)
U-boats submarinos alemanes o "barcos untersee" (pág. 144)

United Farm Workers a group organized to promote the interests of migrant farm workers, it eventually led to the Chicano movement (p. 302)
Trabajadores Agrícolas Unidos grupo organizado para promover los intereses de los trabajadores agrícolas migratorios; con el tiempo, dio origen al movimiento chicano (pág. 302)

United Nations an alliance of nations that attempts to end disputes between countries peacefully (p. 266)
Naciones Unidas alianza de naciones que intenta resolver de manera pacífica las disputas entre los países (pág. 266)

urban renewal a governmental program that attempted to rid innercities of slums and replace them with low- and middle-income housing (p. 279)
programa de renovación urbana programa gubernamental que intentó eliminar las barriadas de los centros urbanos y reemplazarlos con viviendas para personas de recursos bajos y medios (pág. 279)

vertical integration the business practice of owning all of the businesses involved in each step of a manufacturing process (p. 40)
integración vertical práctica empresarial de poseer todas las empresas que participan en cada paso de un proceso de manufactura (pág. 40)

Vietcong the South Vietnam forces that were supported by North Vietnamese Communists (p. 319)
Vietcong fuerzas de Vietnam del Sur apoyadas por los comunistas de Vietnam del Norte (pág. 319)

Vietnamization a policy introduced in an attempt to leave the Vietnam War, in which Vietnamese forces would take over the fighting (p. 330)
vietnamización política introducida en un intento de salir de la guerra de Vietnam, según la cual las fuerzas vietnamitas se harían cargo de la lucha (pág. 330)

Vietnam Veterans Memorial a war memorial in Washington, D.C., dedicated to the veterans of Vietnam (p. 333)
Monumento a los Veteranos de Vietnam monumento conmemorativo de la guerra en Washington D.C. dedicado a los veteranos de Vietnam (pág. 333)

Voting Rights Act of 1965 provided new powers to the federal government to protect African Americans' voting rights (p. 299)
Ley de Derecho al Voto de 1965 dio nueva autoridad al gobierno federal para proteger el derecho al voto de los afroamericanos (pág. 299)

War Powers Act (1973) a law that requires a president to get Congressional approval before sending troops into combat (p. 333)
Ley de Facultades de Guerra (1973) ley que requiere la aprobación del Congreso para que el presidente pueda enviar tropas a la guerra (pág. 333)

War Production Board a government agency set up to oversee production of war materials during World War II (p. 230)
Junta de Producción de Guerra agencia creada por el gobierno para supervisar la producción de materiales de guerra durante la Segunda Guerra Mundial (pág. 230)

Watergate a scandal in which President Nixon resigned over accusations of illegal activity (p. 349)
Watergate escándalo que provocó la renuncia del presidente Nixon por acusaciones de actividades ilegales (pág. 349)

weapons of mass destruction chemical, biological, or nuclear weapons that can kill thousands (p. 377)
armas de destrucción masiva armas químicas, biológicas o nucleares que pueden matar a miles de personas (pág. 377)

World Trade Center a complex of several office buildings that were attacked by terrorists (p. 376)
World Trade Center complejo de varios edificios de oficinas que fue atacado por terroristas (pág. 376)

Yalta Conference a meeting between the leaders of the Allied powers that resulted in a plan for peace after World War II (p. 264)
Conferencia de Yalta reunión de los líderes de las fuerzas aliadas que produjo un plan de paz después de la Segunda Guerra Mundial (pág. 264)

yellow journalism the reporting of exaggerated stories in newspapers to increase sales (p. 117)
prensa amarillista publicación de noticias exageradas en los periódicos para aumentar las ventas (pág. 117)

ENGLISH AND SPANISH GLOSSARY

Zimmermann note a telegram from Germany to Mexico offering Mexico a return of territory in exchange for declaring war on the United States (p. 146)
telegrama Zimmermann telegrama de Alemania a México en el cual se ofrecía a México una devolución de territorios si le declaraba la guerra a Estados Unidos (pág. 146)

zoot-suit riots a series of riots during which Mexican Americans were attacked by whites (p. 233)
disturbios *zoot-suit* serie de disturbios durante los cuales personas de raza blanca atacaron a mexicano-americanos (pág. 233)

Index

C

INDEX

INDEX

INDEX

Credits and Acknowledgments

CREDITS AND ACKNOWLEDGMENTS

For permission to reproduce copyrighted material, grateful acknowledgment is made to the following sources:

Chusma House Publications: from *Soldados: Chicanos in Viet Nam*, edited by Charley Trujillo. Copyright © 1990 by Charley Trujillo.

Doubleday, a division of Random House, Inc., www.randomhouse.com: From *The Diary of a Young Girl: The Definitive Edition* by Anne Frank, edited by Otto H. Frank and Mirjam Pressler, translated by Susan Massotty. Copyright © 1995 by Doubleday, a division of Random House, Inc.

Hill and Wang, a division of Farrar, Straus & Giroux, LLC and electronic format by permission of *Georges Borchardt, Inc., for Les Editions de Minuit:* From *Night* by Elie Wiesel, translated by Stella Rodway. Copyright © 1958 by Les Editions de Minuit; English translation copyright © 1960 by MacGibbon & Kee, renewed © 1988 by The Collins Publishing Group. Originally published as *La Nuit*. All rights reserved.

Alfred A. Knopf, a division of Random House, Inc., www.randomhouse.com; electronic format by Harold Ober Associates Incorporated: "I, Too, Sing America" and "Dream Deferred" ("Harlem") from *The Collected Poems of Langston Hughes*. Copyright © 1994 by the Estate of Langston Hughes.

The Metropolitan Museum of Art, New York, NY: From "Introduction" from *American Paradise: The World of the Hudson River School*, Introduction by John K. Howat. Copyright © 1987 by The Metropolitan Museum of Art, New York, NY.

W. W. Norton & Company, Inc., www.wwnorton.com, electronic format by McCall Corporation: Thirteen Days: A Memoir of the Cuban Missile Crisis by Robert F. Kennedy. Copyright © 1968 by McCall Corporation.

Norwegian-American Historical Association: From quote by Gro Svendsen from *Frontier Mother: The Letters of Gro Svendsen*, translated and edited by Pauline Farseth and Theodore C. Blegen. Copyright © 1950 Norwegian-American Association.

Persea Books, Inc.: Bread Givers by Anzia Yezierska. Copyright © 1925 by Doubleday & Co., Inc.; copyright renewed 1952 by Anzia Yezierska, transferred to Louise Levitas Henriksen in 1970. Revised edition copyright © 1999 by Persea Books, Inc. Foreward and Introduction copyright © 1999 by Alice Kessler-Harris.

Saint Martin's Press: Quote by Sarah G. Bagley from *The Belles of New England: The Women of the Textile Mills and the Families Whose Wealth They Wove* by William Moran. Copyright © 2002 by William Moran.

Scribner, an imprint of Simon & Schuster Adult Publishing Group: From *The Great Gatsby* by F. Scott Fitzgerald. Copyright 1925 by Charles Scribner's Sons; renewed copyright 1953 by Frances Scott Fitzgerald Lanahan.

Viking Penguin, a division of Penguin Group (USA) Inc.: From *The Grapes of Wrath* by John Steinbeck. Copyright 1939 and renewed © 1967 by John Steinbeck.

Sources Cited:

Quote by Harold Bryant from *Bloods: An Oral History of the Vietnam War by Black Veterans* by Wallace Terry. Published by Ballantine Books, New York, 1985.

From *Keeping The Faith* by Jimmy Carter. Published by Bantam Books, New York, 1982.

Quote by Maya Lin from "Architect Maya Lin Describes the thoughts Behind the Vietnam Veterans Memorial" by Fernando Quintero from *The Berkeleyan*, 1995.

Quote by Philip Caputo from *CNN Cold War: Interviews*, accessed at http://www.cnn.com/SPECIALS/cold.war/episodes/11/interviews/caputo/

From "The Fall of Saigon" by Ken Moorefield from *To Bear Any Burden: The Vietnam War and Its Aftermath in the Words of Americans and Southeast Asians* by Al Santoli. Published by E.P. Dutton, Inc., 1985.

From quote by Henry Fenner from *You Must Remember This: An Oral History of Manhattan from the 1890s to World War II* by Jeff Kisseloff. Published by Harcourt, Inc., Orlando, 1989.

From *Yesterday: A Memoir of a Russian Jewish Family* by Miriam Shomer Zunser, edited by Emily Wortis Leider. Published by HarperCollins Publishers, New York, 1978.

Quote by a Hungarian immigrant from *This Was America* by Oscar Handlin. Published by Harvard University Press, Cambridge, Mass., 1949.

From "Now I Lay Me Down to Sleep" by Diana Dwan Poole from *Chicken Soup for the Veteran's Soul* by Jack Canfield, Mark Victor Hansen, and Sidney R. Slagter. Published by Health Communications, Inc., Deerfield Beach, FL, 2001.

From *A Life is More than a Moment: The Desegregation of Little Rock's Central High* by Will Counts, Will Campbell, Ernest Dumas and Robert S. McCord. Published by Indiana University Press, Bloomington, 1999.

Quote by Dave Reinemen from "60 Years Later, Okinawa Memories Still Burn" by Tom Berg from *Orange County Register*, 2005.

Quote by Frank Hall from "Hundreds tread site of bloody battle" by Steve Limtiaco. Published in *Pacific Daily News*, accessed at http://www.guampdn.com/apps/pbcs.dll/article?AID=/20050314/NEWS01/503140301/1002.

Quote from *Hard Times: An Oral History of the Great Depression* by Studs Terkel. Published by Pantheon Books, New York, 1970.

Quote by Lawrence Svobida from "Farming the Dust Bowl" from *The American Experience, Surviving the Dust Bowl*, accessed at http://www.pbs.org/wgbh/amex/dustbowl/sfeature/eyewitness.html.

Quote by Louis Ortega from *WWII: The People's Story* edited by Nigel Fountain. Published by Reader's Digest, Pleasantville, NY, 2003.

Quote by Boris Pilnyak from *Our Times*, edited by Loraine Glennon. Published by Turner Publishing, Inc., Atlanta, GA, 1995.

Quote by Michiko Yamaoka, interviewed by Mitsuru Ohba from *Voices of A-Bomb Survivors* web site, accessed at http://www.csi.ad.jp/ABOMB/Hibakusha/h03.html.

Illustration and Photo Credits

Cover: © PCL/Alamy.

Frontmatter: vii (c) © Canadian Musem of Civilization, artifact no Ill-L-100 a-b, photo no. D2003-18042; xix The Granger Collection, New York; xxi From the Collections of Henry Ford Museum and Greenfield Village; xxix © Charles R. Ritzmann/CORBIS; xxxv © Dallas and John Heaton/CORBIS; xxxviii © Reuters/Stan Honda/POOL/CORBIS xxiii (t) © Flip Schulke/CORBIS; xxiii (c) Bizuayehu Tesfaye/AP/Wide World Photos; xxxvi TIME Inc./Courtesy of the general libraries, The University of Texas at Austin/HRW photo by Victoria Smith; xxxvii © Arthur Schatz/Time Life Pictures/Getty Images;

Prologue: NY0 © Museum of Fine Arts, Boston, Massachusetts, USA. Gift of Maxim Karolik for the M. and M. Karolik, Collection of American Paintings, 1815-65; NY1 (br) The Granger Collection, New York, (bc) Marilyn Wynn/Nativestock Pictures; NY2 © SuperStock; NY3 Courtesy of the Massachusetts Historical Society; NY4 (c) © Francis G. MayerCORBIS, (bc) New York State Archives, NY5 (bl) The Granger Collection, New York; NY6 (c) The New York Public Library/Art Resource, NY, (bc) Print Collection, Miriam and Ira D. Wallach Division of Art, Prints and Photographs, The New York Public Library, Astor, Lenox and Tilden Foundation; NY7 (cr) © Wolfgang Kaehler/CORBIS, bc) Courtesy of the Massachusetts Historical Society, (cl) The Granger Collection, New York; NY8 (bc) Library of Congress, Manuscript Division, (cr) © Bettmann/CORBIS; NY9 (cr) The Granger Collection, New York, (bl) Library of Congress/PRC Archive, (br) The Granger Collection, New York; NY10 (bl), (c) © CORBIS, NY10 (br) © Joseph Sohm, Chromosohm, Inc./CORBIS; NY11 (cr) The Granger Collection, New York, (bc) © Bettmann/CORBIS; NY12 (bc) [neg. #40578] ©Collection of The New-York Historical Society; NY13 (bl) The Granger Collection, New York, (br) © Underwood & UnderwoodCORBIS; NY14 (bc) The Granger Collection, New York, (br) Copyright The New York Public Library / Art Resource, NY; NY15 (bl) © Bettmann/CORBIS, (bc) The Granger Collection, New York; NY16 (bc) © Blank Archives/Getty Images, (br) Time Life Pictures/Getty Images, (c) © Arlie Scott for POV; NY17 (cr) Photo by Thomas E. Franklin/The Bergen Record/Getty Images, (b) © Bernd Obermann/CORBIS

Unit 1. Chapter 1: Pages 2–3 © James L. Amos/CORBIS; 2 (b) Courtesy Wells Fargo Bank; 3 (bl) The Art Archive / Musée d'Orsay Paris/Dagli Orti, (cl) Southern Pacific Lines/PRC Archive, (cr) © CORBIS, (br) The Granger Collection, New York; 7 (tr) © Collection of the New-York Historical Society, [neg. 41800]; 8 (l) Denver Public Library, Western History Collection; 8–9 (r) Nebraska State Historical Society, Photograph Collections; 9 (inset) Bob Boze Bell, True West Magazine; 10 (inset)

© James L. Amos/CORBIS; 11 Union Pacific Historical Collection; 12 (t) The Granger Collection, New York; 12–13 (b) SuperStock; 15 (t) George Lane/AP/Wide World Photos; 16 (t) © Bettmann/CORBIS; 17 (t) Western History Division, National Museum of American History/Smithsonian Institution, Washington, DC; 18 The Granger Collection, New York; 19 (l) (art Reference) all LOC -no credit needed, (r); 21 (b) Western History Collections, University of Oklahoma; 22 (bl) Library of Congress, (tr) Elias Carr Papers, East Carolina Manuscript Collection, J.Y. Joyner Library, East Carolina University, Greenville, NC. Photo by Dewane Frutiger., (br) Nebraska State Historical Society; 23 (l) Culver Pictures; 24 (art reference) LOC/PRC No credit needed; 25 (t) © CORBIS, 28 (bl) Sam Dudgeon/HRW. **Chapter 2:** Pages 30–31 (t) PRC Archive; 31 (bl) © Bettmann/CORBIS, (br) Archives Larousse, Paris, France/ Bridgeman Art Library, (c) George Meany Memorial Archives; 34–35 (b) Library of Congress; 36 (r) [neg. #40578] ©Collection of The New-York Historical Society, (l) Whittier Museum; 37 (l) Property of AT&T Archives. Printed with permission of AT&T., (r) © Hulton Archive/Getty Images; 38 (l) © CORBIS, (r) Library of Congress/PRC Archive; 39 (b) Montgomery County Historical Society; 40 (b) © CORBIS, (inset) Courtesy of the Rockefeller Archive Center; 41 (t) [#71880T] © Collection of The New-York Historical Society; 43 (l) (Art Reference) AP/Wide World Photos & © Bettmann/CORBIS, (c) (Art Reference) AP/Wide World Photos, (r) (Art Reference) Photo courtesy Union Pacific Historical Collection; 45 (b) (Art Reference) © Bettmann/CORBIS, (t) Brown Brothers. **Chapter 3:** Pages 52–53 (t) © Bettmann/CORBIS; 53 (cl) © Joseph Sohm, Chromosohm, Inc./CORBIS, (cr) © CORBIS, (br) © Ted Spiegel/CORBIS; 57 (t) PictureHistory/NewsCom; 58 (cr) Shades of L.A. Archives/Los Angeles Public Library, (cl) National Archives, #90-G-152-2038; 59 (tc) Col. Ernest Swanson Papers, Swenson Swedish Immigration Research Center, Augustana College, Rock Island, IL, (cl) © CORBIS; 60 (bl) Library of Congress, Arnold Genthe Collections, #LC-G403-T01-0363, (br) Library of Congress, Arnold Genthe Collections, #LC-G403-T01-0363; 63 (t) Lake County (IL) Museum /Curt Teich Postcard Archives; 64 (bc) New York State Historical Association, (br) © David Bell/CORBIS; 67 The Granger Collection, New York; 68 Jane Addams Memorial Collection (JAMC neg 227), Special Collections, University Library, University of Illinois at Chicago.

Unit 2: 76–77 Courtesy of the U.S. Naval Academy Museum. **Chapter 4:** 78–79 (t) Elizabeth Cady Stanton Trust; 79 (cl, cr) Janice L. and David J. Frent Collection of Political Americana, (b) The Granger Collection, New York; 83 (t) The Granger Collection, New York; 84 (tl) PRC Archive, (tr) PRC Archive, (cl) PRC Archive, (cr) PRC Archive, (bl) PRC Archive, (br) PRC Archive; 85 (t) © Bettmann/CORBIS; 88 (t) Barnes & Noble, Inc.; 89 (t) Library of Congress/PRC Archive; 91 (b) National Archives/PRC Archive; 93 (t) Courtesy of Steve Latham; 96 (b) © Bettmann/CORBIS; 97 (b) Library of Congress; 101 (tc) Leroy Radanovich/Yosemite Museum, (tl) © W. Perry Conway/CORBIS; 102 (br) White House Collection, copyright White House Historical Association, (bl) White House Collection, copyright White House Historical Association, (bc) White House Collection, copyright White House Historical Association; 107 (t) Library of Congress. **Chapter 5:** Pages 108 (b) © Charles Sleicher; 108–109 (t) © Bettmann/CORBIS; 109 (bl) Press Information Bureau of India, (c) Denver Public Library, Western History Collection; 114 (c) © Douglas Peebles/CORBIS; 115 National Portrait Gallery, Smithsonian Institution/Art Resource, NY; 116 Trustees of the British Museum; 118 (b) © Bettmann/CORBIS, (c) PRC Archive; 120 (tr) Library of Congress; 121 (bl) © Richard Cohen/CORBIS; 123 (br) © CORBIS; 124–125 (b) Library of Congress; 127 The Granger Collection, New York; 128 (inset) © Bettmann/CORBIS; 130 (b) © Bettmann/CORBIS, (c) © Bettmann/CORBIS; 131 (tr, b) © Bettmann/CORBIS. **Chapter 6:** Pages 136–137(t) © Bettmann/CORBIS; 137 (cl) Culver Pictures, Inc., (br) Collection of Colonel Stuart S. Corning/Courtesy of PRC Archive, (bl) Stock Montage, Inc.; 141 The Granger Collection, New York; 144 (t) © CORBIS; 146 ©SuperStock; 148 (t) © Underwood & Underwood/CORBIS, (b) © Patrick BazGetty Images; 149 (t) © K.J. Historical/CORBIS; 151 Sam Dudgeon/HRW; 154 (c) © Hulton/Getty Images, (t) ©Dorling Kindersley Ltd./Courtesy of Spink & Son Ltd., London; 156 (bl) © Michael St. Maur Sheil/CORBIS.

Unit 3: 166–167 Everett Collection. **Chapter 7:** Pages 168 (b) HRW Photo by Lance Schriner; 168–169 (t) The Great White Way, Times Square, 1925 (oil on canvas), Thain, Howard A. (1891-1959)/© New-York Historical Society, New York, USA,/Bridgeman ARt Library; 169 (bl) Egyptian National Museum, Cairo, Egypt/SuperStock, (cr) Brown Brothers, (bc) © Bettmann/CORBIS, (c) The Granger Collection, New York; 173 The Granger Collection, New York; 174–175 (b) From the Collections of Henry Ford Museum and Greenfield Village; 176 (c) From the Collections of Henry Ford Museum and Greenfield Village; 177 (tr) Janice L. and David J. Frent Collection of Political Americana, (tl) Janice L. and David J. Frent Collection of Political Americana; 179 (t) Library of Congress, (b) TIME Inc./Courtesy of the general libraries, The University of Texas at Austin/IIRW photo by Victoria Smith, (c) © Underwood & Underwood/CORBIS; 180 Library of Congress; 181 © Bettmann/CORBIS; 183 The Phillips Collection, Washington, D.C.; 186 (bl) © Bettmann/CORBIS, (br) The Negro Leagues Baseball Museum; 187 (cl) The Granger Collection, New York, (bl) © Hulton/Getty Images, (cr) The Granger Collection, New York; 188 © Getty Images; 189 © Georgia O'Keeffe Museum, Santa Fe / Art Resource. **Chapter 8:** Pages 194 (b) The Granger Collection, New York; 194–195 (t) © Bettmann/CORBIS; 195 (cl) Janice L. and David J. Frent Collection of Political Americana, (cr) Courtesy Everett Collection, (bl) © Bettmann/CORBIS; 199 (t) © Bettmann/CORBIS; 200 (br) Milton (Pete) Brooks/The Detroit News; 201 (t) Brown Brothers; 206 (t) © Bettmann/CORBIS; 208 (br) Library of Congress, (bl) Library of Congress; 211 (b) NOAA George E. Marsh Album; 212 Library of Congress; 213 (t) Twentieth Century Fox; 215 The Granger Collection, New York. **Chapter 9:** Pages 220 (b) (c) Bridgeman Art Library; 220–221 (t) © CORBIS; 221 (tr) Reuters/HO/Hulton Archive/Getty Images, (bl) AKG-Images, London, (bc) © MPI/Getty Images; 225 © Hugo Jaeger/Timepix/Time Life Pictures/Getty Images; 226 © CORBIS; 228 (cr) © CORBIS; 229 (t) © Brooks Kraft/Corbis; 231 (bc) Picture Research Consultants & Archives, (br) Library of Congress; 232 (bl) © U.S. Air Force/Collection of David Ethell, (t) CORBIS/Bettman; 233 (tr) © Seattle Post-Intelligencer Collection; Museum of History and Industry/CORBIS; 235 (b) Everett Collection; 236 © Bettmann/CORBIS; 237 (tl) Bettmann/CORBIS, (tcl) Bettmann/CORBIS, (tc) Bettmann/CORBIS, (tcr) Bettmann/CORBIS, (tr) Bettmann/CORBIS, (bkgd) Bettmann/CORBIS; 238 (tl) © CORBIS, (cr) Library of Congress; 238–239 (b) © Keystone/Getty Images; 241 National Archives (NARA); 243 (bl) © Hulton-Deutsch Collection/CORBIS; 244 ©PHOTOGRAPHER/SuperStock; 246 © CORBIS; 247 © H. Miller/Hulton Archive/Getty Images; 248 © Bettmann/CORBIS; 251 Bantam Books.

Unit 4: 258–259 (bkgd) © New York Times Co./Hulton Archive/Getty Images, 259 (inset) © Lazlo Willinger/SuperStock. **Chapter 10:** Pages 260–261 (tc) © Bettmann/CORBIS; 261 (bl) © Bettman/CORBIS, (cr) AP/Wide World Photos, (bl) © Carl & Ann Purcell/CORBIS, (cl) © Hulton Archive/Getty Images, (cl) © Bettmann/CORBIS; 261 (c) Civil Defense Museum; 265 (bl) © Hulton-Deutsch Collection/CORBIS, (br) UPI/Corbis-Bettmann; 266 (tc) © CORBIS, (tr) AP Photo/United Nations; 267 (cr) Editorial cartoon by Tom Little, 1948; courtesy of the Nashville Tennessean.; 268 The White House, Courtesy Harry S. Truman Library; 269 The Granger Collection, New York; 271 (bl) The Granger Collection, New York; 273 (tc) © ohn Florea/Time & Life Pictures/Getty Images; 274 "FIRE!" From Herblock: A Cartoonist's Life (Times Books, 1998) Library of Congress; 276 (cl) © Bettmann/CORBIS; 279 (tr) Image courtesy of The Advertising Archives; 280 (tl) © Bettmann/CORBIS, (cl) © Ben Martin//Time Life Pictures/Getty Image, (c) Courtesy Elvis Presley Enterprises, (bl) © Bettmann/CORBIS. **Chapter 11:** Pages 286 (br) Photo by Hank Walker//Time Life Pictures/Getty Images; 286–287 (t) © Flip Schulke/CORBIS; 287 (bc) © Bettmann/CORBIS, (cr) AIMovement, (bl) Sovfoto/Eastfoto; 291 (br) AP/Wide World Photos; 292 (cl) Photos by Will Counts from A LIFE IS MORE THAN A MOMENT; 292–293 (c) Photos by Will Counts from A LIFE IS MORE THAN A MOMENT; 297 (tl) © Bettmann/CORBIS; 298 (all) © Bettmann/CORBIS; 299 (t) LBJ Library Collection; 300 (cl) Gene Herrick/AP/Wide World Photos, (bl) Wisconsin Historical Society; 301 (cl) Bill Hudson/AP/Wide World Photos, (bl) AP/Wide World Photos, 303 © Arthur Schatz/Time Life Pictures/Getty Images; 304 (all) © Bettmann/CORBIS; 305 William Philpott/REUTERS/NewsCom. **Chapter 12:** Pages 310–311 (t) AP/Wide World Photos; 311 (bl) © Hulton Archive/Getty Images, (br) © Dirck Halstead/Getty Images, (c) © Blank Archives/Getty Images; 317 (r) NASA, (bl) © 1996 CORBIS; Original image courtesy of NASA/CORBIS; 320 AP/Wide World Photos; 322 (br) © Sygma/CORBIS, (bl) © LARRY DOWNING/Reuters/Corbis; 323 Courtesy of Charley Trujillo/Chusma House Publications; 325 © CBS Photo Archive/Getty Images; 327 (tr) National Archives (NARA); 329 (tcl) © Leif Skoogfors/CORBIS, (tcr) © Dick Swanson/Time Life Pictures/Getty Images, (tl, tr) © David J. & Janice L. Frent Collection/CORBIS, (bkgd) © The Image Bank/Getty Images; 330 © Paula Bronstein/Getty Images; 331 (tr) © CORBIS, (tc) © Bettmann/CORBIS; 332 (b) © James P. Blair/CORBIS, (cl) © Richard Howard/Time Life Pictures/Getty Images.

Unit 5: 340–341 © Jose Fuste Raga/CORBIS. **Chapter 13:** Pages 342 (cl) © Bill Pierce/Getty Images, (b) © Bettmann/CORBIS; 342–343 (t) Wally McNamee/Woodfin Camp & Associates; 343 (cr) Tim Shaffer/AP/Wide World Photos, (br) Lehtikuva Oy/Woodfin Camp & Associates; 347 (t) Jason Laure/Woodfin Camp & Associates; 349 (t) Republished with permission of Globe Newspaper Company, Inc.; 351 AP/Wide World Photos; 353 (t) Bernard Gotfryd/Woodfin Camp & Associates, (c) Janice L. and David J. Frent Collection of

Political Americana; 354 (bl) White House Collection, copyright White House Historical Association, (bc) White House Collection, copyright White House Historical Association; 355 Courtesy, Jimmy Carter Library; 356 (t) AP/Wide World Photos, (inset) © Bettmann/CORBIS; 358 Leste Sloan/Woodfin Camp & Associates; 359 (inset) © Bill Gentile/CORBIS; 360 Joh Ficara/Woodfin Camp & Associates; 361 (br) Courtesy Ronald Reagan Library, (br) © Robert Nickelsberg/Getty Images, (bc) NASA, (bl) Chuck Nacke/Woodfin Camp & Associates. **Chapter 14:** Pages 366 (b) Smithsonian Institution, Washington, DC Harold Dorwin 2004-55788; 366–367 (t) © Jeff Greenberg/PhotoEdit; 367 (cl) © Peter Turnley/CORBIS, (bl) David Modell-Katz/Woodfin Camp & Associates, (br) © Derrick Ceyrac/Getty Images; 372 (c) © AFP/Getty Images, (b) © Shelly Katz/Time Life/Getty Images; 373 The White House; 375 (all) © Brooks Kraft/CORBIS; 376 (bl) © Ricky Flores/CORBIS, (bc) © Oleg Nikishin/Getty Images; 377 (bl) © Mirrorpix/Getty Images, (cr) Hasan Sarbakhshian/AP/WideWorld, (bc) Al-Jazeera via APTN/AP/Wide World Photos; 378 Courtesy the White House/Photo by Eric Draper; 380 (bl) © Richard Ross/CORBIS,

(br) Custom Medical Stock Photo; 382, © REUTERS/John Gress; 381 (br) Zuma Press/NewsCom; 384 (br) © Elise Amendola/AP/Wide World Photos; 385 (bl) © Chabruken/Getty Images, (br) Bizuayehu Tesfaye/AP/Wide World Photos, Rob Schoenbaum/AP/Wide World Photos.

Back Matter: R0-R1 (bkgd) © Royalty-free/CORBIS; Presidents: Pages R29–R33, White House Historical Association (White House Collection); R33 (last) The White House, photo by Eric Draper. R30, ©PhotoDisc/Getty Images; R35, The Granger Collection, New York; R37 © Tom Brakefield/Digital Vision/Getty Images;

State Facts: R33 (b) © James L. Amos/CORBIS, (t) © Royalty-FreeCORBIS

Staff Credits. The people who contributed to *United States History,* **New York Edition** are listed below. They represent editorial, design, intellectual property resources, production, emedia, and permissions.

Lissa B. Anderson, Melanie Baccus, Charles Becker, Jessica Bega, Ed Blake, Gillian Brody, Shirley Cantrell, Erin Cornett, Rose Degollado, Chase Edmond, Mescal Evler,

Rhonda Fariss, Marsh Flournoy, Leanna Ford, Bob Fullilove, Matthew Gierhart, Janet Harrington, Rhonda Haynes, Wilonda Ieans, Cathy Jenevein, Shannon Johnston, Kadonna Knape, Aylin Koker, Cathy Kuhles, Debbie Lofland, Bob McClellan, Joe Melomo, Richard Metzger, Cynthia Munoz, Holly Norman, Nathan O'Neal, Karl Pallmeyer, Chanda Pearmon, Shelly Ramos, Peter Reid, Curtis Riker, Marleis Roberts, Diana Rodriguez, Gene Rumann, Annette Saunders, Kay Selke, Ken Shepardson, Michele Shukers, Chris Smith, Elaine Tate, Jeannie Taylor, Joni Wackwitz, Ken Whiteside